Joseph E. Campbell, Th.D.

THE PENTECOSTAL HOLINESS CHURCH
1898-1948

The Pentecostal Holiness Church

1898 - 1948

ITS BACKGROUND AND HISTORY

Presenting complete background material which adequately explains the existence of this organization, also the existence of other kindred Pentecostal and Holiness groups, as an essential and integral part of the total church set-up.

BY JOSEPH E. CAMPBELL, TH. D.

WIPF & STOCK · Eugene, Oregon

Wipf and Stock Publishers
199 W 8th Ave, Suite 3
Eugene, OR 97401

The Pentecostal Holiness Church
1898 - 1948
By Campbell, Joseph E.
ISBN 13: 978-1-4982-8311-3
Publication date 3/21/2016
Previously published by Pentecostal Holiness Church, 1951

This volume is affectionately dedicated to my loving wife, whom God gave me as a real helpmeet. Her constant devotion and enthusiastic words of encouragement have been to me an abiding inspiration and challenge to do my best as a servant of Christ my Lord.

THE PENTECOSTAL HOLINESS CHURCH
ITS BACKGROUND AND HISTORY
1898-1948

An Abstract of the Thesis

The following presentation of the background and history of the Pentecostal Holiness Church is divided into three main parts.

PART I, "Why the Pentecostal Holiness Church and Other Kindred Pentecostal and Holiness Groups Exist." An attempt is made to explain and justify the existence of these groups. This explanatory background material has been divided into two sections.

Section I deals with "The Divisive Forces Giving Rise to New Sects." This section has been sub-divided into five chapters, each of which deals with some underlying factor present in society, which tends to give rise to and foster the existence of successively rising sects.

Section II deals with "The Evolution of Denominations" and presents historic examples of the recurrent cycle in the development from a despised outcast group which gradually evolves to denominational "respectability."

PART II is concerned with the formal history of the Pentecostal Holiness Church and is divided into three sections as follows:

Section I, entitled "Background and Early Beginnings" presents the early history of the Church, indicating its parent stem and ancient roots, and its early beginnings as an organization until its consolidation with the Fire-Baptized Holiness Church in 1911.

Section II deals with its "Organized Efforts and Expansion," showing the various eras of its historical development in the following named chapters—"Consolidations"; "New Developments"; Growing Pains and Reverses"; "Coordination and Cooperation" and "Organizational Developments."

PREFACE, *Continued*

Section III, called "Departmental Developments in Summary," is a series of separate chapters summarizing in a more comprehensive manner some of the material which has been previously mentioned.

PART III gives special attention to two important phases of the history of the Church, The History of Education and Publications in the Pentecostal Holiness Church.

Section I presents "The History of Education in the Pentecostal Holiness Church."

Section II deals with "The History of Publications in the Pentecostal Holiness Church."

Because of the relative importance of the developments in these two fields of endeavor a more comprehensive account of these historic developments has been presented.

TABLE OF CONTENTS

Abstract XIII

Part I

WHY THE PENTECOSTAL HOLINESS CHURCH AND KINDRED GROUPS EXIST

SECTION I

DIVISIVE FORCES GIVING RISE TO NEW SECTS

Chapter   Page

     Introduction 1
- I The Theological Factor as a Divisive Force 8
- II The Theological Factor as a Divisive Force, Continued:
  1. The Social Gospel 27
  2. The New Phychology of Religious Education . 42
  3. Ecumenicity 55
- III The Psychological Factor as a Divisive Force 66
- IV The Social Factor as a Divisive Force 75
- V The Economic Factor as a Divisive Force 83
- VI The Political Factor as a Divisive Force 94
- VII Why Pentecostal Holiness? 100

SECTION II

THE EVOLUTION OF DENOMINATIONS

     Introduction 113
- I Religious Radicals 120
- II Religious Radicals (Continued) 134
- III Evolutionary Phases in the Denominational Cycle ... 146
- IV Why Pentecostal Holiness? 161

TABLE OF CONTENTS *Continued*

Part II

THE FORMAL HISTORY OF THE PENTECOSTAL HOLINESS CHURCH

Section I

BACKGROUND AND EARLY BEGINNINGS

Chapter	Page
I The Parent Stem and Background	179
II The Fire-Baptized Holiness Church	192
III The Fire-Baptized Holiness Church, 1898-1910, Continued	206
IV The Pentecostal Church, 1900-1910	216
V The Pentecostal Holiness Church, 1900-1910 Early Conventions	233

Section II

ORGANIZED EFFORTS AND EXPANSION

I Consolidations, 1911-1916	254
II New Developments, 1917-1924	270
III Growing Pains and Reverses, 1925-1932	285
IV Coordination and Cooperation, 1933-1944	297
V Organizational Developments	309

Section III

DEPARTMENTAL DEVELOPMENTS IN SUMMARY

I Home Missions	318
II Home Missions, Continued	326
III Foreign Missions	344
IV Orphanage and Eleemosynary Institutions	360
V Youth Society, Sunday School, and Vacation Bible Schools	377
VI Woman's Auxiliary, and Radio Broadcasting	388

TABLE OF CONTENTS *Continued*

VII Camp Meetings, and Bible Conferences 397
VIII Service Pastor, Chaplaincy, and Statistical
 Information 406
IX Bishops 411

Part III

HISTORY OF EDUCATION AND PUBLICATIONS IN THE PENTECOSTAL HOLINESS CHURCH

SECTION I

EDUCATION

Chapter	Page
I Holmes Bible College, Greenville, S. C.	423
II The Emmanuel College, Franklin Springs, Ga.	477
III Some Educational Projects Which Were Attempted and Have Failed	502
IV The Educational Institutions in Western Territory	510

SECTION II

PUBLICATIONS

I Periodicals and Sunday School Literature
 Since 1899 522
 The Importance of the Printed Page 522
 Publications in Interest of Pentecostal Holiness
  Church 525
 Other Publications 532
 The Official Organ 535
 Other Publications in the Pentecostal
  Holiness Church 555
II Books, Booklets, Tracts and Pamphlets 559
 Bibliography 567

THE PENTECOSTAL HOLINESS CHURCH
ITS BACKGROUND AND HISTORY
1898-1948

by Joseph Enoch Campbell, A.B., B.D., Th.M. Th.D.

This book is the largest, and one of the most outstanding volumes ever to be published in the ranks of the Pentecostal Holiness Church. It contains a rich treasure-house of facts concerning trends, issues and personalities involved in the beginning and development of the Pentecostal Holiness Church. The reader's interest will be greatly stimulated as he follows the author's unique presentation of a religious movement that fights its way up from obscurity to recognition.

The author answers the question as to why various Pentecostal and Holiness movements came into being and justifies their continued existence. For this reason the volume will meet with wide acceptance among the membership of all full-gospel churches, both Holiness and Pentecostal.

He makes the heroes of faith to relive in the rather voluminous historical data that he has carefully scanned from many source materials. These materials, along with the author's travels, contacts and personal interests, add zest and authenticity to the volume.

It comprises verbatim the thesis written by the author as a part of the requirements for his Doctor of Theology Degree. This degree was awarded him in 1948 by the Union Theological Seminary of Richmond, Virginia, where the thesis has been placed on file. Because of its academic endorsement, it will therefore be in demand as a reference volume in seminaries and in Bible colleges.

The volume will be especially appreciated by those who know and those who would like to know about the Pentecostal Holiness Church. Those who are members and know the church will

INTRODUCTION *Continued*

want to become acquainted with their organization, and those who do not know, but desire to, will enjoy learning what is here written about it.

Therefore, being a close personal friend of the Reverend Joe E. Campbell for many years, I take great pleasure in introducing *The Pentecostal Holiness Church, 1898-1948, Its Background and History* to the English reading audiences of the world.

      R. O. Corvin, President
      Southwestern Pentecostal Holiness College
      Oklahoma City, Oklahoma

Part I

WHY THE PENTECOSTAL HOLINESS CHURCH
AND OTHER KINDRED PENTECOSTAL
AND HOLINESS GROUPS EXIST

Section I
DIVISIVE FORCES GIVING RISE TO NEW SECTS
Introduction

There are at present 256 separate religious sects extant in the United States. These variegated religious movements have found in American soil a fertile place in which to grow. The national policy of religious liberty for which we stand has created this congenial atmosphere. Elmer T. Clark has this to say about it, "The principles of religious freedom, untrammeled, access to the right of individual interpretation of the Holy Scriptures, and the privilege of worship according to the individual conscience, which were promulgated by the Protestant Reformation and found their fullest expression in America, have given rise to a multitude of religious sects in this country."[1] Mormonism and Christian Science are the only distinctively American contributions. Clark also points out the noteworthy and significant fact that only a comparatively few of the many existing denominations are really indigenous to American soil; but that the vast majority of them are exotic religions which have been imported from Europe, at least in the parent stem. Such information is contrary to the conventional idea among many who regard sectarian diversity as a peculiarly American phenomenon.[2] It is also significant to note that practically all of these sects are geographically localized. According to Clark, "Only eight are represented in each State by at least one Church, and only 58 are so represented in half of the States; 70 are found in from one to six States, and 18 are concentrated in one State only. No State has all of the denominations. Illinois leads in this regard with a representation of 144 of the 212 organizations."[3] (Since Clark's book, the total number of organizations has increased to 256, as noted above.) Differences of opinion have often caused these groups to split. These differences have at times been absurdly trivial. Strange and fatu-

---
[1] Elmer T. Clark, **The Small Sects in America**. (Nashville: Cokesbury Press, 1937), p. 7.
[2] Ibid., pp. 13, 14.
[3] Ibid., p. 14.

ous teachings have been concocted and made to represent the most extreme vagaries of the human mind. Apparently anything that simulates the truth is time and again espoused by a goodly number of devotees who are often more zealous and zestful than those who are the votaries of the real truth. This fact has been glaringly demonstrated in such cults as the Jehovah's Witnesses, Seventh-Day Adventists, Mormons, and Christian Science. In each of these "isms" their respective leaders have written books to supplement the Holy Scriptures, which books have been accepted by their followers as being divinely inspired, on a parity with the Holy Writ. Wyrick puts it in somewhat crude but descriptive language in these words, "The American people are dumb; tie a bell to an idea, and they will follow it."[1] This is particularly true if such an idea is centered around some outstanding personality with leadership qualities.

While it is true that religious freedom gives birth to many sects which would be better unborn, it is also true that it prevents the truth from becoming static. It gives opportunity for neglected truths to be emphasized when needed. Vagaries in religious thought challenge the Church to present the orthodox position. In that sense the Church owes a debt to heretics who have helped it to formulate its creeds. When the Church has failed to emphasize its doctrinal position new sects have had their inception in order to take up the neglected task. Pierson Parker avers that, "The very name of 'Protestant' means one who testifies, on behalf of a forgotten truth. That was the meaning of the Reformation, and in turn has been the motive behind the rise of every Protestant denomination since the sixteenth century.

"The same process is going on today. Christian truth is never embraced in its totality by any individual, nor by any group however large. Something is almost certain to be overlooked. When the neglect grows too glaring, voices will be heard in protest and, especially under today's religious freedom, groups will withdraw to form their own institutions wherein to promulgate the newly discovered emphases. True, such a movement nearly always overstresses its particular teaching. This is why we call it a cult.

---

[1] Herbert M. Wyrick, **Seven Religious Isms.** (Grand Rapids: Zondervan Publishing House, 1941), p. 65.

Always, however, the cult stands as a reminder to the Church at large of a task which the Church itself ought to be about."[1]

Latourette expresses somewhat the same view: "Some sects," he says, "were born of envy, strife and personal ambition, but of the larger ones the great majority sprang from fresh expressions of the Christian impulse."[2] His view appeals as being a more nearly accurate and comprehensive analysis of the problem of a divided Christendom. To offer any one of these factors, however, as a sufficient interpretation of the rise and growth of sects would be a gross over-simplification. Each of these factors, and still other interpretations have in them valid elements which an adequate explanation cannot afford to ignore. The perennial problem of divisiveness among denominations has increasingly challenged the best intellect of the Church to provide some workable solution to promote Protestant unity. In more recent years Church leaders have openly lamented this unfavorable situation and have sought through a widespread ecumenical movement to consolidate various denominations. The possibility of such denominational unity is a consideration which will be dealt with more directly and comprehensively in a later chapter, after we have first come to recognize the principal root-cause which activates this ecumenical movement.

In the chapters which immediately follow in this section an attempt will be made to analyse the root-causes which tend to produce new sects, and to demonstrate the necessity of such new religious groups. The Catholic Church usually makes the charge against the Reformation that it has been the source of all kinds of evil in producing disunity and discord. The Roman hierarchy, however, has never been willing to make any allowance for those who may differ or take issue with any of their autocratic, dictatorial policies. No justification is allowed for any deviation from their prescribed course—mapped out according to papal design. Such an attitude no doubt arises out of either ignorance, personal bias, or an attempt to cover personal guilt. All good Catholics, to be good Catholics, must surrender their right to do individual religious thinking and submit to the corporate body

---

[1] Randolph Crump Miller, Editor, **Interseminary Series**, Volume II, (New York: Harper and Brothers, 1946), p. 181.
[2] Kenneth S. Latourette, **History of the Expansion of Christianity**, IV, p. 41.

of the Roman Church to do their religious thinking for them. It is therefore only natural that Roman Catholic criticism would lack the symmetry of a well-rounded appraisal. The Reformation was somewhat the occasion but not the cause of the existence of multifarious church groups. Not merely for the purpose of recrimination but in the interest of the whole truth the fact should not be overlooked that spiritual decay and disintegration were already manifest before the time of the Reformation and constituted the root-cause which necessitated reform. Encyclical letters have been issued intermittently through the years to justify Romanism by condemning the Reformers' motives. It is an historical fact, however, that separations from the Catholic Church occurred before and since the Sixteenth Century Reformation, even as late as 1870.[1] The point is that the Roman Catholic Church in spite of her complacent attitude could well discover a lack of unity, peace and harmony within her immediate ranks rather than attempting to assign the total responsibility to Protestantism.

The Catholic Church and the Reformers clashed at two points concerning the doctrine of the Scriptures: the veneration of tradition to supplement the Scriptures and the decisive authority assigned to tradition. If tradition has greater authority than the Scriptures, the corrollary of this particular church view would be to give greater authority to the Church than to the Scriptures, though they be the very word of God. The Catholic Church insists that there are three infallible entities in the realm of religious authority: (1) the Church, (2) the Scriptures, (3) and the Church's interpretation of the Scriptures, i. e. Tradition. Their contention is, that the Pope speaking ex-cathedra is infallible and allows for no glosses. The Church, they say, cannot err and if she did err, then those who should follow her in the error would not be held accountable.[2] Further comment at this point would not be directly relevant to the immediate problem before us.

As a helpful working basis from which to enter into a fuller discussion of these divisive forces it seems pertinent to make use of a list of these causes as tabulated by Francis Curran in the first

---

1 N. J. Monsma, **The Trial of Denominationalism.** (Grand Rapids: Wm. B Erdmans Publishing Co., 1932), p. 27.
2 **Ibid.,** p. 23 ff.

chapter of his book, *Major Trends in American Church History*. For the convenience of the reader, this material is presented in the same form in which it appears in the original source, instead of following the customary technique of using smaller type for long quotations. He lists the following causes:

1. Class divisions, as exemplified in the evolution of Evangelical sects, have been frequent occurrences in our religious history. As the original lower-class Methodists separated from the Anglicans, so the Holiness sects broke away from the later middle-class Methodists.

2. Nationalism has produced a large number of denominations. American, German, Danish, Swedish, Norwegian, Finnish, Icelandish and Slovak Lutherans all have their independent synods in this country.

3. Debates over the languages to be used in divine worship have occasioned new sects. The German Albright Methodists and some Lutheran groups owe their origin to this cause.

4. Sectionalism has produced its sects. The Mason-Dixon line divides the northern Baptists and Presbyterians from the schismatic sects of the same denominations in the South.

5. Racialism has caused an almost complete separation of colored and white Christians. Over 90 per cent of all Negro Christians are enrolled in exclusively colored denominations.

6. Immigration has carried with it large numbers of new sects. In recent years England alone has sent us Darbyites, Irvingites, and other small groups. Other immigrants found the branch of their sect, established in this country by previous immigrants, changed beyond recognition; therefore they founded their own sects. The Christian Reformed Church is an example of this type.

7. The problem of polity has partitioned sects. The Evangelical tendency toward congregational polity has caused many schisms from the Methodists.

8. Administration of the "Sacraments," particularly Baptism, has caused friction within sects, and has resulted in their final fracture. The River Brethren with their singular doctrine of the "Sacrament" of footwashing, broke into factions over its administration. One sect insisted that the same man should wash and dry the feet; the other that one man should wash and another dry.

9. Quarrels over the forms of worship have ended in schism.

The "unscriptural" use of organs in the Church was a major cause of separation of the Churches of Christ from the Disciples of Christ.

10. Disputed "moral" questions have broken sects asunder. The Mennonites have proved especially susceptible to fine distinctions in settling moral problems. New Mennonite sects have originated in disputes over the morality of top buggies, horse trades, even the cut of the minister's coat.

11. Opposition to "unscriptural" novelties, such as Sunday Schools, missionary societies, and an uneducated ministry have caused schisms, particularly among the Hard Shell or Landmarker Baptists.

12. Individual church leaders, moved by ambition or even less laudable motives, have led their personal following out of the established sects and have founded new denominations according to their own taste. A number of holiness sects have been established by such leaders.

13. Theological disputes have precipitated a number of schisms.

The unity of churches has always been destroyed by arguments on the relative merits of Calvinism and Arminianism, Unitarianism versus Trinitarianism, Fundamentalism versus Modernism.[1]

While this list of causes is on the whole an adequate expression of the various reasons for Protestant divisions, they are nevertheless presented from a Roman Catholic viewpoint. Hence, for that reason they fail to justify any division, even such divisions as would result in constructive benefit. No allowance is thus made for legitimate expression of valid individual differences. Father Curran has yielded to the inclination to make one man an exact copy of another. Monsma, assuming a counter position, aptly points out that, "Different men have interpreted the Bible differently. And here lies the fountain head of denominationalism. As the rays of the same sun cast different hues through the varicolored panes of the cathedral window, so the Word of God is not reflected identically by different souls. Indeed the cause of this variation is not to be looked for in God, nor in His Word, but in the different mind structures of human beings. Human beings are

---

[1] Francis X. Curran, **Major Trends in American History.** (New York: The American Press, 1946), pp. 14-16.

endlessly variegated. As no two blades of grass, nor two leaves, are exactly identical, so no two human beings are exactly alike."[1] The logical conclusion which he reaches is that the Reformation made way for the Bible to be reflected by a host of individuals, instead of by a coagulated and uniform tradition. The difference, therefore, did not lie in a failure to accept the great truths of the Scriptures but rather in the significance attached to these truths and the emphasis placed upon them. While it may appear that our differences would thus become more apparent; actually, as we make our particular denominational emphasis, we are thus coming to express the whole truth of God more accurately.[2] To emphasize these differences would also tend to express the whole truth of God more adequately.

The crux of Monsma's conclusion is stated as follows:

> It is true that present day denominationalism took its inception from the Reformation and its principles. It may seem as if Protestantism has made a muddle of ecclesiastical authority upon which it insisted. Still—aside from excresences for which Protestantism cannot be held responsible—denominationalism and not Roman Catholicism works for the unity of the Church.[3]

We might well add that no church has a right to exist as a distinct body unless good and legitimate reasons justify its existence. It should either augment the corporate body of divine truth by emphasizing some neglected doctrinal truth or by introducing some legitimate phase of revelation. Such a norm can well be applied to measure every denomination's right to exist.

We shall now turn to a more extended consideration of these divisive forces, each in their turn, to establish the necessity of the existence of various sects or religious groups. We will deal first with the factor of theological differences, which necessarily tend to produce new sects. In the closing chapter of this section summary reasons will be advanced to explain and justify the presence of the Pentecostal Holiness Church, based on the pertinent observations which have thus been made.

---

1 Monsma, op. cit., pp. 42, 43.
2 Ibid., pp. 43-48 et passim.
3 Ibid., p. 48.

Chapter I
THE THEOLOGICAL FACTOR AS A DIVISIVE FORCE

LIBERALISM, A DIVISIVE FORCE

"In 1890 the 'liberal' was debating whether there were two Isaiahs; in 1930 the extreme 'modernist' was debating whether there was a personal God."[1] This striking declaration by Dr. Atkins, in his book, *Religion In Our Times,* serves to introduce the important subject which we propose to treat in this initial chapter. The presence of "modern religious liberalism" is indubitably the root-cause for the spiritual apathy and indifference which characterizes a major segment of the church world which we know. The purpose of this chapter would likely be made more perspicuous if we were to assign to it the sub-title, "Chaotic Conditions in Contemporary Christendom."

Theological factors of various types, shades and colors have always been present to divide Christians into separate groups throughout the history of the Church. Such has especially been the case since the time of the Protestant Reformation. It may, therefore, appear that undue emphasis is being placed upon liberalism as a divisive factor and too little emphasis upon other causes which also deserve attention. While these other causes are recognized, this particular cause for division will be somewhat amplified because of its peculiar relationship to the inception of the Pentecostal Holiness Church and other kindred groups.

It is true that *modern liberalism,* at the time Holiness and Pentecostal sects had their inception, had not come to be recognized as prominently as we view it today. But it is also true, however, that this new theology was in its inchoate stage of development. Such a conclusion is based on the fact that the Social Gospel, The New Psychology of Religious Education, and the trend toward Ecumenicity were at the time each an incipient force in the Church. While all three of these manifestations have a valid emphasis, it will be demonstrated in our later analysis and appraisal of them that these new trends root in liberalism. It is not our contention,

---
1 Gaius Glenn Atkins, **Religion In Our Times.** (New York: Round Table Press, Inc., 1932), p. 86.

however, that either the parent groups or the new sects produced by them were able at the time to discern the influence of liberal theology as a divisive factor. This is a conclusion which is possible only as we view them in the perspective of history. So, while this particular factor is admittedly not the only theological factor which enters into the picture, it will be emphasized as the principle root-cause for division. This emphasis will be better understood when we come to consider the closing chapter of this section.

A Definition

The term "Liberalism," as it will be used herein serves a multiple purpose in that it will be used loosely to include *rationalism, humanism, naturalism* and *modernism*. The use of any of these terms may be understood as substantially including all or any of the others.

The Importance of Considering Liberalism

This subject, in the sober judgment of many thinking Christians, constitutes a grave problem of far greater magnitude perhaps than any of us fully realize. Liberal theology has, since its inception, tended to destroy the historic beliefs of many Protestant churches. This is an admitted fact, admitted even by those who espouse its teachings as will be seen in the following quotations. "The philosophy of religion has within the last generation undergone a revolution," says Professor Edward Caldwell Moore, of Harvard University.[1] George Holley Gilbert, a defender of modernism, speaks of the vast transformation which the Christian faith is surely and in part silently undergoing.[2] Dr. K. C. Anderson, pastor of a liberal church writes: "Liberal Christianity is a radical departure from the creed of Christendom."[3] It is the common knowledge of all those who possess even a meagre amount of spiritual discernment that there is patent within the church some subtle force which seems to attenuate and emasculate our Christian witness and rob us of that spiritual vitality and virility which symbolized Christianity in its pristine form.

---

[1] Edward Caldwell Moore, **The Spread of Christianity in the Modern World.** Chicago: University of Chicago Press, 1919), p. 84.
[2] George Holley Gilbert, **The American Journal of Theology.** (Chicago: The University of Chicago Press, 1910), Vol. XIV, p. 271.
[3] John Horsch, **Modern Religious Liberalism.** (Chicago: The Bible Institute Colportage Ass'n., 1924), p. 12.

Men Repeat Old Errors

Dr. John R. Moose, Professor of Church History at the Lutheran Theological Southern Seminary, in the course of one of his lectures, made a simple but strikingly significant statement which this writer has never forgotten and has had occasion to verify repeatedly. He said, "Churchmen would not fall into as many errors as they do, if they were only familiar with church history." He meant, of course, that many of our errors are a repetition of the self-same errors which others in the history of the Church have made.

These "old errors" are often disguised by an unfamiliar garb and are therefore not recognized. Sometimes they are couched in specious terminology and at other times traditional terminology is used to convey erratic ideas which are quite foreign to those ideas customarily thought of. In other words, liberalism utilizes the terminology of orthodoxy and reads into evangelical speech a content which is often the very opposite of its evangelical significance. The teachings of modernism manifestly demonstrate this tendency. "The most offensive feature of religious liberalism," says Horsch, "is that it uses, as a rule, the old Biblical expressions and claims to be Christian theology—an improvement on the old faith; all this in the face of the fact that modernists, as we have seen, recognize the great chasm which separates them from Biblical Christianity. It is as if within a political party which was founded on the principle of protective tariff there arose a new party which defended free trade, but insisted on retaining the old party name and connections, advancing the excuse that the protective tariff principles, when properly interpreted, mean free trade."[1] Horsch further adds these timely comments:

> It would indeed be useless to deny or belittle the radical contrasts between the old Bible faith and religious liberalism. So great and fundamental are these differences that, if one is Christianity, the other must be something else. It has been said that modernism has changed all the doctrines of the old faith as held by Christendom from the beginning. The fact is—modernism sets aside doctrines and disowns them. Indeed Christianity has more in common with Judaism and some other non-Christian religions than with modernism.[2]

---

[1] Horsch, Op. Cit., p. 17.
[2] Horsch, op. cit., p. 16.

Machen plainly charges that modern liberalism is diametrically opposed to Christianity.[1] Ernest Gordon in his book, *The Leaven of the Sadducees*, aptly and ingeniously sets forth the fact that modern criticism and modern theology are largely a recrudescance of the eighteenth century deism. In parallel columns he shows that the ideas of the deists are the same as those of present-day modernists. Dr. Fosdick's and Tom Paine's writings are shown in parallel. Similar comparisons are made of the writings of other modernists with those of other deists.[2] In each instance these writings are shown to represent man's attempt to work out his own salvation independent of God and His revealed plan of redemption.

MEN ATTEMPT TO SAVE THEMSELVES

In a recent address delivered at the Union Theological Seminary of Richmond, Virginia, Dr. John A. MacKay, a man of eminent qualifications and great profundity of thought, said, in effect:

> Sin has always manifested itself in man to cause him to seek to elevate himself to the level of God and thereby dispense with the need of God to effect his salvation. Man is prone to absolutize things about him rather than to accept God as the Absolute. Hitler sought to absolutize 'power', some seek to absolutize 'beauty', others 'culture' or 'refinement', still others 'race' or 'economic class'. Man is constitutionally disposed to seek some summum bonum other than God Himself. He persists in the attempt to make his final goal of living something other than God. When we view the abyss of our day we discover that all these absolutes have been tried and have failed. There is left no other absolute which has not already been demonstrated as worthless. There is, therefore, left no absolute upon which man can depend. He has through his rejection of God, thrust himself into void and outer darkness. He has no standard and no sense of values. He does not know where he is, nor the way out of where he is. He has abandoned the real God for some human god. It is the task of the Church to show him the way out.

The sum total of his remarks adds up to saying that throughout history man has attempted to substitute rationalism, humanism and naturalism for God's revealed plan to achieve his salva-

---

[1] J. Gresham Machen, **Christianity and Liberalism.** (New York: The Macmillan Company, 1924), p. 5.
[2] Ernest Gordon, **The Leaven of the Sadducees.** (Chicago: The Bible Institute Colportage Assn., 1926), pp. 212 ff.

tion. He has sought something to "do" that through his own efforts he might gain eternal life. We have before us an age-old example of this common error in the experience of Cain. He was a religious man, but his worship was made to accord with his own ideas instead of God's plan. He brought an offering unto the Lord from the field. It was the fruit of his own labors. God rejected it because it was a *"bloodless"* offering. It seems to the rational thinking man that Cain's offering of the fruit of the ground, might have been more acceptable, but it was not. It constituted the *"way of Cain,"* and not the *"way of ₁God."*[1]

Before continuing a further development of the subject, a word of explanation may avoid the possibility of giving offense. It is recognized that those who are in error are often men of sincere religious convictions who are prompted by an ardent desire to do good, but have unwarily been led into devious paths. They, like Cain, are religious and on the whole are sincere worshipers, but they have substituted their man-devised way for God's way. "There is a way that seemeth right unto a man, but the end thereof are the ways of death."[2] Some have referred to all modernists as apostates. We often use the word "apostates" indiscriminately and with too little consciousness of its derogatory implications and condemnatory meaning. Churchmen should seek to emulate the example of Christ who hated sin but loved the sinner. But while He was never activated by animosity, He was never perfidious in failing to speak the unvarnished truth regardless of whom it involved.

RATIONALISM, AN OLD ERROR

Since the time of Christ, the Church has unfailingly been threatened with and molested by those of various circles who, under the guise of true religion, have opposed the simple gospel of salvation by faith as set forth in the Holy Scriptures. Out of a sense of self-sufficiency, and sometimes arrogance, divine authority has been rejected and the attempt has been made to provide salvation on some rational basis.

The rationalists (or modernists) of Jesus' day were the Sadducees. They rejected everything of a supernatural nature. This

---

1 Genesis 4:3; Jude v. 11.
2 Proverbs 16:25.

is evinced by their disbelief in a corporeal resurrection. They sought to adjust themselves exclusively to the natural forces about them. They would, therefore, accept nothing that they could not verify with rational proof. They reduced faith to embrace only those things which they could intelligently apprehend. Such an attitude takes the heart out of religion and limits it to the finite capacities of the human intellect. God is reduced to the finite concept of human limitations. This is the essence of humanism.

The Judaizers, in Paul's time, sought to substitute the keeping of the Law (their works) for salvation by faith. Paul set forth the futility of such an idea. He taught them that their works were an adjunct to their faith and not the essence of faith itself. Works are the evidence that saving faith has been exercised. In other words, our faith is shown by our works.

The Gnostics in subsequent times, also, sought by their own works to substitute knowledge for simple faith. This philosophico-religious movement is but another manifestation of rationalism. Its central doctrine advocated emancipation through knowledge.

Take another example, that of Erasmus and his humanistic teachings in the sixteenth century. He began at the same place Luther began and admittedly wielded an influence of recognized value for the amelioration of society. But Luther parted company with his program when he perceived that he sought to bring about man's salvation by other means than those divinely instituted in the doctrine of justification by faith. Learning is a vehicle to produce faith, but is never to be used as a substitute for it.

Deism, an eighteenth century teaching, also attempted to dispense with the need for God. Deists laughed at the idea of personal religious experience and a personal fellowship with the Supreme. Muncy writes:

> In all sections of colonial America the light of true religion was all but snuffed out. Immorality was rife in all classes of the population and there was corruption in both church and state. The appearance of deism in America and social life. This philosophy denied the revelations of the Old and New Testaments and taught that the voice of nature was sufficient to guide men in religion and morals. The deists taught that God is, that He created the universe, but that He withdrew himself from it. He is above His creation, they said, but not in it. He is related to His creation as the dot is to the 'i'.

Such a conception of God's relationship to the universe makes Him of very little account in the lives of men, neither His blessing nor His judgment upon human conduct is possible. That he could or would enter into fellowship with man is unthinkable according to this conception.

This type of philosophical thought spread over the colonies during the last quarter of the seventeenth century. Many prominent Americans held this view when George Whitefield made his evangelistic tours of America just prior to and during the Great Awakening. Decadence in religion and immorality in daily life were the moral fruitage of it.[1]

LIBERALISM ANALYSED

In this cursory and somewhat superficial manner we have attempted to cite these historical instances of rationalistic and liberalistic religious thinking which have occurred repeatedly since the time of Christ. We now come to the consideration of the latest recrudescence of such teachings, manifested in the form of German rationalism which made its appearance, roughly, about the middle of the nineteenth century. Because this consideration is one of prodigious proportions with respect to its vital relationship and importance to our generation, we must of necessity allocate to it a deserving amount of space and attention. It would, however, be beyond the limits of our purpose to do more than consider in a general way some of the aspects of the nature and fruit of this teaching, noticing particularly how it acts as a theological divisive force among Christians. Such an investigation is fundamental to a clear understanding of current religious trends. Special attention will be given in a separate chapter to the "shoots" of liberalism which are distinct manifestations of this common root-cause, e. g., in The Social Gospel; The New Psychology of Religious Education, and The Ecumenical Movement; pointing out how these influences are diametrically opposed to revivalism and personal religious experience. In conclusion, some suggestions will be made in each case as to the Christian attitude which should be maintained toward modern liberal theology and its advocates. With patience, let us make a somewhat careful study and analysis of these latent influences which demand our solemn thought and attention.

In humble recognition, it is acknowledged that many of the most profound scholars of our day are numbered among the ex-

---

[1] W. L. Muncy, Jr., A History of Evangelism in the United States. (Kansas City: Central Seminary Press, 1945), p. 26.

ponents of modernism. Among them are many men of sterling character and unimpeachable morality. On the whole they possess a most magnanimous, tolerant and brotherly attitude, especially toward those who hold opposing views. It should be kept in mind, however, that "God hath chosen the foolish things of the world to confound the wise; and God hath chosen the weak things of the world to confound the mighty."[1] And that "the natural man receiveth not the things of the spirit of God, for they are foolishness unto him: neither can he know them, because they are spiritually discerned."[2] Paul encountered intellectual giants in his day who sought to reach God through rational, intellectual achievement and were unable to understand the simple story of a Cross, Vicarious Sufferings, and a Blood Atonement which was to be appropriated by simple faith. He said to them, "For after that in the wisdom of God the world by wisdom knew not God, it pleased God by the foolishness of preaching to save them that believe."[3] "Having therefore boldness to enter into the holiest by the blood of Jesus, by a new and living way, which he hath consecrated for us, through the veil, that is to say his flesh; And having a high priest over the house of God; let us draw nigh with a true heart, in full assurance of faith, having our hearts sprinkled from an evil conscience, and our bodies washed with pure water. Let us hold fast to the profession of our faith without wavering; (for he is faithful that promised)."[4]

LIBERALISM'S IDEA OF SALVATION

Liberalism presents an entirely different way of salvation, a salvation found in man and not in the act of God. It ridicules what they term "subtle theory of the atonement." That, to them, is foolishness. Elaborate modern efforts have been made to get rid of this Bible doctrine in the interest of human pride. The Cross is thought of as a convenient symbol, and Christ's death as a mere example of self-sacrifice for man to follow. These teachings contain an element of truth but fail to reveal the real meaning of the Cross. They also fail to show how God hates sin and how we too should hate sin. The Cross displays God' love in giving His Son

---
1 I Corinthians 1:27.
2 Ibid., 2:14.
3 I Corinthians 1:21.
4 Hebrews 10:19-23.

for our sins. Liberal theology ignores the dreadful reality of guilt and makes persuasion of the human will all that is needed for salvation. Liberalism speaks with disgust of those who believe in the shed blood for remission. In contrast, the Bible teaches that "Without the shedding of blood there is no remission."[1] And that "It is the blood that maketh atonement for the soul."[2] Sin to the modernist is a trifling matter. They make no atonement necessary and no sacrifice necessary to pay the debt of retribution we owe for our unrighteousness. They affirm that real moral order already exists and that society and man can save themselves independent of outside help by stimulating into action the resident good inherent in them and thereby overcome evil. To them there is no fear of hell, for God is a God of love. They fail to recall that Jesus spoke of "everlasting fire and outer darkness." Heaven, to them, is actually reduced to a place where sin is. In reality heaven is practically dispensed with entirely by virtue of the fact that they reject the supernatural teaching of the resurrection which precludes the necessity of such a place being in existence.

Because they reject the Creation Work of God and the Supernatural, they reject also the necessity of the New Birth, since it is part of the creative work of God and is supernatural. But man is not merely "sick"; he is "dead." Life must be given to him in the New Birth, after which he must grow and develop. It is a matter for the individual and not for the corporate body of society as a unit. Modernism seeks to effect through natural means a renaissance. *This is plainly the old error of Erasmus.* Liberals say that Christians isolate themselves and that they should discard the time-worn idea of "other-worldliness" and come to recognize with them that religion should be the function of the Community or State. It should deal with business men, politicians, "Christian Americanization" of immigrants, industrial relations, and international peace. Religion has come to be regarded more and more as a means to a higher end. Missionaries desired at one time to save men from eternal damnation but now they seek to change the social order, to make a better world. This present world is the center of thought of the modernist.

---
1 Hebrews 9:22.
2 Leviticus 17:11.

LIBERALISM'S IDEAS OF GOD

Modern liberalism rejects the teachings of Jesus who taught that we become acquainted with God through nature, moral law and through the Scriptures. They insist that a knowledge of God is realized only by feeling His presence. The universal fatherhood of God through this teaching, in the sense which they have in mind, is not taught in the New Testament. Such a peculiar and intimate relationship is the prerogative only of those who are His children by redemption. Liberalism teaches an immanence of God which, in its final analysis, is sheer pantheism. Man is thought of as part of a mighty world process which in the aggregate is God, ranging from minuscule units of earth to massive units in the heavenly sphere. The Incarnation, to them, is a symbol of the general truth which they teach that man, at his best, is one with God. This concept of deity represents still another attempt on man's part to bring God to his own level and to achieve his salvation somewhat independently of God's help.

LIBERALISM'S IDEAS OF MAN

Man is thought of as righteous and having no need of repentance. To him is ascribed no creature limitations. No gulf therefore is thought of as existing between the creature and the Creator. Man is not a sinful creature under condemnation; for there is, they say, actually no such thing as sin. They ignore the disturbing fact of sin. (The denial of the fact of original sin is manifestly the same error into which Pelagius fell and serves as another example of the fact that men are prone to repeat the errors of their predecessors. A clear knowledge of this error in church history would obviate the necessity of repeating the same error). They reject the work of the Supernatural and thus fail to account for a consciousness of sin—the removal of which would require a supernatural act. It is the preaching of the law of God in word and deed that reveals transgressions, but it takes the supernatural Spirit of God to produce conviction and effect regeneration.

LIBERALISM'S IDEAS OF THE SCRIPTURES

Modernism denies the divine inspiration and authority of the Scriptures; it denies that the Bible is of a supernatural origin, and that its avowedly supernatural contents are true. In support of its naturalistic attitude, modernism denies the infallibility of

Christ who most clearly attests the inspiration of the Scriptures. There are, of course, degrees of liberalism ranging from the Kenosis theory to rank Unitarianism. The former would rob Christ partially of His divine nature.

LIBERALISM'S IDEAS OF PERSON OF CHRIST

Modernism denies the essential deity of Christ. To substantiate such a denial, it repudiates the cardinal doctrine of the Virgin Birth, thus reducing him to the level of man, making him at best only an emasculated ideal. It rejects His vicarious death and the fact of His corporeal resurrection with all the implications of these tremendous facts. It rejects the doctrine of the personal return of the Lord Jesus in like manner as He went away. It substitutes human reason for divine revelation, and the wisdom of man for the Wisdom of God.

LIBERALISM'S IDEAS OF DOCTRINE

In short, it removes all the objective standards, and current need of doctrine, either of truth or of morals, and makes man a law unto himself. Not all modernists have accepted the logical implications of modernism; but they are all on the way and in due course of time will arrive at the stage known as Unitarianism, and that is only about one station this side of agnosticism.

The absence of strong and vigorous doctrinal teaching has opened the way for Eddyism, Spiritualism, etc. Liberalism has robbed the supernatural in religion and has substituted the guesses and conjectures of science. The vagaries of Fosdick or Vedder or Shailer Matthews or of any other modernist can never dispel the vagaries of Mary Baker Eddy. The Liberals' denial of a corporeal resurrection and a life beyond the grave opened the way for Spiritualism. It is the natural child of rationalism and unbelief. When Saul rejected the word of divine revelation he then turned to the witch of Endor. Indifferentism about doctrine makes no heroes of the faith. It would never produce a Luther nor a Niemoller nor any of the martyrs of the Christian faith. When Luther was called into question at the Diet of Worms and offered the opportunity to recant, he firmly and steadfastly said, "Here I stand, I cannot do otherwise, God help me, Amen." He had doctrinal convictions which he refused to abandon.

In our day we are passing through a period of church history which might well be termed an "era of watered-down theology." It is considered distasteful by many and impious by not a few for churchmen to assume firmly any avowed theological position. To possess a strong, virile, lusty faith is no longer considered a virtue to be extolled. In modern circles one is considered uncharitable to manifest any disposition to be dogmatic about his or her religious beliefs. It is sometimes feared that to assume such an attitude might inhibit progress toward denominational unity, or that it might cause a poor showing to be made in the column of church statistics. Needful controversy is often avoided in the interest of denominational unity and ecumenicity. While these are unquestionably worthy objectives to seek to achieve, they become of relatively insignificant value when once we awaken to realize the enormous and terrific price involved in their procurement. It would be of negligible value to gain the material advantage and intellectual acceptance of the modern-day scientific mind at the tremendous cost of violating our faith or stifling our time-tried convictions. Biblical doctrines cannot, and must not, be abandoned in the interest of peace. There is a conspicuous absence of doctrinal preaching which is directly traceable to the influence of liberalism.

Dr. B. R. Lacy, in his book, refers to a significant incident in the outstanding ministry of Dr. John L. Giradeau who preached about the middle of the nineteenth century. He writes of him:

> One evening while leading the people in prayer, he received a sensation as if a volt of electricity had struck his head and had diffused through his whole body. For a while he stood speechless under the strange physical feeling. Presently he began exhorting the people to accept the Gospel. They began to sob, softly, like the falling of rain; then, with deep emotion, to weep bitterly, or rejoice loudly, according to their circumstances. It was midnight before he could dismiss the congregation. The meeting went on night and day for eight weeks. He was accustomed to say that he could always count on those who were converted in that meeting.
>
> His sermons during the meeting, as shown by his notes, were very instructive. He dealt with the great doctrines of sin, regeneration, faith, justification, repentance, and such subjects. None of those who went through these meetings ever forgot his wonderful preaching.[1]

---

1 Benjamin Rice Lacy, Jr. **Revivals In The Midst of The Years.** (Richmond: John Knox Press, 1943), pp. 113, 114 et passim.

While this is a remote incident relating to a comparatively obscure individual whose ministry was somewhat localized; it, however, serves to bring into focus an example of the kind of doctrinal preaching which is on the whole so tragically neglected in our times. Carroll states that "The evangelical Christianity of today is not polemic."[1] The modernists of our day never deal with these great and vital doctrines of the Christian faith. Such teaching as Dr. Lacy describes once characterized the ministry of the preachers who lived before the baleful influences of German rationalism had come to affect current religious thought.

We have stooped to conquer in that we have sought to harmonize an Infinite God's Word and divine revelation with finite man's theory and postulates in the realm of his scientific discovery and exploration. Some are content to hear the pious sound of traditional phrases without making any inquiry as to their implications. In short, the Church, in part, has developed into what some have come to regard with a somewhat boastful intellectual pride as, liberal.

Christianity in some quarters has been enervated and emasculated and perverted and watered-down. It no longer advocates the pristine dogma "once delivered to the saints." By the process of rationalism some have darkened their conscience in telling themselves that the "old time" religion of Paul needs a new interpretation adapted to the modern thinking of our scientific age. Some have come to consider themselves "too intelligent" to accept God's Word as infallible. By the application of scientific methods of exegesis as employed by higher criticism, liberals have become smug in their own conceit—"increased with goods and having need of nothing." Thus we see the picture of the Laodicean church which the ascended Christ described as being neither cold nor hot, but wretched, naked and blind. The great redemptive religion hitherto known as Christianity has become diluted and lukewarm, devitalized and impotent.

Not a few churchmen have come passively to acquiese in a vague, vapid, undogmatic belief. They have relinquished the older orthodoxy and admitted liberal theology which embraces certain

---

[1] H. K. Carroll, **The Religious Forces of the United States.** (New York: Charles Scribner's Sons, 1912), p. lxxxiii.

subtle, underlying, basal tendencies that mold indefinite attitudes and vitiate vigorous doctrine. A spirit of laxity and indifference prevails. Such a spirit disparages definiteness and authority and fosters an attitude of spineless, watered-down passivism. There is hence no animated life and fecundity but a formal deadness and inactivity. It is significant that most dead churches are opposed to fundamentalism. Curran makes this observation:

> The recent history of Protestantism in the United States is particularly noteworthy for two major developments. The first is the final abandonment of the older Protestant Orthodoxy, in some instances by the official declaration of the sects. The second, to which the jettisoning of the Protestant creeds contributed, is an ecumenical movement which aims at the consolidation of all denominations in a single church and which has already effected mergers of a number of Protestant denominations.
>
> The rejection of Protestant dogma was the culmination of the latest struggle between orthodox and liberal Protestants for the control of the sects. The last phase began with the issuance in 1910, of the orthodox publication 'The Fundamentals', whence the orthodox received the new name Fundamentalists. The Fundamentals was a series of twelve books at the expense of two Protestant laymen who distributed, free of charge, 3,000,000 copies of the volume to ministers and lay leaders throughout the world. The series stressed five basic doctrines, the chosen field of battle of the orthodox. The fundamentals are:
> 1. Inerrancy and the divine authorship of Holy Writ;
> 2, The Divinity of Christ;
> 3. His Virgin Birth and Physical Resurrection;
> 4. His substitutionary Atonement;
> 5. His Imminent Second Coming.[1]

ROOTS OF PRESENT DAY TRENDS

The church world has not arrived at this stage of "development" by mere chance. This is not a fortuitous happening. The rise of naturalistic liberalism had its inception because of concomitant changes which have currently come about in the modern society of which we are a part. The root of the various manifestations of so-called liberalism is in "naturalism," which denies that the creation of the world in which we live is to be attributed to anything beyond natural ordinary causes. Such a teaching rejects the Genesis account of Creation and seeks to rob God of His prerogative of Creator. Such assumptions emanate from Darwin's theory of evo-

---
[1] Curran, Op. Cit., pp. 148, 149.

lution. His "Origin of Species," published in 1859, made little immediate impression upon the American mind outside scientific circles but through the medium of Herbert Spencer's writings came to be more widely read. Darwin's later work, "The Descent of Man" set forth in a clearer manner the implications of the first work so that even the non-scientific mind could grasp it.[1]

SCIENTIFIC ADVANCES

Modern inventions have been produced in abundance during the past century. Visible achievements are before our eyes to bear testimony to our scientific thinking. No department of knowledge is exempt from the modern lust of scientific conquest. Every inheritance from the past, including our traditional religious convictions, has been subjected to searching criticism. In the process, unfortunately, many of our traditional convictions have been abandoned. Traditions are no longer sacred. We are demanding the new in religion—a religion which harmonizes with scientific development.

From what source have we derived our new theological concepts? This question is broached in order that we may be better able to appraise the worthiness of these liberal influences and to evaluate better the fruit of such teachings. Garrison draws attention to this root-cause in his comments relating to "Broken Ramparts of Custom and Creed." He says,

> The influence of German liberal thought was making itself felt through the return of American students from their studies abroad. The migration of American students to German universities had already begun before the war, though the stream was a very thin trickle. But before the American university had developed a graduate school of any importance, hundred of young people had gone to Germany and brought back the methods and results of German scholarship. The influence of German thought on philosophy and theology soon far surpassed that of either England or France.
>
> Most notable of all, perhaps, was the new position which science began to occupy in the minds of non-scientists. Darwin's 'Origin of Species' was published in 1859 and the Duke of Argyle's 'Reign of Law' was a new book in 1867. Not less significant than the new ideas which these gave to scientists was the new place that they gave to science in the minds of philosophers and theologians and all who were

---

1 Winifred Ernest Garrison, **The March of Faith.** (New York: Harper and Brothers, 1933), p. 90.

attemping to construct a religious view of the world. Taking these influences together, there was enough dynamite in them to blow up the bulwarks of the old order.[1]

To note additional influences of continental Europe and German rationalism we have but to consider Garrison's further comment in this connection. He states:

Perhaps Christians of the evangelical tradition were as much shocked by the tendency to give up the old fashioned observance of Sunday as anything. The coming of the 'continental Sunday' in place of the Puritan Sabbath was viewed with alarm. The influence of the immigrants, the increase of Roman Catholic population in the cities and the general loosening of standards after the war, all contributed to the breakdown of Puritan practice, the increase of drinking tended to make this breakdown more odious to many, though the Puritan mind had always been more sensitive about Sunday than about liquor The spectacle of German communities spending their Sunday evenings in beer gardens—which were often, in fact, pretty respectable places of family resorts according to present standards—served as a symbol of moral degeneracy.[2]

The first stage of the new era of science put the Christian apologists in the somewhat difficult position of having to defend religious concepts which were themselves about to undergo change through the application of scientific methods to the study of the documents upon which they were based. The results of the work of German Biblical scholarship began slowly to filter in and the study of the Bible by new methods, which treated it as a collection of literature whose date, authorship, and character were to be investigated critically, rather than as a book known in advance to be the inerrant product of inspiration, presently found a place in the minds of many of the entire course of the changing attitude towards the Bible is that given by William Newton Clarke is his 'Sixty Years with the Bible,' in which he narrates autobiographically the development of his own views through six decades.[3]

These deplorable spiritual conditions are to be lamented particularly in view of their more pronounced manifestation evident now in a more advanced stage of development. It seems apropos that other reliable evidence should be brought into focus to emphasize properly this deleterious, devisive factor operative in the field of theological thinking. Hence, we call attention to the following information presented by Dr. Atkins. In speaking of the Church he says,

---

[1] Garrison, Op. Cit., pp. 8, 85.
[2] Ibid., p. 85.
[3] Ibid., p. 93.

It was already conscious that it had to reckon with science. It was still gravely teaching in its Sunday schools the essential cosmogony of Babylon interpreted and moralized through the ancient Hebrew sacred books, while science was assembling through patient investigation a massive body of facts and, with evolution for a key word, slowly fashioning a new geology, biology and astronomy. These challenged at every point the old creation stories of the Bible carried with them implications with which inherited religion would have to reckon. Whether the mass religious mind of America was then at all penetrated by what was going on is a question hard to understand after thirty-years—very likely not.[1]

In speaking of the baneful effects of higher criticism he continues with the following information:

Few great religions have been more dependent upon their sacred books than Christianity. All its recognized backgrounds were in the Old Testament, its validity was tied up with the New Testament. It has been invested with infallible authority, every verse carried—if one could understand it—an equal accent of the Holy Ghost. The reverences and associations of the years hallowed its pages. It was religion, history and science. Preaching was the elucidation of its texts, prayer claimed its promises, and faith was sustained by its revelation. It had been however since the middle of the nineteenth century under examination, mostly by German scholars, and its parts were beginning to be traced to their sources and appraised by the historical conditions under which they were written. By the end of the century the more advanced American theological seminaries began to add to their faculties young men 'who had studied in Germany' and brought back the contagion of such ideas.

The engagements they precipitated began in less strategic sectors—the Book of Jonah, for example, which the more advanced as a foreign missionary tract of a 'vivid and dramatic sort'. George Adams Smith's studies of the prophets began to be read by thoughtful young ministers. Prophecy had always been one of the structural supports of the Christian faith. Isaiah's foretelling of Cyrus two hundred years before he appeared was proof text of the prophet's inspired infallibility. Smith assigned parts of the book to a much later author who knew about Cyrus because he was already marching upon Babylon. The theory of the two Isaiahs roused an amazing spiritual belligerency.[2]

By 1890 disturbing rumors were abroad. The work of a long generation of German scholars, whose conclusions challenged or recast the inherited conceptions of the Bible, reached America indirectly through Scotland, or imported directly in the mental baggage of young theo-

---

1 Atkins, Op. Cit., pp. 38, 39.
2 Ibid., pp. 39, 40.

logical students who h~d studied abroad. The best of them became the teachers of a new generation.[1]

Young people came home from college distressed—or—puzzled— their parents by erudite references to 'J' or 'E' and such ministers who had no use for 'J' or 'E' began to preach about the godless tendencies of modern education.[2]

Dr. W. W. Sweet avers that in no period in the history of the American church has there ever been so rapid a change in the theological scene as we have witnessed in our generation. He attributes this fact to the revolutionary changes which have taken place in the political, social, economic and religious climate. He points out, with others, the disturbing fact that American theology is more or less sterile. Denominationalists have come to share the general opinion that theology only served to keep Christians apart, and a religion "of" Jesus rather than a religion "about" Jesus has come to be the great vogue. Thus has the social gospel emerged upon the scene in greater prominence.[3]

We of this scientific age have unconsciously come to rely upon our own ingenuity and creative strength to provide for ourselves nostrums to cure sick society. We have lost sight of the power of God as an indispensable factor necessary in our social set-up. As Dr. John R. Large, Pastor of the Episcopalian communion of Wilmington, Deleware, stated recently in a personal interview, "Churchmen have come to worship scientific gadgets and are no longer conscious of their need of a Higher Power." Religion has come to rely upon scientific pathological procedure which issues from man's effort to save society.

Men, with an elevated conception of their own abilities, and feeling their own self-sufficiency, living in the age of the comfortable, have designed their own fair-weather theology. They have not only exalted themselves but have reduced the Creator to some sort of vague impersonal being instead of the transcendant Being whom Isaiah, in a vision, saw as high and holy and lifted up. Then, in turn, he saw himself in utter dependence. Hence, we have resorted to psychiatry, social sciences, and variegated types and colors of means for social cures. While these sciences

---
1 **Ibid.**, p. 90.
2 **Ibid.**, p. 105.
3 William Warren Sweet, **The Story of Religion in America.** (New York: Harper and Brothers, 1939), pp. 585, 586.

occupy a valid place as sciences, they are not to be used as substitutes to take the place of God's spiritual work in the New Birth. "Ye must be born again." This dictum applies, not to society, but to individuals in society.

To enter into a full treatment of the subject of modernism would comprise a thesis of considerable dimensions within itself. While our discussion of this subject of such grave importance has been necessarily limited; it is the author's hope that its readers will be able to comprehend a sufficient portion of its far-reaching implications to safeguard themselves from the subtle onslaught of its encroachments which threaten to undermine and destroy the very foundation of our Protestant faith.

Billy Sunday was stern in his denunciation of "liberal preachers." Though we may not appreciate altogether his invective pronouncements against them, we cannot but admire his zeal for what he believed to be truth and right.

Atkins writes of him,

> The Rev. William A. Sunday, whose infinite variety age apparently, cannot wither, nor custom stale, said in Memphis, Tennessee, in January, 1932 that: 'The liberal ministers are a lot of Judases and deserve the fate of Judas.... They are a lot of pussy-footing, white-livered, yellow softies.... If the church would teach the virgin birth, the literal resurrection and the second coming of Christ, the evangelistic fires would burn once more and do more good in this Christ-hating, God-blaspheming world than all the disarmament conferences and league of nations.[1]

Atkins, in commenting on the wide chasm between these two factions in the Christian world, says, "No bridge of words, or dispositions either, strong enough to bridge the traffic of a united Church has as yet, been built across the gulf. Doctrinal differences have furnished evangelical Protestantism with cleavages of its own. The gulf between the 'modernist' and the 'fundamentalist' is actually as deep as between the sacramental and evangelical churches, and the interchanges from opposite sides far from irenic."[2]

---

1 Atkins, **Op. Cit.**, p. 149.
2 **Loc. Cit.**

Chapter II
THE THEOLOGICAL FACTOR AS A DIVISIVE FORCE
(Continued)

A. THE SOCIAL GOSPEL

In the preceding chapter we have sought to bring into focus and to emphasize some of the serious implications resulting from modern liberal theology. Now, in the present chapter, it will be our purpose to indicate and consider three significant manifestations which are largely the outgrowth of certain of these liberal teachings. When comparison is made with the old theological concepts which have previously guided our religious thought, it is evident that these new views are definitely tainted by the unsavory influences of German liberalism. We will first analyse the bases and relative value of what has come to be designated, The Social Gospel.

THE CONCEPT OF GOD

Our theological concept of the nature of God and man's relation to Him largely determines the doctrinal system to which we subscribe. It is only natural to expect that man's doctrinal concepts will tend to center around the basal idea as to the nature of God. Dr. Sweet points out the significant fact that economic conditions and the changes in our economic order cause some corresponding change in our attitude toward God and our conception of Him. He illustrates this idea in the following statements:

> Theology is not final truth handed down from above, but grows out of man's condition; it comes out of human background. It is what men think about God and their relationship to Him; and this is conditioned on man's feeling of need. In times of prosperity we are liable to over-emphasize man's part in salvation; when all human efforts fail and wars, famine and pestilence sweep the world, then we tend to empasize the need of a great God who can do all things man finds himself unable to do.[1]

It is a patent fact that with the advance of scientific knowledge which has brought with it improved living conditions and the

---
[1] Sweet, **Op. Cit.**, pp. 584, 585.

comfort of modern conveniences, man has come to feel somewhat independent of God and has virtually come to think of himself as his own God. Sweet also makes this observation:

> The emphasis in theology during the immediate post-war years was an entirely different kind than that noted before. There was then much talk of the scientific approach to religion and 'scientific religion' was much extolled from many a cultured pulpit. Those were days when every branch of learning coveted some tie-up with the word science. It was indeed the charmed word. Belonging to this emphasis upon scientific religion was the emergence of the New Humanism. The extreme New Humanist abolished the supernatural and denied the existence of any God other than the God resident in 'the human will-to-goodness'. A recent interpreter of current theology has suggested that this was a natural reaction to the experiences through which the past generation had passed and that it grew out of 'a certain healthy impatience' and indignation with too easy cures for the pains of the world. In other words, the Humanist was not willing to trust any other cure for the world's evil and pain than the will-to-goodness in the soul of man.[1]

He points out further, how the prosperous twenties affected religious bodies just as it did business, they overexpanded. Costly churches were built as well as denominational colleges. Congregations vied with one another in erecting churches of size and elegance on important corners. It is only natural that such lavish expenditure would create new worship atmospheres. Pulpit robes and robed choirs along with new liturgical emphases and formal services became more common. Personal religious experience ceased to occupy the prominent place it had once held. There came to be a growing feeling that Protestants must recover the art of objective worship if it was to invoke in its worshippers the awareness of reality. The emphasis upon the social gospel turned many a Protestant pulpit into a "soap box" for the proclaiming of social issues. People became emotionally starved and increasingly drama-minded. Mention is made of Professor Fred Eastman's survey of religious drama activities in the United States. It seems that among 451 churches, because of the changing architecture and liturgical emphasis, ninety-one per cent of them utilized dramatic plays to hold the interest of their people.[2] This new emphasis rep-

---

[1] Ibid., p. 587.
[2] Ibid., pp. 578, 580 et passim.

resents a transfer of religious fervor from the erstwhile individual religious experience, which has been virtually outlawed to an emphasis on social ethics.

KARL BARTH'S CONCEPTION

The name of Karl Barth came to be popular in America during the last years of the prosperous era with the appearance of his "Word of God and Word of Man" in an American translation. Barth, by some, is considered too extreme and reactionary in his theological thinking; while by others he is characterized as the greatest thinker since Schliermacher. He is credited with having saved Protestantism in Germany. At the center of his theology stands a God high and lifted up, totally apart from man. The wide acceptance of this exalted view of God, Sweet says, is but the natural reaction against a watered-down God. Books began to be written which were calculated to check the sliding of Protestant teaching and preaching into humanistic paths. Without these writings and their influence it is feared that the Protestant church would have been doomed. Barthian teachings tended to bring into fresh focus, the neglected emphasis upon personal religion. He held that the transcendant God is still concerned about saving individual souls, but allows the world for the most part to shift for itself. God alone, he contends, can transform the structure of society; but He is not interested in society, His concern is to attend and assist the individual soul in its passage into eternity, for the victory of God is achieved "not in history, but beyond history." In contradiction to the liberal views, Barth considers every attempt to correct evil conditions and to right wrongs in human society as "not only futile but presumptuous." The liberal's doctrine of Divine Immanence is thus seen to be directly opposite to the unknowable of God of the Barthians.[1]

Thus, it is seen that our view of God definitely determines our doctrinal thinking. The influence of liberal theology has measurably manifested itself in the emphasis on the Social Gospel. But this tendency to preach a social gospel was incipient and was an inchoate force several decenniums prior to the decades since the twenties, as will be pointed out.

---

1 Sweet, Op Cit., pp. 584-590 et passim.

Atkins states that "the nineteenth Christian century bequeathed to twentieth century Christianiy four distinct tasks: (1) the adaptation of the inherited faith to the conclusions of science, (2) critical history and the new psychology, (3) the examination and re-interpretation of its sacred books, (4) the discovery of a changed appeal, the Christian recasting of society."[1] "Anyone of these four," he adds, "was challenging enough to demand the whole force and intelligence of Christianity."[1]

SOME CHARACTERISTIC TRENDS

Here is as good a place, perhaps, as any for this writer to affirm that there are many distinctly valuable teachings associated with the social gospel which are a needed emphasis in Christendom. Its emphases cannot be wholeheartedly accepted, however, since a dominant portion of its advocates are indisputedly liberals who reject the New Birth as a supernatural experience and deny the fact of personal or original sin. It has been demonstrated that their teachings of the Immanence of God are the outgrowth of their own sense of self-sufficiency and elevated conception of themselves. Its votaries reflect an attitude of being able to work out their own salvation somewhat independently of God's help. Their disbelief in a literal resurrection and the personal appearing of Christ in a second advent has caused them to over-emphasize this present world and to neglect the needed emphasis upon, "other-worldliness," which has characterized the teachings of best saints of all previous ages. Because the resurrection and future advent of Christ are cardinal doctrines, and are vital to genuine religious experience, they cannot be relinquished for the sake of unity nor for any other reason.

Atkins' comments are significant here. He says:

> The doctrinally conservative were suspicious of the social gospel or positively hostile. It was associated with a theology they suspected and tarred with the same stick. It was, they thought and did not hesitate to say heatedly, a deflection from the true gospel, a devise of those who had no essential religious message to find something to preach about. Which was true enough to have an edge to it.[2]

---

1 Atkins, Op Cit., p. 46.
2 Op cit., p. 65.

Principally due to the fact that liberals have rejected the supernatural and have therefore neglected to teach the necessity of the supernatural new birth, they have been forced to look in various directions to find something about which to preach. Atkins points out that the social gospel has thus been a life preserver for twentieth century preaching. Ministers, sensitive to the bearing of science and psychology upon their inherited beliefs, were getting hard pressed to find anything to preach which bore creatively upon life. The curricula of seminaries were recast to train social gospel ministers and hymn books were revised to coincide with this new emphasis.[1]

He illustrates the changes made in the conventional-type hymns which are interesting examples of this changed emphasis:

'There is a land of pure delight' has gone from up-to-date hymn books. The devout no longer stand on 'Jordan's stormy banks'; they wait for the green light
 'Where cross the crowded ways of life
 Where sound and cries of race and clan.'
And something has gone. The old hymns sung by quivering voices and read by dim eyes which had no need of the text were the marching music of pilgrims for whom earth and its shadows were only a stage on the road to heaven, there eternal day would exclude the night and pleasure banish pain. This confidence in one form or another has hitherto been the sustaining power of all religion.[2]

Dr. T. T. Shields, in an address on Modernism delivered at the Calvary Baptist Church of New York City, of which William Ward Ayer is pastor, stated, "I believe that it would not be an exaggeration to say that not more than one per cent of the ministers who have accepted the modernist's position have originated the ideas they have espoused." Mention is made here of his remark in order to add the statement that there are many fine Christian brethren of excellent character who have doubtless become the exponents of the social gospel without having recognized the destructive force of modern liberalism in which it roots; and who should not be severely criticized but patiently informed in the spirit of Christian love and brotherliness. Reason and persuasion should take the place of sternness and rebuke.

---
1 Atkins, **Op. Cit.**, pp. 60, 65.
2 Ibid., p. 61.

CONTEMPORARY APPRAISALS

Dr. M. R. DeHaan makes the following categorical statements in his stern denunciation of the Social Gospel,

There is not one verse in the scripture which states that this age will end in a revival that will see all men saved. There is not one verse in the Bible to give the faintest encouragement to the unbiblical teaching that the so-called 'leaven' of the Gospel will finally permeate society and the teachings of Christ, the Golden Rule and the Sermon on the Mount will so change the hearts of men that they will all come to know Christ and the millennium will be here. This has never been the program of God. Instead, according to Acts 15, He is calling out a people. The very word 'church' in the Greek means a 'called out company.' The word is ecclesia, from two other words: ek, meaning 'out' and kaleo, meaning 'to call.' God is calling out a few here and there to make up the body of His elect Church. There is no wholesale salvation. At Pentecost there were 3,000 saved but this was only a 'drop in the bucket' compared with the tens of thousands who were celebrating the feast in Jerusalem on that day.

Many people believe the gospel has failed because after nineteen hundred years of Gospel preaching the world is yet unconverted, yea seems to be farther from God now than ever before. They imagine that something must be wrong because nineteen hundred years after the Prince of Peace came we are engaged in the greatest and most demoniacal war of all time. The Post-millennialist who had been preaching a so-called gospel and education and reform has abandoned his dream and taken refuge in the rickety and still more untenable theory of Amillennialism. This results from his failure to understand the mystery of the body of Christ. It was never God's program to convert the world in this dispensation. On the contrary, the Bible teaches clearly that this age will end in apostasy and wickedness, war and destruction. God's program does not call for conversion of the world now, but the opposite. This is the very point of James' speech at the first council at Jerusalem. Though we have quoted him before, look at his words again:

> Simeon hath declared how God at the first did visit the Gentiles, to take out of them a people for his name (Acts 15: 14).

This verse says nothing about the conversion of the world. Rather, He is taking out some from among the Gentiles. These are members of the body of Christ. They are the mystery members, from every tribe, race and nation who by faith in Jesus' shed blood are made partakers of His grace and constitute that comparatively small group of true born-again believers in every age. Then He tells us that after that body has been taken out He will return.

> After this I will return, and will build again the tabernacle of David, which is fallen down; and I will build again the ruins thereof, and I will set it up (Acts 16:16).

Following the taking out of the Church, the Lord will restore the kingdom of David and Israel, and then will come world revival and conversion, as is plainly stated in the next verse:
That the residue of men might seek after the Lord, and all Gentiles, upon whom my name is called, saith the Lord, who doeth all these things. Known unto God are all his works from the beginning of the world (Acts 15: 17-18).

How strange that men with open Bibles should still dream of a better world and federation of nations and universal peace without the re-establishment of the kingdom after the personal return of the King.[1]

While Dr. DeHaan has apparently not recognized any value at all to be derived from the preaching of the social gospel, it is fair to add that he would perhaps be willing to admit its relative value, but that he is bitterly opposed to the liberalism out of which it emanates.

Earle V. Pierce has this to say against the watered-down theology of the liberals:

The Church can and must proclaim sound doctrine if it is to have revival and life for its evangelistic and ethical tasks. The coldness of the dead theology which Dr. Cutten deplored is not its greatest evil. It was cold because it was dead. It has denied the very truths which are the life of Christianity. Liberalism in religion has had long enough time to prove its nature and power or lack of it, and it is the lack which has been proved. Evangelism and the services of prayer have dwindled and have disappeared under its blighting influence, as many have confessed. Many times in the history of the Church there has been a cold and sterile orthodoxy, but that has been because of spiritual decadence of the people; the truth has been there, but it has lacked life. But where truth as well as life has been lacking, the Church has made a sorry exhibition of paralysis of its vital functions.

For many years doctrine has been decried. It is a healthy and hopeful sign of returning sanity that quite generally it is being recognized that doctrine is the very soul of life. Next to prayer, the need for today is a reproclaiming with great conviction the basic, cardinal, fundamental dogmas of the Church of the supernatural (or superphysical, if you please) powers of God, as manifested in the production of His Word, the Bible, as exhibited in the person and work of His Son, as shown in the regeneration wrought by the Holy Spirit. People are manifestly hungry today for a true sincere, and earnest exposition of the great truths of sacred Scriptures.

The philosophy of unproved and unprovable evolution has developed the poison of materialism until the "soul of society" is stagnated.

---

[1] M. R. DeHaan, **The Second Coming of Jesus.** (Grand Rapids: Zondervan Publishing House, 1944), pp. 109-111.

There needs to be a great transfusion of the blood of Christ, for bloodless theologies have brought on a pernicious religious anemia. T. R. Glover, before he left us, sent forth an alarm that those hymns exalting "the blood of the Lamb," which he says is "the central point of all history," have largely disappeared from our hymnals. For great revival there is needed great preaching, and great preaching is the proclamalation of the great truths of God and of His redemption of us through His Son. Every great revival has come through the re-emphasis of great neglected truths. There has been a woeful decadence in the preaching which produced the victorious Church of former days. Men can eloquently ring the changes of the day and of social cures, but this can never take the place of preaching the great word of redemption through the crucified and risen Son of God. The evangelists of the world have been the evangelists of the Word.[1]

While these quotations are unusual in length they are deemed as essential for an adequate and clear understanding of the subject.

ITS ASSOCIATIONS AND UTILITARIAN ASPECTS

In the complex society of current times we have unconsciously, but gradually, come to emphasize those aspects which tend toward socialism. Socialism seeks to narrow the range of human personality and accommodate it to fit the total program of society. In the process, our individualism is being submerged. Private initiative is stifled by the utilitarianism which came into vogue in the middle of the nineteenth century as an adjunct to German liberalism. Higher aspirations are being lost. Such is reflected in the evident scarcity of truly great Christian leaders of equal calibre to those of past generations. Our spiritual decline seems to be inversely in proportion to our material and scientific advancement. The social gospel appears to encourage in the realm of religion this same tendency to submerge the individual and utilize him as a cog in the wheel which turns the social community of which he is a part. The emphasis of the social gospel is thus seen to be not on the individual's worth, nor on individual salvation or ethics, but it is almost exclusively on society as a corporate unit.

We Americans have observed continental Europe on the march as they, with blind enthusiasm, have followed the "lock-step" political philosophies advocated under dictatorships. Communism

---

1 Earle V. Pierce, **The Church and World Conditions**. (New York: Fleming H. Revell Company, 1943), pp. 117, 118.

in Russia, Nazism in Germany, and Fascism in Italy represent types of socialism in which the individual has become a mere cog in the wheel. He exists merely to extend the total program of utilitarianism designed to bring the greatest happiness to the greatest number in society. Their aims were realized substantially by means of the best time-proved method, the state-controlled public-school system where their constituency came to know and revere their particular political philosophy.

All this may seem rather remote but it is fundamental to any understanding of religion in our times. For it was in this manner that liberalism came into vogue among our religious institutions which were destined to produce such manifestations as the social gospel. As has been pointed out, before we had developed respectable graduate schools our students habituated themselves to these new ideas by repairing to German universities where they imbibed German liberalism. These more highly educated graduate students were naturally chosen to occupy chairs in our institutions of higher learning, where they wielded their academic influence and molded an unwary generation into patterns according to their own design. A gradual infiltration of liberal theology came to crystalize into theological concepts which ultimately have produced the status quo of current times with its damaging effects which virtually defy alteration.

THE SOCIAL GOSPEL'S INADEQUACY BEGINNING TO BE RECOGNIZED

Studious observers in the conventional churches are coming to recognize the advances which are being made within the ranks of competitive sect groups which have been heretofore looked upon with a somewhat disdainful attitude. They have begun to study their policies and techniques in the hope that their findings will point the way out of their spiritual dilemma. While pursuing this course of action of research and inquiry they have overlooked the basic underlying fallacy, which if it goes uncorrected, will persist in retarding their spiritual progress and will ultimately spell failure, disintegration and death. Undue emphasis has come to be placed upon the physical well-being of man at the sacrifice of his spiritual need which only God can satisfy through faith on the part of the individual—not through the mere physical betterment of society.

Muncy presents a fine summary of the inadequacy of the social gospel. He writes:

There are some grave dangers in present trends. The greatest danger lies in shallow thinking that men may fit into a Christian social order who are not themselves Christians. Unregenerate men are not stable foundation stones for the new structure. Another peril is that Christians and Christian leaders may lose sight of the individual in an effort to deal with men en masse. A prominent leader said recently, that there is very little conviction for personal sin in society of today and there is much conviction for corporate sin. Men as individuals are not directly responsible for much of the evil of our time. This leader concludes that preachers ought to condemn the sins of groups—the capitalists or labor organizations or political parties. This is true but our Lord's witness must never forget that men as individuals are sinners against God and must repent and believe individually. It is well to condemn corporate sin but it must be remembered that corporate sin is. but the sum of sins of all members of the group. One may preach about sins of capitalism with earnestness and convincing logic but no capitalist will repent until he faces the fact that the sin of his own life is the root of the whole matter.[1]

THE SOCIAL GOSPEL TENDS TO CHANGE AN UNCHANGING GOSPEL

The methods of presenting the gospel are necessarily revised and altered to adapt the gospel to an ever-changing society but the essence of the gospel itself remains the same. Dr. Archie Ray in his thesis, "Sowing In Many Waters," on file at the Union Theological Seminary, centers his whole discussion around the theme—that there are many ways of presenting the gospel but the gospel itself is constant. The gospel is as immutable as the God who gave it by inspiration. It is intended for men of all ages, climes and races. This fact does not close the mind to new truth but insists that the corporate body of Biblical truth itself never diminishes or increases. Man has no prerogative whereby he is licensed to add to or take from God's revelation. When man has disregarded this simple law which God has enacted to preserve His redemptive truth, others have been chosen who will faithfully prosecute His program.

Garrison, in referring to the various forms of evangelism resultant from efforts to adapt it to the changing demands of the public ear, mentions a number of evangelists to illustrate the widely differeng types of appeal but adds that:

---

[1] Muncy, Op. Cit., pp. 184, 185.

Evangelism not only revived the methods that had been effective in pioneer days but freely adopted new methods to catch the public ear; but it stood fast against any invasion of modern thought into the area of Christian doctrine. In general, the evangelists have resisted the 'new view of the Bible' and emphasized individual salvation by obedience to its commands and belittled and often denounced the newer stress upon the social gospel.[1]

THE SOCIAL GOSPEL IS BASED ON LIBERAL THEOLOGY

While there are conflicting differences of opinion as to the jurisdiction of such criticism, it would seem that the liberals' repudiation of vital Christian doctrine would necessitate a firm counteracting of its teachings. John Horsch makes a sweeping summary statement which commends itself as being worthy of quoting here. He says:

Modern theology rejects the Bible teaching on man's sinfulness and the Biblical conception of the world. The 'exceeding sinfulness of in,' the existence of Satan and his kingdom, and the need of supernatural salvation are denied. For the Bible message of 'personal reconstruction' the social gospel substitutes the call to social reconstruction. For true spiritual religion we are offered a substitute having no other purpose than to make the world a decent place to live in. The new gospel is the gospel of eternalism. It is assumed that favorable external conditions will bring about the moral regeneration of society and that human nature will respond automatically to its better environment. Salvation is to come through civic, economic, social and political remedies. (Certain defenders of the social gospel tell us that until man's economic desires have been satisfied, it is both useless and illogical to preach to him morality and spirituality.) To Christianize the social order, rather than the individual, or in other words, to make the world a decent place to live in, is supposed to be the great task of the church.

The social gospel therefore lays enormous emphasis on a man's physical and material well-being. Religion is held to be nothing more than a plan for social welfare. Christianity, being considered a scheme of social improvements, is reduced to humanitarian and social endeavors. It is interpreted in terms of materialistic humanitarianism. Education and sanitation take the place of personal regeneration and the Holy Spirit. True spiritual Christianity is denied.

The social gospel is in fact religiously indifferent. It holds that the difference between Christianity and other religions is in degree, not in kind. Yet the social gospel comes under the cloak of religion. We are told that the spirit of loyalty and devotion shown toward modern

---

1 Garrison, op. cit., p. 78.

social endeavors deserves the name of religion and Christianity. "The man who enters thoroughly into the social movements of his time," says Professor Edward Scribner Ames, of the University of Chicago, "is to that extent genuinely religious, though he may characterize himself quite otherwise (i. e., though he may be an avowed unbeliever).[1]

Such liberal teachings would allow a Bob Ingersoll, or any other man who might have made some contribution to social welfare, to be admitted into the Christian fellowship and become, therefore, a constituent part of the "body of Christ." Such teachings are, of course, inadmissable among orthodox worshippers. While there are varying degrees of liberals and hence notable exceptions, in the main, its advocates to some degree, as a rule, fall into the class described.

THE SOCIAL GOSPEL DESERVES A LEGITIMATE EMPHASIS

Atkins points out that there are some who blame the reformation for the creation of capitalism and an acquisitive society. This, however, is untenable.[2] There has been, however, considerable neglect of social conditions on the part of the church and a failure to understand the needs of society. No careful study of this problem had been made until recent years by the Church as a corporate unit, though some sporadic efforts have been expended in isolated instances. Garrison states that eagerness for wealth in the prosperous era which followed the Civil War period of reconstruction relatively blinded the minds of both secular and religious leaders to the needs of the workers.[3] The people were more shocked by strikers than by the conditions which caused the strikes.[4] The question was whether a thing was profitable or unprofitable rather than whether it was right or wrong.[5] There was manifestly a definite relationship between the rise of Labor Unions and the attitude of the Church in its failure to wield a wholesome and telling influence in behalf of the working men.

Washington Gladden and Rauschenbusch were pioneers in the placing of emphasis on the church's social task.[6] Garrison con-

---
1 John Horsch, op. cit., pp. 127, 129 et passim.
2 Atkins, op. cit., p. 47.
3 Garrison, op. cit., p. 63.
4 Garrison, op. cit., p. 64.
5 Atkins, op. cit., p. 47.
6 Garrison, op. cit., p. 64.

THE SOCIAL GOSPEL   39

tributes the following information relative to the introduction of
this social task of the Church. He says:

Washington Gladden, born in 1836, one of the editors of the Independent from 1871-75, did his great pastoral work for the First Congregational Church, Columbus, Ohio, but a greater work still as a leader in the new movement for the socialization of religion. Theological thought was not his primary interest, but his liberal tendencies coupled with his devotion to social enterprises as not merely humanitarian but as an essential function did much to win followers of the newer views.[1]

Atkins calls our attention to the more mature developments of the Church's social mission. He writes:

The lines which Gladden and Rauschenbusch opened were followed by an increasing number of religious leaders and followed deeper and more analytically. Such as these began to draw the outlines, at least, of what a Christian society ought, according to their mind, to be. In December 1908, The Federal Council of Churches of Christ in America adopted what has come to be known as 'The Social Creed of the Churches.'

This was a highly significant document for three reasons. For the first time in the history of Christianity an attempt was made to define Christianity in terms of the ethics of Jesus instead of the theological speculations of the fourth and fifth century Greek-Church councils. The Creed represented the maximum agreement of the churches composing the Council on the contours of a right Christian social order. And leaving out 'Christian'—which provocative word is not in the Creed at all—it is, as far as the writer knows, one of the earliest coherent programs of social amelioration to be realized through education, legislation and industrial readjustment submitted in America. (Atkins lists the social creed in full).[2]

Sydney G. Dimond, in his scholarly and significant work dealing with "The Psychology of the Methodist Revival" sanely appraises and analyses the social value of the work of John Wesley. He writes:

Society is nothing but individuals in relation, and 'the proposal to banish the thought of personal salvation in the name of advancing spirituality or social progress is strange folly.'

Philosophy and psychology alike are suffering from an over-emphasis upon social evolution. It would be futile to say that the group mind or the common will would have recovered living religion in the

---
[1] Ibid., p. 95.
[2] Atkins, op. cit., p. 56, 57.

eighteenth century without the work of John Wesley, or that the general effort of the community would have liberated the mind of Europe in the sixteenth century if the counsels of Erasmus had prevailed instead of the explosive methods of Luther. History has its own logic, and there is a salt and salutary quality in the religious conviction which sustains Athanasius or Antigone against the world. Moreover spiritual illumination is individual, and while the matter of Methodist church history may be social and moral, its form is individual and religious.[1]

While we can never fellowship with the extreme liberal and accept teachings which are diametrically opposed to those of the orthodox, historical Christian Church, this should not blind us to the valid emphases of the social gospel which are designed for the amelioration of society. We can cooperate as a Church with any agency whose purpose it is to help our fellowman, whether it be secular or religious. The social gospel does have a legitimate place in the program of the Christian Church, but it should never be substituted for the divine and supernatural work of the Holy Spirit to produce conviction and conversion of individuals. Though it be cliche, it is ever needful to say, "Ye must be born again"!

This challenging subject with which we have dealt is almost inexhaustible in its scope and invites extended treatment; but this is not possible nor perhaps needful for our present purpose. It would seem well, in conclusion, to quote Dr. B. R. Lacy's rationally sound and impartial apprasial of both sides of the question. He says that,

> The so-called Social Gospel made its appeal to many individuals and organizations which formerly had devoted their time, thought and efforts in converting the individual, building him up in the Christian graces, and extending the Kingdom through missionary efforts. Conferences and conventions which at one time consisted of addresses on evangelism, missions, and personal piety now were taken up with the consideration of the problem of race, industry, war, and other matters involving man's relationship to man in the social, political and economic order. Many think that much ground was lost in evangelism by the disputes between the advocates of the Gospel of Personal Redemption and the enthusiasts of the Social Gospel. The former deplored any preaching and effort that went beyond a Gospel for the Individual,

---

[1] Sydney C. Dimond, **The Psychology of the Methodist Revival.** (Nashville: Whitmore and Smith, Agents, 1934), pp. 265, 266.

while the enthusiasts for the Social Message had little patience with those whose primary interest was the salvation of the soul of the individual. The mutual understanding and the adjustment of these two groups to the ideas and aims of each other may be prophetic of a new revival in which both elements will be preserved.[1]

Parallel with Dr. Lacy's remarks might well be added those of Dr. W. W. Sweet who writes,

Revivalism, as it has run its course in America, has been primarily the individualizing of religion. It has often been blind to the sins of society, sins that cannot be reached by merely converting individuals. But if religion is to continue as a vital force in America, it must not lose the personal and individual emphasis. At the same time it must concern itself about the sins of society.[2]

Such an attitude, in the estimate of this writer, is the only one which the Christian should maintain. It must be recognized that there are Christian brethren who advocate each of these types of religious programs. But, as a solemn warning to those who have fallen onto the fatal error of rejecting the new birth, we would quote the pertinent words recorded in John 1:12, 13; "But as many as received him to them gave he power to become the sons of God, even to them that believe on his name: which are born, not of blood, nor of the will of the flesh, not of the will of man, but of God."

We come to analyse, next, the bases of The New Psychology of Religious Education and attempt to appraise its relative value as an instrument for the promotion of the kingdom of God.

---

[1] Lacy, **Op. Cit.**, p. 156.
[2] Sweet, op. cit., **Revivalism in America**, p. 182.

B. THE NEW PSYCHOLOGY OF RELIGIOUS EDUCATION

It would be needless to enter into a lengthy discussion to set forth the merits of educational evangelism and its Scriptural validity. It is common knowledge that the Christian Church has always recognized the value of teaching in the home, in the Sunday School, and in specialized types of Bible study. Great strides have been made in the field of Christian education. An intelligent presentation of Christian doctrine and truth is of incalculable value and of permanent benefit in preparing an individual to make an intelligent commitment as well as to bring about a mature development in the Christian way of life. There are doubtless no differences of opinion nor controversy in regard to these accepted facts. Christian nurture and education are one of the chief interests of the Christian Church.

But according to Horsch, "Modern liberalism has substituted 'religious' education for 'Christian' education."[1] Niebuhr points out that there has been a substitution of education for conversion.[2] Machen also discusses the relative value of the right and wrong use of religious education. His approach commends itself as being a worthy evaluation of these two types of education prevalent in the Church. He explains:

> At the beginning of every Christian life there stands not a process, but a definite act of God. That does not mean that every Christian can tell exactly at what moment he was justified or born again.... But on the other hand it is a mistake to demand that it should be universal. There are Christians who can give the day and the hour of their conversion, but the great majority do not know at exactly what moment they were saved. The effects of the act are plain but the act itself is done in the quietness of God. Such, very often, is the experience of children brought up by Christian parents. It is not necessary that all pass through agonies of soul before being saved; there are those to whom

---

1 Horsch, **Op. Cit.,** p. 158.
2 H. Richard Niebuhr, **Social Sources of Denominationalism,** p. 13.

faith comes peacefully and easily through nurture of the Christian home.[1]

It is a fact, as Machen observes, that some do come into a genuine Christian experience through Christian nurture who are never able to point to a definite time element involved in the change. It is also true that the wrong type of religious education has resulted in the reception of many into the fellowship of the Church who have been inadequately prepared to take so vital and important a step. Sunday school classes have been garnered into the Church prematurely and without possessing an intelligent conception of the meaning of Christianity. Clark, in speaking of the conversion experience, states that modern religious, education has to an extent failed to recognize that the psychological processes such as conviction, repentance and emotional reactions are produced by God and are preparatory to conversion and regeneration. His explanation of the "new type" of conversion experience is well worth reading and challenges the serious thought of all those who are interested in the spiritual welfare of the Church. He says:

Conversion is assumed when it has never occurred—at least when nothing has occurred which is covered by any reasonable or accepted definition of that experience. This is true not only of sects but of the great denominations. Most of the latter also hold in theory to the necessity of conversion and insist theoretically on a converted membership; at least few would care to admit that they welcome unconverted persons into the fold. But relatively few of their members, certainly the younger members, have experienced conversion in the New Testament sense or even in the plain English meaning of the term. A study of more than two thousands individuals, mostly young people, of the major Protestant groups has shown that above 66 percent never underwent any kind of experience that could be called conversion, but attained to such a degree of religious consciousness as they possessed by a process of gradual growth unmarked by any recognizable emotional features; more than 27 percent had no experience other than the slight emotional stimulus involved in joining the church or responding to a 'decision day' appeal; and only 6.7 percent remembered a definite crisis type. The same study showed that the percentage of those in the last group was much larger among persons above forty years of age, those taught the older and sterner 'heaven and hell' theology, and those whose religious training had been inadequate.

---

[1] J. Gresham Machen, **Christianity and Liberalism**, (New York: The Macmillan Company, 1924) pp. 140, 141.

Thus the trend is definitely away from the crisis conversion experiences under the influence of a milder theology and modern religious culture. To preserve the theory of a definite conversion as essential to Christian life it has been necessary to so define conversion as to empty it of its former accepted meaning.[1]

Because of this unbalanced emphasis the moderns which such a culpable technique has produced are devoid of that religious vitality which is exhilirating enough to issue in serious Christian service. Conversion experiences which were once normal and easily discerned by commonly recognized standards of behaviour have, today, become extremely difficult to discern. The lax and somewhat loose standards set for the conversion experience have opened wide the gate for worldliness to flood the Church, and to virtually erase the line of demarcation which had formerly separated between the Church and the world. The average communion admits men who smoke, drink, gamble, lie, attend places of worldly amusement and retain practically every other worldly habit but who boldly claim to be Christians. Actually they are only church members. They know nothing of the new birth and exhibit scarcely any scriptural evidence of Christianity. Men are deluded. Elmer G. Homrighausen, in his widely read book, "Choose Ye This Day," refers to this delusion of Christendom in the following quotation:

> The delusion of Christendom of which Kirkengaard spoke is no longer a matter of debate. So called 'Christian civilization' is no longer a reality—if it ever was! The churches are filled with persons who joined the Church but who never had a profound Christian experience. It will no longer do to regard the whole nation as Christian. It will no longer do to think of Christian theology in terms of ideas which are casually accepted and discussed. Such cultural Christianity and Christian theology are today being tested by fire. Nothing less than genuine conversion involving decision and commitment can make a true theologian or true Church. The theologian and the Church must believe utterly in the gospel.[2]

It is not possible to understand these current trends without giving some attention to the underlying causes which lie beneath the surface. These new trends are directly traceable to the in-

---

[1] Elmer T. Clark, op. cit., pp. 279, 280.
[2] Elmer T. Homrighausen, Choose Ye This Day. (Philadelphia: The Westminster Press), p. 26.

fluences of modern liberal theology which has run parallel with our secular advances in the field of scientific endeavor.

Garrison,[1] in his book, "The March of Faith" chose to deal with the period since the Civil War because of the significant changes in both Church and state when fresh starts were made in both of these spheres or fields. He refers to the impact of modern science and Biblical criticism and the new theology. Reference is also made to the rise of the religious education movement, the quickened social conscience of the Church and the new attitude toward Church unity. These new emphases, as we have already noted, are shown to relate to and root in the rise of modern liberalism and the new theology.

Atkins in his book, "Religion in Our Times," also refers to the same characteristic trend of this period since the Civil War which in actuality represents a conflict between the forces of liberalism and conservatism or, if better understood, the struggle between fundamentalists and modernists. He says:

> Revivalism furnished a technique to which the emphasis upon religious education and nurture, so emergingly evident, began forty years ago to oppose—and of which Northfield schools were themselves an anticipation. It fixed and heightened the theologies about which rather thunderous controversy of the 'fundamentalists' and 'modernists' have carried on.[2]

The rising interest in religious education perhaps grew largely out of a religious situation which had been created as a result of what had come to be considered as faulty revival technique. With the passing of the American frontier it was thought that the revivalistic methods which had been employed advantageously among these rugged pioneers was no longer needed in a more intellectually advanced society which was fast becoming urbanized. In this dominantly urban population there was no longer seen a need for vigorous emotional expression nor a necessity to furnish diversion from the dull and isolated life which had hitherto colored these hordes of westward-moving rural masses. In spite of this new trend in thinking, Moody[3] and his successors continued to pack the largest halls in the largest cities and won

---

1 Garrison, op. cit., p. viii.
2 Atkins, op. cit., p. 18.
3 Garrison, op. cit., p. 78.

converts by the thousands. It is fair to mention here that some claim that those converted in Moody's services were largely composed of derelict church-members and others of adult ages.

Men in some church circles, however, began to look with suspicion upon these methods of mass-evangelism and because of the defections of many of the converts, began to question the validity of the emotional type of conversion. They saw in at least some of these religious experiences emotional extravagances to be avoided. This trend toward the "right" resulted in a study being made of the conversion experience in the hope that a more sane type of evangelistic approach could be developed. The relative value of such a study is to be appreciated, but in its swing to the right it has come to exclude the necessary and valid emotional experience which should attend the conversion experience in some degree if it is to be genuine. Garrison states, "Just how much emotion is excessive is a question upon which judgments will always differ."[1]

Harry C. Munro, in his book, "Educational Evangelism" well states the case as follows:

> Christian education needs to know and take account of the important place of feelings in religious life. Evangelism needs to know and take account of the many other phases of experience involved in consistent Christian living. They need each other. All Christian education needs a deep and warm undertone of feelings. All Christian evangelism needs a rich content of Christian teaching and ethical living. The closer these two phases of work keep together, the stronger and better balanced they are.[2]

Dr. Donald W. Richardson, Dean of the Graduate Department of Union Theological Seminary of Richmond, comprehends the need of the same type of well-balanced program in his terse but meaningful definition of Christianity. He declares that, "Christianity is a message to be proclaimed; a teaching to be understood; a life to be lived; and an experience to be felt. No one of these elements should be neglected. The teaching is the foundation upon which the life is to be built. There are great facts and truths that need to be taught if we are to have religiously literate Christians."

---

[1] Garrison, **op. cit.**, p. 295.
[2] Harry C. Munro, **Educational Evangelism**. (Chicago: Published by the National Christian Teachers Mission), p. 5.

This writer knows of no better summary of the whole matter than these lines from Dr. William Warren Sweet, an outstanding contemporary historian whose works have been widely accepted in many quarters. In his thrilling book, "Revivalism in America," he says:

> Revivalism has been responsible for over-emphasizing the emotional and underestimating the rational element in religious experience.... Christianity has never been simply emotional fervor, much less.... fanaticism or superstition. To use Davenport's words. 'It becometh not religion to disparge reason.' On the other hand religion is more than reason and intellect; it is fundamentally a great emotion and a plan of life. Most of our decisions are made emotionally. In certain realms of life, emotion is a better guide than reason. And that is more true in the higher realm of life than in the lower. Our homes are built on the basis of a great emotion; men and women undertake the great sacrificial duties of life carried forward by a great emotion.[1]

The lack of emphasis on a clear-cut conversion experience with a reasonable amount of emotional content is better understood when we come to recognize that much of our present emphasis on religious education is, quite unknowingly to many, influenced and governed by liberal forces. When we take into account that liberalism rules out the supernatural, rejects the new birth, ignores the fact of sin both personal and inherited, makes no place for the confession of sin and has in it no definite doctrinal content; we need not be surprised at the discovery of the inadequacy and impotency of much of this method to produce real Christians. The corollary to such a body of teaching is a minimizing of the work of Christ and His substitutionary atonement. While the liberal's program does possess some merit, it unquestionably lacks a saving quality.

To validate the claims of this writer we have but to consider the historic facts involved in the inception of the modern's liberal program of religious education. Garrison, in his discussion of the subject calls attention to these regnant influences in the following succinct statement:

> With the rising interest in child psychology and the problems of education, the hope of the Church came to be placed in Christian nurture rather than in the short-cuts to glory which revivalism has held out to hardened sinners. This substitution of growth in grace as

---

[1] Sweet, **Revivalism,** p. 145.

a normal aspect of human development in the place of the cataclysmic conversion was not in itself an absolutely new discovery. Horace Bushnell has stated it in his 'Christian Nurture' in 1857, a volume almost as revolutionary in its implications as far as the popular churches were concerned as the 'Origin of Species' by Darwin which appeared two years later. By the beginning of the twentieth century the cult of the child acquired new popularity, the index of which was a growing interest in religious education and the diminishing reliance of the churches upon revivalism.[1]

These were onslaughts of modern thought against the cherished teachings of the Church which caused no little concern. Garrison's further comment focalizes our attention on the liberal teachings upon which these new emphases are based. The reader will be amply repaid to incorporate the following statements into his body of thought. Garrison continues:

> Horace Bushnell, of Hartford Connecticut, has started a trend of thought with his 'Christian Nurture,' revised and republished in 1861. Unitarians had, to be sure, long ago challenged the conception of original sin, human depravity and miraculous regeneration, but it had challenged so many other things besides that its arguments carried little weight in orthodox circles. Bushnell was a Congregational minister of high repute, working in the very center of orthodoxy, for Hartford Seminary had been established in 1834 because Yale was not Orthodox enough. Revivalism in the period before the Civil War, as well as in the period immediately after, and to a large extent down to now, was based on the assumption that the normal process of conversion involves a violent internal revolution and sudden change in the nature, status and character of the convert. The gist of Bushnell's teaching was that the child of the Christian community and the Christian home ought to develop naturally into a Christian without realizing that he was ever anything else, and without any shattering emotional experiences of conversion. The implications of this humane idea were these: First, it laid stress upon the responsibility of the church and the home for Christian education, and gave a rational basis for that work of religious education which had already been started in the Sunday School movement. Second, it intensified and rationalized the opposition to the revivalistic method of conversion, especially as applied to the young. While the great revivalists like Finney and Moody had had their most spectacular success in winning sinners who obviously were sinners, the popular churches had come to rely very largely upon revivals as a means of harvesting the young who grew up within them and never became prodigals. The tendency was to treat all persons, young and old, who were not for-

---

1 Garrison, op. cit., pp. 78, 79.

mally enrolled in the church as though they were prodigal sons. And third, it affected theological thought by stressing the moral in contrast to the substitutionary theory of atonement, and by introducing a certain naturalism into the whole religious process. The fact that Bushnell was rated by many as a heretic and that his own church, in standing by him, was finally moved to withdraw from the Congregational consociation to which it had belonged, probably increased rather than diminished his influence in the long run, and he continued until 1876 to be a potent and beneficent influence upon the thinking and practice of the church. The view held by Bushnell and delivered by him to a local congregation and to the ministers who read his book were popularized by Beecher, who had the nation for his audience, and by other liberal-minded thinkers and writers who commanded smaller constituencies.[1]

Atkins in his discussion of "New Forces and Old Faith" says plainly of Bushnell, "His leveling and enlightening intellect greatly influenced liberal preaching of a generation later."[2]

Garrison refers to the subsidizing of religious liberalism. In subsequent paragraphs, apparently without attaching any particular significance to his statements as relating to the influences of such liberalism, he enumerates what he terms "a multiplicity of problems which if not new were at least presented in more complex form." He mentions shift of population to urban areas; social problems; experiments in religious education and the secularizing of our denominational colleges to compete with the rapid growth of state universities. The Carnegie Pension Fund is also mentioned as making provision for teachers of colleges not under denominational control.[3]

Moody Bible Institute and The Bible Institute of Los Angeles were organized as bulwarks against modernism. The Niagara Bible Conference organized in 1876 formulated the famous "five points of fundamentalism" in 1895. Such well known men as A. J. Gordon, Arthur T. Pierson, C. I. Scofield and James M. Gray were its leaders. Bible Conferences sprung up here and there; Moody at Northfield; Torrey at Montrose, Pennsylvania, Sunday at Winona Lake, etc., wielded their influences. While these developments may largely have been to combat liberalism, they also were no doubt the result of the influences of this "child of

---

[1] Garrison, op. cit., pp. 88, 89.
[2] Atkins, op. cit., p. 18.
[3] Garrison, op. cit., pp. 134, 231, 232, et passim.

liberalism" the New Psychology of Religious Education. Moody and other far-sighted evangelists sensed the need of teaching their converts, but it is very doubtful that any of them would have incorporated these new techniques as a substitute for the conversion experience. It is feared that in this new emphasis is to be found one reason for the ever-pyramiding increase of people in the Church who have never been born again.

Niebuhr makes a very revealing observation which is a definite contribution toward the understanding of these liberal trends. His words forcefully bring into the open the root-cause to be found in rationalism and humanism and nineteenth century science. He states:

> Finally, Calvinism was modified so as to assume a more definitely middle-class character through the influence of humanism and rationalism, and nineteenth century science. The middle classes developed their interest in liberal movements of thought because of the education which their economic circumstances enabled them to afford, because of the close relationship existing between rationalism and social philosophy of modern business enterprise and, in later times, because of the technical interest which industry and commerce were required to take in the development of modern science . . . . Religious attitudes combined with rationalist appreciations of progress in the conquest of nature and of the value of human reason to liberalize the strict teachings of early Calvinism. The supreme doctrine of the sole sovereignty of God had lost its significance as the rather considerable sovereignty of man over nature came into light and his imperial instincts were aroused in the competition of economic life.[1]

Thus, we see again the now patent reason for the appearance of the social gospel and the new religious education movement in that they are seen to root in liberalism; being the renewal of a characteristic propensity in man to seek to achieve salvation somewhat independent of divine aid.

Liston Pope, in his unique study of Gastonia, North Carolina, makes a similar observation showing that the town churches, made up principally of the middle-class communicants, preferred religious education to the revival type of evangelism; and that the mill churches preferred the opposite. He also points out differences in liberal and conservative theological content of the sermons presented to these different types of congregations.

---
1 Niebuhr, op. cit., pp. 102, 103, et passim.

Denominational popularity is shown to vary inversely in proportion to the professional education requirements made of their respective ministers. A comparison is made of the educational requirements of various denominations with the suggestion that over-education has tended to produce a ministry which lacks the humility and consecration necessary to qualify them to minister to under-privileged classes.[1]

"The kind of education," Dr. Donald W. Richardson wisely states, "rather than education itself, isolates professionally trained clergymen from the industrial masses."

Stewart G. Cole, in his "History of Fundamentalism" refers to seminary after seminary which went over to the liberal side and how new schools of orthodoxy were established to train ministers in the "old time" religion.[2] This has already been pointed out in our discussion but is mentioned again here to emphasize the importance of the need of the right kind of education properly based upon Scriptural standards.

The present-day lack of emphasis on doctrine, the ignoring of the fact of sin and the need of the new birth, has inaugurated this new program of religious education which has little affinity with the type of teaching program advocated by the New Testament writers.

In a brochure circulated by the Child Evangelism Fellowship comment is made on J. Edgar Hoover's statements regarding the problem of juvenile delinquency of our day. In referring to the break down in the home and other attendant evils it is suggested that we are presenting the wrong type of religious education. The following significant statement appears:

> Added to the breakdown of the home is, of course, the apostasy of the Church. Those who do go to Sunday school and Church often get very little that can help them. Time is wasted. Modernism is taught. Reform is offered instead of regeneration, and thus we find ourselves in the plight described by the head of the Bureau of Investigation.

Dr. Lacy takes a somewhat optimistic outlook as he sums up

---

[1] Liston Pope, **Millhands and Preachers.** (New Haven: Yale University Press, 1942), pp. 85, 95, 107-112, 115, et passim.
[2] Stewart G. Cole, **History of Fundamentalism.** (New York: Richard R. Smith, Inc., 1931), p. 42.

the situation relating to religious education and evangelism. He says:

> Advocates of the new psychology captured large areas of the Christian Education field and there was a time when apparently Religious Education was taboo to large numbers of evangelistically minded ministers who thought they saw in the movement an effort to save men by character building apart from the operation of the Spirit. Many old methods of evangelists were anathema to a large number who adhered to and led in the Religious Education movement. Again, however, there has been a rapprochement of these two elements, and our next revival may profit by and advance greatly Christian Education in our Church.[1]

Such a prediction, of course, could result in nothing more than wishful thinking as long as we allow liberals to emasculate the content of our teaching material by injecting their liberal theology and teaching technique, which teach the child no definite doctrinal standards but leave it to the judgment of the child himself to determine his own doctrine according to his individual choice. This teaching technique is based on the same principle which J. Edgar Hoover criticizes and blames for the juvenile delinquency. He blames the lack of discipline in the life of the child on the fact that "the youngsters" are left to their own devices and the tragic fallacy in the theory that self-discipline "just grows" is being demonstrated day by day.

The real fallacy in our thinking might well be explained by the deleterious influences of our scientific age of rationalism. The later work of Starbuck in the field of psychology supplied a psychological basis for Bushnell's insight and insistence upon Christian nurture. He published in 1899, his "Psychology of Religion" which began with this epoch-making sentence: "Science has conquered one field after another, until now it is entering the most complex, the most inaccessible and of all the most sacred domain—that of religion." Since we have subjected God's work of the new birth to the scrutinizing eye of science we wonder if, perhaps, we will not soon include in our program the attempt to subject God to a similar scientific analysis. While it is legitimate to make some investigation, we should not forget our finite capacities and the fact that God, in His infinite wisdom, has so

---

[1] Lacy, op. cit., pp. 156, 157.

revealed Himself and His plan of salvation that a wayfaring man, though he be a fool, shall not err therein.

George Barton Cutten, in his outstanding and scholarly work wisely makes the following statement in his discussion of conversion. He says: "In this chapter it will be the aim to examine the effects upon the individual of all contributing influences in conversion, but no attempt will be made to analyze, describe or explain the divine element."[1] In the midst of a world that has gone too far afield in this direction Cutten's technique is worthy of universal acceptance.

To give the reader some idea as to the dominance of this new educational emphasis we quote Elmer T. Clark whose book has come to be recognized as a classic in its field. His statements, on the whole are very accurate. He states,

The great Protestant bodies commonly insist that a well-developed and scientifically based system of religious education is necessary to the life and growth of the Church. It is almost their sole method of propaganda at the present time; it is commonly asserted that 90 or 95 percent of all new members come through the Sunday schools, and the success of their programs of religious education is attributed largely to the fact that they have incorporated the finding of modern educational psychology. The leaders in this field are firm in the belief that without this sort of religious education the churches would decline and perhaps die.[2]

Without meaning to be invidious this writer would repeat a former statement that such rational emphasis as this, and lack of emotional emphasis, has served to fill the Church of today with many people who know nothing of the new birth. Clark's further statements are profoundly significant and challenging because of their serious implications. The following sentences should by no means be overlooked:

The emotional element has all but passed from the religion of the great Churches, to their very great loss; it is somewhat pathetic to watch them developing puny 'worship programs' and impotent 'decision day services' and 'religious emphasis weeks' in an endeavor to make up for the passing of great emotional experiences that plumbed the depths of men's souls, changed lives, emotionalized conviction and attitude, and left an irreducible appreciation of spiritual values.[3]

---

[1] George Barton Cutten, **The Psychological Phenomena of Christianity.** (New York: Charles Scribner's Sons, 1908), p. 232.
[2] Clark, op. cit., pp. 287, 288.
[3] Ibid., p. 27.

Clark does not mean to ignore the value of the right kind of teaching program to prepare individuals to make an intelligent commitment but deprecates a program which tends to substitute natural human means for the work which belongs solely to God.

W. W. Sweet taps the root of our trouble in the following summary statements. In referring to the rapid change of the theological scene and liberal influences, he says:

> It was the general opinion that theology only served to keep Christian people apart, and 'a religion of Jesus rather than a religion about Jesus' became the great vogue. It was in this period of theological sterility that Religious Education stepped into the limelight and, perhaps for this reason, got an unfortunate start.[1]

The lack of the proper doctrinal emphasis in our teaching is everywhere evident.

---

1 Sweet, Story pp. 585, 586.

Part III
ECUMENICITY

The current tendency toward confederation, merging, consolidation, union and ecumenicity has been in the air for some two hundred years, since the first union between the Lutherans and the Reformed Church in Germany in 1822.[1] Ecumencity has, however grown to its present dimensions, and come to be a popular trend among people of different religious faiths, principally during the present generation. The tendency toward ecclesiastical amalgamation has followed a parallel trend in the fields of politics, industry, and commerce. Noteworthy efforts have been made and have met with some success in these various fields of endeavor. The ecumenical movement has so far been restricted exclusively to Protestantism. Ecumenical conferences have been held at Stockholm, Lausanne, Oxford and Edinburgh during the course of the twenties and the thirties. The leaders desired ultimately that union might be effected. Such union would, however, be an unnatural and forced union to form one great colossal organization of churches holding to variegated doctrinal views. There are national, racial, economic, sociological and psychological differences which cannot be indifferently ignored but which must be taken into account. Atkins makes the following statements relative to the possibilities of forming a super Church:

> A super-Church in a democracy, so given as American democracy to seek moral ends through legislative action, is not an unqualified ideal. Denominationalism variations have contributed to the total wealth of religious expression and have been the useful instruments of a very necessary liberty. A spirit of accommodation, a generous permission of the right to differ in any department of American life, would be needed in an organically united American Church if it were not to break beneath the strains to which its structure would have to adjust itself. But church union has not yet become evident enough to jusify such apprehensions. The principal stain so far has been getting any at all. And the denominations have commissions or committees there for diplomatic 'conversations' have been held and reports of progress—or the contrary—made.[2]

---
1 Monsma, op. cit., p. 53.
2 Atkins, op. cit., pp. 147, 148.

There have been three major attempts toward ecumenicity and Church union in the United States within recent years, namely, The Federal Council of the Churches of Christ in America which advocates cooperation on a basis of faith in Christ as the divine Lord and Saviour, which means a belief in His divinity and redemptive work. They refuse admission to the Universalists who would not accept this basic creed. Second, we have a group of Fundamentalists who are organized as the National Association of Evangelicals, who hold to the inerrancy of the Scriptures, the virgin birth, the bodily resurrection, the blood atonement and the divinity of Christ as the essential elements in the Christian Creed. Then, the American Council of Churches, which is still more provincial and conservative in its outlook, and is composed chiefly of a rabid group who have ostracized and stigmatized as unchristian all which is contrary to their own prescribed creedal position. They plan a World Counc l to meet at Amsterdam next year in competition with the World Council of Churches and at the same time the "liberals" meet for an ecumenical council. It is quite generally thought that the protagonists of this group have, in their zeal for what they believe to be the truth, assumed an attitude so truculent that they have thus circumscribed their usefulness and limited their influence.

And now we come to a more direct discussion of ecumenicity in its relation to historic Protestantism. Protestantism is itself potentially divisive. Protestantism places truth above unity. If it were merely unity that was to be desired at the expense of sacrificing truth, then the Reformation would have been unnecessary. It has however been a distinguishing characteristic and motif of Protestantism to sacrifice unity for the sake of truth.

Theological truth is truth as found in the Bible. Such truth is inevitable for when we open the Bible we come naturally to put an interpretation upon it. Interpretations vary with individuals. Any religious belief we have involves a theology. If we believe in prayer, that is to some extent a disclosure of our theology. Luther broke with the Roman Catholic Church at Worms because he advocated justification by faith and not by works; he insisted on the universal priesthood of believers and the individual right to interpret the Scriptures. Luther was unwilling to have an external extra-biblical authority to dictate to him his beliefs, because he believed that the interpretation of Scripture was the individual right of all. There was ecumenicity existing in the Roman Church but he refused such unity in favor of truth.

The Universalist and extreme liberal advocate getting rid of theology in order to have unity. They say it makes no difference what a man believes, and that theology itself is a divisive factor which we need to throw overboard. Their claim is justified for it is true that theology is potentially divisive. This is evidenced by the presence of 256 different religious sects, which exist because we interpret the Bible differently.

The Universalists say, do away with the Bible. Other groups say, the Bible is our creed. Such is the claim of the Disciples of Christ, the Baptists and the Plymouth Brethren. But to say, we believe in the Bible, doesn't eliminate theology. To believe in the Bible is itself a theological position or doctrine. Catholics and Protestants differ. There are manifestly three other groups within the Church which differ, the rationalists, the mystics and the supremacy-of-the-Church group. The rationalists advocate reason and subjective personal experience as the criteria which should guide our spiritual life and determine our creedal position. The mystics advocate, as did the Puritans, an "inner light" revelation which comes through a personal and direct contact with the Divine. To them this inner light is the standard of conduct and belief. The group which makes the Church the supreme standard of faith assert that the Church wrote the Bible and was in existence before the Bible was written, and thus should be our authority rather than the Word of God which was written by the Church. They believe that the Christian community and not denominations should decide on the norm and course of action for the Christian.

It is of notable significance that those who agree that the Bible itself should be our guide and supreme authority interpret the Bible differently. We naturally present "our" point of view. To incorporate your view and modify mine adds more to the divisiveness of the Church and opens the way for others to exercise the same privilege. Luther and Calvin both believed in the absolute authority of the Scriptures but differed on the sacraments.

Others have parted company on baptism, and so the story endlessly continues. There are the theological, historical and experimental differences which must be allowed for if we open the Bible to interpret its precepts. There will naturally always be interpretations of the Bible and if the Bible is not interpreted it must remain a closed book.

There comes next the question as to what laws of interpretation we shall adopt in making our interpretation. Shall Genesis 1-3 be interpreted literally or symbolically? Who can say which to use since the Bible itself is silent on this point? There is therefore no such thing as the Bible uninterpreted. We have the Book and its interpreters. When we interpret the Bible we have theology and creed regardless of how strong we affirm that the Bible alone is my creed and I have no other. We all have creeds automatically when we open the Bible to consider its pages. Luther at Worms and Calvin at Geneva each took their stand.

The desire for Church union may in itself indicate a weakness of those organizations which advocate and propose it to save themselves from possible disintegration and to meet the competition of other groups. Ostensibly these groups desire unity in order that they might be better able to promote the interests of the whole Church but, in reality, it may be to cover their own spiritual weakness.

Curran suggests that the great migration from the countryside to urban areas has so emptied the pews of many rural churches that it has become necessary to close the doors of many of them; and that in a desperate attempt to keep organized Christianity alive, many groups have abandoned their particular creeds and united in federated or community churches. Other groups merged their diminishing numbers with neighboring congregations of the same denomination.[1]

Garrison interprets the trend toward unity as being motivated by economic considerations and desire for greater efficiency. He says:

Economic considerations have also had their weight in driving churches together, for it had been observed in many fields that they must combine or collapse. But in general they have been drawn

---

[1] Curran, op. cit., p. 130.

rather than driven into these more cooperative attitudes and the impulse to unification has gained more from the desire of the churches to increase the efficiency of their work than from fear of losing their own lives.

The multiplicity of denominations, each carrying on its work independently through a period of rapid territorial expansion and numerical growth and a period of new complicated problems presented by an urban and industrialized society, produced a situation that, when the whole field and the religious forces at work in it were broadly surveyed, there appeared to be a vast amount of zeal and energy expended with no general plan whatever.[1]

In spite of the progress that has been made by individual denominations these surveys reveal the confusion of disunited Protestantism and that the churches speak with no united voice. Efforts have been duplicated and failure to coordinate efforts has seriously lessened the force of what might have been a united witness. According to the estimate of church leaders of eminent reputation and broad outlook we are nearer such unity than ever before. And yet there is a terrific danger of seeking to achieve a false unity which would eventuate in a vitiated doctrine and an emasculated Church which would not be worthy of being called a Christian Church. Church unity of the right sort is to be desired and worked for. It is pathetic and is indeed humbling to acknowledge that those outside the pale of the Church have justifiably criticized Christians for their lack of cooperation and have been cynical in their attitude because of it. Yet it would be folly to fail to recognize that much of the trend toward ecumenicity roots in modern liberalism.

As the writer has pointed out the social gospel and religious education have a valid place in our Christian mission but these cease to be worthy agencies if or when they violate the Scriptures and ignore the precepts which demand a new birth for every individual who names the name of Christ. So likewise any unity which may be achieved or sought that is activated by those of extreme liberal views which would lower Christianity to the same level as other world religions is not to be desired. Garrison aptly draws attention to the influences of liberalism in these current trends. He writes in his Chapter on Protestant Unity and the Federal Council these noteworthy facts:

---

1 Garrison, **op. cit.**, p. 215.

The three great movements which have characterized the American Church in the last half-century have been, first, a widening and deepening interest in social problems in the light of which divisive doctrines have lost much of their importance; second, a liberalized view of religion in which they have lost much of their certainty; and third, a tendency toward cooperation and unity among the sundered families of faith. The first of these furnished the motive power for the third and the second has removed many obstacles to it.[1]

The social gospel has been shown to ignore the need of personal salvation and the new birth. If Garrison's conclusion is correct that the ecumenicial movement is largely activated by the social gospel-advocates, it is then true that both root alike in liberal teachings which ignore the supernatural new birth; and, as Garrison observes, the lack of emphasis on doctrine opens the way for denominations to merge on a basis so unsound that their union would spell disaster.

Dr. Charles E. Jefferson, with a clear perception, somewhat ironically appraises the ecumenical movement. His book was written at the beginning of this century. Since that time this trend has become increasingly dominant among Christian leaders and groups. We are striving masterfully for unity and much is being said about ecumenicity and worldwide Christian brotherhood. (This thoroughly accords with the social gospel emphasis of the brotherhood of man.) We have much room for improvement and development along this line but the solemn question is, "To what extent can we afford to yield?" It is definitely possible to lose our Christianity in trying to be Christian. He writes:

> The spirit of our times cries out: Let us have peace. Let us forget the points on which we differ and think only on those points in which we all agree. Let all the evangelical churches come together and let the Unitarians come too, and let the Jews come in also, and let us receive also the disciples of ethical culture—let us throw away the dogmas on which we differ and let us think henceforth and forever only on the things in which we agree. This means, of course, throwing overboard the distinctive dogmas of the Christian religion—but let them go, if only by casting them away we can have peace. Our good nature extends even to the ends of the earth. We are no longer the critics of Oriental religions. We are willing to admit that Confucianism and Buddhism and Mohammedanism and Shintoism are earnest

---

1 Garrison, op. cit., p. 215.

strivings of human spirit after God; that they all have in them many beautiful and noble sentiments and precepts, and why should not the followers of all religions of the earth get together and sit at one another's feet, culling out of these and constructing the one universal and final religion? This means, of course, letting the distinctive dogmas of the Christian religion go—but why not let them go if we can have peace? So men are saying.[1]

Curran, in his book, writes a chapter which he titles, "The End of Protestant Creeds" in which he states:

> The recent history of Protestantism in the United States is particularly noteworthy for two major developments. The first is the final abandonment of the older Protestant orthodoxy, in some instances by the official declaration of the sects. The second, to which the jettisoning of the Protestant creeds contributed, is an ecumenical movement which aims at the consolidation of all denominations in a single church and which has already effected mergers of a number of Protestant denominations.[2]

His discussion continues with some pertinent information relating to the conflict between the liberal modernists and the orthodox fundamentalists, demonstrating how denominations and seminaries have one by one succumbed to liberalism. "The domination of Modernism among the Methodist churchmen" he says, "was further illustrated by the merger, in 1939, of the Methodist Episcopal Church with the majority of the membership of the Methodist Church, South, and the Methodist Protestant Church on a creedless basis."[3]

In a recent issue of the Pentecostal Evangel, published by the Assemblies of God the following statement appears in a section captioned "The Passing and the Permanent." It is strikingly significant and may be considered at this juncture since it relates to the organizing of a super-church:

> Having accomplished church union in South India, Dr. E. Stanley Jones has been addressing mass audiences all over America on the need of uniting all Protestant churches in one super-church organization. Liberal leaders are all for it. One day there will be such a union of apostate religious powers, and it will be allied with the Antichrist.[4]

---

1 Charles E. Jefferson, **The Minister As Prophet**. (Grand Rapids: Zondervan Publishing House, 19), p. 172.
2 Curran, op. cit., p. 148.
3 Ibid., p. 154.
4 Editorial in **The Pentecostal Evangel**. November 8, 1947.

Dr. M. R. DeHaan, teacher of the Radio Class Bible Class World-wide Gospel Broadcast, in his book, "The Second Coming of Jesus" holds to a like opinion as will be seen in the following account:

Still more ready for the coming of the Antichrist is the Church in its organized form today. Men are weary of the splitting which has characterized the organized Church of all ages, both the Catholic and the Protestant. Movements are on foot in almost every group to form a union. The governing bodies of most of the denominations are considering now overtures from other groups offering a common basis of union. Much has already been realized. The Federal Council of Churches in America is one of the first members of this product of hell. Hence those who still have a little love for the good old gospel of the blood are slowly being squeezed and compelled to withdraw from the Church systems and denominations. Within a few years, if the Lord tarries, it will be impossible to remain together. A great many of the fence straddlers of this day will have to get off on one side or the other. Just recently the Pope issued a statement that there is but one thing for the Protestant churches to do and that was to get back in the mother church where they belonged! You may laugh at this, but the time is not far hence when this will occur. The Church of England is already Catholic, with the exception of its name. The liturgical churches are adopting confessionals and forms of absolution, while the rest are slipping into a boneless type of Modernism.

The present agitation of the churches looking toward union may be scoffed at, but it is coming. No one can stop it. It has been prophesied that it will come. Once more the scarlet woman of Revelation will realize her dream of holding the world under her sway. This is her Catholic dream and it will be realized. We have reached the Laodicean period of this dispensation and the Master says, 'Behold, I stand at the door and knock.' In the previous ages the Son of Man stood and walked among the candlesticks, but in the Laodicean period he is outside the door and calls for individual separation unto himself.[1]

We will leave it with Dr. DeHaan to assume responsibility for his scathing denunciation of The Federal Council of Churches in America, except to say that there are multiplied thousands who share with him a similar attitude toward all those who reject the blood atonement as a necessary element in our redemption.

Now to get to the crux of the whole matter of ecumenicity, according to the knowledge of this writer, Dr. Monsma submits the best running account of factual information to substantiate

---

1 DeHaan, op. cit., pp. 146, 147.

the claim that the ecumenical movement finds its principal roots in modern liberalism. Our discussion of the subject has already assumed sizeable proportions. It will therefore serve our purpose briefly to refer to the highlights which are presented in this magnificent work.

In referring to denominationalism and liberalism Monsma points out that where one holds sway the other cannot exist. They are at variance in doctrine and no effort can ever bring them together. Liberalism regards denominationalism as an anachronism, a relic of the past and out of harmony with present day thinking. Liberalism has always worked for unity and in opposition to denominations. The extreme liberals discard the infallible Word to accept man's authority to develop truth, even eternal truth. In the seventeenth century, as previously noted, church union was advocated and came to a degree of consummation in 1822. Such men as Calixtus, Molanus, Grotius and Spinola, while not strictly liberals in the modern sense, were liberals in comparison with the Protestant view of the Scripture and its authority. There was an undeniable kinship between them and the modernists of our day. They were willing to make most any sacrifice for the sake of union. Since Modernism is actuated by liberalism it follows that it is also interested in unity.

The Federal Council, he points out, has come to the kingdom for such a time as this; seeks to bring about cooperation and finally federation and church unity. Liberalism is in control of the Federal Council of Churches of America. Liberalism denies objective truth and advocates subjective truth. Its doctrine is humanistic in character, being interested primarily in man and not in God. Doctrine is frowned upon as unimportant and nonessential. Theological differences are treated casually. Authoritative statements and dogmas are shunned. Subjectivism has made man the puppet of his own and his fellowman's ideas and hypotheses.

The question is asked, "Who knows the truth?" To disregard the objective standards of the Bible leads to agnosticism and dark pessimism. Truth, to the liberal modernist, may be everywhere and nowhere. Its validity is made to depend on one's experience. Hence Allah and Buddha may be classed with Jehovah. The main task of the Church, if not the only task, is to improve social conditions—Freemantle is quoted as saying, "To teach the young, to promote culture among rough and rude lives, to inculcate temperance and thrift, to prevent cruelty to animals, to regulate the conditions of labor, to make charity tend to moral and economic progress, to insure provision in old age to all, are coming to be recognized not merely as a part, but as the main part of the religion of the future."

Liberalism advocates a universal atonement and the brotherhood of all men. Spiritual, racial, international and social boundaries are all to be erased. Monsma avers that to form a union with liberalism would mean a separation from God and that separation would mean utter destruction.[1]

There is a union, however, which is Scriptural and which constitutes a legitimate objective to be achieved. This writer, in a recent conference with Dean Donald W. Richardson discussed the subject of ecumenicity as to its Scriptural grounds and validity, and the extent to which we can afford to cooperate and lend our Christian influence to it. His statements form a splendid summary of the whole matter and are imbued with the fine and genuine Christian spirit which prompted them. He said, in effect:

> To my mind there is a very real ecumenicity and this idea of ecumenicity has been found throughout the history of the Church, and is embodied in the commonly accepted Apostle's Creed and expressed in the phrase 'communion of the saints.' The whole of the Epistle of the Ephesians centers around this idea of the oneness of Christians in Christ. "There is one body and one Spirit.... one Lord, one faith, one baptism, one God and Father of all, who is above all, and through all, and in you all." In this sense there is a worldwide fellowship of Christians and there ought to be this ecumenical spirit among those who are united in Christ. But there is no real ecumenicity between us and the Jews because the Jews do not accept the deity of Christ; and there could not be any spirit of ecumenicity between us and the Unitarians, nor could there be any ecumenicity between the evangelical Christians and the liberals who reject the deity of Christ.
>
> We should cultivate this real spirit of ecumenicity and while we should win men to the idea of the 'communion of the saints'—the fellowship of all true believers in Christ—we should be on our guard

---

1 Monsma, op. cit., pp. 51-60, et passim.

against a false ecumenicity which would bring into this evangelical fold men and women who do not believe those things which, according to the New Testament teachings, are essential to this kind of ecumenicity. Ecumenicity in Ephesians all centers around the deity and atonement of Christ. Within these limits you and I, belonging to different communions, know the communion of the saints; but we could not know it with a group of Universalists. There are many different denominations with many emphases but so long as we are one in Christ we should be able to fellowship one with the other. We joyfully recognize each other as fellow Christians, and we commune together around the Lord's table; we still have our differences, yet are still members of the true Church, and it is an ecumenical Church, i. e., a world-wide Church.

We, of different denominations, who are characterized by this oneness in Christ can cooperate to promote the interest of the Church. We cannot fellowship with those who do not accept the things we believe are the very essence of truth concerning Christ. We cannot fellowship with them in the realm of religion but we can fellowship with them in good works—feeding the hungry, clothing the needy, looking after the sick and destitute, etc. There is no room, however, for fellowship in matters of religion with those who do not accept the central verities of the Christian faith.[1]

It should be recognized that increased massiveness cannot produce growth and increase in the kingdom of God. When individuals have in their own way incorporated into their life the Word of God there will be a unity in Christ, not attempting to erase differences or violate peculiarities of soul structure, leaving unrestricted opportunity for every mind to assert itself in its own way.

Cutten suggests that, "The aim must be to furnish guidance so that individual characteristics may be developed; variety in unity, not homogeneity, is the ideal of the Kingdom of God.[2]

---

[1] Dr. Donald W. Richardson, Dean of the Graduate Department of Union Theological Seminary, Richmond, Virginia.
[2] Cutten, op. cit., p. 10.

Chapter III
THE PSYCHOLOGICAL FACTOR AS A DIVISIVE FORCE

God is not limited to one model nor to one method of working. He has, for example, set up in the church nine gifts and designed that these varied types of abilities might develop a Church that is not one sided. Romans 12 and I Corinthians 12 enlarge on this idea. There is variety amid unity. There is "one body" and we are many members. Just as individuals differ, so also denominations differ. If we think of the kingdom of God as being composed of different types of individuals with varying psychological make-ups, then why is it not also reasonable to think of the kingdom of God as being comprised of different types of denominations?

Cutten draws the following analogies which illustrate our natural differences, and yet at the same time our striking similarities. He says:

> The trees in the oak grove, the nestlings in the robin's brood, the cattle upon a thousand hills, and the children around the family table indicate very clearly that individuals of the same species are very much alike and yet quite different. Not only the bodies but the minds of men show these two characteristics. These striking similarities and concomitant wide divergencies are the marvel of God's universe. To the former fact is due the possibility of a common religion, to the latter, the necessity of different denominations.
>
> The dream of the idealist, that denominations at some time will be a memory of the past, is a will-o-'-the-wisp. It recedes as one advances, and at the moment you catch it, behold it is lost. Supposing the possibility of one church, what conditions would exist? It would be in name and no more in reality than at present. The Methodists would still cling to his methods, the Presbyterian to his presbytery, the Baptist to its baptism, the Episcopal to its episcopus, and the Congregationalist to his congregational government. Birds of a feather would continue to flock together, and the real conditions would not be changed.
>
> Why not have one church? Are the perversity and stubbornness of mankind to blame? Not that; men are psychologically constituted so that different things appeal to different persons, and religiously these things are represented by different denominations.[1]

---
1 Cutten, **op cit.**, p. 456.

To persist in these so-called petty differences does not necessarily reflect disloyalty to the cause of Christ; especially if to hold to these differences is, to us, holding to the truth. We as citizens of the same country are no less patriotic because we espouse the principles of different political parties, unless we happen to be living under some form of socialistic regime or a dictatorship.

Cutten aptly points out that it is not the moulder, nor the metal, but the mould that makes the difference. His chapter, "Through the Human Mould," refers to the human mind. The science of psychology and the laws of mental action permit us to study religion. Science may destroy some of our theories and dogma, but the residue which remains is solid rock upon which we can build. Theology endeavors to prove what mental states the religious person must have. Psychology now assumes the task of observing what these mental states actually are. The psychological data form a foundation on which theology must build. As we examine the products of the moulds (minds) we better understand the material and the design of the Moulder. While it is true that the laws governing mental phenomena are more illusive and obscure than those governing material science, we have nevertheless made sufficient advances to recognize that psychological differences definitely adapt us to varying types of religious expression.[1]

Curran, in writing of "The Frontier" brings into focus an illustration of this fact. He writes:

> The frontier provided an environment most suitable for the rapid growth of Evangelicalism. Frontier life was rough, passions were elemental, reactions were emotional rather than intellectual. Frontiersmen generally were of the lower economic classes, poor and poorly educated. Their means of recreation, of emotional outlet, were limited. They were ripe for revival.[2]

Atkins, in referring to the frontiersmen has this to say:

> Their general morality offered plenty of occasions for very elemental religious correction, their highly emotional temperament furnished brush-wood for the revivalists' fire, their extreme suggestibility and lack of poise have supplied examples of religious hysteria hardly to be paralleled. And mixed through all the frontier populations at the beginning of the last century were foot-loose adventurers, criminals,

---

[1] Cutten, op cit., pp. 3-10, et passim.
[2] Curran, op cit., pp. 67, 68.

and degenerates who had themselves been sent over from Europe to the Southern tide-water regions, or were the descendants of such ancestors.[1]

While these may be considered extreme examples they serve to illustrate forcefully the fact that psychological differences determine religious choice. Additional comment on the frontier will be made in our later discussion.

One person may say, "I am a Baptist because my parents were before me." This is just another way of saying that such a person is psychologically conditioned to accept the tenets of that church because of heredity. He is constituted like his parents.

Take another example, one might say, "My parents were Baptists, but after their decease in my early childhood I was brought up in a Presbyterian family and taught Presbyterian doctrines. Therefore, I am a Presbyterian." This is the statement of another psychological fact, we are different persons psychologically because we have reacted to different environments.

Cutten says, "Men from their very natures belong to certain denominations, and can never receive the most from their worship until they find their proper niches. . . . If we know that men cannot worship with us in the way that seems best to them, we should be willing and even rejoice that there are congregations with whom they can worship in sincerity and truth."[2]

Binder, in discussing the phenomena of religious cults, begins by saying that "the student of religious phenomena cannot but be impressed with the fact that ever since the Christian Church was fully organized, their infinite diversity of intellectual equipment impelled men everywhere to emphasize disproportionately certain aspects of the Christian faith which were originally regarded as common property of all believers."[3] He adds further that "The psychological make-up of men is often so strange that they find even the commonly accepted standards unsatisfying. The result, inevitably, is the creation of a religious mode or expression which does satisfy—and a schism is effected or a new sect created."[4]

---

1 Atkins, op. cit., p. 15.
2 Cutten, op. cit., p. 463.
3 Louis Richard Binder, **Modern Religious Cults and Society.** (Boston Richard G. Badger, The German Press, 1933), p. 21.
4 Ibid., p. 23.

Some are mentally so constituted that they find happiness in worshipping in a congregation that lays emphasis on the beauty of worship. Their souls yearn for aesthetic satisfaction. At the same time another person would not appreciate the appeals to the finer feeling and would be miserable in a communion which stressed ritualistic practices. He would find himself better satisfied in a more austere worship atmosphere which would require rigid bodily discomfort.

Some men are so psychologically constituted that they require that someone tell them exactly what to believe so that they might accept this dictum as final and infallible, rather than having to exercise their own reasoning faculties to make their choice. Such men are constitutionally adapted to the Roman Catholic Church. Others who want to think their way through and arrive at independent conclusions would not be at home in this church. There are those who are naturally more emotional than others, and do not experience satisfaction in worship unless they can find opportunity to give free expression to their emotions. Since revivals have always been characterized by intense emotion, such individuals will discover greater happiness in worshipping among the revival sects. Liston Pope makes the following interesting observation. In discussing the various explanations for the emergence of sects he says:

> Another credible diagnosis ascribe psychological deficiencies to most members of the newer sects. Frenetic religious services represent release from psychological repression, it is said, fulfilling a need for self-expression and for identification of one's self with a greater power.[1]

Niebuhr, in his chapter, "The Churches of the Disinherited," makes the following statements which will be seen to coincide with Pope's conclusions:

> The religion of the untutored and economically disfranchised classes has distinct ethical and psychological characteristics, corresponding to the needs of these groups. Emotional fervor is one common mark. Where the power of abstract thought has not been highly developed and where inhibitions on emotional expression have not been set up by a system of polite conventions, religion must and will express itself

---

[1] Pope, op cit., p. 134.

in emotional terms. Under these circumstances spontaneity and energy of religious feeling rather than conformity to an abstract creed are regarded as the tests of religious genuineness. Hence also the formality of ritual is displaced in such groups by an informality which gave opportunity for the expression of emotional faith and for a simple, often crude, symbolism. An intellectually trained and liturgically minded clergy is rejected in favor of lay leaders who serve the emotional needs of this religion more adequately and who, on the other hand, are not allied by culture and interest with those ruling classes whose superior manner of life is too obviously purchased at the expense of the poor.[1]

Niebuhr further emphasizes this psychological difference in his discussion of Presbyterianism. He says:

The abstract terminology of Presbyterian confessions and sermons were not only unintelligible to them, they were irrelevant.... Presbyterianism was intellectualistic. it was authoritarian, it was aristocratic; the disinherited required an emotionally experienced and expressable faith, and one which contained some promise of social amelioration.[2]

It was thus that sects came into existence to supply a legitimate psychological need created by the mode of living necessary in their particular environment. Niebuhr compares the religion of the western frontier with that of the socially disinherited, demonstrating how the psychology of the frontier corresponds in many respects to the psychology of the revolutionary poor. Davenport, in a very able discussion of the Scotch-Irish Revival in Kentucky in 1800, goes to considerable length to describe the type of mind which was psychologically fitted to participate in the kind of revival which characterized those times. It was, in fact, this type of mind that created the revival rather than the mind that was effected by it. In this new wild country conventionalities and law gave place to an unrestrained freedom which removed the rational restraints of religion. The environment which necessitated one's being alert to savage attacks of Indians and wild animals created an atmosphere of fear and apprehensiveness. These factors developed in these Scotch-Irish people a high degree of certain motor and emotional tendencies already in the blood through heredity. Both their hereditary and environmental in-

---
1 Niebuhr, op cit., p. 30.
2 Ibid., p. 43.

fluences combined to produce their psychological make-up. Of them, Davenport writes:

> The primitive surroundings once more fanned into a flame the primitive traits. They were not only a sturdier but a far more excitable and sanguine population in 1800 than their brethren in the north of Ireland, and when at last there was brought to bear upon them in the course of events that most powerful species of 'crowd' psychology, a protracted religious camp-meeting, and they were suddenly halted and aroused by the most fervid, imaginative and reiterative appeals to the sense of their apostasy and everlasting doom if they should not repent, there resulted a perfect combination of conditions....[1]

Tracy, in his novel and epoch-making historical account of "The Great Awakening" writes a paragraph which is a very definitive account of the psychological background which produced the type of mind which made possible the revival which swept the New England Atlantic seaboard during the times of Edwards and Whitefield in the preceding century. Tracy writes:

> It was a time, too, of agitable nerves. There had been two centuries of tremendous nervous excitement. There had been the Reformation, the peasant's war, and the religious wars in Germany and the times of the Covenanters in Great Britian; the rise of Protestantism, the religious wars, and the persecution of the Hugenots in France, ending with the appearance of the 'French prophets' in the Cevennes some of whom were still holding forth among their followers in London. New England sprung out of some of the strongest, deepest, and most permanent of these excitements; and, to say nothing of her religious history, her contest with boisterous seas, and gloomy, unexplored forests, and savage foes, the arrow from an unseen hand by day and the warwhoop that startled her sleepers by night, had kept her spirit ready for excitement.[2]

In addition to the combined effect of two centuries of such influences as Tracy describes must be taken into account also the fact that the unseen world of spirits was to the people of Edwards' day much more real than to men today. The strong belief in witchcraft prevalent in the minds of that day opened the way for preaching about the devil and hell. People fainted and fell, screamed and were thrown into convulsions. Some few committed

---
[1] Frederick Morgan Davenport, **Primitive Traits in Religious Revivals.** (New York: The Macmillan Company, 1917), p. 64.
[2] Joseph Tracy, **The Great Awakening.** (New York: Dayton and Newman, 1942), pp. 317, 218.

suicide. Cutten, in his chapter on witchcraft has this to say: "Two centuries ago, both in Europe and in America, witchcraft was held to be more essential to Christian doctrine than demoniacal possession is today. Disbelief in witches was synonymous with infidelity, so thought Luther and John Wesley."[1] During the 16th and 17th centuries 300,000 people lost their lives from the witchcraft crusade. Children as young as the innocent age of five and even dogs lost their lives by being charged with witchcraft.[2]

And so the minds of men are so differently constituted that we find it is unavoidable to express our beliefs except in a plurality of creeds. The cause of such diversity is not to be found in God, nor in His Word. God is one, and His Word is an organic whole. It seems that it is God's will for men to be different and at the same time that they should appreciate and understand one another, so it does not follow that these divisions are necessarily sinful or a sign of human weaknesses. An orange seed planted in Florida will ultimately become a tree and bear oranges while the same seed planted in Alaska would die in the frigid soil without ever sprouting out of the ground. The difference is, obviously, in the soil and the environment and not in the seed itself. The seed of God's word finds lodgement in varying types of soil (souls) and produces fruit according to the environment into which it enters. Individual differences demand individual expression. Monsma's account of these differences is embodied in the following statements:

> The ideal is, of course, one creed. A creed in which all Christians can unite and which serves as an adequate expression of the beliefs of every Christian. In heaven, the Church Triumphant has such a creed, though it need not express it in the form we must needs employ. But we are not in heaven, we still belong to the Church Militant. We must still struggle to grasp as best we can and to express ourselves as perfectly as possible.
>
> In this struggle it is impossible to deny ourselves and our idiosyncrasies of character and race to such an extent that we shall be able to produce a creed in which we can all agree. It will at least require a long time before such can be possible. The differences are so great and so various. There are national differences, sociological differences, and more subtle than any, psychological differences.[3]

---

1 Cutten, op. cit., p. 89.
2 Ibid., p. 199.
3 Monsma, op. cit., p. 91, 92.

McComus and other psychologists have set about to classify all individuals as to their particular aptitude for certain types of denominational worship. He uses somewhat the same basis of classification as suggested by Hippocrates, dividing individuals into four general classes—choleric, melancholic. sanguine and phlegmatic. He then divides all churches into six great bodies each of which is suited to some particular type of psychological make-up.[1]

Such a mechanical arrangement is readily seen to be impracticable since men are endlessly variegated. It is, however, a widely attested fact, as we have seen, that men's worship practices are determined largely by their psychological make-ups and intellectual constitution. While it is recognized that sin has played a prominent part in causing denominational cleavages, it is also true that there are legitimate differences which issue from the fact that we are individuals and have individual differences.

Niebuhr's statements which follow constitute a fair summary of the fact that men possess varying religious needs which are determined by their environment and personal make-ups. He says:

> Out of the religious movement on the frontier in the eighteenth and early nineteenth century there arose, in this way, a considerable number of sects which divided from their parent bodies because divergent social and economic conditions have emphasized different religious needs and expressions.[2]

It seems pertinent that we call attention briefly to three other instances which Myrick mentions as psychological influences that opened the way for the reception of Christ-Science, Buchmanism and Spiritualism, of Christian Science, he says:

> There is a factor often ignored, which explains the success of Christian Science. It gives a chance to every man to be a philosopher and a scientist. In its ranks we behold the amusing spectacle of thousands of moderately informed persons being called scientists and being regarded as metaphysicians. We breathe an atmosphere of science today, and everyone is hankering to be a scientist or a philosopher. Mrs. Eddy got her movement under way when the first wave of scientific thought struck America. Hence Mrs. Eddy caught the popular imagination and desire with the phrase and flattered her disciples

---

1 Henry C. McComus, **The Psychology of Religious Sects.** (New York: , 1912), pp. 217-235.
2 **op. cit.,** p. 163.

by making scientists and philosophers out of them at the time when these two classes were most celebrated.[1]

Buchmanism, he points out as having had its inception at the same time that house-parties began to be held. Since it moved among those engaged in house-parties and hotel gatherings, etc., it is readily understood why it possessed a particular psychological appeal. Its claim to direct revelation and a mystical relationship were also significant.[2]

Myrick accounts for the rise and growth of Spiritualism as follows:

> It started in a day in which skepticism and Higher Criticism had done much to discredit the older theology and the orthodox churches. It was a day in which religious novelty was the vogue. Spiritualism reached its height in the early years of the movement and then gradually slumped. The World War produced a revival of interest that greatly increased its numbers and influence.

The Unity School of Christianity, New Thought and other religious isms are also definitely traceable to psychological trends prevalent at the time. The emphasis on material advancement coupled with an emphasis on physical well-being in a material universe has paved the way and given impetus to these religious cults.

Various other types of divisive factors are closely interwoven with the psychological factor and will be seen in their relationship to it in the chapters which follow in this section.

---

1 Myrick, op. cit., pp. 49, 50.
2 Ibid., p. 51.

Chapter IV
THE SOCIAL FACTOR AS A DIVISIVE FORCE

Professor Niebuhr's book dealing with the "Social Sources of Denominationalism" has come to be considered by many as a classic in its field. He views the Church as an institution in society which was designed to control other institutions but which has come to be controlled by the others. "In dealing with such major social evils as war, slavery, and social inequality," he says, "the Church has discovered convenient ambiguities in the letter of the Gospels which enable it to violate their spirit and to ally itself with the prestige and power those evils had gained in their corporate organization. . . . This proneness to compromise which characterizes the whole history of the church, is no more difficult to understand than is the similar and inevitable tendency by which each individual Christian adapts the demands of the gospel to the necessity of existence in the body and in civilized society."[1] In other words, the Church is unquestionably influenced immensely by world institutions and standards, however hard it may endeavor to avoid such influences. In spite of honest effort to maintain an untainted relationship to the world about us, we are destined to discover the utter futility of realizing such an ideal.

To illustrate this fact Niebuhr makes use of two powerful analogies which help to demonstrate that it is impossible to incorporate an ideal without the loss of some of its ideal character. He states that "When liberty gains a constitution, liberty is compromised; when fraternity elects officers, fraternity yields some of the ideal qualities of brotherhood to the necessities of government. And the gospel of Christ is especially subject to this sacrifice of character in interest of organic embodiment."[2]

He sees in denominationalism a compromise between Christianity and the world. "It represents the accommodation of Christianity to the caste-system of human society."[3]

---
1 Niebuhr, op. cit., pp. 3, 4.
2 Ibid., p. 4.
3 Ibid., p. 6.

The inner nature of our Lord revolted against the Jewish class distinctions. He ignored the nationalism of Jews and Romans as He ministered to the Roman centurion and others. Paul allotted an appreciable amount of space in his epistles to enforce the teaching that "with God is no respect of persons" and to show the Christian relationship which should exist between men of different social levels and races. Paul discouraged the religious factions which existed in the Corinthian Church and also corrected the disorders which arose in connection with the observance of the Lord's supper. This church as well as other New Testament churches, had in it a large proportion of slaves and men from various walks of life who were socially inferior. These social differences were doubtless responsible for the preferences expressed in the ministers at Corinth. James also condemns heartily the distinctions between the rich and the poor in the conduct of the religious services.[1]

Clark observes that Christianity itself was 300 hundred years old before it attracted considerable numbers of the socially well-placed. This came about, of course, as a result of Emperor Constantine's influence by being baptized into the Christian faith. As denominations come to receive and develop more and more a class of socially higher-ups they cease to appeal to the religiously neglected poor. These social differences come to be so accentuated that the poorer classes withdraw and seek to form another group in which they can feel more comfortable.

Niebuhr calls attention to the findings of Weber and Ernst Troeltsch who have demonstrated how important are the differences in the sociological structure of religious groups in the determination of their doctrine.[2] It is commonly thought that the various denominations have found their way into the total Church picture primarily as a result of some doctrinal or theological controversy. There is a measure of truth in such a conclusion, but a closer analysis of the problem of denominationalism reveals that these ostensibly theological differences root in other more profound divergencies. Niebuhr offers a very plausible explanation in the following quotation:

---

[1] I Corinthians 1:12; 3:5-7; 2:14; 4:3-6; 6:1ff.; James 2, etc.
[2] Niebuhr, op. cit., p. 17.

The orthodox interpretation of denominationalism in Christianity looks upon the official creeds of the churches as containing the explanation of the sources and of the character of the prevailing differences. Roman Catholics are defined, from this point of view, as Christians who hold to a semi-Pelagian view of sin and grace, believe in the innately effective character of the sacraments, recognize the primacy of the Roman bishop and hold to other cognate principles of faith and practice. Lutherans are distinguished, the interpreter of the creed tells us, by their belief in justification by faith alone, by their exaltation of the word of God as the primary means of grace, and by their profession of the priesthood of all believers. The Calvinist is marked by his views on predestination, on the legal character of the Bible, and on church discipline. Baptists are members of their denomination because they are convinced that believers' baptism by immersion is alone justifiable. Methodists are what they are because they temper an underlying Calvinism by Arminian modifications. As for the many sub-groups to be found among Lutherans. Calvinists, Bapists, these also vary from each other on one or another point of doctrine, which, it is said, explains their division and accounts for their antagonism. This mode of explanation has been popular since the time when Josephus described the Pharisees as a school of philosophers who maintained belief in the resurrection from the dead and in oral tradition, while the Sadducees were defined as those who held the opposite doctrines. The inadequacy of the explanation in this instance is patent. Certainly the Sadducees were not distinguished from the mass of Jewish people, or from the Pharisees, primarily by any religious opinions they held or failed to hold but their social character as the members of the Hellenistic aristocracy; while back of Pharisaic ideas one looks for the fundamental element, for the racial loyalty which had its source in resistance to the Seleucid attempts to Hellenize Jewish civilization. Differences of opinion were surely present between Pharisees and Sadducees, but these differences had their roots in more profound social divergences. So it is with the Christian sects.[1]

Social differences are thus seen to account for corresponding difference in doctrine and ethics. In Protestant history, as we observed from Clark's statements, the sect has ever been the child of an outcast minority and with the development and change in the sociological character of sectarianism compromise begins and the ethics of the sect begin to approximate that of the institutional church. When the church world as a whole rises to the point of denominational respectability and becomes smug and

---

[1] Niebuhr, op. cit., pp. 12, 13.

complacent the conditions come to be like those which Sweet describes as existing prior to the Great Awakening. He writes:

> Up until the third decade of the eighteenth century the lower classes in the American colonies were little influenced by organized religion and only a small percentage of the population were members of the colonial churches. On the other hand, in nations of western Europe, where state churches commonly existed church membership came about as a matter of course. Even in the Puritan colonies only a comparatively small proportion of the total population were members of the church, while in Virginia at the opening of the eighteenth century not more than one in twenty were church members, and the proportion was undoubtedly smaller in the southern colonies. Thus there came to be more unchurched people in America, in proportion to the population, than was to be found in any other country in Christendom. It was this situation that made it necessary to develop a new technique to win people to the church, and this new method, peculiar to America, was revivalism.[1]

Niebuhr emphasizes the fact that the "Half-Way Covenant" of the New England churches which is paralleled by the "birthright membership" in the Society of Friends necessitated just such a catastrophic religious upheaval as that which characterized the Great Awakening.[2] Muncy writes that "not more than one in twenty of the citizens in Virginia was a member of the Church in 1700. The lower classes were neglected almost entirely, having no practical interest in religion."[3]

In such times of spiritual decadence and moral lethargy among a socially elite church God again brought about a revival among the poor. According to Niebuhr, "the rise of new sects to champion the uncompromising ethics of Jesus and 'to preach the gospel to the poor' has again and again been the effective means of recalling Christendom to its mission."[4]

Ernst Southerland Bates in his chapter, "The Left Wing of the Reformation" makes a striking observation which deserves special notice, particularly so in view of the fact that it is counter to the customary interpretation of the Reformation. He says regarding the lower strata of society:

> The popular conception that the Reformation began with Martin

---
1 Sweet, Story, pp. 7, 8.
2 Niebuhr, op. cit., pp. 20, 21.
3 Muncy, op. cit., p. 5.
4 Niebuhr, op. cit., p. 21.

THE SOCIAL FACTOR AS A DIVISIVE FORCE

Luther, and was carried with success by Luther and Calvin misrepresents the facts and the significance of the entire movement. Luther and Calvin came late in its development, riding to truimph on the crest of the tide that had been rising for centuries. In many ways they represented a betrayal of the Reformation, a counter-revolution which embodied an unstable compromise with the principles of Catholicism—a compromise eventually left behind in a further resurgence of the original anti-catholic forces. Put in modern political and economic language, the Reformation began as a radical lower class movement which was largely taken over by the rising bourgeoisie under Luther and Calvin, to be followed by a renewed struggled between the two classes within Protestantism itself. This interpretation gives meaning to the otherwise senseless conflicts that developed within Protestantism even before victory of Catholicism was surely won.

There were no less than four essentially Protestant sects of great historical importance—the Cathars, Waldenses, Lollards and Hussites —which arose during the period from the eleventh to the fifteenth century when Roman Catholicism was at the very height of its power. All of them expressed a revolt of the submerged classes in medieval society.[1]

In Bates' interpretation we have an adequate explanation of Luther's attitude toward the Peasants War and the connection between the rise of capitalism with that of Calvinism. It was the Anabaptist who championed the cause of the poorer classes after the Reformation got underway. Curran, in commenting on this fact writes, "In the earliest days of the Protestant revolt, the poor and uneducated found themselves cheated by the new churches. Only the middle and upper classes profited by the new denominations; the lower classes were left to shift for themselves."[2]

Liston Pope, in his exhaustive and scholarly study, "Millhands and Preachers" discusses the Emergence of Class Churches from which we quote:

> Religious ideals in Gaston County do not approve the recognition of class lines within the churches. One minister affirms: 'If we don't get all these social classes together in the church, I don't know how they will ever be brought together. So I try to make no differences as between uptown folks and mill folks.' Despite all such sentiments the churches have adapted neatly to class segregation. Individual churches, when judged by the type of membership attending, have

---
1 Ernst Southerland Bates, **American Faith.** (New York: W. W. Norton and Company, Inc., 1940), p. 34.
2 Curran, **op. cit.,** p. 9.

been almost exclusively either rural, mill or uptown in type . . . . The churches have followed closely the distinctions created by the rise of the mills, and most individual churches are now overwhelmingly affiliated with a particular social class.[1]

Pope, in writing of Religious Denominations and Social Classes has this to say,

The population of Gaston County is divided not only into diverse classes but also into various religious groupings. Religious differences existing in the county before the industrial revolution brought acute social division, and have continued to exist through the decades. They have been modified and increased, however, by economic transformation; other denominations have been changed and newer sects have risen to challenge them. As industrialization proceeded apace, religious denominations, as denominations, were affected as patently as individual churches by which they were represented. Wide social differences appeared between Presbyterians and Methodists, Lutherans and Baptists, with each denomination becoming especially identified with one (or at most two) of the emerging social classes. When the older religious traditions proved too inflexible to meet the needs arising from novel social situations, new sects arose to fill the gaps; the Church of God, the Wesleyan Methodists, the Pentecostal Holiness Church and other neoteric cults.[2]

To submit any additional information to establish the fact that social factors play a definite part in the formation and division of church groups and denominations is perhaps unnecessary. Niebuhr's concluding statements may well serve as a summary of the relation of the Church to society. He says:

Denominations, churches, sects, are sociological groups whose principle of differentiation is to be sought in their conformity to the order of social classes and castes. It would not be true to affirm that denominations are not religious groups with religious purpose, but it is true that they represent the accommodation of religion to the caste system. They are emblems, there, of the victory of the world over the church, of the secularization of Christianity, of the church's sanction of that divisiveness which the church's gospel condemns.

Denominations thus represent the moral failure of Christianity. And unless the ethics of brotherhood can give the victory over this divisiveness within the body of Christ it is useless to expect it to be victorious in the world. But before the church can hope to overcome its fatal divisions it must learn to recognize and to acknowledge the secular character of its denominationalism.[3]

1 Pope, **op. cit.,** pp. 71, 72.
2 **Ibid.,** p. 96.
3 Niebuhr, **op. cit.,** p. 25.

Monsma takes issue with Niebuhr that social and racial difference should be abrogated. These social differences root in the fact that there are psychological differences in men. He does not contend that one class should be allowed to suppress another but that the leveling of social differences would be contrary to the idea that God intended in that He made us to be psychologically different. He also points out that racial differences are not accidental and cannot be abolished at will. God intended it so. Since the time of man's effort to build a tower at Shinar and the confusion of tongues and scattering of men across the face of the earth there has been brought about an endless variety of soul structure. These psychological differences among races again are seen to make racial distinctions necessary. Monsma would not advocate any suppression on account of these racial distinctions. It should be said in Niebuhr's defense that he has set up an ideal which we should work toward, but he is too much of a realist to advocate any fantastic goal, which would violate the basis of God's work in making us as He did. In other words, what he advocates is that we should be controlled by love in the formulation of our attitude toward social and racial distinctions and not allow these differences to destroy the fellowship which should exist between all Christians the world over. Monsma would perhaps agree with this position but would not share in the ideal which Niebuhr sets up as an ultimate goal to abolish these distinctions, and see in them the ethical failure of a divided church.[1]

It seems to be characteristic of Niebuhr to view the darker side of the picture and to criticize the Church in the hope of bringing about a change. While his claims are well based they do not adequately describe the whole picture. Bates' book presents the brighter side which is equally true and is approached from the opposite direction to show how the church has been instrumental in shaping other forces in society. It is a happy consideration of the same subject though it runs counter to the position which Niebuhr takes.

Bates, as a student and writer of numerous books on American history, together with his work in religious fields was particularly well qualified to produce this book on "American Faith" which he

---
1 Monsma, op. cit., pp. 63, 64.

completed just before his untimely death. In it he brings together all his knowledge and experience in a somewhat original achievement. The main articles of the American ideal have their origin in American faith, he shows. Democracy was envisaged in religious terms long before it was expressed politically. Our ideal of local self-government, the separation of church and state, the right of freedom of conscience, the equality spoken in the Declaration of Independence, all are shown to be the outgrowths of religious movements. In the consideration of both of these approaches we have the complete picture. But the fact still remains and for our purpose it should not be overlooked that the social factor is definitely a divisive force in the Church.

Chapter V
THE ECONOMIC FACTOR AS A DIVISIVE FORCE

In our previous consideration we mentioned how the factors which go to make up society are both intermeshed and interrelated. Each contributing factor seems to grow together with every other factor to form a sort of accretion. As we seek to analyze these forces we are faced with the problem of detaching each of them for separate examination and evaluation. Our present problem will be to consider the "economic factor"—one in which certain other factors seem to root. It is an accepted dictum that our economic status to a marked degree determines our social, educational, psychological, and even our theological status. Because of the relative importance of this basic factor, it seems reasonable to assume that it is potentially more divisive than any of the others. Such an assumption finds corroborative evidence in the world about us as well as from reliable authoritative sources. Niebuhr's appraisal of this factor is to be seen in the following quotation:

> One phase of denominationalism is largely explicable by means of a modified economic interpretation of religious history; for the divisions of the church have been occasioned more frequently by the direct and indirect operation of economic factors than by the influence of any other major interest of man.[1]

Sweet states that "our religious development cannot be understood apart from the economic, social, and political changes. In other words the same set of influences has produced similar results in both church and state, and each has exercised a constant influence on the other."[2]

To illustrate this truth, let us suppose the case of a racial group which may enter a given community. We will suppose that they belong to the lower economic stratum and income bracket. Because of their position in the economic scale they are in a correspondingly low social scale. In the course of time these people come to form a church. Such a church can then be dis-

---
1 Niebuhr, op. cit., p. 26.
2 Sweet, Story, pp. 8, 9.

tinguished in at least three different ways—racially, economically and socially. In the process of time let us suppose that these same people rise in the economic scale. What happens then? The result is that these people virtually lose their racial distinction and skyrocket in the social scale in somewhat relative proportion to the economic advancement. Ultimately they would come to develop a church program and adopt doctrinal and ethical standards suited to the new economic and social status. It would be a gross error, however, and would be to miss the point of the whole development, for us to overemphasize any one of these factors to the exclusion of the others. On the other hand, as we have pointed out, all these forces seem to be interrelated and to some degree inseparable. Religion, itself, supplies the energy and the goal and furnishes the motive for sectarian groups. Yet, we should not overlook the fact that those various factors in society determine the form and force which religion will develop.

The salvation of the socially-disinherited, for example, bears a distinct ethical character and moral standard in keeping with the economic standard of such a group. Niebuhr in referring to this class states:

> Hence one finds here more than elsewhere, appreciation of the religious worth of solidarity and equality, of sympathy and mutual aid, of rigorous honesty in matters of debt, and the religious evaluation of simplicity of dress and manner, of the wisdom hidden to the wise and prudent but revealed to babes, poverty of spirit, of humility and meekness. Simple and direct in its apprehension of the faith, the religion of the poor shuns the revelations of ethical and intellectual sophistication and by its fruits in conduct often demonstrates its moral and religious superiority.
>
> When Christianity has become the religion of the fortunate and cultured and has grown philosophical, abstract, formal, and ethically harmless in the process, the lower strata of society find themselves religiously expatriated by a faith which neither meets their psychological needs nor sets forth an appealing ethical ideal. In such a situation the right leader finds little difficulty in launching a new movement which will, as a rule give rise to a new denomination.[1]

To illustrate further how moral standards and standards of dress are determined largely by economic status Pope makes this interesting observation:

---
1 Niebuhr, op. cit., pp. 31, 32.

The newer sects affirm separation from the world; in the face of exclusion on educational, economic and religious grounds, they affirm exclusion from their own fellowship of those who engage in mixed bathing, dancing, card-playing, bobbing the hair, gambling, baseball, county fairs, drinking, and using tobacco. Because they have no jewelry to wear, they make refusal to wear jewelry, including wedding rings, a religious requirement. They transmute poverty into a symptom of grace. Having no money, they redeem their economic status by rigid tithing of the small income they do possess, and thus far surpass members of churches of any other type or denomination in per capita contributions, despite the fact that they stand at the bottom of the economic scale.[1]

It is of course recognized that Pope's conclusions in this regard are based on explanations and interpretations entirely outside the realm of Scriptural requirements which justify such standards of dress and moral conduct or behavior. Such is also true of Clark who makes a corresponding observation. He says, referring to the economically underprivileged:

They elevate the necessities of their class—frugality, humility, and industry—into virtues and regard as sins the practices they are debarred from embracing. Those pinched by economic circumstances look askance at the theater-going, card-playing, and 'putting on of gold and costly apparel' but indulge in the same when their earthly fortune improves. Their standards of conduct are invented from the simple lives they are compelled at all events to lead and which are congenial to their simplicity. They give free rein to their emotions and attribute the pleasant thrills to divine agency. They look for an escape from their hard lot into a haven of bliss and comfort which is foreign to their workaday existence.[2]

Thus we have demonstrated how the ascending economic scale militates against the simple gospel and empties the worship services of those elements which attract men who are at the bottom of the economic ladder. Sweet graphically describes such a situation in the following account:

As the great denominations came more and more to be controlled by business methods, and dominated by men of wealth; as the services tended to become more formal and as ministers and choirs donned their robes, and cushions were placed in the pews, people of limited means began to feel more and more out of place and complaints began to be raised that heart religion was disappearing.[3]

---

1 Pope, op. cit., p. 137.
2 Clark, op. cit., pp. 18, 19.
3 Sweet, Story, p. 505.

To illustrate these contrasting types of worship services, the reader is invited to give attention to the following excerpt selected from a strikingly interesting article by Corinne Pressman which is written in somewhat racy style. She writes the following account of first hand observations:

> Recently, I visited two churches in a typical southern town. Comfortably secure in the valley was a church of stone and stained glass, an old church with a conservative history. Inside the church the merchants, textile mill executives and their families sang hymns softly, worshipped quietly and abided with dignity the gentle message of their pastor.
>
> Up on the hill looking down on the town, was a plain frame building of the Church of God. Inside there was standing room only and the building shook with the din of rebirth as the mill hands and share croppers shouted in the 'unknown tongues.' Meanwhile the less active of the participants sang hymns and clapped their hands rhythmically. As they became reborn converts crowded the aisles, weeping as they danced, moaning as they lay on the floor. The smaller children became frightened and cried; the older children, as used to this as they are fat-back for breakfast, stared with mild interest or fell asleep.[1]

Liston Pope's book, "Millhands and Preachers," presents a commentary on such worship services, and is a classic work completely thorough and interpretative from a psychological and philosophical standpoint. He does, however, miss the mark in failure to completely understand the spiritual value and content in such services due to the fact that he writes as a spectator and not as a participant. For our purpose, his work serves to emphasize the definite divisiveness of the economic factor. He has made a careful and somewhat exhaustive study in which he points to several factors explaining the emergence of new sects. Regarding the economic factor he says:

> It has been popular more recently to explain the emergence of sects primarily in terms of underlying economic conditions. Ordinarily the poorest strata of the community are attracted into membership, and it is urged that an otherworldly emphasis in the newer sects afford compensation for poverty and transcendence of the poor estate. The phenomenal rate of growth during the recent depression argues in favor of a theory of this sort; as economic conditions grew worse, newer sects flourished increasingly.[2]

---

[1] Corrine Pressman, Article on "Southern Revival" **Salute**, November, 1947.
[2] Pope, **op. cit.**, 134.

A. T. Boisen in an article, "Religion and Hard Times" make a simple but brilliant analysis of sectarianism in which he supports Pope's conclusion as to the influence of these underlying economic conditions.[1]

Pope makes the following summary appraisal:

The sect, in summary, represents a reaction, cloaked first in purely religious guise, against both religious and economic institutions. Overtly, it is a protest against the failure of religious institutions to come to grips with the needs of marginal groups, existing unnoticed on the fringes of cultural and social organizations.[2]

It is interesting to note his observation of how individuals change their denominational affiliation as they rise in the economic scale. He says:

A few members of any sect are likely to prosper, partly because of personal qualities (not necessarily virtues), but more often because of loose play in the economic organization. In the vernacular, a few members 'get the breaks.' Becoming more affluent and "responsible,' they either desert their sect as their economic status improves or else help to remould it in keeping with their newer position.[3]

Dimond in referring to these class distinctions among denominations due to the economic status of their constituencies writes:

The middle classes cultivated a very individualistic form of Protestantism, based on Bible and sermon reading and private prayer, which they found quite compatible with the best sort of worldliness. Above them floated a skeptical aristocracy; below lay a neglected heathendom.

In every town, besides the prosperous masters, journeymen, and apprentices, lived a mass of beings, physically corrupt, for whose bodies no one, and for whose souls only the Methodists had a thought to spare. The conditions of existence among the neglected poor, in the eighteenth century as in the first, provided the environment wherein the transforming spiritual power of the Gospel was amazingly manifest.[4]

Curran shows how various denominations appealed to different economic classes. European Lutheranism became and remained

---

1 A. T. Boisen, Article, "Religion and Hard Times," **Social Action,** March 15, 1939.
2 Pope, **op. cit.,** p. 140.
3 **Ibid.,** pp. 119, 120.
4 Dimond, **op. cit.,** pp. 251, 252.

the church of Nordic upper classes. Early Calvinism found its main support among the bourgeoisie. This caste appeal of Calvinism still persists.[1] Professor Niebuhr's statements corroborate Curran's claim. He states, "Calvinism remains the religion of the middle class which excludes from its worship, by character of its appeal, the religious poor as well as those who live within the lower ranges of economic and cultural respectability."[2]

There is another aspect of rel'gious teaching which rises out of the worshipper's economic status. Those who are attracted to certain doctrinal emphases comprise a class made up almost exclusively of those belonging to a lower economic stratum. Their evident lack of opportunity for emotional expression forced upon them in their drab existence creates a desire for a type of worship service which will compensate for this lack in their every-day routine living. Ernest Caldwell and his coadjutor, in their graphic and pictorial representation, *You Have Seen Their Faces,* describe the religion of the southern sharecroppers which serves to illustrate the value of the apocalyptic emphasis of the premillennial second coming of Christ. He gives the following account:

> The backland, pine-barren church-goer is a fervent believer in religion for religion's sake. His religion fits his needs and fulfills his desires. Usually he is a man who, under other circumstances, might have found religion a comforting thought but not a panacea.
> But in the South, in tenant farming regions, he made religion serve as a release and escape. The sermons that are preached to him fulfill his desire for a vision of a different life. Once a week he can hear the minister promise him a new life in another world. It gives him something to look forward to during the other six days of hard labor when he and his family do not have enough to eat. The expectation is that in the life promised by religion, he and his wife and children will not be hungry. It excites a man when he is hungry to be told that, for the asking, he can fill his stomach with food. When a minister does not have to appeal to basic reasoning, he can excite men and women as no one else can. He promises that religion will grant all needs and desires, he appeals to the man who wants to escape from the slavery of labor that wields no returns. He can excite the ignorant who live primitive lives to give vent to their feelings by rolling on the floor, shouting, and dancing in the aisles.
> Many men accept the Church merely to be on the safe side in case there is a life hereafter. They profess to be believers, although their

---

1 Curran, op. cit., pp. 6-9, et passim.
2 Niebuhr, op. cit., p. 105.

motive is to insure themselves against any eventuality. Tenant farmers in the South profess to be believers for a different reason. They have lived a life of hardships, and anything that offered a reasonable reward for their years of hard work would be appealing. It is not strange that many times they are savage in their demonstration of gratitude.

As a mere promise of something in the future, religion has no competitor among tenant farmers in the cotton country. The more **primitive the ritual,** the more exciting the prospect to primitive people. The Foot Washers, the Shouters, and the Holy Rollers are people who not only get excited over the prospect of living a second time, but who also want to celebrate their second life before dying in this one.[1]

Pope aptly points out the same significant facts which we have observed in the above account, as being applicable to the cotton-mill worker as well as the share-cropper. He writes:

Religious services also help the mill worker to transcend his daily life through providing excitement. All ministers acknowledge that mill workers need a strong emotional outlet because of the damming up of self-expression by the conditions amid which they live. The company village system preempts nearly all their fundamental choices, the jobs in the mill are highly mechanical and routine in character. When his day in the mill is over, the worker frequently feels the need of vigorous emotional massage; he finds it in hair-raising movies and emotional religious services, among other outlets. Newer sects, indulging in ecstatic religious emotion, thrive in the villages. Revival meetings have retained their popularity, and the tents of roving evangelists dot the mill hills during the summer months. A revival meeting becomes a community festival, and the astute evangelist provides as much entertainment and induces as much emotional response as possible. Saxophones and string ensembles are favorite props. 'Special music' nearly always includes undisguised appeal to the simpler emotions of the hearers, with the yearning for home as an especially prominent motif—the home from which one came to the mill village, or the home to which one hopes to go after the last spindle has been wound. Many of the favorite songs are in the form of ballads reminiscent of half-remembered mountain ballads, telling a story in a succession of from twelve to eighteen stanzas and adding to nostalgic escape. All parts of the revival service are designed to induce the high emotional crisis of 'being saved'—saved to a personal security that transcends the troubles of the world.

Thus, whether to make this present life more endurable or to escape from it in otherworldliness and emotional excitement, the

---

[1] Ernest Caldwell and Margaret Bourke-White, **You Have Seen Their Faces.** (New York: Modern Age Books, Inc., 1937), pp. 38, 39.

religion of the mill worker is heavily conditioned by the economic and social environment in which he lives. The forms assumed by his religious expression are not determined, however, by economic forces; they are largely religious in character and root principally in religious culture. Economic conditions figure prominently in the environment in the midst of which religious variations occur, and the survival of a particular variation appears to depend, to a considerable degree, on whether it meets needs coming directly out of the economic background. Overtly, religion in the mill churches appears to be indifferent to economic conditions; actually, it is in part a product of those conditions and, in diverting attention from them, is indirectly a sanction to them.[1]

Time and space will not allow us to cite more than a few examples of these typical worship services which Mr. Pope describes, but it will doubtless be interesting and fascinating to read some of them. A composite and impressionistic picture of these extreme types of emotional gatherings is to be seen in the following account. The reader should keep in mind that Pope, like many others, is inclined to look with disdain if not contempt upon the emotional expression of one's religion. He writes:

One traverses a grassless, rutted yard, climbs precarious 2 x 6 steps into a long, bare room filled with crude pews, and takes a seat in the Church of God. It is Sunday night, and the building is filled to overflowing, with about a thousand people present. Many stand in the doors or in the front yard of the church, including a large group of young men watching the girls go in and out. An ice cream vendor has placed his portable refrigerator near the church door, and is doing a thriving business. About 65 per cent of those present are women between the ages of fourteen and fifty-five, many of whom have sleeping babies in their laps. The atmosphere is expectant, and informal; members of the congregation move about at will, and talk in any tone of voice that suits their fancy.

A crude pulpit, a piano, and a section of pews for the choir are placed at the far end of the oblong building. Back of the pulpit to the left is a homemade board on which to register weekly attendance; beneath the board, in sprawling letters, the question:

HOW WILL YOUR
REPORT IN HEAVEN BE?

To the right of the pulpit is another sign:

GOD IS ABLE

A band, including three stringed instruments and a saxophone, plays occasional music.

---

[1] Pope, op. cit., pp. 90, 91.

THE ECONOMIC FACTOR AS A DIVISIVE FORCE 91

The service begins at eight o'clock or thereabouts. Rather, the actions of the congregation become more intense and concerted in character; there is almost nothing by way of formal announcement. The choir, in cooperation with the pastor, breaks into a rhythmic hymn, and the congregation follows suit. The hymn has an interminable number of stanzas, and a refrain, reminiscent of mountain ballards both in music and in narrative form. The hymn looks toward a narrative climax, and the excitement of the congregation increases as the singing proceeds. The stanzas are punctuated with loud shouts of 'Hallelujah,' 'Thank you, Jesus,' 'Glory,' and the rhythmic clapping of hands and tapping of feet. Almost immediately, various members of the congregation begin to 'get the Holy Ghost,' (as the teen-age boy awesomely remarks). One young woman leaves the front row of the choir and jerks about the pulpit, with motions so disconnected as to seem involuntary, weird. A man's head trembles violently from side to side. Another man, tieless and red-faced, laughs boomingly at odd moments, in a laugh resembling that of intoxication.

Half a dozen songs follow in succession. Then comes a prayer, with everybody kneeling on the floor and praying aloud at the same time, each in his own way. Some mutter with occasional shouts; others chant, with frequent bendings backward and forward; the volume of sound rises and falls, without unified pattern of group concentration. The pastor's voice booms out occasionally above all the others. Then as if by a prearranged but unobservable signal, the prayer abruptly ends; the onlooker is amazed to see emerging from the confusion a concerted return to a sitting position. The cacophony of prayer is ended as suddenly as it began.

Then the pastor reads 'the Scripture,' after confessing that he 'ain't had no time to study today,' and after attempting to induce a layman in the congregation to 'say something' without avail, because the layman confesses that he 'ain't had no time to study either' and insists 'you go right ahead, brother,' reluctantly the pastor begins to read, explaining each verse with amazing exegesis and equally amazing insight. Each verse becomes the subject for a homily, and the reader works up to a climax in its hortatory shouts from members of the congregation. Having finished the Scripture lesson, the preacher takes up a collection, counts it, announces that he has to have 'a little more,' and runs around in the congregation to garner proffered contributions, acknowledging each with a receipt 'God bless you, brother,' and finally emptying the collection plate into his pocket.

Then the service moves toward a climax; the taking of the collection has been an emotional interlude. The preacher begins a sermon; more precisely, he enunciates verbal symbols that arouse immediate response from the congregation. Such motifs play through his shoutings as 'sanctification,' 'the Second Coming,' 'the world despises and misunderstands and lies about the Church of God,' 'Jesus can heal your body and soul,' 'Believe the Word,' 'follow the kneeroute.' The Church of God is depicted as a remnant of those who have escaped from the 'coldness' of the Methodist and Bapstist churches. Lay preaching is urged, and personal evangelistic work. Attention is called to a number of prayer meetings to be held at various houses during the subsequent week, and to persons for whom prayer is desired—especially the family of a four-year old girl who has just died, because 'they can't hardly get over it.'

Then there is a testimony meeting in which a large number of the more faithful testify to their personal experience and joy in religion, some mutteringly, some loudly, fervidly. One woman defends her right to wear long-sleeved, high-necked dresses in the summer time, because 'the Spirit told me to.' Nearly all say that they are proud to speak for Christ, and not ashamed to speak out for their Master in church. The man who has been indulging the intoxicated laugh defends his right to laugh in church, saying that his religion makes him feel good all over and is not like the stiff coldness of the Methodist Church. Recurring phrases appear in the testimonies: 'I'm glad I got over bein' too proud to be a Holiness and get all there was of the Holy Ghost'; 'I'm a better wife and I've got a better husband because I joined the Church of God'; 'the Baptists are all right, but I wanted more of the Lord than they had.' Several testify to marvelous cures of physical illness during the past week, through prayer and the 'laying on of hands.'

All the while waves of ecstatic rhythm have been sweeping over the congregation, with the actions of the preacher setting the pace. There are patterns to the rhythmic actions: running around the pulpit, holding trembling hands to the sky, very fast clogging of the feet, swinging the arms, in sharp staccato motions. One girl leaps from her seat as though struck by an electric shock, races four times around the aisles of the church, screaming 'O God . . . do Jesus . . . O God . . . glory, glory, glory . . . give me more . . . more . . . glory, glory, glory'; falling over backward with hands outstretched, her whole body quivering and rhythmically jerking, she collapses at last in a dull heap on the floor, and stays there in comatose conditions for several minutes. Others rise and shout at the top of their lungs for five minutes or bang on something in staccato rhythm. The same persons respond again and again, with perhaps seventy-five individuals represented. Each responds with an individual pattern of motions, but all motions revolve around a few general types. The motions appear to have been culturally conditioned, whether immediately conditioned by the agent or not. One wonders if some form of mass hypnotism is at work.

About ten o'clock the pastor calls for sinners to come to the front and kneel around the altar (constructed of a bench quickly placed before the pulpit). About ten come, including one-five-year old boy. A hundred members of the congregation gather about, and a tremendous tumult ensues as they attempt to 'pray and shout sinners through,' interspersed with wild demonstrations of joy as one is 'saved.'

It is nearly 11 P. M., but one stays and wonders. They cry out, and cry; they are drunken, but not with wine; they stagger, but not with strong drink. . . .[1]

Clark, in discussing the economic influence in the rise of sects makes a striking observation regarding Wesley and Methodism which deserves close attention as a solemn warning. He says:

Wesley, the creator of a typical sect of the poor and ignorant clearly foresaw this evolutionary process. 'I do not see how it is possible in the nature of things for any revival of religion to continue long,' he declared. 'For religion must necessarily produce both industry and frugality, and these cannot but produce riches. But as riches increase so will pride, anger, and love of the world in all its branches.' The process was under way in his time. 'The Methodists in every place grew diligent and frugal; consequently they increase in goods. Hence, they proportionately increase in pride, in anger, in the desire of the flesh, the desire of the eyes, and the pride of life. So although the form of religion remains, the spirit is swiftly vanishing away. Wesley had a formula to prevent this development. He could not and ought not to prevent people from gathering all they could, but 'what can we take, that our money may not sink us into the nethermost hell?' There is one way and there is no other way under heaven. If those who gain all they can and save all they can, will likewise give all they can, then the more they gain the more they will grow in grace, and the more treasure they will lay up in heaven.[2]

We will bring our discussion to a close by saying in Curran's words—"By the thousands and scores of thousands, the lower economic classes abandoned a Protestantism which had first abandoned them."[3]

So, we conclude from the evidence submitted that economic forces more than any other are directly or indirectly responsible for divisiveness in the American Church.

Clark says, "It is the growth in wealth and culture that brings about departures from the early status and standards against which schismatics protest. In several ways the economic influence operates to bring about changes in theological emphases.[4]

---

1 Pope, op. cit., pp. 130-133.
2 Clark, op. cit., p. 20.
3 Curran, op. cit., p. 129.
4 Clark, op. cit., p. 21.

Chapter VI
THE POLITICAL FACTOR AS A DIVISIVE FORCE

In our discussion of the political factor as a divisive force the term "political factor" may be understood to include denominational difficulties which issue from national, sectional and racial causes, and also the divisiveness which grows out of a preference for a different type of church polity.

Dr. Sweet, the celebrated contemporary church historian begins his volume, *The Story of Religion in America,* with a chapter dealing with "The Creative Forces in American Religion" in which he sets forth striking parallels between American political and Church history. His wide knowledge of historical facts enables him to make observations which only a mature student of history could discern. Examples are cited of the frequent connection to be found between the political history of the nation with that of the Church. The reader is invited to take special note of the following quotations which illustrate this parallel trend:

> The American churches were engaged in forming organizations at the very time our constitutional fathers were formulating the federal constitution. Nationalism was in the air, manifested not only in the political activities of the nation, but in the religious organizations as well. Between 1784 and 1800 the Methodists, Protestant Episcopalians, Presbyterians, Roman Catholics, and the Reformed churches were engaged in nationalizing their ecclesiastical organizations. This same emphasis is likewise indicated in the formation of organizations among the churches to carry on certain phases of philanthropy. Thus in the early years of the nineteenth century the American Bible Society, the American Tract Society, and a whole group of similar organizations were formed, which indicate that the churches were viewing their task as one of national scope. 'Thus the church and the nation felt themselves called at the same period to grapple with the same problem,' that of securing harmonious cooperation among the states and among the churches.
>
> The period of nationalism was followed by the period of the growth of sectionalism. In this era slavery divided the nation, and it also divided the church. Churches began to emphasize their own denominational interests, at the expense of interdenominational and national interests. Loyalty to the denomination came now to be the great emphasis, as loyalty to the North and South came to be characteristic

in politics. Interdenominational societies gave way to denominational; churches were divided into anti-slavery and pro-slavery groups, while doctrinal schisms added to the confusion.
In the great American wars, the Revolutionary, the Civil and the World war, the American churches supported the program of government, and were affected by post-war influences. The new nationalism and the new centralization in government and in business arising after the Civil War found expression in the churches in the formation of the Federal Council, the rise of new interdenominational organizations, as well as the emphasis upon centralization and efficiency within the individual churches. During the World War the churches and the nation became internationally minded and built great world programs, to be followed by postwar reaction and a return to narrow nationalism. Thus has the same set of influences produced similar results in church and state while each has exercised a constant influence on the other.1

In this panoramic view we can easily grasp the significant relation which exists between our political and religious history, and can thus come to better understand how the political factor often influences religious trends. The reverse is also true. In the preceding chapter attention has already been directed to the motif of Dr. Bates' book which centers around the fact of how religion has influenced our political philosophies. Edwin Paxton Hood, quotes Mr. Lecky, whose statements regarding the influence of the Wesleyan revival are also valuable to consider here. Lecky writes:

Our splendid victories by land and sea must yield in real importance to this religious revolution; it exercised a profound and lasting influence upon the spirit of the established Church of England, upon the amount and distribution of the moral forces of that nation, and even upon the course of its political history.2

Dr. Lacy makes an interesting and somewhat original observation which will serve to further emphasize these conclusions. He says, "The religious revivals in Europe in the seventeenth century, in France, Puritan England, Scotland, and Northern Ireland, furnished dynamic power to enable thirteen colonies to become a Christian nation."3

Sweet, in his book, *Men of Zeal*, cites two instances which illustrate how individual clergymen have allowed political partisan-

---
1 Sweet, **Story**, pp. 9, 10.
2 Edwin Paxton Hood, **The Great Revival of the Eighteenth Century**. (New York: American Sunday School Union, 1882), p. 10.
3 Lacy, op. cit., p. 62.

ship to govern their religious choice. He mentions how the early Methodist missionaries who were staunch loyalists found it necessary to return to England during the Revolutionary War period; and how Devereaux Jarratt became harsh in his attitude toward the Methodists, ostensibly because he felt their defection from the Church of England was unjustifiable, but in reality because he was himself a slave-owner and objected to the stringent rules on slavery adopted at the organizing conference.[1]

The principal thesis of Muncy's book, *The History of Evangelism in the United States,* is to demonstrate how War has tended to retard or halt spiritual advancement in our nation. Our triumph which later became tragedy in evangelizing the Indians, he explains on the basis that war caused enmity between the two races. King George's War in 1744 sounded the death knell to the Great Awakening—The War of the Revolution brought with it spiritual decline—The period from 1625-1725, he refers to as the "Dark Age."[2]

Let us now notice more specifically how the political factor tends to cause division among sects. In a previous chapter we have designated the economic factor as being the most powerful in causing schisms in the Church; but the political factor offers very close competition as a divisive force. This is largely due to European immigration. America has become the melting pot of many races and in the process the Church has been affected. The patent influence of ethnic and national factors is clearly apparent. To name a few such groups will be sufficient to exhibit their national and racial character. German Seventh Day Baptists, German Baptist Dunkards and Scandinavain Baptists, Albanian, Bulgarian, Greek, Roumanian, Russian, Syrian Orthodox Churches; the Norwegian Lutheran, The United Danish Evangelical Lutheran and so the list might be continued.[3] It is also true that often when these groups drop their national or ethnic title they seldom lose their original character and complexion.

Niebuhr interestingly points out that nationalism came to birth with humanism. The Latin language supplanted the language of the once barbarous native tongues. National literature

---

[1] William Warren Sweet, **Men of Zeal.** (New York: The Abingdon Press, 1935), pp. 47, 118, et passim.
[2] Muncy, **op. cit.,** pp. 16, 37, 46, 73, et passim.
[3] Niebuhr, **op. cit.,** p. 107.

also brought national self-consciousness.[1] Linguistic differences have resulted in debates over the language to be used in divine services and have often ended in the formation of split groups. (It is characteristic of these nationalistic groups usually to follow a liturgical form of service. This fact may also account for the appearance of new sects to provide a different type of worship.)

Another phase of the political factor as a divisive force is to be found in sectionalism which offers another cause of denominationalism. Professor Niebuhr writes:

> America replaced the horizontal lines of European class structure with the vertical lines of a sectional society and continued or originated church schisms in accordance with that pattern of provincial organization of East and West and North and South which underlies its economic and political history. It brought the diverse races of Europe, with their various religious organizations, into a new relationship in which new kinds of accommodation and new kinds of conflict greatly modified the character of their church life.
>
> The Appalachian Mountains drew the first dividing boundary between American denominations; the Mason and Dixon line bisected the two unequal portions which resulted and added churches of the North and South to the Churches of the East and West.[2]

Because these sectional differences are written so plainly in history it becomes unnecessary to dwell at length on their description. It is desirable at this point, however, to give special attention to certain of these basic reasons for the sectional differences between the North and the South because of their far-reaching present-day implications. Ordinarily the slavery issue would have been discussed when dealing with the economic factor. We refrained from introducing it under that heading because it seemed well to reserve it for our present discussion. We customarily think of the slavery issue as a political question, and it is, but under the stress of war it became an ethical question; while actually it will be seen to be an economic question.

Men of the same race who spoke the same language and worshipped the same God were divided politically and religiously because they had different economic interests. The differences in climate, the differences in soil, and natural resources, and in

---
[1] Ibid., p. 121.
[2] Ibid., pp. 135, 136.

types of labor systems all combined to separate these two sections. The South being predominantly agricultural and the North predominantly industrial necessarily created a need for different types of labor. The Republicans wanted a "high-tariff" to protect the North's industrial system while the Democrats championed the cause of the South by advocating a system of "freedom" to create a foreign market for their cotton crops.

Several factors would be involved in full discussion of what caused these sectional differences, but it will serve our present purpose to conclude our treatment of these sectional differences with a needed additional emphasis being placed upon one of the factors mentioned—the rural character of the South and the urban character of the North. It was not until recent years that the South began to develop any appreciable amount of industries. It has remained predominantly rural and agricultural for the most part, while the North has continued its major emphasis on industrial development. The climate, the soil and other factors will perhaps cause these two sections to continue their same characteristic economic trends. These economic sectional differences have so far caused corresponding political and religious differences. "In recent times," Niebuhr writes, "the conflict between rural and urban religion took dramatic form in the theological battles of Modernism and Fundamentalism."[1] Atkins describes the South as "conservative and evangelical." These observations are of paramount importance for the understanding of the theological differences of these sections. Modernism has invaded the ranks of all the larger denominations and a goodly number of the smaller ones in both sections of the country but in the main it has no doubt influenced the urban North more than the rural South. These two religious schools of thought are diametrically opposed to one another and will not mix. The Continuing Methodist Episcopal Church, South, is an example of a sect which grew out of such controversy. According to reliable information from various quarters there are factions within many communions which are voicing their disapproval of the status quo and are contending for a return to old-line funda-

---

1 Niebuhr, op. cit., p. 184.

mental teachings. This trend will possibly issue in the formation of other new sects.¹

What was once a political and economic issue has in our day become a theological issue, and as such it will doubtlessly persist in dividing the two sections religiously. A fuller discussion of these wide-reaching implications will engage our attention in the chapter which follows.

A few brief statements will be all that is necessary as we come to deal with the last two causes of division listed. Above ninety per cent of the sects which have resulted from racial differences have involved the Negro. The Negro as well as the white man has for obvious reasons chosen to worship separately. According to Niebuhr, only a negligible number of colored people belong to churches with a mixed racial constituency. It is significant that the Negro's proneness to become over-emotional in his worship practices is due in part to the white man's failure to provide for him the same educational opportunity which has been offered to other under-privileged classes.

Finally, regarding the choice of church polity as a cause for division, the most outstanding example is to be found in the Methodist Church. Clark states, "Methodism is directly or indirectly responsible for over fifty of the existing American sects. They have a combined membership of nearly 9,000,000 persons." A substantial portion of these groups have resulted from being dissatisfied with the episcopal form of church government.

---

1 Atkins, op. cit., p. 87.

Chapter VII
WHY PENTECOSTAL HOLINESS?

We come now to the closing chapter of this section. Consideration has been given at some length to the various divisive factors which tend to produce new sects. An attempt will now be made to summarize some of our findings and to point out their particular bearing upon the main subject of our discussion. It has been our summary conclusion that new sects are necessary, and that divisiveness among denominations is not altogether undesirable. While it is recognized that many sects have found their way into an already crowded field without any apparent justification for their existence; it is nevertheless true that others have served a useful purpose and have prevented Christian doctrine from becoming static and unproductive.

In entering the discussion of this chapter and introducing the subject at hand it will be helpful to reiterate a portion of what has already been stated in the Introduction, namely, that no church has a right to exist as a distinct religious body unless good and legitimate reasons justify its existence to augment the corporate body of divine truth by emphasizing some neglected truth or by stressing anew some legitimate phase of revelation. If it be true that some of these new sects make their appearance in divine order, and according to many authorities that seems to be a warranted conclusion; the corollary is then that God foresaw a need and designed that they should make some particular and definite contribution to the total Church program.

Principally because Pentecostal and Holiness bodies have had no influential protagonist to give voice to their cause, the Church world has never come to fully appreciate nor to understand the respective contribution these groups have made. As in the case of other new sects these new groups also have been looked upon with contempt and disdain, and on the whole they have been misunderstood and despised. This has not come about altogether because of an unchristian attitude on the part of other churchmen. It has occurred primarily because it seems impossible to understand and appreciate such sects unless they are seen in the perspective of history. We come to understand them when they are viewed retrospectively and an effort is made to ascertain the underlying causes of their origin.

Pentecostal and Holiness groups are by and large still in an inchoate stage of development and therefore cannot yet be completely understood. Up until recent times the established churches have ignored these groups and considered them as fanatical minorities which would sooner or later regain their spiritual equilibrium and return to orthodox folds. But to their surprise, and in some cases their disappointment, these religious radicals have grown much more rapidly than was expected and have come to constitute a major threat to the stability of the large denominations. These groups are relatively small but together their constituencies aggregate hundreds of thousands and still they continue to increase. Many of the big churches have come to recognize in them a wholesome competition and have inaugurated extensive evangelistic programs to meet their competition. But they have thus far been unable to compete with these somewhat insignificant and inferior groups. Explicit and elaborate studies have been made to determine the reasons for their successes. While these are steps toward a desired goal, church historians have not yet offered an adequate explanation for their appearance. In the main, historians have either ignored or misunderstood them. The essential nature of their message and their respective contribution to the divine program have not yet come to be recognized.

It is the cherished hope of this writer that he may be able to unfold here some of the revealing facts which have hitherto been obscured; and that a mutual understanding can be affected between these groups and the established churches. If such an ideal objective could be realized, it would not only give impetus to the cause of the full gospel within these disinherited groups but also within the Church at large. It would be, however, mere wishful thinking to expect the whole church to adopt the teachings and worship practices of these minority groups. To advocate such an objective would obviously violate the very thesis which this section has set forth. Nevertheless the pristine dogma of the apostles needs the emphasis which these sects are giving and such an ideal should be more fully realized in our day.

A just and unbiased consideration and appraisal of the historical facts relating to the inception of these new sects should measurably affect current thinking and produce salutary effects toward realizing "the revival we need" in the whole church. We, as churches, increasingly need to recognize one another's respective contribution to the work of the Kingdom of God. In a chaotic world of uncertainty, misery and woe this writer pleads for a hearing that God's purposes for His Church may be more completely achieved. His church is eternal, its victory is sure, but that fact does not relieve us of our responsibility to know God's plan and to cheerfully cooperate in reaching such a goal and in presenting every man complete before Christ at His coming. The misunderstanding of one another is perhaps the greatest single impediment to hinder God's program.

Let us, therefore, soberly make a more careful study of the underlying reasons for the appearance of these Pentecostal and Holiness sects, and decide whether or not their existence can be justified. To such a task, may we earnestly direct our thought and attention with a conviction that in so doing we may come to serve God's purpose.

THE THEOLOGICAL PICTURE

Garrison aptly points out certain significant facts which have a direct bearing on the appearance of these sects. He says:

> For more than fifty years, there has been a widening gap between the more conservative and more liberal phases of evangelical religious thought. Throughout the greater part of the nineteenth century, the term 'evangelical' was used as a convenient barrier to protect orthodoxy in all its varieties from the contamination of unitarianism. Within the last two or three decades, (Garrison's book was written in 1933) the word has become somewhat vague in its meaning. Its significance, like that of the word 'orthodoxy' itself, depends on who uses it. It has therefore ceased to have much value for the purpose of classifying Christian thinkers into two groups.
>
> The liberalizing of theology within the present generation has been marked by two features. The first of these is a daring modernization of theological thought beyond that which had taken place in the nineteenth century through the influence of evolution and Bible criticism. The new changes have to do with the idea of God, the relation of Christianity to other religions, and the basis as well as the content of Christian morality. It has been influenced not only by the development of physical science but even more by psychology

and sociology; not only by recent types of philosophy, of which pragmatism and its variations have been the most influential in America, but also and perhaps still more by a rather loose and unthinking drift toward secular interests.1

In these two short paragraphs Garrison has embodied an extensive amount of information which we will keep in mind as a sort of working basis or spring board for our present discussion. It was in round numbers about fifty or more years before the writing of Garrison's book in 1933 that holiness groups began to make their appearance principally in the Southland. We are not so much concerned with the fact of their existence as with the causes which necessitated their existence. Calling to mind and enumerating some of the facts which we have discussed at length in earlier chapters will enable us to get the whole composite picture before our minds in an overall fashion.

We have pointed out how American students began to repair to German universities to do graduate work when our graduate schools had not yet reached respectable academic levels. While studying abroad they imbibed the teachings of German rationalism. Upon their return to America they brought their "mental baggage" as Atkins puts it, of German rationalism. These more highly educated men were naturally selected to occupy important chairs of learning in our best educational institutions. Their ideas were gradually transferred to the minds of their students who in turn carried them to congregations over the nation. Our best schools and our very best academically trained theological students have often been those who have sat under the teachings of these men, and their successors, who had also received a so-called superior education. We have already presented a somewhat lengthy discussion of "modern liberalism" and its manifestations in our first two chapters, but the particular point of our present discussion is to emphasize the fact that it began about the middle of the nineteenth century, and is one of the outstanding and significant reasons for the later appearance of Holiness and Pentecostal sects. Muncy, in writing of the influence of these groups says, "Their conservatism in theology has been a constant challenge to liberalism and a protest against any departure from the traditional theology."1 This is likely the first time any

---

1 Garrison, op. cit., pp. 266, 267.
1 Muncy, op. cit., p. 131.

writer of prominence has ever made the same observation. To amplify the significance of this pertinent observation we have but to imagine what the church world of today would have degenerated into without the stern orthodox witness of these sects.

A large number of the institutional churches and their seminaries have been shot through with modernism. Such a statement is not made with any intention of being invidious, but as that which is necessary to adequately depict the true situation which confronts us. As we have quoted Monsma, "Union with liberalism would mean separation from God and that separation would mean our utter destruction." There are admittedly many thousands within the large denominations who have not yet bowed their knee to Baal. However, if we would be fair we must recognize that these new sects have wielded a strong and almost immeasurable influence for truly orthodox, fundamental and evangelical doctrinal teaching. Without their faithful witness it is questionable as to what would have become of the Church. While it may be humbling to concede the correctness of such a claim, it would perhaps be a futile effort to attempt to disprove it. If we accept such a claim as valid, there is then sufficient ground to justify the existence of these "radical" church groups. It is an established fact that these groups present a "united theological front." Within them there is not one modernist. Every minister and every layman, without exception, holds to the same traditional orthodox, evangelical dogma which characterized the teachings of the Church before the infiltration of German rationalism and modernism. None of these groups nor the parent bodies from which they stem were at the time conscious of the indispensability of their witness, but God who knew the need of the future to combat these modernistic trends designed that they should take up the torch of fundamentalism and spread the fire which would keep alive the Christian faith. This is a stupendous claim! But what if the Church had not had their witness?

In the second chapter of this section we have already noted at some length the major manifestations of liberalism in the appearance of the social gospel; the emphasis on the new psychology of religious education; and the ecumenical movement. While we recognized in these new trends certain valid and worthy aspects to be emphasized, they were nevertheless all three shown to root in modern liberalism. Although we have already cited and discussed the principle underlying factors which issued in these new trends, it should be helpful to list them chronologically and call attention to the fact that these developments preceded or immediately followed the appearance of these new sects. In fact, these forces made the existence of these sects necessary. We list some of these forces as follows:

1. 1850, German Rationalism began its infiltration.
2. 1850-1872, 2,000 Spiritualist congregations were formed.
3. 1857, Horace Bushnell's "Christian Nurture."
4. 1859, Darwin's "Origin of Species."
5. 1861-1865, The Civil War.
6. 1866, Mrs. Eddy introduced Christian science.
7. 1870, Labor Movement.
8. 1880, Social Gospel.
9. 1893, The Depression (Panic).
10. 1898, Spanish-American War.
11. 1899, Starbuck's "Psychology of Religion" furnished a psychological basis for Bushnell's conclusions.

In this period great advances were made in the field of scientific development and invention. All ideas and methods of religion were required to justify themselves as scientific. Science came to be so popularized that it was considered the highest compliment to God that some scientiests believed in Him. Modernists sought to explain supernatural phenomena by natural laws and means. Reports of questionnaires which were sent to ministers and theological students were revealing. They disclosed the fact that infidelity and apostasy were everywhere to be found. Extreme liberals were closely allied in their thinking to humanism and completely abolished the supernatural and even denied the existence of a Being that could rightfully be called God. A period of disillusionment and doubt ensued. Labor troubles multiplied; politics were corrupt; science grew less complacent toward orthodoxy; the idea of God changed amid the new economy where men were primarily interested in profits. The lack of emphasis on individual salvation opened the way for the new emphasis on the social gospel. The "consecration of wealth" came to be a favorite topic, etc.

It was to be expected that some reaction to these conditions would be made in the natural course of events. In 1876 the Niagara Bible Conference was formed. In 1895 the famous five points of fundamentalism were formulated. Bible Conferences were organized over vast areas to combat modernistic trends. The Moody Bible Institute was established in 1886 and later the Los Angeles Bible Institute with the avowed purpose of training conservative evangelical ministers.

Curran, in his book, *Major Trends in American Church History* writes a chapter on "The Increase of Unbelief" in which he enumerates a number of these developments which led to these fundamentalist reactions which we have just mentioned, and also led to the formation of Holiness and Pentecostal groups.[1]

Garrison states:

> As Methodism became more urbanized and less revivalistic, there separated from it various groups which laid stress on the idea of 'complete sanctification.' . . . Not less than twenty-five Pentecostal and Holiness Organizations have been formed since 1880.[2]

Muncy presents a fine chapter in his book on "The Evangelization of the Underprivileged" in which he traces the origin and development of holiness sects. It is especially interesting to follow him as he deals with some of the conditions within the Methodist Church in particular that called this movement into being. The first national Holiness Camp Meeting in the United States was held at Vineland, New Jersey, in 1867. At this meeting there was organized the National Camp Meeting Association for the promotion of holiness. John S. Inskip was its first president.[3] Muncy writes of this association:

> The promoters of the Camp Meeting Association did not propose to organize a separate denomination. They decried denominationalism and sought to unite all true Christians. They sought at first to influence the older denominations toward their ideas of Christian perfection but found themselves more and more unwelcome in these groups. They sought to make their impact upon the total Christian population through 'bands' and conventions for almost a quarter of a century. But the movement split into many sects after the first effort at unification. In a period of fourteen years (1893-1907) at least

2 Garrison, op. cit., p. 197.
3 Muncy, op. cit., p. 127.
1 Curran, op. cit., pp. 121-135, et passim.

twenty-five separate Holiness denominations came into being. The state and national associations became sects or the evangelizing agencies of these groups.[1]

Benjamin Franklin Brown, in his thesis on file at Union Theological Seminary in Richmond, Virginia, states that the passing of perfectionism out of the life of Methodism gave rise to two important developments, the exodus of small dissenting groups from Methodism and the formation of the National Holiness Movement.[2] Brown gives to us a splendid summary of the conditions in society and the church prior to the coming of perfectionist groups. He says:

At the close of the Civil War there existed the same social situation as is common after most wars—immorality, secularism, national apostasy, together with an alarm at the reign of lawlessness and the continuance of manifold hatreds. Within the church there was a distinct tendency to compromise with the world. Little stress was placed on emotional experience. Consequently many unconverted people came into the church, and the spiritual vitality of the church reached a low ebb. Almost spontaneously all over the United States there arose a wave of perfectionism.[3]

While Mr. Brown presents an excellent summary of these existing conditions, he does not enter into a discussion of the underlying causes which brought them about. He does, however, list a number of these causes which may seem to be repetitious to quote here, but it is deemed worthwhile for emphasis, especially since he has based his comments on Gaddis' splendid and outstanding dissertation. He writes:

About 1890 the holiness movement entered into the sect-formation stage. In his chapter on the National Holiness Movement and Present Day Holiness Sects, Gaddis finds a number of influences and factors that led to the organization and later combinations of the groups into sects and churches in the late nineteenth and twentieth centuries. These and other influences include the natural tendency of all social movements, after a time, to become more and more definitely organized and institutionalized; the unwelcomed attitude on the part of regular members toward their holiness members; the absolutistic viewpoint of the perfectionists with respect to morality; the appearance of modernism with the scientific method; the rise of the quiet-process theory of conviction and conversion (sponsored by Bushnell

---
1 Ibid., p. 129.
2 Benjamin Franklin Brown, **Perfection Vs. Sanctification.** Thesis on File at Union Theological Seminary, Richmond, Virginia.
3 Ibid., pp. 12, 13.

in his Christian Nurture) as against the crisis experience; the rapid progress of the evolutionary theory; fresh outburst of revivals following the panic of 1893; and the ever-present insistence upon literal interpretation of the Bible—all of which combined to convince these groups that the 'true religion' could only be preserved by new and purged institutions.1

Dr. Clark makes a somewhat parallel observation:

At the close of the Civil War, as at the close of all great conflicts, including the World War, there swept over the country a wave of immorality, secularism and religious indifference. The spirit naturally affected the churches, bringing about what many believed to be a lowered moral tone, compromise with 'the world,' awakening of the insistence on definite religious experience as a condition of membership with the influx of unconverted persons into the fold, and a general decline in vital piety and holiness of life.2

Both Garrison and Atkins' books run somewhat parallel in dealing with events which have happened since 1892, while Garrison begins his account with the close of the Civil War. They both see in the same period a definite trend toward "change" because both the nation and the church had taken a "fresh start" during the periods about which they write. Some of these changes if not most of them within the church have been so revolutionary that these conventicle groups were organized in protest, after they had failed in their effort to alter these conditions within the established churches. If such had not taken place the Church would likely have been utterly doomed. But God ordered that it be preserved through these minority groups.

Robert Evans, Executive Secretary of the International Youth For Christ, when interviewed by this writer recently in Chicago, made certain significant statements which are apropos to explain the place and mission of the Pentecostal Holiness Church and other related bodies. In speaking of how God by-passes existing agencies when they abandon the program He had intended they should follow, he said:

There may be many and varied vehicles of divine truth. God doesn't need agencies but he uses them. They are means to an end. When the 'means' becomes the 'end' then God removes his presence from the midst.

---

1 **Ibid.,** pp. 14, 15.
2 Clark, **op. cit.,** p. 92.

Methodism, for example, was used of God to save England from moral ruin. As long as she continued to serve as a means to accomplish divine purposes God continued mightily to use her. All human movements have a tendency to degenerate from an organism to an organization; from a living, pulsating thing to a skeleton. If godly men succeed godly men God continues His special blessings.

Take another example, the Y. M. C. A. which Moody organized in this country began its work with the idea of using recreation as an instrument to serve in bringing young men under spiritual influence to win them to Christ. Today, recreation is in the forefront and has eclipsed the spiritual.

The Youth for Christ Movement has used legitimate entertainment to attract young people. If it ever becomes just an entertainment we will be in danger and God will withdraw His presence and blessing. We trade in our used car when it ceases to function. God isn't interested in preserving the status-quo but wants to get His work done. He hasn't promised to keep our organization but He has promised to bless us as we honor Him, that's all.

He climaxed these statements by making this thought provoking observation:

There has never been a major revival within the existing denominational set-up. Such was the case during the ministry of Christ, His apostles, Luther, Wesley, etc. They tried first to promote a revival within the Church but couldn't. God raised up other agencies and used them instead.

Bob Evans is, himself, a member of one of the large denominations which he criticizes, but his criticism was made in the right spirit. It is logical, reasonable and usable. The churches since the Reformation out of which these dissenting groups have come are still in existence—The Catholic Church from which Luther came; the Church of England out of which Wesley came, and the denominations out of which Holiness and Pentecostal sects have emerged are all extant. The Catholic Church and the Church of England need have no comment made about their spiritual condition. It is obvious. The inference is plain and sobering—that the present-day denominations will also go the way of their predecessors who persisted in rejecting God's program.

If the multiplied thousands of perfectionists are deluded and have no scriptural grounds for their experience of sanctification; and if the Pentecostalists are also deluded in the same manner and are the victims of a sort of "religious neurosis"; then they should all alike be ostracised from the society of sane people and from the circles of orthodox evangelical Christianity. But, if the reverse is true, and reasonable Scriptural proof can be adduced to establish the validity of their experiences, showing them to coincide with that received by the Apostles and many saints of subsequent periods of church history—if that be true, they are then justified in their existence and to that extent should point the way for others to follow.

Further comment and discussion as to why these sects exist will be made in the closing chapter of the second section after historical evidence has been presented to demonstrate how all major revival movements, out of which the major denominations have come, have followed the same evolutionary pattern cycle which these newer groups have more recently begun.

SECTION II
THE EVOLUTION OF DENOMINATIONS

Section II
THE EVOLUTION OF DENOMINATIONS
Introduction

Thus far in our discussion we have attempted to evaluate some of the causes for divisiveness among denominations. In the series of chapters which comprise Section I, we have analyzed separately these various underlying factors in society which tend to act as divisive forces and which have often given rise to and fostered the existence of successively rising sects. Some consideration was also given to the possibility of achieving Protestant unity and ecumenicity. In the process of our analytical procedure we arrived at the conclusion that denominationalism is not only unavoidable, but that it is to some extent definitely desirable. Some sects, it is true, appear to serve no useful purpose, while others, it seems, are divinely appointed instruments used to preserve true Christian doctrine and to prevent the truth from becoming static. Invariably, when the existing church has failed in its mission to lay proper emphasis on certain phases of truth, new sects have been formed to take up the task. Such a procedure has been in full harmony with God's divine purpose.

Now, as a sequel to the ideas set forth in Section I, in this second section we will attempt to demonstrate the fact that denominations have always tended to follow a set pattern or trend of development as they have evolved from the "sect" stage to the "denominational" stage. As "sects" they have been considered as outcast minorities who have on the whole been despised and have represented an extreme type of religious radicals. Emotional excesses and erratic teachings have characterized these new groups. As their cultural and economic standards have been raised, and as their rational inhibitions have been developed with better educational advantages; these groups of religious radicals have come finally to reach the stage of denominational respectability becoming numerically, socially, economically, and psychologically respectable.

After churches have evolved to the stage of denominational respectability, it will be noted that there is invariably a tendency to enter into the downward phase of this pattern cycle which is characterized by compromise of doctrine and ethical practices which leads ultimately to a definite and pathetic spiritual decline. There is abundant evidence of the fact that denominations are, at the time, conscious of their defection; and yet it seems that their efforts to avert such a disaster are on the whole futile. When decay, corruption, disintegration, spiritual apathy and indifference become perceptible and finally pronounced in their mature stages of development, it is then that these minority groups within the churches begin their demand for a revolutionary change. The denomination's reaction to such a demand is to be seen reflected in their efforts to inaugurate elaborate programs of various types in the hope of averting the inevitable. They seem to be within the relentless embracings of a huge octupus who mercilessly crushes the life out of them. Just as the arms of an octupus hold its helpless victim from many sides, so it is that the arm of social and cultural advancement, educational opportunity, economic betterment and numerous other forces bind the "denominational Samson" who has continued to court the "worldly Delilah" until worldly influences have finally robbed it of the power of God's Spirit. Emotion has been squeezed out so completely that a genuine revival, which is the only remaining hope, is no longer possible. As Dr. Sweet puts it, religion comes to be more and more a matter of learning and less and less a matter of feeling.[1] When the patience of agitating factions is finally worn threadbare and there is no reasonable hope of recovery in sight, it is then that a new sect is born. It is sad but true that, so far, history has not failed to repeat itself. As each new sect develops and grows, it soon becomes more popular and finally becomes respectable and so continues in the pattern cycle until other new sects are eventually formed for the same reasons.

It will be observed that these new sects emerge at a time when spiritual tides have subsided and there arises a divine necessity for a revival of pure religion either to come "inside" or "outside" the Church. When there has been a stubborn refusal on the part of the parent body to adhere to the minority's demand for re-

---

1 Sweet, **Revivalism**, p. 180.

THE EVOLUTION OF DENOMINATIONS 115

vival, a new "denominational child" is born to augment the ever-increasing list of sects and cults.

In the chapters which follow, the chronological phases of this "pattern cycle" will be demonstrated by historic examples which are observed in different eras of denominational church history. Since this same sequence of events has recurred with a noticeable frequency, it should be therefore of highly significant value. It should serve as a solemn warning to all those denominations which are in the process of becoming respectable, lest they should wander into devious paths and follow the same destructive course that others have followed. With such a guide before us we should be able to determine our approximate position or stage of development and be able to govern our attitude and actions accordingly. None of us need despair, regardless of our present condition! There is hope for all—provided we will not only recognize our need, but become willing to meet God's requirements for spiritual rehabilitation. While the pages of history reveal that it has never been done, it nevertheless can be done! If we, like Samson of old, are willing to sacrifice even our own selves that God's cause may go on, then we can accomplish in our death more than we did in our life.

The material presented in this section is intended to furnish also an historic perspective which is prerequisite for an adequate understanding and appreciation of the presence of the Pentecostal Holiness Church and other kindred groups. The relationship of these groups as a constituent part necessary to complete the body of Christ will be considered. The particular contribution which these groups have made to the total Church program will be further emphasized in order to show their indispensable character. In short, a further attempt will be made to explain and justify their existence. But before we turn our attention to an actual working demonstration of this pattern cycle within denominations, let us validate such a procedure by making a few summary observations selected from the authoritative writings of some of those who also have recognized the same characteristic cycle.

Niebuhr points out how differences in the sociological structure of various groups determine their doctrinal teachings and ethical practices. These particular distinctions, he says, determine whether a religious group may be considered a "sect" or a "church." Members are "born" in the church, while in the sect they must be "born again" and join. The institutional church lays primary emphasis on ritualism and symbolism. The means of grace and the liturgical expertness of communicants is emphasized.[1] To give a practical illustration of this distinctive trend—recently, this writer interviewed Dr. John R. Lodge, Rector of St. Andrews Episcopal Church, Wilmington, Deleware. When asked the question as to his idea of recruiting new members, he replied:

> The only evangelism that is effective teaches responsibility. The newly admitted communicant needs to acquaint himself by study and thorough instruction to become familiar with the liturgical framework. He must adjust himself to the required disciplines of worship pertaining to the sacramental acts. He gradually becomes accustomed to the mechanics of the science of liturgical worship.

Niebuhr points out further how the sects have ever been the child of an outcast minority. New sects are seen to champion the uncompromising ethics of Jesus and to serve as agencies to recall the Church to its mission. Denominations are described as sociological groups conforming to different social orders or castes. "Castes make outcasts and outcasts make for castes. The churches of the poor all become middle-class sooner or later. Economic and social factors are recognized ultimately as causes for wide cleavages within the Church. Persecution then follows and a new sect appears. The parent church frantically continues its struggle for existence by substituting religious education for conversion; the social gospel replaces the gospel of personal salvation and a middle-class complacency prevails."[2]

In referring to the characteristic trend of spiritual decline which necessitates a new sect, Niebuhr makes this summary statement:

> [Religious history amply illustrates the process.] An outstanding example is the 'Half-Way Covenant' of the New England churches, which provided for the baptism of the children of the second generation, unconverted parents who had 'owned the covenant' and submitted to discipline of the Church without being able to attain to full fellowship because of their lack of experience of salvation. The

---

1 Niebuhr, op. cit., pp. 17-19.
2 Niebuhr, op. cit., pp. 19, 21, 39, 29, 30, 53, 54, 60, et passim

THE EVOLUTION OF DENOMINATIONS   117

rise of 'birthright membership' in the Society of Friends shows the
same process at work while the histories of the Baptists, Mennonites,
Methodists offer further illustrations. Doctrines and practices change
with mutations of social structure.[1]

In summing up the whole process of the evolution, he says,

One phase of the history of denominationalism reveals itself as the
story of the religiously neglected poor, who fashion a new type of
Christianity which corresponds to their distinctive needs, who rise
in the economic scale under the influence of religious discipline, and
who, in the midst of a freshly acquired cultural respectability, neglect
the poor succeeding them on a lower plane. [This pattern occurs
with remarkable regularity in the history of Christianity.] Anabaptists, Quakers, Salvation Army, and more recent sects of like type
illustrate the rise and progress of the churches of the disinherited.[2]

Curran discusses the same characteristic trend but presents
it in a little more explicit or detailed style. He says:

In the origin of a typical Evangelical sect, the poor and the uneducated found the established sect unsuited to their needs, and so
tended to form within it congregations composed exclusively of lower-class members. Gradually these congregations of the disinherited
drew apart from the parent denomination, established fraternal
relations with other groups experiencing a similar process of evolution, broke relations with the parent sect, and established an independent denomination. Almost invariably, the polity of the new sect
was congregational; its worship, moral teachings, and doctrinal tenets
assumed a form conditioned always by the poverty and ignorance of
its adherents.

While such a new sect manifested the theological proclivities of its
parent denomination, whether Calvinistic or Arminian, Lutheran or
Anglican, it invariably based its theology on the peculiar Evangelical
doctrine of 'conversion.' This dogma taught that man was 'saved,'
not by the justification of faith or by the predestination of God alone,
but by an emotional upheaval through which sinful man is 'convinced of sin,' and 'accepts the Lord.' Apparently the ignorance
of the disinherited, which permitted them to confuse religion with
emotionalism, and the economic disabilities, which forced them to
seek emotional catharsis in their worship rather than in costly
recreation, were important factors in the universal adoption of this
peculiar doctrine by the Evangelicals.[3]

In conclusion Curran summarizes how evangelical mutations
follow a classical evolutional process. He says:

Over a period of years the membership of the new sect, partly
because of emphasis on Puritan morality and thrift, gains in wealth

---

1 Ibid., pp. 20, 21.
2 Ibid., p. 28.
3 Curran, op. cit., pp. 10, 11.

and acquires a degree of respectability. Imperceptibly the sect becomes tinged with a bourgeois mentality, and is somewhat shamefaced about its antecendents. If the doctrine of millenarianism and the "Second Blessing" had been taught, they are now tacitly and tactfully forgotten. Since the new respectability views sensationalism with disfavor, emotionalism in the "conversion" experience and in worship are gradually eliminated . . . .

Often has it happened that sect members who had lagged behind in the acquisition of wealth and respectability find the denomination, in its final stages of evolution, no longer capable of satisfying their peculiar religious needs. Once more, therefore Evangelicalism begins the evolution of a new sect.[1]

Clark gives a most satisfactory summary in which he states, "All denominations begin as sects, and the evolution of a sect into a Church has followed a routine." His summary would be somewhat repetitious to quote but we will mention the high spots. He points out how economic influences have caused persons to become socially well placed. These new acquisitions of wealth and culture cause churchmen to depart from their early status and standards and to change their theological emphases to suit their newly acquired economic and cultural status. Class distinctions emerge and social life becomes worldly. "The favorite taboos of the poor, against dancing, theatre-going, and similar exercises weaken, and the difference between the 'saved' and 'unsaved' becomes less apparent. In the minds of the conservative element, and those debarred by circumstances from participation in the general affluence, the Church has grown apostate and worldly. Revolt ensues and a sect is born."[2]

In a previous discussion in Chapter V of the first section we have already mentioned how Wesley clearly saw this evolutionary process, but with all of his warning he was unable to prevent the inevitable from happening. Although he suggested a potent formula to prevent this development his remedy was rejected by those who had gained wealth. They refused to "give all they could" but "gained and saved all they could." It is easier for a camel to go through the eye of a needle than for a rich man (or rich church) to enter into the kingdom of heaven.

Clark points out how wealth and bigness undermine the democratic spirit. The church becomes a machine and some of the

---
[1] Ibid., p. 13.
[2] Clark, op. cit., pp. 18-22, et passim.

members chafe under its demands, and revolt in protest. He also points out how education modifies doctrinal emphasis and modes of religious expression. The advance of science and the effects of higher criticism cause departure from orthodoxy.[1] His concluding remarks are worthy of consideration and we quote them verbatim. He says:

> Th's modification in belief has been accompanied by an almost total elimination of emotional expression, radical conversion experiences, and the revival method in the great denominations. Religious education has supplanted these phenomena which were fundamental to frontier religion and dear to thousands of simple souls. All this development has been accompanied by uneasiness and protest and has been responsible for many schisms and the creation of many new sects.[2]

With the consideration of this quotation we are brought in our thinking to the point where we should be ready to give attention to the type of religious behaviour which has been peculiar to every outstanding revival of genuine religion in modern times.

It would not be perhaps too far afield for us to say that the two greatest enemies of the church have always been money and education. We need both, but when either or both come to be over-emphasized they have a subtle way of robbing us of the simplicity which is indispensable if we would worship God acceptably. If education sets up rational inhibitions which deprive us of legitimate emotional expression in our religious worship, and if wealth be so increased or economic and cultural standards so raised that we no longer feel the need of God in true worship; then wealth and education have become a curse instead of a blessing. "The love of money is the root of all evil."[3] Wealth brings within our grasp those things which militate against true worship. If we refuse to part with wealth we then love it more than we love God. We cannot serve God and mammon.[4] The love of mammon is then the root of all evil.

In turning now to the main body of our discussion in this section, let us remember from whence we have come, and do our first works over, lest we die.

---

1 Ibid., pp. 22, 23.
2 Clark, op. cit., p. 23.
3 I Timothy 6:10.
4 Matthew 6:24.

Chapter I
RELIGIOUS RADICALS

Without exception the evangelical denominations of our day were born in the midst of great religious awakenings. Such revivals were on the whole characterized by radical preaching, erratic behaviour and somewhat extreme types of emotional expression. Although many of us have forgotten from whence we came, these are facts which admit of no dispute. Dr. Sweet, in referring to the radical nature of those who have pioneered in these religious revivals has this to say: "The one fact, more than any other, which explains American religion in the period of the colonies is that the colonial churches were planted largely by groups of religious radicals."[1] This was somewhat equally true of all the evangelical denominations. In speaking of the Baptists and Quakers, Sweet makes the following statements regarding their radical tendencies:

> The principles of the Baptists and the Quakers struck at the foundations of the seventeenth century state and ecclesiastical organization, were considered in the more conservative colonies, such as Virginia and Massachusetts, as dangerously radical.[2]

Our ecclesiastical forebears, besides being religious radicals, were people most of whom we would class as socially-inferior and economically-disfranchised. They were on the whole the most indigent of the poor. Ernst Troelsch, the astute historian of social ethics of the churches, Niebuhr quotes as saying: "The really creative church-forming religious movements are the work of the lower strata."[3]

The Church since that time has made marked advances in various fields of endeavor. This has been especially true with relation to its foreign missionary program, and also in the realm of its social mission. There needed to be a leveling-off period for practical instruction in the meaning of Christian discipleship and stewardship. They needed to have their religious zeal and enthusiasm tempered by Christian training, and to be relieved

---

1 Sweet, Story, p. 2.
2 Ibid., p. 3.
3 Niebuhr, op. cit., p. 26.

of the extreme emotional excesses which had come to be overdone. Thoughtful church leaders inaugurated programs designed to accomplish such worthy ends and they are to be commended for so doing. We should, however, recognize that the pendulum swings from one extreme to another and that in our effort to avoid one extreme we have, it seems, swung to the opposite extreme.

The established church, in seeking to avoid emotional extremes, has virtually outlawed emotion altogether. In an effort to assume her social task and to point out the evils of society she has neglected the all-important aspect of personal salvation. The undue emphasis which has been placed on the new psychology of religious education and the social gospel has already been discussed at some length. These statements of criticism are not intended to suggest that the established churches have utterly failed, nor is it this writer's opinion that only the smaller sect groups have in them the real church which goes to make up the body of Christ. Such a claim would be unwarranted, unreasonable, un-Scriptural, as well as unchristian. No single church or denomination can rightfully lay claim to God's complete revelation nor to all of the divine truth. Neither can any single church or denomination expect to serve adequately the complete purpose of Christ's program for His Church. We have already demonstrated at some length the necessity for different types of denominations. Each denomination is intended to serve a limited purpose in laying some needed emphasis on a neglected phase of divine truth. Such an emphasis distinguishes it from other denominations and justifies its separate existence. When we, as a denomination, mistake our own denominational "arc" for the "whole circle" we are to be pitied. Each denomination attracts certain types of individuals and social classes which others could never attract; and as such are in a sense indispensable to God's program. True Christians of the Invisible Church are to be found in various communions. The Holiness and Pentecostal sects need to recognize this truth, and to develop a greater appreciation for those Christians who may differ with them in doctrinal emphasis. May we also add that the same rule can well be applied on the other side. Caution should be exercised to avoid any hurtful compromise of one's convictions in the process of making Christian allowances for these differences. Neither should we ignore scriptural standards which are intended to guide our experience and worship, nor the conclusions which issue from valid experiences. By a process of rationalization we might easily justify most any given emphasis. It therefore requires strict honesty lest we fall short of God's scriptural requirements and neglect that which is vital for genuine salvation.

For example, the crisis conversion experience has had its particular emphasis in connection with adults, though it has not been restricted to adults. It has characterized revival periods which have dealt principally with adult types who have been deprived of the early Christian nurture and training which the Christian home affords. Such a type of conversion was to be expected as the natural outcome under such circumstances. It should not be forgotten, however, that there are many others who have come up under different circumstances who became Christians in a milder manner without being able to point to a definite emotional crisis taking place at a definite time. Some of the very best saints of the Church bear testimony to this quiet type of conversion experience which resulted from a lengthy period of Christian training. It should not be overlooked that although these people became Christians through the subconscious work of the Spirit of God in a gradual process, they were no less conscious of their sonship. Their lives bore testimony to the fact that the new birth had taken place.

Denominations naturally embark upon a program of Christian nurture or education when they enter the second generation of their existence, dealing with those of their children whom they have trained with the purpose in view of effecting their salvation in that manner. It is a mistake to expect all persons alike to experience a crisis conversion. But it is an equally great mistake to expect all persons to become Christians without such a crisis experience, through the means of Christian education. We have pointed out in our discussion of the new psychology of religious education the difference between "Christian education" and the so-called "religious education" which the established Church to a large extent has drifted into in its effort to avoid emotional extremes. Many are admitted into the Church who know practically nothing of the meaning of genuine Christian discipleship.

Emotional extremes are to be disparaged, and every legitimate means should be exercised to prevent these excesses but the greater hurt which has come to the Church in our day has resulted from the lack of emotional expression in religion. While this may be considered by some to be a debatable question, this statement is based on the unanimous opinion of more than forty religious leaders of different church organizations in the principal cities ranging from Washington to Boston and Toronto and from Chicago back into Richmond. In recent personal interviews with this writer these men all expressed the opinion that the Church as they knew it had failed in current times to give a legitimate emphasis to the emotional aspect of religious experience.

The character of the times which preceded these early revivals were such that demanded a crisis conversion experience. These times will be described in the closing chapter of this section and a comparison made with our own times which should reveal the necessity of a repetition of this emphasis in our day. It will be in order, perhaps, to make a general statement at this point to affirm that the absence of the family altar, the decline in Sunday schools, and other factors have created a need for fresh emphasis on this older type of conversion experience.

It is hoped that the consideration of the facts presented in this chapter will help the established Church to recognize her failure in unduly opposing the very forces which gave her the power to be born. We moderns have assumed a somewhat supercilious attitude because of our intellectual achievements, and have rejected that which could be used in a saving measure to bring about a genuine revival.

The pages of history are replete with factual information which describes these periods of great awakenings. There is abundant evidence of radical preaching, severe persecution, crisis conversion and emotional expression. It will be impractical for us to enter into an exhaustive discussion of these factors, but in order to serve our purpose it will be necessary to review some of these facts at least in a general way. The Church needs to recognize the distinct value of the contributions which these eras of religious awakening have made. A comparison should be made of the relative value of their revival techniques as compared with those of more modern design. In spite of the so-called extravagances of these early groups we are forced to admit that God was with them and that we would do well to incorporate at least a part of their revival technique.

THE CRISIS CONVERSION EXPERIENCE

Let us notice first the historic trend of the crisis conversion experience in the major revivals of the past. Sweet tells us that "pietism lies at the heart of colonial awakening."[1] Irish Presbyterianism and Pietism together formed a confluence of kindred forces which issued in the Great Awakening and other subsequent revival movements in America. These major revival awakenings have unfailingly stressed the necessity of a vital personal religious experience or crisis conversion. In order to understand and more fully appreciate the emphasis of these movements it becomes necessary to investigate the influences of at least three other revival movements originating in Europe, Ireland and England, viz., The Pietistic Movement in Germany which began in 1670; the revival in Ireland which began in 1642; and the Wesleyan Revival which was contemporaneous with the Great Awakening.

It was when the State Church in Germany drifted away from the moorings of theological safety that it began to expound the creedal statements of the Church as authoritative rather than the Word of God. Nearly one hundred and fifty years had passed since Luther had nailed his 95 theses on the door of the castle church in Wittenburg, on October 31, 1517. This departure from the Word of God to the creedal statements of the Church had produced a meaningless formalism and a generation of church members who knew little or nothing about vital personal religious experience.[2] The Lutheran church continued to exist but God used a new movement to emphasize what they had neglected to emphasize.

In 1670 the Pietistic revival had its inception under the able leadership of Philip Spener who was himself a Lutheran minister.

---
1 Sweet, Revivalism, p. 24.
2 The Encyclopedia Americana, Vol. 22, p. 78.

It was his conviction that to return to the Bible and a vital conversion experience was imperative. He initiated this movement in a very humble way by opening his home for prayer and an earnest study of God's word.[1] Spener later published a book in which he advocated (1) an earnest study of God's word, (2) giving to laymen a share in church government, (3) insistence from the pulpit on a personal religious experience. Walker states that pietism was "an assertion of the primacy of feeling in Christian experience."[2] Spener's ideas came to be widely accepted in many quarters. Among those influenced by the movement were a group of university students at Leipsig. They began a devotional study of the Scriptures and prayer in their rooms much on the same order as Spener had done in his home at Frankfurt. When their meetings aroused more and more interest because of their growing popularity these students were suppressed by University officials. They immediately withdrew and enrolled in the newly formed university at Halli which had been established that year by Spener, Francke and others. Here it was that young men were trained whom God used to spread revival fires throughout Europe and America. The Moravian Church, organized by Count Von Zinzindorf in 1727 was the fruit of the pietist movement. Thomas J. Frelinghuysen was a German Pietist and a product of Halli University. Being a very zealous young minister he attacked the dead formalism which pervaded the Dutch Reformed churches in the colonies. He, like other Pietists, preached the necessity of a genuine moral reformation and a vital conversion experience. These new evangelical doctrines aroused immediate opposition and caused divisions comparable to those factions within the Church which have either opposed or endorsed new methods in subsequent periods of revival. Though he was charged with heresy his ardor did not diminish. Elders and deacons in his four churches professed conversion one after another. The news was spread of these results and calls began to come from various directions inviting Frelinghuysen for revivals. It was in this manner that he withdrew from the pastorate and began an active itinerant evangelistic

---

1 The Encyclopedia Britannica, Vol. 7, p. 919.
2 Williston Walker, **A History of the Christian Church.** (New York: Charles Scribner's Sons, 1945), p. 496.

ministry. According to Muncy, two other innovations were introduced besides itinerant preaching. He led in the formation of groups which, like the Pietists, met for Bible study and prayer. A second departure from the traditional path was the introduction of "lay preachers" as helpers.[1]

Among the many he influenced was a promising and gifted young man by the name of Gilbert Tennent, the first of the famous Tennent family to come into prominence. In a later experience young Tennent fell seriously ill and at the time was strangely impressed concerning his responsibility as a soul winner. As a result he solemnly pledged himself to give all diligence to God's work if Providence would permit him to recover. He was the foremost preacher within the great Presbyterian Church supporting the revival. The biography of his life constitutes an interesting study as one traces the important developments of the Great Awakening. Sweet states that the influence of this illustrious minister's preaching upon the masses was even beyond the immortal Whitefield's.[2] Muncy writes that his farewell sermon in Boston initiated a revival which lasted two years after his departure. In his own words:

> The revival continued unabated for about two years after Tennent's departure. One Boston preacher said that more people had sought personal interviews with him, relative to their spiritual needs, in one week than had come to him in all the twenty-four years of his ministry before Tennent's visit. Another testified that six hundred had sought personal spiritual guidance in a period of three months, still another could count one thousand in the same period.[3]

Special mention is being made of these incidents to emphasize the value of the crisis conversion experience which he advocated. A vital personal religious experience was a characteristic emphasis of the Great Awakening which came about largely as a result of Pietist influences. Sweet refers to this individualistic trend in the following quotation:

> Preaching likewise, among all colonial religious bodies came largely to deal with individual needs. In the stress and strain of colonization, where the facing of hardship was an every-day experience, there

---

[1] Muncy, op. cit., p. 40.
[2] William Warren Sweet, Makers of American Christianity. (New York: Henny Holt and Co., 1937), p. 91.
[3] Muncy, op. cit., p. 33.

was a demand for a type of preaching that would concern itself with everyday needs and individual concerns. Calvinism is a legalistic system and the tendency of early Calvinistic clergy was to devote their sermons to an exposition and defense of the system, but in the course of time the legalistic theology of Calvinism became in the hands of men like Edwards and Tennent a personalized Calvinism searching out the hearts of individuals.[1]

George Whitefield also came under the direct influence of Pietism. The importance of his most outstanding ministry needs no comment. Although the Great Awakening had its inception under Edwards, Whitefield was the principal protagonist in its extension. To further illustrate the individual aspect of the revival technique Muncy refers to one of Whitefield's preaching tours during which he brought ministers as well as laymen face to face with the question of their personal salvation. He writes:

> In the course of this preaching tour, Whitefield raised the question as to whether or not the ministers had been converted. This caused resentment on the part of some of the clergy, but more than twenty ministers professed conversion under the spell of his preaching.[2]

In a day like our own, when preaching has become more and more general and less and less personal, it is not difficult to see the value of a more personal and individual approach that would affect both clergy and laity alike.

It was said of Edwards that "he spoke little of heaven, he cared nothing for this world, but he certainly knew his hell."[3] Men were made to feel a need for their own personal salvation. Others who labored during the Great Awakening and in the Great Revival of 1800 also laid the same emphasis on personal salvation.

Dr. Sweet summarizes in a most able manner the real heart of the Great Revival in his comments which are based on Ola Elizabeth Winslow's statement. He says:

> Miss Winslow has well stated that the central fact in the great upheaval in American life, which we call the Great Awakening, and with which Jonathan Edwards had so much to do, was that religion is a personal matter; that it is an 'inner experience or it is nothing.' In his 'Treatise Concerning Religious Affections' and through his own example of preaching, as well as in his pastoral ministrations,

---

1 Sweet, **Revivalism**, p. 20.
2 Muncy, op. cit., p .31.
3 Grover C. Loud, **Evangelized America**. (New York: Lincoln Mac Veagh. The Dial Press, 1928), p. 21.

Jonathan Edwards made religious emotion theologically and intellectually respectable. This fact is basic to any understanding of the course of revivalism in America.[1]

The revival in Ireland in 1642 perhaps we should have mentioned first, according to its chronological priority. The story goes that Scottish regiments were sent into Ulster, Ireland following their rebellion in 1641.[2] The chaplains of these regiments were Presbyterians under whose ministries a great revival was prosecuted. Conventicle groups withdrew from the Church of Ireland and eventually some of them migrated to America. William Tennent was the most famous of these dissenters. He migrated to New York where he joined himself with the Presbyterian Church. He was a man of wonderful zeal and foresight. It was through his influence that the famous Log College of Neshaminy, Pennsylvania was established in 1727. Gewehr tells us that Tennent's school turned out a group of men eminent for their piety and qualities of leadership. His four sons were among the number. Blair and Finley, two Log College Alumni, also established schools. There is a continuity between the Log College and Princeton. So it is that Tennent's Log College became the germ of Princeton, and was indirectly or directly responsible for many institutions, including Hampden-Sidney and Washington College. The preaching of some of these Log College ministers will be described presently under another caption. It will serve our purpose to close this part of our discussion with saying that the influence of the Irish revival reached far into America and affected the Great Awakening in a sizeable manner—the vital personal conversion experience came to be further emphasized.[3]

As a final consideration of the influences which fostered the crisis conversion revival technique, we refer to another group who were influenced by the Pietists and who in turn exercised a substantial and telling influence in America. The "Holy Club" or "Methodists" were a small group of Oxford students who met regularly for devotional Bible study, prayers, fastings, and worked together in various types of eleemosynary and pastoral

---
1 Sweet, **Revivalism**, pp. 84, 85.
2 The Encyclopedia Britannica, Vol. 22, p. 290.
3 Wesley M. Gewehr, **The Great Awakening in Virginia**, 1740-1790. (Durham, N. C., The Duke University Press, 1930), pp. 222, 223.

activities. In the group were John and Charles Wesley, George Whitefield and others. It was later through Moravian influence that John Wesley became concerned about his own personal standing with God. The extreme poise and calm complacency which the Moravians displayed during a storm on the Atlantic made an indelible impression on Wesley. Although Wesley had been preaching and since the time of his association with the Holy Club, originated by his brother Charles, he had endeavored to serve God, Loud tells us that "it was not until he met Peter Bohler, the ardent Moravian, in the winter of 1738 that John Wesley, though a priest in the Church of England was "convinced" of unbelief, of want of that faith whereby alone we are "saved." Though Wesley wanted to quit preaching Bohler advised him to continue preaching until he got faith and then preach because he had it. We give Loud's account of Wesley's conversion verbatim:

Then came his hour. He marked it. It was quarter to nine on the evening of Wednesday, May 24, 1738. The place was the meeting house of the Methodist society in Aldersgate Street where the leader was reading Luther's preface to the Epistle to the Romans describing the change God works in the heart through faith in Christ. 'I felt my heart strangely warmed,' Wesley said of his experience. 'I felt I did trust in Christ, Christ alone for salvation; an assurance was given me that He had taken away my sins, even mine, and saved me from the law of sin and death!'[1]

Thus it was that his Aldersgate, heart-warming experience came as a direct result of Moravian influence. And keeping in mind that we have already mentioned that the Pietists were directly responsible for the Moravian Church, it is not difficult to understand why Wesley made rigid requirements of his followers that they experience a vital, personal, knowable conversion. Here is at least one example of a man who had the advantage of the very best family training in a Christian minister's home, and a man who had a most saintly mother, but he did not naturally become a Christian because of these influences. He required a crisis conversion. Some maintain vehemently that such a conversion experience takes place only in such cases as those which involve individuals who lack an adequate education and have not set up the rational inhibitions necessary to con-

---
1 Loud, op. cit., pp 81, 82.

trol their emotions. It is strikingly interesting to note Davenport's comment about Wesley. Although he freely criticizes emotional excesses throughout his book he writes:

> He had the best university training of his time, and exhibited a scholarly taste and breadth of culture. Contrary to the quite generally received opinion, he laid great emphasis upon reason throughout his career. If there was one thing above another that he could not endure among his followers, it was unintelligent faith. A distinguished antagonist once asserted that it was a fundamental principle of the societies that all who went into them should renounce their reason. 'Sir,' said Wesley, 'Are you awake? Unless you are talking in your sleep, how can you utter so gross an untruth? It is a fundamental principle with us that to renounce reason is to renounce religion, that reason and religion go hand in hand, and that all irrational religion is false religion.'[1]

It should be of some value to observe that this eminent churchman saw in the crisis conversion experience a place for emotional expression entirely compatible with reason. While Wesley did not encourage emotional excesses he was careful not to speak too strongly against them lest he might hinder the work of God's Spirit. This writer would not suggest by these citations and comments that everyone alike must experience a crisis conversion, but that the Church as a whole has come to regard such an experience as something to be cautiously avoided altogether.

Davenport's further comment about Wesley's attitude toward these manifestations is of particular value as showing the necessity of exercising due discrimination, and at the same time not to discourage legitimate emotion. He writes of him:

> He thinks there was a danger at one time of regarding the extraordinary circumstances as essential. He thinks perhaps now the danger may be of condemning them altogether, of imagining that they are a hindrance, with nothing of God in them. The truth is, that God in the former time did visit lost sinners with such conviction that the natural consequence was outcry and convulsion, that he favored several of them with divine dreams and others with trances and visions. But after a while there was some 'nature' mixed with grace, and finally Satan stepped in and imitated the work in order to discredit it. It was originally wholly from God; it is partly so still, but Satan is now responsible for a share.[2]

---
[1] Davenport, op. cit., p. 145.
[2] Ibid., pp. 173, 174.

There could be perhaps no fairer explanation than that which is offered in this statement. Muncy gives a splendid summary of the value of the crisis conversion technique in the sweeping revivals among southern Methodists. These conclusions have a wider application and are equally true in all similar cases. He says:

> Certain factors besides the operation of the Divine Spirit and the power of the gospel contributed to the phenomenal success of the Methodists during this brief period. They preached the necessity of a vital, personal religious experience. The conversions produced real moral reformation and they found genuine joy in their Christian experiences. Like the Baptists, they ministered to the masses of the people. This gave them a large constituency. Their music was also powerful in winning men to Christ. The hymns of John and Charles Wesley and of others contained gospel truth and made a mighty appeal to the people.[1]

Though it may be of some profit to submit still other facts it appears that sufficient factual evidence has been adduced to establish the valid place of this type of experience in current times. The Great Awakening, the Wesleyan Revivals and thus far in the experience of the church in modern times revival leaders have encouraged and required a vital personal crisis conversion experience. It has only been in recent times, under the influences of Horace Bushnell, Starbuch and others that the program of the new psychology of religious education came into vogue and has gone far toward replacing this older type of conversion. When we recognize that the Wesleyan Revival saved England from moral ruin we must have respect for the techniques which were employed. Pierce, in referring to Lecky's appraisal, writes: "Lecky tells us that the revivals of the Wesleys saved England from vast and horrible industrial and political revolution, such as France suffered; and by doing this Wesley made it possible to save hundreds of thousands who otherwise could not have been saved."[2] Dr. Lacy, in speaking of the value of the Great Awakening states "that it furnished the dynamic power to enable the thirteen colonies to become a Christian nation."[3] With all the good that might be said in favor of the social gospel

---

1 Muncy, op. cit., p. 56.
2 Pierce, op. cit., p. 26.
3 Lacy, op. cit., p. 110.

or the religious education programs, it is, in the humble judgment of this writer, a fact that these newer emphases have not been and perhaps will not ever be able to produce accomplishments comparable to those realized in these major awakenings of former times. Society needs, and the Church needs, periodically, other great awakenings of the Wesleyan and Edwardian type which encourage the older type of experience in addition to its more modern programs. The big denominations are keenly conscious of the inability to appeal to the masses and are earnestly in search of some legitimate and workable plan to overcome their handicap.

As an interested spectator who sincerely desires to offer Christian assistance for the advancement of God's kingdom, may this writer be allowed to make what he believes to be at least a partial solution of this knotty problem which has come to be more and more acute. While it is to be expected that the established churches would naturally lean toward a program of religious education as they initiated new generations into their ranks, they have lost sight of the fact that many prospective communicants are to be found outside the immediate influence of their own families. A more extreme example of the same fallacy is to be found in the religious groups such as Mennonites and others who confine their evangelistic activities almost entirely within their own colonies. While it is admittedly possible to instruct those of our posterity in such a manner as to bring about their conversion in a quiet manner through Christian nurture there are multiplied thousands of others who constitute a major portion of society who are unreachable except by means of a crisis conversion. Many adults who attend the average church service are largely unaffected by these milder methods, and would become Christians if they had the opportunity to experience conversion by being brought face to face with a personal need of salvation through a legitimate appeal to their emotions in addition to receiving proper religious instruction through a Christian education program.

About the only possible way to become a Christian in the average church is to begin as a young person in the Sunday school and arrive at such a status on Decision Day, after a gradual routine process. Adults have little or no chance to become Christians. It is to be lamented that the rejecting of the crisis conversion experience has divested the large denominations of emotional expression and with it has gone in a measurable degree the stately steppings of God's Spirit within their midst. Our modern worship has come to be a more or less perfunctory routine procedure of a static nature. This writer realizes the seriousness of such charges and begs to be heard with tolerance. There is, however, concrete evidence before our eyes of a generation of many who "profess that they know God but in their works they deny him."[1]

Within the average communion there are those who know nothing of the meaning of repentance, restitution, or the new birth. They have never heard of conviction and have a very limited conception of the meaning of true conversion which produces a "new creature in Christ Jesus." They have been "whitewashed" instead of being "washed white." Could it be possible that such groups represent the class of whom Paul spoke as "ever learning and never able to come to the knowledge of the truth"?[2] Splendid, intelligent, and cultured middle class groups have been built up by those who are earnest and sincere in their purposes, but in their effort to be respectable and sane in their worship have robbed themselves appreciably of those elements which make for life and spiritual vitality. "They have a form of godliness but deny the power thereof"[3] are Paul's words. While these words may not apply in the absolute sense there is no doubt a measure in which they do apply.

In interest of self-preservation of both the Church and the State we refer to Dr. Pierce's solemn warning which challenges us to both sober thought and action. He says: "America may as well face the fact that she is in for an industrial and economic revolution unless Christianity does what Wesley's revival did in England."[4] We can hardly expect similar results without adopting a similar technique.

---

1 Titus 1:16
2 II Timothy 3:7.
3 Ibid., 3:5.
4 Pierce, op. cit., p. 110.

Section II
RELIGIOUS RADICALS, Continued

As we turn now to the consideration of a few historical accounts of these great awakenings, we should be better able to understand and appreciate the radical preaching techniques, the pungent conviction, the crisis conversion experiences, and the outburst of emotional ecstasy; especially since we have seen the permanent good which these methods have wrought. Comparing these revival methods with present day techniques, in spite of their admitted defects, they are far superior in effectiveness. They should be appreciated especially when we take into account that present-day evangelical denominations had their inception because of this emphasis. Our primary purpose in making these observations is to encourage a reasonable return to these former revival methods by the larger denominations, and to effect a better understanding of the smaller sects who still use this older method, by reminding the established churches that they too have made similar emphases with success in their inceptive years.

There has been too strong a reaction against these extremes which accounts for the absence of emotional expression in some communions as will be seen from Dr. Lacy's statements. He writes:

> It is distressing to recall in the full tide of her evangelistic efforts the Presbyterian Church has so often been rent asunder. This was true in the Great Awakening in the 'Old Side—New Side' controversy, in the Great Revival of 1800 in the 'Old Light—New Light' division, and was again true in the 1830's when the Church was disrupted by the 'Old School—New School' division. One can see the effects of the heightening controversy as the year 1837 approaches. Less and less space is devoted to revivals in the Narrative of the Assembly. Only a paragraph sufficed for 1835. And in 1836 it is recorded: 'The Assembly cannot resist the melancholy conviction that the last year has been one in which the churches have been deserted by the divine Spirit to a degree unexampled in our former history.' In the fateful year of 1837 one short paragraph again suffices for all references

to revivals, and is taken up in part with deploring the lack of the same.[1]

REVIVAL TECHNIQUES AND EMOTIONAL EXPRESSION

"The Great Awakening," Curran states, "introduced to the American scene one of the most remarkable characteristic phenomena of American religious history, the revival."[2]

Both Atkins and Cutten speak of the Great Revival in 1734 as the starting point for revivalism in America.[3] It is true that the techniques adopted in this revival have persisted with a perceptible degree of uniformity in every major awakening till current times. We will, therefore, give some attention to Edward's type of preaching as an initial observation. Davenport writes of him:

With a tremendous earnestness, a wealth of imagery, a strength and weight of logical argument that, his premises being granted were irresistible, he so presented the chief themes of the Christian religion and the Calvinistic creed that at the end of the winter 1734-35 'there was scarcely a single person in the town, old or young, left unconcerned about the great things of the eternal world.'[4]

Davenport's comments which describe Edward's pulpit manner and the effect of his sermons on his congregations are an interesting side light. He says:

Edwards' method of arousing the sinner had in it very little indeed of the merely superficial art of the orator and rhetorician. There was an extraordinary power of fascination in him, even though his eye never seemed to rest upon his audience, but flashed continually from his manuscript to the opposite wall. . . . By dint of prodigious intellectual strength, by the wonderful vivid imaging forth of premises which seem absurd to us but were as fundamental to his auditors as their own being, by the masterly marshalling of terrible argument, he wrought out an appeal to the fears of his hearers which stirred them to the very depths of their souls. They wept, they turned pale, they cried aloud. Some fainted, some fell into convulsions, some suffered thereafter from impaired health and some lost their reason. Of course he preached on other themes but the sermons which he himself says were remarkably blessed, which truly awakened the hearts of his hearers, were ever those in which he pictures 'the kind of hell an infinite God would arrange who was

---
1 Lacy, op. cit., pp. 105, 106.
2 Curran, op. cit., pp. 49, 50.
3 Atkins, op. cit., p. 6—Cutten, op. cit., p. 175.
4 Davenport, op. cit., p. 106.

infinitely enraged against a human being who had infinitely sinned in rejecting God's infinite love.'[1]

Cutten has this to say about Edwards and his contemporaries:

In 1735 there was scarcely an unconverted person in Northhampton, and most of the recent converts had become such by the only method Edwards preached—a spiritual convulsion. It was not long before the revival spread over the surrounding country, and then over all New England. The Revival thus started was carried on by Davenport, Wheelock, Barber, Parsons, Bellamy, Pomroy, Allen, Bliss and others. Most of them preached the same doctrines that Edwards did but lacked the good common sense. All manner of extravagances were indulged and encouraged. Davenport, especially, was successful in producing tremblings, shriekings, fallings, and faintings. In his method he used not only the passionate appeal, but laying aside his coat he would leap, clap his hands, stamp, and scream until his excited audience would shriek and fall into fits.[2]

Of Edwards' famous Endfield sermon Davenport speaks of an avalanche of woe coming down upon the people from his pulpit. The people cried aloud for mercy until Edwards could not be heard for their cries. They convulsively grasped the benches to prevent themselves from slipping into hell. He had preached from Deuteronomy 32:35, "Their foot shall slide in due time."[3]

Davenport writes of Whitefield, "When the people cried out about him so that they drowned out his voice and fainted here and there, he says he never saw a more glorious sight."[4]

Cutten states also of Whitefield:

The culmination of the Great Awakening took place under the ministry of Whitefield, who traveled from Maine to Georgia several times, frequently speaking many times a day to large crowds, and meeting with much success in reclaiming men. He was assisted by clergymen in different states, not the least of whom were Gilbert and William Tennant in New Jersey. . . . Weeping and crying were not uncommon at his meetings, and less frequently more disorder. It is estimated that at least 50,000 converts resulted from 'The Great Awakening.[5]

Davenport's comparison of Wesley and Whitefield is significant. He writes:

Whitefield addressed great audiences of the common people with all the persuasiveness and magnetic eloquence which he could com-

---

1 Ibid., p. 108.
2 Cutten, op. cit., p. 177
3 Davenport, op. cit., p. 109.
4 Ibid., p. 126.
5 Cutten, op. cit., pp. 177, 178.

mand, but reflex phenomena never appeared until they had first appeared under Wesley and spread by imitation and contagion. But they were common under Wesley during the early itinerant years of his ministry.

Wesley's example of calm self-possession thwarted the outflow in the form of the quieter and saner emotions, while the shock of his dominating and fascinating personality, his plain and searching speech and his demand for instantaneous decision fell with terrific force upon the plastic mental and nervous organization of his hearers. The pent-up energy found vent in almost every conceivable form of muscular reflex action, and finally into cries and groanings and terrors of impending judbment.[1]

The reader, of course, has no doubt readily observed that these interpretations do not purport to deal with anything beyond that which relates to psychology. There is, however, an additional interpretation which involves the Divine element operative through these men. The Spirit of God possesses an infinite knowledge of all types of psychological phenomena and every other factor which goes to make up man's being. Much of what took place, we can be sure is beyond the realm of our finite capacities to comprehend. Satan often injects his counterfeit in order to discredit the genuine. He is also a good psychologist. A further explanation of the divine element in these manifestations is ably presented by Price, who says:

Recent investigations into the infant science of Mental Psychology, led by William Carpenter, M. D., LL. D., of the University of London, and seconded by such men as Sir William Crookes in England, Berheim, Charcot, and Liebeault in France, Hudson, James, Quackenbos, and Hyslop in America, and a host of lesser luminaries, have shed new light on the subject of certain abnormal mental conditions and psychic phenomena. There is a subliminal world of which we know but little, but which sometimes rises above the horizon of consciousness. In this subliminal world there are forces which, under peculiar conditions, produce strange and wonderful phenomena, such as the catalepsies often witnessed amid revival scenes, the jerks, etc. Rapid progress is being made in psychological as well as physical science, and the time will probably come when psychic phenomena will be as well understood as physical phenomena are now. The universe is under law; nothing happens. Psychic phenomena are as surely controlled by law as gravitation, chemical affinity, light, sound, growth, and decay. All natural laws are laws of God, and they therefore exist for the glory of God and the good of his creatures. These laws God uses in the government of the physical, mental, and moral world. The strange

---

[1] Davenport, op. cit., pp. 149, 170, et passim.

exercises of the revival of 1800 occurred according to God's laws, and they evidently took place for the betterment of humanity.[1]

Loud writes that McGready, when preaching, would reach out with a mighty swing of his arm and would pluck up an imaginary sinner from his congregation and would dangle him over the brimstone brink. It was said that his compelling voice and eyes augmented the terrors of his composite Calvinistic hell and Methodistic regeneration.[2]

Catherine Cleveland writes of James McGready: "Such was the excitement caused by his work in South Carolina that fierce opposition was aroused. He was accused of 'running people distracted' and diverting them from their necessary vocations. The opposition went so far as to tear away and burn his pulpit and sent him a threatening letter written in blood."[3]

Cutten's account of McGready and the McGee brothers is as follows:

When Rev. James McGready, a Presbyterian minister, came to Logan County, he brought with him the Edwardian slogan of the awful wrath of God upon impenitent sinners. He would portray hell so vividly that persons would grasp the seats to keep from falling into the burning abyss which they saw yawning at their feet. His meetings attracted great crowds and his fame was wide-spread. In 1799, the two McGee brothers turned aside, while on their way to Ohio, to attend a sacramental solemnity, and incidentally to hear the noted McGready. Both brothers spoke during the meeting that day, at the end of which began the manifestations which made this series of meetings so famous. John McGee said that when the first meeting closed, 'the floor was covered with the slain.'

From here the revival spread over Kentucky, North Carolina, and Virginia with great rapidity. The camp-meetings, however, held at Gasper River, Logan Co., and Cane Ridge, Bourbon Co., Kentucky, eclipsed all other meetings. At the Cane Ridge meeting it was estimated that 20,000 people attended, some driving in carts fifty miles. Everything was forsaken on farms and in villages, and with their families, bedding and provisions in their wagons, men drove to the meetings. On arriving there the wagons were placed in rows, like streets, and the people gave themselves up to excitement and excesses, never thinking of returning home until the provisions were exhausted.[1]

---

1 Price, op. cit., pp. 376, 377.
2 Loud, op. cit., pp.
3 Cleveland, op. cit., p. 39.
4 Cutten, op. cit., p. 180.

In these services large numbers "fell" and would lie breathless for hours. As many as one in six fell at some meetings. The "jerks" seized saint and sinner alike. Others were "barking" like dogs. Groups of men and women were on their all-fours snarling, barking, growling and snapping their teeth. They referred to it as "treeing the devil." Others were doing the "holy laugh."[1]

It is obvious that it would be impracticable to give very many examples of these unusual manifestations but one or two descriptions of them can be mentioned with profit. It is interesting to note the affinity of the "barks" and the "jerks" which Price records:

> The barking exercise, as opposers contemptuously called it, was nothing but the jerks. A person affected with the jerks, especially in his head, would often make a grunt or a bark from the suddenness of the jerk. This name of barking seems to have had its origin from an old Presbyterian preacher of East Tennessee. He had gone into the woods for private devotion, and was seized with the jerks. Standing near a sapling, he caught hold of it to prevent his falling; and as his head jerked back he uttered a grunt, or a kind of noise similar to a bark, his face being turned upward. Some wag discovered him in this position and reported that he had found the old preacher barking up a tree.[2]

There are to be found many unusual cases of the "jerks" recorded by a number of writers, but the highly descriptive account given by Peter Cartwright in his Autobiography is most impressive. Like the case just referred to and many others there seems to be no mistake but what these manifestations, though they may have been aped by the devil, were on the whole of divine origin. The following account is from the famous Peter Cartwright's pen:

> While I am on this subject I will relate a very serious circumstance which I knew to take place with a man who had the jerks at a camp-meeting, on what is called the ridge, in William McGee's congregation. There was a great work of religion in the encampment. The jerks were very prevalent. There was a company of drunken rowdies who came to interrupt the meeting. These rowdies were headed by a very large drinking man. They came with their bottles of whiskey in their pockets. The large man cursed the jerks and all religion. Shortly afterwards he took the jerks, and he started

---

[1] Ibid., p. 181.
[2] Price, op. cit., p. 379.

to run, but he jerked so powerfully that he could not get away. He halted among some saplings, and although he was violently agitated, he took out his bottle of whiskey, and swore he would drink the damn jerks to death; but he jerked at a rate that he could not get the bottle to his mouth, though he tried hard. At length he fetched a sudden jerk and the bottle struck a sapling and was broken to pieces, and spilled his whiskey on the ground. There was a great crowd gathered around him, and when he lost his whiskey he became very much enraged, and cursed and swore very profanely, his jerks still increasing. At length he fetched a very violent jerk, snapped his neck, fell and soon expired, with his mouth full of cursing and bitterness.[1]

Price speaks of women with long braided hair having the jerks and their hair cracking like whips.[2]

The question naturally arises as to whether such physical disturbances will ever again invade the precincts of the modern Church. Davenport's comments at this point could be nothing more than conjecture but they are interesting to consider. He says:

"The Rev. Samuel Doak, D.D. was conspicuous for his outstanding contributions to the Great Revival of 1800. For more than 20 years he was an occasional subject to the 'bodily exercise.' Price describes him as a powerful man in body and mind, a graduate of Princeton College, an excellent scholar and Calvinist of the Scottish Presbyterian School. Gideon Blackburn, one of his pupils in a letter written to a friend describes this revival. He writes in part:

I am constrained to say I have discovered far less extravagance, disorder, and irregularity than could have possibly been expected in so extraordinary an awakening, especially when part of it took place among persons in the back parts and entirely destitute of the means of grace. If crowded audiences, earnest-praying, practical-preaching, and animated singing may be considered irregular, there is a great deal of irregularity. If crying for mercy, if shouting glory to God for salvation are disorderly, then there is some disorder; but I presume not more than on the day of Pentecost.[3]

The entire letter is significant and most reasonable and con-

---

[1] Peter Cartwright, **Autobiography of Peter Cartwright**. (Cincinnati, Cranston and Curtis, 1856), pp. 46, 48-51.
[2] Price, op. cit., p. 376.
[3] R. N. Price, **Holston Methodism**. (Nashville: Publishing House of the M. E. Church, South, 1904), pp. 351, 352.

vincing, but we will only notice one more excerpt; a concluding remark:

> In short, I have not only heard of it and seen it, but have felt it, and am persuaded that it is only to be effected by the immediate finger of God. There are some imposters, there are some extravagances, but these make no characteristic feature of the work, and are held in absolute abhorrence by the pious. The best evidence of a revial is the fruits produced.[1]

Price, in commenting on this revival states, "This was not a man-made revival; an extraordinary power descended upon the preachers and people at a time and in a manner unexpected to them. It was the Lord's doing and wonderful in his eyes."[2] He also adds:

> The doctrines preached in that great season of grace were free, full, and present salvation, regeneration by the Holy Ghost, the knowledge of sins forgiven, the witness of the Spirit, and peace and joy in believing. The doctrines of absolute decrees and unconditional election were left out of sight.[3]

It seems that the Methodists, Baptists and Presbyterians all worked together. Especially is this true of the Methodist and Presbyterians. In fact denominations were so closely allied in their work that it seems difficult for historians to decide which one initiated the first camp meeting. Sweet states that the camp meeting originated among western Presbyterians.[4] Price on the other hand clearly states that camp meetings began among the Methodists,[5] while Muncy claims that camp meetings began with the Baptists at the Sandy Creek Baptist Church.[6]

Since we have just mentioned the Baptists, it will be interesting to note that they were perhaps more bitterly persecuted than any of the other denominations. Muncy writes of them the following account which he bases on Gewehr's statements. He says:

> The Baptist suffered severe persecution everywhere. They traveled at their own expense, sought no remuneration from the people they served, and gave themselves without stint, but the people to whom they preached the gospel subjected them to terrible indignities. In

---
1 Ibid., p. 352.
2 Ibid., p. 363.
3 Loc cit.
4 Sweet, Revivalism, p. 122.
5 Price, op. cit., p. 357.
6 Muncy, op. cit., p. 51.

1771 John Waller was severely beaten. The Anglican clergyman, his secretary and the sheriff led in the attack. The clergyman ran his whip down Waller's throat to silence him and he was given a severe beating. When his persecutors had left, however, Waller continued the sermon which they had interrupted. Others of the itinerant evangelists were kicked, dragged by the hair, and submerged in mud until they were nearly drowned.[1]

Sweet writes of the Separate Baptists that they had the reputation of being an illiterate and ignorant set.[2] Thom says of them that they had objectionable pulpit mannerisms and that they were very noisy and "whooped it up in odd tones."[3] Broadus refers to a peculiar mannerism developed among the Baptist preachers called the "holy shine."[4]

It would be extremely interesting to consider somewhat at length the colorful accounts of these early colonial religious awakenings. A number of splendid books dealing with their description have been written. Some of them are exhaustive and minute accounts of these revivals. Since these books have been widely read and their contents have come to be the common knowledge of even the average layman, we have, therefore, limited our treatment to include only a few quotations selected at random from various sources. A review of these accounts should serve to remind the established Church of its former status and to reflect some ray of hope for present-day "religious radicals" who are much less extreme in their emotional expression. Other more direct comparisons will be made when we come to the closing chapter of this section.

Cutten observes that "revivals have always been characterized by intense emotion. This has been at the same time the source of their strength and of their weakness, of their success and of their danger."[2] Atkins avers that:

> Fervent speech carrying an appeal for immediate decision or action is about the oldest, most direct and effective vehicle for any cause. It needs nothing save the cause, the apostle and the crowd— the wind and the flame soon follow. Religion has through the very nature of it furnished all the elements which make a revival pos-

---

1 Muncy, loc cit.
2 Sweet, **Religion Frontier (Baptists)**, p. 10.
3 W. T. Thom, **Struggles for Religious Freedom in Virginia.** (Baltimore: John Hopkins University Press, 1900), pp. 10-11.
4 Baptist Quarterly Review, IX (1875), pp. 1-20.
5 Cutten, op. cit., p. 188.

sible and has used the revival method consistently. After a long period of neglect, revivalism was reborn in America, developed its technique, became an outstanding characteristic of American Christianity, and supplied the evangelical Protestant churches their principle way of growth.[1]

Davenport, in his remarkable book *Primitive Traits in Religious Revivals* makes the following analysis of crowd behavior:

> The mind of the crowd is strangely like that of the primitive man. Most of the people in it may be far from primitive in emotion, in thought, in character; nevertheless the result tends always to be the same. Stimulation immediately begets action. Reason is in abeyance. The cool, rational speaker has little chance beside the skillful emotional orator.[2]

Imagination may be used to unlock the flood-gates of emotion. A speaker can direct attention to certain common ideas such as the Church, the Scripture, Home, etc., which are calculated to stimulate the emotions of all individuals. Certain methods are recognized as effective in dealing with crowds. Davenport gives a terse summary of those methods which are most commonly employed. He says:

> The means of influencing their audiences upon which skillful speakers universally depend, are appeals to imagination and emotion, direct and indirect suggestion, affirmation and repetition. Repetition is one of the surest means of getting an idea firmly into the mind of a crowd as well as a child or a savage. As Mr. Dooley phrases it in his philosophy—'I believe anything at all, if ye only tell it to me often enough.[3]

It is true that attention can be focused on the human mind, and that through the power of suggestion, imitation, and the like the emotions are moved. There is the possibility of creating extraordinary phenomena as a result of both human and Satanic suggestion. But we should also recognize that there is a legitimate divine source of power functioning to produce God-ordained phenomena in harmony with His divine purpose. Satan endeavors to offer a counterfeit in order to discourage sincere worshippers and cause inhibitions concerning the genuine.

The emotional element in religion is necessary to activate the will. Emotion, if stabilized by rational judgment, is a legitimate and indispensable factor in accomplishing conversion. It is,

---

[1] Atkins, op. cit., p. 6.
[2] Davenport, op. cit., p. 26.
[3] Ibid., pp. 28, 29.

however, dishonest to resort to hypnotic methods to secure spiritual results. Cutten aptly and masterfully summarizes the whole matter for us in the following remarks:

> Thousands have been swept through a revival by the torrent of emotion, some to moral transformation and useful lives, others to moral degradation and loss of respect for religious things. When the sensibilities alone are affected, the intellect and will are neglected, the result is inevitable and disappointing. This emotional method has developed a special explosive type of conversion, and its apologists have frequently assumed that it is the only type. The danger from this is two-fold: those who have gone through such an experience are liable to look upon it as a miraculous rather than a natural process, and they, and others as well, are prone to believe that this is the only method by which a person can be saved. When there is laid down one method which all must follow, and that an emotional and explosive one, those who are temperamentally constituted so as to be unable to experience these sudden changes and overpowering emotions are hopeless of knowing God or obtaining salvation. They are taught to seek something they can never find, and either despair or revolt is the result: they either give up trying, or consider religion all humbug. This grave mistake on the part of many revivalists has done incalculable harm. Feeling, or any other subjective test, cannot be the only one—'by their fruits ye shall know them, not by their roots.[1]

No thoughtful person would offer argument or protest to these sane and valid claims which are without question well-based. Yet this side of the question has been grossly overdrawn. The good which has resulted from emotion in religion has far outweighed any deleterious or baleful effect which may have issued from it. It seems that the devil, himself, has used this argument as a tool to accomplish his unholy purpose of hindering the work of God's Spirit in effecting salvation in the hearts of men. Catherine Cleveland makes the following statement regarding the "Great Revival in the West":

> Making all due allowances for the excessive stress laid upon the emotional side of religious life, yet it remains clear that the Great Revival stimulated the religious life of the country as a whole, and did much to develop the region west of the Alleghanies. A resident of Tennessee, in a letter dated Dixon Springs, Tennessee, May 13, 1843, wrote that he witnessed much of the excitement and, 'notwithstanding all this fanaticism, much good appears to have been done.[2]

---

1 Cutten, op. cit., p. 188.
2 Cleveland, op. cit., pp. 128, 129.

Dr. Pierce, in discussing the value of revivals, refers to a striking illustration used by a fellow minister which is apropos here. He writes:

> Dr. John A. Earl, a number of years ago, in speaking of revivals, said that when he had rung the doorbell of a certain home, he could hear a sepulchral sound within the house. A prim woman came and decorously admitted him. When he went into the living room he perceived everything was in perfect order, and he readily inferred that scarcely a piece of furniture had been moved for years. Why all this primness and preciseness? There were no children in the home. From that place he went to another home. As he rang the doorbell, he heard the cries and shouts of children inside. Soon a woman came to the door, carrying a baby in her arms, with another child clinging to her skirts. She said cheerily, 'Come in, Dr. Earl, if you can get in.' And he went in. He stepped over one child on the floor. Very few things were in the proper place but the house was full of life.
>
> The question is, which do you choose for the Christian Church—the abundant life of youth or the sterile, stereotyped life of senility? A vital young man from the middle West went East for some theological studies. He said that many of the churches of the East were well supported and had dignified service Sunday morning. 'Why,' he said, 'they have the same interest in keeping up the church that they have in keeping up the family burying ground.' Do they need revival? It would either 'kill them' or bring them to life.[1]

While this analogy may be considered a bit extreme, it contains enough truth to cause the average churchman to be uncomfortable when he comes face to face with the fact it suggests. It is imperative that the Church should rethink the matter of crisis conversion and lay a legitimate emphasis on the place of emotion in religious experience.

---

2 Pierce, op. cit., pp. 114 115.

Chapter III
EVOLUTIONARY PHASES IN THE DENOMINATIONAL CYCLE

1. RISE AND RESPECTABILITY

Niebuhr's statement regarding the Quakers is a fair example of the same characteristic trend in all denominations. He says, "The Quakers, no less than their predecessors among the churches of the poor, soon settled down to an equable respectability."[1] In the preceding chapter we have considered at some length a few of the historical facts relating to what we chose to term "Religious Radicals." We observed that the evangelical denominations had their inception amid revivals and that two things stand out prominently, viz., crisis conversion and a free expression of emotion. These groups met with extreme opposition and were severely persecuted, but despite their persecution they grew and multiplied. Just as those of the Early Church were persecuted and were scattered abroad, it was so with these new groups. They were considered "disturbers of the peace" and "perverters of good order." Sweet quotes Leland who states that thirty or more Baptist preachers were "honored with the dungeon" and that the early Baptists who were arrested had the charge brought against them that "they cannot meet a man in the road, but that they must ram a text of scripture down his throat."[2]

Muncy states of the Quakers that although they were persecuted, their persecutions did not dampen their enthusiasm nor squelch their zeal. He writes of them:

> George Fox, the founder of the movement, was imprisoned more than sixty times covering a period of eleven years in England. The first Quaker missionaries to America were women, and they were denied the privilege of disembarking from their ship in Boston. After being permitted to land they were imprisoned for five weeks. Boards were nailed over their windows of their jail to prevent them from speaking to people on the outside and their books were burned.[3]

---
1 Niebuhr, **op. cit.**, p. 54.
2 Sweet, **The Baptists**, p. 12.
3 Muncy, **op. cit.**, p. 9.

Muncy adds that "in spite of this persecution—or more likely because of it—the Friends grew rapidly in all the early colonies."¹ But he further adds:

The disappearance of persecution contributed to this state of apathy. Like many other Christian groups, the Quakers 'went everywhere preaching the Word' and winning men when persecution was rife. But when it was easier to be Christian this earnestness and faithfulness was not in evidence.²

Sweet, speaking of the Quakers says, as numbers increased spiritual life seemed to decline, and that an increase of wealth among them was a definite reason for spiritual decline.³ After 60 years one of these Quakers writes of their early status:

Friends were a plain lowly minded people, and that there was much tenderness and contrition in their meetings. That at 20 years from that date, the society increasing in wealth and in some degree conforming to the fashions of the world, true humility was less apparent, and their meetings in general were not so lively and edifying. That at the end of forty years many of them had grown rich; and made many a specious appearance in the world, that marks of outward wealth and greatness appeared on some in our meetings of ministers and elders, and as such things became more prevalent so the powerful overshadowings of the Holy Ghost were less manifest in the Society. That there had been continual increase of such ways of life even until the present time, and that the weakness that had now overspread the Society and the barrenness manifest among it is a matter of much sorrow.⁴

Sweet, in writing of the state of the Baptists at the close of the Revolution states:

The close of the Revolution found the Baptists in the United States in a vastly different position than they had occupied at the beginning. At the beginning of the War for Independence they were but small persecuted groups, here and there, made up largely of underprivileged classes, economically and educationally. By 1790 a social revolution had taken place. Influential and wealthy members were now counted among them, and their general reputation was equal to that of any other denomination of Christians.⁵

Gewehr, in writing of this trend among the Baptists who have raised their social standing and economic status, says:

In it for the first time the people found an organization, a ministry

---
1 Loc. cit.
2 Muncy, op. cit., p. 12.
3 Sweet, Story, p. 147.
4 Ibid., pp. 147, 148.
5 Sweet, The Baptists, p. 17.

148   HISTORY OF THE PENTECOSTAL HOLINESS CHURCH

and a preaching congenial to their thinking, their emotions, their habits of speech and station in life. . . . We see here a social upheaval in progress. As the masses continued to assert themselves they gained recognition, became more and more like other people, and won respect in the eyes of the world. Along with this progress they threw off odd and disgusting mannerisms, paid attention to education, became more rational and conservative, and gained recruits from the well-to-do classes.[1]

As economic standards have been raised in denominations a better education has been provided, and with it has come a corresponding rise in cultural and social standards, and as Niebuhr points out, there is a compromise of ethics designed to suit the newly emerged classes.[2] With these rises to respectability there invariably comes "compromise and complacency," a sub-topic with which we will deal in our further discussion.

Pope's remarks form a most excellent summary of the "Rise and Respectability" among the newer sects of current times. He writes:

In their desire to surpass rival sects, the newer denominations begin to lose their extreme sectarianism. Increasingly they are building more expensive churches, insisting on greater educational background for their preachers, and cooperating more fully with older denominations and with community leaders, in an effort to achieve prestige and power. One Church of God preacher boasted: 'We have the biggest building program in North Carolina, and are growing so fast we can hardly get enough preachers to keep up with it.' Ministers of the Church of God are very proud that one of their number was selected to deliver the commencement sermon at one of the local high schools recently, 'with several mill owners and preachers of the big town churches setin' right there.' One of the clearest impressions that come from the conversation with sect preachers is of their desire to extend the influence of their sect as a denomination rather than simply as a faith.

Little by little, the newer sects are seeking and winning support from mill management and are coming to occupy a recognized place in the life of mill communities. Previously most employers have discouraged them, on the ground that they upset the routine of the life of workers, and perhaps also lest organization along economic lines, as it has in some instances. More recently, however, subsidies similar to those granted to older churches are being offered a few sectarian groups. One Church of God minister, when asked if he knew an executive of the mill in whose village he was stationed, replied, exultingly: 'Know him! Why, he's my financier! I've got about

---

1 Gewehr.
2 Niebuhr. op. cit., p. 21.

$1,400 from him in the last two or three years. You see, I know something about the income tax, and have had great success with mill officials!' A preacher of the Pentecostal Holiness Church is planning to erect a new building soon; he has inquired, for the first time, concerning possible assistance from the mills, and reports happily that 'the mills will be tolerable to us when we get ready to build!' In many respects the newer sects are tending to make their peace with the world, seeking to conquer it rather than to transcend it.[1]

The pages of church history are often a sad commentary on this evident trend in denominations which have become respectable. There is among them a marked tendency to assume an arrogant attitude of superiority toward the poor and underprivileged classes from which they have themselves emerged. Curran, in writing of the changing financial background of sects says: "Even the Methodist and Baptist faiths, once religions of the poor, now displayed almost frantic solicitude for the spiritual welfare of the rich."[2] Garrison refers to the attitude of the Methodist Church toward the lower classes after it had reached the stage of denominational respectability. He writes:

As Methodism became more urbanized and less revivalistic, there separated from it various groups which had laid great stress on the idea of complete sanctification and which prized the liberty of unbridled expression of emotion and conviction as the Spirit gave them utterance. Not less than twenty-five Pentecostal and Holiness organizations have been formed since 1880. Their members are for the most part rural, poor, ignorant, and emotional. The cultural advance of Methodism has been facilitated by the sloughing off of this element among which a fiery religion is compensatory for the consciousness of financial, social, and intellectual inferiority.[3]

This somewhat supercilious attitude current among some Methodists toward the underprivileged classes is in distinct contrast to the attitude of its founders. Wesley sought out the mean and the debased, the poor colliers and others of the lower economic strata.[4] Such an observation does not apply exclusively to the Methodists, but is also representative of the characteristic attitude assumed by other denominations after they too have evolved to the stage of denominational respectability.

Curran states, "Several of the Holiness sects have already ex-

---
1 Pope, op. cit., pp. 139, 140.
2 Curran, op. cit., pp. 127, 128.
3 Garrison, op. cit., p. 181.
4 Niebuhr, op. cit., p. 60.

perienced the classical evolutionary process of Evangelical Protestantism. The Church of the Nazarene, for example, has marked its arrival among the sects of the middle class by quietly dropping the betraying prefix 'Pentecostal' from its title."[1] Clark also points out in this connection how the Nazarenes have also dropped "holiness" from the title of their schools. For example, the Texas Holiness University has changed its name to Peniel College. Not one institution of the denomination now exposes its doctrinal character in its name.[2]

Pope writes:

> Not all mill workers, of course, belong to sectarian groups; there are class distinctions among mill workers themselves—distinctions largely reflected in religious affiliation. Presbyterian workers feel superior to those belonging to the Methodist and Baptist churches, while members of the latter two denominations regard themselves as definitely higher in the social scale than the Wesleyan Methodists. All, in turn, despise the Church of God and deprecate the social status of its members. . . . As a Presbyterian minister put it, 'the Methodists and Baptists used to care for the ignorant; the Holy Rollers do now and the Methodists and Baptists are left floundering, wondering what to do.' A Lutheran minister expressed pity for the newer symptoms of religious errancy.[3]

It will be unnecessary to extend our discussion further at this point. The examples which have been given will suffice to illustrate this uniform tendency among denominations. In closing this segment of our discussion we quote another relevant paragraph from Pope who says:

> A denomination inclines to move and to settle down with its few leaders who become community leaders also, leaving behind the masses of its members and society. Its position on the scale of transition from sect to Church follows closely after the economic fortunes of its more influential members; its religious character changes as the economic status of its leaders improves. From reflecting the need of a large group of people, it comes to sanction the position of its more respectable members simply because of their position, sanctioned also by the whole weight of existing culture, and this enables them to control the particular religious institution. As time goes on, the emerging Church either raises up its membership from childhood, finds new members from cultural groups to which its fresh but moderate enthusiasm appeals, or else declines in mem-

---

1 Curran, op. cit., p. 132.
2 Clark, op. cit., pp. 96, 97.
3 Pope, op. cit., p. 138.

EVOLUTIONARY PHASES IN THE DENOMINATIONAL CYCLE 151

bership and influence. It cannot go back to the sect form because the unique social naivete and pristine enthusiasm are irrevocably lost. Movement on the scale between sect and Church is, with minor exceptions, in one direction only.[1]

As Mr. Pope has pointed out the Church cannot retrogress to the sect stage. It might well be added, also, that the sect cannot prevent making progress in the evolutionary cycle or rise to respectability, and with it the "attendant evils" are virtually inevitable as will be seen from our further discussion. In the history of the Church, no sect has ever yet become the exception to this characteristic trend.

2. COMPROMISE AND COMPLACENCY

Consequent to the evolutionary rise to respectability in a given denomination, there is immediately a perceptible lowering of ethical standards and worship practices compatible with the newly acquired social and economic status. Persecution ceases, the socially well-placed become increasingly numerous, and with this the feeling of superiority to the poorer classes becomes more pronounced. The communicants of such groups gradually become less emotional and manifest a preference for a more formal and conservative type of service. There is a definite shifting toward a liturgical form of worship. Preaching tends to become general rather than personal. The sermon is stripped of those objectionable elements which could be classified as radical or offensive. Sins are no longer named and brought into critical focus lest the dominant bourgeoisie should withdraw its support. In short, the standards of Christian behavior are made to conform more and more to those of the world. It is to these characteristic compromises that we wish to direct attention in this chapter.

There are always a number of factors which are responsible for the decline from revolutionary fervor. It seems that when persecution ceases denominations become settled social bodies and are content with their place in the conventional scheme of things. The second generation hold their convictions as a heritage while the first generation won these convictions through bitter sufferings.

Niebuhr points out that the most important cause for this

---

[1] Pope, **op. cit.,** p. 120.

decline is to be found in the economic rise to prosperity. He says: that "most important among the causes of the decline of revolutionary churches into denominations is the influence of economic success."[1] Niebuhr, in referring to the example of American Methodism, clearly delineates the compromise which takes place in the transition from a sect to a church. He says:

> This religion of the disinherited became a respectable church of respected classes. Originally urban in character it retained the loyalty of the tradesmen and workers who, rising in the social scale through their thrift and diligence, became the small and later often the great capitalists of the growing cities of the nineteenth century. More than Presbyterianism or Congregationalism, Methodism came to be the religion of the business classes. Methodism left behind the emotionalism of its earlier years and adapted its ethics, never typically lower class in character, to the needs of its rising clientele. It abandoned lay preaching in favor of a regular and theologically-trained ministry; it modified and softened in many ways the original stringency of its methods; it gave up the old program of mutual aid, so typically a feature of the religion of the poor; it left aside the semi-ascetic character of its early communities and arranged its rules to accommodate those whose interests made the world-fleeing ethics even less practical than it was for the poor. Once more a religious revolt, issuing in the formation of a sect, led finally to the establishment of a middle-class church, a yielding servant to the social order.[2]

Niebuhr states that "The Methodist Revival was the last great religious revolution of the disinherited in Christendom."[3] Professor Niebuhr would certainly be willing to recognize the Holiness and Pentecostal revivals and the part they have played to champion the cause of the disinherited groups in current times, but he evidently does not consider that they have made a great contribution. His conclusion, it appears, is either based on superficial evidence or perhaps is the result of a prejudiced appraisal of these neglected groups, which are not yet sufficiently far removed from their inception to permit an unbiased evaluation of their true worth. The self-same statement would likely have been made concerning the Methodist revival if it had been made at a parallel stage of their development. It is true, however, that revivalism has become increasingly unpopular since its

---

1 Niebuhr, op. cit., p. 54.
2 Ibid., pp. 71, 72.
3 Loc. cit.

decline within Methodism, and according to popular current opinion it may be said that the Methodist revival represents the last truly popular type of revival. This characteristic decline in popularity of the revival method has followed the development and increase of modern liberalism since its initial appearance in the middle of the nineteenth century. Atkins aptly makes certain interesting observations which reflect the typical attitude toward revivalism in current times. He writes:

Revivalism furnished a technique to which the emphasis upon religious education and nurture, so emergingly evident, began forty years ago to oppose—and of which the Northfield schools were themselves an anticipation. It fixed and heightened the theologies about which the rather thunderous controversies of the 'fundamentalists' and 'modernists' have been carried on. It conceived and offered religion as a way of salvation, it made conversion the mystic operation of the Holy Spirit, a divinely granted witness that the seeker had passed from death unto life. It created a literature of its own and especially a gospel hymnology which set to music the confessions of the sin-burdened, the offer of salvation, the rapture of the saved, the bliss and glory of heaven and the peace of a life entirely committed to Christ and lived in communion with Him. . . .

It demanded a serious, chaste, church-attending life. It tabooed cards, the theatre and dancing. was laborious, thrifty 'giving of its substance to the Lord,' and fought alcohol in all its seductive forms. . . . The missionary enterprizes of American Protestant churches have grown out of revival awakenings, been motivated by the belief that Christianity alone can save and without it the vast Asiatic and African world, the Negro with his fetish, the Buddhist with his inherited lore of twenty-five centuries, and the Hindu with his wealth of speculation enriched by almost timeless insight of a great race, were alike doomed. The missionary passion has risen to flood-tide power beneath the compulsion of convictions so shaped and tempered. If one adds the influence of Wesleyanism in England to the force and outcome of evangelism in America, one has the religious dynamic of almost two hundred years among English-speaking peoples. To leave that out would be to rewrite their history without any possible way of knowing how to rewrite it.[1]

It naturally follows that with the decline of revivalism there has been a decline of those characteristic features which revivalists emphasized. In other words, to repeat former statements, religious education and the social gospel have been substituted for the crisis conversion and a definite, personal, vital religious experience. To that extent denominations have com-

---

[1] Atkins, op. cit., pp. 18, 19.

promised and have left it with the less enlightened sect groups to perpetuate these older emphases. Atkins' further comments in a later chapter amply illustrate the absence of the former revivalistic trends in Methodism. He states:

> Mysticism was an attempted return to immediate religious experience. Conversion, in the period of revivalism, had furnished a religious experience of which the saved were more sure than anything else in the world. They could date their second birth as definitely as their first. A religion thus validated had sure supports, it could survive the loss of pretty much everything save the encouragement of other people who had like experiences. Methodism at one time would have felt the loss of its bishops less vitally than the loss of its class meetings.
>
> Very likely at no time since the beginning of the eighteenth century has evangelical Protestantism been so inwardly arid as it was in the beginning of the twentieth century. Young people came into the communion of their churches through the 'pastor's classes': a little church history, a little Christian ethics and a good deal of 'what are you going to do with your life?' Older people joined the church through appeals to support 'an institution without which society would go to pieces.' Real estate values, it was said were higher in church districts, and 'how would you like to live in a town without a church?'
>
> It is easy to over-exaggerate this trend. The finer, the quieter aspects of religion were, as always, in existence and action. The supporting church constituencies had an unguessed number of the sincere and devout. But the trend was dominant. The recession of the religion of experience carried 'prayer meetings' along with it. Though the change was less marked in some regions and denominations, all the churches mourned the ebbing tide and with it the habit of public lay prayer began to fail. The drama of the soul which had so long supplied 'testimonies,' confessions, trembling words of hope and appeal for help—'Pray for me that I may prove faithful'—grew remote and dim; the younger generation had very little to say about their souls or were too tongue-tied to say it. . . . How could one testify to an 'experience' he had never experienced? Church people were thinking in other regions, practical, half secular. They began to make a liturgical exercise of the prayer meeting, or else an open forum.[1]

It would seem that no plausible objection could be offered to repudiate a revivalistic method which has proven itself capable of producing such wholesome and salutary results. And yet, as we have seen, it is a patent fact that denominations do compromise their more vigorous and fruitful techniques in favor of

---

1 Atkins, op. cit., pp. 121, 122.

the less disturbing type. It is pathetic to observe that when denominations reach the "respectable" stage of their development, it is extremely difficult for them to perceive their need sufficiently to prompt them to energetic action. They are usually numerically strong and financially independent. Because they have inaugurated their highly developed and well-organized programs which receive the enthusiastic support of most of their constituency, it is damaging to their sense of pride to admit any deficiency. It is thus that a sense of complacency prevails and that compromise becomes more and more evident.

As a sample illustration of the compromise of ethical standards which had once been maintained in two of the larger denominations, we turn to Garrison's chapter on "Denominational Events and Contributions." In commenting on the Young People's Methodist Alliance, he says:

> The Alliance combined a reading course (like Chautauqua), the temperance society technique of the pledge, an evangelistic emphasis, the pietistic fervor which later became the special characteristic of the Holiness groups. Its pledge read as follows: 'I enjoy or will seek the blessing of heart purity as taught in the Scriptures. I promise to abstain from the use of tobacco and all intoxicants as beverages, to refrain from card-playing and dancing, and from attending the theatre, the opera, the circus and all other places of questionable amusements.'[1]

Garrison also mentions how the Reformed Presbyterian Synod at Pittsburgh adopted resolutions advising all of their church officers and members to avoid the use of tobacco and the opposing of prohibition.[2] These standards of Christian behavior are in distinct contrast to those generally advocated in our day. These are specific examples which indicate compromise and complacency. Persons who make any particular issue of these sins today are immediately classed as "old fogies" or "religious fanatics." Dr. Pierce very frankly charges the Church with the responsibility for the repeal of the Eighteenth Amendment. It would no doubt be helpful to enter here a long quotation from his book except for the fact that it might be somewhat irrelevant for our purpose. But to indicate a concrete example of such compromise we quote briefly his following remarks:

---

[1] Garrison, op. cit., p. 180. (Also Niebuhr, op. cit., p. 69).
[2] Ibid., p 185

Multitudes of our churches today want nothing said about the liquor evil, lest it tread on the toes of some of their members. . . . The pastorate of the Methodist church (in a northern city of 150,000) suffered frequent changes because each pastor persisted in speaking against alcohol. The pastor of the Baptist church in this city was asked by the official members to say nothing about this evil, but he persisted, and alienated the beer-drinking element of his church. When the first World War broke out, we had a prohibitionist as Secretary of the Navy, and he dried up the Navy. We had in General Pershing one who had the clear vision and courage to say. 'Banish the entire liquor industry from the United States; close every saloon and brewery; suppress drinking by the severe punishment of the drinker . . . and the nation will find itself amazed at its efficiency. . . . I shall not go slow on prohibition, for I know it is the greatest foe to my men, greater even than the bullets of the enemy.' Where is the Pershing for us today? The Church indeed is raising its voice against the evils attendant upon the easy means for dissipation of the war camps; but from the President down, how many members of the Christian Church are there who propose that the curses pronounced by God against the nation that encourages and profits by drunkenness and the curse which naturally comes from the drinking evil, shall not befall us?[1]

Numerous quotations might be made to further illustrate the compromise of ethical standards which has taken place largely due to the fact that many churchmen have rejected the revival method of evangelizing the Church and the world. Atkins' statements with regard to this evident compromise form a very splendid summary which should be most helpful for contemporary Christendom to consider. No thoughtful reader can afford to overlook his statement. His words are as follows:

Whitefield made seven visits to America and crossed the ocean thirteen times. He never made his last voyage home. He was buried (1770) in the crypt beneath the pulpit of the Old South Presbyterian Church in Newburyport where his bones—wanting an arm—await the general resurrection whose terrors and rewards he had so often proclaimed. He had shaken England and America and left a mark upon America religion it has never escaped . . . . What Edwards, Whitefield and Wesleyanism had vitalized was then nationalized. The communions organized themselves according to temper, tradition and necessity but religion meant for them generally personal salvation, a laborious, orderly, frugal life, faithful attendance upon the means of grace and due watchfulness against the sins of the flesh and the love of pleasure. A religious experience was the general condition of church membership. Revivalism was a recognized (and

---

1 Pierce, op. cit., pp. 86, 87.

greatly desired) method of 'winning souls' and building up the churches. It had created its own technique of conviction, repentance and conversion often through great travail of soul. Often also through great travail of body and with strange accompaniments of hysterias. The system had worked out its own doctrinal supports—an infallible Bible, a lost humanity, the saving power of the Cross, the mystical (though it knew no such word then) reception and sharing of the Christ life.[1]

3. Examples of Fissiparous Groups

When denominations emerge from the status of religious radicals and have gradually made their rise to respectability, and after they have compromised their former standards and accommodated them to suit the newly acquired status of their constituency—it is then that they become complacent. Spiritual decline and decay become more and more prominent until there arises within their ranks minority factions which revolt against such prevailing tendencies and demand a revival. Such groups are never understood or appreciated by the parent body from which they stem. It is also true that leaders of such minority groups are sometimes men who allow their Christian zeal to become vitiated by unchristian attitudes toward those who refuse to give ear to their demands. They become somewhat rabid in their denunciation of their brethren within the parent body and renounce them all as apostates. They are either unable or unwilling to recognize the place or purpose of the larger group's continued existence. There is manifestly a great need for more attention to be given to the thirteenth chapter of I Corinthians, on both sides perhaps.

It would be amiss to conclude that the parent bodies of such fissiparous groups are no longer capable of serving a useful purpose within Christendom. It is an incontrovertible fact that these older groups have among their large constituencies a multitude of staid and tried saints who will occupy many of the places reserved for eminent saints in Heaven. The huge contributions of these conservative groups are legion. One of their most generous contributions is to be seen in their attitude toward the sect groups in opening to them their seminaries and colleges to train ministerial students who would not otherwise have such an opportunity. These brotherly Christian gestures

---

2 Atkins, op. cit., pp. 13, 14.

are not made merely as a duty, but these parent bodies actually are grateful for being able to render such a service. Students from these radical sect groups do not become "ugly ducklings" on the campus nor are they made to feel ill at ease. On the contrary they are extended every possible courtesy and consideration which it is customary to offer students from the larger communions.

Another great contribution which the established Church makes is that it serves as a stabilizing influence to ballast the radical sect groups as they pass through turbulent waters of emotional excesses and erratic teachings and behavior. It seems that each of these groups, both large and small, are essential to color the variagated picture of the whole Church. While we may not be competent to envisage the complex interweaving of the Divine ecclesiastical tapestry we can be sure of the ultimate outcome. Bishop Arthur Moore of the great Methodist Church writes a paragraph in his admirable and inspiring book, *Central Certainties,* which cannot but thrill the heart of any true believer. The optimistic chapter heading is itself captivating, "The Church Is Deathless."

It will be both encouraging and invigorating to read his comforting words which pulsate with a confident certainty. He writes:

At no time has Jesus deserted his church. The compromise and timidity of its members may often sadden his heart, but he stands by in love to quicken them into fresh devotion and more effective service. In the Book of Revelation are pictured several churches. Some of them were tepid, colorless and compromising. They were without moral allegiance, lacking in spiritual discernment. Religion had become a compromise when it ought to have been a passion, a cowardly adaptation when it was intended to become a cleansing fire; but Christ had not counted them as unworthy and faithless. He stood by to restore zeal and courage to their languishing lives. They were still of his church, and not even their sterile worldliness and spiritual apathy could rob them of his affection. He set about to redeem them of their thralldom of worldly environment so that they might go forth with inner peace and outward fortitude to turn the world upside down.

With such encouraging words fresh in our minds it becomes necessary to quote also the words of Jesus as recorded by Luke: "Strive to enter in at the strait gate: for many, I say unto you, will seek to enter in, and shall not be able."[1] These words were

---
1 Luke 13:24.

in reply to the question, "Are there few that be saved?"[1] and were followed by explanatory statements revealing that many who thought they would enter in discover after it is too late that the door has been shut and they are standing without, knocking at the door and making their claims to discipleship and seeking to gain an entrance. While the Church, as the body of Christ, will be drawn from various communions, let no man think that mere church-membership entitles him to a certain admission into the heavenly kingdom. "Many" who are in the church as members are destined to make the sad discovery that they have "strived to enter in" but have failed.

God uses the sect groups, periodically, as agencies to revitalize His Church, and to call it again to its true mission in the world. When spiritual apathy and indifference become dominant, these groups play an indispensable part to revive His Work in the midst of the years. It was true in the Catholic Church when Luther was used of God to protest against the existing evils which had become regnant at the time. We have noticed how the Reformation failed to meet the religious needs of the peasants and other disfranchised groups and how the Peasant's War and the Anabaptist movement both are representative of the revolutionary tendency incipient at a time when the poor had no adequate agent to articulate their cause.[2]

The Pietist Movement, we have also viewed as a reformation within the Reformation calling the Church again to a vital personal conversion experience, prayer and devotional Bible study at a time when Lutheranism had drifted into a meaningless formalism and had substituted the creedal statements of the Church for the Word of God.

Another branch of the non-Roman Church is Anglicanism. Its appeal is yet principally to those of the higher stratum. It is the most ritualistic of the non-Roman sects.[3] The Anglicans, known as the Church of England and also as Episcopalians, have been responsible for the appearance of two fissiparous groups on American soil, viz., American Methodism and the Puritans or Congregational church Each of these denominational groups

---

1 Ibid, 13:23.
2 Niebuhr, op. cit., p. 34.
3 Curran, op. cit., p. 9.

became sects only after they had abandoned any hope of bringing about the needed revival inside the Church of England.

Muncy, quoting Henry Martin Dexter, and A. W. McClure, says:

> The Congregationalists had a vital interest in genuine evangelism. They became Separatists only when they despaired of purifying the Church of England. During the early Colonial period they demanded evidence of regeneration as a prerequisite to church membership. If anyone desired to unite with the church he presented his request to the elders who brought the matter to the attention of the congregation. The procedure was followed in receiving male members, but women were permitted to tell their experience to the elders only. . . .
>
> The early Congregational ministers of New England bore the cross in their attitude toward the unsaved. In an argument against the theory of Apostolic succession, which taught that every minister must be consecrated by a bishop, an early Congregational minister said: 'When we see a man called to the ministry by the Church of God, his mind instinct with the grand truths of revelation, mighty in the Scriptures, fervent in spirit, instant in prayer, BURNING WITH LOVE TO JESUS, AND THE SOULS FOR WHICH CHRIST BLED, laboriously and faithfully dispensing the bread of life to hearts hungering for the heavenly food, where is he who could coldly ask to see his commission to preach the gospel?[1]

The Congregational church in the New England settlements had an almost universal church attendance. Miles Standish and other officials at Plymouth, for example, marched to church on Sundays to the beat of drums but Muncy states that the second half of the century witnessed a sad decline in evangelism.[2] Dr. Sweet, in writing of the Puritans says, "The religion of the Puritans had become unemotional, with a type of preaching unconducive to revivals and conversion."[3]

We have observed the same trend prevalent among the Quakers in our previous discussion.

According to Garrison[4] and Muncy[5] the Methodists gave birth to most of the holiness sects principally because of the relaxed emphasis upon the Wesleyan doctrine of sanctification. While many of the groups spawned by Methodism resulted from a dissatisfaction with the episcopal type of government, the principal reason among holiness groups was of a theological character.

---

1 Muncy, op. cit., p. 6.
2 Ibid., pp. 7, 8 et passim.
3 Sweet, Story, p. 96.
4 Garrison, op. cit., p. 181.
5 Muncy, op. cit., p. 127.

Chapter IV
WHY PENTECOSTAL HOLINESS?

In order to get before our minds the relationship of Sections I and II, and to introduce the material which is to be incorporated in the second of the two "twin chapters" entitled "Why Pentecostal Holiness?" it becomes necessary to recapitulate in a general way some of the main thoughts which have been brought into focus previously.

In Section I we have considered some of the divisive factors at work in society which tend to produce new sects. Each of these factors was considered separately in the following order: "The Theological Factor," and in a supplementary discussion three manifestations of modern liberalism were also considered, then the psychological, social, economic, and political factors were considered each in their turn. In Section II we have set forth representative historic examples to illustrate the evolutionary pattern cycle beginning with religious radicals and finally ending in that compromise and complacency which necessitates revolt and revival. Out of such revivals new sects have usually emerged. Likewise these new groups have followed the same pattern cycle and in time they, too, have become the parent body from which other fissiparous groups stem. In the closing chapter of each of these sections we have chosen to set forth reasons to justify and explain the existence of Pentecostal and Holiness sects.

In the first of these twin chapters we drew our conclusions principally from the theological background, calling attention to the various underlying factors which colored the theological picture and necessitated the appearance of these new groups. Some attention was also given to the distinctive contribution which they have made in forming a bulwark to combat German rationalism or modern liberalism.

We will now continue our discussion by giving additional attention to these factors and to introducing others which are also pertinent. Sections I and II are seen to be very closely related to one another. In the first section we have analyzed why and how new sects come into existence, and in the second section we have observed the fact of their historic appearance in various eras when the spiritual life of the Church had become languid and flagging.

THE ACTIVATING MOTIVES OF NEW SECT GROUPS

These new sects, on the whole, have not sought to set up new denominations but have been actuated by sincere and worthy motives to promote a revival within the established churches of which they were originally a constituent part. Luther was unable to institute a reform in the Roman Catholic church despite the fact that he cried out against the abuses of Albrecht, Johann Tetzel and others who were selling indulgencies and pocketing half of the proceeds.[1] Luther's profound personal experience would not allow him to tacitly acquiesce in these nefarious practices without protest. However, Romanism was by no means willing to receive his criticism nor to amend her ways. Until this day Martin Luther is still considered by Roman Catholics as a rank heretic. It is strange but true that this has been somewhat characteristic in the attitude of the established churches in subsequent times when schisms have resulted. Neither was it Wesley's desire to gain a following at the expense of the Church to which he belonged and served. Not until after his death did the "societies" he had organized become a new sect, and then only because the Church of England stubbornly refused to submit to the revival. Devereux Jarratt, himself a parish minister of the Church of England, in his autobiography writes the following account which illustrates this fact. He says:

The first Methodist preacher I ever conversed with or saw, in Virginia, was Mr. Robert Williams, a plain, simple-hearted, pious man. This I believe was his genuine character. He came to my house the year 1772 or 1773. He staid with me near a week, and preached several sermons in the parish, most, or all of which I heard. I liked his preaching in the main very well, and especially the affectionate and animated manner in which his discourses were delivered. I had much conversation with him concerning Mr. Wesley, and the nature and design of Methodism. He informed me, 'That the Methodists were true members of the Church of England—that their design was to build up, and not divide the church—that the preachers did not assume the office of priests—administered neither the ordinance of

---

1 Walker, op. cit., p. 340.

Baptism, nor the Lord's Supper, but looked to the parish ministers, in all places, for these—that they travelled to call sinners to repentance—to join proper subjects in society for mutual edification, and to do all they could for the spiritual improvement of those societies.[1]

Muncy writes concerning the later appearance of the holiness groups which emerged principally from the Methodist Church:

> The promoters of the Camp Meeting Association did not propose to organize a separate denomination. They decried denominationalism and sought to unite all true Christians. They sought to influence the older denominations toward their ideas of perfection but found themselves more and more unwelcomed in these groups.[2]

Dr. Sweet, in referring to the same historic fact writes the following account:

> As the great denominations came more and more to be controlled by business methods, and dominated by men of wealth; as the services tended to become more formal and as the ministers and choirs donned robes and cushions were placed in the pews, people of limited means began to feel more out of place and complaint began to be raised that 'heart religion' was disappearing. Beginning about 1880 and continuing until the close of the century the so-called 'holiness' question agitated the several churches of the Methodist family particularly. Wesley's doctrine of Christian perfection had become little more than a creedal matter among the main bodies of American Methodism.[3]

Clark's observations, based on information derived from the General Conference Journal are highly significant. No better explanation could be given for the appearance of the Holiness sects. He writes:

> In 1870 the bishops of the Methodist Episcopal Church, South, in their quadrennial Address, deplored the low spiritual state of the people and pleaded for 'an increase of inward genuine, scriptural holiness.' They feared that 'the doctrine of perfect love,' 'a prominent theme in the discourse of our fathers' was being 'overlooked and neglected.' 'Nothing is so much needed at the present time, throughout all these lands,' continued the bishops, 'as a general and powerful revival of scriptural holiness.' But when this advice seemed to be heeded, and thirty years later, a holiness movement was sweeping over the country and through the Church, giving much trouble to the staid leaders, there was a different tone in the Episcopal Address.

---

1 Devereux Jarratt, The Life of The Reverend Devereux Jarratt. (Baltimore: Warner and Hanna, 1806), pp. 107, 108.
2 Muncy, op. cit., p. 129.
3 Sweet, Story, p. 505.

In 1894 the bishops pointed out that Methodism had ever taught the privilege of entire sanctification, though few had attained the experience; 'let the doctrine still be proclaimed, and the experience still be testified.' Then followed a virtual denunciation and repudiation of the 'party with holiness as a watchword' and holiness associations, meetings, preachers and evangelists. The bishops were seeking to bring under control the perfectionist advocates who, true to form, were finding themselves uncomfortable in the complacent congregations which in their sophistication had outgrown the doctrine dear to the naive and ardent rural enthusiasts. The bishops deplored the tendency to 'separate themselves from the body of ministers and disciples' and pointed out that 'the responsibility of appointing and directing religious services belongs to the preacher in charge'; they warned the unauthorized holiness meetings and even went so far as to suggest legislation against 'such interference.' A comparison of the Addresses of 1870 and 1894 tells the whole story of the passing of perfectionism as a vital influence from the great Methodist bodies.

All this is interesting in showing the inevitable beginnings of a new sect, and in the customary manner. With perfectionism definitely eliminated from Methodism, there began first an agitation for its reinstatement, and then withdrawals and schisms on the part of the poor and lowly into congenial groups.[1]

John R. Brooks, in his book *Scriptural Sanctification,* quotes from a Pastoral Address of the Centennial Conference of American Methodism, held in Baltimore, December, 1884, and composed of delegates from eight branches of the Methodist family. It is plainly evident that Methodist leaders realized their defection and were earnestly but hopelessly trying to prevent the inevitable from occurring. The Address says:

We remind you, brethren, that the mission of Methodism is to promote holiness. Holiness is the fulness of life, the crown of the soul, the joy and strength of the Church. It is not a sentiment nor an emotion, but a principle inwrought in the heart, the culmination of God's work in use, followed by a consecrated life. In all the borders of Methodism the doctrine is preached, and the experience of sanctification is urged. We beseech you brethren, stand by your standards on this subject. Our founders rightly interpreted the mind of the Spirit, and gave us the truth as it is in Jesus. Let us not turn from them to follow strange lights, but rather let us believe their

---

1 Clark, **op. cit.,** pp. 78, 79.
2 **Ibid.,** p. 97 (Clark also relates how the Pilgrim Holiness Church came into existence in a similar manner. Martin W. Knapp organized the International Apostolic Holiness Union in his home at Cincinnati. His purpose was to form an interdenominational union which would react helpfully upon the churches which had deserted the Wesleyan landmarks of holiness, divine healing and premillenarianism. Inevitably the union itself became an independent sect.)

testimony, follow their example and seek purity of heart by faith in the cleansing blood, and then, in the steady line of consecrated living, 'go on to perfection.'[1]

These perspicuous illustrations leave no room for misunderstanding as to why or how holiness groups made their appearance. They are merely fissiparous sects which have appeared in the selfsame manner that most of the other evangelical denominations have made their appearance.

Major Forces Requiring Major Awakenings

GERMAN HUMANISM

The Protestant Reformation saved the Church from total moral decay and successfully combated the force of German humanism prevalent in that day. Walker writes:

> The religious and economic situation of Germany at the beginning of the sixteenth century was in many respects critical . . . The clergy at home were much criticised for the unworthy examples of many of their number in high station and low . . . Monasteries in many places were in sore need of reform . . . The peasantry in general were in a state of economic unrest . . . added to these causes of restlessness were the intellectual ferment of rising German humanism and the stirrings of popular religious awakening, manifested in a deepening sense of terror and concern for salvation. It is evident that, could these various grievances find bold expression in a determined leader, his voice would find a wide hearing.[2]

FRENCH DEISM

The Great Awakening was God's way of saving the colonial Churches from spiritual impoverishment, and of combating the deleterious and deadly influences of Deism which had found its way into America from France. Church membership has been made a requisite to citizenship and church attendance was made compulsory by law. Under the economy which involved the union of church and state the churches were supported by taxation. Those who were non-church members were deprived of participation in church business and their children were debarred from all the privileges of the church. To relieve these ecclesiastical disabilities the Half-Way Covenant was adopted in 1662. It admitted non-christians by baptism and even men

---

1 John R. Brooks, **Scriptural Sanctification.** (Nashville: Publishing House of the M. E. Church, South 1899), pp. 157, 158.
2 Walker, op. cit., p. 335.

of lax personal morality who might desire baptism for their children. Gradually the Lord's table was opened to those who owned the Covenant. By 1679 the church had been filled with unregenerated communicants. Thoughtful minds were provoked to serious contemplation. Men began to take inventory of the prevalent evils which they believed were responsible for God's judgments being visited upon them in various ways.[1] Beardsley presents a list of these evils which will give to us an idea of the times preceding the Great Awakening. He writes:

After a careful consideration of these problems, thirteen evils were specified as being the causes of the disasters and calamities which had come upon them. They were as follows: decay of godliness on the part of professing Christians; pride and extravagance in dress; neglect of baptism and church fellowship together with a failure to testify against Quakers and Baptists; profanity and irreverent behavior in the sanctuary; absence of Sabbath observance; lack of family government and worship; back bitings, censures, revilings and litigations of church members, intemperance, tavern hunting and putting the bottle to the lips of Indians, besides adultery, lustful dress and behavior, mixed dancings, gaming and idleness; dishonesty; covetousness and a love of the world; opposition to reformation and leniency towards sin, a want of public spirit in causing schools and other common interests to languish; and finally a general unfruitfulness under the means of grace and a refusal to repent.[2]

These conditions continued to become worse until the time of the Great Awakening in 1734, some sixty years later. We have already quoted from Muncy's book the account of how deism laid the foundation for the decadent structure of religious and social life.[3] Muncy describes colonial America in the following lines which are indeed striking: "In all sections of colonial America the light of true religion was all but snuffed out. Immorality was rife in all classes of the population and there was corruption in both church and state."[4]

Dr. Lacy, in speaking of the Great Awakening says: "He who designated the religious movement in the Colonies during the eighteenth century as 'The Great Awakening' had a touch of genius. Known as the 'Wesleyan Revival' in Great Britain, it

---
[1] Frank Grenville Beardsley, **A. History of American Revivals.** (New York: American Tract Society, 1912), p. 15.
[2] **Loc cit.**
[3] Muncy, **op. cit.,** p. 26.
[4] **Loc. cit.**

was for America an awakening of dead churches and the calling of many sinners from death unto life."[1] While historians and psychologists have been severely critical of the emotional extravagances during this period, it appears that nothing less than such a revolutionary spiritual upheaval would have been adequate and potent enough to produce the same results.

Gewehr, in speaking of the Half-Way Covenant and the prevailing conditions in the churches prior to the Great Awakening says:

> The Half-Way Covenant which permitted morally respectable persons to enter the church although they had not experienced conversion, opened the doors to laxity and worldliness. There also seems to have been no little defection from sound doctrine. Among the Presbyterians, too, little was known of vital experimental religion, and there was much complaint of the lack of zeal and fidelity in the preaching of the gospel, to say nothing of the conviction that many members of the Synod of Philadelphia were in an unconverted state. The Anglicans were no better off, indifference, coldness, formality and lack of spirituality characterizing both clergy and laity. Religious destitution was also great among Lutheran and Dutch Reformed churches of New York, New Jersey and Pennsylvania. In a word, prior to the Great Awakening the evangelical doctrines were obscured by externals, and religion everywhere throughout the colonies.[2]

It would be interesting to read Hood's account of the condition of the times which preceded the Wesleyan Revival.[3] However, it will serve our purpose to state that the times in Great Britain were parallel with those in America and required the same extraordinary type of spiritual upheaval to awaken the people.

A fourth example of a great awakening which served to utterly rout the forces of deism was The Great Revival in the West. Muncy writes of this period:

> From the close of the Revolution to the end of the century, religion was at low-tide in most of America. The only exception to this statement was the brief period of revival in Virginia. These years were characterized by a great migration to the 'new west,' the spread of deism and immorality over the nation. This condition obtained when the Great Awakening of 1800 came to bless and revitalize American Christianity.[4]

---

1 Lacy, **op. cit.**, p. 32.
2 Gewehr, **op. cit.**, p. 3.
3 Hood, **op. cit.**, p. 10 ff.
4 Muncy, **op. cit.**, p. 75.

A tidal wave of evangelism came to the eastern seaboard and flowed to the western frontier settlements of the 'new west' about ten years before the coming of the missionary organizations and numerous religious journals and other literature. This season of revival came to the Congregational churches in Connecticut in 1791 and the Presbyterian churches in the eastern seaboard in 1792. It swept the colleges, beginning at Yale in 1802 and turned back the tide of French Deism.[1]

The wide-spread infidelity which followed the War for Independence was driven from the American scene by the vital evangelism of this era. French Deism was so firmly established in the American mind that many people despaired for Christianity. College students were sure that it was a dead issue, that the Bible was outmoded, and that the 'Age of Reason' had finally come to the world. It was vital evangelism under the leadership of Timothy Dwight of Yale that sounded the death knell of this philosophy. The revival spread to Yale and other centers of learning with similar results. The Camp Meetings on the frontier and the local revivals along the eastern seaboard were effective answers to Deism among the rank and file of the population. The rout of Deism was a notable contribution to the life of the nation in its early years.[2]

Dr. Wilbur Smith of the Moody Bible School, when personally interviewed by this writer recently, made the following statement: "What we need most in our day is to evangelize our educational centers. Men who are scholars and who know God need to do for our generation what Timothy Dwight did for his generation. Modernism needs to be routed."

It will be time well spent for us to consider the thrilling account of Timothy Dwight's epoch-making experience as president of Yale at a time when the light of Christianity in America was all but burned out. Muncy quotes Cunningham and Sweet's account of these eventful days in American Church history. He says:

In 1795, when Timothy Dwight came to Yale as president, only two students would confess that they believed in God.

The morals of college groups were at an extremely low level during the closing years of the century. Lyman Beecher, who was a student at Yale College in 1795 describes conditions there as follows: 'Most of the students were skeptical, and rowdies were plenty. Wine and liquor were kept in many rooms; intemperance, profanity, gambling and licentiousness were common.'

Conditions similar to those at Yale appeared on other campuses.

---

1 Ibid., p. 95.
2 Ibid., pp. 111, 112.

Princeton was a Presbyterian school, but in 1782 there were only two students who professed to be Christians. The General Assembly, meeting in 1798, published the following of theological thought and public morals:
'We note with painful and fearful apprehension a general dereliction of religious principles and practices among our fellow-citizens, a visible and prevailing impiety and contempt for laws and institution of religion, and an abounding infidelity, which in many cases tends to atheism itself. The profligacy and corruption of the public morals have advanced with a progress proportionate to our declension in religion. Profanity, pride, luxury, injustice, intemperance, lewdness and every species of debauchery and loose indulgencies greatly abound.

For such a time as this God raised up Timothy Dwight, a grandson of Jonathan Edwards. He inherited much of the mental acumen of his famous grandfather and was taught Edwardian theology and Puritan morals by his mother. . . . His service in the chaplaincy brought the young clergyman into close contact with the gross immorality usually associated with war and with French deism. . . . He conceived of deism, which had been brought to America by French statesmen and soldiers during the war, as a great danger to the life of the infant nation. He had already begun to fight this menace before he was chosen as president of Yale in 1795.

The students seemed to think that the battle would soon be joined when Dwight assumed the responsibilities of the presidency. They were very certain that Christianity was a dead issue in that 'Age of Reason.' The seniors seized their first opportunity to test the new president. In the list of possible topics to be discussed before him, they submitted the following question: 'Are the Scriptures of the Old Testament and the New Testament the Word of God?' Dwight chose this question for his first 'disputation,' permitting the members of the class to take either side of the debate. Cunningham says: 'Here was an opportunity they never dreamed would be given them. They must make the most of it. When the day of the dispute came, most, if not all came forward as champions of infidelity. Dwight allowed each to state his case fully.

When the seniors had presented their arguments, President Dwight entered the debate personally. He showed them how little they knew about the subject and that many of their statements of fact were either mistaken or irrelevant. He presented the proof of the divine origin of the Scriptures with irresistible logic and commanding eloquence. His biographer says that Dwight's handling of the question 'left the stoutest infidel utterly confounded. His bolts had the effect of lightning on the whole college. . . .'

His preaching was a convincing answer on the intellectual plain to the scoffing deism of the day. His own conversion experience was a laboratory demonstration of the fact that God does enter into the experiences of men. The Holy Spirit used this man and his message to bring a religious awakening to the campus in 1802. One third of the students were converted and more than thirty of the new converts became ministers. The awakening began when some young men who had been converted in local revivals came to Yale.[1]

The closing sentence of this interesting quotation introduces a fact which deserves no little attention. While President Dwight's contribution to Christendom is laudable and noteworthy, the real revival began when the new converts from local revivals came to Yale. This writer would agree with Dr. J. Wilbur Smith that we do need scholarly orthodox witnesses like Timothy Dwight to present the gospel on an intellectual level, yet this method would never reach the masses and produce "the revival we need."

GERMAN RATIONALISM

We have already pointed out at some length how God used the Holiness and Pentecostal sects as a bulwark against German Rationalism. Contemporary churchmen look upon these "radical sects" as being emotionally unbalanced religious extremists. Some even consider them as being mentally unbalanced. These sects are, on the whole, comprised of those classes of persons who are socially inferior, economically disfranchised, and of limited educational opportunity. We gladly accept the charges, realizing that "religious radicals" have promoted every worthwhile revival in history. Also realizing that Jesus came to preach the gospel to the poor and the disinherited groups. The established churches of our day were at one time more radical, more ignorant, poorer, and occupied even lower social strata. The Holiness and Pentecostal groups have never known the "jerks" or the "barks," or "fallings." We only wish we could boast of such phenomenal manifestations of God's presence and power. While it is recognized that the devil tried to ape God's work in many instances, yet, as we have previously pointed out, by and large, these physical manifestations were used of God to awaken a slumbering, dead church to new life, and raise up a generation of devout enthusiasts who would evangelize the world. These radical type revivals have made of America the first ranking Christian nation of the world. Without them we would likely be groping in heathen darkness, superstition and im-

---

[1] Muncy, op. cit., pp. 78-81.

morality and infidelity. This statement may at first seem somewhat overdrawn. But when we consider the damning effects of Deism as has been pointed out in the above quotations we are forced to conclude that Christianity is again being threatened with a similar onslaught of Satan in the form of German Rationalism.

Pentecostal and Holiness groups advocate a vital, personal religious conversion experience and contend for the orthodox evangelical faith. They, also, advocate a free expression of emotion amid a church world where emotion has been crowded out. Pierce states, "The lack of genuine and true spirit of revival has resulted in the promotion of Pentecostalism. Love must have warmth, instead of the atmosphere of an icebox."[1] The biggest objection or criticism directed against these groups has been "speaking in tongues." Elaborate efforts have been made to explain this phenomena from a psychological standpoint. Some have attributed it to the devil, while many others are of the opinion that those who practice it are to some degree demented. Is it not fair to include also those who are listed in Acts 1:13, 14 in the same class? But to make such a charge is a calumny against an eternal God and borders on blasphemy pure and simple. The burden of proof lies upon those who reject the experience of speaking in tongues to show that it is unscriptural and not intended for Christians of our own day. Though the devil may offer his counterfeits, there is a genuine on which the counterfeit is based. More will be said on this point in the discussion of the baptism of the Holy Ghost as a distinctive doctrine of the Pentecostal Holiness Church.

Men's hearts as well as their heads must be convinced and converted. It seems that when the world sinks to low spiritual levels God uses mighty physical manifestations and phenomenal occurrences to coerce men to regain their equilibrium. This seems to be especially true when such spiritual apathy has been the outgrowth of man's egotistical rational attempt to eliminate the necessity of God in human affairs. Humanism, deism and German rationalism have presented the three major threats to the Christian Church in modern times. God used the Protestant Reformation to combat Humanism; He used the Great Awaken-

---

1 Pierce, **op. cit.,** p. 114.

ing, the Wesleyan Revival and the Great Revival of 1800 to combat the forces of French deism, and in our own day God has chosen to use Pentecostal and Holiness groups to combat German liberalism. Of course orthodox Christians in the conventional churches are also being used of God for the same purpose. But humbling as it may seem, these "modern-day religious radicals" constitute the strongest threat against modernism, and also furnish the wholesome competition necessary to stimulate the larger churches to action. Historians of the future will be forced to allocate to these somewhat despised groups just recompense for their noteworthy contribution in preserving the orthodox, evangelical Christian faith when modern liberalism threatened to smother it completely.

OTHER CONTRIBUTIONS OF PENTECOSTAL AND HOLINESS SECTS

Another outstanding contribution which these new sects have made is to deepen the spiritual life and experience of those who have become Christians, and to help many in the discovery that they who thought themselves to be Christians were only church members. Billy Sunday and others who have used high-pressure revivalistic methods filled the churches with many people who had never been born again. The superficial methods of "handshaking" and "card-signing" increased membership enrollments but did relatively little to enlarge the kingdom of God. Swift's statements in this connection deserve serious thought. He says:

> While churchmen, at the release of each new estimate of church membership and the publication of each new series of church statistics, are prone to point with pride to increases in church membership, it is extremely doubtful whether, in the long view, Christianity is maintaining its hold on the people of the United States.[1]

In spite of just criticism of these culpable methods there was a residue of genuine good done which far exceeds the less potent and ineffective methods which have been substituted in more recent times. The Holiness and Pentecostal groups, however, can lay just claim to perpetuating the old-time religion and the revivalistic method which produces conviction, and a vital conversion experience. While these groups do not have a monopoly on this type of experience they are largely responsible for its

---

[1] Arthur L. Swift, **New Frontiers of Religion**. (New York: The Macmillan Co., 1938), p. 74.

continuance. Muncy writes that the greater percentage of church-members from the Civil War to 1930 were added to the Church by the revival method.[2] Since that time the educational-evangelism method has been a regnant influence in the bigger denominations and has substantially replaced revivalism in the conventional Church. This observation has been made previously but is repeated here for emphasis. The admission of non-Christians into the modern-day Church by faulty techniques is comparable to the Half-Way Covenant which vitiated the Church in Edward's day. Muncy writes: "The standards of church membership have been lowered and many are enrolled as church members who show no evidence of vital religious experience."[1] His additional comment is a sane appraisal of the need in the Church and world about us. He writes:

> Some of the leaders of American Christendom have become so alarmed over the low moral standards of church members and the impotency of so many churches in their witness to a lost world that they are insisting on a vital personal religious experience. This is a good omen. The passion for adding names to the church rolls which seized so many evangelists and other Christian leaders a few years ago has brought many unregenerate persons into the membership of the churches. It is to be feared that this condition will stifle evangelism in our day very much as did the Half-Way Covenant and Birthright membership in Colonial times. This is one of the greatest perils to the evangelism of today and tomorrow.
>
> The world of today calls in no uncertain terms for an evangelism which will produce social and economic adjustments upon Christian principles. Such adjustments will be made only through the leavening influence of men and women who have become new creatures in Christ Jesus. The evangelism of the past has been too willing to stop at the new birth, but in so far as it has insisted upon and produced twice born men it has been wise. It has shown lack of wisdom in failing to go on 'perfecting the saints' both individually and in the group.[2]

The Holiness and Pentecostal groups advocate just such a program as Muncy has outlined in these quotations and are stalwart witnesses dedicated to the fulfillment of such purposes. There has been a distinct absence of virile doctrinal preaching in current times, which has opened the way for the encroachments of error. These groups by and large have persisted in a

---
1 Ibid. p. 179.
2 Ibid., p. 183.

strong presentation of doctrinal teachings especially with relation to personal holiness and the baptism of the Holy Ghost.

Psychologically these sects "appeal to types of minds that could never be comfortable in the conventional folds of the great denominations."[1] Clark writes also this enlightening statement which further explains the psychological reason for the appearance of holiness sects and illustrates the contribution they are making in ministering to poorer groups. He says, "the humbler Christians with emotional temperaments and perfectionist leanings began to feel uneasy, to protest against the abandonment of earlier practices, and to seek wherever it might be found the experience of perfect love."[1]

Pope's comments concerning the development of the textile industry are pertinent to note here. He says: "Two decades after the Civil War, cotton mills began to appear in unprecedented number throughout the Southern Piedmont area from Danville to Birmingham."[2] The relation of the textile areas to the geographical centralization of the Holiness and Pentecostal groups is significant. Pope also points out how the professionally educated preachers of the established churches have been ruled out by the mill-hands.[3] He also points out how the industrial system makes for wide social differences.[4] The attitude of premillenarians toward the Second Coming furnishes escape from the drudgery and colorless existence these people are forced to live in.[5]

The times preceding the Holiness and Pentecostal revivals which Atkins describes are of a type which demanded a cataclysmic revival. He writes of the changing times at the close of the 19th century:

All this began to be greatly changed by the end of the century. The plutocrat had come into his own. The older American aristocracies (families who had been rich long enough to get used to it or whose ancestors came over in the Mayflower) were crowded off stage by men and women who made spending a mad caprice. Dogs wore diamond studded collars, cigarettes were wrapped in one hundred dollar bills, chorus girls took the place of blackbirds in a pie and furnished

---

1 Clark, op. cit., p. 92.
2 Pope, op. cit., p. viii.
3 Ibid., p. 108.
4 Ibid., p. 96.
5 Ibid., p. 90.

a pretty dish indeed. Women who once might have done their own laundry wore ropes of pearls. Peacock Alley furnished newspaper headlines. Any gentleman from the interior was proud to know 'Oscar' the chef, and the Bradley Martins gave a ball which brought a replica of Versailles to a New York hotel while hunger stalked the streets outside and misery huddled in alleys.[1]

Such is a description of the "gay nineties" which preceded the Holiness revivals. Atkins adds that "This also affected the churches, their techniques, their interpretation of moral standards and, very greatly, the content of preaching."[2] Thus it is that Holiness and Pentecostal groups have entered the arena to combat the destructive forces of modernism and worldliness and insist upon the revivalistic method and the crisis conversion experience, plus personal holiness as taught by Wesley and the baptism of the Holy Ghost as taught by Jesus and His apostles.

SOLEMN WARNING TO HOLINESS AND PENTECOSTAL SECTS

This writer issues here a solemn warning, though we as outcast groups have so far served a useful purpose there is danger lying ahead. Wealth and education are the two greatest enemies of the Church. The proper use of wealth and education is possible but highly improbable. These two factors have been the downfall of others before us and unless we take warning we will soon go the way of all others. Our place is to work among the poor, the untutored and disfranchised and to follow Wesley's advice to "earn all we can, save all we can and then give all we can" laying up our treasures in Heaven and not on the earth. Wesley's total possessions at the time of his death were his meager personal effects and a silver spoon. He had practiced what he preached. His treasures were in Heaven.

Pope has worked out the following scale to indicate the various facets of the transition from sect to Church, it is listed here in order to serve as a warning to those sects in the process of evolution. Here are twenty-one indications:

1. **From** membership composed chiefly of the propertyless to membership composed of property owners.
2. **From** economic poverty to economic wealth, as disclosed especially in the value of church property and the salary paid to ministers.

---
1 Atkins, **op. cit.**
2 **Ibid.**

3. From the cultural periphery toward the cultural center of the community.

4. From renunciation of prevailing culture and social organization, or indifference to it, to affirmation of prevailing cultural and social organization.

5. From self-centered (or personal) religion to culture-centered religion, from 'experience' to a social institution.

6. From noncooperation, or positive ridicule, toward established religious institutions to cooperation with the established churches of the community.

7. From suspicion of rival sects to disdain or pity for all sects.

8. From a moral community excluding unworthy members to a social institution embracing all who are socially compatible within it.

9. From an unspecialized, unprofessionalized, part-time ministry to a specialized, professional, full-time ministry.

10. From a psychology of persecution to a psychology of success and dominance.

11. From voluntary, confessional bases of membership to ritual or social prerequisites only. (Such as certificate of previous membership in another respected denomination, or training in an educational process established by the denomination itself).

12. From principal concern with adult membership to equal concern for children of members.

13. From emphasis on evangelism and conversion to emphasis on religious education.

14. From stress on a future in the next world to primary interest in a future in this world—a future for the institution, for its members, and for their children; from emphasis on death to emphasis on successful earthly life.

15. From adherence to strict Biblical standards, such as tithing or nonresistance, to acceptance of general cultural standards as a practical definition of religious obligation.

16. From a high degree of congregation participation in the services and administration of the religious group to delegation of responsibility to a comparatively small percentage of the membership.

17. From fervor in worship services to restraint; from positive action to passive listening.

18. From a comparatively large number of special religious services to a program of regular services at stated intervals.

19. From reliance on spontaneous 'leading of the Spirit' in religious services and administration to a fixed order of worship and of administrative procedure.

20. From the use of hymns resembling contemporary folk music to the use of slower, more stately hymns coming out of more remote liturgical tradition.

21. From emphasis on religion in the home to delegation of responsibility for religion to church officials and organizations.[1]

---

1 Pope, op. cit., pp. 122-124.

Part III
A HISTORY OF THE PENTECOSTAL HOLINESS CHURCH

Chapter I
THE PARENT STEM AND BACKGROUND

ANCIENT ROOTS

It would not be possible to adequately understand nor to fully appreciate the existence of the Pentecostal Holiness Church without giving some consideration to the ancient roots out of which it stems.

This church advocates three basic doctrinal teachings out of which grow three definite religious experiences. These experiences go to make up what they choose to designate as "full salvation." The doctrinal teaching regarding the first of these, justification by faith, exactly coincides with the conventional doctrinal position commonly held by evangelicals in all of the established churches. However, there are two major points of doctrinal disagreement which have issued in considerable controversy, viz., their teaching concerning sanctification by faith as a definite experience to be received subsequent to regeneration, and their doctrinal position regarding the reception of the Pentecostal baptism of the Spirit, with the initial evidence of speaking with other tongues as the Spirit gives utterance. Because some have rigidly held those teachings to be associated with these two definite experiences beyond conversion, there has resulted the appearance of the Pentecostal Holiness Church and other kindred organizations.

The existence of any new sect can be justified if it serves the purpose of emphasizing some neglected phase of doctrinal truth which was originally a part of apostolic teachings, or if it serves to minister to the spiritual welfare and happiness of some socially disinherited or economically underprivileged segment of society.

It is neither necessary nor possible to establish the fact that the early disciples were converted by merely pointing to some exact Scripture reference which states, "Here the disciples were converted, or born again." This fact is no less true regarding the experience of sanctification. There is, however, ample scriptural evidence that can be adduced to attest such a claim in both of these cases. Such evidence is also sufficient grounds upon which to establish specific doctrinal tenets. Viewing the matter entirely from an experimental standpoint, there is a host of many witnesses to bear testimony to these separate experiences which were received after conversion.

We know that the early disciples were converted because Jesus definitely states that their names were written in Heaven.[1] This is further substantiated by the fact that Jesus chose them and commissioned them to preach, to cast out devils and to heal the sick. It seems very unlikely that such men would have been unsaved. To draw such a conclusion would be preposterous. It should be observed that these things took place at least three years preceding the day of Pentecost when these disciples received the baptism of the Holy Ghost. Although they had been "born" of the Spirit they had not been "baptized" with the Spirit. It would be an anachronism to place the time of their conversion at Pentecost. Jesus clearly differentiates between the times these experiences were received. After His resurrection and before His ascension he said to His disciples, "John truly baptized with water; but ye shall be baptized with the Holy Ghost not many days hence."[1] Although three years had elapsed since the time of their conversion they had not as yet received the baptism of the Spirit. In this same connection Jesus says to His disciples, "Ye shall receive power after that the Holy Ghost is come upon you, and ye shall be witnesses unto me."[2] The question might well be asked, Had not these disciples received power? Could they not preach, cast out devils, and heal the sick? But here was an additional power which meant ye shall be martyrs, ye shall witness unto death, ye shall have the power of boldness to witness in spite of impending danger. Peter had denied his Lord a few weeks before Pentecost, but after Pentecost he was empowered to witness to the same group which has crucified the Lord. He charged them saying, "Ye denied the Holy One and the Just and desired that a murderer be granted unto you, and killed the Prince of life." They could easily have killed Peter, but he was bold to witness. With this new power at his command more

---

1 Acts 1:5.
2 Acts 1:8.

people were converted under his ministry in one day than had been in the previous three years.

It is the commonly held belief in most of the established churches that the baptism of the Spirit is synonymous with being born of the Spirit. Those who are born of the Spirit, it is contended, are by virtue of the same act baptized with the Spirit. Attention should be given to the fact that the New Testament disciples did not speak in tongues when they were born of the Spirit, but that they did speak in tongues when they were "baptized" with the Spirit. This was the convincing sign which convinced Peter and those with him that those at Cornelius' house were baptized with the Holy Ghost. In referring to that occasion later, he said:

> As I began to speak, the Holy Ghost fell on them, as on us at the beginning. Then remembered I the word of the Lord, how that he said, John truly baptized with water but ye shall be baptized with the Holy Ghost. Forasmuch then as God gave them the like gift as he did unto us, who believed on the Lord Jesus Christ; what was I, that I could withstand God?[1]

Luke's account of what took place is to be found in the following passage:

> While Peter yet spake these words, the Holy Ghost fell on all them that heard the word. And they of the circumcision which believed were astonished, as many as came with Peter, because that on the Gentiles was also poured out the Holy Ghost. For they heard them speak with tongues, and magnify God. Then answered Peter, Can any man forbid water, that these should not be baptized as well as we?[2]

When Peter heard them speak with tongues he was convinced. To suppose that Cornelius was not at the time a Christian would involve one in serious complications. He was a devout man, one who feared God, gave much alms to the poor, and prayed to God alway. An angel came in answer to his prayer. What Christian could boast of such? How much less should we suppose that an unconverted man could be able to measure to such a standard. Jesus taught His disciples saying, "I will pray the Father, and he shall give you another Comforter, that he may abide with you forever, even the Spirit of truth whom the world

---
1 Acts 11:16-17.
2 Acts 10:44-47

cannot receive because it seeth him not neither knoweth him."[1] This experience is exclusively for Christians, not for sinners.

The Pentecostal Holiness Church assumes the position that there is a difference between being "born" of the Spirit and being "baptized" with the Spirit, and firmly maintains that the experience of the new birth is essentially and entirely different from the baptism of the Spirit. They contend that in the natural realm to be "born" does not mean to be "baptized," and that such is also true in the spiritual realm. This difference in doctrinal teaching is, in part, the ground for its separate existence from the established churches. In view of the fact that this teaching is an emphasis of a neglected truth which the apostles taught, this church's existence should therefore be justified on that score.

Another distinctive doctrine which is maintained by the advocates of the Pentecostal Holiness truth as we have noted is that of "sanctification." There seems to be ample Scriptural evidence to justify the claim that the early disciples were sanctified after their conversion, and prior to the time when they were baptized with the Holy Ghost on the day of Pentecost. The high priestly prayer of Christ for His disciples to be sanctified would seem to indicate beyond all doubt that they needed to be sanctified, although they had been converted for three years. He was not praying for the world (sinners), but for those who were not of the world even as he was not of the world. "God so loved the world that he gave his only begotten son that whosoever believeth on him should not perish, but have everlasting life."[2] "Christ also loved the church, and gave himself for it; that he might sanctify and cleanse it by the washing of water by the word."[3]

There seems to be two outstanding evidences of sanctification, both of which are to be observed among the disciples prior to their Pentecostal experience, and after their regeneration experience. One of these is "unity," and the other is a "supernatural joy" which is not dependent on circumstances. Notice the first in the prayer of Christ as He petitions the Father "that they all may be one;"[1] "and when the day of Pentecost was fully come

---
1 John 14:16-17; 3:16.
2 Eph. 5:25, 26.
3 John 17:21.

they were all with one accord in one place."[1] Only a few days before Pentecost they had been quarreling and bickering as to which of them should be the greatest. Now they were in unity, with one accord. Something definite had taken place in their hearts. Now, concerning the supernatural joy, let us observe that when Jesus merely mentioned to his disciples that He was going away, "sorrow filled their hearts."[2] He did not actually go away, but merely mentioned to them that He was going away and sorrow filled their hearts. They were His disciples. They were saved, but sorrow filled their hearts. Now observe, when the day of His ascension came He led them out as far as Bethany and He lifted up His hands and blessed them. And it came to pass, while He blessed them, He was parted from them, and carried up into Heaven. And they worshipped Him, and returned to Jerusalem with *great joy* and were continually praising and blessing God. Amen.[3] This blessing which they received when Jesus lifted up His hands and blessed them was something beyond regeneration. It was a greater blessing because they were able to rejoice instead of being filled with sorrow. This was joy that did not depend on circumstances. This same joy enables sanctified people to rejoice when they are persecuted and reproached for witnessing to the experience. It was this "great joy" at Samaria which had prepared the people to receive the baptism of the Holy Ghost when Peter and John came to pray for them. It also prepared the disciples to return to Jerusalem with great joy where they were continually praising and blessing God until the Holy Ghost came and they were all baptized with the Holy Ghost. The Church of our day needs the genuine power of Pentecost. This experience can only come to those who are sanctified and are thus made ready for the reception of this experience. The Pentecostal Holiness Church emphasizes this neglected truth which the apostles taught. The church's existence is therefore doubly justified. These are the ancient apostolic roots out of which the Pentecostal Holiness Church stems. Jude exhorts us saying, "Ye should

---

[1] Acts 2:1.
[2] John 16:6.
[3] Luke 24:50-53.

earnestly contend for the faith that was once delivered unto the saints."[1] Because the Pentecostal Holiness Church contends for that faith, it is at variance with those who deny and reject these experiences. As long as it continues to maintain its doctrinal position it deserves the right to exist as a separate denomination.

MODERN ROOTS

John Wesley is the father of the modern holiness movement which began in 1729. The germinating center of this great movement was the little group which met at the Holy Club at Oxford including John Wesley, Charles Wesley, George Whitefield and others. R. N. Price, the author of "Holston Methodism" appraises the Wesleyan Movement as "the greatest fact in the history of the Church of Christ since the days of Paul."[2] Clark states that Wesleyan perfectionism has exerted the most far reaching influence of any type of doctrine ever presented; and while it has not remained vital in the great Methodist Churches it has persisted in numerous smaller bodies. In fact, most of the groups today that inculcate holiness are offshoots of the Wesleyan movement.[3] He also states that Methodism is directly or indirectly responsible for over 50 of the existing American sects which have a combined membership of nearly 9,000,000 persons. All of these are perfectionists as far a their official doctrine is concerned and at least 30 of them still emphasize the doctrine of holiness as their cardinal teaching.[4]

The Wesleyan Revival centered around the three principal members of the Holy Club mentioned in the preceding paragraph. Edwin Paxton Hood refers to Whitefield as the Luther of this great revival, and to Wesley as its Calvin.[5] Whitefield, and not Wesley, was the prominent figure in the opening of the Wesleyan revival. It was field-preaching in the open air that gave the first national distinctiveness to this revival, and it was Whitefield who

---

[1] Jude 3.
[2] R. N. Price, **Holston Methodism**, (Nashville: Publishing House of the Methodist Episcopal Church South, 1904), p. 1.
[3] Elmer T. Clark, **The Small Sects in America**, (Nashville: Cokesbury Press, 1937), p. 75.
[4] Ibid., p. 80.
[5] Edwin Paxton Hood, **The Great Revival of the Eighteenth Century**, (Philadelphia: American Sunday School Union, 1882), p. 69.

led the way. This greatest evangelist of his day was most affectionate, amiable, and sympathetic in his attitude toward those among whom he labored. His oratory is yet a mystery in the history of eloquence. The strength of his powerful voice was overwhelming, and yet at the same time its modulations and inflect'ons were equal to its strength. Hood states that it had all the commanding tones of a bell in clearness, and all the modulations of an organ in its variety and sweetness.[1] Whitefield preached to huge crowds which were estimated at from twenty to thirty thousand people. Some have estimated as high as fifty thousand. And yet his voice could be heard. In speaking of his preaching, Hood says that "After one of his sermons, drenched through, he would lie down spent, sobbing, exhausted, death-like; John Wesley, after one of his most effective sermons, in which he also had shaken men's souls, would just quietly mount his pony and ride off to the next village or town, reading his book as he went."[2]

Both Whitefield and Wesley were ordained ministers of the Church of England. When Whitefield was called into question by the Chancellor and charged with preaching false doctrine, he replied that he was preaching what he knew to be the truth and that he would continue to preach it. The Chancellor then threatened to excommunicate him. Afterwards the city churches were shut against him. But if they had all been open they would not have held the crowds that came to hear. Wesley had a similar experience of being excommunicated. He was invited from his father's pulpit, whereupon he walked from the Epworth Rectory into the church cemetery, mounted his father's tomb for his pulpit and preached holiness to the crowd that gathered in the church yard. It was in that sermon that he is reputed to have uttered the famous words, "The world is my parish." They became the motto of his life.

Although Wesley did not intend to organize another church, he did organize "Methodist Societies" which ultimately became church organizations after his death. Whitefield and Wesley came to differ in doctrine after a time, but surprisingly it caused no breech in their fellowship. The two Wesleys were strictly Arminian, while Whitefield became a teacher of the

---
[1] **Ibid.,** p. 75
[2] Hood, **op. cit.,** p. 81.

doctrine that the irresistible grace of God is that which is outside of us, and comes down upon us. He was actively associated with Jonathan Edwards in the Great Awakening that came to America. After crossing the Atlantic 13 times during his colorful ministerial career he died on this side, having literally spent himself in preaching the gospel. His influence did much to give impetus to the Great Awakening and to aid the cause of Methodism by preparing the way for its spread over America under the able leadership of Bishop Asbury.

No greater and more self-sacrificing group of men ever graced the American frontier than did the earnest and zealous circuit riders of the Methodist Church. Many of them died before they reached the age of forty. Their bodies were emaciated. They were gaunt figures from exposure and hardships coupled with fasting and agonizing before God for lost souls. Price in writing of Asbury's great zeal says:

> Perhaps no preacher of the Christian era, not excepting Paul or Wesley, were more industrious and indefatigable than Asbury. He was constant in going rain or shine; constantly preaching in chapels, in courthouses, in school houses, in private residences, outdoors, teaching publicly and privately, praying with families, sitting in conferences and making appointments; and yet all this time he was an invalid. When he should have been in bed he was riding thirty to forty miles a day in inclement weather over hills and mountains, through pathless forests, exposed to savage beasts and more savage men. His journal is a perpetual round of complaints of bodily weakness, fatigue, exhaustion, pain, asthma, low spirits, and medicine taking; and with all these bodily discomforts he was always ready to go to preach, to work, and always be happy in God as his salvation.[1]

Asbury's sacrificial life was the example which most of his preachers sought to emulate. He never married because he felt it would hinder him in his ministerial labors. It is said that he remarked that if he could find a woman who had enough grace of God in her heart to allow him to be gone from home most of the year he might marry her, but on second thought he had decided not to, for fear he would not have enough of the grace of God in his own heart to stay away from home. A great many of the circuit riders followed this example and remained single.

So it was that this modern Holiness movement vigorously con-

---

1 R. N. Price, op. cit., p. 247.

tinued for more than a century to spread the doctrinal teachings which Wesley and his contemporaries had inaugurated. Then ominous signs began to appear. In 1835, an article in the Christian Advocate and Journal deplored the fact that "Christian holiness is at the present time so little talked of and so little enjoyed in the Methodist Church."[1] In 1840 the Bishops stated that it is not enough to have the doctrine of sanctification just as a theory, reminding the clergy that it was the feature of early Methodism.[2] By 1870 the bishops in the quadrennium addresses were pleading for an increase of inward genuine, scriptural holiness.[3] We also cite a paragraph from the Pastoral Address of the Centennial Conference of American Methodism held in Baltimore, December, 1888, being composed of delegates from eight branches of the Methodist family. The address says:

We remind you, brethren, that the mission of Methodism is to promote holiness. Holiness is the fullness of life, the crown of the soul, the joy and strength of the Church. It is not a sentiment nor an emotion, but a principle inwrought in the heart, the culmination of God's work in us, followed by a consecrated life. In all the borders of Methodism the doctrine is preached, and the experience of sanctification is urged. We beseech you, brethren, stand by your standards on this subject. Our founders rightly interpreted the mind of the Spirit, and gave us the truth as it is in Jesus. Let us not turn from them to follow strange lights, but rather let us believe their testimony, follow their example and seek purity of heart by faith in the cleansing blood, and then, in the steady line of consecrated living 'go on to perfection.'[4]

In spite of such warnings and exhortations the spiritual fires continued to die down, and the surging tides of religious fervor subsided. Methodism had deserted the landmarks of holiness and many earnest Methodists were alarmed by the tendency to minimize the doctrine of Wesleyan perfectionism in their Church.

Muncy states that the Civil War and its immediate consequences built other foundations for the holiness movement in the United States.[5] All great conflicts invariably seem to bring with them a wave of immorality, secularism and religious apathy

---
1 May 8, 1835 issue.
2 General Conference Journal, 1840, p. 161.
3 General Conference Journal, 1870, pp. 16, 165.
4 Jno. R. Brooks, **Scriptural Holiness**, (Nashville: Publishing House of the M. E. Church, South, 1899), pp. 157, 158.
5 W. L. Muncy, Jr., **Evangelism in the United States**, (Kansas City: Central Seminary Press, 19 5), p. 128.

which vitally affects the churches. Such is evidenced in a lowering of moral standards, a compromising with the world, and a failure to vigorously demand a definite religious experience as a condition for church membership. With the consequent influx of the hoard of unconverted persons into churches, there was naturally a definite decline in genuine piety and holiness of life. The more pious people of the churches began to feel a corporate conviction for sin, and were of the opinion that the War was the direct result of divine judgment, and that the Almighty had permitted it because of the failure of Christians to do their duty in "going on to perfection," and in not insisting on the doctrine of holiness being taught among them.

With perfectionism definitely eliminated from Methodism, there began first an agitation for reinstatement, and then withdrawals and schisms. The existing spiritual condition in the churches eventually called into being a movement known as the "National Camp Meeting Association for the Promotion of Holiness." The first national Holiness camp meeting in the United States was held at Vineland, New Jersey, in 1867. It had for its purpose to lead believers into a state of holiness. Out of this initial Holiness camp meeting grew the national association just mentioned, of which the Rev. John S. Inskip was elected president.[1] It was believed that the resurgence of the frontier-type camp meeting into American church life would give opportunity for the needed emphasis on the doctrine of holiness to be made.

More than two decades prior to the appearance of this Association Dr. and Mrs. W. C. Palmer of New York City had opened a weekly prayer service which was operated for the express purpose of encouraging Methodist believers and also Christians of other denominations to seek the experience of sanctification as it had been set forth by John Wesley. Both of these fine consecrated people were members of one of the Methodist churches in New York City. God blessed their efforts, and it was not long until this Holiness meeting became widely known. From time to time many people from far and near repaired to this Mission for the purpose of seeking God for this experience which offered deliverance from indwelling sin. Muncy refers to a monthly publication, "The Guide to Holiness," which appeared in 1842 under the editorial

---

1 Muncy, op. cit., p. 127.

supervision of Dr. and Mrs. Palmer. This magazine, he quotes Gaddis as saying, claims to be the original holiness journal of America.[1] Through this agency and by word of mouth this prayer service was publicized.

It was thus that the Rev. John S. Inskip, a noted Methodist minister of the Pennsylvania Annual Conference, M. E. Church embraced the experience of sanctification, often called "perfect love" or "Christian perfection." He was a man endowed with exceptional intellectual faculties, a dynamic personality, a strong courage and an indomitable will. He immediately became engaged in preaching and teaching the truth of holiness which he had received, and in a brief space of time his fame as an exponent of this revived Methodist doctrine became known, especially among the membership of Methodist churches. God seemed to have used him as a divine instrument by which He brought about one of the greatest revivals in the history of American Methodism. It was definitely the great revival in the Methodist Church during the nineteenth century. This great revivalist became the modern apostle of holiness in the Church, extended the field of his labors to include all of the United States. The National Association for the Promotion of Holiness had its inception largely because of the indefatigable and zealous labors of Mr. Inskip. It was due to his wide popularity and leadership qualities that he was elected to head this organization. The Rev. William McDonald was his coadjutor in the work of organizing and spreading these camp meeting associations. He was the theologian of the movement. The Reverends John A. Wood, John Thompson, Sheridan Baker, I. E. D. Pepper, Isaiah Reid, George Douglas Watson, and others whose names are prominent among the people of the holiness persuasion, were raised up as a direct result of this organization. These men also became prominent as exponents of the truth of Bible holiness, and were mightily used of God to promote the cause. Muncy has this to say about the Association:

> The promoters of the Camp Meeting Association did not propose to organize a separate denomination. They decried denominationalism and sought to unite all true Christians. They sought at first to influence the older denominations toward their ideas of Christian per-

---

[1] Ibid., p. 128.

fection but found themselves more and more unwelcome in these groups. They also sought to make their impact upon the total Christian population through "bands" and conventions for a quarter of a century. But this movement split into many sects after the first effort at unification. In the period of fourteen years (1893-1907) at least twenty-five separate Holiness denominations came into being.

It would seem unfortunate that these numerous groups could not have found some common basis upon which to organize themselves. As a single unit organization they could no doubt have exercised a more telling influence. But the glaring fact is they either lacked the cohesive force which was necessary to bind them together, or they were unable to furnish the proper leadership to bring it about. In either event, these facts constitute an embarrassing situation which is unpleasant for holiness people to face, especially in the light of their claim that sanctification makes for oneness, but in all honesty they are forced to admit that oneness had not been realized. It should be recognized, however, that the holiness churches, are made up largely of underprivileged people. That fact in itself constitutes a barrier which naturally inhibits the formation of a large organization. Their limited financial status, educational background and other factors all add up to the conclusion that it was not possible to set up the intricate organizational machinery necessary to operate a big organization. It is not difficult however to understand why God would have allowed this divisiveness to exist, when we have come to recognize that there is invariably a price to pay when denominations become big. With the rise of economic, social and educational standards there also comes a corresponding decline in spirituality, and a consequent departure from the simple standards of holy living. The Methodist church is a concrete example of this trend. It would therefore seem that there is a distinct spiritual advantage in these groups remaining relatively small. In addition there is a wholesome competition created by the presence of other competitive groups. Extreme caution should be exercised in making sure that the existence of these separate groups is not due to any lack of brotherly love and Christian appreciation for fellow-members of the body of Christ. There must be a oneness in Christ! Especially is this true among those who claim and teach the experience of sanctification. There are

THE PARENT STEM AND BACKGROUND 191

doctrinal reasons which absolutely prohibit the possibility of any organizational union between Pentecostal and Holiness Groups. This is however a consideration for a later discussion. Let us confine our present thinking to Holiness groups and exclude all ideas pertaining to Pentecostal groups, for there were no Pentecostal groups in existence until after the latter rain outpouring in 1906. The Pentecostal Holiness Church which we know today did not embrace the experience of the Pentecostal baptism of the Holy Ghost until after it had been in existence several years. Let us think of it now as only a holiness group which knew absolutely nothing about the Pentecostal experience. Think of it as one of the several organizations which re-emphasized the old time Methodist teachings, after the Methodist church had ceased to do so.

The Pentecostal Holiness Church represents a consolidation of the Fire-Baptized Holiness Church and the Pentecostal Holiness Church into one organization. When the two organizations came together and effected a merger they took the name of the younger group. The history of these two organizations was entirely separate until the consolidation took place in 1911. In view of the fact that the Fire Baptized Holiness Church had its inception a year or so prior to the Pentecostal Holiness Church we will now consider its history from 1898 until the time of merger which took place in 1911, at Falcon, N. C. (There were some other smaller organizations which united with the Pentecostal Holiness Church which will be mentioned separately in a later chapter).

Chapter II
THE FIRE-BAPTIZED HOLINESS CHURCH

We have previously noted how the Rev. Mr. Inskip was greatly used of God to preach extensively over wide areas of the United States, and how the "National Association for the Promotion of Holiness" was organized as a direct result of his prodigious labors. In most of these holiness conventions which he conducted there were great throngs in attendance. It was not an uncommon occurrence for from 300 to 1500 believers to be sanctified in one of these conventions. His dynamic preaching was attended by wonderful manifestations of God's presence and power which gripped the hearts of these vast audiences. The people who attended these conventions soon found themselves more and more unwelcome in the established churches. It thus became necessary to organize themselves into more congenial groups. A number of holiness denominations and holiness associations stemmed from this national association among which were: The Church of God of Anderson, Indiana, The Church of the Nazarene, The Christian Missionary Alliance, The Pilgrim Holiness Church, The Iowa Holiness Association, The Holiness Church of North Carolina, and quite a few other Annual Conference Associations in North Carolina, South Carolina, Georgia, Florida, Tennessee, Kentucky, Mississippi, and other states as well. Concerning the the largest of these groups, Clark furnishes the following information which is an interesting sidelight that indicates the ultimate trend of holiness denominations. He says:

> The largest of the sects emerging from the National Holiness Movement is the Church of the Nazarene, which has approximately 1800 churches and 85,000 members (Clark's book was published in 1937) and is represented in all of the states. Its history is somewhat complicated. It is the product of several mergers among holiness groups and associations of the East, South and West; one of its aims is to bring together all such groups into one large denomination and it has a permanent committee to negotiate such mergers.[1]

---

1 Clark, op. cit., p. 94.

Clark interestingly points out that in spite of the doctrine subscribed to, there are already signs that vital perfectionism is on the decline in the Church of the Nazarene.[1] Concrete evidence of this trend is to be seen in the following lines:

> Already there have been revolts within the body; as early as 1917 one of these rebellious groups in Pasadena withdrew into the Pilgrim Holiness Church. The Nazarene schools especially, have been embarrassed by the holiness label and all of them have elided the designation from their names; the Texas Holiness University changed to Peniel College, Illinois Holiness University changed to Olivet College. . . . Not one institution now exposes its doctrinal character in its name. Such straws indicate the blowing of the wind in the inevitable direction taken by the large Methodist bodies.[2]

This is an illustration of the fact that it seems virtually impossible for a denomination to become big and at the same time to maintain the standards of Bible holiness, which excludes worldliness and demands purity of life, dress and conduct. This note of warning should serve to prevent other Holiness denominations from wandering into devious paths.

The Iowa Holiness Association became the largest of the national associations for the promotion of Holiness. It was not confined exclusively to the state of Iowa, but extended its borders of operation to include a major segment of Missouri and Nebraska as well. The National Holiness Movement was almost exclusively a Methodist phenomenon, led by Methodists and appealing mainly to Methodists. But in some sections of the country the impact of the Methodist influence was sufficient to encompass substantial numbers of churchmen in other denominations, particularly among the Baptists. Some of them were quite prominent people.

One of the ministers of the Baptist communion whose name was Benjamin Hardin Irwin, came under the influence of the Iowa Holiness Association which had extended its operations into the section of Nebraska where he lived. The Rev. Mr. Irwin heard, with eagerness, the messages of these fiery preachers of holiness, and it was not long until he had accepted the truth of sanctification and had received the experience. He became the founder of the Fire-Baptized Holiness Church as will be seen.

---

1 Ibid., p. 96.
2 Loc. cit.

Mr. Irwin was born and reared in Mercer County, Missouri and was educated for the law profession. Although he was able to achieve an average amount of success in this field of endeavor, he did not continue to practice law for any extended period of time. The exact time of his conversion is not definitely known, nor is there any information available as to the exact time he entered the ministry. It seems evident that he was likely converted after reaching manhood, perhaps it was not long before he quit the law practice. He most likely underwent some sort of catastrophic conversion experience that may have caused him to decide to change his profession to that of the ministry. Concerning these details we are left to rely on mere conjecture as to what the real facts were. It is certain, however, that he was an ordained minister of the Baptist Church at the time he became associated with the advocates of holiness teachings, and it was under their ministry that he embraced the experience of holiness. It was not long until his labors were rejected among those of the Baptist communion, but Mr. Irwin found an open door to preach among the holiness people with whom he soon became identified.

Mrs. William "Granny" Bowers of Royston, Georgia, who is now ninety-one years of age described Mr. Irwin when she knew him and entertained him as a guest in her home as being a "fine looking man, of large frame, possessing an unusually strong voice, and very interesting to listen to." The late Bishop J. H. King described him as a man of brilliant intellectual powers, a magnetic personality, an ardent nature, a bold, fearless soul, and a disposition which made it natural and easy for him to throw himself whole-heartedly into any task he might choose to undertake.

After B. H. Irwin began his career as a holiness minister he applied himself to the reading and study of holiness literature in order to be able to give an answer to those that asked for a reason for the hope that was in him. His brilliant, analytical and legally-trained mind caused him to delve into the profound depths of the teachings relating to the experience of sanctification he had received. He made a careful and thorough study of a vast amount of literature in the field of Methodist theology. It was while he was studying John Fletcher's writings that he discovered this writer clearly taught there was some sort of experience beyond sanctification which the fully cleansed sanctified believer could receive. This was described as a "baptism of burning love," an inflow of Divine fullness which was intended exclusively for those who were pure in heart and sanctified. The Rev. Mr. Irwin was profoundly impressed with Mr. Fletcher's writings, especially concerning this "baptism of fire," which Fletcher and others of the early Methodist movement are reputed to have sought, experienced and taught. Eventually Mr. Irwin sought and claimed to have received a "baptism of fire," and began to teach and preach the experience. Holiness people at that time believed and taught that when one receives the experience of sanctification he has in the same act also received the baptism of the Holy Ghost. The two experiences were thought of as being one and the same, and the two terms synonymous. This is yet the doctrinal position held by the Nazarene, Pilgrim Holiness, Wesleyan Methodist, Free Methodist, The Church of God of Anderson, Indiana, and various other holiness groups who have not yet embraced the experience of the Pentecostal baptism of the Holy Ghost. It might be added that these groups are bitterly opposed to the Pentecostal experience and some of them very unwisely have attributed such an experience to the power of the devil.

It is not difficult to conceive of the possibility of Mr. Irwin's running afield in his sincere and earnest attempt to reach out for an experience beyond sanctification for which his soul thirsted. Like other holiness people he was of the opinion that he had come into possession of the baptism of the Spirit in sanctification. He thus conceived of a "baptism of fire" as being that which John the Baptist spoke of in connection with the "Holy Ghost and fire" which Jesus would baptize with.[1] The experience which he taught was a harbinger of the Pentecostal baptism of the Holy Ghost which did actually appear a short time later. The baptism of fire vaguely foreshadowed, as a sort of adumbration, the real Pentecostal outpouring which had not that time taken place.

Other sanctified people shared the same desire for a fuller experience. It was this unfulfilled desire which prompted some other good sanctified people to pray for weeks at a time, asking for what they thought they needed, the gifts of the Spirit. They likewise thought they had received the baptism of the Spirit

---
1 Matthew 3:11.

196 HISTORY OF THE PENTECOSTAL HOLINESS CHURCH

and were seeking for the "gifts of the Spirit" just as others were seeking for the "baptism of fire." The esteemed and venerable N. J. Holmes speaks of these seasons of prayer in his autobiography as follows:

In the Institute at Columbia in the term of 1904-1905, a spirit of prayer came upon us, for a world-wide revival, and for a month or so, we almost suspended the daily studies under the burden of protracted prayer for a revival, for the manifestation of the Holy Ghost in Pentecostal power for the gifts of the Spirit as promised in I Cor. 12; and the signs following as in Mark 16. We saw these things in the Bible and believed they were for the church now, but did not know how to look for the fulfillment, or realize what Pentecost was. We believed that we had received the baptism with the Holy Ghost in sanctification, and that it was all one, and what we were praying for was not Pentecost or the baptism with the Spirit, but the gifts of the Spirit and the signs following.[1]

Because of this prevalent attitude among holiness believers Mr. Irwin was given a receptive hearing in every direction he turned. Multitudes of holiness people eagerly sought for the "baptism of fire." Great and mighty demonstrations of power were manifest in his meetings. In spite of the fact that he possibly did not intend to initiate a new movement, he did so. This "baptism of fire" movement swept over Iowa, Nebraska, Kansas, Oklahoma and Texas in the Southwest. It also invaded the Southeast, through the states of North and South Carolina, Georgia and Florida. It had spearheaded parts of two or three other States and into the provinces of Ontario and Manitoba, Canada, where a few had accepted of this new teaching.

There was manifested a disposition by many people of the holiness ranks which was inimical to this anomalous religious experience. It came to be designated as the "Third Blessing Heresy" and was vigorously opposed as a "doctrine of demons." Some were rabid in their denunciation of his teachings. Many doors were closed to him and his teachings in all quarters of the holiness movement. This, however, did not seem to hinder the progress of his movement which came to be known as the "Fire-Baptized Movement" by those who favored it. The persecution which was engendered by those who thought it heretical actually gave impetus to the movement instead of retarding its

---
1 N. J. Holmes and wife, **Life Sketches and Sermons**, (Royston, Georgia: The Press of the Pentecostal Holiness Church, 1920), p. 135.

progress. Because those who accepted the "baptism of fire" were no longer welcome in the holiness ranks, it soon became necessary to provide some sort of church-home to take care of them. Thus another sect was born.

THE FIRST STATE AND LOCAL ORGANIZATION

In the year of 1895 the first local organization of the "Fire-Baptized Holiness Association" was organized at Olmitz, Iowa. Later that year other local organizations were formed at Coolfield and at Ontarioville, Iowa. During the same year the first State organization had its inception, known as the Iowa Fire-Baptized Holiness Association. On the occasion of this state organization being effected, the General Overseer, B. H. Irwin assumed the authority to appoint the Rev. Oliver Fluke as the official leader to direct the work of the Association in that territory. This somewhat undemocratic method of procedure established an unfavorable precedent as will be seen. Others who composed the Iowa Ministerium were the Reverends John E. Dull, Stewart Irwin, William Elisha Stevenson, John Nelson, Charles Lescault, J. A. W. Wilson and Miss Mary McKeown. Reports were made, testimonies were given, congratulatory addresses were made, and fervent prayers were offered asking for divine guidance and blessings. Those present were exhorted to take up the torch and launch out into the white harvest fields to preach the "baptism of fire" for sanctified believers, repentance for the unsaved, and sanctification for the saved. This small beginning was the first step toward later inaugurating a national organization.

It was not long before other local and state organizations were set up according to the same order in Kansas, Oklahoma and Texas. The Rev. J. F. Wolford was appointed to oversee and direct the ministerial work in Kansas. Some of those who made up the Ministerium of Kansas included the Reverends Harry Sallenburger, Isaac Hershey, Noah Hershey, Benjamin Young, and Ezra Sheets. This list includes the ministers who were the most prominent preachers of that state. The Rev. J. H. Henson was appointed by the General Overseer to head the work which was organized in Oklahoma. The most outstanding ministers who labored under his direction included the **Reverends A. B.** Bissey, Andrew Vausant, John Alloway, and Mrs. Anna Simmons.

Other State Organizations along the Atlantic Seaboard

In the state of Georgia, the famous Rev. Richard Baxter Hayes was appointed as the state overseer. (A more detailed account of his ministerial activity will be found in the chapter on Home Missions). Working under his direction were the Reverends Joseph Hillery King, Andrew Cauthen Craft, George Oliver Gaines, James H. Jordan, Jonah Starr, Thomas Putnam, Thomas A. Carey, J. T. A. Gaines and others. The Rev. George Oliver Gaines was later elected to superintend the work of the Georgia Conference, and served in that capacity for more than a decade. His outstanding ministry was a benediction to hundreds. The South Carolina organization was headed by the Rev. W. S. Foxworth who had been appointed General Overseer. Some of those who composed the Ministerium of South Carolina were the Reverends James A. Williams, Allen W. Brooks, S. J. McElroy, W. Bino Harris, Ralph Taylor, Irwin Cannon, George Cannon, F. M. Britton, G. R. Thomas and Mrs. B. L. Hill. In North Carolina, the Rev. Edward Kelly was appointed as president of the State Association. Working with him were the following ministers; the Reverends Samuel Daniel Page, John Carter, M. D. Sellers, Jacob King, Jerry M. Howell, John Pate, Sarah Minerva Payne, Cornelia Allen and others. The Rev. John W. Wine spearheaded into Virginia. The Rev. N. G. Pulliam was the head of the Ministerium of Florida. Mr. Albert Ernest Robinson of Toronto represented the Ontario Provincial Association. Fire-Baptized ministers also spearheaded into parts of Tennesee, Ohio and Pennsylvania but they were able to attract only a limited number of followers, insufficient in number to warrant the forming of any state organizations.

The General Organization

During the interim from 1895 to 1898 there had been organized state associations in nine states and spearheads were made in four other states and two provinces of Canada. Each of these associations functioned as a unit organization due to the fact that there existed no organic bond which drew them together. It was true, however, that Mr. Irwin exercised jurisdiction over each association; taking the authority to appoint the state presidents, to ordain all preachers, and to dismiss or expel anyone who showed any disposition to ignore or fail to cooperate with the policies which he dictated. To facilitate matters for himself he decided to bring these Associations into a closer organization which would make them less difficult to supervise. More or less as a matter of form he submitted the matter of centralizing these state organizations into one national organization to the respective president of each Association. They, in turn, took the matter to their state Associations and true to form there was voiced no objection, but they all voted unanimously to comply with Mr. Irwin's request. Pursuant to this action he then called for the First General Convention to open its session on July 28, 1898 and to continue until August 8, 1898 at Anderson, South Carolina. The following prominent leaders of the various state associations, and some from the outlying regions where the movement had extended, were in attendance: The Reverends B. H. Irwin of Nebraska; J. F. Wolford of Kansas; J. M. Henson and B. Bruce Boroughs of Oklahoma; Allen Hodges of Texas; R. B. Hayes of Georgia; I. C. Ogle of Florida; W. S. Foxworth of South Carolina; Edward Kelly, S. D. Page, and Misses Sarah M. Payne and Cornelia Allen of North Carolina; the Reverends John H. Wine of Virginia; Joseph H. King, A. K. Willis, J. A. Williams, D. R. Brown, S. J. McElroy, Daniel Awrey, A. C. Craft, A. E. Robinson, W. B. T. Looney (layman), Misses Estelle Gaines, Mattie L. Cockran, Mrs. Sarah M. Penney, Mrs. C. L. Hines of South Carolina, Georgia, and Ontario.

On August 5, 1898, the formal organization took place and was called the Fire-Baptized Holiness Association. A Discipline had been formed and published by the Rev. Mr. Irwin, and after a few minor changes were made it was adopted by the Convention. One particular section of the Discipline is strangely significant in that it provided for the election of a General Overseer for life tenure, vesting him with the authority to govern and exercise control over all of the activities and work of the organization. Since that time it has been difficult to understand, even by those who were present and by their vote adopted such rule, why any intelligent group would have agreed to it. No person, however, seemed to feel that it was contrary to wisdom to delegate such power to their chief officer. During the three years since Mr. Irwin had been head of the state organizations he had always exercised unquestioned authority, it therefore came only natural for them to confirm what they had previously condoned without protest. To grant him such a prerogative for life simply meant to make permanent a hitherto temporary agreement.

At this general session it was decided to designate the state leader as "Ruling Elder" instead of the "President" of the State Association. The General Overseer continued to exercise his prerogative to appoint these leaders instead of having them elected. He also continued to license and ordain all ministerial candidates, and to dismiss them or revoke their credentials if he judged it necessary. The following were appointed by him to serve as Ruling Elders for the ensuing year:

South Carolina—W. S. Foxworth.
North Carolina—Edward Kelly.
Georgia—R. B. Hayes.
Florida—I. W. Ogle.
Oklahoma—J. M. Henson.
Kansas—J. L. Wolford.
Texas—Allen Hodges.
Iowa—Oliver Fluke.
Ontario—Albert E. Robinson.
Manitoba—(none appointed).

The next General Council was called to convene at Royston, Georgia, April 1-10, 1899. Mr. Irwin presided over its sessions and a sizeable amount of business was transacted but no minutes were kept of these proceedings. It is therefore impossible to record the facts, except to state that there was no action taken to curtail the authority of the General Overseer. (In October of 1899 the first issue of the "Live Coals of Fire" was published at Lincoln, Nebraska. The details of this project appear in connection with the history of publications).

THE GENERAL OVERSEER'S DEFECTION

Following this General Council session some of those who were in attendance accompanied Mr. Irwin to conventions which he held in Fayetteville and Dunn, N. C., in Beaver's Dam, N. Y., and in Toronto, Canada. Mr. King was appointed as pastor of the Toronto church and Ruling Elder of the Ontario Conference at this convention. From Toronto Mr. Irwin went to Manitoba and various other points West.

About a year later, in April 1900, Mr. Irwin wrote Mr. King to come to Lincoln, Nebraska, to assume the duties as Acting

Editor of the "Live Coals of Fire" publication of which he was editor. The Rev. Richard Waters was assigned the Toronto work to serve in Mr. King's stead.

Mr. Irwin had traveled incessantly since 1895 and it was natural that such a strenuous schedule would draw heavily on his physical reserve. He therefore decided to take a rest and repaired to Pittsburg for several weeks to relax his worn body. The scope of the territory he had covered ranged from the Middle West to the Atlantic Seaboard, as far North as Canada, and as far South as Florida. The complete detailed facts with regard to Mr. Irwin's intimate private life are not known, but it seems evident that the strenuous schedule which he maintained in connection with his itinerant preaching ministry must have caused him to grossly neglect his private devotion. Since he was a man endowed with rich natural gifts and a brilliant, sparkling personality, he perhaps came to rely upon sheer human ability and ceased to depend upon Almighty God for spiritual power. Such a fact is to be lamented, but it is commendable to say that he was still man enough to acknowledge his unworthiness to continue in his place of leadership in the ministry. So, in June 1900, with a tired worn body and a smiting conscience he wrote Mr. King to take over the full editorship of the paper, and notified him that he was also resigning as General Overseer of the church he had founded and organized. It is not known whether Mr. Irwin later entered the ministry in some other church or not, but it is definitely true that he was no longer associated with the Fire Baptized Holiness Association.

THE NEW GENERAL OVERSEER

The Rev. J. H. King then called a special session of the General Council to convene at Olmitz, Iowa, June 30—July 2, 1900, for the purpose of electing another General Overseer. After some preliminaries the ballots were prepared. Three distinct ballotings were made but with no election being declared. Then, it was that these brethren felt impressed to observe a period of fasting and prayer on Sunday, July 1. As the Council convened on Monday, July 2, 1900 the ballot was unanimously in favor of J. H. King. The acting editor thus was elected the General Overseer of the Fire-Baptized Holiness Association of the United States and Canada.

Mr. King was at the time 31 years of age, being born on August 11, 1869. He was converted on August 11, 1885, his sixteenth birthday, and on August 17, six days later, he felt a definite call to preach. He was later sanctified, on October 23, 1885. He entered the ministry of the Methodist Church when he was twenty years of age, where he served until he united with the Georgia Fire-Baptized Holiness Association at Royston, Georgia in January, 1898, at the age of twenty-eight. In spite of his youth he was a man of somewhat sober judgment and was very conservative in his religious behavior. He possessed the appropriate dignity to be expected of a high church official.

CHANGES IN CHURCH GOVERNMENT

In a sense it seems providential that a man of his temperament and personal qualifications should have been available to assume the responsibilities of leadership in this infant organization. There were changes necessary to be made in church polity and there were religious extravagances to be corrected. In all the General Councils which he conducted after being elected to the office of General Overseer he voluntarily began to inaugurate certain changes which would democratize the existing method of church government and limit the authority of the General Overseer. At the first General Council meeting he conducted after being elected to this office he suggested two changes which would substantially curtail his power. For the first time in the history of this church it became the corporate responsibility of the Council to examine and pass the ministerial character of those holding their clerical membership in the body. The Council was also to take the initiative in licensing and ordaining ministers. These prerogatives had been previously exercised exclusively by the General Overseer. After Mr. King called the third General Council to meet at Sanford, N. C., in September, 1901, he suggested that a law be passed governing the frequency of these sessions instead of allowing the General Overseer to call them at will. It was voted at that session that in the future the General Council meetings should come every two years. In subsequent conventions which met at Lamont, Oklahoma in 1902; at Royston in 1904; at Toccoa in 1906 other changes were made to democratize the dictatorial policies of government.

A significant change took place at Lamont, Oklahoma when the Council met in 1902. The name of the national organization was changed from Fire-Baptized Holiness "Association" to "Church." Miss Pearl Fluke was appointed as the General Council secretary and served for two years until 1904 when the General Council met at Royston, Georgia and A. E. Robinson was elected to take her place. Miss Fluke was the oldest daughter of the Rev. Oliver Fluke who was appointed by Mr. Irwin as the first State President (Ruling Elder) of the Fire-Baptized Holiness Association, to supervise the ministerial activities in Iowa. Miss Fluke later became the wife of the Rev. B. Bruce Boroughs who was a charter member of the national organization of the Fire-Baptized Holiness Association which was organized at Anderson, S. C. in 1898. They labored in the ministry together for a number of years in Oklahoma and Texas. Some years after Mr. Borough's decease she was united in marriage to the Rev. C. B. Strickland who has been a faithful member of the Pentecostal Holiness Church since 1900. Since his retirement in recent years they have lived at Falcon, N. C.

Specific information regarding the detailed happenings in others of these early General Council sessions is not available. No minutes of these sessions seem to be extant.

RELIGIOUS EXTRAVAGANCES CORRECTED

Amid the wonderful manifestations of God's Spirit in any organization there invariably appears some fanaticism or extravagances. This was true among the Methodists, Baptists, Presbyterians, and many others. Davenport makes reference to religious extravagances in connection with Mr. Wesley's great work. He says of him:

> He thought there was a danger at one time of regarding the extraordinary circumstances as essential. He thinks perhaps now the danger may be in condemning them altogether, of imagining that they are a hindrance, with nothing of God in them. The truth is, he says, that God in former time did visit lost sinners with such conviction that the natural consequence was outcry and convulsion, that he favored several of them with divine dreams and others with trances and visions, but after a while Satan stepped in and imitated the work in order to discredit it.[1]

---

[1] Frederick Morgan Davenport, **Primitive Traits in Religious Revivals**, (New York: The MacMillan Company, 1917), p. 173.

This explanation commends itself as being cogent reasoning. It is often true that the devil apes the power of God. The thing that makes it so very difficult to discern between the manifestation of the genuine power of God and the counterfeit of fanaticism is that the two are so closely associated that only a few men are able to discern the difference. Unfortunately some religious extravagances also crept into this new organization as we will now observe. It became necessary to prove all things and to hold fast to that which was good.

As we have previously observed, sanctified people everywhere were prayerfully asking for more of God's blessings because many of them realized there was something they needed beyond what they had received. Mr. Irwin's ministry had therefore been eagerly received because he offered something to sanctified believers beyond the experience of sanctification. However, it is true that after they had received this "baptism of fire" which he taught they were still unsatisfied, for this was not the baptism of the Holy Ghost for which they really longed but did not know how to receive; nor did they recognize they needed to receive it. Some of these honest, sincere, earnest Christians went overboard in their zealous attempt to satisfy this unfulfilled desire. The Rev. Mr. Irwin had taught that there were also additional "baptisms of fire" called "dynamite," "lyddite" and "oxodyte." This commercial, chemical jargon was to designate the varying degrees of "fiery baptisms." This was like eating inferior quality foods in an attempt to satisfy the desire for real nourishment. The new General Overseer set about to correct this erroneous teaching in as discreet a manner as possible, and in time this was accomplished.

In addition there were other religious extravagances to be corrected which included the following ideas: that an open public confession of all grades of sin was necessary to evidence genuine repentance; that restitution must be made of the most minute and insignificant things; that the wholly sanctified could not succumb to temptation; that those who were filled with the Spirit needed no one to instruct them; that doctors should be denounced as imposters and their remedies as poisons; that swine meat and other foods which were condemned as unclean under the Levitical dietary laws should not be eaten; and that neck ties and all other so-called worldly ornamentation should not be worn.

It took time, patience, courage and wisdom to correct these incongruous behaviors and erratic ideas, but by the grace and help of God it finally came to be realized. These religious extravagances, however, did not constitute the major problem which threatened to dissolve the young organization. It was when the news had spread abroad of Mr. Irwin's defection that the whole national set-up was virtually paralyzed and all but vanished away. This was partly due to the fact that Mr. Irwin had built the work around himself and his magnetic personality. When he withdrew the people were scattered like sheep without a shepherd. Another reason for this wholesale defection can be assigned to the fact that Mr. Irwin had been so very courageous in proclaiming the truth, and had made no compromise with sin or Satan; and now for him to withdraw from the race made his followers feel there was no use for them to try to continue. A short time after the new General Overseer had come into office every state organization in the West had disappeared and there remained only Georgia and North Carolina left intact on the Eastern Seaboard. The work in Canada also disappeared. A pall of discouragement and despondency settled over the entire organization. For a time it looked as though the little church would evanesce completely. But, by the help of God the infant organization was rebuilt on a more solid foundation. Under the wise and sane leadership of men like J. H. King, George M. Henson, S. D. Page, F. M. Britton, Harry P. Lott, A. E. Robinson, G. O. Gaines and others God confirmed His word with signs following and helped them gradually to retrieve some of what had been lost.

The "baptism of fire" does not seem to have had a valid scriptural basis, although many good people professed to have received such an experience. It was an honest attempt to satisfy an unfulfilled desire resident in the heart of the majority of those who have been sanctified. This desire was fully satisfied when the Pentecostal baptism of the Spirit came to be recognized and received. It was the reception of that experience which saved the day and enabled a discouraged group to come back in triumph.

Chapter III
THE FIRE-BAPTIZED HOLINESS CHURCH, 1898-1910
(Continued)

HOW THE CHURCH WAS RE-ESTABLISHED IN OKLAHOMA

As a typical example of the conditions which were prevalent over the church at this time, we will turn our attention briefly to some of the details connected with the re-establishment of the State Association in Oklahoma which took place in September, 1909, after some eight years of struggle.

Bishop Dan T. Muse graphically describes the thrilling experiences of some of these early pioneer ministers in the following account. He says:

> The early pioneer workers met with determined opposition from many religionists and endured much suffering and privations. Persecution was rife. Many were rocked and had eggs thrown at them. Others met with red pepper being thrown in the straw to bring discomfort to the worshippers. Tents were slashed, and doors were locked on them. Some were threatened with death by hanging, and others were arrested and spent a night or two in jail. Some towns attempted to bar the preaching of this great gospel truth.
> The support of the pioneer minister was negligible, and many times preachers were forced to walk from one meeting to another, and at times were compelled to sleep on the straw under the brush arbors and tents, and some were forced to eat wild berries for noon and onions for breakfast. Other places were more considerate and saw that ministers were provided for.
> Those who were sanctified and filled with the Spirit were turned out of the conventional churches and were forced to form small groups here and there over the Territory.
> Miracles accompanied the preaching of the full gospel. Many were slain by the power of the Lord. Some lay prostrate under the power of the Holy Spirit for hours, others for days. At the Pleasant Valley the Rev. A. J. Finklenbinder's father, an unsaved man, was slain under the power of God and lay in that condition for hours. Others spake in tongues for several days. Near Stratford, Oklahoma, under the ministry of the Rev. Iva Hayes, one man who mimicked the Holy Spirit suddenly fell prostrate and began foaming at the mouth and died under a curse.[1]

---

[1] The majority of factual information relating to the early history of the church in the West was kindly furnished by Bishop Dan T. Muse.

THE FIRE-BAPTIZED HOLINESS CHURCH, 1898-1910

Mr. Henson was able by sheer hard work and earnest prayer to salvage a few faithful members at the Lamont, Oklahoma local church despite the fact that the State Association itself had been discontinued. The General Council meeting which convened in 1902 conducted its sessions in this church. There may have been at the time some semblance of a state organization, but it is definitely a fact that no such organization existed in Oklahoma after 1902 until the Conference was reorganized in September of 1909 by the Acting General Overseer of the Fire Baptized Holiness Church, the Rev. F. M. Britton. This Conferenece was organized with only the one local church at Lamont, Oklahoma. The following Christian workers comprised the ministerium of Oklahoma when the Conference was reorganized. The Reverends H. P. Lott, Frank Adams, Effie Adams, A. T. Kersey, Alonzo Jackson, F. E. Short, J. M. Warner, Mrs. J. M. Warner, and L. A. M. Taylor. The Rev. N. T. Morgan united with the church at this time, but did not unite with the Conference until 1910.

THE PENTECOSTAL OUTPOURING

During the interim from 1902 to 1909 when there was no longer a state organization of the Fire Baptized Holiness Church in Oklahoma, there still continued a considerable amount of activity among at least a few people who had leanings in that direction. Nevertheless, it is perhaps a justifiable claim to state that likely there would have been no reorganization of this conference except for one fact—the Pentecostal outpouring of God's Spirit furnished the boon necessary to bring it about.

We have noted that for years sanctified people had taught that the baptism of the Holy Spirit was identical with sanctification, but it was more or less general that these people evinced a latent desire for something beyond that experience. Some had sought for the "gifts" of the Spirit and others for the "baptism of fire." But in due time, according to God's clock, the real thing came—the Pentecostal baptism of the Holy Spirit.

James speaks of the "early" and the "latter" rain for which the husbandman waiteth and hath long patience. The "early" rain as in Old Testament times was intended to cause the seed to spring forth and grow. That is what took place at Pentecost when three thousand were saved, and on subsequent occasions when great numbers were swept into the kingdom and the gospel carried into heathen lands. Between the time of the "early" rain and the "latter" rain there were intermittent sprinklings of rain but no copious showers fell until the time of the "latter" rain. This rain served to mature the grain and make it ready for the final harvest. So it has been with the spiritual rain of which James speaks, there have been intermittent sprinklings down through the centuries since the Pentecostal early rain. There have been people who have received the Pentecostal experience in every age since Pentecost, but it was not until 1906 that the "latter" rain outpouring actually took place. Then in short order it circled the globe and has continued to gain momentum as the years go by. Now, after a little more than forty years Pentecostal groups have come to compete with the established churches which look on in amazement and wonder at the phenomenal growth of these new sects.

Just prior to the "latter" rain outpouring it is only natural to expect that a sprinkling would come to announce the oncoming showers. That is what took place before 1906. There were certain indications which tended to suggest rain. We will notice a few of these indications:

On January 1, 1890 the famous missionary, preacher and teacher, Daniel Awrey attended a prayer meeting where voluntary prayers were being offered. When it came his turn to pray the Spirit suddenly came upon him in the midst of his prayer, and he began to pray in an unknown tongue. (Mr. Awrey was later connected with a Holiness Bible school where a number of people received the baptism and spoke with tongues, further mention of which will be made presently).

Another person to receive this experience was Miss Agnes Ozman (later Mrs. P. M. LaBerge) in Topeka, Kansas, January, 1901. Several others received their baptism immediately following her experience. When the Fire-Baptized Holiness Conference was reorganized after the latter rain outpouring, Mrs. LaBerge became a member of the Conference and served both as a pastor and an evangelist for several years.

Another such incident occurred at Billings, Oklahoma, in 1905, during a great revival meeting which was being conducted jointly by the Rev. Harry P. Lott and a Free Methodist preacher. One night during the meeting a man and his wife who were seeking God for a deeper experience came forward for prayer and were baptized with the Holy Ghost and spoke in tongues. These two preachers were both amazed and perplexed for neither of them had at the time received such an experience. Their large congregation was so awed by this unusual manifestation and the powerful demonstration of the Spirit that they broke into a disorderly retreat from the building. These are a few sporadic instances but they were sprinkles which preceded the showers.

Later, in the fall of 1906, the Rev. Glenn A. Cook came to Lamont, Oklahoma and conducted a meeting in which twelve or more people received this same experience. Mr. Cook was one among the numerous host of people who visited the Azuza Street Mission in Los Angeles where the "latter rain" outpouring of the Spirit began to fall in great abundance. These people arranged for the General Overseer of the Fire-Baptized Holiness Church to conduct a meeting for them the following May, 1907. He had received the Pentecostal experience on Feb. 15, 1907, at Toccoa, Georgia under the ministry of another who had been to Los Angeles, the Rev. G. B. Cashwell. Harry P. Lott visited this meeting, also a delegation from the Beulah Bible School, as well as many people from various states. Scores of people were blessed and carried the news to their own communities.

OKLAHOMA CITY REVIVAL

The combined reports of these various happenings served to sharpen the faith and whet the spiritual appetites of sanctified people in all directions. Just as we noted N. J. Holmes' account of how classes were suspended during 1904-1905 term at the Altamont Bible and Missionary Institute to engage in special prayer for more of God's Spirit, so it was in many other places. Several devout, consecrated women, mothers in Israel, covenanted together to pray that God would somehow make it possible for a Pentecostal Mission to be opened in Oklahoma City. Week after week they met together in earnest prayer. Their experience is in some measure comparable to that of devout Cornelius whose prayers resulted in the appearance of the Apostle Peter and a great Pentecostal revival. In answer to their earnest petitions three young preachers felt impressed to go to Oklahoma City. The Rev. R. B. Beall came on January 18, 1906, and by April 4th had opened a Sunday school on South Robinson Street not far from where these women had been meeting to pray. Mr.

Beall was encouraged by his successes and was prayerfully considering the possibility of opening a down-town mission when another young minister whose name was O. C. Wilkins came to the city from Colgate Indian Territory. Shortly thereafter a third young preacher arrived. He was the Rev. Harry P. Lott who had conducted the revival with the Free Methodist minister when a man and his wife had received the baptism of the Spirit and spoken in tongues. By Feb. 6, 1907 these young men had rented the old Blue Front Saloon building at No. 7 Grand Street for $40.00 per month and opened the down-town mission. They had only $13.00 in view, but agreed to rent the building and to pay the first month's rent the next day. God miraculously supplied the need, and by April, Mr. Lott had begun a revival in the newly organized mission.

These young men had been reading of the much publicized Azuza Street Pentecostal outpouring in Los Angeles through the pages of J. M. Pike's holiness periodical called the "Way of Faith," published at Columbia, S. C. Mr. Lott possibly was selected to lead the revival because of his former experience at Billings, Oklahoma with the Free Methodist minister. He preached as best he could about this new experience, and then the three holiness preachers would join the other seekers in the altar to seek God for this Pentecostal blessing. Mrs. Mary A. Sperry graciously opened her home for a daily "tarrying service" to be conducted to give opportunity for those who desired this blessing to seek for it. The revival continued, interest increased and the daily tarrying services were still in progress and by August, 1907, R. B. Beall and Harry P. Lott had received the experience. A few weeks later O. C. Wilkins had also received it. People poured in from far and near who likewise received the same experience.

LAMONT REVIVAL

In May, 1907, the Rev. J. H. King had also begun a revival at Lamont, Oklahoma where scores of people from various states and localities received Pentecost and returned to their home communities carrying the Good News!

It was the success of these two meetings that revived the Fire-Baptized Holiness work in Oklahoma which for a time had all but disappeared. The gracious Pentecostal outpouring had come in answer to the prayers which had risen from the hearts of these earnest Christian women and others. The Christian workers who went out from these two revivals, according to the Rev. H. P. Lott, established churches at Yukon, Drummond, Billings, Perry, Pawnee, Muskogee, Mazie, Witchita, McAllister, Quinton, Cowen, Hart, Stratford, Paul's Valley, Castle, Swan Lake, Manitou, Faxon, Tipton and many other places in Oklahoma. Other churches were established in Kansas, Nebraska, Texas, Arkansas, Iowa and Arizona. In addition, foreign missionaries had carried the Good News to both China and India. All of this took place by the end of 1911.

THE BEULAH HOLINESS SCHOOL REVIVAL

During the latter part of 1906, under the leadership of the Rev. Frank T. Alexander an independent group of holiness people called the Indian Creek Band purchased a tract of land at Beulah, Oklahoma and established the Beulah Holiness Bible School. We have mentioned that a delegation from this school attended Mr. King's meeting at Lamont in May, 1907. Those who received the experience of Pentecost there had created a great desire in the hearts of others at the school who were hungry for the fulness of blessing which they had received. During the summer of 1907, a Pentecostal Church of the Nazarene minister whose name was Robinson came to Beulah to conduct a revival meeting. He had received the Pentecostal baptism although his church refused to embrace the teaching. Under the ministry of this fiery evangel the power of God came down like rain. More than a hundred men and women, boys and girls received the experience and spoke in tongues. The first person to receive was a godly elderly woman whose name was McClung. The attitude of this godly woman toward the "new" experience influenced others. One entire family of eleven people received the baptism of the Holy Spirit.

Dan and Dolly York who were members of the Holiness Church of Christ rented their farm and headed West in their farm wagon in the old Methodist camp-meeting style to attend the services at Beulah, but they received the experience during the following summer in 1908, in a meeting conducted by Mr.

Alexander at Foss, Oklahoma. During the summer of 1908 the Rev. Francis Marion Britton from South Carolina, who was the Assistant General Overseer of the Fire-Baptized Holiness Church, came to Beulah as the invited camp meeting speaker. Brother Britton was a "pioneer of the pioneers" who hit sin with all of his might. Under his ministry a substantial work was done. This independent holiness group never became a part of the Fire-Baptized Holiness Church although many individuals did. Today, many members of the Pentecostal Holiness Church in western Oklahoma can trace their spiritual beginnings to the Beulah Holiness Bible School. Among them are the Dunlaps, the Robert Aarons, the Chesters, the Reeders, the Taylors, the Starks, the Odens, the Hills, the Knights, the Bealls, the Rankings, the Millers, the Kenneys, the Andersons, the Dodds, the Moores, the Bridges, the Kerns, the Starches, the Martins, the Davis's, the Peters, the Kerseys, the Powells, the Greshams, the Nix's, the Sparks, the Melvins, the Neals, the Boles, the Quintals, the Colliers, the Higginbothams, the Stewarts, the Thurmans, and many others.

THE OKLAHOMA CONFERENCE RE-ORGANIZED

Following each of these great revivals a number of Christian workers began to go as the early disciples after the day of Pentecost carrying the glad news. During 1908 the Rev. Joseph H. King had also held a meeting at Snyder, Oklahoma, where literally scores were saved. On the closing night 22 people were genuinely born again. Soon after this revival closed a devastating western tornado swept many people of this little town into eternity. It seemed that God was miraculously confirming the ministry of the new General Overseer and helping him to regain what had been lost because of the former Overseer's defection.

By September 1909, the Rev. F. M. Britton reorganized the Oklahoma Conference of the Fire-Baptized Holiness Church which had been dissolved since 1902. This Conference had only a small beginning, being organized as we have seen with only one local church at Lamont, Oklahoma, and five ministers and four mission workers who were named in an earlier paragraph. Harry P. Lott was appointed Ruling Elder. In October, the following month, Mr. Lott brought the Oklahoma City Mission which he had organized in 1907 into the Fire Baptized Holiness organization. This church was organized in spite of the protest of some of the group who were opposed to all types of organization, feeling that it would be detrimental to their spiritual welfare and take away their liberties. Their mistaken idea was soon corrected, however, and most of them came into the organization during the following year. The church was organized with 39 charter members. Mary Edy is the only remaining charter member whose name is still on the church roster. G. W. Thompson is a member of the Bethel Pentecostal Holiness Church, while Grace Wofford is a member of the Agnew church. Mother Lay, Mrs. Mary A. Sperry, Terrie J. Walker, Mrs. J. T. Ellis, Mrs. Shomp, Mrs. Harry P. Lott (the former Miss Lizzie Schomp), Grace Bergle Keller, Effie Allen, Mrs. Roe, Newton Taylor Morgan, Oscar C. Wilkins, J. F. Hughes and Brother Miller have all been transferred to the Church Triumphant. Some are living in California and other places, and possibly others are deceased. This First Pentecostal Holiness Church of Oklahoma City bears the unique distinction of being the oldest organized church in the Conference and perhaps is the oldest Pentecostal church of any denomination in the mid-west.

Due to the fear of organization and the natural tendency among Western peoples to be free and independent, many loosely organized groups could not be brought into the new organization which otherwise would have made strong outposts to promote this full gospel truth. Because these independent groups lacked proper discipline and were not adequately shepherded a large percent of them were either disbanded or lost to fanaticism or erroneous teachings. This accounts for the slow growth of the Conference in comparison with the rapid appearance of these new local church organizations.

In 1910 Mr. Lott was appointed again to serve as Ruling Elder when the Second Conference met. On August 30, 1911 the Third Annual Convention convened at Capital Hill Park in Oklahoma City. This was the first annual convention of the Oklahoma Conference after the Fire-Baptized Holiness Church had been consolidated with the Pentecostal Holiness Church at Falcon, N. C. on January 31, 1911. The state Ruling Elder, Mr. Harry P. Lott, presided over this Conference in the absence of the Rev. S. D. Page who had been elected as General Superintendent (name changed from "Overseer"). The Rev. F. M. Britton of the North Carolina Conference and the Rev. R. B. Hayes of the Georgia Conference were present as visitors, having just closed the camp meeting.

A letter from J. H. King, the Superintendent of Foreign Missionary work was read. He was at the time on a world tour and had just organized the missionary work in India.

It was at this convention that the Conference officers were elected for the first time instead of being appointed. Harry P. Lott was elected as Superintendent of the State. Richard B. Beall was elected as his assistant. F. Earl Short was elected as Secretary and Treasurer and J. W. Cooper and L. L. Wentz were elected to complete the Conference Board. Twenty-five missions and churches were listed. Most of these were only mission churches.

Familiar names of others which have not been mentioned are: A. I. Shannon who was assigned the church at Mazie; Miss Mary K. Davis was assigned the church at Manitou. (Later these two were united in marriage). J. M. Warner was sent to Pleasant Valley; N. T. Morgan went to a Mission Church in Muskogee; A. T. Kersey was assigned a work in Tipton; Dan and Dolly York were placed at Stratford, Hart, and Paul's Valley; Annie Aston (mother of Almyra and Ogla Aston) was assigned to Quinton; and Austin Hatcher (brother to Mary Foy) to Perry. The following were designated for evangelistic work: O. C. Wilkins, Willard Short, Daniel W. Evans, Charles E. McPherson, B. B. Boroughs, Agnes La Berge, Arthur Martin, Pearl Burroughs and S. M. Bradstatt.

Among those present at the 1911 Convention who are now deceased are the following: Newton Taylor Morgan, Francis Marion Britton, Richard Baxter Hayes, J. M. Warner, Emma Warner, Mary K. Davis, L. L. Wentz, O. C. Wilkins, B. B. Boroughs, Agnes La Berge, P. M. La Berge, and S. M. Bradstatt.

The facts which relate to the reorganization of the Fire-Baptized Holiness Church in Oklahoma will serve as a typical example of what took place in some of the other states where organizations had originally existed under Mr. Irwin's leadership.

Further mention of these other developments will be made in connection with the Consolidation at Falcon, N. C.

Since 1924 several other Annual Conferences have been carved out of the Oklahoma Conference among which are the East Oklahoma, Texas, and Pan Handle. In addition it has been indirectly responsible for about all of the work in the West, and yet the Pentecostal Holiness Church population of Oklahoma is greater than the combined population of the Church in all the other western states.

Chapter IV
THE PENTECOSTAL HOLINESS CHURCH
The First Decade 1900-1910

The Pentecostal Holiness Church emerged from the same general background which produced the Fire-Baptized Holiness Association. Since we have already given due attention to the parent stem and background of the Holiness "conventions" and "bands" which have appeared in connection with the Holiness Movement in the United States, it therefore becomes unnecessary to reiterate all of the details concerning the work of John S. Inskip who headed the National Association for the promotion of Holiness. It will be sufficient to say that under his direction and supervision numerous State Holiness Conventions were organized some of which later became Holiness Churches. The original intention of these associations was not to organize separate denominations but to influence the existing denominations toward their ideas of perfection. This, however, could not be realized, and eventually it became necessary to organize more congenial groups to take care of the sanctified people who were being ostracized from fellowship and excommunicated from the conventional churches.

SPIRITUAL CONDITIONS

Frequently during the history of the Christian Church there have been recurrent periods of spiritual lethargy and lukewarmness which have emasculated the Church of her spiritual strength and have weakened her witness for Christ. During these periods of spiritual declension God has unfailingly raised up a faithful few to call the Church back to its mission. Unfortunately it has often become necessary for new sects to be brought into existence before this could be realized. The circumstances which necessitated the appearance of the various holiness groups is no exception to this rule. Bishop J. H. King, in writing of his early boyhood describes the spiritual temperature of the churches in his community. He says:

During the period of my life from 1874-1882 when I needed to have the most favorable and effective influences thrown around me, sad to say, I had the least. There were but one or two genuine Christians in all the country. Few others did live a moral life. Vice, filth, uncleanness, foul language and gross immoralities abounded. The use of whiskey was universal. Some were only dram drinkers, and in our immediate community these were in the majority. However, there were some who drank heavily. All church members drank, with but one or two exceptions, and some even were drunkards; but no steps were taken to expell them from the communion to which they belonged. Dram drinking was looked upon as consistent with Christian living, and no one would think of preferring charges against a member for such a practice; and those who were drunkards were regarded with pity for their drinking to excess. No word was ever heard from the pulpit in condemnation of intoxicants so far as I can recall. Many of these who occupied the pulpit would occasionally take a dram of what was regarded as pure whiskey.

A high state of Christian life was absolutely unknown, or if known was never mentioned. To have an assurance of salvation beyond reasonable doubt was looked upon as an impossibility in this life. No one could know they were saved until they had reached Heaven. The Methodists received those into the fold who had just 'a desire to be saved,' and the Baptists did not require one to declare that they were saved as a condition of membership in the Church. If you professed to have some kind of a hope of Heaven and wanted to live with God's people you were eligible for membership. And the Presbyterians had no higher standard than the Methodists and Baptists.

What passed as the Gospel in these churches was almost no Gospel at all. Regular prayer services at any church in all the community I never heard of during the years we lived in that vicinity. Only one or two in any church would pray in that vicinity. One had to be somewhat called, or endowed with the gift of prayer in order to pray in public, was the view of the people of all faiths. Sunday schools would be conducted for a few months during the spring and summer seasons. There were no Bible students, and hence no one qualified to teach the Sunday School lessons. In fact, many looked upon the daily reading and study of the Bible as an evidence of mental weakness. You would 'lose your mind' if you gave attention to careful study of the Scriptures. Darkness covered the masses mentally and morally.[1]

Bishop King was not a man given to exaggeration, nor was he a preacher who delighted in making invidious remarks, and indulging in vituperations regarding other religious sects. He began his ministry in the Methodist Church and would have remained in it if it had been possible. He never lost his respect and ap-

---
[1] J. H. King, An Unpublished Manuscript—Autobiography.

preciation for that church, although he was coerced into leaving its ranks because he received and taught the experience of sanctification. When interviewed by this writer the Rev. Ralph Taylor, who was reared in the same community, described contemporary conditions as being the same as Bishop King has described them. This was typical of other communities.

The Rev. G. F. Taylor in describing the conditions in his neighborhood writes:

> It was considered to be a fearful thing to claim to be sanctified. One or two people who were considered to be Bible readers in our community declared that they had read the Bible through twice in the last forty years, and that the word 'sanctify' could not be found in the Bible anywhere. One old man said he had read the Bible through seven times, and that 'sanctify' was in there; but others said he was a liar, because no man on this earth had ever read the Bible through seven times. There was also a great discussion as to what 'sanctify' meant. Some said they would not believe in sanctification until they could learn what it meant.
>
> Now I had an uncle who was an almost graduate, and he was taken as very learned by all our community, and his statements were taken as final on every question. He lived in another community, but he came to see us right often, and it was decided that when he came he could settle the question. Soon after he arrived, he was asked what the word 'sanctify' means. Why, he said, the word 'sanctify' means 'to make holy.' Then he told us it was impossible to be sanctified in this life, for the Bible says we cannot be made holy. Well, well, that settled it forever. Surely no one would be such a fool as to believe that we can be sanctified when a man who knows Latin like that says it is impossible.[1]

The nominal church members and preachers were in bitter opposition to holiness preachers, and any who identified themselves with their meetings. Some churches turned out their ministers by the dozens after they had been brought to trial and condemned for heresy. They excommunicated all those who claimed to be sanctified. Some were expelled for going to the holiness altar and others were expelled even for attending their meetings. Others were turned out because they had a favorable attitude toward holiness. Mr. Taylor comments:

> One Baptist church I knew of attempted to turn out all the holiness members, but found that they were in the majority, and so

---

[1] G. F. Taylor, Advocate, op. cit., Jan. 20, 1921, p. 10.

gave up the job. In the light of these facts you can see there were many holiness people without a church home.

Another mighty force in the opposition was the presiding elders of the Methodist Church. You see many of the Methodist pastors were sanctified in these meetings. Some of them were saved for the first time in their life. It soon became evident that the higher authorities of the Methodist church were bitter opponents to this doctrine. The preachers were taken to task about it. Some of them were tried in the district conference and expelled. There was a continual conflict between the elders and these pastors. Many of the pastors seeing the conflict, and fearing the results, gave up to the dictates of the elders, and soon lost their experiences. And many of these pastors became bitter opponents to the truth of holiness. If a sanctified pastor had holiness revivals on his work one year, the next year an anti-holiness pastor would preach it out of the members. I think the elders and the bishops made it a business to follow every sanctified pastor with an anti-holiness pastor, so as to keep the work beat down.

In October 1899, the Rev. A. B. Crumpler, father of the holiness movement in North Carolina, was tried in the Methodist Church under the charge of immorality, for preaching the doctrines of Methodism, when asked not to do so by a Methodist preacher. He was found not guilty of the charge. but he afterwards withdrew for the sake of peace and harmony. There were others of the sanctified Methodist preachers that followed his example.[1]

The Founder and His Early Ministry

Mr. Crumpler's statement as to his experience of sanctification which resulted in his withdrawal from the Methodist Church of which he was a minister is as follows:

I was sanctified in 1890 at Bismark, Mo., at the District Conference, under a sermon preached by Beverly Carradine, D.D. I came to North Carolina, my native state, to preach the blessed doctrine of full salvation to my own people, and in 1896, the great holiness movement broke out in North Carolina chiefly under my own ministry, in which hundreds and thousands came into the experience of salvation. In October 1899 I was tried under the charge of immorality, for preaching the glorious doctrines of Methodism when asked not to do so by a Methodist preacher, after which I withdrew from the Methodist church for the sake of peace and harmony, and with others organized the Holiness Church,[2] that those who had been saved and sanctified many of whom belonged to no church, and many who had been turned out of their churches for professing Holiness might

---

[1] G. F. Taylor, **Advocate, op. cit.,** Feb. 10, 1921, p. 9.
[2] The Holiness Church was originally called the Pentecostal Holiness Church, but from 1901 to 1909 it took the name of Holiness Church and since 1909 has been called the Pentecostal Holiness Church.

have a congenial church home. This organization was formed in the Spring of 1900 at Fayetteville, N. C.[1]

A spirit of controversy continued for some time after these holiness groups had been organized. Both sides took part but it is only fair to say that most of it was provoked from the established churches. They were severely critical of these new sects. An example of these criticisms is to be seen in an article called "Wildfire at M. E. Church Conference" in which those who had been sanctified were ridiculed as having gone off into wildfire.[2] In a later issue of the same paper another article appeared about the attitude of Bishop Candler, who was speaking on the subject of Charity and yet showed an uncharitable attitude toward Holiness people.[3] A little later another article appeared entitled; "Holiness or Sanctification, the Methodist Armour," in which an attempt was made to show that this experience of sanctification was not introduced by the holiness movement but that it had been an old Methodist doctrine which had been revived.[4] Much writing was done both pro and con and for a long time it continued to be a live issue. The more these new groups were persecuted, the more they thrived and multiplied, and the more people were attracted to their services.

After Mr. Crumpler was sanctified in 1890 he felt definitely impressed that God would be pleased for him to return to his home community in Sampson County, North Carolina, that he should confine his ministerial labors to his native State. He had been saved in North Carolina and had entered the Methodist ministry there before he had moved to Missouri. When he returned, he began his holiness ministry in and around Clinton which was the county seat of Sampson County. In 1896 a great holiness movement was inaugurated in the state of North Carolina, chiefly under his ministry, and principally in the Methodist Church to which he still belonged. So the Rev. A. B. Crumpler was the father of the present-day Holiness movement in North

---

[1] A. B. Crumpler, **The Discipline of the Holiness Church**, (Goldsboro, N. C.: Nash Brothers, Book and Job Printers, 1901), preface, pp. 3, 4.
[2] A. B. Crumpler, **The Holiness Advocate**, (Clinton, N. C.: Published and Edited by A. B. Crumpler, later published at Goldsboro, N. C., Sept. 16, 1901), p. 3.
[3] A. B. Crumpler, **The Holiness Advocate**, op. cit., Jan. 1, 1902, p. 2.
[4] A. B. Crumpler, Ibid., June 1, 1903, p. 6.

Carolina. Following the same method of procedure which had been customary in other states, he called for a meeting of sanctified people in a great holiness convention and on May 15, 1897, he organized a State Holiness Association at Magnolia, North Carolina. As has already been explained, these Associations were not intended for permanent organizations but were a somewhat temporary expedient which existed for the purpose of conducting annual meetings which would offer mutual help and fellowship for holiness people of all denominations, and would encourage the spread of this Bible truth.

His Personality

The Rev. A. H. Butler, who knew Mr. Crumpler intimately and was closely associated with him in his work for a number of years, describes him as being an outstanding orator who seemed to be endowed with an unusual unction and power in declaring the truth of the Gospel. His voice could be heard on a clear night for a distance of three and one-half to four miles; it could be heard distinctly for two miles. It was a common occurrence for people to fall under conviction in his services. Others who heard him from a distance would become convicted of their sins and come to the services and be converted. W. B. Godwin, a prominent layman who lived near Falcon, N. C. describes him as a stout man who had a pleasing appearance, an attractive personality, a splendid voice, and a fine preacher whom God blessed with wonderful meetings.

His Meeting and Successes

Under his ministry there were scores of Methodist preachers sanctified, among whom were Duncan A. Futril, W. A. Jenkins, Add Royals, Galloway, Perry, Kelly, Ethridge, Martin and a host of others. Many Baptist preachers were also sanctified and a number from other denominations as well. Laymen were saved and sanctified by the hundreds from all denominations, and in rapid fire order a great host of people from all over eastern North Carolina came to be followers and admirers of this powerful preacher. He conducted meetings in Clinton, Warsaw, Roseboro, Mount Olive, Goldsboro, Faison community, near Goshen Church, and in many other communities especially in Sampson, Duplin and Wayne Counties. These were the greatest revivals which the people in those localities had ever known. No church or community where he went could ignore his ministry, for it commanded attention and demanded some sort of recognition. It was reported that he was tearing up churches as he went. Many Methodist churches were divided over the question of sanctification. This was also true among other denominations.

THE REPORTS AND CRITICISMS

All sorts of reports were scattered abroad about these meetings. Some said that sanctified preachers carried along women who were emotionally inclined, and when the preachers would slap their hands and jump into the air, these women would yell and scream at the top of their voices. This, they said, would be kept up until many nervous people would become excited and join in with the rest. All of the leaders of these holiness meetings were accused of carrying some kind of magic powders with them, and that just at the psychological moment they would shake these powders on excited people who would then fall as dead under the powerful effects. This was called going into a trance. Many people were deathly afraid of getting too near these people for fear they would be brought helplessly under some kind of strange spell. Many said that the preachers and people who were attracted to these services were the scum of society and that no decent persons would have anything to do with these meetings except to laugh, scorn or ridicule them. They said that nobody but poor white people and negroes would have anything to do with such religion. Some people reported that these preachers were preaching that it was a sin to dance, to drink whiskey, wine, beer, and such like; and that it was affirmed that it was an actual sin to use tobacco. The attitude was that when a preacher started preaching against tobacco he had quit preaching and had gone to meddling; and that it was none of his business. Holiness preachers and holiness people were accused of about every mean thing that could be thought of or imagined. It made people mad for any person to say they were sanctified. Others made a joke of the whole affair and some said it was all the best side-show they ever attended.

But many lives were changed, drunkards and harlots were converted; drug addicts, and cigarette and tobacco fiends were completely and instantly delivered.

CONTROVERSIES

Holiness preachers in their zeal to denounce sin were sometimes unduly critical of other churches, but most of what they said was true, and that is where the rub came. Articles were written to justify both sides. Mr. Crumpler's paper, "The Holiness Advocate" carried all the news of these controversies, and people from all directions avidly devoured every word of them. One of these was entitled, "Another Preacher Expelled," and gave an account of another such occurrence in the Methodist Church. Another article called "Bride and Bridegroom" vindicated the Holiness people's right to indulge in "holy manifestations," explaining that they were divinely wrought. Another powerful article which excited considerable controversy was written by Mr. Crumpler, called "The Church of the Holy Refrigerator," in which he scored worldly church members who had not been born again. In it he quoted Bishop Candler's remarks in which he ridiculed "perfect love" while "theatre-going, card-playing, godless church members showed their approval by laughing aloud, and to think Mr. Candler gets paid $3,500.00 per year to fight holiness." Quite a bit was said about tobacco. In a quite lengthy article called "Tobacco," is related a story of a little seven year old girl who went to a storekeeper and asked for a can of "snuff." He refused to sell her the snuff and told her it was a sin to use it, and an unclean habit. She then naively replied, "If it is a sin for me to use it, it looks like you would not sell it in your store. That is a sin too." It is not difficult to see that Holiness churches had to exist separate from the established churches.

Thus it was that the Pentecostal Holiness Church was organized in the early part of 1900. The Rev. A. B. Crumpler, W. A. Jenkins, and W. F. Galloway met at Fayetteville, N. C., where the organization was effected. There were perhaps others there also, among whom were Duncan Futril, J. A. Rouse and others. There was not at the time an adequate discipline drawn up which would accurately define the relation of clerical and lay members, nor clearly set forth the doctrines for which the church stood. After Mr. Crumpler had prepared a more acceptable discipline in 1901 he refers to the first discipline in the following statement:

> There was a discipline framed which did not well represent our doctrine and polity, and at our last Convention which met at Magnolia, N. C., November, 1901. I was appointed by the brethren to frame one which would truly represent our doctrines and polity, as they were agreed upon in that Convention. . .[1]

The Discipline

This discipline was divided into four sections as follows:

Section I Articles of Faith (This section included statements regarding the Trinity; the Scriptures; Man; Repentance; Saving Faith; The Witness of the Spirit; A Holy Life; Entire Sanctification; Growth in Grace; Divine Healing; The Second Coming of Christ; The Destiny of Man; The Church; The Sacraments; Water Baptism; The Lord's Supper; The Ministry).

Section II Government (This section provided for a Congregational form of government; rules to govern Christian behavior among the laity and clergy; rules for the organization of the official Church Board, Board of Trustees and Sunday School officers; rules were also made governing and restricting the methods whereby the church was to be supported).

Section III Forms and Ceremonies

Section IV Qualifications of Officers and Their Duties.[2]

This first discipline has continued to form the basis of each future discipline although a number of revisions and changes have been made from time to time when varying circumstances have required such.

What is now called "Conference" was then called "Convention." The church polity has gradually become more and more episcopal and may thus be described as being a combination of congregational and episcopal forms of church government. What is now called a "Conference Superintendent" was then called "President" of the Convention.

---

[1] A. B. Crumpler, The Discipline of The Holiness Church, op. cit., p. 4.
[2] Ibid., pp. 59, 60, et passim.

The Articles of Faith or Doctrines Taught

In listing the four sections of the Discipline we have already mentioned in the first section what the church believed and taught, but it will be well to make some brief statements concerning each of these teachings. This is especially necessary at points which were emphasized, or which were at variance with the conventional teachings of the established churches.

Trinity. The Holiness people taught the doctrine of the Trinity in the regular established fashion: three distinct persons in one Godhead of one substance, co-equal and co-eternal. These three were seen to cooperate in bringing about man's salvation.

Man. Concerning all men, they are fallen sons of Adam and all have sinned and fallen short of the glory of God, and are utterly helpless to save themselves, being dependent upon God's love and mercy which have been set forth in the plan of Redemption.

Scriptures. The Scriptures contain the revealed will of God and are the only sufficient rule of faith and practice. They include books of the Canon, and reveal the plan of redemption whereby sinful men can be justified before the Father on the basis of the vicarious sufferings and death of the Saviour, His Son, if or when man exercises faith in the Word. The Holy Spirit then applies the atoning blood of Christ and transforms the sinner into a new creature in Christ Jesus.

Repentance is genuine when it is produced by godly sorrow for sin, and the penitent sinner makes full confession, forsakes his sins and is willing as far as possible to make restitution for his sins, straightening out everything he can between himself and his fellowman.

Saving Faith cannot be exercised except as one has truly repented. It is believing with the heart and not merely with the head.

The Witness of the Spirit comes to all those who have repented and believed according to the above described standards, and a person will know unmistakably that he is God's child, by feeling God's Spirit bearing witness with his spirit that he is a child of God. The catastrophic, crisis conversion is made the rule and not the exception in determining one's knowledge of salvation.

A Holy Life is required of all those who name the name of Christ. They must depart from iniquity, or they automatically forfeit their right to continue to be sons of God. This teaching was emphasized.

Entire Sanctification. This doctrine was also emphasized. The Holiness people taught that there remains in the born-again believer's heart a "root of sin" which is born in every child's heart, being inherited from Adam. That all actual guilt is removed and sins are forgiven in justification, but there must also be removed the "sin in our nature." This is realized by faith when the justified believer appropriates through the blood of Christ his sanctification. The "old man," carnal nature is thus destroyed, and a person is then made ready to serve God with an undivided heart, being ridded of the inbred sin. This is the state of "perfect love" or "perfect holiness" or perfect freedom from sin inward and outward. This doctrine is opposed to the idea of growth into sanctification. Such a theory is interpreted as being achieved by "our works" instead of "faith" in God. This experience was considered the same as receiving the baptism of the Holy Ghost until 1907, after the "latter rain" outpouring of the Spirit.

Growth in Grace is seen as a development in the experiences of justification or sanctification, after they have first been received by faith. The Holiness people taught that it was no more possible for a person to grow into sanctification than it was possible for a person to grow into the conversion experience.

Falling from Grace was taught as a possibility for any person, regardless of his experience with God, and that unless repentance took place the person would be lost.

Divine Healing was taught as the privilege of every believer who would call for the elders of the Church, according to James 5:14-16. It was not considered an evidence of sin or a mark of divine displeasure because a person was sick or employed medical aid.

The Second Coming of Christ was emphasized as being premillennial, at which time the dead would be raised, the ready living ones translated, a great tribulation set up through which those who were left would pass, after which the devil would be chained while the saints reign during the millennium with

Christ, after which the devil is loosed for a season and then judged, and the unrighteous dead are raised and judged and with him cast into the lake of fire.

The Destiny of Man is determined by the attitude he may assume toward God's Son, and the provision he has made for salvation. Those who rebel will be punished everlastingly, while those who accept God's provision will enjoy eternal happiness and blessedness in His presence.

The Church, the Sacraments, and the Ministry are viewed in the same conventional orthodox way, except that the Holiness Church believed that people of either sex may be called to the work of the ministry; and that water baptism was not compulsory for church membership nor salvation—candidates who desired it could choose the mode of baptism they might prefer.

There has been substantially no change made in these doctrinal tenets, except in the teachings which relate to the baptism of the Holy Ghost. This change will be noted in connection with the history of the "latter rain" outpouring which will be a consideration in a later discussion.

The principal points of disagreement which distinguished the Holiness sects from the established churches was their teaching of a holy life as the standard for believers, and of the possibility of receiving the sanctified experience, the same as formerly had been taught by Wesley and the Methodist Church which he founded. Their emphasis on the imminent Premillennial Second Coming, and their refusal to condone worldliness was also singularly significant.[1]

THE FIRST CHURCHES

Antioch

The first local church of the Pentecostal Holiness Church organization in North Carolina was called Antioch. It was organized as a result of a tent-meeting which was conducted by the Rev. W. C. Galloway in the spring of 1900, in a community six miles east of Four Oaks, North Carolina. Some of the most prominent charter members of this little church were Mr. Nelson Lee, who was the father of the Rev. R. H. Lee, who for more

---

1 A. B. Crumpler, The Discipline, op. cit., pp. 5-13, et passim.

than 25 years was connected with the Publishing House of the Pentecostal Holiness Church, and for a major portion of that period was the Associate Editor and Business Manager of the Advocate. Mr. R. E. Lee, a brother of Nelson Lee, was also a charter member and was elected as secretary of the new organization. His daughter, Miss Eva Lee, was another of the first members. She served faithfully as a linotype operator during the early history of the Publishing House at Franklin Springs. The Rev. C. B. Strickland, who was for years the Superintendent of the North Carolina Conference, was also one of the first members of Antioch Church.

For a time during 1907-1908, the Rev. G. F. Taylor was assigned as pastor of Antioch. When he announced the meeting of a church conference soon after his pastorate began, he discovered they had kept no record since the time the church was organized. Mr. Taylor in referring to the occasion wrote:

One of the charter members said that he remembered the names were taken down on a bit of paper at the time of the organization, and that is all that could be established. They had been receiving and turning out members, holding church conferences, appointing delegates, calling pastors, and doing all the work of a church for eight years, and there was not the slightest record of any of it. We got all the old heads together, and soon made a roll of the charter members to the best of their memory, and then struck out those who had been dismissed in any way, and began a system of good records. If the present pastor of Antioch can find that book today he will find that the first minutes of church conferences was recorded while I was pastor in 1908. I trust they have kept good records since then. The purpose of this paragraph is to inspire our secretaries to keep good records.[1]

MAGNOLIA

The second local church was organized at Magnolia, N. C., by the Rev. A. B. Crumpler in the old public school building which was located on College Street. This was the home community of the Rev. G. F. Taylor, and was the first school he ever attended. On the same spot where he had recited his A B C's Mr. Crumpler stood to organize the second Pentecostal Holiness Church, after he had successfully conducted a few nights of revival services in the same building. Mr. Taylor was

---

1 G. F. Taylor, Advocate, op. cit., Feb. 17, 1921, p. 9.

present at the time of the organization but did not join until later. He was at the time a member of the Methodist Church. Some of those who did unite as charter members were Mr. Sylvester West, the local blacksmith, Mr. M. A. Culbreth, the photographer, Mr. George Gaylor, who was the father of Mrs. George Kelly, who went as a missionary to China under the Assembly of God Mission Board, Miss Bertha Sellers, who was the sister of the Rev. M. D. Sellers, once a member of the North Carolina Conference, Miss Pearl Elmore, now the wife of the Rev. E. L. Parker, a minister in the Free Will Baptist Church, and a few others.

Mr. Taylor, in referring to this church in later years, tells the following story which is deemed worthwhile to record here. He says:

The Magnolia Church failed to demand a deed to the property before they built the church. One of the members began the building in his collard patch, and the people joined in and helped him build the church until it was finished. The story is a long one, but to make it short, the deed has not yet been secured, the church bursted up a long time ago, and we have no organization there until this day. The banner of the church has there trailed in the dust, and great reproach there fell upon the cause we represent. My point is to beg, to beseech, to plead, to request most earnestly, that no Pentecostal Holiness Church, neither in the present nor future, invest one cent in a church building until you have first legally secured the land. It makes no difference how good a man is, how faithful he is to his promise, how much people think of him, how he can preach or testify, never build a church on his personal property. Please do not let yourselves be trapped at this point into thinking a certain man will be an exception to the rule. Take my advice at this point, and you will never regret it. The facts are, if he will not do this, you had better not build.[1]

GOLDSBORO

Goldsboro was the place where the third local church was organized in North Carolina during the spring of 1900. This was decidedly the most important church of the new organization, because it came to be a sort of center around which most of the church's activities revolved during the first seven years of its history. It therefore seems well that we accord to it a somewhat greater amount of attention.

---
1 G. F. Taylor, Ibid., pp. 9, 10.

To begin with it had a better and bigger building than any of the other early churches. One of its parishioners happened to be a man of considerable financial ability, who offered to loan the congregation the amount they needed to construct a building 60 x 90. This plan was considered unwise by some, while others felt that it would be none too big, in view of the increasing interest which they anticipated when a church building could be erected.

The Rev. A. B. Crumpler was called as its first pastor and everyone was delighted with his ministry. He soon moved from Clinton to Goldsboro, and while the membership enrollment of his church was slightly more than one hundred the regular congregations he preached to were much larger. Mr. Crumpler invited men like the Revs. L. L. Pickett, G. D. Watson, Seth C. Reese, Sam Jones and others to come to conduct revival services at frequent intervals, and by and large this work was very encouraging.

Mr. Crumpler was the proprietor and editor of the Holiness Advocate as long as it was published. This paper was in a sense the official organ of the Pentecostal Holiness Church. He had previously published it at Clinton, but when he moved to Goldsboro it was entered at that office. He was also elected President of every convention as long as he remained with the organization. So it was that the President of the Convention, the editor of the official organ, and the pastor of the strongest local church was one and the same person, all at Goldsboro. Unfortunately the Goldsboro congregation had assumed more financial responsibility than they were comfortably able to handle, and it soon became necessary for Mr. Crumpler to visit other churches and call upon them to help with these payments. This was recognized virtually as the church's headquarters, and for that reason he had a basis of appeal whereby to raise money from other churches. The churches responded very liberally but in spite of every effort to prevent losing the building it was eventually sold to a Quaker congregation.

There were several factors which entered into the picture to retard the progress of this church. They are mentioned here for what they may be worth as historic examples, which are worthy of close attention and should be sanely analyzed. In 1903 Mr.

Crumpler decided it would be wise for him to be relieved of his pastoral duties, at least partially so, in order that he might be free to visit among other churches to raise funds for the Goldsboro indebtedness. He therefore secured the services of the Rev. E. L. Parker to fill his preaching appointments on Sundays at the church. There were some lay members in the church who were selling tobacco. When Mr. Parker discovered it, he allowed his zeal in preaching against this evil to be exercised unwisely and not according to knowledge. The congregations soon fell off in large numbers. He took a similar attitude toward the divorce question, and it seems that in both instances, his attitude was without Christian tolerance and devoid of scarcely any measure of divine love or wisdom. Things began to look dark. The atmosphere was clouded.

In 1903 the Rev. W. H. McLaurin was assigned this church. After learning of the existing situation he should have exercised greater wisdom than his predecessor, but with the bare facts staring him full in the face, he entered the arena with his gloves off and attacked in his own strength the tobacco and divorce questions. He seemed to be blinded to the fact that he was dealing with the souls of individuals for whom Christ died. Although Mr. McLaurin may have had good intentions, he failed to exercise prudence and judiciousness in dealing with these matters. He evidently forgot that although sin should be preached against it should be condemned in the spirit of love, and that finite human beings ofttimes err in their fallible judgment of others. He soon had things worked up to a white heat.

There were in the church at Goldsboro two members, a man and his wife, both of whom had been previously divorced from former companions. The question was raised as to whether they should be allowed to remain in the church; and Mr. McLaurin insisted that they should be expelled, while Mr. Crumpler held that there were no grounds for their expulsion. The question was argued and debated by both sides without end in Goldsboro, and gradually the same issue was raised in all parts of the (Conference) Convention. At the 1904 Convention the matter was thoroughly thrashed out and was decided in Mr. Crumpler's favor, but the damage was already done. Mr. Parker withdrew from the Church and went back to the Methodist Church, and Mr. Crumpler again was assigned to pastor the Goldsboro church. He hoped to gather up the fragments but was unable to do so, and during the year he moved back to Clinton where he has remained since. In 1905, the Rev. A. H. Butler was sent to pastor the church. He took this work at its worst, rented an old store building, and attracted an entirely new group of people. Interest grew, and in time the church was completely reorganized after a long, hard battle. There stands at Goldsboro today one of the best churches in the Conference.

It is to be lamented that this infant organization became involved in unnecessary controversies which deflected their attention from the all-important task of evangelizing the world. Had it not been for such internal dissensions, it seems certain that a considerably greater amount of good could have been accomplished. The cause of Christ often suffers when His Church allows other things to obscure her vision and prevents her from seeing the real mission for which it exists. Sin should be dealt with, but dealt with wisely, and not allowed to retard the work of reaching the lost. An indiscreet minister can tear down in a single sermon what it will take years of sedulous labor to restore. Some losses are often sustained which can never be recovered. These losses involve the most precious thing on earth, the human soul.

It would be extremely interesting as well as beneficial to know all of the facts which related to the founding of all of the churches of this new organization, but such an exhaustive treatment would require volumes to be written. By the end of 1907 there were other churches or mission points as follows: Beulah, Bethel, Bethlehem, Burgaw, Canaan, Duke, Dunn, Ebenezer, Falcon, Fayetteville, Godwin's Chapel, Goshen, Howard's Chapel, Jamestown, Lebanon, Manly, Mount Pelier, Mayodan, Nebo, Raeford, Princeton, Rockingham, Phoses' Chapel, Sharon, St. Matthew, St. John, St. Stephen, Spring Hill, Sinai, Stony Point, and Thunder Swamp.

Chapter V
THE PENTECOSTAL HOLINESS CHURCH 1900-1910
Early Conventions

As we have noted, the annual representative gatherings of the Pentecostal Holiness Church were first called "Conventions" instead of what is now designated as an "Annual Conference."

THE GOLDSBORO CONVENTION, 1900

The first of these Conventions held its session in Goldsboro, North Carolina in the fall of 1900. A good number of the former Methodist preachers withdrew and returned to the Methodist church. Some went to the Episcopal church. W. A. Jenkins, W. F. Galloway, D. A. Futril, T. M. Lee, J. A. Rouse and others either left at this time or soon thereafter. The principal reason for their withdrawal grew out of the extreme difficulty that holiness ministers experienced in those days of securing a livelihood from their ministerial labors. Some of them had to drink branch water, eat wild berries, and sleep on the benches with their Bible for a pillow—sometimes for days before they had homes opened to them. Some of these pioneers had more faith than others who felt forced to drop out. The Rev. C. B. Strickland, who later became Superintendent of the Conference, and several others joined to take the places of those who left.

THE MAGNOLIA CONVENTION, 1901

The second convention was held at Magnolia, North Carolina in November, 1901. The reader will recall that the North Carolina Holiness Association was organized by the Rev. A. B. Crumpler in this little town, on May 15, 1897; and early in 1900 he organized the second local church of the Pentecostal Holiness organization here, in the school house on College Street.

Mrs. Bertha Maxwell was among the number who was received at this convention as a preacher. She later became the primary teacher at the Falcon Holiness School. After serving in the Conference until 1919 she then asked that her name be dropped as a preacher, but continued her membership as a lay member in the Pentecostal Holiness Church. The Rev. T. J. Smith who was also received as a minister continued to serve in the conference for more than twenty-five years. Others who became members of the Convention at this time did not remain for very long.

Name of Church Changed to "The Holiness Church"

One of the significant things which occurred at this meeting was a debate which arose about the name of the Church. One of the preachers contended that the name ought to be changed on the ground that there was not enough reproach connected with it. He argued that when members were asked to what church they belonged, they would reply, "to the Pentecostal Church," to avoid the reproach of holiness. Although Mr. Crumpler and others took the opposing view, a majority agreed with the other preacher and it was voted that the name be changed to "The Holiness Church," dropping the word "Pentecostal." It will be well to add that at this time the Pentecostal experience had not come and there was no stigma attached to the name "Pentecostal" which later came to be associated with it. The church retained this name from 1901 to 1909 when the name "Pentecostal" was again taken, the details of which will appear presently. (The Holiness Church was sometimes referred to as "The Holiness Church of North Carolina," though this was never the official name but came about because it operated principally in North Carolina).

It was also at this convention that Mr. Crumpler was authorized to enlarge the original discipline. This revised discipline was used until 1909.

The LaGrange Convention, 1902

In 1902, the next annual Convention convened at LaGrange, North Carolina. The Rev. E. L. Parker, who was mentioned in connection with the Goldsboro church was received at this convention. Glowing reports were made of successes in preaching the gospel; fervent prayers were offered; the brethren rejoiced in the Lord and on the whole this was a very harmonious and blessed Convention.

The Dunn Convention, 1903

The next Convention met at Dunn, North Carolina. One thing of particular interest was the presence of the great evangelist and singer, the Rev. L. L. Pickett. His marvelous preaching and Spirit inspired melodious gospel singing brought a real revival in connection with the Convention. He preached several sermons on the theme of the Second Coming of Jesus, and sold hundreds of his books to the clergymen and laymen who were in attendance. His presence and preaching and the permanent deposit which he made with his books wielded an influence among the members of this new organization which has continued to some extent even until this day.

Holiness Singing

It is perhaps apropos to interject here an account of the singing in connection with the Holiness Convention which the Rev. G. F. Taylor attended in 1897. Over the years this type of singing among holiness people has persisted, and is mentioned here because it is typical, although in more recent years there has come to be some perceptible lack of zest and spirit which has usually characterized holiness singing. It is just such singing that has played a conspicuous part in winning many people to its ranks. Mr. Taylor, in referring to that meeting writes:

> The singing in this meeting, as well as in many others, was led by 'Uncle Jim' Crumpler. The song book used was Revival No. 2 edited by Charles D. Tillman. Among the many leading songs were the following: 'All Taken Away,' 'Leaning on the Everlasting Arms,' 'More About Jesus,' and 'I'm at the Fountain Drinking.' During the testimonies and altar services they sang: 'The Old Time Religion,' 'By the Grace of God I'll Meet You,' 'I'm Nearer Home,' and 'I Can, I Will I Do Believe.' The people sang in the Spirit, and such singing as we had never heard before. (This occurrence was seven years before Mr. Taylor became a member of the Pentecostal Holiness Church, and can be seen as being a major factor which influenced him to join the holiness group.) The very air was laden with the spirit of these songs; and as we returned home from the meeting that night, we could hear the different crowds going their respective roads singing
>
> 'More about Jesus would I know,
> More of His love to others show.'

Far away in another direction we could hear:
'Did you hear what Jesus said to me?
They are all taken away, away:
Your sins are pardoned, and you are free,
They are all taken away.'

Another company would be singing:
Where'er I am, where'er I move
I'm at the fountain drinking
I meet the object of my love
I'm on my way home.

It was during this meeting that the beautiful Miss Ella Catherine Brown received the glorious experience of sanctification. Mr. Taylor later became acquainted with her and won her for his wife. No finer or greater woman ever graced the Pentecostal Holiness Church with her presence than this great saint who still lives to bless and inspire the thousands who know her.

THE PREACHERS RECEIVED

At the Dunn Convention there were six preachers received from other organizations and ordained. From the Free Will Baptist was received the Rev. Willie Pope who continued a member until 1918; the Rev. G. B. Cashwell who became a prominent exponent of Pentecost as will be seen. From the M. E. Church was received the Rev. W. H. McLaurin who was connected with the organization for the brief period of only one year. His name and an account of his work which proved to be unsatisfactory has already been mentioned in the early history of the Goldsboro Pentecostal Holiness Church. Another of those was the Rev. E. H. Blake, who remained in the Convention until 1909, when he withdrew and united with the Fire-Baptized Holiness Church. When these two churches united in 1911 Mr. Blake continued with the organization until 1919 when he then withdrew and joined the Pentecostal Fire-Baptized Holiness Church, a continuing faction of the former Fire-Baptized Holiness Church. He became the editor of "Faith and Truth," a paper published in Toccoa, Georgia in interest of the Toccoa Orphanage. The Rev. M. J. Sterling was also one of the six ordained, and remained with the Conference until his withdrawal in 1920. Another of these was the widely known and dearly beloved Rev. A. H. Butler, who has faithfully performed the work of a true minister of Christ until this writing. He was saved under the ministry of the Rev. W. A. Jenkins while he served as a Methodist minister on the Newton Grove Circuit in Sampson County, North Carolina. He was later sanctified under the ministry of the Reverend D. A. Futril. Both of these ministers united with the Pentecostal Holiness Church and later withdrew and reunited with the Methodist Communion for reasons already mentioned in an earlier discussion. Mr. Butler served as Superintendent of the North Carolina Conference. At this time was also received the eminent Reverend G. F. Taylor who made perhaps the greatest single contribution to the cause of Pentecostal Holiness of any of his contemporaries. He was the founder of the Emmanuel College, the father and founder of the Pentecostal Holiness Publishing House and at one time a Bishop (then called General Superintendent) of the Church. The inspiration of this Convention and the influence of L. L. Pickett, a true man of God, no doubt contributed to the future success of these men in no small way.

The Tobacco Question Introduced

The discipline of the Church at this time forbade its preachers to use tobacco, but no restrictions were made with regard to laymen. At the Dunn Convention the Reverend J. A. Culbreth introduced a resolution which had for its object to forbid laymen to use, raise or handle tobacco. This issue caused considerable controversy later, as will be seen.

Conference Register

Another thing which was decided at this Convention was to prepare an alphabetical list of the names of the preachers, their addresses and the time and place where they entered the conference, to appear on the last page of the minutes of each convention. This plan was later adopted as the regular format for other conferences which have come into the church over the years.

The Fayetteville Convention, 1904

Tobacco and Divorce Questions

The Fayetteville Convention was characterized by a somewhat turbulent session due to the *"tobacco"* and *"divorce"* questions which had been growing issues for a period of two years, especially at Goldsboro which was a strategic church, being thought of as the organization's center. It was at this convention that the divorce question was brought to a head and settled in favor of Mr. Crumpler's side. Mr. McLaurin then withdrew as we have noticed. Then there was also a rehashing of the tobacco question. When the minutes of the 1903 Dunn Convention were printed something had been changed. Nobody seems to know just what happened, unless the printer may have made a mistake, but it caused no little controversy and dissatisfaction. The bulk of the sentiment was against the use of tobacco and there were some who were determined to agitate the matter almost beyond measure, feeling it was their Christian duty. Some members withdrew on account of it. In the course of three or four years those who favored absolute prohibition of the use of tobacco won out, but over the years this question has periodically re-emerged and has caused no little trouble especially in those sections where it is a principal crop.

REGULAR DATE FOR FUTURE CONVENTIONS

It is of some historic significance to note the fact that the Reverend G. F. Taylor, who had been a member of the Convention for only a year at this time, offered his first motion which was carried. The motion, which related to the time for the next Convention and all subsequent ones, provided that all future conventions should meet between the third and fourth Sunday in November. This date continued until 1929 to be the regular meeting time for the North Carolina Conference every year except 1908. The reason for the change that year will be revealed presently in our further discussion.

FIRST FOREIGN MISSION BOARD

At this Convention there was elected perhaps the first Foreign Mission Board of the Pentecostal Holiness Church. The personnel of this Board was composed exclusively of women. Mrs. Hannibal Bizzell of Dunn, North Carolina was the secretary and treasurer. There were at the time no official church missionaries in the field, but this step does evince the fact that there was at least some consciousness of the missionary task in which the

Church should be engaged. A little money began to be raised for that purpose, and in this small way a start was made.

MAGNOLIA, 1905

The sixth annual Convention convened at the same place where it had met for the second convention in 1901, at Magnolia, North Carolina. To express the actual status quo at that time we quote a passage found in Acts 9:31 as follows: "Then had the churches rest throughout all Judea and Galilee and Samaria, and were edified; and walking in the fear of the Lord, and in the comfort of the Holy Ghost, were multiplied." This conference was pleasant to attend and edifying in that there was unbroken fellowship, and no live issues of any controversial nature arose to cause any anxiety or perturbation of mind. At least the tobacco question and the divorce question which had caused grave concern in 1903 and 1904 at Dunn and Fayetteville had subsided for the time. The Reverend A. H. Butler stated that he had counted twenty-eight shouting at once during a conference meeting at Magnolia. It could have been at this pleasant session.

LUMBERTON, 1906

Cashwell's Letter

The next Convention which met at Lumberton was even more harmonious than the one the preceding year. Not a ripple disturbed the placid sea of harmony and fellowship. The business sessions began on Tuesday and closed on Saturday afternoon, which indicates a considerable amount of business, though there is nothing of special interest in a historical way to report, except to mention that there was an interesting letter read which was addressed to the members of the Convention, from the Reverend C. B. Cashwell who was an absent member of the Convention. He was at the time on his way to California to attend the great Pentecostal Revival at the Azuza Street Mission in Los Angeles. Many of those present were already quite interested in the Revival and had read of it in J. M. Pike's paper, "The Way of Faith," and had heard of it from many sources. It was a more or less generally observed fact that all of the Holiness people in North Carolina and elsewhere were praying that God would pour out His blessings upon them in like manner.

There were a number in the Convention who had grievances against Mr. Cashwell, and in his letter there were words of apology asking all those whom he may have injured to forgive him. Though Mr. Cashwell was a talented man with many good qualities he also had his faults, the chief of which was that he was temperamental. It is to his credit, however, that he was willing to apologize and was earnestly endeavoring to remove everything that might hinder his faith and prevent him from receiving the Pentecostal experience.

It did not seem to occur to any of the Holiness Church constituency that the experience which people were receiving in the California revival would in any way be at variance with what they believed and taught. The Holiness Church, as we have seen, taught that the experience of sanctification included the baptism of the Holy Ghost. They had seen in sanctification both a filling and a cleansing in one act, i. e., the Holy Ghost filled the justified believer and cleansed him at the same time and in the same act. (This is yet the teaching of all holiness groups which reject the Pentecostal experience, viz., The Wesleyan Methodist, Free Methodist, Nazarene, the Church of God of Anderson, Indiana and others.) Members of The Holiness Church knew that the people in California were speaking in tongues but they did not recognize such as an evidence of the baptism of the Holy Ghost. They looked upon it as one of the "gifts" of the Spirit in addition to the baptism and were therefore in full harmony with it.

THE PENTECOSTAL OUTPOURING IN NORTH CAROLINA

Mr. Cashwell received the Pentecostal experience while he was in California and word had been circulated that he had returned from California. It had also been announced that he would begin a revival meeting at Dunn, North Carolina on the last night of the year in 1906. The Reverend G. F. Taylor had spent Christmas night and the next day in the home of the Convention president, Mr. A. B. Crumpler. The subject naturally arose as to his attitude toward the new experience and toward Mr. Cashwell's prospective meeting. He expressed himself by saying that if Mr. Cashwell intended to preach that "speaking with tongues" was the evidence that one had received the baptism of the Holy Ghost that he was going to oppose him. (For reasons which were never expressed Mr. Crumpler did not have any confidence in Mr. Cashwell, and though Mr. Cashwell was for a period mightily used of God, in the end Mr. Crumpler's misgivings seemed to have been justified. Mr. Cashwell did grievously fail God and bring reproach on the cause of the full gospel of Pentecostal Holiness. Ministers of all denominations have failed God and brought hurt to His cause, but the hurt is infinitely greater when such failure occurs within the ranks of those who teach and profess the highest standards. Mr. Crumpler soon left the Church as we will see. He refused to accept the Pentecostal truth largely because he had no confidence in Mr. Cashwell. It is likely that a different chapter would have been written in his life had some other man brought the Pentecostal message to him).

In a day or so Mr. Crumpler went to Florida to conduct a revival, and on December 31, 1906 Mr. Cashwell's revival began. A large warehouse was rented for the meeting, and the people filled it. People came from every direction and from all over the South. There were people present from all denominations. A considerable portion of the preachers and many of the laymen of The Holiness Church were there. Many also were in attendance from the Fire-Baptized Holiness Church. Nothing like this meeting has ever struck that town or country before or since. Great and marvelous manifestations of God's presence filled the warehouse and all the town. The best and most spiritual people of all the churches came and many of them received the baptism of the Spirit and spoke in tongues. The meeting continued for about a month, and from it the same truth was spread in all directions through the instrumentality of both clergymen and laymen. Many who received the experience also received and responded to a definite call to preach.

Scores of the preachers of The Holiness Church went down to the altar in Mr. Cashwell's meeting with all the earnestness of their souls and it was not long until they were rejoicing in the new found experience. Some were speaking in tongues, singing in tongues, laughing the holy laugh, shouting and leaping and dancing and praising God in much the same way that the Methodists and Baptists and Presbyterians did in the early history of their churches, especially during the frontier camp-meeting days. The Pentecostal fires were burning and these preachers took up the torch and carried it hither and yon with which to kindle other fires in their respective communities. Some of the people who attended took no part in it, but for the most part the majority readily accepted the truth that was preached and received the experience, among whom were men like G. F. Taylor, A. H. Butler, J. A. Culbreth and others. A genuine God-sent revival had come and no human or satanic force was able to quench these Pentecostal fires. It was not long until a major portion of the members of The Holiness Church had received the baptism of the Spirit and spoke in other tongues.

Many of those who received the experience sent in their testimonies to Mr. Crumpler's paper. Likewise there were reports sent in of the various revivals which had taken place and almost simultaneously all over North Carolina. Other articles setting forth the doctrine of the Pentecostal baptism were also published. The editor who was at first silent soon became openly hostile, bitter and acrimonious in his denunciation of this new experience. Most of the year of 1907 his writings were colored with polemic tone in his effort to curb what he evidently felt was heretical teaching, but onward surged the mighty tide of Pentecost and the Pentecostal element was daily gaining strength.

FANATICISM

As we have previously observed there has been no great revival in the history of the Christian Church which has not had with it some fanaticism and extravagances. But the counterfeit proves there is a real which is being imitated. Believers were instructed to first seek God for a cleansed sanctified heart. After they had been justified by faith all their sins had been forgiven, but there remained the root of sin which was cleansed in sanctification. Sanctified people were then instructed to praise God and wait for the promise of the Father just as the people at Pentecost were waiting in the upper room and were continually praising and blessing God. Many followed these instructions and received the experience.

The fanaticism came in when some who were over-zealous in their desire to see others receive the experience began to instruct them to say "glory," "glory," "glory" as rapidly as their tongues could do it. The result was in many cases people who were not sanctified and ready to receive the experience said "glory" so fast that their tongue got tangled up and they muttered some sort of gibberish and jabbering of unintelligent speech which was in no wise the genuine manifestation of the Spirit of God. Some good and well-meaning people instructed others to follow such a method of seeking for their baptism. It was true, however, that some did receive the real blessing of Pentecost after this fashion, but fortunately there were sane people who began to question the Scriptural warrant and the rationality of following such a procedure. Such a method was therefore abandoned in due time. There has persisted the same such technique among some Pentecostalists, but by and large the Pentecostal Holiness people have vigorously condemned and refused to tolerate any such method. It is the devil's good pleasure to disgust thoughtful and intelligent churchmen with the whole Pentecostal movement on account of such spiritual irregularities which are nothing short of disgusting and detestable to the nth degree. And yet extreme caution must be exercised in order not to prevent or discourage a free expression of legitimate emotion and earnest seeking of the genuine Pentecostal baptism of the Holy Ghost which God intended for every individual of His Church to receive just as the apostles received it on the day of Pentecost.

The LaGrange Convention, 1907

As would naturally be expected, the 1907 Convention which met at LaGrange was the scene of conflict and debate between the factions which had resulted because of this "new" experience, although there was no harshness or bitterness. There could be detected, however, some hidden resentment which awaited a favorable opportunity for complete expression if necessary. Preachers from both sides when asked to speak were not hesitant about declaring their position. It became obvious that a distinct dividing line was being clearly drawn.

One of the anti-Pentecostal preachers offered a motion that a committee be appointed to examine every preacher in the Convention to determine his doctrinal position. Mr. G. F. Taylor was quick to second the motion. It could be seen that all others of the Pentecostal faction were heartily in accord with the idea. In fact they welcomed the opportunity and considered it a distinct privilege to bear testimony for Jesus' sake. When the chairman discovered this attitude and realized this faction was definitely in the majority he discreetly ruled the motion out of order.

It was the custom at that time to elect the Convention officers at the beginning of each annual session. Mr. Crumpler was nominated and elected without a dissenting vote, just as he had been each year since the Church was organized. A. H. Butler was re-elected as vice-president, and likewise Willie Walker was re-elected secretary.

The Dunn Convention, 1908

The historic 1908 Convention held its session at Dunn, North Carolina where the Fourth Convention had also met in 1903. This Convention in some respects was in distinct contrast to the earlier Convention when the famous L. L. Pickett was present, and wielded such a telling influence. As the time drew near for the Convention to meet the people were at a loss to know where it would meet. Because Mr. Crumpler had begun to use the Holiness Advocate to voice his harsh disapproval of the Pentecostal experience he soon discovered that the subscription list had so shrunken that it became necessary to discontinue its publication during the year prior to the 1908 Convention.

In 1904, at the Fayetteville Convention, as we have indicated it was decided that in the future these annual sessions would meet each year between the third and fourth Sundays in November. This much was understood, but the place for the meeting was uncertain since the Holiness Advocate was no longer being published, and no announcement of the meeting place had been made through any other medium. Mr. A. H. Butler wrote Mr. Crumpler making inquiry as to where it would meet. Mr. Crumpler's reply to him was that the "tongues people" could have their Convention wherever they liked but The Holiness Church would have theirs at Dunn, North Carolina beginning on Thursday after the fourth Sunday in November. This was the only change in the time of the North Carolina Convention from 1904 until 1929, when it was voted to hold its sessions in October instead of November.

When the Dunn Convention opened its sessions both sides were in attendance as usual in spite of what Mr. Crumpler had written to Mr. Butler. The Convention met in Dunn Holiness Tabernacle on Thursday, November 26, 1908 at nine-thirty. Mr. Crumpler called the session to order and the following preachers answered the roll: A. B. Crumpler, A. H. Butler, C. B. Cashwell, H. R. Martin, O. J. Owen, W. M. Pope, Zebb B. Pratt, J. D. Wiggins, W. J. S. Walker.

On motion Mr. Crumpler was unanimously re-elected as President for the ninth consecutive time. A. H. Butler was chosen as Vice-President and W. J. S. Walker was elected as Secretary. The reports were called for from the various churches and pastors, and also evangelists. Prayer was offered by J. D. Wiggins and just before the first day's session adjourned the Reverend Zebb B. Pratt arose and announced that he was withdrawing from the convention and with him was to go the church at LaGrange, North Carolina. During the day it appeared as if the President wanted things to come to a head. About everything that was introduced seemed to terminate in something that related to Pentecost. It is not known whether Mr. Crumpler and Mr. Pratt had planned to withdraw as they did or not, but after Mr. Pratt withdrew Mr. Crumpler then announced that he was also withdrawing from the Convention. Following this the secretary, W. J. S. Walker, withdrew, then the Beulah Church withdrew. As we have noted Section II of the Holiness Church discipline provided for each local congregation to exercise the right to exist independently of other religious bodies, unless a majority of the congregation voted otherwise. Hearts were saddened and the sudden defection created a perplexing atmosphere, and in the confusion of the moment the Convention elected the Reverend C. B. Strickland as President and the Reverend A. H. Butler as Secretary, and the session then adjourned.

By the time the next day's morning session was opened everybody had come to realize that they had made a mistake the evening before in electing a new President when rightfully Mr. Butler, as Vice-president should have taken the chair when the President resigned. The Convention rescinded their action and the Chairman called for a new election. A. H. Butler was then elected as President, G. F. Taylor, Vice-President and C. B. Strickland, Secretary.

246   HISTORY OF THE PENTECOSTAL HOLINESS CHURCH

THE COMMITTEES

On motion the President was empowered to appoint the committees which might be needed to transact the regular conference business. Among the most important of these committees was a committee of five who were commissioned to revise the discipline. The new President, Mr. Butler, appointed the following: G. B. Cashwell, G. F. Taylor, J. H. Sutton, H. R. Martin, and A. T. Herring.

THE DISCIPLINE COMMITTEE

This Committee on Revision of Discipline recommended the following changes to be made in Article X in the Articles of Faith in the Holiness Church Discipline:

X-a—Our own hearts as well as the Scriptures teach us that even in the hearts of those who are justified and regenerated there remains something that 'is not subject to the law of God, neither indeed can be.' That something is variously termed in the Scriptures the 'carnal mind,' 'our old man,' 'the sin that doth so easily beset us,' and 'the flesh that lusteth against the Spirit.' The Christian finding himself in this condition and desiring to escape the corruption of the 'old man,' consecrates himself definitely and wholly to God (Rom. 12:1) with all that he has or ever expects to have or be and then is able to exercise sanctifying faith in Jesus, who sanctifies him with the blood (Heb. 13:12) through the Spirit (I Pet. 1:2) witnessed by the Holy Ghost (Heb. 10:14, 15).

The Pentecostal Holiness Church has since recognized that the Scripture referred to in Romans 12:1 does not apply to persons desiring to be sanctified, but to those who are already sanctified. The exhortation is to "present your bodies 'holy' (sanctified) which is your reasonable service." This Scripture refers to the sanctified person presenting himself for the baptism of the Holy Ghost that he "may prove that which is the good, and acceptable, and perfect, will of God," which embraces the experiences of justification, sanctification and the baptism of the Holy Ghost. A further change which was made in the Discipline was in Section X as follows:

X-b. The Scriptures teach us that after we are cleansed (John 15:3; Acts 10:15, 44) with the blood we then need to receive the filling of the Spirit, the baptism with the Holy Ghost, the abiding Comforter, that which was promised by John the Baptist (Matt. 3:11) and corroborated by Jesus Christ (John 14:15-17) that on receiving the baptism with the Holy Ghost we have the same evidence that followed Acts 2nd, 10th and 19th chapters to wit: The speaking with other tongues as the Spirit gave utterance.

Respectfully submitted,
G. B. Cashwell
G. F. Taylor
J. H. Sutton
H. R. Martin
A. T. Herring

The following resolution was also passed:

Resolved, that this Convention request all pastors and officers of the churches to admit no preacher or teacher into any of the churches who preach or teach against the baptism of the Holy Ghost as taught in our revised Discipline.

C. B. Cashwell
D. J. Williams
J. M. Stevens

All ministers who had withdrawn from the Church were to be notified to surrender their credentials.

FOREIGN MISSIONS

It is interesting to note that at this Convention Mrs. J. A. Culbreth makes her report as secretary and treasurer which showed a grand total of $254.70 had been received and paid out. The Reverend John T. Benson received $22.35 of this amount. The remainder of it was sent to the Reverend T. J. McIntosh who had been received into the Convention at Lumberton in 1906. He later went around the world two times preaching the gospel. Mr McIntosh was not fully supported by this Board as the small amount well indicates. The story of this man's adventuresome and colorful missionary career would read like fiction. God miraculously had strangers to put the necessary amount for his fare to China in his pockets on the streets of San Francisco as he sang in the Spirit the old song, "I'm a Child of the King." It is with regret that it must be said that after a time Mr. McIntosh became lifted up and destroyed his usefulness because of his aberrant decorum. Mr. McIntosh was present at this Convention and received $12.75, one Testament and one Bible which was given him to help finance a religious paper which he said God had laid on his heart to publish in China. From the record it appears that Mr. McIntosh was the first member of either the Holiness Church or the Fire-Baptized

Holiness Church to go to the foreign field. He went in 1907 and again in 1909, each time traveling around the world before he returned. However, it was not until 1911 that the Pentecostal Holiness Church officially sent out any missionary. Additional information regarding the missionary activities of the Church can be found in the chapter on Foreign Missions.

A Foreign Mission Board was appointed which was composed of three sisters in Christ, Mrs. J. A. Culbreth, Bertha Maxwell and Ella Flowers. Only women continued to make up this Board.

First Home Mission Board

According to reliable information it appears that the 1908 Convention appointed the first Home Mission Board of the Holiness Church. The Reverends C. B. Cashwell, A. H. Butler and R. B. Jackson were appointed to serve on this Board. All three of them were well qualified to serve from the standpoint of experience in that they had all been unusually successful as evangelists. An offering of $13.12 was taken for the purpose of missions and on motion it was divided between the Home and Foreign Mission Boards. The pastors and churches were instructed to send in their offerings earmarked for the field desired.

Eleemosynary

The Reverend C. B. Cashwell spoke in the interest of the Wilmington Rescue Work and later the Reverend G. F. Taylor offered a resolution that this institution be recognized as worthy of support. An offering was taken which amounted to $12.80 and one Teacher's Bible.

The New President

This Convention may be said to have been one of the best in the history of the Church up to that time. The Pentecostal faction had not in any unethical way tried to protect their interests or to make any encroachments on the rights of the other side. They had unanimously voted for Mr. Crumpler to continue in his office as President of the Convention. It seems that God Himself governed and controlled the circumstances in their favor. By actual comparison it seems that this Convention did more constructive work and inaugurated more workable programs than any previous Convention had been able to do. Mr. Butler took over his new duties as President of the organization and obviously demonstrated his ability as a leader.

It would seem that the infant organization might have become discouraged after Mr. Crumpler and others withdrew, and along with them some of the local churches. But when this writer inquired of Mr. Butler if the little groups were not discouraged, he replied, "Not in the least, we were happy in our new experience and felt that we were in God's will, and that He would be with us in all of our ways."

To the Reverend A. H. Butler is due much credit for the continued existence of the Pentecostal Holiness Church. There were, of course, prominent men who were stalwart exponents of the Pentecostal Holiness truth, but Mr. Butler's indomitable spirit and sane spiritual leadership, coupled with a personal demonstration of what could be done in preaching the full gospel is responsible in no meagre way for guiding the Church in a critical period of its history. Mr. Butler, being the humble servant of God that he is, is yet unable to recognize that he was so greatly used of God. The Pentecostal Holiness Church owes to Mr. Butler a great debt and will come to recognize it more and more as they are able to view his work in the perspective of history.

The year that followed was a wonderfully good one. Well may it be said of this Church as it was said of the Early Church, "The word of God grew and multiplied." Many new churches were established. The new President traveled incessantly over the entire Convention territory and through the favor and help of God was able to build up the work, "and so the churches were established in the faith, and increased in number daily;" as Luke would say it.

CONSOLIDATION CONSIDERED

In the same territory all the while were two other Holiness Church organiations operating, viz., The Fire-Baptized Holiness Church and the Free Will Baptist Church. We have already noted at some length how the Fire-Baptized group came into existence and later embraced the experience of Pentecost. When the Holiness movement came to North Carolina in 1896 and 1897 a large number of the Free Will Baptist members were sanctified just as were many people in other churches. They, however, were not excommunicated from their church as had happened in the other established churches. Some of the people who were turned out of the other churches joined the Free Will Baptist. When the Pentecostal Holiness Church was organized in 1900 there arose some feeling of resentment because of the competition which was thus created. A large part of the holiness element in the Free Will Church received the experience of the baptism of the Holy Ghost when the "latter rain" outpouring came to North Carolina in 1907 and subsequently. Hence there were three organizations which believed the same fundamental doctrines working separately in the same territory. In many cases their work overlapped one another. Mr. Butler knew a great many of the leaders in both of these groups and exerted a powerful influence among them. There were some in these organizations who desired that the churches should be brought together.

With regard to the Fire-Baptized group there existed a few impediments which seemingly might prevent a consolidation, but they did not actually constitute any serious hindrance. Mr. Crumpler and others of the Holiness Church had vigorously opposed the "baptism of fire" which B. H. Irwin taught and had labeled it the "Third Blessing Heresy." Naturally this attitude had provoked some measure of reaction from the other side. When the Pentecostal revival came these differences were gradually swept away and forgotten. Most of the people of the Holiness Church did not subscribe to the Fire-Baptized Holiness doctrine of "no ties and no hog-meat," though some in the Holiness Church did contend for these teachings. The majority, however, looked upon them as non-essentials which should be left for each individual to decide personally.

There appeared to be even less difficulty which might prevent forming a union with the Pentecostal element in the Free Will Baptist Church. Circumstances seemed to indicate that something might be done to bring these organizations together, and during the next Convention steps were taken and plans formulated which gave promise of bringing about such a union.

The Falcon Convention, 1909

The Convention of 1909 held its sessions at Falcon, North Carolina. The Discipline which was revised at the previous Convention had been printed and circulated. All preachers who were not in harmony with the Pentecostal baptism of the Spirit and who had withdrawn had been asked to send in their credentials. No ministers or lay members expected to remain in the organization unless they were in harmony with the teaching concerning the baptism of the Holy Ghost with the initial evidence of speaking in tongues as the Spirit gives utterance.

THE CHURCH TAKES ITS ORIGINAL NAME

After the members of The Holiness Church received the Pentecostal experience and spoke with tongues they began to recognize the fact that they had the wrong name. They were no longer just Holiness people but were Pentecostal Holiness people. Hence it was voted at the 1909 Convention to take again the word "Pentecostal" and thus the Church took its original name, "The Pentecostal Hoiiness Church" and has been called that ever since.

TOBACCO AND DIVORCE LAWS

A law was incorporated into the Discipline forbidding any Pentecostal Holiness member to use, grow, sell or handle tobacco in any form. A law was also enacted which forbade any church member to have more than one wife or husband at the same time.

WATER BAPTISM

Prior to the 1909 Convention The Holiness Church had received members into the church without requiring them to receive water baptism. If they desired to be baptized they had the choice of any mode they might choose. The Quakers do not believe in water baptism and the Holiness Church had made it optional with its members. At this Convention it was voted that water baptism should be required but the candidate was still free to choose the mode he preferred.

CONSOLIDATION COMMITTEE

The most important thing which happened at this Convention was a motion introduced by the Reverend G. F. Taylor that a committee of three be appointed to confer with a like committee from the Fire-Baptized Holiness Church to draw up a mutual agreement to be submitted by these committees for adoption by each body, looking forward to a proposed union. The Reverend G. B. Cashwell offered an amendment to the motion which was accepted, providing that this motion be extended to include the Free Will Baptist.

The Pentecostal Holiness Church appointed as its representatives A. H. Butler, J. A. Culbreth and G. F. Taylor. The Fire-Baptized Holiness Church appointed five men instead of three. They were as follows: S. D. Page, A. E. Robinson, F. M. Britton, M. D. Sellers, and E. D. Cannon. These eight committee members met in the rough tabernacle at Falcon in April, 1910. Although the discussions were necessarily lengthy, they lasted for only two days. A Basis of Union was formulated and adopted which has remained substantially unchanged since that time. In view of the fact that the Fire-Baptized Holiness Church had come to recognize their error in teaching the "baptism of fire" as a separate experience, it was decided that the name "Pentecostal Holiness" would be best suited for the new consolidated organization, if it were actually effected. This committee changed the name of the General Overseer to General Superintendent and the name of President or Ruling Elder to Superintendent. All annual state gatherings were to be called Conventions, and the general gatherings were to be called a General Convention. Other minor changes were suggested. Copies of this agreement were printed and circulated among the churches and preachers of both organizations. The majority voted in favor of the consolidation.

THE KINSTON CONVENTION, 1910

When the next Convention met at Kinston, North Carolina in 1910, the report of these joint committees was adopted. It was then decided that this Convention should appoint a committee of one to meet a like committee of the Fire-Baptized Church, and that these two should choose a third member, and the three were then to be commissioned to formulate a complete Discipline for the proposed new church. The Convention appointed the Reverend G. F. Taylor to act as its representative. The Reverend A. H. Butler was again elected as President, and J. A. Culbreth was elected as Secretary.

In the late fall of 1910 the Reverend J. H. King had left on a tour around the world and had appointed the Reverend Francis

Marion Britton as Acting General Overseer of the Fire-Baptized Holiness Church and had delegated to him the authority to act in his stead. Since the Fire-Baptized group had no general meeting planned in the immediate future in which a committee could be appointed, the Reverend Mr. Britton assumed the responsibility to act for that Church. Mr. Taylor then asked that Mr. Britton select the third man, and he named J. A. Culbreth, a man well known and acceptable to both men. During the Christmas holidays in 1910 these three men met in the home of the Reverend G. F. Taylor and in a short time drew up a complete Discipline covering the main points.

This Convention brings to a close a complete era in the history of the Pentecostal Holiness Church. It also brings to a close Section I in which has been presented "The Background and Early Beginnings." With the beginning of Section II the Church takes on a different character. It is no longer provincial, but from henceforth it assumes larger proportions and broadens its horizon as an organization.

Section II
Organized Effort and Expansion

Chapter I
CONSOLIDATIONS, 1911-1916

Introduction

It seems fitting and proper that before we enter into the consideration of the material which will comprise Section II it will be well to recapitulate what has been presented in the previous section, "Background and Early Beginnings."

We observed that the Pentecostal Holiness Church, as we know it today, represents a merger of two Holiness groups: The Fire-Baptized Holiness Church, and the Pentecostal Holiness Church. (The details of that merger will be an immediate consideration in this new section.) The history of each of these two organizations was entirely separate until the time of their consolidation in 1911.

In dealing with the background of both of these organizations, attention was called to the ancient Apostolic roots out of which they have stemmed. New Testament Scriptures were cited in an attempt to establish the validity of the doctrine and experiences of sanctification and the baptism of the Holy Ghost. We also noted that the modern Holiness movement roots in the Wesleyan Revival and Methodism. We have noted that when the Methodist Church deserted the landmarks of holiness and lost their religious fervor there was the appearance of the National Association for the Promotion of Holiness, which had its inception largely as a result of the fiery evangelistic labors of the Rev. John S. Inskip, who became the first president of the Association.

The history of these two organizations was seen to have issued directly from certain of the State Associations which were a part of the National Association. With the outpouring of the Pentecostal baptism of the Holy Ghost in 1906 and the immediately following years these two organizations discovered an affinity for one another which made it easy for them to be merged into a single body. Such preliminary steps as were necessary had been made during 1909 and 1910, the details of which we have already recorded. (We will turn presently to consider the actual consolidation.)

With the consolidation of the Fire-Baptized Holiness Church and the Pentecostal Holiness Church there begins a new epoch in the history of the Pentecostal Holiness Church. We may divide the history of the Church into two general periods, viz., "Early Beginnings" which included the history of the separate organizations from 1898 and 1900 respectively until 1910; and a second General Period which might well be designated as a period of "Organized Efforts and Expansions," from 1911 to 1948. A suitable sub-title would be "General Conferences and General History." The first section covers a period of 12 years, while Section II extends over a period of 37 years. This section is conveniently divided into five chapters each of which deals with a certain phase of the historical development. The subject matter of which these separate chapters treat makes for a natural grouping of certain of these General Conferences, because of the similarity of the type of work accomplished during a given period of history. The chapter headings which indicate these various stages of historical development will appear as follows: "Consolidations"; "New Developments"; "Growing Pains and Reverses"; "Coordination and Cooperation"; and "Organizational Developments." The subject matter which appears in these various chapters is not necessarily confined to that which the chapter heading suggests, but the principal portion of it falls in that category. A third section in the history of the Church is devoted to "Departmental Developments in Summary."

THE FIRST GENERAL CONVENTION, FALCON, NORTH CAROLINA, 1911

Consolidation Effected

After the 1910 Kinston Convention met the Rev. G. F. Taylor was appointed as a committee of one to represent the Pentecostal Holiness Church. The Rev. F. M. Britton acted as the member of the committee from The Fire-Baptized Church, and the two agreed for Mr. J. A. Culbreth to act as a sort of referee to complete the committee of three. These three men then drew up a Discipline which was to be the basis upon which the consolidation should take place, provided a majority of the representatives from each of these Churches should vote to adopt the same when they met together for the General Convention.

A general representative gathering of each of the Churches was called to meet the last days of January, 1911. The representatives of the Pentecostal Holiness Church met at night in the school building, while those of the Fire-Baptized Holiness Church met at the same time in the home of the Rev. S. D. Page. Each of these bodies had before them a copy of the proposed Discipline which was read critically and discussed as to the merits and demerits of various items. The Pentecostal Holiness Church body suggested some minor corrections in the punctuation and wording, but the document itself was adopted without question. The Fire-Baptized Holiness Church however wanted to make some changes.

The following morning on January 30, 1911, both groups met in the historic octogan-shaped tabernacle. This was a memorable occasion. Christian brethren who had worked in the same neighborhoods, teaching the same doctrine, were now about to consolidate their efforts by uniting their organizations. Godly men whose hearts were anxious for the cause of the Full Gospel were eagerly hoping for the best. The Rev. A. H. Butler was elected as chairman pro tem to preside over the meeting. J. A. Culbreth was elected as Secretary pro tem. The Convention opened by singing No. 11 in the "Bread of Life Songs," followed by a prayer which was led by the Rev. F. M. Britton. The Pentecostal Holiness Church reported that it was ready to unite on the basis of the entire document asking that the minor changes in grammar and punctuation be made. The Fire-Baptized group said they would unite on the grounds that the officers be elected first, and then that the Discipline be adopted. It seemed for a time that the consolidation would not be possible because of the unwillingness of each side to yield. After considerable discussion Brother A. E. Robinson offered a motion that the document be adopted verbatim et literatim and the motion was carried by a majority of 36 to 2 on a rising vote. They then sang together "The Old Time Religion" and "Blest Be the Tie that Binds" shook hands, hugged one another and shouted the high praises of God. Heaven seemed to look down and confirm the transaction.[1] Prior to the Consolida-

---

[1] A. E. Robinson, General Secretary, **Minutes of the First General Convention of the Pentecostal Holiness Church.**

tion a number of the principals involved had come to Falcon, N. C. to enjoy the revival blessings under the ministry of the Rev. A. G. Canada which were then in progress. The spiritual preparation which resulted from these services no doubt played a large part in bringing about the consolidation. In an interview with J. A. Culbreth he stated that any lack of oneness which might have existed before the consolidation all had completely vanished and perfect harmony prevailed after the consolidation was effected which made everyone feel that God was pleased.

The Enrollment

The roll of the members of the General Convention was as follows:

From the Fire-Baptized Holiness Church: F. M. Britton, G. O. Gaines, J. J. Carter, M. D. Sellers, H. P. Lott, E. D. Reeves, C. M. Wheeler, Mrs. F. M. Britton, J. H. Blake, S. D. Page, Ralph Taylor, A. E. Robinson, J. H. Inman, J. M. Howell, J. H. Spain, J. T. Crumpler, C. O. Daniels, Howard Sellers, J. A. James, H. M. Israel and others making a total of 32 in all who were present on the occasion.

From the Pentecostal Holiness Church were: A. H. Butler, G. F. Taylor, J. A. Culbreth, R. B. Jackson, J. T. Herring, B. B. Pleasants, and others.

Election of Officers

A motion was offered to elect a General Superintendent and two Assistants. It was passed unanimously and the following were nominated for General Superintendent: J. H. King, S. D. Page and G. O. Gaines. On the first ballot J. H. King received 16; S. D. Page, 17; G. O. Gaines, 3. On the second ballot S. D. Page received 19; J. H. King, 17. The Rev. S. D. Page was declared elected, and by motion his election was made unanimous, and he came to the chair.

Mr. A. E. Robinson was then unanimously elected as General Secretary, after which the Rev. A. H. Butler was elected as Assistant General Superintendent to direct the work of Home Missions, and the Rev. J. H. King was elected as the other Assistant and placed in charge of the Foreign Missionary work. (He was at the time on a world tour in the interest of Foreign Missions).

Mr. J. A. Culbreth was then unanimously elected as General Treasurer. A motion was carried which called for the election of S. D. Page, G. O. Gaines, H. P. Lott, J. A. Culbreth and A. E. Robinson as General Trustees.

In view of the fact that this consolidation brought together two sections in North Carolina it was decided that the respective Superintendents of each section should continue their work until the meeting of the next Annual Convention.

New credentials were issued to all members of the new organization, signed by the General Superintendent and General Secretary.

The Church Incorporated

The Pentecostal Holiness Church was never chartered prior to this time, but according to the public records at Carnesville, Georgia, the Fire-Baptized Holiness Church was chartered in Franklin County, Georgia, by the Superior Court, during its September term in 1905.[1] After the union of the two churches the General Officers who comprised the Official Board of the new organization petitioned for an amendment of the 1905 charter. The amendment was granted, changing the name of this church to the Pentecostal Holiness Church, and making some other minor changes. This is the charter under which the Church still operates. Carnesville is not far from Franklin Springs, the present headquarters of the Pentecostal Holiness Church.[2]

The Conventions in 1911

The Annual Conventions in 1911 at the time of the First General Convention were as follows:

1. Eastern North Carolina and Lower South Carolina, J. J. Carter, Superintendent (1910).

2. Georgia and Upper South Carolina, G. O. Gaines, Superintendent.

3. Florida, H. A. Smith, Superintendent (1909).

4. Virginia, E. D. Reeves, Superintendent (1909).

5. Oklahoma, H. P. Lott, Superintendent (1909).

---
[1] Superior Court Record, **Book of Charters**, (Franklin County, Carnesville, Georgia) pp. 75, 76; also **Book of Minutes, Book "B,"** p. 471.
[2] Ibid., **Book of Charters**, pp. 100, 101.

6. Tennesseee, C. N. Wheeler, Superintendent, (during 1911 R. L. Todd from Columbia went to Memphis to assist Mr. Wheeler 1910).

All of the above named men were connected with the Fire Baptized Holiness Church. It seems that the Pentecostal Holiness Church had up until this time confined their efforts principally to the state of North Carolina. (It was sometimes referred to as "The Holiness Church of North Carolina.") The Rev. A. H. Butler was the President of the Pentecostal Holiness Church at that time and G. F. Taylor and J. A. Culbreth were also prominent leaders in the Church.

THE SECOND GENERAL CONVENTION, TOCCOA, GEORGIA, 1913

The Second General Convention met in Toccoa, Georgia, opened its sessions on Tuesday, January 28, 1913, two years after the First General Convention had met at Falcon, North Carolina. All subsequent general meetings have held their session at the end of each quadrennium. The Convention was opened with a song which all joined heartily in singing, after which earnest prayers were offered invoking God's blessings upon those present and upon the church business to be transacted. The Rev. S. D. Page then read an appropriate passage of Scriptures from I Timothy and exhorted the brethren of the Conference to conform their lives and ministries to those standards therein outlined for those who would be faithful in Christ Jesus.

The Enrollment of Delegates and Conventions

The ministerial roll of the Convention was called and delegates were enrolled. A motion was passed which provided that substitute representatives be elected to take the place of those persons who were absent and should have been present. There appears to have been two Conventions added since 1911: a Colored Convention and the Western North Carolina Convention. The Colored Convention was short-lived, however, since a motion was offered in this Convention to drop it from the roll. The Pentecostal Holiness Church has since that time done no work among the colored brethren excepting the large missionary work in Africa. Concerning the Western North Carolina Conference we have already explained that after the Consolidation it was voted that the state leaders of both merging bodies should continue their work in their respective fields. For the sake of convenience the Pentecostal Holiness work which had extended into the western part of the state was technically treated as a separate convention, although it was not actually a separate convention until the formal organization of the Western North Carolina Conference in 1915.

Officers Elected

The Rev. G. F. Taylor was elected as General Superintendent to succeed the Rev. S. D. Page, who was then elected as Assistant General Superintendent. A. E. Robinson was elected as General Secretary and Treasurer. The following were elected as General Trustees: J. H. King, G. F. Taylor, S. D. Page, A. E. Robinson and R. E. Lee.[1]

Invitation Extended to the Tabernacle Presbyterian Church

The Revs. N. J. Holmes and L. R. Graham of the Tabernacle Presbyterian Church and the Rev. C. H. Culclasure of the Palmetto Baptist Church were voted a seat of welcome and a voice in the Convention. On the next day, Wednesday, January 29, 1913, the Revs. N. J. Holmes and L. R. Graham, fraternal delegates from the Southern Pentecostal Association and the Tabernacle Presbyterian Church, greeted and addressed the Convention, stating that while they did not see their way clear to unite with the Pentecostal Holiness Church at that time, the body they represented was desirous of cooperating as far as possible in the spread of Pentecostal truth, especially in the foreign field. (The Tabernacle Church had been extended an invitation to merge with the Pentecostal Holiness Church, by their official Board sometime just prior to the General Convention.) The Convention then voted to return these greetings and to assure this body of its desire to cooperate in any undertaking which would aid them in spreading the "full gospel." Mr. Holmes accepted an invitation from the Devotional Committee to preach that night. His wonderful Scriptural message thrilled the hearts of all who heard him.

---

1 After the 1913 General Conference the General Officers were elected at the close of the Conference instead of at the beginning as had been the custom.

Divorce Question

We have observed how the divorce question came to be a live issue in the Goldsboro church in 1902 and how it was finally settled in Mr. Crumpler's favor at the Fayetteville Convention in 1904. In the meantime this question was agitated considerably over the entire Church body and actually diverted energies which should have been utilized more constructively. To view these matters retrospectively drives one to the conclusion that this issue must likely have been a trick of Satan to hinder the spread of holiness in the infant organization, at that time only two years old, and definitely still in an inchoate stage of development. For a time after 1904 the question remained quiescent but it was again brought into sharp focus at the time of the Consolidation, and was a divisive factor which threatened to make the merger impossible. After a time the Discipline was adopted verbatim et literatim as we have noted, but it was not long after the Consolidation until this matter was given fresh emphasis. There were some who interpreted the Scriptures as teaching that under no circumstances could any person remarry, whatever had been the grounds of their divorce or previous marital status. Others believed that if a person were separated from a former companion on "Bible grounds," he or she then had a Bible right to remarry an eligible person. In the two year interim between the meeting of the First and Second General Conventions this question continued to be agitated increasingly, and by the time the Convention met the divorce question had become a very prominent issue.

On Thursday morning, January 30th, a motion was introduced to discuss the following query: "Resolved, That a person who has been divorced for the cause of fornication has a Scriptural right to remarry." Each side was allowed one and one-half hours to present their views. It resulted in the divorce clause in Section LV., paragraph 10 of the Discipline being amended to read as follows: "No one shall be admitted to membership in the Pentecostal Holiness Church who has two living companions, or is living with a wife or husband who has two living companions, except it be for the cause of fornication." The vote for the adoption of the motion to amend the clause showed 20 affirmative to 19 negative votes. After the Convention it was apparent that both sides were somewhat dissatisfied with the way the ballots read. The General

Superintendent then wrote out a petition to the General Secretary to the effect that the divorce clause be left out of the Discipline. This petition was sent for the signatures of all General and State Convention Officers, all but two of which voted to leave it out. It would seem that mortal man with his finite limitations is not competent to set an arbitrary rule which will apply to every case. It is Satan's business to cause divisions over any matter possible, and to distract our attention from the great work of the Kingdom by causing us to focus our attention on things which will cause a cleavage and destroy the unity wherein rests our strength. Such matters need attention but should not be over-emphasized.

Discipline

Several changes were made in the Discipline, the most significant of which were a definite plan of procedure for the conducting of the business of the Annual Conventions; the setting forth of the requirements for ministers making their reports to their respective Conventions; stipulation that the General Convention shall meet every four years; and the numbering of the various Conventions according to location as follows: 1. Virginia; 2. Western North Carolina; 3. Eastern North Carolina and Lower South Carolina; 4. Georgia and Upper South Carolina; 5. Florida, Alabama and South Georgia.

Foreign Missions

The report of the Committee on Missions provided for the election of a General Mission Board by the General Convention which would have the oversight of all the missionary work of the church, and would cooperate with the Missionary Boards of the various Annual Conventions; the examining of candidates and assigning them to their fields of labor; and the disbursing of funds. The following men were elected officers of the General Mission Board; J. H. King, Pres.; A. H. Butler, Vice Pres.; A. E. Robinson, Secretary; G. F. Taylor, Treasurer; F. M. Britton, S. D. Page, G. O. Gaines, R. E. Lee and J. A. Culbreth, Directors. The Foreign Missions Board of the Pentecostal Holiness Church had heretofore been composed exclusively of women, except, as we noted that in 1911 the two Assistant General Superintendents were placed in charge of both Home and Foreign Missions.

Books and Periodicals

The Rev. G. F. Taylor after being elected to the office of General Superintendent at this Convention made an address in the interest of publications in the Church, but was unable to stimulate any noticeable response. There was, however, a report of the Committee on Books and Periodicals, which suggested a course of study for young preachers and recommended that all the constituency of the Church should give careful and prayerful study to the Word of God.

TABERNACLE PRESBYTERIAN CHURCH

The Organization

After the Rev. Nickels John Holmes had served several years as a member of the South Carolina Synod of the Presbyterian Church, he received the experience of sanctification and was led to trust God for the healing of his body independent of medical means. He was eventually brought into question by members of the Presbytery and for the sake of peace withdrew from that body and united with the Brewerton Independent Presbyterian Church which had unanimously withdrawn from the jurisdiction of the Presbytery, because it held the same doctrinal views. Mr. Holmes was then called as pastor of this church. Associated with him in his work was the Rev. S. C. Todd who shared his views and who had also withdrawn from the Presbytery. Mr. Todd became associated with Mr. Holmes in the work of the Altamont Bible and Missionary Institute which began on November 1, 1898.

In the course of time, in 1909, Mr. Holmes erected a cross-shaped tabernacle building on what is now the campus of Holmes Bible College in Greenville, S. C. which he desired to organize into a church. A commission from the Brewerton Independent Presbyterian Church was appointed for this work, and on July 10, 1910, the Tabernacle Presbyterian Church was organized.

Following the Pentecostal "latter rain" outpouring in 1906 there came a great Pentecostal revival to the Bible school principally under the ministry of the Rev. G. F. Taylor, in June 1907, during which time Mrs. N. J. Holmes and quite a number of the students received the baptism of the Spirit. During the month of April preceding this revival the Revs. L. R. Graham, O. E. Taylor and N. J. Holmes had also received this experience. During the following summer Mr. Holmes conducted a meeting at Clinton with the Rev. C. B. Cashwell around whose ministry largely centered the "latter rain" outpouring in the Eastern part of the United States. Their meetings were exceedingly fruitful during that summer, and in the years which immediately followed quite a number of people received the baptism of the Spirit. These people were misunderstood and unwelcomed in the midst of the established churches, and felt that they would like to belong to some organization where this "full gospel" could be preached, and others could also be brought into the experience they were enjoying. Among the number of the ministers who became charter members of The Tabernacle Presbyterian Church at the time of the organization in 1910 were: the Revs. N. J. Holmes, S. A. Bishop, Luther R. Graham, W. Ray Anderson, O. E. Taylor, Richard Anderson and Paul F. Beacham.

The Doctrinal Position

The Brewerton church which had operated for a period of about eleven years made the following amendments to the larger and shorter catechism to harmonize those documents with the doctrines for which they stood:

Chapter VI, Section V, Page 43
Chapter X, Section III, Page 66
Chapter XIII, Section I, Page 75
Chapter XIII, Section II, Page 76
Chapter XIII, Section III, Page 77
L. C. Q. 75, Page 221
L. C. Q 75, Page 221
S. C. Q 35, Page 392
S. C. Q 82, Page 412

Confession and Catechisms changed at Brewerton Church, Charter VI, Section V. Insert between the words "regeneration" and "And" the phrase "Until wholly sanctified through faith in Christ."

Chapter X, Section III, Strike out the word "elect" before the word "Infants."

Chapter XIII. *Sanctification*, Section I, strike out the words "More and more weakened and."

Section II, strike out all after the word "Man" and insert the words "Wrought by the Holy Ghost through faith in this life."

Section III, strike out all between the words, "In which" and "And so," and insert in lieu thereof the words, "Sanctification the believer is enabled through the sanctifying grace of the Holy Spirit to reckon himself to be dead indeed unto sin and alive unto God, through Jesus Christ our Lord."

Longer Catechism, 75, What is Sanctification? A. Strike out the words "More and More." Q 77, A. Strike out the word "subdued" and all thereafter and insert in lieu thereof the words, "Done away with in the crucifixion of the Old Man."

Shorter Catechism Q 35, What is Sanctification? A. Strike out the words "More and More." Q 82 Is any man able perfectly to keep the commandments of God? A. Insert between the words, "Man" and "Since" the clause "Without the power of the Holy Ghost."

The Change in Name

When the Church embraced the experience of Pentecost certain other amendments were made to harmonize with that experience. Consequent upon a great number of the members of the Tabernacle Presbyterian Church receiving the Pentecostal baptism it was decided that this organization should indicate its doctrinal position by changing its name to "The Tabernacle Pentecostal Church."

The Consolidation

In 1915, at the annual meeting of the Georgia-Upper South Carolina Convention, this organization was consolidated with the Pentecostal Holiness Church. Mr. Holmes and the Greenville church which he pastored did not become a part of the consolidated church, since for justifiable reasons he felt that because of his connection with the interdenominational Bible School which he headed it would be best not to unite. He was, however, in full harmony with, and continued to work in full cooperation with the Pentecostal Holiness Church. More details of Mr. Holmes' work and his relation to this Church organization may be seen in connection with the History of Education in the Pentecostal Holiness Church. The remainder of the churches which comprised the Tabernacle Pentecostal Church were taken into the Pentecostal Holiness Church, among which were local churches at Brewerton, Easley, Gum Springs and others.

THE UPPER SOUTH CAROLINA CONVENTION ORGANIZED, 1915

When the Tabernacle Pentecostal Church organization finally became a part of the Pentecostal Holiness Church and brought into that body several new local churches in South Carolina, it became evident that there needed to be a geographical separation of the Georgia and South Carolina work. Thus it was decided during the 1915 Convention to form a new Annual Convention to be called the Upper South Carolina Conference. The Rev. Thomas L. Aaron, who was present on that occasion and was there licensed to preach, tells of the ministers being allowed to come forward and take their stand at the front of the Church on either side to indicate the Annual Convention which they wished to join. This meant separation from the fellowship of brethren who had labored and sacrificed together over the years in what was one of the oldest Conventions in the Church. Mr. Aaron says as he watched these older brethren as they came forward there were no dry eyes and some had tears coursing down their cheeks, but for the sake of progress they were also able to shed some tears of rejoicing. Some of those who were present were the Revs. Perry Sexton, R. B. Hayes, W. J. A. Russum, W. H. McCurley, W. L. Myers, Hugh Bowling, Watson Sorrow, Ralph Taylor, G. R. Thomas, N. J. Holmes, F. L. Bramblett and others.

The Rev. Ralph Taylor was elected as the superintendent of the Convention and served until 1919, when the Rev. F. L. Bramblett was elected to succeed him and served until 1943, the longest term of any Conference Superintendent in the history of the Church. Mr. Ralph Taylor was again elected as Superintendent and served until 1947, when the young Rev. James H. Taylor succeeded him. This Conference has for a long time been a prominent part of the Pentecostal Holiness Church and under the progressive leadership of its present Superintendent should continue to make rapid strides of advancement.

THE WESTERN NORTH CAROLINA CONVENTION ORGANIZED, 1915

As a result of the consolidation of the Fire Baptized Holiness Church in 1911, it immediately became necessary to technically divide the work in North Carolina as we have noted. The division was actually effected in November, 1915, when the Western North Carolina Convention was organized by G. F. Taylor. The boundaries included all territory west of the Seaboard Air Line Railroad from Richmond to Hamlet, and this division was established by the General Conference in 1917 as Conference No. 3 of the Pentecostal Holiness Church. The Rev. F. A. Dail was elected as the first Superintendent and the Rev. J. H. Capps was elected Secretary. Mr. Dail served until 1922, when the Rev. C. A. Stroud was elected to succeed him. Mr. Stroud served for a long period during which the Conference became the largest in the Church. He was succeeded by the Rev. T. A. Melton in 1943. Mr. Melton served in that capacity until 1946. At the General Conference in 1945 he had been elected as a Junior Bishop and following the death of Bishop J. H. King he resigned his position as Conference Superintendent on June 15, 1946, to enter the general work of the Church and to supervise the ministerial activities of the Third District.

THE ALABAMA CONFERENCE ORGANIZED, 1915

(Details of this organization appear in a later discussion.)

THE LOWER SOUTH CAROLINA CONVENTION—NORTH CAROLINA CONVENTION, 1916

The name of the Eastern North Carolina and Lower South Carolina Convention was changed to the "Lower South Carolina" and the "North Carolina" Conventions after the Convention met in 1916. Both of these Conventions date from the same time in 1911, when the Church was consolidated; and because of the growth during the years up to 1916 it became necessary to separate the two Conferences. So it was that by the time the General Conference met in 1917 there had been added three additional Annual Conventions making a total of nine. There were seven Annual Conventions listed in the 1913 General Conference Minutes, but as we have observed there were actually only six, the Western North Carolina Convention technically existed after the Consolidation but was not actually organized until November 1915, as has been pointed out.

THE GIFT MOVEMENT IN VIRGINIA, 1916

In 1916 there was initiated in the Virginia Convention a movement which came to be designated as "The Gift Movement." Some of the very best, and most conscientious and spiritually reliable people of the Church allowed their zeal for spiritual things to lead them into what afterward came to be recognized as heretical. The word "heretical" is used advisedly and with no intention of being offensive.

There was a great amount of good which came out of this movement but in time it came to be good which was evil spoken of. What had begun with the best of intentions soon went beyond the boundaries of sane spiritual behavior, principally because there had been no defined Scriptural limits incorporated into the thinking of those who were involved. It was thus that an unharnessed movement swept good people from the stable moorings of rational religious expression.

In the decade which had lapsed since the "latter rain" outpouring of the Spirit in 1906 it was quite natural that the spiritual tides should have subsided to some extent. The more deeply spiritual people interpreted this as a sign of declension, which they thought could be eliminated. The diminishing fervor they believed had resulted because of their failure to seek from God the "gifts" of the Spirit, after having received the "gift" of the Spirit. After people began to seek God, even those who had never received the baptism of the Spirit over the years since they had been members of the Pentecostal Holiness Church, began to receive the experience. Others who were seeking for the gifts of the Spirit had miraculous healings to take place under their ministries. Some seem to have been able to exercise the gift of discernment, and time proved the soundness of their statements. There were those who claimed that demons which were literally cast out had actually been seen, appearing like a cloud filling the room; and that they were rebuked in the name of the Lord and driven from the building. On several occasions it seems that the Spirit led certain ones to be prayed for. The leaders in these services would say to such people, for example, "You came to the service this morning to get healed." Strange to say this was actually the case. In many instances they were miraculously healed instantly before the eyes of large congregations. These services centered around Pulaski, Radford, Bluefield, and Roanoke. Honorable and sincere people, like the Rev. and Mrs. J. B. Daugherty and the late Rev. E. D. Reeves and many others, were associated with this movement.

Mrs. J. B. Daugherty was one of the leaders. She and Mr. Daugherty were married at the close of a six weeks revival campaign at Pulaski, Virginia. The two of them then went together to the other places mentioned. When they went to Roanoke the renowned minister, Rev. E. D. Reeves, declared "This is of God." It seems that quite a number of people claimed to have had it revealed to them by the Spirit that certain persons were supposed to get married. Astounding prophecies began to be made. Much of what was prophesied was never fulfilled. Other things occurred which tended to bring this movement into question and finally into disrepute. When the news spread over the Church some of the leaders went to Virginia to make an investigation. The Rev. F. M. Britton, who bore the reputation of boldly speaking his mind, denounced the whole affair and was instrumental in securing a called meeting of the Conference which was presided over by the Rev. G. F. Taylor, who was less outspoken but who also denounced the movement.

It is the opinion of some that these men should have attempted to correct the disorders, and in proving all things should have held fast to that which was good. It is gratifying to know that most of those who were brought into question were afterwards fully reinstated and some rose to high official places in the church. The Rev. Reeves became an Assistant General Superintendent and his outstanding ministry proved a blessing to hundreds in the Church before he passed to his final reward in 1936. The Rev. and Mrs. Daugherty are prominent and tried members of the Pentecostal Holiness Church, and enjoy the reputation of being second to none anywhere in their spiritual demeanor and Christ-like spirits.

Such facts as these should not be interpreted in such a way as to discredit the work of God, but should be viewed as the normal occurrence naturally to be expected among a people who had not developed to the point of being able to exercise mature spiritual judgment. This should be interpreted sympathetically as being the result of dealing with a new experience which the modern Church world had not previously encountered.

Chapter II
NEW DEVELOPMENTS, 1917-1925

In the preceding chapter we have considered the principal consolidations which have taken place in the history of the Pentecostal Holiness Church, viz., The Fire-Baptized Holiness Church and the Tabernacle Holiness Church. There have been a few other groups received into the Pentecostal Holiness Church from time to time since 1911, but they have been so insignificant in size that to give the details regarding the history of their consolidation with the Pentecostal Holiness Church would be unwarranted. Suffice it to say that with the opening of this new chapter we can begin to view the Pentecostal Holiness organization as a more unified group which had overcome the difficulties usually to be associated with the establishing of a new church body.

THE THIRD GENERAL CONVENTION, ABBEVILLE, S. C., 1917

It was decided at this meeting of the General Convention to cease using the word "Convention" in referring to the business sessions of the Church, and henceforth to use the word "Conference" instead. In all subsequent references made to these meetings, either before or since the Third General Convention, they will be referred to as "Conferences."

With the beginning of the Third General Conference and extending through the Fifth General Conference, the History of the Pentecostal Holiness Church may be characterized as a period of "New Developments," as is indicated by the chapter heading above. In some sense the Third General Conference may be considered the most important General Conference in the entire history of the Church. It was unquestionably the most important one up to 1917. The total Church membership by that time was still relatively small, being less than 5,000 in the United States. There were ten Annual Conferences, the membership of which in the Pentecostal Holiness organization was as follows:

Virginia, 441; North Carolina, 1192; Western North Carolina, 605; Lower South Carolina, 368; Upper South Carolina,

519; Georgia, 737; Florida, 425; Alabama and Memphis, (no figures given) and Oklahoma, 551; a total of 4,838.[1] The membership in Alabama and Memphis Conferences would likely not swell the total to as much as 5,000 members. So although the Church was yet weak in numbers it had reached a stage in its development where it was better organized and was therefore ready to undertake certain new developments as will be seen.

1. Virginia: States of Virginia and West Virginia.

2. North Carolina: State of North Carolina east of S. A. L. Railway from Richmond to Hamlet, S. A. L. Railway east to Wilmington, N. C.

3. Western North Carolina: Bounded on the east by S. A. L. Railway from Richmond to Hamlet, on the South by South Carolina, on the west by Tennessee, on the North by Virginia.

4. Lower South Carolina: State of North Carolina not mentioned in above boundaries of North Carolina and Western North Carolina Conferences, and State of South Carolina east of and including Columbia, S. C.

5. Upper South Carolina: Northern portion of State of South Carolina, west Columbia, S. C.

6. Georgia: State of Georgia, except extreme southern portion.

7. Florida: State of Florida and southern extremity of State of Georgia.

8. Alabama: State of Alabama.

9. Memphis: All of State of Tennessee west of the main line of the L. and N. Railway, all of State of Mississippi north of V. S. and P. Railway, all of State of Arkansas north and east of Arkansas River, and all of State of Missouri south of a direct line running from St. Louis to Kansas City, Mo. (This Conference was called the Tennessee Conference from 1911 to 1914, and in 1924 it was again called the Tennessee Conference until 1926, when it was consolidated with the Missouri Conference and called the Tri-State Conference.)

10. Oklahoma: State of Oklahoma.

---

[1] A. E. Robinson, Minutes of the Third Session of the **General Convention of the Pentecostal Holiness Church** (Abbeville, S. C., Jan. 23-29, 1917), p. 24.

(The Missouri Conference held its first annual Conference meeting in 1924 and was consolidated with the Tennessee Conference in 1926 to form the Tri-State Conference.)

According to appointment the General Conference met with the Abbeville, S. C. Pentecostal Holiness Church beginning its session on Tuesday, January 23, 1917, at 9 A. M. For the first time in the history of the Church there was a full representation at this meeting of the General Conference. There were 51 members of the General Conference and all but 7 of this number were present. Proxies were then elected to take the place of the absent members. It was gratifying to see so many lay delegates present along with the clerical delegates.

A new program was adopted for the conduct of the Conference business and for the first time it took on the character of a legislative body, in a manner worthy of its purpose. This meeting of the General Conference was accorded a place of importance in the Church which it had not previously enjoyed. There existed a greater spirit of unity than had been manifest on any other like occasion. Each Annual Conference seemed to be aware of the fact that it existed as an integral part of a whole and the delegates of these Conferences reflected a willingness to yield their own wishes as soon as they came to recognize the need of their cooperation for the benefit of the whole Church. In spite of all debates and differences of opinion the spirit of brotherly love and fellowship was unbroken. Everyone seemed to feel proud of being part of something that was prospering and promising.

The legislative enactments of this Conference might in a sense be called radical, but the influence of that which became law was far reaching in effect. One thing that led to the making of changes was a request made by the Rev. G. F. Taylor, who was General Superintendent, for suggestions to be submitted advocating changes which any member felt would be profitable. This seems to have created a spirit of cooperation which otherwise would not have existed, although it might be added that very few of these suggestions were accepted.

A few of the most important new developments were as follows: First, we have already mentioned the substitution of the word "Conference" for "Convention" in referring to all annual and general meetings. On the surface this may not be considered an important change, but actually it created considerably more respect for these sessions, and tended to give to them a dignity which they had not previously possessed.

One General Board

Second, a General Board was created which was designed to represent the whole Church and was delegated power second in many respects only to the General Conference. For the preceding four years there had been two General Boards, one to carry on the work at home while the other directed the work of the foreign field. Now the General Board does the work of the General Mission Board. This made for better coordination and eliminated unnecessary red-tape.

Quarterly Conferences Inaugurated

For a number of years the Rev. G. O. Gaines, Superintendent of the Georgia Conference had successfully employed the quarterly conference as an instrument to facilitate the conduct of Conference business. Those extra sessions had helped to bring the work of the Church under closer supervision and had promoted a unity and fellowship which otherwise would have been impossible. The General Conference was made to recognize the value of making this method of procedure universal. The Church has since been made to realize the debt it owes to G. O. Gaines who was largely responsible for this new development.

General Superintendents to Preside

Prior to this Conference it had been customary for the General Superintendent to be elected as chairman pro tem if he presided over the business sessions of a Conference. He might travel for miles to attend a Conference and then be disappointed or embarrassed to sit through the session and never be called upon to direct its business. This did not give to the General Superintendent any recognition beyond that of the State Superintendent, and in a sense not as much. This General Conference ordered that in the future the General Superintendent should preside at each Annual Conference when he was present. It was expected that he should direct the business of all such sessions. This new development made for a greater uniformity in the transaction of church business and it also helped to make the church more of a single corporate unit. The General Superintendent was also made ex-officio Chairman of the General Board.

In referring to the first Annual Conference which the late Rev. J. H. King conducted after being elected General Superintendent, he makes the following statement which reveals the attitude that was afterward assumed by all of the Annual Conferences toward the General Superintendent as the presiding officer at these sessions. He writes:

> At the close of Beulah Heights camp meeting I journeyed westward and came to Oklahoma City where I attended the closing services of a camp meeting in that city conducted by Rev. S. A. Bishop. The annual camp meeting of the Oklahoma Conference followed by the sessions of the Annual Conference, held in Drummond, Oklahoma, followed upon the close of the Oklahoma City Meeting. This was the first session of an Annual Conference that I attended after my election to the position of General Superintendent, and I had, to some degree, a feeling that perhaps my service in presiding over the deliberations of the Conference would not meet with full acceptance. But I was most gladly surprised at the reception given and the appreciation of the services I rendered in the ministry, and also as presiding officer of the Conference. Rev. S. A. Stark was Superintendent, and he was most congenial in spirit, in cooperating with and endorsing my work.

The Church Organ

The Conference also authorized the publication of an Official Organ to be known as the Pentecostal Holiness Advocate, to be begun May 1, 1917. The Rev. G. F. Taylor who had been General Superintendent of the Church during the preceding quadrennium was elected Editor of the proposed periodical, which was to appear weekly at the cost of $1.50 per year. Its publication was begun on May 3, 1917. A fuller account of this phase of the church's work may be seen in the History of Publications in the Pentecostal Holiness Church.

General Officers

The General official Board elected at this Conference included the following: J. H. King, Superintendent; S. D. Page, Assistant Superintendent; A. E. Robinson, Secretary; G. F. Taylor, Treasurer; R. B. Beall, S. A. Bishop and G. O. Gaines, Trustees.

Ministerial Standards

Still another new development worthy of mention is the setting of more rigid standards for licensure and ordination. It was ordered that no one should be granted license to preach who could not recite in consecutive order the Books of the Bible, and who had not read it through at least once. Candidates for ordination were required to have read the Bible through twice, and in addition were to read at least 1,000 pages of other suggested books in harmony with the doctrines of the Pentecostal Holiness Church.

Bible Conferences Begun

The 1917 General Conference also ordered a Bible Conference to be conducted once each year within the bounds of each Annual Conference. The first of these Bible Conferences to be conducted was at Durham, N. C. The late Bishop King in referring to the occasion writes:

> I had been appointed at the General Conference to conduct Bible Conferences in harmony with the act requiring such to be held in all conferences annually. I did not ask for this work to be done, but no appointment was ever given me that pleased me so well in all my life. I have never asked for an appointment in my ministerial life covering a period of 44 years, but if it should be the will of God and the Pentecostal Holiness Church I should be pleased to have this work given me for the remainder of my life. The first Bible Conference was held for the Western North Carolina Conference at the invitation of Rev. F. A. Dail, Superintendent, and it convened at Durham in May, 1917. The attendance was small, but we had a blessed time studying the subject of the Atonement.[1]

Church Headquarters

By 1918 there was a general feeling among the leaders of the Church that some suitable site should be selected where a Church headquarters could be located. For a number of years the beloved Rev. G. O. Gaines had prayed that the abandoned health resort property at Franklin Springs, Georgia, might some day belong to the Pentecostal Holiness Church. The eighty-seven acres, with the hotel buildings thereon were purchased in 1918 for the sum of $9,000.00. This property was easily adaptable for a school, an orphanage, a publishing house, and a gathering place for Annual

---

[1] J. H. King, **Autobiography**, (Unpublished manuscript).

and General Conferences, and other large assemblies, such as camp meeting or Bible Conferences. Full information regarding the purchase of this property is given in connection with the Emmanuel College in the section dealing with The History of Education in the Pentecostal Holiness Church.

Franklin Springs Camp Meeting Organized

The Franklin Springs Camp Meeting was conducted for the first time in August, 1918, prior to the opening of the school. Other information appears in the chapter on Camp Meetings in Section III which follows.

Emmanuel College Opened

On January 1, 1919 the Rev. G. F. Taylor opened the Franklin Springs Institute which has since become the Emmanuel College. Miss Blanche Moore, who later became Mrs. J. H. King, and Miss Ruby Gates, who was later married to the Rev. W. W. Carter, Superintendent of the Virginia Conference, were the first teachers assisting Mr. Taylor. The section on the History of Education in the Pentecostal Holiness Church gives the detailed information concerning this institution.

Franklin Springs Orphanage Opened

In April of 1919 there was also inaugurated an orphanage project which was intended to care for the orphan children of the entire Pentecostal Holiness Church. The Rev. J. H. King was elected by the General Board to serve as Superintendent of this new development. Mr. King had also been instrumental in initiating the orphanage work which was begun in Falcon, North Carolina ten years previously. It would appear that the Church had assumed more than it was financially able to support in opening the Franklin Springs Institute, building a publishing house and purchasing a church headquarters all in the course of so short a time. Attempts were made to secure sufficient support from the Church to finance the orphanage work, but with these other pressing obligations it proved to be impossible. At one time there were about 30 children in the orphanage, but in 1921 the project had to be abandoned, and most of the children were transferred to the Falcon Orphanage, which was not at that time church-owned.

Publishing House Built

Another new development was the erection of a publishing house for the Church. During 1919 a modest size building was constructed on the Franklin Springs property and with the October 16, 1919, issue of the Advocate, for the first time, the Church Organ was printed in its own home. The History of Publications in the Pentecostal Holiness Church contains full factual information about this new development.

CONGREGATIONAL HOLINESS CHURCH ORGANIZED, 1920

Among other new developments in this area of the Church's history is the defection of a major portion of the Georgia Annual Conference which formed the Congregational Holiness Church. The facts are that a bitter controversy arose in the Georgia Conference over the doctrine of divine healing as provided in the atonement. One faction contended that the provision in the Atonement for the healing of the body was all-sufficient, and that it was unnecessary to supplement any human means to assist God in effecting a healing. This faction admitted the therapeutic value of any effective remedy, but did not deem such as necessary for God to perform a healing in the body. The other side, which finally withdrew to form the Congregational Holiness Church, insisted that since God had placed remedies here He intended that these remedies should be used if a person expected to be healed. In other words they contended that we are healed by faith and works combined. The orthodox faction viewed the matter of insisting upon means to supplement faith in the atoning sacrifice as a denial of the all-sufficiency of Christ's provision for the body and that "by his stripes we are healed." They held that although means are permissible they are unnecessary. They believed that Jesus Christ is the same, yesterday, today and forever and will still heal independent of any human means all those who will trust him. The faction also advocated variant views regarding the Second Coming. The Rev. Watson Sorrow and quite a few other ministers and laymen withdrew under his leadership and formed the Congregational Holiness Church. The name of the Church indicates that they also objected to the leanings in the Pentecostal Holiness Church toward Episcopal church polity.

278 HISTORY OF THE PENTECOSTAL HOLINESS CHURCH

THE BALTIMORE CONFERENCE ORGANIZED, 1921

(Since 1944 this Conference has been called the Eastern Virginia Conference.)

In April, 1921, the Rev. J. H. King organized the Baltimore Conference in the city of Baltimore, Maryland. The eastern part of Virginia, Delaware, and one or two churches in the northeastern section of North Carolina were included in the territory of this new Conference. It was unfortunate that those of this Conference who were sincere lacked stability while others who were leaders were corrupt, and it finally became necessary to expel them from the Conference. This was done after an extended period of controversy and dissatisfaction.

The Baltimore Conference, since 1944 called the Eastern Virginia Conference, under the able leadership of men like J. A. Synan, and in recent years J. H. Mashburn, has made rapid strides. They have set the pace in good business policies which have been adopted from time to time, especially with regard to their Conference budget. Able pastors like the Revs. L. B. Edge and his wife, Byon A. Jones, A. D. Beacham, Lindsay Synan, T. K. Howard, Irving Baccus, E. L. Boyce and others have built up substantial churches which are among the best in the entire Pentecostal Holiness Church movement. This Conference has recently spent $35,000.00 in providing a Conference camp meeting grounds between Richmond and Hopewell.

THE FOURTH GENERAL CONFERENCE, ROANOKE, VA., 1921

The Fourth General Conference opened its sessions on Tuesday, May 3, 1921, at 9 A. M., and continued for a period of 7 days. On the whole this Conference was a good one, although it cannot be said that as many important and far-reaching items of business were transacted as had been at Abbeville in 1917. The General Superintendent opened the meeting with a sermon which was followed by a communion service and a testimony meeting.

The Enrollment

The afternoon session opened at 2 P. M. at which time the delegates were enrolled. There arose considerable controversy and debate because of a protest which came from the members of the North Carolina Conference concerning an alleged irregularity in the organization of the Baltimore Conference. A "Committee on Boundaries" was elected to settle the matter, and reported that the preachers and Official Boards of each North Carolina local church involved should have granted the North Carolina Conference Officials the courtesy of consulting them regarding their intended actions and thus have sought to arrive at some mutual agreement. This committee suggested a dividing line, subject to approval of both conferences. After a time the delegates of the new Conference were duly enrolled. More than fifty delegates were present in all. The Baltimore Conference was the only new Annual Conference added during the quadrennium, but the Alabama Conference had been merged with the one in Georgia. There were therefore ten Annual Conferences, the same number which were in existence at the time of the Third Conference.

General Board Increased

The Rev. J. H. King was reelected General Superintendent for the coming four years. It was decided at this time to elect two Assistant General Superintendents. The Revs. S. A. Bishop and E. D. Reeves were elected as these Assistants. The Rev. L. R. Graham was elected as General Secretary succeeding Mr. A. E. Robinson; and the Rev. G. F. Taylor was elected General Treasurer. The following ministers were added to complete the General Board: The Revs. Paul F. Beacham, Ralph Taylor, F. L. Bramblett, A. H. Butler, R. B. Beall, and F. M. Britton. There were some who felt that there was no need for two General Assistants. There were now approximately 6,000 members, which was an increase of about 1,000 during the quadrennium, but the increase perhaps did not justify the increase in the number of officials. It is true, however, that such made for a more democratic set-up.

The Rev. S. A. Bishop who had been elected as one of the General Superintendents was sent to preside over the Oklahoma and Memphis Conferences. He also was the Oklahoma Camp Meeting speaker, which runs concurrently with the Oklahoma Conference. Since 1913 there have been four Annual Conferences which have conducted a camp meeting in connection with their annual Conference. This works considerable hardship for one man to do this combined work. The Rev. E. D. Reeves was sent to preside over the Oklahoma Conference in 1922.

Printing Office Debt

The matter of the printing office debt was presented by Mr. G. F. Taylor and it was suggested that 60 cents per member (6,000) would raise the needed $3600.00 and the indebtedness could thus be retired without difficulty.

Miscellaneous

Various committees were elected and reports made which called for a few minor changes in the Discipline governing the organizational machinery of the Church, the sale of church property and the membership of missionaries on the foreign fields; the imperative need of education in the Pentecostal Holiness Church was stressed, and at the same time a warning was sounded to caution against unconsecrated education. Especially were the people of the Church urged to support the new Franklin Springs Church school and at the same time not to overlook the commendable work and definite place of the Falcon School and Holmes Bible Missionary Institute. This Conference also did much to encourage reading and study, raising the standards and making more rigid requirements of ministerial candidates. In addition the Rev. G. F. Taylor and J. H. King were selected and commissioned to write a book on theology, which was to be included in the required list of books for ministers wishing to qualify for ordination to the ministry. This volume, however, was never published.

South Georgia Conference Organized, 1922

The South Georgia Conference was organized in 1922 and continued to exist until after 1925 General Conference. The Revs. G. Sigwalt and H. W. Hampton served as Superintendents of this Conference which later became a part of the Florida Conference.

East Oklahoma Conference Organized, 1924

In 1924 the Rev. J. H. King organized the East Oklahoma Conference which was to some extent the result of a faction which had developed in the Oklahoma Conference because of differences in opinion as to the amount of emotional manifestation which should be encouraged in religious expression. Some, it seems, were over zealous and were demanding unrestrained expression which had climaxed in somewhat extravagant behaviour. It should be remembered that the people of the West are accustomed to the wide-open spaces and it comes natural for them to revolt against anything that would curb their traditional liberty. This case furnishes just another example in a measure comparable to the "gift movement" which was mentioned in an earlier paragraph. Those who were involved are not to be unduly criticized, but sympathetically understood and appreciated. Their zeal for spiritual attainments should have been tempered by more knowledge, but what live church organization has not in time had to correct such disorders among the best of its people? The maturity which is acquired through experience has since that time been developed, and has produced one of the most progressive Conferences in the entire Church. When unrestrained expression has yielded to the restraint of rational control it becomes a constructive force which is unmatched.

MISSOURI CONFERENCE ORGANIZED, 1924

The Missouri Conference of the Pentecostal Holiness Church assembled for its first Annual meeting with the Manila Church, Manila, Arkansas, August 7, 1924, 4 P. M. with the Rev. J. H. King, General Superintendent in the chair. After reading from I Thessalonians he brought an instructive and inspiring message, after which the conference was called to order and duly organized. Mr. E. I. King was elected as Superintendent. This Conference was short lived, being consolidated with the Tennessee Conference in 1926. The combined organization took the name of the Tri-State Conference.

ALABAMA CONFERENCE DISAPPEARS IN 1918 AND REAPPEARS, 1924

The Alabama Conference, which had been organized in 1915, was discontinued after the 1918 meeting because of the fact that there was not a sufficient number of churches to warrant its continuance. It became a part of the Georgia Conference until 1924 when it was revived. The Rev. S. A. Bishop was the Superintendent for the first three years. The Rev. J. W. Gaines was Superintendent in 1924 when it was revived. The Rev. O. N. Todd, Sr., headed the Conference from 1925 to 1928. He was succeeded by the Rev. C. B. Till who served from 1929-1932 and was succeeded by the Rev. R. L. McGougan being followed by the Rev. J. W. Cato who served from 1933-1938. After Mr. Cato, the Rev. Mr. Till again became its head from 1938-1940 when the Rev. O. N. Todd, Sr. was elected for a second term serving one year and being succeeded again by the Rev. C. B. Till who served from 1941-1943 when the Rev. L. T. Pressley was elected and served one year. In 1944 the Rev. V. V. Pate was elected to head the conference, and has energetically directed its work until the present time.

It seems well that special mention should be made of the fact that, in 1930, the Rev. C. B. Till and the Rev. S. D. Page received the Free-Will Holiness Church into this communion. This organization included three local churches and five ministers, and it may be said to be the beginning of the Pentecostal Holiness Church in Southern Alabama.

PENNSYLVANIA CONFERENCE ORGANIZED, 1924

On November 5, 1924 the Rev. Mr. King organized the Pennsylvania Conference at Sharon, Pennsylvania. It was begun with two churches and eight ministers. J. H. Mashburn and James F. Eppes were transferred from the North Carolina Conference. Mr. Eppes was elected Superintendent, Mrs. Jerome Plummer as Assistant and J. H. Mashburn as Secretary and Treasurer. A motion was adopted providing that a Camp Meeting should be organized in connection with the Conference, and Greenville was the place selected for these meetings which began in 1925. Through the years the Pennsylvania Conference has made some progress and now under the determined and able leadership of the Rev. Marvin Parrish it is destined to make even greater strides in the future. Under the leadership of J. E. Knapp, Charles A. Bailey, G. H. Montgomery, E. E. Howard, O. E. Sproull and others the Conference has steadily grown since its organization.

BUFFALO CONFERENCE ORGANIZED, 1924

United Pentecostal Association

After Mr. King had organized the Pennsylvania Conference, he went to Conneaut, Ohio, where he also organized the Buffalo Conference. What actually took place was that another church organization was consolidated with the Pentecostal Holiness Church. For the sake of charity it will be necessary to give some attention briefly to the history of the church group which was received.

For several years prior to 1915 the Rev. Mr. Erdman had preached among independent Pentecostal churches in and around Buffalo where he lived. Some had expressed the desire to create a central organization. In 1915 Mr. Erdman who was the recognized leader of this independent movement called a council meeting for the purpose of forming an organization. He was elected chairman pro tem and, after setting forth the purpose of the meeting, he called for the delegates to make their reports and express their desires. A motion was then offered that the United Pentecostal Association be organized and incorporated. Mr. Erdman was elected as its head. The churches which were brought into the organization were scattered through southwestern New York, northeastern Ohio, and western Pennsylvania, but the principal church membership was localized around Buffalo.

During the time this Association had been in existence Mr. Erdman had preached among Pentecostal Holiness people at the Falcon and Piney Grove Camp Meetings and was well known to many of them. He had also invited Pentecostal Holiness ministers to preach among the churches of his organization. And thus it was that he was instrumental in having Mr. King bring these churches into what was called the Buffalo Conference of the Pentecostal Holiness Church. But when Mr. Erdman died in 1927 all of these churches withdrew except those at Greenville, Pennsylvania, and Conneaut, Ohio, which were received into the Pennsylvania Conference and the Buffalo Conference was thus dissolved. In 1947 the Rev. James F. Epps was asked by certain people in Buffalo to return to preach among them in the hope that there could be reorganized a Pentecostal Holiness Church in Buffalo. As a result of his efforts an organization was effected and according to recent reports from the Rev. Marvin Parrish, Superintendent of the Pennsylvania Conference of which the new church is a part, this work is one of the most promising. Perhaps it should be added that the reason for the defection of most of the churches in this group after Mr. Erdman's death can be assigned to the fact that the people of this Association were not well-grounded in the doctrine of sanctification as a second work of grace. They withdrew and became independent rather than yield, but have since seen the fruit of a Pentecostal movement which fails to emphasize this experience, and are glad to have a second opportunity to become identified with the Pentecostal Holiness Church which stresses this doctrinal teaching.

(From 1932 to 1934 the Pennsylvania Conference was consolidated with the Baltimore Conference but they were again separated because of the widely scattered churches which made it infeasible to continue as a single conference and it was decided to divide them again. This time the dividing line was set at the Potomac River which took the Baltimore, Washington and Rahway (New Jersey) churches out of the original Baltimore Conference. Although this caused some dissatisfaction among the brethren of the old Baltimore Conference, in time they reluctantly yielded.)

TEXAS CONFERENCE ORGANIZED, 1925

Still another new development is to be seen in the organization of the Texas Conference. The Rev. J. H. King effected this organization on August 7, 1925, at Healdton, Oklahoma. This conference was created by the authority and consent of the Official Boards of Oklahoma and East Oklahoma Conferences each of which gave a portion of their territories in Southern Oklahoma and Texas. The Rev. F. M. Kidd was elected Superintendent, K. E. Jolliff as Assistant, C. F. Kennedy as Secretary and Treasurer, C. W. Gaither and D. P. Thurman to complete the Board.

This brings us to the close of a period in the history of the Pentecostal Holiness Church which is marked by "New Developments." Some of these developments were doubtless premature, which has already been suggested, and as a result there developed "growing pains," the consideration of which will occupy our attention in the following chapter.

Chapter III
GROWING PAINS AND REVERSES, 1925-1932

The laws which govern the progress and growth in any field of endeavor seem to demand that after a period of rapid growth there must also come a levelling-off period. Out of those plateau experiences of arrested development there comes, as a consequence what may be called "growing pains." Certain phases of the programs which have been initiated we discover have to be discarded because they fail to weather the pragmatic test. This is discouraging. In this settling down period an organization becomes conscious of its faulty and inadequate organizational machinery and it takes time to discover wherein the trouble lies, but this must be done in order to prescribe a potent remedy which will effect a cure. During such periods it is extremely easy to become critical of one another while making an attempt to analyze the problems which have emerged unexpectedly from what seemed to be a placid sea.

When an organization is small and is passing through the inchoate stage of its development only a few individuals are willing to risk the chance of inaugurating new developments which are essential for the promotion of a given enterprise. Since this is true, it is also true that such new developments become centered around a few individuals who possess an intrepid spirit to dare and do. Through the gruelling process of hard toil and severe sacrifice resolute persons are able to achieve some measure of success. They gain the good will and confidence of the members of their organization and are enthusiastically eager to attempt even greater achievements to accomplish the desired goals. They succumb to a human weakness and yield to the temptation to "plunge." The discovery is then made that a sizeable debt has been incurred and those who had cheerfully supported other such projects became discouraged and less willing to give. This causes a "growing pain."

An organization which has been thus developed naturally comes to depend heavily upon the individuals around whom it has been built. To remove such persons calls for readjustment, and that readjustment involves "growing pains." Yet it should be recognized that these individuals assumed the responsibility when no one else was willing to take it, and they became the victim of circumstances, having become unconsciously involved in unavoidable situations. Their success causes some to become jealous, while others have their misgivings, and come to question the intentions of such individuals. As the process of organization develops the individuals around which an infant organization is built must eventually recede into the background and give way to organized groups of men. Projects which have previously been individually-owned and almost individually-operated become church-owned and church-operated. This transition cannot be realized without "growing pains."

This is an accurate description of what took place in the Pentecostal Holiness Church. The esteemed Rev. G. F. Taylor began the publication of the Sunday school literature in 1913 when neither the Church itself, nor any other individual in the Church, was willing to do it. Through untold sacrifice and toil from early until late he labored, not to build up something for himself, but to promote the cause he loved. His faithful wife willingly joined him in the sacrifice which meant many deprivations for their growing family. Then someone had to edit the Church Organ which was begun May 3, 1917. He was elected to do it at no salary. A publishing house business must be begun. He began it and built it from nothing to the point where in 1929, when the literature was purchased from him by the Pentecostal Holiness Church, it was paying a net profit of $2,000 a year. Somebody had to start a church-school and when Franklin Springs Institute was opened on January 1, 1919, Mr. Taylor was its founder. In the meantime, in 1918, the Franklin Springs property was purchased for a church headquarters. G. F. Taylor took the major responsibility of raising the necessary funds to pay this indebtedness. The same is true concerning paying for the Publishing House and machinery in 1919. These funds were raised through appeals made through the Church Organ, the Advocate. All of these projects involved Mr. Taylor. Fate seems to have chosen that he should take the initiative in going ahead. Eleven years of strenuous work and sacrifice were spent from January, 1907, until December. 1918, at Falcon, North Carolina, connected with the Falcon Holiness School and the Falcon Publishing Company, and beginning in 1919 we have just noted some of his manifold activities. Then beginning in 1922, until 1926, the Franklin Springs Institute was operated as a faith school.

Everything moved along with a fair degree of smoothness and in 1924 a new building was erected to provide adequate classrooms for the rapidly increasing enrollment of students who were attracted to an institution which was operated by faith and made it possible for even those without means to be admitted. It was also near the time for the General Conference to convene in 1925, which was scheduled to hold its sessions at Franklin Springs. The new building had been built with a dual purpose, to provide both classrooms and an auditorium for the student body and also to be able to entertain such general gatherings of the Church. It has already been related elsewhere in connection with the History of Education how Mr. Taylor made substantial personal contributions to avoid embarrassment of not having this building ready and seated for the General Conference. In order to provide this building a debt was incurred which took a long while to liquidate, for reasons which have been suggested, and for additional reasons which will be seen presently. Again, these were growing pains. We will now turn our attention to the Fifth General Conference and note some of the developments at that meeting. (All of the aforegoing facts are more comprehensively treated in the sections which deal with the History of Education and the History of Publications in the Pentecostal Holiness Church).

THE FIFTH GENERAL CONFERENCE, FRANKLIN SPRINGS, GA., 1925

The Fifth General Conference of the Pentecostal Holiness Church was held at Franklin Springs, Georgia from May 5-11, 1925. The General Superintendent, Rev. J. H. King, expressed for the Franklin Springs community, a hearty welcome to all the visitors and delegates, calling attention to the answered prayer as evinced by the property and improvements in and around the Springs. Remarks were made to encourage unity and to erase any possible sectional barriers which might exist in an expanding church.

During the quadrennium since the last General Conference there were brought into existence seven additional Annual Conferences, making a total of 17 in all. It was not until after 1937, twelve years later, that the total number of Annual Conferences exceeded seventeen. The Alabama Conference which had existed from 1915 to 1918 was revived in 1924; The Pennsylvania, East Oklahoma, Buffalo, and Missouri Conferences were organized in 1924; the Texas in 1925, and the South Georgia in 1922. This represents the greatest number of Annual Conferences to be added during any quadrennium in the history of the Pentecostal Holiness Church. The increase in total church membership, however, was a little less than three thousand, and yet this represents about a 50% gain. During this four year period Mr. King reported that he had conducted 32 Annual Conferences and had assigned 10 to his Assistants. He had conducted 28 Bible Conferences, attended 8 camp meetings and had traveled approximately 60,000 miles and had received between six and seven thousand dollars for his services during the quadrennium. Others of the General Officers reported they had also been very busy in their work. With each of their reports a statement was made with regard to their relationship to the Ku Klux Klan, which indicates there was considerable controversy about the attitude a Christian should take toward that organization.

Foreign Missions

The Missions report indicates that each of the Conferences made at least some contribution for Foreign Missions, which contributions together aggregated $77,639.56. The Western North Carolina Conference led, giving more than $14,000.00 of this amount.

Education

The Report of the Committee on Education is significant for two reasons: first, because of the emphasis which is laid on the need of education among the ministry, and second, because of the recommendation to create a Pentecostal Young People's Society. In the preamble of this report are the following lines which definitely indicate that the denomination had by this time made perceptible progress away from the "radical sect" stage and was moving in the direction of becoming what is commonly termed a "respectable" denomination. The committee report reads:

> We your committee on Education beg to submit the following report: Having gone over the field with its needs, we find that the education demands upon us are great; we find that Greenville, Falcon and Franklin Springs Schools have done great good in the past, for which we highly commend them. We note with profound pleasure the work that has been accomplished in the schools at Greenville, S. C. and Falcon, N. C. We give our unqualified endorsement, and wish to express our sincere gratitude to the faculties of these schools for their unselfish and untiring labors in their respective fields, and we desire to express further the hope that our people will take advantage of the services these schools offer and will assist this worthy cause.
>
> We are not unmindful of, or ungrateful for the work which has already been accomplished by some of our brethren in the field of education; they have wrought faithfully and well; nor do we forget the fact that hundreds and thousands of people have been blessed under the ministry of our noble workers in the past; but today finds us facing a new era. We feel that Jehovah God has committed to us a message which alone our ministry can supply.
>
> (The dignity of such a position demands, that our preachers be prepared to so present this message that it will appeal to the cultured as well as the crude.)[1]

Since that time some have come to question the advisability of continuing the emphasis on education lest the Church should in the process divest herself of those rugged characteristics which make an appeal to the untutored and socially-inferior groups to which in the purpose of the Almighty it was commissioned to minister. Although educational standards have been raised in our day there will always be a preponderance of the simple common people, and those, with little exception, are the only type of people who will receive the gospel which the Pentecostal Holiness Church was brought into existence to preach.

Young People's Society

The thing of particular note which transpired during this Conference was the creation of the Pentecostal Young People's Society, which was to have its headquarters at Franklin Springs, and to have three general officers, viz., a President, Vice-President, and Secretary and Treasurer, who were to be elected by the

---

[1] **Minutes of the Fifth General Conference of the Pentecostal Holiness Church,** (which convened at Franklin Springs, Ga., May 5-11, 1925), pp. 16-17.

General Official Board of the Church. The duties of this General Board of the Youth Society were to formulate a constitution and by-laws by which the various societies were to operate. Similar Boards or Committees were to be organized in the Annual Conferences and the local churches, all of these organizational set-ups were expected to cooperate with one another and were subject to the jurisdiction of the General Committee. This organization, like others which have appeared from time to time, was the natural outgrowth to be expected with the increase in church enrollment, but it constituted a "growing pain." It made but little progress in the years immediately following its inception. More will be found concerning its development in a separate chapter.

New Editor for the Advocate

Some changes were made in the Discipline, among which an important one had to do with the Official Organ and the work of Publications, providing for the election of an Associate Editor and Business Manager in addition to the Editor who had previously handled this work without such aid. The Rev. G. F. Taylor asked to be relieved of his editorial work because of other pressing duties in connection with the Franklin Springs Institute and various other work which engaged his attention. The Rev. J. H. King was elected as Editor, and Mr. R. H. Lee was elected as Associate Editor and Business Manager of the Publishing House.

General officers

The following General Officers were elected for the coming quadrennium: J. H. King, General Superintendent; S. A. Bishop and E. D. Reeves as Assistant General Superintendents, L. R. Graham, General Secretary and A. M. Taylor, General Treasurer. R. B. Beall, P. F. Beacham, A. L. Jackson, F. L. Bramblett, Ralph Taylor and A. H. Butler were elected to complete the Board.

Summary and Outlook

The Conference on the whole was a good one but the years which followed were filled with disappointments and pain. Such were the inevitable outcome to be expected at this stage of development and growth, for reasons which have already been given in the beginning of this chapter. A number of reverses which God allowed to come aggravated and accentuated these natural developments. There were a number of reverses which God permitted to come.

During the period which intervened between the Fifth and Sixth General Conferences, from 1925 to 1929, there was no change in the total number of Annual Conferences but there were considerable changes in the appearance and disappearances of Conferences. The South Georgia Conference which had been organized out of the Florida Conference in 1922 was again incorporated in that Conference in 1926. The Missouri and Tennessee Conferences which appeared in 1924 were consolidated to form the Tri-State Conference in 1926. The Buffalo Conference, which had been organized when the United Pentecostal Association became a part of the Pentecostal Holiness Church, became a part of the Pennsylvania Conference in 1927. The West Virginia Conference was organized out of the Virginia Conference in 1925 and continued to exist until after 1929 when it again became a part of the Virginia Conference. The Arkansas Conference was organized in 1928 and continued to exist until 1930. The Kansas Conference was organized in 1926. The South Georgia, Buffalo, Missouri and Tennessee Conferences ceased to exist, but the Tri-State, Kansas, Arkansas and West Virginia Conferences were brought into existence and thus the total number of Conferences remained the same during that quadrennium.

REVERSES[1]

G. F. Taylor Resigns to Continue Education

On January 19, 1926, after the Fifth General Conference, the Rev. G. F. Taylor tendered his resignation, stating that he desired to continue his education that fall, in the hope that he could later establish a Junior College for the Church. Mr. Taylor returned to the University of North Carolina where he was awarded the Bachelor of Arts Degree in 1928. When he left the Franklin Springs Institution it was immediately changed

---

1 A more detailed historical account of all these "Reverses" will be found in the separate sections which deal with the History of Education and History of Publications in the Pentecostal Holiness Church.

from a faith school as it had been operated since 1922, and was operated on a regular board and tuition basis. Professor A. M. Taylor who had been a member of the school's faculty was chosen in G. F. Taylor's place as head of the institution. This constituted one of the most severe "growing pains." G. F. Taylor had operated the school by faith for four years. There were naturally more students to attend under those circumstances. He had erected a new school building, as has been noted. There was a considerable debt still against the building. No one could well fit into his place since he had necessarily built the work around himself and had assumed the greatest portion of the responsibility. No one else was quite as willing to make the same sacrifice, nor was there another person who could readily win the confidence and support of the constituency of the church. His absence involved all these things and more. He was also missed as Editor of the Advocate.

Dormitory Burns

The school's next term had barely begun when early on Saturday morning, October 23, 1926, the Upper Hotel or Boys' Dormitory at Franklin Springs caught fire and in a few minutes was razed to the ground. There was no insurance to cover the loss which was sustained. The meagre enrollment, the heavy indebtedness and other discouraging factors were climaxed by Mr. A. M. Taylor's resignation at the close of the school term.

From 1927-29 the Rev. Byon A. Jones served as President of the Institution, and made a desperate attempt to promote the interest of the school until such time that G. F. Taylor might finish his education and return to his post as President.

Other Dormitory Burns

Another great reverse came to the Church on March 23, 1928, when the only remaining dormitory was also reduced to ashes. The General Board of the Church met at Franklin Springs on the 24th of April and adopted a motion to build another dormitory. It was extremely difficult to raise funds from a discouraged Church which was already chafing under the burden of the indebtedness which remained on the building that had been erected in 1924-25. The Rev. Byon A. Jones deserves a great deal of credit for the hard work and sacrifices which he made during these difficult years in attempting to build a new dormitory and carry on the school work.

KING'S COLLEGE, CHECOTAH, OKLAHOMA (1925-1932)

To augment these heavy church obligations another school was opened at Checotah, Oklahoma in 1925, called King's College. While this school was not sponsored by the whole Church it naturally took some support from the Franklin Springs Institute that might have come from the Conferences in the West, which were financing this project. Each section, East and West, was struggling to found a school. King's College was later moved to Kingfisher, Oklahoma where it operated until 1932, when it was closed because of a fire which destroyed the main building. Here was another reverse, combined with a "growing pain."

THE SIXTH GENERAL CONFERENCE, OKLAHOMA CITY, 1929

As a climax to all of these reverses there were developed two propositions which were intended to solve the problems which had thus arisen. During 1926, when Mr. A. M. Taylor was head of the school, because of the dormitory-fire and other complications which resulted while Mr. G. F. Taylor was away finishing his education, the General Board of Administration voted to sell the property, but were disappointed to learn that the prospective offer was not bona fide. The news of their decision caused Mr. J. A. Culbreth to make the Church a very attractive offer just before time for the General Conference to meet, in the hope that that body would vote to accept it. He offered to turn over to the Pentecostal Holiness Church the Falcon Holiness School and Orphanage, if they would agree to perpetuate these works which he had begun at Falcon, North Carolina several years previously. His offer was published in the Advocate to acquaint the whole Church with all of the details. Then another article appeared which was written by the Rev. J. H. King in which he set forth a number of reasons why the Church should not accept Mr. Culbreth's offer.

Church Buys G. F. Taylor's Literature Business

Still another proposition came from the Rev. G. F. Taylor which was also published in the Advocate before time for the

General Conference to meet. He had just completed his work at the University of North Carolina, being awarded the Bachelor of Arts degree in 1928. He was anxious to devise some plan whereby he could realize a life's ambition to be able to establish a Junior College. His proposition was rejected, but the General Conference made him a counter offer which he immediately accepted. This offer stipulated that the annual profits from the sale of Sunday school literature should be used to subsidize the educational work of the Church after he had been paid $8,000.00 for his literature in quarterly installments of $500.00 each.

COMMITTEE RECOMMENDATIONS*

Publications

The first Year Book of the Pentecostal Holiness Church was published and distributed at a minimum price. A Board of Publications was created to investigate the merits of all proposed publications, such as books, booklets, pamphlets, and tracts, and to supervise their issuance and distribution. This Board was also commissioned to produce such tracts as would set forth the doctrines of the Pentecostal Holiness Church. A separate department of the Advocate was also recommended, for the publicizing and emphasizing of the Pentecostal Young People's Society; a similar department was to be devoted to the announcement of revivals, camp meetings and evangelists' schedules of their meetings. Also adequate provision was made to acquaint and inform the Church of the work of the Falcon Orphanage.

Discipline

The Disciplinary Committee made several corrections and improvements in the Discipline, the most important of which was the "Articles of Faith" section inserted between the Basis of Union and the General Rules.

Foreign Missions

A Bible training school, a home for the missionaries, and the general expansion of the African work was authorized. In India

---

*In 1929 was the first time the Pentecostal Holiness Church elected a Committee on Nominations delegated to select the personnel of other committees.

a home, industrial school, and church were ordered built. Similar improvements were recommended for the China work at Shaukiwan, Pakhoi, Yanchow and elsewhere.

Election of Officers

The Rev. J. H. King was re-elected the General Superintendent and the Revs. S. A. Bishop and E. D. Reeves were elected as his Assistants. The Rev. L. R. Graham was elected as General Secretary and the Rev. Paul F. Beacham was elected General Treasurer. The following were also elected to complete the General Board: A. L. Jackson, C. A. Stroud, Ralph Taylor, Dan T. Muse, S. E. Stark and J. A. Culbreth, making a total of eleven.

The Rev. G. F. Taylor was elected in the Rev. J. H. King's place as Editor of the Advocate, and also as Superintendent of the Franklin Springs Institute. The Rev. T. L. Aaron was elected President of the Pentecostal Young People's Society, and also as Editor of the Pentecostal Young People's Quarterly. Mr. R. H. Lee was re-elected as Associate Editor and Business Manager of the Official Organ and Publishing House.

ONTARIO CONFERENCE ORGANIZED, 1929

After the Oklahoma City General Conference in May, 1929, the Ontario Conference was organized at the first Pentecostal Holiness camp meeting near Markham, Ontario on July 6, 1929.[1] The first Annual Conference was held in the Toronto First Church, October 27, 1929. The Rev. Edward D. Reeves was elected as the first Superintendent and the Rev. Alpheus Noseworthy was elected as the first Secretary of that Conference. Since that time the Ontario Conference has grown to include 9 churches, the largest of which is the First Church of Toronto, of which the Rev. Alpheus Noseworthy is pastor. This church several years ago purchased a handsome building on East Gerrard Street which had formerly been occupied by the Presbyterian Church, which had become a part of the United Church of Canada. This edifice is one of the finest in the entire movement.

---

1 The Minutes of the Second Annual Session of the Ontario Conference of the Pentecostal Holiness Church reveal that the Second Conference met on October 21, 1931, which indicates the first annual conference was in October, 1930. Since Mr. Noseworthy was Secretary and furnished the above information there must have lapsed two years between the first two conferences.

Franklin Springs School Closed, 1931-1933

As we have noted the Rev. G. F. Taylor was again elected as head of the Franklin Springs Institute in 1929. The old debt on the building which he had erected in 1924-25 was still hanging over the Church. In addition to this there were financial obligations which had been incurred in erecting and furnishing the dormitory during the Rev. Byon A. Jones' administration from 1927-29. The profits from the sale of Sunday school literature, which had been allocated to subsidize the educational program, were being used to pay off the quarterly installments due Mr. Taylor for his literature business. For some reason the General Board saw fit to place the raising of funds for the school in other hands besides those of G. F. Taylor. The new dormitory was not sufficiently completed nor adequately furnished to receive students if they had come and the 1929 Depression hindered students from coming, and would have hindered their staying if they had come. All these factors combined to make it absolutely impossible to continue the school. There was a definite lack of cooperation and coordination within the Church, especially was this true regarding its educational program. When Mr. Taylor lost all hope of being able to remedy the situation he resigned, on July 2, 1931 and the school was ordered closed. In the meantime the installments which were due Mr. Taylor for the publishing house business were all paid by 1933 when the General Conference met at Marion, North Carolina.

Other Reverses

The Ozark Industrial College which had operated at Monte Ne, Arkansas since 1928 was forced to close in 1931, when all efforts failed in a desperate attempt to finance the project. The Triangle College and Emmanuel College of Milford, Texas, were also attempts to open schools which never materialized. And with these was the King's College which we have noted was closed in 1932 after a fire had destroyed the main building.

From 1925 to 1933 the Pentecostal Holiness Church passed through a period of "Growing Pains and Reverses" such as has been unprecedented in the history of the organization. We turn now to consider the events which transpired beginning with the General Conference in 1933.

Chapter IV
COORDINATION AND COOPERATION, 1933-44

From 1925-29 the Pentecostal Holiness Church passed through the hardest quadrennium in its history. It had reached a stage in its development where necessary adjustments had to be made. Such adjustments caused what we have chosen to term "growing pains." To augment these natural developments there came a number of reverses which taken all together threatened the organization's very existence. In 1925 there was a total church membership of 9,574 and by the end of the quadrennium, in 1929, there were 8,794 which represents a decrease of roughly a thousand members.

During the quadrennium from 1929 to 1933, however, there was a substantial increase, from 8,794 to a total of 15,447 members. This increase did not result so much from the fact that the Church had actually improved its organization machinery, but because of the depression years. The chief emphasis in the preaching of this Church and other related sects is upon heaven as the future abode of the righteous, and the eternal doom of the unrighteous. The emphasis is on "other-worldliness," therefore, during depression periods when social and economic conditions are in a sense favorable the Pentecostal and Holiness groups grow numerically, while other churches often show a decrease.

SEVENTH GENERAL CONFERENCE, MARION, N. C., 1933

By 1933 the leaders in the Pentecostal Holiness Church as a whole began to analyze their problems, and to make some deductions which proved to be helpful. In short, they came to realize the importance of coordinating their efforts and cooperating together if they were to achieve their goals, especially with relation to their endeavors in the field of educational developments. With an increase in total church membership of almost 70% there were indications which were encouraging, if some feasible plans could be formulated whereby there could be secured the general cooperation of the Church. The organization ceased to be "individual centered" in leadership, and had come to be operated as a more democratic organization. In other words what individuals had previously assumed the responsibility to undertake was now undertaken by the Church as a corporate unit.

General Conference Opens

The Conference opened on June 1, 1933, and continued until June 9. A lovely reception of welcome was extended the General Conference by representatives of the city of Marion, N. C. and the Ministerial Alliance of McDowell County on the evening before the Conference opened. This is an indication that the Pentecostal Holiness Church was becoming what is commonly designated as a more "respectable denomination." This can be interpreted as either favorable or unfavorable, according to the way it may be viewed. It was gaining worldly favor which has its advantages, but it also indicates that perhaps it had lost a degree of its spirituality. Various denominations invited Pentecostal Holiness ministers to fill their pulpits all over the county.

The Rev. J. H. King, General Superintendent, read Scriptures from Philippians 2:1-10; Eph. 1:15-22 and John 17:20-23. These were appropriate selections to exalt Christ and to promote a spirit of unity and cooperation. Mr. King, a few months before, had suffered a broken limb and was not too well in body. The Rev. S. A. Bishop, Assistant General Superintendent was called upon to preside frequently during the Conference.

There were still a total of 17 Annual Conferences although the Gulf Mission Conference was not represented at the 1933 General Conference. In 1930 the Arkansas Conference had been consolidated with the Oklahoma Conference; in the latter part of 1929 the West Virginia Conference had been consolidated with the Virginia Conference. These losses were offset by the organization of the Ontario Conference in June 1929, and the Gulf Mission Conference in 1932.

COMMITTEES

Connectional Societies and Administration

The usual type of committees were appointed to serve with one exception, a "Connectional Societies and Administration" committee was elected to formulate a "Sunday School Constitution" and a "General P. Y. P. S. Constitution." In the preamble to this Committee's report were the following statements:

> Recognizing the authority with which the Master Teacher instructed His Church, and further recognizing that the obligation contained in His parting message to "Teach all nations" is incumbent upon us as a Pentecostal Holiness Church in promoting a program of religious instruction in the Sunday School and P. Y. P. S., and further recognizing that these organizations maintained by the church for its constituency offer an opportunity for instilling Scriptural truths in the hearts of those who are young and tender, and instruction in doctrine to those who make up its membership, we, your committee, offer the following program of organization.[1]

These recommendations are too lengthy to present here, except to say that rules were set forth to govern membership, administration, election of officers and their duties, the duties of teachers and the divisions and departments of the Sunday School. In the General P. Y. P. S. Constitution various Articles were incorporated as follows: name, object, membership, officers, duties of officers, general convention, delegates, amendments, etc. The Annual P. Y. P. S. Convention was organized in the same manner.

These recommendations made for an over-all program which was coordinated, and which called for the cooperation of the whole church in an all-out effort. It also made for uniformity of procedure. In this committee's report we see reflected the characteristic trend which largely characterizes the history during this period beginning in 1933.

Evangelism (Home Missions)

In the report of the Committee on Evangelism there is to be seen reflected the same church-wide outlook, recommending a uniform program for raising funds and evangelizing in the Annual Conferences and also in the local churches. Emphasis is also laid upon the need of the united prayers of the whole Church which is seen in the following recommendation:

> Our evangelistic work, to meet with the success it ought to, must have the united prayers and encouragement of the (whole church) and this will require the cooperative efforts of all our people, from the

---

[1] **Minutes of the Seventh General Conference of the Pentecostal Holiness Church,** (Marion, N. C., June 1-9, 1933), p. 15.

General Superintendent down to the most humble individual member, working together harmoniously for the purpose of calling out a people for His name to be prepared by the full gospel which we preach, through the abundant grace of God for the coming of the Lord.[1]

Foreign Missions

Another example of "Coordination and Cooperation" is to be seen in the report of the Committee on Missions, part of which reads as follows:

We earnestly recommend that there be regular missionary meetings held every month in every one of our churches; that our pastors awake to the need of the non-Christian world, and take the lead in the missionary activities of their churches, and that they be a source of missionary information and inspiration; that they use their young people to forward this great work, and endeavor to interest the local Pentecostal Young People's Society in the missionary task; that their Sunday School be used as a medium for the dissemination of missionary interest; that they give to the monthly missionary meetings one of their prominent services, and that they urge their people to practice self denial in all departments of life, ever keeping the needs of the mission fields before their eyes.[2]

It is evident from these lines that the Church had grasped the importance of coordinating the various departments of the church's activity in all-out efforts for Foreign Missions as well as for Home Missions.

Educational Program

The most pronounced evidence of this characteristic trend, as we have noted, is to be seen in the developments made in the field of education. For the first time there was elected a General Educational Board separate from the General Official Board. They were as follows: T. L. Aaron, I. H. Presley, G. F. Taylor, W. J. Nash and R. H. Lee. This Educational Board was given the authority to formulate the educational program, making some sort of opportunity for those students desiring to work their way in cases where they were unable to pay. It was decided to reopen Franklin Springs if at all possible. A Secretary and Treasurer was elected to take care of all funds, this person being required to furnish an indemnity bond. The Educational Board also were to employ and dismiss teachers.

---

1 Ibid., pp. 29, 30.
2 Ibid., p. 28.

The responsibility which had been assumed almost entirely by individuals was now placed in the hands of the Educational Board. In this manner people over the Church generally began to feel that the Church school belonged to them in a more real sense. Of course the president of the institution continued to be an important person around whom revolved the major portion of the activities, but he was cleverly able to secure the cooperation and support of the church as a whole. King's College which had operated from 1925-32, and the Ozark Industrial College which was operated from 1928-31 were no longer in existence to create competition nor to divide the interests of the Church, which had only limited financial ability. Through the Advocate's pages and by word of mouth new interest was stimulated and the Franklin Springs Institute was immediately brought into sharp focus. God's favor seemed to have been upon this program, in that people took heart and regained confidence, and also because substantial revivals came among the student body resulting in the conversion of practically all of the unsaved students each year.

The Rev. T. L. Aaron was elected as the new president of the school by only a small margin. His name, with that of the Rev. G. F. Taylor, was placed in nomination and when the votes were counted some of Mr. Taylor's were thrown out because they had no initials on them. The Chair ruled that they could not be counted due to the fact that there were two other Taylors present. Had it not been for this technicality, which some interpreted as an unfair ruling, G. F. Taylor would have been elected president instead of T. L. Aaron. Mr. Aaron would have become president the following year anyway, for Mr. Taylor was unexpectedly called to his heavenly reward, which would have left the president's chair vacant.

Mr. Aaron took the school with its old debt, finished the dormitory, and has prosecuted a progressive program remarkably well in spite of many handicaps. While his administration has not been the sensational type, it has been stable and dependable.

Up until this time the Holmes Bible School had furnished the large majority of ministers and missionaries of the Church as is to be seen in the following motion:

In view of the fact that approximately 98% of our foreign missionaries, and a large per cent of our ministers have come from the

Holmes Institute, Resolve that we as a General Conference express our deep appreciation for its fine work and service to the Pentecostal Holiness Church.[1]

Subsequently, however, under a new educational program which was designed to function by coordination and cooperation, the Franklin Springs Institute began to make substantial contributions to the missionary and ministerial personnel. Mr. Aaron was also elected President of the Pentecostal Young People's Society, which gave him an excellent opportunity to coordinate this program with that of the school.

NEW CONFERENCES DURING QUADRENNIUM, 1933-1937

Panhandle Conference

On August 27, 1934, the Panhandle Conference was organized by the Rev. J. H. King with ministers and churches out of the Oklahoma Conference. The Rev. A. T. Kersey was elected as Superintendent and served until 1944 when the Rev. J. M. Lemmon became his successor and has guided the conference in a sane progressive program.

California Conference

The Rev. Mr. King also organized the California Conference out of the Oklahoma Conference churches and ministers on March 9, 1936. It might be said here that every Conference in the Midwest and West, excepting the British Columbia Conference, came either directly or indirectly from the original Oklahoma Conference which was organized in 1909 by F. M. Britton, Acting General Overseer of the Fire Baptized Holiness Church.

EIGHTH GENERAL CONFERENCE, ROANOKE, VA., 1937

In the quadrennium from 1933 to 1937 there still remained no change in the total number of Annual Conferences. The two new Conferences just mentioned above were offset by the loss of the Gulf Mission Conference and the Texas Conference, making the total stand at 17 Annual Conferences. The quadrennium was somewhat a levelling-off period in which the gains of the previous four year period were conserved and amalgamated. In 1933 the total church membership was 15,447, and in 1937 the

---
1 Ibid., pp. 33, 34.

total was 16,400, which shows an increase of less than 1,000 members.

The Eighth General Conference of the Pentecostal Holiness Church convened in the Roanoke, Virginia church at 9 A. M., Thursday, June 3, 1937, with the General Superintendent, J. H. King presiding. Scripture was read and followed by appropriate remarks after which the General Superintendent led in prayer. Due to the fact that the Rev. E. D. Reeves, Assistant Superintendent had passed to his reward on Feb. 4, 1936, and because the Rev. S. A. Bishop had not arrived for the Conference, the Rev. O. E. Sproull was elected as chairman pro tem. During the meeting he presided over some of the sessions, as did Mr. Bishop after his arrival.

Bishops Instead of General Superintendents

Corresponding to the church polity of the Methodist Church, which has largely influenced that of the Pentecostal Holiness Church, it was voted to change the title of "General Superintendent" to "Bishop," in 1937, 39 years after its inception in 1898. The Methodist Church which grew out of the Holy Club in the University of Oxford in 1729, did not make their change until 59 years later, in 1788.[1] The term "Bishop" is taken from the Greek; the term "Superintendent" is derived from the Latin, while both mean the same thing, "overseer."

Another significant change is to be seen in the fact that for the first time in the history of the Church there were elected two General Superintendents and one Assistant, instead of the customary one General Superintendent and two Assistants. To the General Board of Administration was delegated the authority to assign the work of these two General Superintendents. This actually amounted to an additional step toward better coordination and organization of the work of the Church. The Revs. J. H. King and Dan T. Muse were elected to fill these places, and the Rev. O. E. Sproull was elected to the office of Assistant General Superintendent. The Church therefore had two Bishops and one Junior Bishop to preside over the work for the ensuing quadrennium.

---

1 R. N. Price, op. cit., p. 16.

Evangelist General Elected to Direct Home Missions
(Evangelism)

As further evidence of coordinating the efforts of the Church in the work of Home Missions, an Evangelist General was ordered elected by the General Board whose duties it would be to plan and supervise the work of evangelism in the various Annual Conferences. The report of the Committee on Evangelism in this connection is significant in its entirety. It was as follows:

In order to solve the problem of evangelization the General Board shall elect an Evangelist General who will be sent out by this Conference to outline evangelistic programs in each Annual Conference in collaboration with the Official Boards of the Conferences. Your Committee specifies that the man elected to the office of Evangelist General shall be a man of competence from the standpoint of calling and successful experience in evangelistic work.

Let each Annual Conference elect a competent person to set in motion a Conference evangelistic program adaptable to its particular needs.

Let each local church organize an Evangelistic Society to operate on the same principle as our local Missionary societies.

We deplore the activities of incompetent, and often unscrupulous, evangelists whose work is detrimental to the cause of true evangelism, and urge all Annual Conferences to strive to counteract their unsavoury influence by organizing intelligent, Conference-wide campaigns to promote the principles and policies of Pentecostal Holiness.

Pursuant to the above recommendation there were elected "Conference Evangelists" in each of the Annual Conferences, and "Evangelistic Societies" in most of the local churches. In the process of a short time there came a somewhat church-wide revival from Canada to Florida and from the East to the West, wherever there were Pentecostal Holiness Churches. Through the medium of the Advocate, and through the ministry of these Conference Evangelists and others, the entire Church was called to prayer in behalf of this all-out revival effort. The Rev. J. A. Synan, being assisted by the Pentecostal Trio, the Frazier Brothers, conducted a very outstanding revival at the Danville, Virginia Church, in which scores were blessed, many receiving the baptism of the Holy Ghost. The news of this revival success seemed to sharpen the faith in other quarters, where revivals also broke out. The Rev. J. Louis Coward, Pastor of a church in Honea Path, S. C., was instrumental in promoting a revival under his ministry which affected the whole town and nearby country. There were other such revivals in the West about the same time. From 1937 to 1941 there was an increase in the total church membership of 6,349 as compared with less than 1,000 increase the previous quadrennium, and 1,760 increase during the quadrennium which followed from 1941 to 1945. There was also an increase of three Annual Conferences from 1937 to 1941. There seem to have been some of the Conference Superintendents who interpreted the Conference Evangelist's activity as a possible threat to their jobs and they were soon instrumental in having themselves elected to do this work, in addition to superintending their Conference. It was therefore not very long until the interest had subsided, and a somewhat different program was inaugurated, as we will note in a subsequent chapter.

New Editor of Advocate

The Rev. G. H. Montgomery was elected as Editor of the Advocate to succeed the Rev. J. H. King, who had taken that work after the Rev. G. F. Taylor's death in 1934, more as a matter of duty than by choice. Mr. King's heavy duties as General Superintendent of the Church were sufficient to occupy his time, and the editorial position worked on him a severe hardship, although he did an admirable job as editor. Since 1937 Mr. Montgomery has served as editor of the Church Organ, and by virtue of this position he has through his influence established a liaison between different departments, helping to coordinate them. The office of evangelist in the Church had for some years come to be thought of as a sort of "junk-heap" into which were cast those men who were not in demand as pastors. Mr. Montgomery did much through his writings to elevate the evangelist's position and to bring his work into prominence as it had been in the early history of the Church organization, at the same time discouraging the "unsavory influence" of the wrong kind of evangelist.

NEW CONFERENCES

Missouri, Maryland, and Colorado Conferences

Between 1937 and 1941 there were three new Conferences organized, viz., the Missouri Conference was organized in 1937, the Maryland Conference in June, 1940 and the Colorado Conference on September 20, 1940. This made a total of 20 Annual

Conferences, the first increase in Annual Conferences since the 1925 General Conference which had also met at Franklin Springs 16 years previously. (The name of the Baltimore Conference was changed to "Eastern Virginia" Conference in 1940).

NINTH ANNUAL CONFERENCE, FRANKLIN SPRINGS, GA., 1941

The Ninth General Conference of the Pentecostal Holiness Church met at Franklin Springs, Ga., June 5-12, 1941, with Bishop J. H. King presiding.

It was announced by the Chairman that the Rev. O. E. Sproull had withdrawn as Junior Bishop from the Pentecostal Holiness Church, and it was also announced that the General Secretary, Rev. I. H. Presley, had withdrawn from the Church. The Rev. Hubert T. Spence was elected as Secretary pro tem, with the Rev. Oscar Moore to assist him, to serve during the Conference. (Since that time Rev. Sproull and Rev. Presley have again united with the Church and are doing successful work as pastors in Florida and Alabama respectively).

General Officers Elected

In 1941 the Rev. Dan T. Muse received the highest number of votes for the office of Bishop, and for the first time since the Rev. J. H. King was elected as General Superintendent, in 1917, he failed to be elected as top Bishop but was elected as second highest official. The Rev. J. A. Synan was then elected as Junior Bishop, the Rev. Oscar Moore as General Secretary, and the Rev. Paul F. Beacham as General Treasurer. The Revs. Alpheus Noseworthy, H. T. Spence, B. R. Dean, T. A. Melton, W. W. Carter and T. L. Aaron were elected to complete the General Board.

The two most important happenings at this General Conference were the recommendations relating to "Home Missions" and those relating to "Education," both of which called for the continued cooperation and coordination of the work of the Church in these fields of endeavor.

Home Missions

At the previous General Conference, in 1937, a similar Home Missions project had been set up, called the report of the "Committee on Evangelism," which provided for the election of an Evangelist General to be elected by the General Board of Administration. Bishop King had been selected for this work and had met with some success, but it was felt that there should be a Superintendent of Evangelism elected who was not a Bishop, and who could give his full time to evangelistic work. Provision was made by the Finance Committee to pay the Superintendent out of the Evangelistic Fund which was to be created. The Rev. G. H. Montgomery was selected for this work. A Home Missions Board was created by the General Board, comprised of members of its own personnel, who were to direct and supervise Home Mission work. The Board under whom Mr. Montgomery worked was composed of the Revs. J. A. Synan, Hubert T. Spence, W. W. Carter, T. A. Melton and B. R. Dean. As a gesture to set an example for others, each of these men contributed $1.00 each to begin this fund, which was the first General Home Mission Fund to be created in the history of the Church. The primary object of this general church effort was to promote the interests of new field work in virgin territory, in the hope of enlarging the boundaries of the Church. This work had heretofore been conducted by Conferences or individuals without the corporate backing of the whole church in achieving their desired goals.

Education

There was an additional $6,000.00 per year recommended for the Emmanuel College, over and beyond the Publishing House profits which accrued each year from the sale of Sunday school literature. The West and other sections were anxious to develop educational institutions in their own territories, but it was agreed at that Conference that they would not attempt any such project, and that no funds would be diverted from the Franklin Springs school until it could become an accredited senior college. This was an evidence of the spirit of cooperation which existed in the Church at that time.

NEW CONFERENCES

British Columbia, Maritime, Mississippi, and West Oklahoma Conferences

In the four years which lapsed from 1941 to 1945 there were several new Conferences organized, among which were the British Columbia Conference which was organized by Bishop J. H. King; the Maritime Conference which was organized on Nov.

10, 1944, by Bishop Dan T. Muse; the Mississippi Conference; and the West Oklahoma Conference which was also organized by Bishop King on Aug. 28, 1944. (At the ninth meeting of the Texas Conference held at Sulphur, Oklahoma, August 8, 1933, the Texas Conference voted to consolidate with other Conferences, part going to the Oklahoma Conference, part to the East Oklahoma Conference and part to the Gulf Mission Conference. In 1933 the Gulf Mission Conference changed the name of the Conference to Texas). By 1945 there were a total of 24,509 members in the Pentecostal Holiness Church. This was an increase of 1,760 during the quadrennium.

Orphanage

On April 7, 1943 the Falcon Orphanage property was transferred to the Pentecostal Holiness Church, the details of which will appear in the chapter on "Orphanage and Eleemosynary Institutions."

Service Men's Commission

On June 10, 1943 the Service Men's Commission was set up in a meeting called for the Home Mission Board by Bishop J. A. Synan, in Cumberland, Maryland. Their action was followed by the General Board. This Commission was made up of ten men as follows: The Home Mission Board, with Bishop J. A. Synan as Chairman, the four general officers of the Pentecostal Holiness Youth Societies and the Rev. G. H. Montgomery, Superintendent of Evangelism. The Rev. Samuel J. Todd was then appointed Service Pastor and began his work on July 15, 1943. Further details will be found in the chapter captioned "The Chaplaincy and Service Pastor."

Woman's Auxiliary

On May 10, 1944, Mrs. John W. Berry called for a meeting of minister's wives of the North Carolina Conference with the idea of organizing a sort of preachers' wives club. The Rev. Eddie Morris, Superintendent of the North Carolina Conference, presided and organized the women of that Conference, Mrs. J. W. Berry being elected to head this organization. Laymen were also included. At this meeting the Rev. T. A. Melton was invited to address this group. Additional details appear in a separate chapter.

Chapter V
ORGANIZATIONAL DEVELOPMENTS
TENTH GENERAL CONFERENCE, OKLAHOMA CITY, 1945

The tenth General Conference of the Pentecostal Holiness Church met at Oklahoma City at 9 A. M., Thursday, June 7, 1945, with Bishop Dan T. Muse presiding. After a song and prayer, Bishop Muse and Bishop J. A. Synan read portions of Scripture and made appropriate comments. When the clerical and lay delegates were enrolled there proved to be representatives from twenty-five Annual Conferences besides the two conferences of the Mexican work in Texas and Mexico.[1]

With the period beginning in 1945 the Pentecostal Holiness Church entered upon a distinctly new era in its historical development which can well be described as a period of "Organizational Developments." The dry details of facts are interesting mainly as exhibiting the steady evolution of business methods in the church. This improvement was evidently due to an increase in experience and a growing intelligence among the preachers. There had come to be a consciousness of the need for setting definite objectives, and for organizing various groups so as to develop the greatest possible efficiency in an all-out coordinated effort. As evidence of the greater efficiency which had been developed in these General Conference Sessions, there was transacted about twice the usual amount of business in the same length of time. The Minutes of the 1945 General Conference required eighty pages as compared to an average of less than half that number in other General Conference meetings. The outlook was no longer provincial but Church-wide in extent, as will be seen in the examples which follow.

Service Pastor's Report

Mention has already been made of the Rev. Samuel J. Todd's assignment as Service Pastor, whose duties it was to visit Pente-

---
[1] Minutes of The Tenth General Conference of the Pentecostal Holiness Church (Oklahoma City, July 7-14, 1945), p. 30.

costal Holiness men in uniform all over the nation, and to raise funds in the various churches to carry on this work. In making his report to the 1945 General Conference there is reflected this church-wide outlook. He says:

> Let me take this occasion to thank the entire Church for every honor extended in placing me in the position of National Service Pastor and for the inspiring support given the Service Men's Commission. I thank God for the Pentecostal Holiness Church, her faith, her doctrine, and her standards. My life has been molded by her hands. My heart is vitally interested in her growth and expansion. I am happy to be a part of those who are committed to serving Christ and man through this Church.

These remarks not only reflect a church-wide outlook as an individual who is part of a denomination, but an ecumenical outlook viewing the Pentecostal Holiness Church as a unit in the mystical body of Christ, the whole Church. A more extended discussion of this phase of activity is reserved for separate treatment.

Woman's Auxiliary

Another example of General Organizational development, and a preview beyond local church or Conference boundaries which encompassed the whole denomination is illustrated by the report of the Woman's Auxiliary as follows:

> Inasmuch as we have groups of women who are organized under various names, and in view of the fact that we have no general organization of our women, we are asking this General Conference to organize the women as a church-wide group to be known as the Woman's Auxiliary of the Pentecostal Holiness Church.

More will be said about the Articles of Constitution and other information in the chapter which deals with this subject.

Pentecostal Holiness Youth Society

The Constitution Committee in its report recommended certain significant changes, which reflect church-wide organizational developments. The objectives of the P. H. Y. S. were to include five major emphases, viz., Christian experience, worship, study, service and fellowship. To help to realize these objectives the following recommendation was made:

> As an aid to realizing these objectives (a General P. H. Y. S. appears necessary) because it gives an opportunity for better cooperation,

more efficient coordination, and a means of helpful integration of all P. H. Y. S. activities in the Pentecostal Holiness Church.

A more extended discussion of this church-wide organizational set-up will appear in a separate chapter.

Committee on Resolutions

As an example of the improved business methods which were adopted in 1945, and to show something as to the ecumenical outlook of the Pentecostal Holiness Church, i. e., the ability to recognize the value of cooperating with and belonging to an organization of evangelical denominations, the following report is given here:

We, your Committee on Resolutions, offer the following recommendations:

1. That the General Board employ a Certified Public Accountant and have the books of the Publishing House, and the books of the following treasuries audited for the past quadrennium within ninety days:
    Board of Education
    General Treasury
    Home Mission Board
    Service Men's Commission

Also the books of the Falcon Orphanage for the past twenty-six months.

2. That said books be audited annually thereafter.

3. We recommend that the General Conference ratify the action of the General Board to place the Pentecostal Holiness Church in affiliation with the National Association of Evangelicals; that we pledge one thousand dollars a year to the support of the Association.

                Respectfully submitted,
                      Signed:
                      J. W. Berry
                      J. W. Kelly
                      R. E. Powers
                      J. V. Shipley
                      A. T. Kersey
                      P. W. Oxley
                      Lee Hargis[1]

Foreign Missions

The report of the Committee on Foreign Missions reveals the same trend toward a definite church-wide organization, and an

---

[1] Ibid., pp. 34, 35.

administrative set-up similar to that in the Home Mission Board. This makes for a coordinated program, a closer supervision, and a more equitable distribution of missionary funds, as well as for better cooperation generally in the Conferences and local churches in interest of foreign missionary work. The report reads as follows:

Viewing the signs of the imminent end of the age and the coming of the Lord, the increasing need of speedy world-wide evangelization, coupled with the fact that many of our consecrated young people are offering themselves for service, we feel it incumbent upon us to take forward steps. To this end we recommend:
1. That a Foreign Mission Board be elected by the General Conference.
2. That this Board shall consist of five members, one of whom, to act as chairman, shall be chosen from the Executive Board of administration.
3. That this Board shall have the supervision of foreign mission work of our Church, receiving and disbursing funds raised for foreign missions; examination and approval of candidates, and such other business as may arise in connection with foreign mission work in our Church.
4. That we have a full time corresponding secretary of Foreign Missions, chosen from the membership of this Board.
5. We request a minimum budget of seventy-five thousand dollars annually for foreign missions, aside from the postwar balance now on hand in the General Treasury.
6. That Sec. VIII, par. 2 in our Discipline be amended to read 'all candidates for the foreign mission field shall be examined by this Board as to their qualifications for foreign missionary work, having been recommended by the Board of the Annual Conference in which they hold membership.'
7. That this Board shall establish a standard of qualifications for prospective missionaries.
8. That this Board shall determine the length of service between furloughs for missionaries, and provide for their financial support while on furlough, placing all on equal basis as far as practical.
9. That this Board shall review conditions as to prevailing standards of living and adjust allowances to missionaries in accordance therewith, that they may give their full time to missionary work.
          Signed:
          J. H. King, Chairman
          A. E. Robinson, Secretary[1]

Sunday School Committee

The Sunday School Committee also recommended that the 1945

---
1 Ibid., p. 35.

General Conference elect a General President, Vice President, and Secretary-Treasurer to head the Sunday School work throughout the Church and that such officers should be elected each quadrennium. Provision was made for a similar organizational set-up to be inaugurated in the local Annual Conferences over the whole Church. The Sunday School work was also to be coordinated with the various other branches of work throughout the church. More details will appear in the separate chapter dealing with the subject.

Finance

The Finance Committee encouraged tithing on a church-wide basis: the church members in their local church treasury; the local churches in their Annual Conference treasury and the Annual Conferences and General Officials in the General Treasury. Stipulated sums were recommended to be spent in various departments as follows:

Foreign Missions, $75,000.00.
Education, $15,000.00.
General Fund, $35,000.00 (For support of General Officers, etc).
Falcon orphanage, $18,000.00.
General Evangelism, $25,000.00.

In summary the following recommendation was submitted and adopted:

Believing that God's plan of tithes and offerings for carrying on the work of God cannot be improved upon, we recommend that all our members, both ministerial and lay, be faithful in bringing all tithes and offerings into the treasury of the local church and conference. We advocate a church-wide, unified financial program which will include every general interest of the Church. We recommend the following:

(a) That an amount equivalent to ten per cent of all regular income of the local church treasuries be sent to the General Treasury through the Annual Conference treasury or direct, on a monthly basis.

(b) That there be a seasonal emphasis put upon each department of general interest with offerings received for designated departments being given wholly for the same.[1]

These recommendations are in full harmony with the organizational developments in other departments, as is readily seen.

---
[1] Ibid., p. 42.

Education

The recommendations of the Committee on Education also reflect the same church-wide organizational trend, as will be seen by the following lines:

From the information our committee has received we are of the opinion that there is a desire on the part of the leaders of the Pentecostal Holiness Church for a centrally located college and Theological Seminary. In the light of these facts the members of the Board of Education of the Southwest have agreed to unite their efforts and resources with the general educational program of the church on the CONDITION THAT THE Church College and Theological Seminary shall be located in a geographical center that will best serve the church.

It would be redundant for us to present here the recommendations which were submitted in view of the fact that since that time entirely different plans have been made. It will suffice to say that a cooperative and coordinated church-wide program was set up, the details of which are discussed in connection with the History of Education in the Pentecostal Holiness Church.

Publications

For the first time the 1945 General Conference elected a separate Board of Publications and specified that a full time resident Editor-in-Chief should be elected. The editorial staff in consultation with the Board of Publications was authorized to determine the policies of the Advocate. Such an organizational set-up had not previously existed in this department of the Church's work. This phase of church work was definitely tied in with the phases of work to which it could make helpful contributions, such as, the Sunday School work, Daily Vacation work and Teacher Training work.

Radio

The church-wide trend was likewise reflected in the agitation for a National Radio Broadcast. The Rev. Byon A. Jones, who for a number of years has conducted radio broadcasts in connection with his pastoral activities at the Portsmouth, Virginia Church, was granted the privilege of addressing the General Conference relative to the need and possibility of a church-wide broadcast designed to acquaint the general public with the doctrines and mission of the Pentecostal Holiness Church.

The General Board of Administration

By 1945, the Pentecostal Holiness Church had grown to be an organization of somewhat respectable size, which required more than a mere simple rudimentary type of church machinery to carry on its business. There were nearly twenty-five thousand members scattered throughout more than twenty-five Annual Conferences. There were in addition a total of 21,083 members of the Church in foreign mission areas, making a grand total membership of 45,592. We have noted the pronounced organizational developments in every department of church work which were recommended and adopted at this meeting of the General Conference. In order that this work should be properly supervised it became necessary to make corresponding improvements in better organizing the work of the General Board. Part of the report of the Committee on Church Polity which relates to these organizational developments will be listed here in order to show the relation of the General Board to the other Boards. Some of the recommendations were as follows:

The General Board shall be called the General Board of Administration. The officers of the General Conference shall consist of four General Superintendents, an Assistant General Superintendent, the General Secretary, and the General Treasurer. The General Board of Administration shall be composed of the Officials of the General Conference, together with the members of the Board of Education, the Board of Publication, the Board of Foreign Missions, the Board of Home Missions, and the Orphanage Board; and that no member shall serve on more than one Board with the exception of the Executive Board. The General Officials shall constitute the Executive Board of the General Board of Administration.

(a) The Boards of Foreign Missions, Home Missions, Education, Publications, and Orphanage shall be elected by the General Conference, with the exception of their Chairman, who shall be selected by the General Board of Administration immediately after the General Conference from the personal of the Executive Board.

(b) The Board of Foreign Missions, the Board of Home Missions, the Board of Education shall consist of five members each, four of whom shall be elected by the General Conference. The Board of Publication and Orphanage Board shall consist of three members, two of whom shall be elected by the General Conference.

316   HISTORY OF THE PENTECOSTAL HOLINESS CHURCH

(c) Immediately following the election of the General Superintendents, there shall be elected from among them a Chairman and Vice-Chairman of the General Conference, the same to be Chairman and Vice-Chairman of the General Board of Administration and the Executive Board. The one receiving the highest number of votes shall be Chairman and the one receiving the next highest shall be Vice Chairman.

(d) The work of the General Superintendents and the Assistant General Superintendent shall be determined by the General Board of Administration.

(e) The General Board of Administration shall meet annually, date and place of meeting to be determined by said Board and shall transact the following business:

(1) Receive the reports of the General Officers.

(2) Receive the reports and pass upon the work of the following Boards:

Executive Board, Foreign Mission Board, Home Mission Board, Board of Publications, Board of Education, and the Orphanage Board.

We recommend that the General Conference authorize the Chairman to appoint a Nomination Committee of six to serve with him to prepare nominations for the Boards of Foreign Missions, Home Missions, Education, Publications, and Orphanage, providing equitable representation on these Boards.

General Officers

Four Bishops were elected as follows: The Revs. J. H. King, Dan T. Muse, J. A. Synan and Hubert T. Spence. The Rev. T. A. Melton was elected as an assistant or Junior Bishop. Mr. Spence at a later date when the General Board of Administration met asked to be relieved of his duties as a Bishop, and since that time he has most commendably performed the work of General Treasurer. The Rev. Paul F. Beacham, who had been General Treasurer for more than twenty years, was then elected by the General Board of Administration to take his place. When the Rev. J. H. King died in 1946, the Rev. T. A. Melton was elected a Bishop. The work of these officers was divided as follows:

Bishop J. A. Synan has jurisdiction over the diocese known as District No. 1 which includes the Pennsylvania, Eastern Virginia, Maritime, Virginia, Ontario, Maryland and Western North Carolina Conferences.

Bishop Paul F. Beacham, District No. 2 which includes the Florida, South Carolina, Georgia, North Carolina and Upper South Carolina Conferences.

Bishop T. A. Melton, District No. 3 which is made up of the Missouri, Tri-State, East Oklahoma, Alabama and Mississippi Conferences.

Bishop Dan T. Muse exercises jurisdiction over District No. 4 which includes the following Conferences: Texas-Mexican, Texas, West Oklahoma, Colorado, Oklahoma, California, Arizona, Panhandle and British Columbia.

The personnel of the various General Boards is as follows:

Foreign Mission Board: Paul F. Beacham, Chairman; A. Noseworthy, J. T. Baker, J. H. Taylor, G. A. Byus.

Board of Education: J. A. Synan, Chairman; C. H. Williams, T. L. Aaron, R. O. Corvin, W. J. Nash.

Orphanage Board: T. A. Melton, Chairman; F. A. Dail, W. W. Carter.

Home Mission Board: H. T. Spence, Chairman; G. H. Montgomery, Harold Paul, R. L. Rex, A. E. Robinson.

Board of Publications: Dan T. Muse, Chairman; L. J. Oliver, T. T. Lindsey.

General P. H. Y. S. Officers: Virgil Gaither, General President, T. M. Oliver, Secretary-Treasurer.

Regional Presidents, P. H. Y. S.: Southwest, Alfred Spell; Pacific and Western Canada, J. D. Nunn; Eastern Canada, Mrs. M. E. Hutchinson; Northeastern, Bane T. Underwood; Southeastern, Don S. Whitfield.

General Sunday School Officers: Dan T. Muse, President; T. L. Aaron, Vice President; D. M. Tarkenton, Secretary-Treasurer.

Woman's Auxiliary: Mrs. J. W. Berry, President; Mrs. Dan T. Muse, Vice President; Mrs. J. H. King, Secretary-Treasurer.

Through the agency of these various organizational set-ups the machinery of the Church should function smoothly and efficiently. An intelligent appraisal of these new organizational developments cannot be made, however, until after the General Conference meets in 1949.

Section III
Departmental Developments In Summary

Chapter I
HOME MISSIONS

General History

The earliest extant record of a Home Mission Board in the Pentecostal Holiness Church is found in the minutes of the Annual Convention of 1908 which met at Dunn, North Carolina. This was the year after the great Pentecostal outpouring of the Spirit which began in North Carolina in 1907. It was at this Convention that the Rev. A. B. Crumpler withdrew from the organization and the Rev. A. H. Butler was elected in his place. In the record of the business transacted are these words: "The following appointed as a Home Mission Board: Brothers G. B. Cashwell, A. H. Butler and R. B. Jackson, moved and seconded that the mission money paid today be equally divided between Home and Foreign Missionary Boards. Amount $13.12."[1] So, there was $6.56 contributed for the purpose of Home Missions when the first Board was appointed. There was considerable home mission activity in the Church from the time of its inception, but this was likely the first home mission board.

In 1911 at the First General Convention of the Pentecostal Holiness Church there was no board elected or appointed but the following information reveals a separation between the work of home and foreign missions:

> The election of Assistant General Superintendents was taken up, resulting as follows: A. H. Butler, home field; and J. H. King, foreign work.[2]

In 1913 at the Second General Convention in the report on Missions is the following brief reference to home missions:

---

1 Procedings of the Ninth Annual Convention of the Holiness Church of North Carolina, Nov. 26-29, 1908, Dunn, N. C.), p. 7.
2 Minutes of First General Convention of the Pentecostal Holiness Church (Dunn, N. C.: January 31, 1911), p. 3.

HOME MISSIONS 319

We, your Committee on Missions, beg leave to submit the following report and recommend that:
1. There shall be a General Mission Board elected by the General Convention, which shall have the oversight of all the missionary work of the Pentecostal Holiness Church in foreign lands, and this Board shall cooperate with the Missionary Boards of Annual Conventions in carrying forward the work of missions in the home and foreign fields . . .[1]

In this casual reference to home missions it is not difficult to see there was no definite program in operation. A similar reference appears in the minutes of the Third General Convention in 1917 as follows:

Feeling the great burden and responsibility that is upon us of spreading this glorious gospel; and having the great commission: 'Go ye into all the world and preach the gospel to every creature,' therefore we recommend:
1. That every pastor, evangelist, Sunday school superintendent and teacher shall advocate, stress and preach foreign as well as home missions . . .[2]

In 1921 and 1925 practically nothing was done in the interest of home missions at the General Conference meetings. There were, of course, many individuals who were working in the interest of home missions, but no organized effort was being promoted according to these records. By 1929 there seemed to be a general feeling that this phase of work in the Pentecostal Holiness Church was being sorely neglected, and for the first time in its history this church elected a Committee on Evangelism which submitted a report worthy to be presented here because of the fact that the total membership of the Church jumped from 8,994 in 1929 to 15,447 in 1933. This splendid report is no doubt largely, if not entirely, responsible for this increase. It reads as follows:

In obedience to the command of the Son of God, Matt. 28, we His Church, are in duty bound and solemnly obligated, to carry the gospel of the cross to all states, peoples and nations. So far, we have failed to make the advancement in new territory that has been our privilege, and by neglecting this primary phase of the work of the Church, every department of the Church has been made to suffer.

---

[1] Minutes of the Second General Convention of the Pentecostal Holiness Church (Toccoa, Georgia: Jan. 28-30, 1913), pp. 10, 11.
[2] Minutes of the Third General Convention of the Pentecostal Holiness Church (Abbeville, S. C.: Jan. 23-29, 1917), p. 7.

The time has come when the General Conference should be first in action in reviving the evangelistic zeal, that one time pervaded the Pentecostal movement. Therefore, we your Committee on Evangelism beg leave to submit the following:

1. We earnestly insist that all our Annual Conferences and local churches, in a way best suited to their locality, create a fund for the purpose of purchasing tents, renting buildings, or any necessary equipment, to stand by the God-called evangelists in opening up work in new territory, and thus to accomplish the great work for which the Son of God gave His life.

2. That the Committee on Discipline incorporate such a clause in the Discipline as will place before our people the great importance of aggressive evangelism.

3. We advise that wisdom be used in conducting revivals everywhere in regard to law and order in the state or city.

We advise and urge all our preachers to preach more frequently on the fundamental doctrines of our Church, i. e., regeneration, sanctification—a second definite work of grace, the baptism with the Holy Spirit, divine healing, and the second coming of our Lord, and endeavor to make the unsaved feel the reality of a personal devil, and an eternal, burning hell.

> D. Wiley
> A. H. Butler
> J. L. Kesling
> S. D. Page
> W. Ray Anderson
> Committee

In 1932 the Rev. S. A. Bishop conceived of an idea of organizing an Evangelistic Association, which was endorsed by the General Board, as is indicated in the following article which appeared in the Advocate during the spring of 1932:

Fervent and fiery evangelistic effort is the supreme need of the Pentecostal Holiness Church. Everything cries out for it. It is imperative, and we must do our utmost to promote it. It is our very life. To fail is to die. As servants of God, as ministers of His Word, as representatives of the entire church we call upon every minister and member in the name of our Lord Jesus Christ to fall in line with the will of God in carrying out the following as a means of promoting Pentecostal evangelism throughout our land.

1. Each individual church is urged to do all in its power to extend the full Gospel in the communities surrounding its location.

2. Each church is urged to pray and work for the greatest revival that has ever occurred in its own history.

3. Conference superintendents, pastors and evangelists, are urged to bring before each Quarterly Conference and church the duty and importance of evangelizing the entire territory that the Conferences embrace.

4. We commend the Evangelistic Association organized at Greenville, S. C. in the month of May, 1932, to the favorable consideration and cooperation of the ministers and members of all the Conferences throughout the Church. This will enable many to go into new fields and carry the Pentecostal Gospel to those who have never heard it.

Mr. Bishop was later elected as Chairman of the Committee on Evangelism when the General Conference met at Marion, N. C. in 1933. It was here that he advocated substantially the same program which was embraced in that of the Evangelistic Association. Because of a general lack of confidence in the program throughout the Church it was soon abandoned.

In 1937 an Evangelist General was elected by the General Board upon the recommendation of the 1937 General Conference.

On June 13, 1941 for the first time since 1908, there was organized at Franklin Springs, Georgia, a Home Mission Board in the Pentecostal Holiness Church, composed of five members as follows: The Rev. J. A. Synan, Chairman, and the Revs. H. T. Spence, T. A. Melton, B. R. Dean and W. W. Carter. Mr. G. H. Montgomery was elected Superintendent of Evangelism and plans were discussed and adopted tentatively. These six men contributed one dollar each to begin the Home Mission Fund. It was decided that Mr. Montgomery should actively begin this new work by September 1, 1941 at which time he would be paid a salary of seventy-five dollars per month plus three cents per mile traveling expenses.

When the Home Mission Board met on December 18, 1941, in Richmond, Virginia at the Central Pentecostal Holiness Church, the Superintendent of Evangelism reported that he had conducted eight evangelistic rallies and had arranged for three more, and that one church had been organized at Wichita, Kansas as a direct result of his Home Mission activities. The Superintendent of Evangelism was instructed to devote his time as far as possible and practicable to promotion work in the interest of home missions, by contacting Conference Boards relative to possible developments in their new territory, and by visiting Quarterly Conferences, Annual Conferences, revivals, camp meetings and other such gatherings to present the cause of home evangelism and when possible to raise funds for that purpose. Five thousand "Home Mission" pamphlets were ordered published which were to be used in publicizing this work. Mr. Montgomery's salary was ordered raised to eighty-five dollars per month. When the Home Mission Board met again on June 9, 1942, at Central Pentecostal Holiness Church in Richmond Mr. Montgomery reported a church-wide interest in this work, and that another church had been organized at Mobile, Alabama. The "Home Mission Department" which had been conducted in the Advocate was ordered to be continued. A motion was adopted requesting the General Board to allow the Home Mission Board to employ certain missionaries who were home on furlough at thirty dollars per month plus transportation to do home mission work in virgin territory. Miss Effie Barker and Miss Laura Hylton were later contacted by the Rev. W. W. Carter and sent to Kansas City, where they opened a mission and conducted prayer services in preparation for evangelists who might come later to organize a Pentecostal Holiness Church.

It was decided at this meeting to arrange with Evangelist Joe E. Campbell and his party to go to Johnson City, Tennessee to conduct a campaign with the purpose in view of organizing a church, allowing him twenty-five dollars per week and fifty dollars for transportation of his equipment. Because there were already four tent campaigns being conducted there by ministers of other communions, Mr. Campbell turned to other fields where the one hundred and fifty dollars which had been appropriated was used to sponsor two other campaigns resulting in the organization of churches at Cherryville, N. C. and Rock Hill, S. C. These campaigns were conducted in collaboration with the Western North Carolina and South Carolina Conferences respectively. In the summer of 1943 this evangelist organized churches at East Radford, Floyd and Gretna, Virginia, being both summers assisted by the Wells family of Danville, Virginia.

On April 6, 1943, the Home Mission Board met again at Falcon, N. C. The Superintendent of Evangelism submitted important information regarding evangelism in each section of the Church. His salary was ordered raised to one hundred and twenty-five dollars per month, plus four cents per mile traveling expenses.

The Rev. Henry Maxwell was called before the Board to arrange for his employment in home mission work. He was assured of twenty-five dollars per week, and sent to Kansas City to begin evangelistic services in the mission which had been opened there by Misses Barker and Hylton. At the same meeting these two workers were granted a raise in their salaries equal to the cost of their room-rent. Appropriations were ordered made to the Florida, Texas, Upper South Carolina, Alabama, Tri-State, Maryland, Baltimore, Virginia and Georgia Conferences which aggregated $1,025.00.

About two months later, on May 27, 1943, in another meeting it was decided to purchase a gospel tent from the Rev. N. N. Perkins for the sum of $325.00. The Gospel Trio composed of the Revs. Doyle Zachary, Harry Correll and Paul Taylor were employed to use this tent in East Tennessee, in the hope that a new conference could eventually be organized. In a personal interview with Mr. Correll he related the following account of their activities, along with the activities of other parties, who labored in this field in 1943 and 1944:

In the early summer of 1943 the Gospel Trio was sent to Johnson City under the auspices of the Home Mission Board. After prayer we felt led to go to Greenville, Tennessee where we came in contact with a Methodist evangelist whose name was C. E. Whitson, and who lived near Kingsport where he was also in the dry cleaning business. He befriended us in every way possible and through his help and influence we were able to get started in Kingsport after about two weeks. We set up our tent on a lot where other evangelists had previously set up, although the owner of the lot could not be learned. We stayed there for eleven weeks and as a result of our efforts a church was organized, and a building built during the year while I was pastor of the newly organized church. We continued our friendship with Mr. Whitson and sang for him on his radio program over WKPT, the Kingsport station, also visiting with him in a tent campaign he was conducting at Greenville, Tennessee. The Rev. C. B. Till, who had been employed by the Home Missions Board, came to Tennessee and for a time worked among the new churches there.

While we were at Kingsport Brother Paul Nance and his wife, Billy Hutcherson and Miss Florine Freeman went to Elizabethtown, Tennessee to organize a church, but they were soon forced to close because of a lack of interest among the people of that community. They moved then to Mt. City, Tennessee where they organized and built a nice church. This building was erected before the organization was actually effected. The Western North Carolina Conference and other Conferences, churches and individuals paid for this church. The people of that community were very poor and would have been unable to assume that much responsibility. Brother Bill McKenzie was sent there to serve as pastor after Brother Nance left.

In the summer of 1944 the Gospel Trio set up in Greenville, Tennessee, on the same lot where Brother Whitson, the Methodist Evangelist had conducted his tent campaign. We already knew many of the people there, being introduced and recommended by Mr. Whitson. In seven weeks we had organized a church and Paul Taylor was sent there to pastor that work.

In the meantime that year Brother G. Ray Taylor had gone to Knoxville, Tennessee, to work on a defense job. Largely with his own funds, he rented a building and conducted cottage prayer meetings until he was finally able to organize a church and has built a respectable church building himself, with the aid of those few whom he could get to assist him.[1]

This is the most outstanding single project which the Home Mission Board has sponsored thus far in the history of its existence, since 1941. This Mission Conference is expected very soon to become an Annual Conference. The Rev. R. L. Rex has also done most commendable work in establishing churches in the Mid-west, while a number of others have made sizable contributions laboring in many quarters.

In the course of five years, by 1946, this Board had supervised or sponsored the work of establishing no less than ten churches, and in each instance there has been provided acceptable places of worship, the total value of which is approximately $75,000.00. There have also been organized eight other churches in Annual Conferences where the Home Mission Board has furnished financial aid by making cash appropriations to supplement that supplied by the Conferences. During the same five year period there was spent less than $60,000.00 for both general evangelism and the Service Men's Commission.[2] (The facts which relate to the Service Men's Commission will be found in a separate chapter.)

Since the General Conference meeting in 1945 the Home Mission Board has been one of the five boards which go to make up the General Board of Administration, as we have noted, and there is allocated $25,000.00 annually for this purpose. The Chairman of the Home Mission Board, the Rev. Hubert T. Spence, has

---

1 Harry B. Correll, Personal Interview.
2 Hubert T. Spence, Pamphlet (dealing with Home Missions and Church Extension in the Pentecostal Holiness Church), p. 6.

since that time been director of general evangelism. According to Mr. Spence:

This Board works in collaboration with the various annual Conference Boards in conducting evangelistic meetings in communities, towns, and cities mainly where we have no established churches.

The Home Mission Board is also authorized to organize Home Mission churches and conferences in sections of our country where we have not as yet organized and established Annual Conferences. Full authority is given the Home Mission Board to examine candidates for the ministry and to receive them, subject to appointments in Home Mission work, also to engage evangelists, who are already members of Annual Conferences, for new field evangelism.

However, as a result of our experience we have found that the most constructive work is done in collaboration with the Annual Conferences, thereby turning the newly organized churches over to those Annual Conferences which in turn become responsible to supply them with pastoral supervision.

The Home Mission Board is authorized to purchase property, and also to lend money to local congregations for the purpose of buying, building or remodeling property.

This work of general evangelism and church extension is not intended to take the place of local church and conference evangelism, but rather to supplement the same, and to keep evangelism ever before the whole Church. We believe that as a Church our main mission is to evangelize and that it is either "evangelize or fossilize." The work of general evangelism does not in the least relieve the local church and Annual Conference of their responsibility along that line.

The Home Mission Department is to supplement and assist local evangelism, and to supervise the work of pioneering in those areas, both rural and urban, where our Annual Conferences have not as yet evangelized.[1]

In summary, it might well be said that the Pentecostal Holiness Church in reality had no Home Mission Board from 1908 until 1941, and that such a Board did not actually become part of the General Board of Administration until 1945. There was no "Committee on Evangelism" report until the General Conference in 1929. But this does not mean that this church has not been actively engaged in evangelistic work. Evangelism has always been a major emphasis, but this responsibility has until recent years been assumed by individuals, and not by the whole church. We therefore turn now to observe a few examples of such individuals who pioneered in this work.

---

1 Ibid., pp. 4, 5.

Chapter II
HOME MISSIONS—Continued
Some Early Pioneers

It would require volumes to record the multiplied activities of the host of evangelists who have been actively engaged in evangelistic work in the Pentecostal Holiness Church. Since its inception just before the turn of the century its history has been replete with examples of individuals who have zealously spent themselves for the cause of spreading the full gospel truth for which it stands.

Throughout the history of the Pentecostal Holiness Church, evangelistic services have been conducted in private dwellings, barns, school houses, store buildings, abandoned churches, tents, brush arbors, warehouses, street corners, courthouses, and every other place where people could be gathered. It is true however, that most of this type of preaching took place in the pioneer days when few churches were in existence. These Spirit-filled fiery evangels were for the most part crude and unlettered, but they were possessed with an unconquerable determination to carry this gospel in spite of all opposition. They had little favor with man but God was on their side to confirm His Word with signs following. It would be indeed a fascinating and thrilling story to relate the details of the experiences of many of these men, but it will serve our purpose to give a running account of how some of the churches were established and some limited description of a few of the men God used to establish them.

SOUTH CAROLINA AND GEORGIA

R. B. Hayes

One of the most eccentric and one of the most outstanding of the pioneer preachers of the Pentecostal Holiness Church was the Rev. Richard Baxter Hayes. He was born in Oconee County S. C. on November 15, 1858. His father and two of his father's brothers were Baptist ministers. He was given the name of one of these uncles who had been named for the famous Richard Baxter, a Baptist minister of Kidderminster, England.

"Brother Hayes," as he was affectionately known to his many friends, was a member of the Baptist Church at the time of his conversion which he experienced two years after he had joined. He laughingly referred to his joining the Church as a "pasteboard" conversion, just signing a card and going on living and acting like the world. For some time he remained in that Church, feeling that he would like to receive something more of God, but was handicapped by what he called an "ecclesiastical grazer" which limited him. His father was sanctified in a Holiness meeting and invited the minister to come to Walhalla, S. C. where his son, Richard Baxter was in the mercantile business and was a deacon in the First Baptist Church. He and a prominent Presbyterian elder, who was also a widely known and successful physician were among the great number who were sanctified in the meeting at Walhalla. Both of them later gave up their secular work and entered the ministry and became members of the Wesleyan Methodist Church.

When the Rev. B. H. Irwin of the Fire-Baptized Holiness Church came to Piedmont, S. C., advocating the Holy Ghost and fire as an experience subsequent to sanctification, Brother Hayes accepted the teaching and became identified with the Fire-Baptized Holiness Association and was afterwards appointed the first "State overseer" or Ruling Elder of that Church in Georgia. He held tent meetings in Seneca, Denver, Fellowship, Craft's Ferry, Bull Snort, and other places in South Carolina, and in Hartwell, Elberton, Reeds Creek Settlement, Canon, Mount Olive, Royston, Iron Rock, New Bethel, Bowersville, Carnesville, Dewey Rose, Athens, Toccoa, Gainesville Atlanta and numerous other places in Georgia. He had several tents burned, was stoned and on occasions had rotten tomatoes, eggs, etc. dripping from his coat-tail and many other persecutions but nothing quenched his zeal or stopped his mouth from preaching the gospel. One of the tents was burned by a Baptist preacher who was tracked to his home and convicted. Another Baptist minister confessed on his deathbed that he had burned another of his tents. (Baptist ministers in their early history were even more severely persecuted). In a biography compiled and edited by his son, W. M. Hayes he relates the following incident which occurred at Athens, Georgia:

His first tent meeting at Athens, Georgia, stirred the old devil and sinning preachers. One afternoon my father preached on the street. After the service he went into crockery store owned and operated by Brother Huggins, one of my father's best friends. A Baptist preacher followed my father and when they stopped, he turned to my father and said, 'I did not like what you said in your sermon at all,' and before anyone knew what was happening, he hit my father in the face with his fist. Father went down on his knees praying for him and when he arose, the fellow sneaked out. The next day the daily paper picked it up and crowds enlarged until the tent wouldn't hold the people. They wanted to see the preacher who was hit by the Baptist preacher, who wouldn't fight back but prayed for his enemy. This advertized the meeting more than anything that could have happened. Scores of souls were saved, some sanctified and healed . . .[1]

Everywhere he went scores were saved and sanctified. He organized several churches, one of the most outstanding of which was one at Canon, Georgia, which was organized with one hundred and twenty members. Brother Hayes was a strong believer in divine healing and on one occasion spent a day and night in a murderer's cell for standing true to his conviction when his small son was ill. Scores of his converts were called to preach. In conversation with this writer several years ago he told of many nights using the Bible for his pillow and a bench for his bed, then seriously he mused, "The Master had not a place to lay His head." Then he would praise God, perhaps because He counted him worthy to suffer a little bit for Jesus' sake. He made his earthly departure in great triumph during the month of July, 1937.

The Rev. G. O. Gaines, Josiah Allen, James A. Argo, Dr. J. T. A. Gaines, Ralph Taylor, G. R. Thomas, J. H. Barton, F. L. Bramblett, D. R. Brown, Bert Todd, O. M. Hilburn, J. J. Carter H. D. Wiggins, J. W. Kennedy, J. H. Wiggins, D. D. Causey, W. S. Foxworth, J. H. Jordan, C. A. Jordan, Sr., and many others were prominent in *pioneer Pentecostal* Holiness work, either in Georgia or South Carolina.

F. M. Britton

The name of Francis Marion Britton will perhaps always be

---

[1] W. M. Hayes **Memoirs of Richard Baxter Hayes** (Philadelphia Dunlap Printing Co., 1945), pp. 1-44, et passim.

a familiar one among people in the ranks of the Pentecostal Holiness Church. He was the outstanding doctrinal preacher of the early pioneers, and wielded an influence which was felt throughout the entire movement. He was born January 21, 1870, and went to his reward in recent years. The place of his birth was in the eastern part of South Carolina, on a farm midway between the Indian Town Presbyterian Church, five miles to the north and the Union Methodist Church five miles to the south. His father was F. Marion Britton, the son of Benjamin and Sarah Britton, whose parents had come from Europe and settled at Britton's Neck between the big and Little Pee Dee rivers. Sarah Britton was the daughter of Dr. Thomas Britton. F. M. Britton's mother was a devout Christian who had two brothers in the ministry. Through her prayers and influence, Mr. Britton was called to preach. He tells the following story of his call to preach as a small boy:

I was by my Mother's side holding her right hand, and Mother was praying as she walked along, and I saw her mouth working, and the drops of tears running down her cheeks. I said, 'Ma, what are you crying about, and who are you talking to?' And she prayed on as though she did not hear me. I kept watching her very eagerly, and all at once she commenced laughing the 'holy laugh.' I then commenced pulling her hand, saying, 'Ma, Ma, What are you laughing about, and who have you been talking to, and why do you cry so?' At that time she stopped in the road and looked at me and said, 'I have eleven dear children, and I have been praying for them all to be saved ever since the first one was born into the world, and you asked who I was talking to just now; I was talking to my heavenly Father, praying for you children, and I never heard of a Britton being a preacher; but it runs in my family to be preachers. I have two brothers who are preachers, and I have been asking God to make one of my six boys a preacher, and I laughed because he gave me the assurance that one of my boys would be a preacher.' At that time she pulled her hand loose from mine and said, 'I believe you are the one!'

When she did I felt a strange tingling go all over me from head to feet, and from that day I had an assurance that I would have to preach. I don't know how old I was at the time, but I had to reach up to hold my Mother's hand. From that day on I often went to the altar seeking God. I was converted when about eighteen years of age in a meeting conducted by the Rev. W. B. Bakerman, a Methodist Episcopal preacher. I joined the Methodist Episcopal Church under the preaching of Old Uncle S. I. Brown, the Presiding Elder, in the

Quarterly Conference, at Union Church, where my parents are buried.[1]

Mr. Britton was sanctified in his own home and later began to preach the experience in the Methodist Church and continued to do so until they passed strict rules against holiness teaching, forbidding *all* unauthorized evangelists, local preachers, exhorters or laymen to conduct meetings in churches, school houses, tents, or private homes, anywhere in the bounds of the South Carolina Conference, unless they had a special invitation from the pastor in charge of the circuit, or a written recommendation from the Presiding Elder. He then joined the Baptist Church, which he was invited to join, but in a short time he was turned out for what they called "heresy." In speaking about this occasion, and later experiences in the ministry, he says:

But none of these things moved me. I went on and was used of God for the salvation of many, many precious souls. Many were sanctified, and scores were divinely healed . . . I bought a tent of my own and went out, wife and I had two children, through many toils and snares and persecutions, we lived on, suffered hunger and cold, a lack of proper clothing, and blazed the way for Holiness, where there are Holiness churches today. I lived hard, and tried to 'endure hardness as a good soldier of Jesus Christ.' I remember eating huckleberries for dinner all alone in the woods, when I did not have an invitation for dinner. I remember eating persimmons for dinner while Brother Gregg and I were walking through the country to hold a meeting. I walked twenty-four miles and preached three times on Sunday many a time to get Holiness established in South Carolina. Well do I remember walking seventy-five miles to hold a meeting in a 'new field' where poor people were begging me to go, and after the meeting was over and many were saved and sanctified, I rode a short distance so the people would not know but what I rode all the way home. But when I remembered my wife and children at home and I knew how little money I had and how much they needed at home, I got off the train and walked more than sixty miles so I could have something for them to live on while I was holding another meeting, and I walked all day and only ate ten cents worth of crackers, and a rain came up about night and I went into a church tired, hungry and happy in Jesus, put my Bible and song-books under my head and stretched out on a hard bench and went to sleep praying, and got up the next morning at the dawn of day, and after I had walked eight miles and stopped and ate breakfast with a brother, and he said he was too busy to take me

---

[1] F. M. Britton **Pentecostal Truth**, (Royston, Ga., The Publishing House of the P. H. Church, 1919), pp. 220, 221.

home, which was twenty-two miles. I was so tired I did not see how I could ever get home; but I walked off down the road and hid myself, where only God could see me, and poured out my heart to God, and told him how I loved Him, and also how I loved my precious wife and children and how I wanted to see them, and I said, O Lord, see how sore my poor feet are, and have mercy on me, and help me to get home today, and I remembered the verse in the Bible, 'As thy days so shall thy strength be,' and I got up and walked home before I ate dinner. When I got in sight of home and saw my good, patient, sweet wife look out and see me, and she and the children came running to meet me—Oh, how glad I was no mortal tongue can tell.[1]

Such experiences as these which the Rev. Britton relates were common among all of the early pioneers of the Pentecostal Holiness preachers. Many miraculous healings took place under his ministry, including his own child who had a broken leg, his wife of spinal meningitis, pneumonia and influenza, and many other people of influenza, rheumatism, epilepsy, pellegra, cancer, and various other diseases. Dozens were called to preach under his ministry, and when the "latter-rain" outpouring of the Spirit came he was one of the strongest advocates of this experience. Prior to that time he was an ordained minister of the Fire-Baptized Holiness Church and for a time he was the Assistant General Overseer of that organization. He was active in Florida, Virginia, and Oklahoma, organizing the Annual Conferences in Oklahoma in 1909, and in Virginia in 1910, as will be seen in an immediately following section.

FLORIDA

The Rev. B. H. Irwin of Lincoln, Nebraska, was among the first to preach Holiness in Florida. At that time he was head of the National Fire-Baptized Holiness Association. State Associations were formed, as we have previously noted, in most of the States in the South and Middlewest, among which was Florida. After Mr. Irwin's defection there came to Florida the Rev. and Mrs. C. M. Wheeler from Grand Rapids, Michigan. Before their marriage at Grand Rapids, Mr. Wheeler practiced law in Chicago, Illinois, but because of illness had gone to Grand Rapids on a pleasure trip in an effort to regain his health. He wandered into a Mennonite mission where he was converted, sanctified and

---

[1] Ibid., pp. 225, 226.

divinely healed of a paralytic stroke, under the ministry of a Miss Ritter who soon became his wife. He was then fifty-four and she was in her early thirties. She is still a resident of Bristol, Florida, being an octogenarian, and he only recently died as a centenarian, having reached the ripe old age of one hundred and one.

When they came to Tallahassee in 1900 they began to conduct street services, soon becoming acquainted with a Methodist minister, the Rev. Mr. McManning, who had already come into the experience of sanctification which they were preaching. He invited them to conduct revivals in the churches of his circuit. A marvelous revival broke out which spread all over that vicinity, and it was not long until Conference Officials of the Methodist Church forbade their preaching in Methodist churches and made it necessary for Mr. McManning to withdraw, whereupon he organized a Wesleyan Methodist Church in Tallahassee.

The Wheelers continued their preaching in and around Tallahassee and after a time organized an independent Holiness church at Bristol, Florida, the county seat of Liberty County. Shortly thereafter they also organized an independent work at Wetumpka. This church was organized after a revival meeting which had been held in the Wetumpka school house by the Rev. Mr. McManning and Rev. and Mrs. Wheeler. Camp Meetings were also organized and conducted at both of these places.

In 1909 the Rev. J. H. King, General Overseer of the Fire-Baptized Holiness Church, organized the Florida State Convention and thus brought these two churches into that Church which was later consolidated with the Pentecostal Holiness Church in 1911. Among the ministers who joined the Conference at that time were the Revs. C. C. Chester, H. A. Smith, C. M. Wheeler and Mrs. C. M. Wheeler. As we have noted in the history of the Fire-Baptized Holiness Church, the Rev. H. A. Smith was elected as Superintendent or Ruling Elder of the Florida Convention.

In the beginning most of the churches were established in the north and north central part of the State, but by 1911 the Rev. and Mrs. Clark Eckert joined the Florida Conference and brought the Coconut Grove (Miami) church into the Pentecostal Holiness Church. (Since Mr. Eckert's death Mrs. Eckert

HOME MISSIONS, continued

has recently married Mr. R. E. Lee, a charter member of the Pentecostal Holiness Church.) She still directs the work of this same church. For years she was also the beloved and esteemed leader of the young people's work in Florida. The Rev. and Mrs. J. D. Jowers of Waycross, Georgia, brought their work, a Wesleyan Methodist Church, into the Pentecostal Holiness organization in 1912. The Rev. J. A. Killebrew united with the Conference in 1911, the Rev. G. Sigwalt, in 1913, and the Rev. Joel E. Rhodes, who became the famed missionary to Africa, united with the Conference the same year. Mr. Sigwalt was the second Superintendent, and since then the Revs. J. A. Killebrew, L. J. Oliver and S. E. Franklin have served the Conference as Superintendents. Mr. Oliver faithfully served for eighteen years, and in later years his successor, Mr. Franklin, has enthusiastically continued the work of the Church in this area.

From 1907 to 1909 the Rev. F. M. Britton held great revivals in Orlando, Palatka, Tampa, Largo and Arcadia and elsewhere, but did not organize churches, because of the fact that he belonged to no church at that time himself. These people were brought into other Holiness and Pentecostal movements. He united with the Pleasant Grove Fire-Baptized Holiness Church, which was organized by the late Bishop J. H. King in May of 1908. Mr. Britton had previously been a member of that organization but left them when they drifted into the heretical teachings of experiences known as "dynamite, lyddite and oxydite" baptisms, but they had by this time denounced that heresy. He became one of the greatest preachers and organizers of the Pentecostal Holiness Church movement. More than one hundred persons received the baptism of the Holy Ghost under his ministry at the Pleasant Grove Camp Meeting, seventeen miles east of Tampa.

From 1911 to 1916 churches were established in Tallahassee, Ocklocknee, Ft. Braden, Greensboro, Cody, Inwood, Shady Grove, Wausau in West Florida and Jacksonville in East Florida, and other places. Other prominent ministers of the Florida Conference who have not been mentioned are the Revs. R. H. Chason, Z. B. Adams, Claude Smith (missionary to Hawaii,) J. E. Till, C. B. Till, I. H. Simpson, G. W. Sorrow, Hugh

Bowling, J. V. Yon, B. H. Osteen, B. V. McDaninel, S. J. Hopkins, J. L. Bartholf and many others.

The Revs. J. H. King, S. A. Bishop, G. F. Taylor, J. A. Synan, W. H. Turner, H. T. Spence, P. F. Beacham, T. A. Melton, O. E. Sproull, L. H. Fortson, Dan T. Muse, G. H. Montgomery, Virgil Gaither and a host of other able ministers have from time to time conducted evangelistic campaigns in Florida. The Revs. Jake Till Cary Forehand, Emmett Hartsfield, Fred Sanders, Albert Barfield and other young ministers have in recent years brought the Florida Conference into prominence.

THE MID-WEST

J. H. King

Bishop J. H. King, while General Overseer of the Fire-Baptized Holiness Church, conducted a number of revival meetings over the State of Oklahoma. In April and May of 1905 he was at *Snyder* in the southwestern portion of the State. This meeting closed on May 5, 1905 and on that night twenty-two people were genuinely converted; and in a few days a terrific tornado wiped out most of the town, killing scores of people.

In 1907 he conducted the famous Lamont Church revival which was mentioned in connection with the History of the Fire-Baptized Holiness Church. A number of people from distances received the baptism of the Spirit here, and went into their communities where they were responsible for extending this revival which was exceedingly far-reaching in its effect.

F. M. Britton

From 1905 to 1918 the much-talked-of F. M. Britton conducted numerous revival meetings, particularly in the western and central sections of Oklahoma. His outspoken and fearless type of ministry was attended by severe persecution. At one meeting he suffered a broken jaw from a flogging he took for his invective pronouncements against sin. He was active in meetings in western Oklahoma near the Texas Oklahoma line, and was unusually successful in the camp meeting he conducted at the Oklahoma Conference, then called the Oklahoma State Convention of the Fire-Baptized Holiness Church.

HOME MISSIONS, *continued* 335

Oscar C. Wilkins and Harry P. Lott

The Revs. Oscar Wilkins and Harry P. Lott will be remembered as the young preachers who came to Oklahoma City in 1906, and were jointly responsible for the organization of the First Pentecostal Holiness Church there. Mr. Wilkins came from Campbell, Missouri, was saved at Coalgate, Indian Territory, where he was employed in a coal mine. In 1905 he quit his job and entered the ministry. He became a charter member of the church he helped to organize and later united with the Annual Conference in 1910. Mr. Wilkins was among the most active pioneers and fiery evangelists in Oklahoma, establishing numerous churches. Mr. Lott came from Long's Peak, Colorado feeling led of God to go to Oklahoma City. He was preaching with a Free Methodist preacher at Billings, Oklahoma, in 1905, when a man and his wife received the baptism of the Holy Spirit and spoke in tongues, causing quite a sensation, due to the fact that the "latter-rain outpouring" had not yet begun in California and people were alarmed at this unusual happening. He pastored the Oklahoma City First Church for the first three and one-half years after its organization, was the first Ruling Elder of the Fire-Baptized Holiness Church's Oklahoma Convention, and was mightily used of God in pioneer work in establishing new churches.

R. B. Beall

The Rev. R. B. Beall received the baptism of the Spirit on August 4, 1907, and became one of the leading pioneer preachers, establishing new churches in the Oklahoma Conferences.

Newton Taylor Morgan

The Rev. Newton Morgan became a member of the Fire-Baptized Holiness Church at Lamont, Oklahoma, in 1909, pioneered in the central and western parts of the State, becoming Treasurer and later Superintendent of the Conference.

W. Dan York

The Rev. W. Dan York and Miss Dolly Fagan, who later became his wife, were among the first to receive the baptism of the Spirit, were used to bring hundreds into the Kingdom, and were responsible for the organizing of quite a number of churches among which were Ada, Stratford and Seminole. The Rev. Grover Waterfield, one of their converts, also became prominent as a pioneer preacher.

Kersey and Powell

The Rev. Tom Kersey, Miss Lela Mae Cook, who became his wife, and the Rev. J. G. Powell received the baptism of the Spirit in a great revival conducted by the Rev. F. M. Britton and R. B. Hayes at Tipton, Oklahoma. All three of them pioneered in southwestern Oklahoma.

Mrs. Willard Armstrong Earl Short

Miss Willard Armstrong, who became Mrs. Earl Short received the baptism of the Spirit in 1907 while she was a student in one of the Oklahoma schools. Professor Baker was present and heard her speak in Greek as plainly as a college professor, a language she had never studied. He and others marvelled. In 1908 Mrs. Short came to be known as the girl preacher, became a successful evangelist, and joined the Conference in 1911, serving both as an evangelist and pastor.

A. I. Shannon and Wife

The Rev. A. I. Shannon and Miss Mary K. Davis, whom he later married, also became members of the Oklahoma Conference in 1911.

Dan W. Evans and Wife

The Rev. Dan W. Evans and Miss Rexie Gilbert, who later became his wife, were filled with the Spirit in 1909, moved to Oklahoma City in 1910, and were largely responsible for the starting of the Bethel Church near Seminole. They became members of the Conference in 1911, Mr. Evans later serving as Conference Superintendent.

Luther Chilcoat

The Rev. Luther Chilcoat and his wife were brought into the experience of Pentecost in the Oklahoma City Camp Meeting in 1912. He later became actively engaged in pioneer preaching.

HOME MISSIONS, *continued* 337

Dean Smith and Lillie Bourland Smith

After receiving the baptism of the Spirit in 1909, the Rev. Dean Smith and his wife were mightily used of God as Pentecostal Holiness evangelists in eastern Oklahoma and western Arkansas and other sections in the East, including Florida and Georgia.

S. E. Stark

One of the outstanding figures in Oklahoma is the Rev. S. E. Stark who was among the number to receive the baptism of the Spirit in 1908, becoming a member of the Oklahoma Conference in 1911. He is responsible for many churches in Oklahoma. Because of his fine spirit and leadership qualities he was elected as Conference Superintendent for twelve years during the interim between 1915 and 1932. He has also served seven years as a member of the General Board of Administration. He married Miss Fay Reinking, who united with the Conference in 1912 and was also a prominent pioneer preacher.

J. M. Warner and Wife

The Rev. and Mrs. J. M. Warner were charter members of the Oklahoma Conference, organized in 1909, and were responsible for the organizing of the Pleasant Valley Church between Drummond and Waukemis. Several ministers, missionaries and active members of the Pentecostal Holiness Church were converted in this church.

James A. Campbell

The Rev. James A. Campbell and his wife, Jessie Olive Campbell, were filled with the Spirit in 1912, joined the Conference in 1913, pioneered in central and western Oklahoma and in Denver, Colorado. Mr. Campbell is responsible for leading Bishop Dan T. Muse into the experience of Pentecost.

Others

Quite a number of others whom God used mightily as pioneer ministers of the Pentecostal Holiness truth and prominent laymen were as follows: Albert J. Finkenbinder and wife, Mrs. C. L. Smith, Claude Stone and his wife, the former Miss Myrtle Keener, Martin Luther Dryden and his wife, the former Miss

Mamie Myrtle Beatty, Miss Annie Carmack, Arthur and Belle Martin, Callie Winters, A. D. Rice, S. J. Hickey, W. W. Marrs, John G. Bond, L. M. Taylor, Lula Melvin, Samuel M. Brandstatt, Charles J. Phipps and many others. A number of these deserve as much space as any that have been mentioned but it would not be practical to devote more attention to them in the limited space of one volume which demands many considerations.

NORTH CAROLINA AND VIRGINIA

A. H. Butler

The Rev. A. H. Butler is one of the oldest living members of the original Pentecostal Holiness Church which was organized in 1900 by the Rev. A. B. Crumpler. He became the President of the organization when Mr. Crumpler withdrew in 1908, and served in that capacity until the Church was consolidated with the Fire-Baptized Holiness Church in 1911, and formed the Pentecostal Holiness Church which we know today. He was the Chairman pro tem at the consolidation meeting when the Rev. S. D. Page was elected the first General Superintendent.

Mr. Butler only finished the seventh grade but he has kept his mind active through the years. He was teaching school in North Carolina at the time he entered the ministry. His ministry from then until now has been sane, spiritual and straight from the shoulder. There is not one blot against his unimpeachable character. He has always been a Christian minister with firm convictions. In a recent conversation with the writer, when discussing some of the early preachers who started out in the Pentecostal Holiness Church but for financial reasons withdrew and compromised their message, he said, "I made up my mind before I started that I would drink branch water, eat huckleberries and beg bread before I would compromise."

He was saved under the ministry of the Rev. W. A. Jenkins, a Methodist minister, and was sanctified under the ministry of another Methodist minister, the Rev. D. A. Futril. Mr. Butler received the baptism of the Spirit at home by himself and was awake all night rejoicing. He has one great thing in his favor, that many other ministers have lacked, a wife who was just as determined in her convictions as he, and who was willing to make any necessary sacrifice to help him carry the gospel.

HOME MISSIONS, *continued* 339

There were quite a number of zealous ministers responsible for the spread of Pentecostal Holiness in North Carolina, but the Rev. A. H. Butler without a doubt ranks among the greatest, and in the opinion of many was the greatest. Since he is a man not given to talking very much about himself, it was difficult to secure more than some general information about the church organizations with which he was familiar, and it was not learned which of them he actually organized.

He went to Mayodan in 1903 and followed up the work of A. B. Crumpler, conducting a great revival there; then to Jamestown, 22 miles north of Mocksville; at High Point meetings were conducted in a store building, and in two tents with remarkable results; at Leaksville a building was rented from Charlie Martin, a Baptist merchant, and services were also conducted in private homes. The present church in Leaksville was erected on the same lot where services were originally held. Here it was that Mr. Butler met the Rev. F. W. Gammon who also became prominent in pioneer preaching. At Sanford, N. C. the Revs. J. B. Williams and George Stanley were instrumental in organizing that church; at Aulander a tent meeting was conducted which resulted in a church being built on the property donated by a Christian brother by the name of Peale, who also gave the property for a parsonage and a camp meeting grounds. In 1907 the Hodges Chapel church was organized by Mr. Butler, and property was donated for the Piney Grove Camp Meeting which began in 1908. The first year a tent was used and later a tabernacle was built which is still in use. At St. Paul, N. C., services were begun in the living room of a large two story dwelling. J. B. Williams donated the property for the church to be built. At Greenville, N. C., the Rev. Mr. Butler began by preaching in the Courthouse yard. City officials became interested in his message and invited him to come into the courthouse where he conducted two meetings, then several tent meetings and a church was organized. The same thing occurred at Wilson, N. C. At Danville, services were begun in a store building. Schoolhouses, storehouses, brush arbors and tents were used by those who spearheaded into various communities preaching Pentecostal Holiness. At Kinston, N. C., a revival was begun which lasted in spirit for eleven years. Literally hundreds of people were saved,

340 HISTORY OF THE PENTECOSTAL HOLINESS CHURCH

sanctified and filled with the Spirit during that time. Other churches were organized at Winston-Salem, at Parmalee, Scotland Neck, Rocky Mount, South Norfolk and other places. Some of the ministers besides Mr. Butler who took part in helping organize these were the Revs. M. D. Sellers, R. B. Jackson, Bill Gurganus, J. G. Crocker, P. F. Robinson and others.

G. W. Stanley

Another outstanding pioneer minister of the first order is to be seen in the Rev. George W. Stanley of Siler City, North Carolina, who began his ministry about 1902. He was first licensed in the Wesleyan Methodist Church, but after receiving the Pentecostal Baptism he united with the Pentecostal Holiness Church in 1911. Mr. Stanley's ministry has been indeed fruitful. He is quiet, sweet-spirited and unassuming, but has been unusually successful in being able to establish a number of churches, some of which are among the best in the movement. In North Carolina he began churches at Star, Maple Grove, St. Marks, Altamahaw, Mt. Holly and Siler City. In Virginia he organized churches at Dry Fork, Danville, Buena Vista, Swansonville, Altavista, Grit and Skyler. In referring to his ministry, he says:

I have seen thousands saved and dozens of preachers have gone out from my ministry. I have prayed for many who were healed of various diseases: blind received their sight, deaf to hear, cancers healed, and tuberculosis. I have been trusting the Lord for my body for 45 years and was healed instantly of tuberculosis.[1]

J. B. "Jake" Williams

The Rev. J. B. "Jake" Williams is still another outstanding pioneer preacher whose work and sacrifice deserve special mention. He was the father of four sons and five daughters all of whom are prominent citizens and most of whom are Christians, one of them being the Rev. Floyd Williams, a prominent young minister of the North Carolina Conference. He, with the help of his sister, Mrs. G. H. Lewis and others of the relatives and friends have continued to carry on the work of the Aulander Camp Meeting which their father founded, thereby perpetuating it as a memorial to their faithful Christian parents, and at

---

1 G. W. Stanley, Letter dated April 7, 1948.

the same time maintaining a full-gospel witness in that section of the State. In fact, they feel definitely called to continue this work which God has signally blessed.

"Brother Jake" as he was known, packed his seventy-year allotment in a brief forty-one years, finishing his work for the Master and passing to what will no doubt be a rich reward on December 7, 1927. He left a permanent deposit of influence, which, like Abel of old it can be said of him, "he being dead yet speaketh." Through his sacrifice and toil early and late, and with the help and cooperation of an understanding and godly wife he was able in addition to this camp meeting to either build or establish thirteen churches principally in North Carolina, some of which were: the Millennium Pentecostal Holiness Church at Aulander and others at Shiloh, Scotland Neck, Lamb's Grove, Moore's Chapel, Shelmerdine, Happy Home, Hopewell, N. C., St. Paul near Greenville, N. C., and Pike's Cross Roads.

Being possessed with unusual talents as a business man, he was a successful building contractor, and also in the wholesale and retail meat business. These interests, however, were only secondary and were used to implement his greater work of the ministry which lay close to his heart. It was a normal occurrence for him to drive fifty miles or more and preach at night after spending hard days at secular work in order to be able to take care of his large growing family in the days when these pioneer holiness preachers were poorly paid for their services. This faithful and illustrious soldier of the Cross now has these churches to stand as a monument to his memory to memoralize his labor of love and sacrifice.

S. D. Page and W. W. Avant

When the Fire-Baptized Holiness Church was consolidated with the Pentecostal Holiness Church in 1911 the Rev. S. D. Page was elected as the first General Superintendent. Mr. Page was a merchant at Blakely, Georgia, at the time of his conversion. He was saved at a Methodist Church there, after which he immediately felt a call to preach and an urge to return to his home community at Green Sea, S. C. in Horry County. He was soon licensed by the Fire-Baptized Holiness Church. After he had tried to farm for a year he decided to give up all secular activity and enter the ministry full time. Mr. Page's ministry is usually mentioned by those who knew him as being associated with that of the Rev. W. W. Avant, who was connected with the Free Will Baptist Church. In referring to details of how they became acquainted Mr. Avant writes:

> A man by the name of Robert Riggins told him about B. T. Skipper, H. B. Johnson and myself who had been carrying on cottage prayer-meetings for more than two years. He drove his buggy about twenty miles to see me. This prayer meeting had attracted the attention of people for miles and miles around. It was from house to house for thirty miles broad and seventy miles long. He asked me if I would go with him in meetings which I agreed to do. Our first meeting was at Gaddy's Mill, S. C. in a meeting-house my father had built. From there we went to Serro Gordo, N. C.[1]

These men conducted meetings in North Carolina at Evergreen, Chadburne, Boardman, Whiteville, Abbottsburg, Dublin, Tar Heel, Bluefield, Fayetteville, Kelly and many other places where Pentecostal Holiness Churches were organized. Their services were attended by people who walked or rode for miles. The power of God was manifested by solemn conviction resting upon the people. Many drunkards, harlots and other dissolute persons were swept into the Kingdom of God under their fiery preaching, as well as many people who were morally good but had not been born again.

E. D. Reeves

The Rev. Edward Dulany Reeves was the son of the Rev. James T. Z. Reeves, and the brother of a Methodist minister. He was born on August 17, 1874 at Front Royal, Virginia, and was converted in the St. James Methodist Church at Roanoke, Virginia, when he was twenty-two. He was advised to sever his connection with that church after he became interested in sanctification and was sanctified in 1900. He received the baptism of the Holy Ghost in 1909 near Dublin, Virginia. In 1910 he was ordained by the Rev. F. M. Britton, Assistant General Overseer of the Fire-Baptized Holiness Church, when the Roanoke Church was organized, as was also the Virginia Convention. He was the Ruling Elder of this Convention at the time of the Consolidation in 1911. Mr. Reeves was elected as Assistant General Superin-

---

[1] W. W. Avant, Letter written to G. F. Taylor in 1934.

HOME MISSIONS, *continued* 343

tendent of the Pentecostal Holiness Church in 1921, and served in that capacity until his death in 1936. He was not only actively engaged in pioneer work in the Virginia Conference but also in the Ontario Conference where he labored after 1927. (The Revs. George Fisher, Sr., Alpheus Noseworthy, A. C. Ward, John MacMillan, G. F. Legge, J. H. Hutchinson, Miss K. I. Reid and others were pioneers in the Ontario Conference.)

Others

The Rev. E. M. Clower, E. R. Clower, D. H. Clower, J. B. Daugherty, D. M. Whiteneck, J. W. Vaughan and a number of others were prominently engaged in pioneer preaching.

GENERAL EVANGELISTS

There is quite a host of evangelists and evangelistic parties which have been active in evangelistic work over the Church during recent years, especially since 1937. Their work for the most part has not been under the Home Mission Board but has been conducted as individuals. The record of their full accomplishments cannot be written until their works have been finished, which will be reserved for some future historian to write. It will therefore suffice to merely mention the names of some of the most outstanding ones whose slates have appeared in the Advocate from time to time. They are as follows: J. A. Synan, G. H. Montgomery, Roy, Clarence and Taylor Frazier, comprising the Pentecostal Trio, Misses Blonnie Johnson, Marie Houser comprising the Johnson-Houser Party; J. A. Wells and his family comprising the Wells Evangelistic Party; Misses Irene Gaskins and Jessie Faircloth, comprising the Gaskins-Faircloth Party, Fred Sanders, S. J. and O. N. Todd comprising the Todd Evangelistic Party, and later Miss Evelyn Klefsaas and Mrs. S. J. Todd joined S. J. Todd after O. N. Todd began teaching school; Fannie Mae Morris Jones, Lee F. Hargis, W. H. Turner, Oral Roberts, Alice and Eddie Wilson, J. E. Knapp and wife, Philip Genetti, James F. Eppes, I. D. Dickens, Edgar Gourd and Bryan McClain, his singer; Oscar Moore, S. E. Pringle and many, many others who have made equally great contributions.

Chapter III
FOREIGN MISSIONS
The Holiness Church[1]

The earliest record of a missionary board in the Pentecostal Holiness Church was at the Fayetteville Convention in 1904. There may possibly have been some earlier activity of that sort, but there is no concrete evidence to warrant such a conclusion. The infant church had been busily engaged in organizing new churches since the time of its inception three years previously in 1900. In 1906 at the Lumberton, N. C. Convention the Rev. T. J. McIntosh was received into the Holiness Church, as an ordained minister. Mr. McIntosh was the first missionary to receive any support from the Pentecostal Holiness Church, although he did not go out under the board of the Church. He went to China in 1907 and traveled on around the world, and in 1909 went around the world a second time. The minutes of the 1908 Convention which met in Dunn, N. C., reveal that $164.75 in money was sent to Mr. McIntosh and $67.60 to another missionary by the name of John T. Benson, but where he labored is not stated. There was elected at that Conference a Foreign Missions Board. There were no official missionaries sent out by the Pentecostal Holiness Church until after the consolidation with the Fire-Baptized Holiness Church in 1911. Although the above mentioned missionaries and others were active members of this organization, their missionary activities were not church-sponsored. Other missionaries were members of other Church organizations, as will be seen, but they were in harmony with the Pentecostal Holiness Church in doctrine.

THE TABERNACLE PENTECOSTAL CHURCH

The Tabernacle Pentecostal Church, first called the Brewerton Independent Presbyterian Church, and later called the Tabernacle Presbyterian Church after it came to embrace several

---

1 The Pentecostal Holiness Church changed its name in 1901 and was called "The Holiness Church" until it again took its original name in 1909. This explains the references made to "The Holiness Church."

other independent churches of like faith, was founded by the Rev. N. J. Holmes who was also the founder of the Altamont Bible and Missionary Institute in 1898. The Church later took the name of "Tabernacle Pentecostal Church" and was consolidated with the Pentecostal Holiness Church in 1915. It therefore becomes necessary to mention its missionary activities as a contributing part of the history of foreign missions in the Pentecostal Holiness Church. Miss Lucy Jones was perhaps the first missionary to serve in the ranks of those churches which have gone to make up the Pentecostal Holiness Church as we know it today. Mrs. Holmes refers to her in 1916 as one of the students who had spent 14 years as a missionary to China and was then on furlough recuperating. Another of these early missionaries she also mentions was the Rev. Conway Anderson. He spent several years in an unhealthy section of Central America, which cost him his life.[1] Miss Carrie Casey likewise spent several years in Central America, and by 1916 had returned to the States and served as matron of the Holmes Bible and Missionary Institute.[2] In 1909 Miss Fay Watson was called to the mission field, and that year she accompanied the Rev. Richard Anderson and his wife (her sister) to Central America.[3] The Rev. Homer Owings was also an early missionary to China, having gone perhaps at approximately the same time that Miss Lucy Jones went, about 1902.[4] Miss Anna Deane, a distinguished educator from New York, who later moved to Birmingham, Alabama, went to China in 1909 where she founded a mission at 118 Main Street, Shaukiwan, Hong Kong, China. About two years later Miss Anna Deane Cole, the daughter of the beloved Mrs. J. B. Cole who was the sister of Miss Deane, went to China to join her aunt there. Miss Jane A. Shermerhorn, who also had taught at White Plains, N. Y., for twenty-seven years, joined Miss Deane and her niece in November, 1914. These three pioneer missionaries were being supported by the Tabernacle Pentecostal Church when it was consolidated with the Pentecostal Holiness Church at Canon, Georgia, in 1915, and thus became

---

1 N. J. Holmes and Wife, **Life Sketches and Sermons**, (Royston, Georgia: Press of the Pentecostal Holiness Church, 1920), p. 259.
2 **Ibid.**, p. 257.
3 **Ibid.**, p. 177.
4 **Ibid.**, p. 100.

Pentecostal Holiness missionaries. Although it is not definitely stated that all of the missionaries mentioned were connected with Mr. Holmes' Church, it seems perhaps that they were.

FIRE-BAPTIZED HOLINESS CHURCH

Oklahoma

Soon after the outpouring of the Spirit in Oklahoma in the Fire-Baptized Holiness Church there arose an urge among some of them to become witnesses unto the uttermost parts of the earth. The first to respond was Mrs. Adell Harrison and her daughter, Golden, who were sent to China, and supported by the Oklahoma State Convention, of that Church. A large work was developed at Sai Nam. She tells of an interesting incident when 24 girls, some of whom were blind, who were accustomed to gather in a prayer-room to tarry for the baptism of the Holy Ghost, after they had received the experiences of conversion and sanctification under Mrs. Harrison's ministry. One morning she was awakened by the noise of shouts in the prayer-room, and when she had gone to the prayer-room and opened the door she made the discovery that these 24 girls had gotten up during the night, gone to the prayer-room, and by morning all of them had received the baptism of the Spirit. The blind as well as the others were leaping, dancing and speaking in tongues as the Spirit gave utterance. Soon Miss Almyra Aston was also ordained by the Oklahoma Conference which met at Oklahoma City August 25, 1911 and sent to India. She had only ten dollars toward her fare when she started for California, but God miraculously supplied her need and on January 3, 1912 she sailed for Hong Kong. Here she intended to stay until God saw fit to provide passage to India, which He did, and in due time she arrived at her destination where she labored for several years.

Georgia

In 1910 Miss Della Gaines, the daughter of the famous Rev. G. O. Gaines went to India from the Georgia Convention of the same Church. She returned in 1912.

King's Tour of the World

In 1909, before the late Bishop J. H. King began his world tour in interest of foreign missionary work, it was arranged

FOREIGN MISSIONS 347

through Mr. A. E. Robinson for him to visit with the Rev. and Mrs. A. G. Garr (his first wife died shortly afterwards) who were then engaged in revival services at the Oliver Gospel Mission in Columbia, S. C. (Mr. Robinson was at the time living in the Mission and working in the printing office of "The Way of Faith," a publication sponsored by J. M. Pike, who was also director of the Oliver Gospel Mission.) The Garrs has spent several years as missionaries in China and gave Mr. King information regarding mission stations in China and India which he decided to visit. He set sail from San Francisco on September 20, 1910, and was gone two years on his tour around the world. (Mr. King was at that time the General Overseer of the Fire-Baptized Holiness Church, and it was while he was away that his church consolidated with the Pentecostal Holiness Church on January 31, 1911, at Falcon, North Carolina). He visited China, India, Ceylon, Palestine, and parts of Europe, and returned to the United States in 1912. While in China he received into his Church Miss E. May Law who had been an independent missionary there about three years. While in India the Revs. R. E. Massey and D. S. Mahaffey, who were also independent missionaries, were received into the Fire-Baptized Holiness Church. Mr. Massey returned to America in 1913.

Initial Developments After the Consolidation

At the North Carolina Convention of the Pentecostal Holiness Church which met at Fayetteville in November, 1911, there was begun more definite church-action in regard to foreign missionary work. This Convention decided to assume the responsibility for the support of Miss Law in China, and to send what money they could to the Rev. Mr. King to aid him on his trip around the world. Each local church was requested to contribute $2.00 per month for these purposes. The Rev. G. F. Taylor was chosen as Treasurer of the Foreign Missionary Board which was then elected. The General Superintendent, Rev. S. D. Page, was authorized to urge the other Annual Conventions to follow the good example set by the North Carolina body, and assume responsibility for the support of some of the missionaries who have been named. The Georgia Convention naturally chose the

Georgia missionary, Miss Della Gaines, while other Conventions chose other missionaries.

At the State Convention, in 1910, at Kinston, N. C., the Rev. H. C. King was accepted by the Foreign Mission Board to be sent to Africa. In 1912 he went to Liberia, West Africa, but remained only one year and returned to his home at Faison, North Carolina. In the Spring of 1912 Miss E. May Law came home from China on furlough. Before she returned that fall she visited various local churches in North Carolina in the interest of her work. Miss Ollie Mae Maw, of Ninety Six S. C., who was endorsed by the Georgia and Upper South Carolina Convention, returned with Miss Law to China. Sometime in 1912 the Rev. Amos Bradley and his wife, who had been missionaries to Central America, became members of the Pentecostal Holiness Church and, in 1913, they were sent again to that field, and were to be supported by the North Carolina Convention. The Rev. J. C. Lehman, who had been to Africa several years as an independent Holiness Missionary, returned to America in 1907 and received the Pentecostal baptism of the Spirit, and about 1912 he united with the Pentecostal Holiness Church and returned to Africa, but was promised no support. He came home in 1914 on furlough and returned late that year. On the way back he came in contact with the Rev. K. E. M. Spooner, further mention of whom will be made presently.

By 1913 when the General Convention met at Toccoa, Georgia, the Pentecostal Holiness Church had about a dozen missionaries on the field. Some of these were partially supported and others received no support at all. They were as follows: The Rev. J. O. Lehman in South Africa; the Rev. H. C. King in Liberia, West Africa; Misses Ollie Maw, and E. May Law and Mrs. Adell Harrison and her daughter Golden Harrison were in China; Miss Almyra Aston, the Rev. R. E. Massey and the Rev. D. S. Mahaffey were in India. The Rev. and Mrs. Amos Bradley were in Central America.

Kenneth M. Spooner and Geraldine M. Spooner

During 1914 Mr. Lehman returned to America on furlough, but by December he had embarked again for South Africa. Before his departure he chanced to contact two other missionaries who were going out for their first time, and who had been unable to get any missionary board or society to consent to sponsor their work in South Africa. They were the Rev. Kenneth E. M. Spooner and his wife Geraldine M. Spooner, who were well educated and cultured colored people. Mr. Spooner was born in the British West Indies and educated in this country, while Mrs. Spooner was a native of Port Lemon, Central America. Mr. Lehman enlisted them as missionaries for the Pentecostal Holiness Church, but for sometime they did not receive any support from that organization.

The facts are that immigration laws in South Africa were at that time very strict regarding the admission of any colored people. Some years before when God spoke to Mr. Spooner calling him to South Africa, he then asked God three different times to confirm His call by having some person speak to him about Africa. After this happened in such an unmistakable fashion each time, he no longer doubted but began to pray earnestly that God would supply his needs in order to be able to go. His wife, who had led him to Christ before they married in 1905, after a two year courtship, was altogether pleased to go with him. They sent their baggage to the dock by faith the day before their departure, not as yet having the necessary funds for their passage. That night a lady handed Mr. Spooner a roll of bills. The next morning at the boat a minister handed them another roll, and they departed hurriedly without passports, securing the same when they arrived in England. Mr. Spooner, in referring to the occasion of their arrival at Cape Town on January 15, 1915, is quoted as saying:

Owing to the fact that we had our passport, we met with no molestation. Let me say right here, it was a miracle we ever got into the country. I was told by an official five years afterward that it was the fault of the officer at the port that we were permitted to land. 'There is,' he said, 'a law that the colored population of South Africa must not increase from without.' This is the reason why no mission board would undertake to send me to South Africa.[1]

Mr. Spooner is without question the greatest missionary whom the Pentecostal Holiness Church has sent to Africa, in spite of

---

[1] Mrs. K. E. M. Spooner, et al, Sketches in the Life of K. E. M. Spooner, (Franklin Springs, Georgia: Pentecostal Holiness Publishing House, 1940), pp. 100, 101.

the fact that some of the purest gold in human talent and consecration have represented this Church on that dark Continent. He is responsible for establishing more than 60 churches during his life time, which ended on February 28, 1937.

Summary Showing the Remaining Missionaries by 1915

By 1915 the Lehmans, the Spooners, and Bradleys were the only remaining missionaries which the Pentecostal Holiness Church had in the field. H. C. King had returned in 1913, after going out in 1912. Miss Ollie Maw became involved by contrary doctrines, which required that she be dropped as a missionary. Miss E. May Law expressed her desire to work independent of the Church. Miss Della Gaines had returned in 1912, after being in India since 1910. Miss Almyra Aston asked to be independent and withdrew. The Masseys returned from India in 1913; the Mahaffeys withdrew, also desiring to be independent. Mrs. Harrison and her daughter likewise chose to be independent. There remained no Pentecostal Holiness Church missionaries in China or India. But in November, 1915 the Tabernacle Pentecostal Church organization was consolidated with the Pentecostal Holiness Church, thereby adding the following missionaries: the Rev. Conway Anderson at Zacapa, Guatemala, Central America; Miss Willie Barnett in the province of Guatemala; Miss Anna M. Deane, Miss Anna Deane Cole and Miss Jane Schermerhorn. Miss Deane died on the field April 12, 1918. Miss Anna Deane Cole sailed for America on her first furlough the same month.

First General Mission Board and Subsequent Developments

When the Second General Convention met at Toccoa, Georgia, in 1913, there was elected the first General Mission Board of the Pentecostal Holiness Church. The report of the Committee on Missions recommended that:

> There shall be a General Mission Board elected by the General Convention, which shall have the oversight of all missionary work of the Pentecostal Holiness Church in foreign lands, and this Board shall cooperate with the Missionary Boards of the Annual Convention in carrying forward the work of missions.[1]

---

[1] **Minutes of the Second General Convention, Toccoa, Georgia,** 1913 pp. 10, 11.

The Rev. J. H. King was elected as chairman of this Board, and the Rev. G. F. Taylor was elected Treasurer. This was the first step toward properly organizing the Foreign Missionary work which has continued to grow with a remarkable degree of success since that time. At the 1917 General Conference, pastors were urged to stress and to preach Foreign Missions. Tithing was recommended as a means of raising the necessary funds for both home and foreign work. A more rigid set of rules was set up for the requirements of out-going missionaries, to determine their doctrinal soundness and sincerity, as well as their natural qualifications, such as health and general aptitude for missionary work. At the General Conference in 1921 the Conference was asked to endorse the recommendations of the General Board authorizing the immediate purchase of lot and building for the providing of a Missionary Home for the missionaries in China.

There was raised $8,000.00 for this purpose, which amounted to 30,000 Chinese dollars. A new mission station was authorized to be opened in the interior of China. Recommendations were made also for the work in Africa. In 1925 requests were made to meet the demand for the immediate expansion of missionary activities, and the General Board was asked to survey and consider, annually, the needs of the various mission fields. By 1929 the missionary endeavor may be said to have reached a "high-water" mark. The Rev. W. H. Turner was home on furlough and at this General Convention was chairman of the "Committtee on Foreign Missions," and largely through his influence recommendations were made for sizeable expansions in Africa, India, and China alike. Missionary Rallies were inaugurated and special prayers were urged. In 1933 the Mexican work was recognized and placed on the same status as other missionary work in the Church. A General Secretary was elected, who was also to act as Corresponding Secretary to edit the Missionary Department of the Advocate. Tracts, programs and literature were to be scattered among the church constituency to create and stimulate interest in the foreign missionary work. The Young People's Society was urged to take part in giving impetus to the missionary work. In 1937 there were pressing financial needs; and it was recommended that they be met by enlisting the aid of the Sunday School, the Young People's Society, and a special missionary service to be conducted every month in every local church. A goal was set at one cent per day as a minimum for every member of the organization. Special prayer was urged that people would give liberally and systematically. In 1941 the Missionary Evangelists whom the General Board had appointed were recommended by this General Conference to continue their work. It was ordered that the missionary efforts be continued to the fullest extent, in spite of the war. Furloughs were urged when needed in order that the health of the missionaries should not become impaired. In 1945 the Foreign Mission Board was elected by the General Conference to be composed of four members, and a fifth member, who was to act as chairman, was to be appointed by the General Board of Administration. The budget for foreign missions was set at $75,000.00 which, on January 22, 1948, at the General Board of Administration meeting was raised to $100,000.00.

In the general summary given above it can be seen that there has been a growing interest in foreign missionary efforts, especially since 1915. We will now give more specific attention to the more detailed developments which have been made in the various fields since 1915, considering each field separately, and in conclusion give an over-all summary of the status of all the missionary work as a unit whole.

Some Later Developments

China

Miss Anna Deane had planned to return to America on furlough with her niece in 1918, but on April 12, 1918, she went to her eternal reward, having spent herself for the Chinese people before a much needed furlough could be granted. Miss Anna Deane Cole, however, sailed for America the same month and left Miss Schermerhorn to take care of the work in her absence. There was at that time, in China, a well-organized mission work and a day school of more than fifty students. There was also in operation a night school for men and boys who had to work during the day, who wanted to learn the English language. Most of these men were transient laborers, and as a consequence there was a continual turn-over in the night school's enrollment.

In 1919 the Rev. and Mrs. W. H. Turner and the Rev. and Mrs. T. H. Rousseau went to China to join Miss Schermerhorn.

In the fall of 1920, after a two-year furlough, Miss Cole returned to China, accompanied by the Misses Mary Wilkes Andrews, Pearl Loftin, and Julia Payne (Now Mrs. H. H. Morgan). As we have noted, during the year of 1920 a missionary home was provided for the missionaries in China. While Miss Anna Dean Cole was home on furlough she had opportunity to present the need of a Gospel Boat. Funds for this project were made possible principally through the beneficence of Mr. and Mrs. A. L. Jackson of Tallapoosa, Ga. In 1921, this boat, 19' by 60', was constructed and launched on Shaukiwan Bay. It was built with no machinery to make it mobile, but remained anchored near the shore among 7,000 to 9,000 "boat people," i. e., those who live in small boats in the Bay. In a short while there were more than one hundred of these people who had become Christians. In 1923 the Rev. Mr. Turner began work in the Pakhoi field, and later opened the Shanghai work in Central China. Miss Laura Hylton went to China in 1924. Since then other very able missionaries have been sent to that field, including the Rev. and Mrs. G. C. Legge, the Rev. and Mrs. Clyde H. Herndon, Miss Mavis Lee Oakley, Miss Ethel Strickland, Miss Leona Causey, Miss Eleanor Deane Cates, niece of Miss Anna Deane Cole, and Misses Evelyn and Sybil Rousseau.

North China (Hangchow)

After the British Columbia Canadian Conference had been formed in 1942 out of an independent work directed by the Rev. Harold Paul, the Chinese missionary work of this organization was also received in 1945. This work during the 30 years of its existence had spread in all directions over the Yangtse Valley, having its main base at Hangchow. The Rev. and Mrs. Harwood, Miss Florence Hamilton, the Cartmell sisters, Miss Milley and a number of others have been connected with this missionary project.

Central China (Shanghai)

The Rev. W. H. Turner, now on furlough, is Superintendent of the Central China work, which is based at Shanghai. There are at present 6 missionaries on the field, 4 on furlough and 6 accepted as outgoing missionaries. A Chinese Bible school is already started in this section. There are approximately 20 churches and a substantial number of native workers. The present needs in this area are tremendous, growing out of the recent inflation and the terrific losses which have resulted from the war. (No accurate statistics have been available since the war). The Turners spent two years in a Japanese concentration camp as prisoners of war, returning to America in December, 1943.

South China (Pakhoi)

The Pakhoi District of which the Rev. C. H. Herndon is head, has 3 missionaries in the field, and 6 more are awaiting the opportunity to be sent. The Pentecostal Holiness Church has here a valuable piece of property and should make rapid progress in this missionary endeavor. Mr. Herndon was also a prisoner of the Japanese and spent some time in a concentration camp.

India

After 1913, when Mr. Massey returned to America, and Mr. Mahaffey, and Miss Aston had withdrawn to become independent missionaries, there was no Pentecostal Holiness missionary work in India until the Rev. and Mrs. J. M. Turner were sent there in late 1920. They arrived on January 19, 1921, and by October 28, 1922, had opened the Jasidih Station. They were located at Bihar, East India, some 200 miles from Calcutta. The Turners spent two terms of service, from 1921-1927 and from 1931 to 1941. Mr. Turner has been on the field without his family for a third term since 1945. There are two schools and two orphanages and other property, such as dwellings, etc., in India, which together are worth well over $100,000.00.

The Rev. T. L. Robertson and his wife were sent to India, in 1924, and remained until 1930, when because of poor health he came home, alone, working his way back on a ship, peeling potatoes. They were the only missionaries in that field from 1927-1930. The Robertson family were brought home in January 1931. When the Robertson family were on their way home, in crossing the Red Sea they passed the boat which was bringing the Turners back to India, and exchanged Christmas greetings. Miss Effie Barker accompanied the Turners to the mission field, and is responsible for the Madhupur school and orphanage for girls which were begun in 1938. The Rev. George Byus and his wife (he married on the field) were in India from 1927-1931, when he returned on account of poor health, having contracted a fever. This left the Turners and Miss Barker on the field from 1931 until 1937, when the Rev. M. E. Parrish and his family were sent to India, and with them were Miss Emma Yeatts and Miss Emma Britton, the daughter of the renowned Rev. F. M. Britton. The Parrishes opened the Giridih Station. By 1937 a Conference had been organized. In 1940 Miss Barker returned on furlough, and in 1942 the Parrishes and Miss Britton came home, leaving Miss Yeatts to stay by the stuff during the war period. Miss Yeatts came home on furlough in 1946, after Mr. Turner had gone out to relieve her in 1945. With him also went Miss Emma Britton and Miss Effie Barker. In 1948 the Robertson family also have just returned to India. So there are now 4 missionaries on the field in India, 7 are on furlough, and 10 are on the accepted list. There are now 5 mission stations in the Conference which was organized about 12 years ago.

South Africa

After the Rev. Kenneth E. M. Spooner and his wife had landed at Capetown on January 21, 1915, they came up by train to Johannesburg with the Rev. J. C. Lehman, and shortly thereafter the Spooners had an opportunity open to them at Phokeng, District of Ruestenburg which they interpreted as an act of Divine providence. On January 21, 1917, exactly two years later, the Rev. and Mrs. Joel E. Rhodes, originally from the Florida Conference, arrived at Capetown. They also came up by train to Johannesburg and settled 21 miles west of that town in Krugersdorp. Sometime that Spring they met Mr. Spooner and were particularly drawn to him. In 1920 Mr. Lehman suddenly decided to go to America and without any notice he left, and since then has not returned. The Revs. Rhodes and Spooner discovered there was no organized body of the Pentecostal Holiness Church in Africa after his departure, and in 1922 at the Sophiatown church at Johannesburg these men and a few native workers were organized into the African Conference of the Pentecostal Holiness Church, Mr. Rhodes being elected as Superintendent and Mr. Spooner as Assistant Superintendent, in which capacity he served until his death in 1937, excepting the year he was in America on furlough. (In fairness to Mr. Lehman it should be said that through his influence, jointly with Mr. Rhodes, the first property for the Church was acquired in the Transvaal). Besides the 60 churches which we have previously mentioned that Mr. Spooner organized, he is responsible for opening the Phokeng Preparatory School in 1916. This school has made steady progress and was in process of being enlarged at the time of his death in 1937.

The Rev. and Mrs. D. D. Freeman and the Rev. and Mrs. J. W. Brooks were sent to Africa in 1924, Mr. Freeman locating at Johannesburg and Mr. Brooks at Krugersdorp. The Rev. and Mrs. J. W. Warren were sent a little later. Miss Verdie Lee Johnson, Miss Mildred Reynolds, Miss Helen Dunkerly have also served as missionaries in Africa. There are at present 9 missionaries in the field, including the Rev. and Mrs. J. E., Rhodes, the Rev. and Mrs. D. D. Freeman, the Rev. and Mrs. H. B. Johnson, and the Rev. and Mrs. George E. Fisher and Misses Irene Orser and Ann Lyon. Mr. Freeman is the present Superintendent of the South African Conference, which is the largest and most progressive of the missionary Conferences in the Pentecostal Holiness Church. In 1945 it had a total membership of 13,251. It has twenty-eight day schools with an attendance of nearly 3,000 and six night schools. There were 175 churches and mission points. Eight missionaries are at home on furlough and 12 are accepted as outgoing missionaries. A self-supporting White Conference was organized in 1947 with three churches, one of these has under construction a $30,000.00 church plant. It is being predicted that the colored work in South Africa will soon be self-supporting also.

Central America

The Rev. Conway Anderson, who was received into the Pentecostal Holiness Church in 1915, with the consolidation of the Tabernacle Pentecostal Church at Canon, Georgia, died of a fever in 1916. Miss Willie Barnett came home in 1917, and the Rev. and Mrs. Amos Bradley also came home in 1918. Since that time the Church has had no missionary work in Central America.

South America

Miss Janet Hart is in charge of the Pentecostal Holiness Church work in Concepcion del Uruguay, Argentina, South

America. She is assisted by Miss Jean Munn. (Miss Mary Watson accompanied Miss Hart when the station was opened in 1931, and afterwards Miss Hazel Childers worked with her). The missionary work in this area is 17 years old and has not moved with very great progress, but there are four missionaries scheduled to sail for that field during the fall of this year. Two others are accepted as outgoing candidates.

Mexico and Texas-Mexican Work

The Rev. Botello Alanis is Superintendent of the Pentecostal Holiness missionary work in Mexico. This work was accepted on the regular missionary basis in 1933. There are 50 churches and nearly 100 ministers in that country. There is also a native Bible school. Mr. Alanis' work has been most outstanding, and he enjoys an excellent reputation in the Pentecostal Holiness Church movement because of his enviable record and deep sincerity.

The Rev. Estaban Lopez of Weslaco, Texas, is also doing a creditable work in Texas among the Mexican people in South Texas, the state of Colorado, and two points in California.

Hawaiian Islands

The Pentecostal Holiness Church first opened this field on October 1, 1936, under the direction of Miss Mildred Johnson. In a short while, the Door of Faith Mission was opened in Honolulu, and in addition work was carried on in the leper camp and other places. The prospects were for opening stations on all of the islands. Because of some marital difficulties in which Miss Johnson innocently became involved, the General Board of the Church felt it would be unwise to continue to sponsor her work.

It was not until 1947 that the Pentecostal Holiness Church reentered this field, sending the Rev. and Mrs. Claude W. Smith as their missionaries. Mr. Smith had been converted under Miss Johnson's (now Mrs. Brostek) ministry while she was in Florida. The Smiths located at Oahu in the Hawaiian Islands.

During the first half of the year Mr. Smith solved the housing problem for himself and his family by securing a government quonset hut, which he erected with a little help from a kindly neighbor, on the rear of the property which he had selected for a church site. Since then he has secured a 30' x 30' government warehouse which has been attractively transformed into a handsome little church building on the front of this lot. This building which cost the Pentecostal Holiness Church approximately $1500.00, when completed will be worth $10,000.00.

In five months time, with practically no one to help him, this enterprising young missionary has set an unprecedented example for other ministers everywhere to emulate. There are encouraging prospects that this field will yet be extended to all parts of the Hawaiian Islands.

Summary and Outlook

There are at present 34 missionaries in the foreign fields, and 23 on furlough. Three of those on furlough will return to the field, and 4 new ones will be sent out during 1948, while two in the field will be returned. A total of 39 will be in the field by the end of 1948. There are 45 on the waiting list, plus those on furlough (22), making a total of 67 prospective missionaries, and 39 in the field.

The Pentecostal Holiness Church is the oldest organized Pentecostal Denomination. According to its size the Pentecostal Holiness Church enjoys the unique distinction of having the largest and most progressive foreign missionary work of any other Pentecostal group. Its growth in this country has been third highest. This can be readily accounted for by comparing the emphasis which has been placed on foreign missions with that of home missions.

The Church for example had no "Home Mission Board" from 1908 until 1941, while it has had a "Foreign Mission Board" every year since 1904. In every General Conference since 1911 there has been a report submitted by a "Committee on Foreign Missions." There was no such "Committee on Evangelism or Home Missions" report until 1929. The present Church Budget calls for an expenditure of $100,000.00 annually for Foreign Missions, as compared with $25,000.00 for Home Missions. In the face of these indisputable facts, those leaders of the Church who have become familiar with the facts are beginning to question the wisdom of this unbalanced emphasis. It is expected that there will be some change made at the next General Conference in 1949, which will correct this maladjustment, and it is predicted that there will be inaugurated a more satisfactory program which ultimately will promote the interests of both of these fields of service, by strengthening the home front.

The General Conference Minutes for 1945 reveal that at the end of 1944 there were 24,509 members of the Pentecostal Holiness Church in this country, as compared with 21,083 members in foreign lands, making a total combined membership of 45,592. It would appear from these figures that the immediate need is to enlarge and strengthen the home front before other expansions and developments are made on foreign soil.

Chapter IV
ORPHANAGE AND ELEEMOSYNARY INSTITUTIONS

BACKGROUND OF THE FALCON ORPHANAGE AND RELATED
INSTITUTIONS

The Founder

Mr. J. A. Culbreth is one of the best known and best loved men connected with the Pentecostal Holiness Church. No person even superficially acquainted with the orphanage work of the Church would fail to associate the name of Culbreth with that work. Mr. Culbreth was born and reared in the community where the Falcon Orphanage, the Falcon Camp Meeting, the Falcon Holiness School, and the Falcon Pentecostal Holiness Church are now located. He was born on December 28, 1871, and has remained in the same community all his life. He lives there now and expects to be buried there, next to his first wife, in a handsome vault provided for that purpose, "provided," he says, "that Jesus does not come during my life time." A good portion of the property of the above named institutions was inherited by Mr. Culbreth from his father's estate and dedicated for the purposes mentioned.

Location

Falcon is a village 9 miles south of Dunn, N. C. and 20 miles west of Fayetteville, just off of 301 Highway, 3 miles from Godwin. It is level rural country with arable land, and because it is sparsely settled it affords a quiet environment which adapts itself as a suitable place for all the activities associated with the church institutions named above. When Mr. Culbreth was 10 years of age, in 1872, the nearest neighbor was a quarter of a mile away. Today it is a small village of three or four stores and a post office.

Names Town

His father owned a store in this farming community. One day while government officials were in the store arranging for a post office to be located there, there was some question as to what the post office should be named. Young Culbreth glanced toward one of the store shelves and seeing the name "Falcon" on a box of Falcon Pens said, "Let's call it Falcon," so it took that name.

Marries

A few days after his 21st birthday he married Miss Venie Bizzell of Johnson County, North Carolina, a beautiful and talented young girl who inspired him throughout her life to accomplish things for God. Mr. Culbreth, since her death and his retirement, wrote a little poem which he entitled, "A Love Tribute to My Wife," the first verse of which seems apropos to quote here:

> I loved her not only for what she was,
>   But for what she inspired me to be.
> I loved her not only for what she made of herself
>   But for what she endeavored to make of me:
> I loved her because she seemed to see in me
>   Some better things that might be brought out;
> And for the faith and trust she showed in me
>   To put forth her efforts to bring it about.

Miracles

In 1899, seven years after their marriage, Mrs. Culbreth became seriously ill with appendicitis, and because of her weak physical condition it was not advisable to operate. The two doctors who were attending her anxiously waited for some sign of improvement in the hope that an operation might be performed to save her life, but no improvement came. Mr. Culbreth was praying day and night for her recovery but it seemed that he was unable to exercise faith. He and his wife had read in "The Way of Faith" of remarkable healings that had taken place in Oklahoma and other places in the West, under the ministry of the Rev. B. H. Irvin, General Overseer of the Fire-Baptized Holiness Church. One day during Mrs. Culbreth's illness she expressed her desire to have Mr. Irwin pray for her healing if he could be prevailed upon to come to her bedside. In one week's time, much to their surprise, Mr. Irwin had pitched his gospel tent in Dunn, N. C. On the first Sunday morning when the meeting opened on April 23, 1899, Mr. Culbreth attended the service, and immediately after the service Mr. Irwin and a man by the name of Harper from Durham went with him to pray for his wife. Before prayer Mr. Irwin asked all present to leave the room who did not believe in divine healing, and that God would heal Mrs. Culbreth independent of human remedies. Her father and mother, Mr. and Mrs. Hannibal N. Bizzell, quietly retired from the room. Then Mr. Irwin anointed her with oil in the name of the Lord, according to James 5:14. She was instantly and miraculously healed and in a few minutes had dressed herself and was in a rocking chair on the front porch when both doctors having heard of her healing came to investigate. One of them ordered her back to bed, but Mr. Culbreth paying them for their services, thanked them and told them they would be no longer needed.

Mr. Culbreth had asked that God allow her 15 more years to live, like Hezekiah of old, but she lived exactly 44 years, being called to her heavenly reward on April 23, 1943. This miraculous occurrence dates the beginning of a series of miracles which have characterized the entire history of the Falcon work. On the top of the slightly sloping gable topped double vault, appearing as an open book is to be found the inscription, which we quote on the following page, and which gives in outline form the important dates, and miraculous events, connected with the orphanage and school.

The Falcon Camp Meeting

The history of the Falcon Camp Meeting, The Falcon Holiness School and the Falcon Orphanage are so closely interwoven that it is not possible to discuss them apart from one another. These were all begun as interdenominational projects, intended to benefit people of all denominations.

After Mrs. Culbreth's healing which occurred in 1899, both she and Mr. Culbreth desired to make a "thank-offering" unto the Lord for His goodness and mercy, and decided to spend $250.00 in sponsoring a Camp Meeting at Falcon. The Rev. S. C. Todd, mentioned in connection with the history of the Holmes Bible College as the Presbyterian minister with whom the Rev. N. J. Holmes was associated, had at his disposal a large gospel tent, and had agreed to make use of it for this purpose. Gasoline lanterns, torches and outside fires were used to illuminate the tent in those days. Fifty army tents which had

"Her children arise up and call her blessed, her husband also, he praiseth her."

	1896 MEMOIRS 1943
Purposes	FORTY-SEVEN YEARS OF SERVICE TO HONOR GOD TO THANK FRIENDS, TO GIVE TESTIMONY
1896	Born again, Sanctified wholly, Dedicated for service.
1899	Wife seriously sick, two Doctors said she would die, God instantly healed and added 44 years to her life.
1900	With gratitude to God we gave a thank-offering of $250.00 and arranged for first Camp Meeting at Falcon. A sermon at Camp Meeting on feeding the 5000 with five loaves and two fishes given by a lad to Jesus inspired us to deny ourselves and give of our means to God to be multiplied in His hands to feed hungry thousands with the Bread of Life. The lad's lunch fittingly represented all we had to give, but thousands have been fed and filled, and holy influences of Falcon Camp Meeting have spread worldwide.
1902	Falcon Holiness School opened, many of its graduates have filled honorable and holy callings and rendered valuable services in this Country and abroad.
1909	The Falcon Orphanage was incorporated, has operated 34 years and accumulated a plant worth about $100,000.00. Operations for these years and expenses of 43 annual camp meetings have cost more than $300,000.00. These funds of more than Four Hundred Thousand Dollars came in answer to prayers through many friends without organized effort or direct solicitation.
	To God Be All the Glory
1943	The entire plant was held in the name of Falcon Orphanage, Inc. and on April 7 was transferred to the Pentecostal Holiness Church, an organization of about 25,000 members. In consideration of the transfer the Church obligated itself to perpetuate and expand the work in harmony with, and according to the principles of the certificate of incorporation of The Falcon Orphanage, Inc. The orphanage was free from debt and had a Bank Balance of $5,000.
Miracles	These Memoirs had their beginning in a Miracle of healing. The inspiration to faith and courage to follow on came through the miracle of feeding more than 5000 people with 5 loaves and 2 small fishes multiplied by God's blessing, and agrees with a small gift of 14 cents, among the first made to us, and increased in the same manner to thousands of dollars since then. The transfer of Plant and cash balance represents the fragments taken up by the Disciples at the command of Jesus and committed to them for conservation. Such a trust honors the Trustees, and increases their opportunities; but places them under sacred and solemn obligations, both to God and man.

been used during the Spanish American War, in 1898, were rented to take care of those who came from distances and camped on the grounds. The famous Rev. George D. Watson was invited to conduct these special camp meeting services which took place during the last of July. (Since that time they have been conducted during the "full Moon" in August, and this year will make the 49th consecutive year).

Mr. Watson preached one powerfully appealing sermon on the lad with five loaves and two small fishes, which so profoundly impressed Mr. and Mrs. Culbreth that they decided to give to God what little they had and asked Him to bless it in providing the spiritual Bread of Life for hungry multitudes. This Camp Meeting alone has been the source of spiritual blessings and food for literally multiplied thousands. Sometime afterwards Mr. Culbreth had built a 48 room, three-story dormitory according to his own design. There is an outside entrance to every room leading to a partially enclosed veranda which completely encircles the building on all three floors. It is good naturedly called the "Ark" because of its similarity in appearance and size to that ancient vessel. This building was erected specifically for the campers and was designed for summertime use only. Rooms rent for a nominal sum of 50c. per night. It can accommodate 180 persons, and has a kitchen and restaurant in the basement.

The first offering for the Falcon work was the small sum of 14 cents which was given by a woman missionary who visited the first camp meeting. In referring to this occasion Mr. Culbreth writes:

The Falcon Camp Meeting was launched as a work of faith and all the phases of work ever sponsored by it have been on the same basis.

We had no organization under any obligation to support our work, except whatever moral obligations, motivated by a sincere personal interest they voluntarily assumed, but such as desired to have part in the work to promote and perpetuate its blessings to mankind and to render service in the name of the Lord. Among the first contributions made to us for the purpose of promoting the work, was the amount of fourteen cents given us by a woman missionary to the Negroes in the South, it being the full amount that the woman had left after allowing for her expenses to her next meeting. A small amount, but we appreciated it enough that we shall never forget it, and the increase of that amount to an approximate sum of $400,000 which the Lord provided and permitted us to use since that time in carrying on the work of the Camp Meeting and operating the Orphanage, proves to us conclusively that God's blessings and approval were upon our efforts, as the feeding of the five thousand men besides the woman and children, with five loaves and two small fishes, proved that God's hand could multiply the least of our offerings into the superabundance for our needs in any emergency.[1]

In 1926, a large auditorium 120 feet square was built to accommodate the large crowds which throng the camp meeting each year. The acoustics in this building are excellent, and the speaker can be seen without difficulty from any part of the congregation. This is the only camp meeting in North Carolina which has a permanently constructed tabernacle building.

In 1947, the North Carolina Conference finished a new concrete block dormitory which has 50 rooms and will accommodate 180 guest preachers, delegates, or members of their families. The kitchen and dining room in the basement are equipped to serve 110 persons at a single sitting.

Falcon Holiness School

In 1902, two years after the Falcon Camp Meeting began, Mr. Culbreth and his wife decided to open a non-denominational Holiness School i. e., those of all denominations were invited to attend. It was begun as a private school with only a few students, and was the first rural high school in Cumberland County. At one time it was a 10 teacher high school having 80 students. Later, after the orphanage was founded in 1909, it was financed through that medium, when the State withdrew its support due to an insufficient enrollment. The high school department was finally discontinued in 1942. Since that time it has been a seven grade elementary school until recently, in 1948, the 8th grade has been added and some subsidy has again been obtained from the State. The school was accredited in 1929. Present plans call for discontinuing the high school department at Franklin Springs, Georgia, when the Emmanuel College has been developed into a fully accredited Senior College, and transferring that phase of educational activity to Falcon, making it a fully accredited High School.

---

[1] J. A. Culbreth, **Our Children**, (Falcon, N. C.: Published monthly Falcon Orphanage of the Pentecostal Holiness Church, April, 1947), p. 2.

The Principals

Beginning sometime after the school opened and continuing until January, 1907 a man by the name of McCuller from Georgia was principal of the school. He withdrew when the people of that community began to receive the baptism of the Holy Spirit in 1907. The Rev. G. F. Taylor, who was conducting the revival there, and who was at the time principal of a school at Bethel, North Carolina, accepted Mr. Culbreth's offer to take Mr. McCullen's place and served from 1907 until 1916. The Rev. A. C. Holland served from 1916 to 1926, and was succeeded by the Rev. I. H. Pressley who served from 1918 to 1929. Mr. J. O. Humphries served from 1929 to 1942 with the exception of one year, 1933-34, when Mr. Nickles R. Beacham was principal. From 1942 to 1945 Mrs. W. H. Randall was principal and after a time Mr. Humphries again came to head the school.

The Alumni

In 1943 the Alumni Association was organized. This organization has been active in its efforts to improve the school building at Falcon, and has also served to stimulate enthusiasm among the alumni. In 1947 the Association elected Mr. Rufus R. Edwards to direct its activities. Mr. Edwards, who is Superintendent of the Rural Electrification project near Falcon, saw fit to donate a barbecue dinner for the Alumni meeting and gave the proceeds of $1.00 each which was charged the guests to the institution. Some of the outstanding graduates of this school are as follows: The Revs. A. C. Holland, present Superintendent of the Falcon Orphanage; W. H. Turner, veteran missionary to China; J. W. Brooks, also a veteran missionary to Africa; T. H. Rousseau, missionary now in China; J. W. Berry, Jerome Hodges, W. E. Morris, J. H. Marshburn of the North Carolina Conference; I. H. Pressley of the Alabama Conference, and S. E. Franklin of the Florida Conference; Dr. John W. Messick, President of the Eastern North Carolina Teachers College; Dr. R. S. Turlington; Dr. P. C. Chan, Chinese; T. D. Lee, Chinese, and quite a number of others.

School Buildings

The classes which were begun in the small local church are now conducted in a ten-room brick school building having an auditorium which seats 1,000. In this building are also the offices of the faculty and Superintendent of the Orphanage.

THE FALCON PENTECOSTAL HOLINESS CHURCH

The historic octagonal-shaped church building was built about the time the school was opened. Mr. Culbreth designed it to appear like the first camp meeting tent, and on occasions it was used for camp meeting gatherings before it became a Pentecostal Holiness Church. It was here that the consolidation of the Fire Baptized Holiness Church with the Pentecostal Holiness Church took place. The lumber which went into this building was donated by a Presbyterian elder, who had a number of trees blown down on his property by a wind-storm. Recently, in 1945, three Sunday school rooms have been added to the rear of this building. The congregation more recently purchased a Hammond electric organ which was paid for in five months by the "Venie Culbreth Ladies Circle." A new 8-room parsonage has also just been completed and is practically without debt.

THE FALCON ORPHANAGE

The Falcon Orphanage like the Falcon Holiness School and Church has grown directly out of the Falcon Camp Meeting. It is therefore a child of the Camp Meeting. In 1935 the Falcon Camp Meeting, the parent institution, gave up all its property-holdings to the orphanage. The orphanage assumed a $6,000 debt which was against the camp meeting property. In a newspaper write-up which appeared in the August 31, 1947, issue of the Raleigh News and Observer the following statement is made about the Falcon School and Orphanage:

Culbreth and his wife opened the non-denominational Holiness School. . . . To it came orphans whom the Culbreths had taken to rear, and children from the surrounding area.

The Orphanage was incorporated in October, 1909. The number of children grew, until today it has a home for 37 girls, two homes for 43 boys, and a dairy barn on its 200 acres.

Culbreth served as its Superintendent from 1915 to 1945 when he became Superintendent emeritus. While associated with the orphanage, he worked several years as a bank clerk in Dunn and also with the Cotton Growers Cooperative Association in Raleigh.

Most of the above facts are correct but according to the information given this writer by Mr. Culbreth in a personal interview there were no orphan children received until March 9,

1909, when they were brought to Falcon by the late Bishop J. H. King. Bishop King was the first Superintendent of the Falcon Orphanage which was incorporated on October 22, 1909, under the laws of North Carolina, application having been made for its charter by J. A. Culbreth, J. H. King and F. M. Britton, as the original incorporators and Trustees. Mr. King was at that time head of the Bible department of the Falcon school, of which the Rev. G. F. Taylor was head. In speaking of the founding of the Falcon Orphanage and bringing the first two children, he says:

The time had come according to the revelation of God's will for the orphanage to be opened. I was definitely led to take the initial step. I felt that I, of all persons on earth, was least qualified to open and take charge of the orphanage. But though I viewed it in this light, and felt as if I did not know how to begin, yet the Lord led me step by step until arrangements had been made to start the work. I employed Mrs. M. D. Sellers as the first matron, and rented the home in which they were living for an orphanage.

After several weeks had passed I was notified that a woman who lived in Bethel, North Carolina, had two children whom she desired to put into the orphanage. I arranged to go there to see about receiving them. Her two children, Mary and Thomas Ward, were quite small and she wanted them to have a home. . . . I went to the Ward's home, i. e., where they were staying with an aunt. There was an atmosphere of sadness in the home. It seemed as if someone were dead, and arrangements were being made for the funeral. . . . We arose early the next morning, prepared what little there was for the children, and rode to the station for the early train to Rocky Mount. . . . The children seemed to be able to endure until the train left, and then little Mary began to cry most bitterly. I could do nothing to quiet her. All the passengers on the train seemed to be affected. Some came to inquire what was the matter with the little child. I replied that I was taking them to an orphanage, and they seemed very sad. It made some of them weep. . . . She cried most all the way to Rocky Mount but finally ceased. As the train stopped at the station I took the two children into the waiting-room, and as I sat down little Mary looked up into my face and said so anxiously, appealingly, 'Do you love us?' Then I put my arms around her and said, 'Yes, I do.' There it seemed that the Lord put a special love in my heart for orphan children. They both said, 'Well, we love you!' And it seemed as if their sadness was gone, and that they felt as if they were in the hands of those who loved them. . . . That was the ninth day of March, 1909, and it will be one of the great days in life stored up in memory. It was not long until almost everybody in Falcon came to see the first children received into the Falcon Orphanage. We soon purchased forty acres of land as the beginning of the orphanage farm.[1]

---

[1] J. H. King. Unpublished manuscript.

Bishop King continued his work as Superintendent for a short while until September, 1910, when he began his tour around the world in the interest of foreign missions. He arranged with Mr. J. A. Culbreth to assume these duties as well as the editorship of the revived Apostolic Evangel which had been begun on March 15, 1909. When he returned in 1912 he discovered that Mr. Culbreth had built a Girl's Home. This original building which Mr. Culbreth had built in Mr. King's absence has since been named "The J. H. King Cottage" in honor of the founder of the Orphanage. Mr. King took over his duties as Superintendent again for a short while, and then the Rev. C. B. Strickland succeeded him and also served for a brief period until 1915. J. A. Culbreth then became the Superintendent and served nearly thirty years until July 1, 1943, when he retired because of failing health, and was succeeded by the Mr. A. C. Holland. (The Rev. W. W. Carter served temporarily from July 1, 1943 to August 15, 1943.) The name of J. A. Culbreth will never cease to be held in high esteem, and will be immortalized as long as there is a Pentecostal Holiness Church organization. He is now Superintendent emeritus, is much improved in health, was married on September 8, 1946 to Miss Mollie Thornton, a faithful employee of the Orphanage, and looks much younger than his 76 years.

The Present Superintendent

Mr. A. C. Holland, as we have noted, served as principal of the Falcon Holiness School after his graduation from 1916-1926. Mr. Holland loves the orphanage work and is eminently qualified in every respect to do it. He is a graduate of the Presbyterian College in Clinton, S. C., and perhaps will receive his Ph.D. degree at the University of North Carolina, where he majored in "child welfare." He was the first B. A. and M. A. and will be the first Ph.D. in the ranks of the Pentecostal Holiness Church. He was Superintendent of the Jones County Schools when he was elected to superintend the Falcon Orphanage work.

The Printing Press

As a most commendable gesture of appreciation for the Falcon work, Mr. Holland last year donated a $2500.00 printing press which is now being used to print the monthly periodical known as, "Our Children," and other necessary printing in connection with the Falcon work.

In referring to the acquiring of the printing press and the uses to which it will be put Mr. Holland writes:

> The most important piece of news we have this week is that the Orphanage is the possessor of a printing press. Your superintendent and editor is donating it to the orphanage plant. It will not only take care of printing the orphanage paper, but will take care of the orphanage printing and some of your printing, later on, if you want some done. . . . The most important phase is that our orphanage boys and possibly girls who show an aptitude in this direction will have a chance to learn the printer's trade.
> It is a sad story that our Church is lacking in people who are skilled in the printer's trade as well as writers. Our Church will never grow and make the progress it should until we begin turning out our Pentecostal Holiness books and literature in much greater volume. Tragic is it that we do not have more writings by our pioneer leaders. It is to be hoped that we can begin to inform the world through books and other literature in a greater way.[1]

Mr. A. E. Robinson, who was the first printer in the Pentecostal Holiness Church, and who has done most outstanding work in that field of endeavor, has been given charge of this work. A fuller account of his lengthy service and sacrificial contributions to publications in the Church will be seen in the section dealing with the History of Publications.

Orphanage Publications

From March 15, 1909 until 1929 the "Apostolic Evangel" was published at Falcon, N. C., in the interest of the Falcon work, when it then turned over its subscription list to the Advocate. Other details will be found in the section dealing with the History of Publications in the Pentecostal Holiness Church. The Orphanage had no voice after 1929 until March, 1946 when Mr. Holland began to edit "Our Children" a periodical which has served a very worthwhile purpose in publicizing the orphanage work.

The Property and Buildings

In addition to the J. H. King Cottage for girls there have been

---

[1] A. C. Holland, **Our Children**, op. cit., p.. 2.

other buildings added which include the J. A. Culbreth Home for small boys; the S. D. Page Cottage for large boys and the F. M. Britton Cottage for babies. Three of these are named in honor of those who were the original incorporators, and the fourth in honor of the late Rev. S. D. Page who donated his home, built in 1911, to the Orphanage. He was the first General Superintendent of the Pentecostal Holiness Church, since the time of the consolidation in 1911. All other property connected with the School and Camp Meeting was given to the Orphanage as we have noted, in 1937. Recent recommendations for 1948 provide for the Brooks' house, which was donated to the orphanage to be moved on Mr. Culbreth's lot, and that the building he now occupies may be repaired and alterations made so as to adapt it for use as a home for small girls. (Another recommendation also requests that $25,000.00 be set aside for orphanage work instead of the usual $18,000.00 as heretofore. By actual comparison with the orphanage work of other denominations the cost per child to operate the Falcon Orphanage is considerably lower. The budget of the Falcon Orphanage is fixed by the North Carolina Welfare Department at $400.00 per child and it takes close figuring to get by on that amount. The Duke Foundation contributed more than $2,000.00 to the Orphanage in 1946.)[1] Other property includes a farm, a dairy-barn and a Grade "A" dairy.

Becomes Pentecostal Holiness Church Property

In 1929 Mr. Culbreth offered to the Pentecostal Holiness Church the Falcon property, after the Franklin Springs project had virtually failed, but that offer was rejected. The details concerning this appear in connection with the History of Education in the Pentecostal Holiness Church. It is the opinion of some that when the Franklin Springs project was originally begun, in 1918, that a much better plan would have been to have developed the publishing house, college, and church headquarters and all at Falcon. It is likely true that the apparent dissatisfaction which terminated in moving from Falcon to Franklin Springs could have been avoided had it not been for possible jealousy or misunderstandings between leaders. It would seem

---

A. C. Holland, **Annual Report of Falcon Orphanage for 1947.**

that those who were trustees of the Falcon work could have gotten together and worked out some mutually agreeable proposition. In that case a fully accredited four-year College and other Church projects could have no doubt been realized long ago, and without anything like the expense and sacrifice which have been entailed in the other program of procedure. At least this is the opinion of some in the Church.

Mr. Culbreth continued to operate all of the Falcon work on an interdenominational basis, and it was privately owned, until March 30, 1943, when a deed was drawn up transferring the Falcon Orphanage and all of its holdings to the Pentecostal Holiness Church. This deed was accepted on or about April 8, 1943, and recorded in the Fayetteville, Register of Deeds office, Cumberland County, N. C., July 1, 1943. The total assets in 1948 were $112,412.50, and there are now some 80 children in the institution.

Adoption Plan

During 1947, Miss Ruby Manuel was placed in charge of the "Adoption Plan," which was inaugurated as a means of securing clothing and Christmas gifts for the children. This plan is not meant to take the place of the regular type of offerings ordinarily received for the orphanage. In writing of the growing interest in this phase of the work Mr. Holland says:

> The interest in the 'Adoption Plan' is nation-wide, from Texas, California, Canada and New York to Florida, and other Southern States. Churches from all Conferences have responded. Up to the present most of the children have been taken by some group, but we still have others eligible for adoption under the plan.
> It is wonderful to see how the plan is progressing and God is blessing. It has taken such a burden off the Orphanage and the workers in the matter of purchasing and obtaining clothing. It is so difficult to obtain clothing in many instances in quantities. Travel is difficult and time is limited and we are located in a small town away from shopping centers.[1]

Tours and Offerings

Periodically tours of various Conferences, not too far away, are made by groups of talented children who are able to render

---

1 A. C. Holland, **Our Children, op. cit.,** Nov. 1947, p. 2.

a special program in the interest of the Orphanage, after which offerings are taken for the orphanage work. A typical appeal at Thanksgiving is to be seen in the following lines which appeared in the November, 1927, issue of "Our Children":

> The best way to express our thanks is to share our blessings with those who are not so fortunate. Among the people of all denominations Thanksgiving suggests remembrance of the Orphanage. The Falcon Orphanage, owned and operated by the Pentecostal Holiness Church, is caring for approximately 80 children who were homeless until they found one in our institution. The Thanksgiving and Christmas seasons have been set aside by our Church as a time to remember the Falcon Orphanage. Regular support is necessary to meet the needs of the Orphanage, but at this season it is the desire of the authorities to make a special effort to raise funds for the improvement of the Orphanage.[1]

The Orphanage Board

At the 1945 General Conference the Orphanage Work of the Church was brought under the supervision of the General Board of Administration, and made to function in the same capacity as the various other programs of activity such as Home Missions, Foreign Missions or Education. The Orphanage Board at first consisted of three members, with T. A. Melton as chairman, W. W. Carter as Secretary and F. A. Dail to complete the Board. Since that time Mrs. J. W. Berry and W. E. Morris have also been added, making a total of five members.

The Staff

The staff of workers for 1948 is as follows: A. C. Holland, Superintendent; G. H. Carter, Farm Manager; Mrs. G. H. Carter, matron; Mrs. Fonnie Leake, Matron; Miss Ruby Mathews, Class Director of the 8th Grade; J. A. Culbreth, Superintendent Emeritus; Miss Ruby Manuel, Secretary and Director of "The Adoption plan" work; Miss Nellie Fay Fowler, Matron and Mrs. Lucile Cooper, Music Director. Mrs. A. C. Holland was recently placed on the State teachers payroll and added to the faculty.

THE FRANKLIN SPRINGS ORPHANAGE, 1919-1921 . . . . . .

During January of 1919 the Official Board authorized the Franklin Springs Orphanage to be opened. It was actually opened

---
[1] Loc cit.

in April of that year. The Rev. J. H. King was selected to head this work and afterward wrote an article which appeared in the Advocate, part of which reads as follows:

> The General Board of the Pentecostal Holiness Church, at its recent session at Franklin Springs, near Royston, Ga., established an orphanage on the property at the Springs, to be known and owned as the Orphanage of the entire Pentecostal Holiness Church. It is not an institution of the Georgia Conference but of the entire church. The Oklahoma Conference owns as much in the Orphanage as the Georgia Conference; that is, legally. It will be run under the auspices of the General Board of the Church, and that for the church as a whole, one member will have as much in it as another, and one conference will own as much as another. We want this point clearly understood.
>
> The Board elected the writer as Superintendent of the Orphanage. A building has been secured. . . . We will need hundreds of dollars to furnish the home complete, and we sincerely urge every church in the various Conferences to send us a donation for this purpose.[1]

It is evident from these lines that Mr. King realized that it would be difficult to secure the united support of the Church, due to the fact that there was already an orphanage work at Falcon which had received children from the Pentecostal Holiness Church, and would continue to do so. Another reason he may have had some misgivings about the matter was that the Church was already heavily obligated with the School which was opened on January 1, 1919, and the Publishing House which was built the same year, and with the Franklin Springs property which had been purchased in 1918.

All these factors add up to saying that it was impossible to finance an orphanage at this time, and that there was no real need for such in the Church as long as the Falcon Orphanage was still in existence. There was, however, some doubt as to what would become of the Falcon property if Mr. Culbreth died, and for that reason more than any other, perhaps, the orphanage work was begun at Franklin Springs.

At one time there were about 30 children in this institution but, in 1921, it was forced to close, and most of the children were transferred to the Falcon Orphanage, according to the opinion of some, where they should have been sent to begin with. No other such attempt has been made since that time, but the Falcon

---

1 J. H. King, **Advocate, op. cit.,** January 23, 1919, p. 7.

Orphanage has continued to serve the Church, both before and since it came to be church-owned.

THE BETHEL HOME FOR GIRLS

Before 1929, Mrs. J. H. Hutchinson had opened the "Bethel Home for Girls."[1] This work has for some years been in fellowship with the Pentecostal Assemblies, although Mrs. Hutchinson is a member of the Pentecostal Holiness Church, and the Home is operated under the Ontario Pentecostal Holiness Church Charter. It is located at 375 Parkside Drive, Toronto, Canada. Mrs. Hutchinson has done a very creditable and noteworthy work in helping fallen girls to escape from their disgrace and despondency. All of them appreciate Mrs. Hutchinson's motherly kindness and Christian consideration, and for the most part these girls become Christians before leaving the home. Although this work has never been included in the General Budget appropriations of the Church it has nevertheless been recognized and appreciated as will be seen from the following recommendation included in the report of the "Committee on Evangelism" at the 1945 General Conference:

> Your committee takes notice of the fine work being done by the Bethel Rescue Home for Girls, under the direction of Mrs. J. H. Hutchinson in Toronto, Canada. We recognize in this work a fulfillment of the spirit of compassion as manifested by our Lord and Saviour toward the lost and fallen. We commend this work to your prayerful and sympathetic consideration.[2]

EARLY RESCUE HOME PROJECTS IN OKLAHOMA AND NORTH CAROLINA

In a letter from Bishop Dan T. Muse he relates the following account of a rescue work in Oklahoma City about 1908:

> Under the leadership of Pastor H. P. Lott of the Oklahoma City First Pentecostal Holiness Church there was started a Rescue Home in the northwestern outskirts of Oklahoma City. Mrs. A. L. Warsham and Fannie Waterfield served as matrons, and many fallen girls were rescued from lives of sin. Some left the Home changed into new creatures. One girl who had been rescued from the slime pits

---

1 **Minutes of the 1929 General Conference, p. 6.**
2 Minutes of the 1945 General Conference held at Oklahoma City, Oklahoma, June 7 to 14, 1945, p. 46.

of sin, sanctified and filled with the Spirit, later died, and left this world speaking in other tongues as the Spirit gave utterance. Her baby girl grew up under Pentecostal Holiness influence and the last time she was in this writer's home visiting, she was a fine Christian woman.[1]

The minutes of the 1908 Holiness Church Convention reveal that there was a Rescue Home in Wilmington, North Carolina. The Rev. C. B. Cashwell made an appeal in its behalf and received an offering of $12.80 and a Teacher's Bible. Although there was not at that time a Pentecostal Holiness Church in Wilmington, this work may be considered in some sense as part of the history of the Church, in that it received support from the Church at least on this occasion.

---

[1] Dan T. Muse, Letter dated March 10, 1948.
Acknowledgement is also hereby made to Bishop Dan T. Muse, who generously furnished the bulk of the information relating to the church west of the Mississippi River.

Chapter V
YOUTH SOCIETY, SUNDAY SCHOOL AND VACATION BIBLE SCHOOLS

YOUTH SOCIETY

The Name and Some Objections

The youth society of the Pentecostal Holiness Church was called the "Pentecostal Young People's Society" when it was first organized in 1925. At the 1941 General Conference, the Rev. J. M. Jewell offered a motion which had for its purpose to give to the youth society a more suitable name, more in harmony with the name of the Church itself. The name was changed from the "Pentecostal Young People's Society" to the "Pentecostal Holiness Youth Society." There is apparently no objection to this name at present, but for a long time there was an element in the Church who were somewhat rabid in their denunciation of the word "Society," feeling that the use of such a term would lead to worldliness. The word, to some, carried with it certain evil connotations which they felt for sure would destroy the sanctity of the Church and worship services. Instead of interpreting "society" to mean the "voluntary association of individuals for a common end," they thought of it as meaning only one thing, "that part of the community which marks itself apart as a leisured class, with much time given to formal social affairs, fashionable sports, etc."[1]

This attitude was more prevalent during the years immediately following the time of its inception as a general organization in the Church. The young people's work met with vigorous opposition especially in some quarters. Older people who ordinarily would not have objected to certain types of recreation among young people, became outspoken in their denunciation of the same things they ordinarily would have endorsed and condoned. But because it was instigated by that new "Society" group in the Church they objected to it. This attitude of course has suggested other

---
1 **Webster's Collegiate Dictionary, Fifth Edition** (Springfield, Massachusetts: G. and C. Merriam Co., 1937).

imaginary objections, particularly on the part of older people who are overly conservative, or who imagined that the youth of the Church, if allowed to organize themselves, might become recalcitrant or contumacious and even threaten to become a church within the Church. Because of sane spiritual leadership among the young people of the Church this attitude is gradually changing and those who were the most unfriendly in their attitude are now making friendly gestures which indicate a reconciliation. If daring youthful enthusiasm is tempered with the mature judgment and sobriety of older people, it can prove to be an invigorating force to prosecute many constructive programs for Christ. The young people's program, so far, has proved a far greater blessing to the Church than it has been a hindrance.

Early Beginnings

Before the general organization in 1925 there were some attempts made within certain local churches in Tallahassee, Florida and Atlanta, Georgia, to organize the young people and to foster some sort of planned program. The Rev. and Mrs. O. N. Todd, Sr. were perhaps the first pastors to inaugurate youth programs in the local church when they pastored the Atlanta Church in 1921. According to the Rev. T. L. Aaron, perhaps one of the earliest attempts in this direction was made by Miss Margaret Conley of Atlanta, Georgia. He says she is largely responsible, more than any young person, for organizing the youth of that church. She was particularly talented and was ingenuous in planning worship programs for the young people and enlisting them to participate. Miss Conley unfortunately left the Pentecostal Holiness Church, and has since become a prominent leader among the women of the Methodist Church, speaking on one occasion before Bishop Candler and other renowned churchmen.

The General Organization, 1925

When Mr. Aaron went to be pastor of the First Church of Oklahoma City just prior to the meeting of the 1925 General Conference, he inaugurated a young people's program. His church requested that the church-bulletin include a young people's program. These successes and others led to the following recommendation being made in the report of the "Committee on Education" at the General Conference:

We recommend that there be created for the Young People of our Church a society to be known as the 'Pentecostal Young People's Society,' with headquarters at Franklin Springs, Georgia, the General Officers of which shall be a committee of three: President, Vice-President and Secretary-Treasurer, to be elected by the General Board, to serve annually, whose duties shall be to formulate constitutions and by-laws for all such societies; that there be elected at each Annual Conference a committee to cooperate with the General Committee, and in each local church a committee which shall cooperate with the committee of the Annual Conference.

Committee:
A. M. Taylor
J. A. Killebrew
Dan W. Evans
Burton A. Hall
J. H. Mashburn
W. L. Patterson
O. E. Sproull

Mr. A. M. Taylor was elected as the first General President. He was also elected as General Treasurer of the whole Church, and was a member of the faculty at the Franklin Springs Institute. Mr. Taylor resigned in 1927 and the Rev. T. L. Aaron succeeded him to finish the quadrennium. The period which ensued during the quadrennium from 1925 to 1929 was a stormy period for the Young People's Society for the reasons already mentioned, and because some pastors felt that these Societies in the local churches were creating an unwholesome competition.

Young People's Quarterly, 1930

When the General Conference convened in 1929, in spite of the opposition which had been encountered during the preceding quadrennium, the committee for the Pentecostal Young People's Society recommended that such a Society should continue to be maintained; and further recommended that a Young People's Quarterly be prepared, suggesting such material as would be helpful in carrying on young people's work. The Rev. T. L. Aaron who had been elected as General President of the Young People's Society was also elected as editor of the Pentecostal Young People's Quarterly which was first issued in 1930. The net income from this publication was to be given in support of the Franklin Springs Institute. Another significant recommendation was that the local societies should be pastorally supervised. This may be interpreted as a gesture on the part of the young people to eliminate the opposition from those pastors who felt that they were in competition with their programs in the local churches.

Constitution Outlined

At the next General Conference, in 1933, a "Committee on Connectional Societies and Administration" was elected. This committee presented a somewhat elaborate and explicit Constitution governing the organizational set-up of the young people's work and providing for both an Annual and a General Convention, the latter to meet every four years. Rules were adopted which governed the proportionate representation. The relationship of the Society to the General Board, the Annual Conference Board and Local Church Board was carefully outlined, so as not to conflict with or cause any opposition to the regular Church program, being made subordinate to and subject to the governing powers of the Church, itself. This was another step toward defining the limits of operation in order to effect a more smoothly functioning relationship between the Church and this connectional society in the church. Mr. Aaron was selected as head to the young people's organization; J. W. Butler was elected as Vice-President and Byon A. Jones as Secretary-Treasurer.

Closer Cooperation, Integration

At the 1937 General Conference there were no significant changes made except to tie in more closely the society, providing that it should be considered not as an independent unit, but as an integrated part of the General Conference, Annual Conference, and the Local Church programs. The General President was to be recognized as an ex-officio member of the General Conference, and the Conference P. Y. P. S. President should receive the same recognition as a member of the Annual Conference. It was also decided that the Young People's Constitution should be incorporated in the Discipline.

Innovations

By the 1941 General Conference certain innovations were introduced which were calculated to give new impetus to the young people's work in the Church. As has been mentioned the name of the society was changed to the "Pentecostal Holiness Youth Society." There were elected four Regional Presidents who are authorized to preside over the Annual Young People's Conventions in their respective regions, or to designate some person to do so. The Regional Director who was elected as chairman was to preside at General Conventions and at General Committee meetings, and likewise the Regional Presidents were to preside over Annual Conventions in their respective regions or to appoint someone to do so. The Secretary-Treasurer was to act as substitute for the Chairman in his absence or by request. The following were elected: T. L. Aaron, General President; Virgil Gaither, Western Region; Byon A. Jones, Eastern; Mrs. M. E. Hutchinson, Canadian Region. Conference Presidents were elected in practically all of the Conferences. It was suggested that a Junior P. H. Y. S. be organized in every Church where possible, with age limits up to 11 inclusive. It was also decided to have the next General Convention to meet at the same time and place and in connection with the General Conference.

General P. H. Y. S. Board

In the 1945 General Conference the Young People had their Convention separately. This time there were elected four Regional Presidents in the United States and two in Canada. Those elected to serve were as follows: Alfred Spell, Southwest; J. D. Nunn, Pacific and Western Canada; Mrs. M. E. Hutchinson, Eastern Canada; Bane T. Underwood, Northeastern and Don S. Whitfield, Southeastern, Virgil Gaither was elected General President and T. M. Oliver General Secretary-Treasurer. These seven officers constituted the General P. H. Y. S. Board. Their work consists of providing for a uniform administration of the young people's work in all regions; to hear reports of regional presidents; and to plan means and methods of attaining the five-point program which includes emphases on Christian experience, Worship, Study, Service, and Christian Fellowship. This Board meets annually at the same time and place with the General Board of Administration.

Youth Training Schools

Pursuant to these recommendations there have been organized very effective Youth Training Schools in a number of the Annual

Conferences. These are conducted under the direction of the Conference Youth Boards, and in cooperation with the Annual Conferences. Training schools usually last from 5 to 10 days. Three fields of activity are emphasized during this period, viz., Classroom, Recreational and Evangelistic.

Classroom Work

In the Training School four or five subjects are usually taught which may include classes in Personal Evangelism, Youth Problems, Church Doctrine, Teaching Younger Children, and Christianity in its relationship to Youth or whatever subject matter may be deemed worthwhile. Music is taught with directing, rudiments, etc. Group participation is urged, believing this to be a form of instruction in singing. Competent teachers are chosen for all this work, with the object in view of securing those persons who are interested in youth and who have a particular appeal to youth. Various teachers also lead round-table and panel discussions. These training schools are expected to be opened soon for adults to attend as well as those of adolescent age, and are designed to train church-workers in various fields of activity. The Conference President usually acts as president of the school, and as a rule directs various other activities.

Recreation

The classes are usually in the morning and during the afternoon following the dinner hour recreation is given a prominent place. Supervised sports include foot-races, calisthenics, softball, croquet, horse-shoes, tug of war. The value of recreation is emphasized, and the young people are instructed as to the rightful place of wholesome recreational activity.

Evangelistic Services

The evenings are spent in an atmosphere of revival, directed usually by some live-wire youthful evangelist, whose presence and ministry will inspire other young young people to emulate his example. Youth choirs, special singing by youth, personal testimonies and fervent seeking of God characterize these special services where decisions are made that change the entire course of young lives and direct them in channels of usefulness. Consecration services are emphasized.

Youth Conventions

The Young People's Annual Conventions are usually conducted immediately following their Training Schools, although there is no particular connection between the two except that the time is an opportune one. Programs are outlined for the coming year, in much the same fashion that the Annual Conference conducts its business. In fact, the whole organizational machinery of the young people's work in the Church almost exactly parallels that of the Church itself. Sometimes these Conventions are conducted separately from the Annual Conference, but in each instance their programs must be ratified by their respective Conference, and their work done in collaboration with it.

Separate General Convention

In 1945 the Young People's General Convention met separately from the General Conference, and while their Minutes appear in the same book, they are entirely separate. There is a natural inclination among youth to want to have something they can call their own. They do not resent supervision, nor do they object to being "chaperoned," but they do desire the opportunity of making their own choices and setting up their own programs, which in any event are to be endorsed by the Church of which they are a part. It was decided that they would have another General Convention in 1947, two years after the General Conference and entirely separate from it. The time and place were set when the General Board met in Charlotte in 1946, but when the time came for it to convene there arose serious objection. The General Board of Administration under which the Young People's Society operates in the same capacity as any other branch of general Church activity, ruled that they would not be allowed to conduct their General Convention, but did allow that such a convention might be planned to meet one week preceding the General Conference of the Church which will meet at Jacksonville, Florida in 1949.

Full-Time General President

The Rev. Virgil Gaither was elected in 1945 as the first "full-time" National or General President of the Pentecostal Holiness

Young People's Society. Mr. Gaither had previously served as Conference President of the East Oklahoma Conference from 1938 to 1941 when he was then elected as Regional President of all the territory west of the Mississippi. He gave one-half of his time to young people's work and one-half to his pastorate, proving himself to be specially adept in doing this work. As General President he was placed on a salary of $175.00 per month and was allowed four cents a mile for traveling expenses. If during any month his offerings did not amount to that much, his salary was to be supplemented from a general fund. This fund was to be created by asking the various societies to contribute thirty cents a member each year into the general treasury of the Young People's Society. If his offerings exceeded his set salary any month he would not be required to apply the excess amount to another month. It was later decided to raise his salary to $200.00 a month and traveling expenses at 4c a mile; and require him to turn in or report all offerings. According to a recent statement which Mr. Gaither made to this writer the young people are in debt to him $1,355.47, after he had cancelled $569.00 which he had spent for telephone calls. This statement was not made by way of complaint but in answer to a question asked.

His work, like that of every other person engaged in pioneer work, has required sacrifice, but he has willingly made it. Mr. Gaither travels incessantly in his indefatiguable labors. He has broken down much prejudice and has gained the favor of a host of people who did not fully appreciate or understand the young people's work. Best of all a gain from 12,000 society members in 1945 to 17,000 in 1947 had been made, and many precious souls and lives have been saved for the Kingdom.

Sunday School

The Pentecostal Holiness Church has throughout its existence had an organized Sunday school, and has used it as a means of instructing the unsaved concerning the way of salvation, and for the purpose of edifying believers. There has been a constant exhorting of Christian disciples to study to show themselves approved unto God, workmen that need not be ashamed, rightly dividing the word of truth. The first "children's card," which the Rev. G. F. Taylor published in 1913, was the beginning of Sunday school literature to be printed by the Pentecostal Holiness Church, and in a year or so a complete line of graded lesson material was made available. Prior to that time either the Bible itself or literature published by other organizations was used. From time to time laymen and preachers have been exhorted to help increase Sunday school enrollment, etc., but there was no formal Sunday School Committee report made until the General Conference in 1929. The Committee on Sunday schools submitted the following report at that time:

1. That every pastor see that a Sunday School is organized and maintained in every church under its jurisdiction.

2. That teachers and officers in Sunday schools be consecrated Christians, and able to stress the need of a personal knowledge of Christ, urging each child to accept Christ as their personal Savior.

3. We see the need of teacher-training work, and whereas this training is necessary to meet the needs of the church; we recommend that there be a Sunday School Superintendent or General Officer in each Annual Conference to promote the interest of this work, who shall be elected by each Annual Conference.

4. We recommend that we adopt a standard for our schools in excellence, the course of study to be decided by the Superintendent with the cooperation of the pastors.

5. That our Sunday schools use literature edited and published by Rev. G. F. Taylor. (Now published by the Pentecostal Holiness Church.)

Respectfully submitted,
F. G. Bailey
O. N. Todd
Mrs. Grace Henderson
T. O. Evans
Mrs. O. N. Todd
Committee

It is evident from the aforegoing recommendations that the Pentecostal Holiness Church had become more definitely Sunday school minded, and with it began to recognize the value of teacher-training, and the merits of a well-planned and well-organized program and the setting up of definite objectives.

Constitution and Manual

In 1933 the "Committee on Connectional Societies and Administration" submitted a Sunday School Constitution outlining in detail all the necessary basic elements which go to make up a well-organized and smooth functioning Sunday School organization, such as duties of officers and teachers; divisions and departments; the election of a Sunday School Board, etc. In 1937 it was recommended that the Sunday School Constitution be published in the Discipline and that the Committee on Church Publications prepare and publish a manual outlining the duties, responsibilities, opportunities, and methods to be used in organizing and conducting the Sunday school.

General Organization

In line with all the other departmental agencies of the Church, in 1945, the Sunday School was made a general organization and set up to function under the direction and supervision of the General Board of Administration. Bishop Dan T. Muse was elected as General President, the Rev. T. L. Aaron as Vice-President, and the Rev. Dallas M. Tarkenton as Secretary-Treasurer. The Sunday School and the Youth Society have come to be considered somewhat as a combined agency for Christian Education. A Sunday School Association was ordered formed in each Annual Conference and that a President, Vice-President and Secretary-Treasurer be elected at a Sunday School Convention. The organizational set-up may again be seen to correspond to that which exists in the Church itself, as well as in the other Departments as we have observed.

Duties of the Sunday School Association

It is the duty of the General Sunday School Association to encourage the local Sunday school in addition to meeting at its discretion also to call together once each month all its teachers and departmental heads for the purpose of training workers and discussing matters pertaining to the progress and work of the Sunday school; to encourage each Annual Sunday School Association to promote an annual Teachers' Training Course, and that they in turn encourage each local church under their jurisdiction to sponsor Daily Vacation Bible Schools. The Board of Publications has ordered to be prepared and published suitable literature for a Teachers' Training Course and Daily Vacation Bible Schools.

DAILY VACATION BIBLE SCHOOLS

In a recent personal interview with the Rev. Harry B. Correll, who has been actively engaged in youth programs in various sections of the Church, he gave in effect the following information relative to the Daily Vacation Bible Schools, which is a comprehensive and yet concise account of the work being done:

Generally speaking, there has been very little organization in the field of Daily Vacation Bible Schools. Their existence has been left almost entirely to the individual churches. This is considered a local thing and handled locally. It is true that the Sunday School organization and Youth organization have endeavored to promote these to the extent that they encourage them, and even suggest courses of study and workers. Recently, in some cases, they have been conducted solely by the Sunday School Department.

These schools are held during the summer months for the younger children. They are organized as to age and the study corresponds. One would find a vast difference in the study of one such school as compared to another. Since the last General Conference in 1945, however, the trend has been toward a more uniform study course. But although the courses may differ, yet the purpose remains the same: arousing interest, pursuing recreation, encouraging crafts and Bible study. Materials have usually been secured from any number of sources and used to fit the group.

Where local teachers are available and qualified, they are used. Also certain teams of workers spend their summers working with said schools, going from church to church as the demand might be. These organize the local workers and are having considerable success.

Chapter VI
WOMAN'S AUXILIARY, AND RADIO BROADCASTING

Women have always played an important role in the carrying on of various types of activity in the Pentecostal Holiness Church. For that matter the same has been true of all organized Christendom during every church age. The preponderance of the total church membership in all denominations is invariably female, and were it not for the faithful work of women, the Church of Jesus Christ could not have survived.

The Pentecostal Holiness Church has always given women a prominent place within its ranks, even to licensing some to preach, believing that both sons and "daughters" shall prophesy. Quite a few women of this communion have entered the ministry because they felt the Divine urge to carry the message of glad tidings. Some have made the mistake of thinking that they were called to preach when actually they were not. The fact that some have made the mistake of merely thinking they were called indicates there was within them an inner urge to do something for God, though it may not have been to preach.

Loyal women have served God in various capacities, some have faithfully fulfilled the oftimes thankless task of being a good pastor's wife, which is no easy and unimportant work. Others, who have been "Mothers in Israel," have held up their pastor's hands by entering the secret chambers of their prayer closets. Still others have toiled early and late at menial tasks, in an effort to obtain some meager amount of money in order to be able to make some small contribution to their church.

Then there came to some the idea that if some sort of organized effort could be promoted, ideas could be exchanged, resources could be pooled, and efforts could be combined to accomplish greater things. "Ladies Aid Societies" began to be organized in various local churches.

Among the first women to realize the possibilities of such an organization was Mrs. Nina Holmes, of the Holmes Memorial Church in Greenville, S. C. It was not until recent years that more extended Conference-wide efforts have been made in that direction, and by the General Conference in 1945 there was inaugurated a national or general organization known as The Woman's Auxiliary of the Pentecostal Holiness Church. The Woman's Auxiliary may be said to have actually had its inception on May 10, 1944, when a small group of women and nearly as many men met in the historic octagonal shaped church at Falcon, North Carolina. This was the identical place where the consolidation of the Fire-Baptized Holiness Church with the Pentecostal Holiness Church took place 33 years before. Mrs. Lila W. Berry, the wife of the Rev. John W. Berry, was elected as the first Conference President of the North Carolina Woman's Auxiliary, and later became the General President of the church-wide organization also. In speaking of the organization she says:

On May 10, 1944, a small group of women (nearly as many men) met in the historic little church in Falcon for the purpose of organizing something. I hardly think any of us knew just what we wanted, but out of a yearning heart to do something to help the Church and with a determination to find our places in God's great harvest field, we met to plan and exchange ideas. We invited Brother T. A. Melton of Durham to speak to us. When he had finished we had no trouble getting started and with our Conference Superintendent, the Rev. Eddie Morris, acting as chairman we had soon organized THE WOMAN'S AUXILIARY OF THE NORTH CAROLINA CONFERENCE OF THE PENTECOSTAL HOLINESS CHURCH. Sister Melton and some of her friends from Durham came from Durham with Brother Melton and they said, 'We are going to have an auxiliary in the Western North Carolina Conference, and soon they were organized. I hardly know how it all happened, but Brother Muse gave place in the General Conference in Oklahoma City in 1945, and it was there we became a real Woman's Auxiliary of the Pentecostal Holiness Church. Now we have twenty-one conference auxiliaries and I am sure others will organize this summer.[1]

The second Annual Conference to organize a Woman's Auxiliary was the South Carolina Conference, under the leadership of Mrs. R. O. Corvin, and a third was organized in the Western North Carolina Conference, headed by Mrs. R. N. Williams. Her sparkling personality and talented speaking ability have won for her unusual success in her own Conference, and have made her services to be in demand as a speaker at annual gatherings of Woman's Auxiliaries in other Conferences. A number of other women have been prominent in this work, some of whom are: Mrs. Dan T.

---

1 Lila W. Berry, **Advocate, op. cit.,** May 8, 1947, p. 2.

Muse, Vice-President; Mrs. Blanche King, Secretary-Treasurer; Mrs. O. N. Todd, Mrs. L. B. Edge, Mrs. Carl Thurman, Mrs. S. E. Franklin, Mrs. D. M. Tarkenton, Mrs. Bane T. Underwood, Mrs. W. J. Nash, Mrs. M. E. Parrish, Mrs. Roy Johndrow and others. There are now Woman's Auxiliary organizations in 23 of the 26 Conferences in the Church, and without exception the women who have led these groups have done outstanding work according to reports. Membership is voluntary and is extended to all women who are members of the Pentecostal Holiness Church. Those outside this communion can become associate members, and men may join as honorary members. No person is eligible for office except those who are members of the Church, however, associate members are permitted to serve on committees and to vote.

Objectives

The avowed object of the Auxiliary is to promote the welfare and spirituality of home, church, and community. The various Conference organizations have undertaken different projects, such as furnishing kitchens at camp meeting grounds, guest rooms at schools, colleges, or reception rooms at the orphanage, or to help in any other way possible to promote the general welfare of the Church. They raise money to paint churches, to carpet or furnish them, or to buy an organ or piano, or any number of other things to help the local church, the Conference, or even a church-wide project. For example there is a general project on foot now to raise $1,000.00 to buy and erect a monument in memory of the late Bishop J. H. King. The Venie Culbreth local church Auxiliary at Falcon, N. C., as we have noted, raised $2,000.00 in five months time to pay for a Hammond electric organ.

The Woman's Auxiliary had its inception in a most opportune time psychologically, due to the fact that the Pentecostal Holiness Church had become "organization-minded" by 1945, i. e., the General Board of Administration was then brought into existence, and the various Departmental Boards were brought under its supervision and jurisdiction. The value of organized efforts had been demonstrated in the young people's work, missions, Sunday school, etc., and this paved the way for the Woman's Auxiliary work to be inaugurated on somewhat the same scale.

RADIO

Twenty-five years ago on May 23, 1923, Dr. Ralph Sockman began broadcasting religious programs over the facilities of the National Broadcasting Company, and in 15 years it is said that more than 7 million responses were elicited from the 48 states. Two years later, in 1925, the Moody Bible Institute had its first experience in radio broadcasting over station WECS when one of their cornetists was invited to play. Free time was given the Institute, then time was bought, and then more time on WENR. In 1926 a license was obtained to operate their own station WMBI from two towers on top of the Woman's Building, with a 600 watt transmitter, from that to a 5,000 watt in 1928, and in 1938 a new 490 foot vertical radiator was erected. Now there is a 50,000 watt frequency modulation sister station WDIM. No commercial announcement, no jazz, no cigarette or liquor business has been advanced through these facilities.[1] In 1928 Charles E. Fuller began his Old Fashioned Revival Hour over KGER of Long Beach, California, which now has more outlets than any other religious or commercial broadcast costing him more than $2,000,000 annually.[2] Percy Crawford began his Young People's Church of the Air in Philadelphia, Pennsylvania, in 1931.[3] He estimated from eight to ten thousand are converted annually. In 1933 Dr. Walter Maier began the Lutheran Hour Broadcast which had 224 stations over Mutual and 350 local stations in nine years time, with an estimated 15 million listeners. Many other programs such as M. R. DeHaan, Dale Crawley, J. Harold Smith and others too numerous to mention have opened the eyes of a few Pentecostal Holiness ministers to the value of radio evangelism, although their activities in this field have been indeed meager in comparison with those which have just been mentioned.

It would not be practicable nor desirable to present here a detailed account of what has been done in the field of radio

---
1 Brochure furnished by Moody Bible Institute.
2 Statement made by Mr. Fuller in Madison Square Garden where this writer heard him speak in November, 1946.
3 Personal interview with Mr. Crawford in November, 1946.

broadcasting by individuals in the Pentecostal Holiness Church. By way of example, however, some facts will be given relating to one or two of these broadcasts to demonstrate what is being done by a considerable number of others over the Church.

Washington, D. C. Broadcast.

Some time during 1940 the young people of the Pentecostal Holiness Church in Washington, D. C., became particularly interested in the possibilities of radio broadcasting and were desirous of sponsoring such a program to publicize the work of their church and to acquaint the people in that section with the doctrinal teachings of Pentecostal Holiness and minister to shut-ins. They approached their pastor, the Rev. Hubert T. Spence, about the matter, and on Feb. 16, 1941, at 8:30 A. M. their first broadcast went out over station WINX. On the first anniversary of this broadcast it was decided to celebrate the occasion by arranging for a special broadcast from the church, preceding the evening service. The name of the program was then changed from "Youth on the March" to "The Pentecostal Revival Hour." Because of increased interest, evidenced by responses from listeners, there was begun the first Sunday in 1944 a 55 minute broadcast at a very desirable hour from 11:05 to 12:00. It was felt that this opportunity was opened by the hand of God. This was an indication of the confidence and favor of the radio station management which arose out of the fact that hundreds had written that this broadcast had been of special help and blessing to them. Quite a number have been added to the Kingdom as a result of these efforts, and others who were Christians have been deepened in their spiritual life.

An outstanding contribution has been made by the young people of the church, not only by helping to finance this program, but by faithfully giving of their consecrated talent in helping with the choir and special singing, and also with the orchestra work. These programs have been underwritten by the local church almost entirely, however, hundreds of dollars have been sent in by those who have felt impressed to do so. Such offerings have created a fund which is used in taking care of any deficit from time to time. No one has received any remuneration for services rendered in connection with staging their broadcasts.

Mr. Spence continued this program during four years of his five-year pastorate at the Washington, D. C. Church, and as a climax to this work he prepared and published "Twelve Radio Messages," which have been widely circulated among his listeners, and also among many members of the Pentecostal Holiness Church who have never heard the program. The Rev. Dallas M. Tarkenton who succeeded Mr. Spence as pastor has admirably continued this work and there is now under construction a beautiful new church which has been made possible largely as an outgrowth of this radio ministry.

The Portsmouth, Virginia Broadcast

The Rev. Byon A. Jones, after a varied experience as Superintendent of the Franklin Springs Institute for two years, and then traveling several years in the interest of the General Young People's work of the church, was assigned as pastor of the Portsmouth, Virginia Church in 1936. On the first Sunday morning there were only ten of the 24 members and two visitors out to hear him, and there had been only 19 in Sunday school that day. Because the people were not coming to hear his message he decided to resort to the radio to carry the message to them. In speaking of his experience he says:

Since the people would not come to the little church to hear me I decided to go to them.

I first went over to the Seaboard Shops to conduct a service at the noon hour, which I have continued to do on each Wednesday for more than twelve years. Some of them began to come to church, and then I felt I should speak to all of them about sponsoring a radio broadcast which they agreed to do. That was 11 years ago that these men helped me to begin my radio ministry in the Tidewater area. They still sponsor my "Friendly Visit" Sunday morning broadcast over WSAP.

Then I started a daily early morning program known as "Smile a While." This broadcast continued for 3 years, or until I went abroad to travel in Europe and the Middle East.

The question has been asked many times, "Does it pay?" My answer is an unequivocal, "Yes." It pays even financially and in many, many other ways. The radio ministry has been largely responsible for the increase of our ministry to one of the largest and busiest of any in all the Tidewater, Virginia.

Though we are very strict in membership requirements, we have increased in church membership from 24 to 141 at the present time. The Sunday school has increased from 19 to a peak attendance of 333.

As I write these words our average attendance for this quarter is 272. The General Superintendent of the Seaboard Railway Shops who joined my church was later elected Superintendent of our Sunday school and is now a leading churchman in Portsmouth.

To give an example of the good a radio ministry can perform, I have never asked for anything over the radio to help needy families but what I received it. I have received thousands of dollars in money and items of supplies for destitute people. One man who was crippled for life and had no insurance beyond a small pittance was brought to my attention, and after appeals to my radio listeners a small home was bought and furnished.

In almost every service there are those who are present because they heard the radio broadcast. The radio work has done more than any one thing to give the Pentecostal Holiness Church its rightful place among other churches of our city. I have been Secretary-Treasurer of the Ministerial Union of the city for several years, and am now Vice-President and am in line for the presidency next year. Our London Street Church has had the privilege of bringing one of our outstanding men to the city for special services sponsored by the Ministerial Union each year. A great open door is now ours in our city and it was largely opened by radio allowing this pastor to enter and minister to thousands of people.[1]

A few of the other ministers who have been actively engaged in radio work are the Revs. L. H. Fortson, F. A. Dail, C. F. Noble, Oral Roberts, D. D. Freeman, Carl Simpson, N. J. Lynch, P. F. Beacham, Louis Coward, T. K. Howard, W. B. McKay, O. E. Sproull, Alpheus Noseworthy, L. J. Oliver, T. T. Lindsey, and R. N. Williams who has been unusually successful in his radio ministry over the Asheville, N. C., station, having been invited to preach in the churches of various denominations all over that section.

At the 1945 General Conference, as we have noted, the Rev. Byon A. Jones was given opportunity to speak on the need of a National Radio Broadcast sponsored by the Pentecostal Holiness Church. His remarks were received enthusiastically but nothing has been accomplished as yet toward realizing such an objective. There are other Pentecostal denominations which have initiated progressive activities in the field of radio, the most outstanding of which the Rev. Stanley H. Frodsham writes about in a thrilling article which appeared in a recent new publication which is edited and published by the widely known Rev. Donald

---

[1] Pastor Jones furnished the above information upon request, in a letter dated April 9, 1948.

Gee at the request of the World Conference of Pentecostal Churches held in Zurich, Switzerland, in May, 1947. He writes:

Three Pentecostal young men have caught the vision of broadcasting the gospel in the Far East. A few weeks ago, I heard John C. Broger, who served for four years as radio radar officer in the U. S. Navy, tell his story. For nine years he and Bob Bowman, who for thirteen years has been singing every day on a splendid gospel broadcast in Los Angeles, have been praying. After Broger was retired from the Navy, he and Bob each put five hundred dollars of their own savings into a fund, and Broger went on a prospecting tour. He discovered that because of the dominant spirit of nationalism in China, it will be impossible for Americans to erect a station there. He went to the Philippines and arrived two days after these islands had been given independence. His first application for the erection of a broadcasting station was rejected. But God overruled in a wonderful way, and enabled him to have an interview with the judge to whom all radio matters had been committed; and the result has been that a station franchise has been given to erect two radio stations with four frequency assignments. A site of 12½ acres, just outside the city of Manila, has been secured, the work of erecting the stations with the housing of workers has already started, and it is announced: 'We hope to go on the air soon after the beginning of 1948.'

From these stations will be beamed gospel broadcasts to the three million who own receiving sets along the coast of China, to many millions who own radio sets in Japan, to the three million who own them in India, and to the nine hundred thousand who have shortwave sets in Russia. This should prove a marvelous outlet for Pentecostal missionaries of all nations. The Assemblies of God in America have already appointed their first two missionaries to the staff of this radio station—Brother and Sister Kenneth Short, who have been denied re-admittance to Borneo, but who can reach a far larger audience in these islands through the facilities of these stations.

Incidentally, it might be said that a Christian business man in Chicago is attacking the problem of manufacturing inexpensive receiving sets, also an inexpensive hand-cranked phonograph. Miss Joy Ridderhoff, a returned missionary who lives in Los Angeles, is having a unique ministry. She has produced nine hundred master records in seventy-eight languages, on which there is a gospel message. We are planning to make similar recordings to hers in Springfield.

About eighteen months ago the American Assemblies of God began broadcasting on a national scale. The weekly program, 'Sermons in Song,' on which our General Superintendent Ernest S. Williams, gives a brief message, and on which a special radio choir from Central Bible Institute sings old-fashioned gospel songs, is now going out from ninety-five different stations. Two of these are in Alaska, one in Chunking (The Voice of China), two in Cuba, two in Hawaii, and one in Labrador. A series of thirteen records has recently gone to station HCJB in Quito, Ecuador, to be used in days to come. Thos. F. Zimmerman, our Radio Director, said to me a few minutes ago: 'Every broadcast reaches a larger audience than Dwight L. Moody preached to in all his large audiences combined.'[1]

In a personal interview with Mr. Reuben E. Larson in Toledo in December, 1946, this writer heard the story of, and has since read the complimentary copy of the book containing the written story of how Mr. Larson and Mr. Clarence W. Jones came to contact one another and erected the world's strongest radio station HCJB in Quito, Ecuador. Their mission is to "Herald Christ Jesus' Blessings." The "Voice of the Andes," as the station is called, according to a recent letter from Mr. Larson, has had its license extended to 1980. An excerpt from his letter regarding the matter of the chancellor's decree is as follows:

You as a partner in the work of the 'Voice of the Andes,' share in the honor thus bestowed. The citation of His Excellency Sr. Don Carlos Julio Arosemena Constitutional President of the Republic of Ecuador, states the following: 'Whereas . . . that on the 25th of December, 1947, Radio Station HCJB, 'The Voice of the Andes' completed 16 years since its founding; that during this time it has continued working actively and without interruption for the cultural advance of the country; and at the petition of the Chancellor . . .

DECREES

FIRST—Confer the Decoration of the National Order 'for Merit' in the Degree of Knight upon the Radio Station HCJB, 'The Voice of the Andes.'

SECOND—Charge the Minister of Education, now acting minister of Foreign Relations, with the execution of this Decree

Given in the National Palace; in Quito, the 26th of December 1947.

Signed
C. J. Arosemena[2]

Mr. Larson and Mr. Jones were led of God to establish this radio station in an area which radio experts in that day said would be uncongenial, because of the metal deposits in the Andes, and because of the close proximity of the equator. Since that time greater developments in radio have confirmed God's orders in that experts have discovered this section of the world is the very best possible location for a world-wide short-wave broadcast.

---

1 Stanley Frodsham, **Pentecost**, (London: Victory Press, Oct. 1947), p. 9.
2 Letter received from Reuben Larson, April, 1948.

Chapter VII
CAMP MEETINGS AND BIBLE CONFERENCES

The "camp meeting" appeared on the American frontier and played a vital role in the Christianization of the young nation. There is difference of opinion and conflicting evidence as to which denomination can claim the right of having introduced this technique in evangelism. The Baptists claim that Samuel Harris is responsible for the camp meeting's inception, in 1774, in connection with his evangelistic preaching in Culpepper and Orange Counties, Virginia.[1] The Methodists point to John McGee as somewhat the originator of the camp meeting before the Rehoboth church was erected in Lincoln County, N. C., when the congregation was accustomed to worshipping in the grove in the midst of where the church was built.[2] Associated with him later was his brother, William, a Presbyterian preacher. There is also indication that the Presbyterians initiated this camp meeting movement under Gilbert Tennent's ministry, as will be seen in the following statement:

> Under the preaching of McCready the great Cumberland revival began in 1798 and continued with increasing power for some three years. The crowds were soon so large that meetings had to be held in the fields, just as in the days when George Whitefield and Gilbert Tennent preached. People came in wagons on horseback, and on foot for miles and camped on the scene that they might attend the meetings. It was here that the famous 'camp meeting' came into the life of the American frontier.[3]

The fact is that camp meetings originated on the frontier, and Methodists, Baptists, and Presbyterians were all engaged in what some consider the greatest revival which has ever come to America. It no doubt had the most far-reaching effects of any revival movement in American history, especially as a means of preparing the way for the missionary enterprises. The practice of encamping on the ground was introduced partly by inclination

---

[1] W. L. Muncy, Jr., **Evangelism in the United States**, (Kansas City: Central Seminary Press, 1945), p. 51.
[2] R. N. Price, **Holston Methodism**, (Nashville: Publishing House of the M. E. Church, South, 1904), p. 355.
[3] Muncy, op. cit., p. 83.

and partly by necessity. The congregations were too immense to be received by any common neighborhood, although everything was done which hospitality and brotherly kindness could do to accommodate the people. Public and private houses were opened, and free invitations were given to all persons who wished for rest. Farmers gave up their meadows before they were mown to supply the horses. Yet it was manifestly impossible for the people to be accommodated. Whole families came from distances as great as fifty to one hundred miles or more, bringing their camp wagons loaded with provisions, cooking utensils, and some simple bedding, and set up camp. It sometimes became necessary to return home for provisions when their loved ones came to be effected by the "fallings" and would remain in an unconscious state sometimes for days at a time. Besides these people were unwilling to suffer any interruption in their devotions, and they formed an attachment to the place where they had been blessed or where they were continually seeing so many sinners being converted and hearing so many deists who were constrained to call on the formerly despised name of Jesus. They felt like Jacob that, surely the Lord is in this place; this is none other than the house of God, and this is the gate of heaven."

The camp meeting era lasted for some fifty years and had begun to wane in its influence by the time of the Civil War because of the developments which had taken place. The frontier became a settled society with churches, schools and a normal community life which made the camp meeting less necessary. It was succeeded by the large tabernacle and local revival type which still prevails, but is also definitely on the wane in more recent years, especially in some sections. This declining interest in revivalism in the established churches may also be accounted for by the absence of true spirituality which has issued from the teachings of Modernism and the constant influx of worldly and secular interests. There was a resurgence of the camp meeting movement, however, when the first national Holiness camp meeting was held at Vineland, New Jersey, in 1867. Since that time the Holiness denominations which grew out of this movement have continued to emphasize this revival technique, but generally speaking camp meetings have never enjoyed the same degree of popularity as during frontier days.

Camp Meetings in the Pentecostal Holiness Church

Throughout the history of the Pentecostal Holiness Church camp meetings have continued to be popular, and it can be said of a truth that they have become more and more popular. Fervent prayers offered by many people praying at the same time; shouting, sometimes by great hosts of people which can be heard for miles; zealous and spirited testimonies; good, hearty—"amens"; dancing in the Spirit; speaking in tongues as the Spirit gives utterance; and various types of bodily manifestations, are still to be seen and heard at camp meetings conducted by Pentecostal Holiness people. Emotional expression on the whole, however, has never been as pronounced as that which appeared among Baptists, Methodists, and Presbyterians in their early history. A large percent of what has been said in criticism of the Holiness and Pentecostal people has come frequently from those of the established churches who were jealous of them, and in the final analysis much of what has been said has been unwarranted and cannot be proved. This is the natural reaction to be expected from the established churches out of which the Holiness groups and Pentecostal groups have come. It might also well be added that these groups have been unduly critical and belligerent in their attitude toward the established churches out of which they came. In recent years the trend on both sides has been to have a more sympathetic understanding and Christian appreciation of one another.

It would be virtually impossible to mention all of the camp meetings which have been attended by Pentecostal Holiness people, and we will therefore limit our attention to just those which have been sponsored by the Church and have been the most widely attended.

North Carolina

The Falcon Camp Meeting was begun in 1900 and is discussed in chapter IV. In 1909 the Rev. A. H. Butler was instrumental in founding the *Piney Grove* Camp Meeting near Chocowinity, N. C., which is the second oldest one in the state. The Rev. J. B. Williams established another camp meeting at *Aulander*, N. C., in in 1914. The *Rockingham* Camp Meeting was organized largely under the influence of the Rev. F. A. Dail who was Conference

Superintendent. The *Happy Home* Camp Meeting was also organized near Elizabeth, N. C., in 1925.

Florida

The *Bristol,* Florida Camp Meeting, which according to the Rev. L. J. Oliver began about 1905, is the second oldest in the Pentecostal Holiness Church organization, and is strictly speaking the oldest, since Falcon was not at that time conducted under the auspices of the Church. It was organized largely as a result of the ministry of the Rev. and Mrs. C. M. Wheeler. Another camp meeting was organized soon afterwards at *Wetumpka,* near Quincy. Several years ago the Pentecostal Holiness people largely controlled the Pleasant Grove Camp Meeting, an independent Pentecostal camp meeting, and in recent years, since 1941, has sponsored it again. It is located 18 miles west of Tampa, near Durant, Florida, and is one of the largest attended camp meetings in the entire South.

The Mississippi

The Mississippi Conference has a camp meeting which began in 1909.

Oklahoma Conference Camp Meeting

The Oklahoma Conference Camp Meeting is one of the oldest in the Church, having been organized in August, 1909. This was the first camp meeting to be conducted concurrently with the Annual Conference, but since that time a number of other Conferences have adopted the same plan and have their annual sessions in connection with their camp meeting. The permanent camp grounds is located 4 miles west of May Avenue, Oklahoma City, but for a number of years these services were conducted in various places over the State including Lamont in 1909, Oklahoma City in 1910, 1911 and 1912. It was at this camp meeting in 1912 when the Rev. Luther G. Chilcoat and others received the baptism of the Spirit. He was so overjoyed that he ran from the tent and threw his arms around a nearby tree. Newspaper reporters publicized the incident with headlines, announcing that Pentecostal people were climbing trees in their emotional ecstasy, and as a result enormous crowds came and some received the truth who otherwise would not have heard it. Other Oklahoma Conference camp meeting sessions were conducted at Stratford, Wagoner, Drummond, Seminole, Shawnee, and West Sulphur, At the latter two places the attendance was among the largest in the history of this camp meeting. In 1921, at West Sulphur the people came by train, automobile, horse and buggy and wagon from all directions, some traveling in wagons as far as 200 miles, many others from 50 to 100 miles. There were 85 wagons and 50 tents used for camping purposes. This medley of men milling about was reminiscent of frontier camp meeting days. At Shawnee, in 1924, the renowned Rev. Paul F. Beacham preached for his first time west of the Mississippi River. His presence and powerful, sane, Scriptural preaching caused quite a sensation and contributed much to the success of the camp meeting.

In 1912 the *Holmes Bible School* Camp Meeting was begun, the details of which are given in connection with the History of Education in the Pentecostal Holiness Church.

The *Franklin Springs* Camp Meeting began in 1918, and is held each year near the opening of Emmanuel College. Many successful meetings have taken place here, the most outstanding of which was in 1919.

The *Pennsylvania* Conference Camp Meeting, called Hickory Grove, was begun at Greenville, Pa., in 1925.

The *Texas* Conference Annual Camp Meeting began in 1925, but has no permanent camp grounds.

The *East Oklahoma* Camp Meeting was established in 1925, and since that time there has been erected a large, modern tabernacle on a roomy acreage situated about 2 miles east of Ada, Oklahoma.

The *Kansas Conference* Annual Camp Meeting had its beginning in 1926, and has its permanent camp grounds located at Pawnee and Greenway Boulevard, Wichita, Kansas.

Panhandle Camp Meeting

The Panhandle camp meeting was begun in 1935, the next year following the Conference organization at Carnegie, Oklahoma. For the first several years the camp meeting was conducted in various localities on borrowed property wherever suitable arrangements could be made to accommodate the project.

Then, in 1944, a ten acre plot was purchased, situated on the east side of Highway 87 two miles north of the city limits of Amarillo, Texas. Under the leadership of their Conference Superintendent, the Rev. J. M. Lemmon, this property has steadily been improved, beautified and developed from year to year. It is now a credit to the zealous, sacrificial labors of the cooperative-spirited people of the Panhandle Conference. Having begun on land where there was neither bush nor building, they now have their own water-system, fourteen cabins and two duplex apartments with bedroom, study and private bath, and hot and cold water to house their camp meeting speakers. There is also a small dormitory consisting of eight rooms in one unit. Two bath houses are provided with modern plumbing, including also facilities for necessary laundering.

Trees have been planted. Six acres have been cut into streets and named for Bible towns such as: Jericho, Bethlehem, Jerusalem, etc. Adequate space is provided for house trailers, tents, and other means of camping. The people of this section of the country by and large are still possessed by the inherent pioneer spirit which characterized their forefathers in frontier days, and they more or less prefer camp-life and enjoy it.

In the center of the plot on a commanding knoll the tabernacle has been located. Including the wings of this building it is 68 x 84 feet in size and except for brief intervals during the day there are services from 6:30 A. M. until late at night. An adequate size and well-equipped dining room and kitchen is also centrally located, and nice meals are served to campers free of charge.

The Conference Superintendent's home is also located on the grounds, and there is a possibility that sometime these cabins can be utilized as tourist cabins for Christian tourists during seasons when they are not being used for Conference purposes. Being located on the Highway and having been built according to definite plans, this is seen as a possible way of subsidizing the work of the Conference, and is mentioned here as a suggestion for other such conference camp meeting projects which can possibly be made to serve a dual purpose. It would not only provide a salary for a caretaker but also provide a fund to keep the buildings in repair. Any surplus which might accumulate could well be used to promote and sustain the work of evangelizing the Conference.

The *California* Camp Meeting, which began in 1936, has its permanent camp grounds on No. 99 Highway, two miles north of Madera, California.

The *Missouri* Annual Conference Camp Meeting was established in 1939 at Mt. View, Missouri.

The *New Covenant* Camp Meeting near Mt. Airy, N. C. was organized in 1940.

The *Tri-State* Conference Annual Camp Meeting has a camp ground near Memphis, Tennessee.

The *Alabama* Conference has their Camp Meeting at River Springs, Alabama, near Evergreen, Alabama. It had its beginning in the early thirties; as did also the *South Carolina* Conference Camp Meeting at Lake City, S. C.; and the *Beech Springs* Camp Meeting, 18 miles southeast of Greenville, near Pelzer, S. C.

The *Colorado* Camp Meeting was begun in 1941, and is located in Woodland Park on the east slope of the Rockies, 20 miles from Colorado Springs. The camp is at an 8,000 feet altitude and affords a lovely view, and is 29 miles by road from the top of Pike's Peak.

The *West Oklahoma* Conference Camp Meeting began in 1945, but as yet has no permanent camp grounds. This camp meeting is held at Clinton, Oklahoma, each year in a city park.

The *Arizona* Conference Camp Meeting was begun in 1946, but likewise does not have any permanent camp grounds.

The *British Columbia* Canadian Conference Camp Meeting was also begun in 1946 but owns no permanent grounds.

The *Alberta District* Annual Camp Meeting in Canada has a permanent camp ground 20 miles from Calgary, Alberta.

The *Ontario Conference* Annual Camp Meeting, called *Pine Grove*, is located a few miles from Toronto, near Markham, Ontario, and was begun about 1929.

The *Virginia Conference* has two camp meetings within its bounds, the *Wytheville*, near Wytheville; and the *Piedmont*, near Shawsville, where they have recently purchased the Alleghany Health Resort which has a large building, a colonial home, camp meeting houses and a spring creek. This beautiful property was purchased for $15,000 and will be one of the finest camp grounds in the Church.

The *Portsmouth* Camp Meeting was founded in 1947 by the Portsmouth, Virginia Church largely through the influence of their progressive pastor, the Rev. Byon A. Jones. This camp is located just outside the city limits of Portsmouth and is easily accessible from all the churches of the Tidewater area. The property was formerly a tourist camp and adapts itself readily for camp meeting purposes, is in a nice grove, and from all indications promises to be one of the best camp meetings in the Church.

The *East Virginia Conference* Camp Meeting is located on the highway between Richmond and Hopewell, not far from Hopewell. It will be opened for the first time on June 17, 1948. This camp ground, which is nearing completion, has on it a $35,000 tabernacle, 70 x 97', a dining room, and kitchen equipped with $2500.00 worth of modern devices to promote efficiency, and a small dormitory. Adequate space is available and lots are being sold to a number of individuals who are planning to construct camp houses on the property very soon. This will be, without question, one of the nicest camp grounds in the Church.

There has been a camp meeting at *Mountain Gap,* Georgia, for several years, but until recently the Georgia Conference have had no camp grounds which they could call their own. According to reports however, negotiations have just been made, providing for the purchase of a very desirable site near Atlanta, Georgia.

BIBLE CONFERENCES

At the 1917 General Conference it was recommended that a Bible Conference be conducted within the bounds of each annual conference once during each year if possible. The late Bishop J. H. King was appointed to carry on this work. With the greatest enthusiasm and personal satisfaction he began this work in May, 1917, at the Durham, N. C. Church of which the Rev. F. A. Dail was pastor. The interest in Bible Conferences during the first year was not so encouraging, but since that time it has creased from year to year. They have now come to occupy a prominent place in the life of the Church, especially among the ministry. Other able Bible scholars have lectured to ministerial fellowship groups conference gatherings, and in local churches, among whom are the Revs. Bishop Paul F. Beacham, Bishop J. A. Synan, Bishop Dan. T. Muse, Bishop T. A. Melton, G. H. Montgomery, H. T. Spence, T. L. Aaron and others. The North Carolina Conference recently reported that they had "just closed the most successful institute (Bible conference) ever held in Falcon." It was conducted by Bishop Muse.

"Joint-Conference Ministers Fellowship Conventions" have recently come into vogue, and by pooling their resources adjoining conferences can provide a most excellent opportunity to hear several invited speakers during the period of a week. They also provide an opportunity for conference leaders to make valuable comparisons. These conferences also afford an unsurpassed opportunity for fellowship, comparable to that to be found at camp meetings, but without the distractions of a mixed-multitude.

The first Ministers' Fellowship Convention was held in Washington, D. C., at the Russian Bible House in February, 1948. The announcement of the convention appeared in the Advocate, part of which was as follows:

The Eastern Virginia and Maryland Conferences are sponsoring a great Ministerial Fellowship in Washington, D. C., Feb. 2-6, 1948. This is the first of such conferences to be held within our ranks of such magnitude. Such outstanding men as Bishop Synan, Bishop Beacham, Senator Clyde Hoey, Dr. Clinton Howard, editor of Progress Magazine, Mr. L. B. Nichols, assistant director of the F. B. I., Pastor Basil Malof, president of the Russian Bible Society, the Rev. H. T. Spence and others will appear on the program.[1]

Since then the Ontario and Pennsylvania Conferences have had a joint Ministerial and Sunday School Convention from March 23-26, 1948, at the First Pentecostal Holiness Church of Toronto, Canada, at which the Revs. J. A. Synan and D. M. Tarkenton were the principal speakers.

Another Joint-Conference Ministers' Fellowship group met in Oklahoma City recently. The Rev. Paul F. Beacham was the Bible lecturer and principal speaker for the occasion.

These Bible conferences reflect the prevalent growing tendency within the Church to produce a better trained and more efficient ministry.

---

1 D. M. Tarkenton, **Advocate, op. cit.,** Jan. 22, 1948, p. 9.

Chapter VIII
SERVICE PASTOR, CHAPLAINCY, AND STATISTICAL INFORMATION

At the meeting of the Home Mission Board at Greenville, S. C., on May 27, 1943, there was at first a general discussion of the home mission work, which included Military Evangelism, then later there was a lengthy discussion of the need of arrangements being made for the appointment of a Service Men's Pastor to visit army camps and to contact men and women from Pentecostal Holiness homes. The Rev. H. T. Spence was selected for this work, but was unable to secure release from the Washington, D. C., Church which he pastored.

On June 5, 1943, the Rev. J. A. Synan, Chairman of the Home Mission Board and the Rev. H. T. Spence, Secretary, met at Cumberland, Maryland, and decided to set up the Service Men's Commission. After contacting the Rev. T. A. Melton, another member of the Home Mission Board, by telephone the plan was made legal and effective immediately. It was decided that this Commission should be comprised of 10 persons, the 5 members of the Home Mission Board with the Rev. Mr. Synan as Chairman were to constitute the Executive Committee, four General Officers of the Pentecostal Holiness Youth Society, and the Rev. G. H. Montgomery, Superintendent of Evangelism. The entire Commission was composed of the following: Bishop J. A. Synan, the Revs. H. T. Spence, T. A. Melton, W. W. Carter, B. R. Dean, and G. H. Montgomery, and the Rev. T. L. Aaron, General P H. Y. S. President, Byon A. Jones, Vice-President, James W. Butler, Promotional Secretary and Virgil Gaither, Young People's representative in the West. The Rev. Sam Todd was selected as Service Men's Pastor and placed on a salary of $50.00 per week with traveling expenses figured at 4c a mile. The Rev. G. H. Montgomery and Mr. J. W. Butler were authorized to prepare and publish suitable tracts to be distributed among servicemen. Later the Church Military paper was named "Forward" and Mr. Montgomery was elected to edit the same. Tens of thou-

SERVICE PASTOR, CHAPLAINCY, STATISTICAL INFORMATION 407

sands of copies were distributed during the period from 1943 to 1945.

The newly organized Commission was immediately registered with the War Department and given official recognition, and the Rev. Mr. Todd reported his work to the General Conference in 1945 and was highly commended for his services. Part of his report was as follows:

The work of Military Evangelism for the Pentecostal Holiness Church officially began on July 15, 1943. The first service conducted by the Commission was at Seymour Johnson Field, Goldsboro, N. C., July 16, 1943, and since then the road of service has led through some 35 states and more than 130 camps.

One source of rich blessing has been the service men's paper, "Forward," published under the able editorship of Rev. G. H. Montgomery. 145,000 copies of "Forward" have been printed and with very few exceptions, all have been mailed to our Armed Forces.

Another service the Commission is rendering in an increasing measure is that of keeping in touch with the families back home. Dozens of men write, requesting that we write to their wives and mothers. Mrs. Todd is maintaining correspondence with approximately 150 to 200 of these homefolk. To them go letters, cards and folders bringing encouragement and cheer with an offer to serve in any way possible. Here again, we are going to find a softer place in their hearts for the Church after the war is over. In this field, we along with other churches have failed.

Summary

Camps Visited	130 (plus)
Miles traveled (approximately)	60,000
Individual visits to camps	255
Men visited personally	Hundreds
Number of letters sent service men	19,000
Pieces of literature	225,000
Funds raised in services	$12,500

S. J. Todd[1]

Mr. Todd worked hard and long and is not to be criticized personally, but there was a general feeling over the Church that the results obtained and the actual good accomplished did not justify the expenditure of Home Mission funds in that channel. It was felt by many that pastors near the various army camps could have been paid to do the same work with much less ex-

---

[1] Minutes of 1945 General Conference of the Pentecostal Holiness Church (Oklahoma City: June 7-14, 1945), pp. 21, 22.

pense, and in all likelihood the boys could have been visited much more frequently.

THE CHAPLAINCY

Bishop J. A. Synan and the Revs. G. H. Montgomery and H. T. Spence were elected to serve as an Examining Committee to place eligible candidates before the War Department for possible appointment to the Chaplaincy. The Church was first given a quota of two chaplains, then five, then eight and finally twelve. (In January, 1948, at the meeting of the General Board of Administration the Home Mission Board, which as we have noted is the Executive Committee of the Service Men's Commission, was authorized to act as Commission of Chaplaincies, with D. M. Tarkenton, the local Washington, D. C., pastor elected to act as Secretary of the Commission.)

On August 18, 1943 the Rev. J. Vinson Ellenberg was examined and recommended for the chaplaincy and soon thereafter was sent to the Chaplain's School at Harvard, after which he was given an assignment. For some reason Mr. Ellenberg was unable to adjust himself to Army life, and stated that he had a feeling he was violating his personal convictions in performing the duties required of him. He was finally given a discharge before he went overseas. The Rev. T. E. Myers was accepted in the meantime and went to France and Germany where he saw active service, and is still in Germany, having been promoted to the rank of Captain. The Rev. Julius W. Green also served in the Army as a chaplain and since the war has been continuing his work as a Hospital chaplain in the Veteran' Hospital at Memphis, Tennessee.

The Rev. Freeman Mashburn also received an appointment to the Corps of Chaplains June 15, 1945, and entered on active duty June 30, 1945, at Hampton Roads Port of Embarkation, Newport News, Virginia. After attending Chaplain's school at Fort Oglethorpe, Georgia until August 25, 1945, he was assigned as transport chaplain aboard the S. S. WESTMINISTER VICTORY, making eight crossings of the Atlantic on that vessel ferrying troups from Europe to the United States and returning war prisoners. One June 3, 1946, he was transferred to the Pacific, which he crossed twice and was relieved from active duty Dec. 3, 1946.

The Rev. E. L. Shirey also received an appointment to the Corps of Chaplains on May 26, 1945, and entered active service June 15, 1945, being sent to Fort Oglethorpe, Georgia where he graduated at the same time with Mr. Mashburn. He was then assigned to the Westbrook Victory S. S. as transport chaplain making several trips across the Atlantic, and traveling in Egypt and northern Africa, parts of Europe and in England. In November, 1946, Mr. Shirey was transferred to another ship which went through the Panama Canal to the west coast and to Japan. Because of his outstanding service the Rev. Mr. Shirey received three letters of commendation, one of which came from the Chief of Chaplains, and on January 31, 1946, he was promoted to the rank of Captain.

Because of the meritorious service rendered by Pentecostal Holiness men during the second World War, there will no doubt be an increased demand for more such men if and when another war comes.

STATISTICAL INFORMATION

Total Number of Conferences and Total Church Membership

There were 6 Annual Conferences in the Pentecostal Holiness Church in 1911, and a total membership of approximately 3,000; in 1913 there were still 6 Annual Conferences and approximately 3,500 total membership; in 1917 there were 10 Annual Conferences and a total of 4,838 members; in 1921 there were 16 Annual Conferences and a membership of 5,494; in 1925 there were 17 Annual Conferences and 9,574 members; in 1929 there were 17 Annual Conferences and a jump in total church membership to 15,447; in 1937 there were 17 Annual Conferences and a total church membership of 16,400; in 1941 there were 22,749 members in 20 Annual Conferences; in 1945 there were 26 Annual Conferences and a total church membership of 24,509. In 1947 there were the same number of Annual Conferences, and an increase in total church membership to 28,614. These figures do not include the church membership on foreign fields, which totaled 21,083 in 1945, making a total over-all membership of 45,592 in 1945.

---

1 This statistical information was taken largely from Bishop Dan T. Muse's January, 1948, report to the General Board.

Ministerial Membership

During 1947 there were a total of 144 ministers received into the various annual conferences which raised the total ministerial membership to 1,616, of which 76.9% or 1,243 were men; and 23.1% were women.

Churches, Church Buildings and Property

Of the 822 churches reported in the United States and Canada in 1947, there are 682 church buildings, 241 parsonages, 15 churches with living quarters in church buildings, 7 Conference parsonages for Conference Superintendents and 27 camp grounds equipped for camp meetings.

Sunday Schools

Twenty Annual Conferences reported an increase of 2,008 in their average Sunday School attendance over 1946, four Conferences reported a decrease of 331, making an over-all net increase of 1,677. Of the 694 Sunday schools reporting there is a total enrollment of 48,565, with an average attendance of 35,686. Nineteen of the 24 Annual Conferences making reports have an average Sunday school attendance larger than their church enrollment, while five Conferences reveal an average attendance less than the local church membership.

Pentecostal Holiness Youth Society

The 446 Societies which reported reveal a total membership of 17,524, and an average attendance of 13,545, indicating an increase of 2,559 average attendance over 1946 figures.

Pastors' Salaries

Out of 804 churches, 758 report an average salary of $964.98 annually. The 758 churches report salaries in the following brackets:

One church paid its pastor more than $4,000.00; ten churches paid their pastors between $3,000.00 and $3,999.00; thirty-four churches paid their pastors between $2500.00 and $3,000.00; fifty-nine churches paid pastors between $2,000.00; and $2500.00; seventy-nine churches between $1500.00 and $2,000.00; one hundred eighteen churches from $1,000.00 to $1500.00; one hundred seventy-one churches from $500.00 to $1,000.00; and two hundred and eighty-six churches paid their pastors under $500.00.

Chapter IX
THE BISHOPS

The title of "General Superintendent" was changed to "Bishop" at the 1937 General Conference, i. e., it came to be an honorary title conferred upon the General Superintendents. The head of the Pentecostal Holiness Church before the consolidation was called "President," and the head of the Fire-Baptized Holiness Church was called the "General Overseer." The Revs. A. B. Crumpler and A. H. Butler were the only two Presidents of the Pentecostal Holiness Church from 1900 until the consolidation in 1911, while the Revs. B. H. Irwin and J. H. King were the only two General Overseers from 1898 until 1911. The Rev. S. D. Page was elected as the first General Superintendent of the consolidated group in 1911, and served until the Second General Conference met in 1913. The Rev. G. F. Taylor was elected to serve from 1913 until the Third General Conference met in 1917. A short biographical sketch of Mr. Page's life appears in the second chapter dealing with Home Missions. A biographical sketch of Mr. Taylor's life appears in the section dealing with the History of Education in the Pentecostal Holiness Church.

Bishop J. H. King (1869—1946)

From the standpoint of service Bishop J. H. King is without question the most outstanding General Officer who has served the Pentecostal Holiness Church. He served in official capacity longer than any other man, more than twice as long. From 1900, when he was elected to succeed the Rev. B. H. Irwin as General Overseer of the Fire-Baptized organization, until the time of his death, in 1946, he either served as the official head or as assistant-head of the Church. At the time of the consolidation Mr. King was on a tour of the world in the interest of foreign missions, but he was elected as the first Assistant General Superintendent. He served in that capacity until 1917, when he was elected as General Superintendent and served in that office from 1917 until his death in 1946.

He possessed the air and dignity of a bishop, and in all fairness it deserves to be said that, in spite of any fault or error in judgment he rendered a service to the Pentecostal Holiness Church which was of incalculable value, and for the most part was beyond any just criticism. He was a man of strong convictions and of commanding presence and because of these character traits he was able to guide the Pentecostal Holiness Church through various vicissitudes which threatened its existence as an organization. His name with unanimous consent will go down in history as one of the greatest men and sanest leaders which the Church has ever produced.

Bishop King was born on a farm in Anderson County, South Carolina, near Alford's Bridge on the Savannah River, on August 11, 1869. On his sixteenth birthday, Aug. 11, 1885, he was converted under the ministry of the famous William Asbury Dodge in a Methodist Camp Meeting near Carnesville, Georgia. He often said, "That made it a double birthday to me." Then, on Aug. 17, 1885, he felt a call to preach. On October 23, 1885, he received the experience of sanctification under the ministry of the Rev. F. S. Hudson, a Methodist minister who was associated with the Revs. A. J. Jarrell and William A. Dodge who were President and Vice-President respectively of the North Georgia Holiness Association. The Association meeting was being held at the Carnesville, Georgia, Methodist Church. He was licensed to preach by the Methodist Church in March, 1891, and the following May was assigned as an assistant pastor in the Atlanta district. At the next Conference he was given an assignment as pastor of a church. He afterwards entered the School of Theology of the U. S. Grant University of Chattanooga, Tennessee. In 1898 he came in contact with the Fire-Baptized Holiness Association, and because of an uncongenial atmosphere in the Methodist Church toward sanctification and divine healing he decided to join the Fire Baptized Holiness Association and was soon afterwards elected as Assistant General Overseer. After B. H. Irwin, the General Overseer's defection, in 1900, Mr. King was elected as the General Overseer, as we have noted. In the early spring of 1907 the Rev. G. B. Cashwell came to Toccoa, Georgia, preaching the baptism of the Holy Ghost with the evidence of speaking in tongues as the Spirit gives utterance. This experience was indeed difficult for Bishop King to harmonize with the doctrine of sanctification which he had been taught, and with the baptism of the Holy Ghost and fire which B. H. Irwin had taught. After fasting and praying for some ten days or more he saw the truth of Pentecost and sought and received the experience.

During his long term of office, among many other things, he was responsible for the organizing of the Falcon Publishing Co., in 1909; and the organizing of the Falcon Orphanage in October, 1909; in April, 1919, he opened the Franklin Springs Orphanage. He was editor of the Live Coals of Fire from 1904 to 1907, and on Feb. 15, 1909 began the publication of the Apostolic Evangel. He also edited the Advocate from 1925 to 1929, and from 1935 to 1937. With his passing in 1946 there disappeared a prominent figure who has been missed in all quarters of the Church, but God has seen fit to furnish other capable men to take his place.

Bishop Dan T. Muse (1882-

One of the most loved men in the Pentecostal Holiness Church is Bishop Dan T. Muse. This is largely due to his spirit of true humility. No one feels ill at ease in his presence. The youngest or the most inexperienced minister can occupy a chair next to him on a speaking platform and feel no different than he would by the side of any fellow-minister of his own calibre. Bishop Muse rose from "church-janitor" to the office of a bishop in such a dramatic way that the story of his life reads like fiction.

Mr. Muse was born at Booneville, Mississippi, on March 15, 1882, and when he was at the age of three his family moved to Texas. At four years of age his grandfather called him to his death bed and laying his hands on his head asked God to make him a minister of the gospel. Although little Dan knew little of what took place he was mightily affected by it, which is evidenced by the fact that when he was six to eight years of age he gathered his playmates around him on Sunday afternoons and rehearsed the sermon he had heard at church that morning. He did not become a Christian, however, until some years later.

After his Mother's death in his early youth he decided to go to Oklahoma Indian Territory and try his lot, at about the turn of the century. He was engaged as a printer in a newspaper office, and in 1905 made the acquaintance of a fellow-worker whose name was James A. Campbell. Mr. Campbell and his wife formed a special friendship with Mr. and Mrs. Muse, but after a time they were separated. In 1912 the Campbells both became earnest Christians, and it was not long until Mr. Campbell and Mr. Muse were again working for the same newspaper office, of which Mr. Muse had become foreman. This was God's way of leading Bishop Muse into the way of salvation. During the noon hour Mr. Campbell arranged to conduct a Bible study service, making it optional for the men to attend. In a short time no one attended these services but the foreman, Dan T. Muse, while the other workers were engaged in playing cards or some other type of diversion. Mr. Muse went through a long period of conviction during which time he cried and prayed, asking that God would save him. Every way he turned he seemed to hear the voice of God and feel his need of God. He had a "graphophone" which he tells about how God used a song to convict him. He says:

In the year 1912 a deep longing possessed my being to find God. I had an old graphophone and a record with the song, 'Lord I'm Coming Home.' I would play that song and walk the floor under conviction. I could not resist playing it over and over again. I walked the floor and wondered how I could find God. My body was sorely afflicted. I would lay out under the stars and say to myself, 'Somewhere beyond the stars is God, I wish I knew him.' I would slip off into the nearby woods and cry out to God for mercy. At night I would hide myself in the midst of the clothes in the closet and say over and over again, 'Lord have mercy on me, a sinner.' . . . The Lord sent James A. Campbell to work in the shop near me. That was a great relief for Jim was a Christian. There was a revival meeting in progress at the Olivet Baptist Church, and on Friday night, Jan. 17, 1913, I attended. I was heavily under conviction, and said to myself as the congregation stood to sing the invitation hymn, 'If they sing Lord, I'm Coming Home I am going forward tonight.' When they actually began to sing that hymn I shook like a leaf, but did not keep my promise and go forward.[1]

The next day, on Saturday, a large concern had placed a large order for a special printing job which required that someone work on Sunday, but Mr. Muse refused to comply with the management's request, even if it cost him his job, but he and another man did work all Saturday afternoon. That night at 8:30, Jan. 18, 1913, he was able to make an unconditional surrender to God and started to the next room to tell his wife. He found her there weeping and praying and soon she had made her surrender too. In February he was sanctified and testified to the

---

1 Personal letter from Bishop Dan T. Muse, dated March 11, 1948.

fact in the Baptist Church, announcing that he wanted to receive the baptism of the Holy Spirit with the evidence of speaking in tongues as the disciples did at Pentecost. On May 1, 1913, he went to his first Pentecostal Holiness service, and on May 13, 1913, Mr. Muse received the baptism of the Holy Ghost. In referring to the occasion he writes:

> James A. Campbell had led me into the experience of Holiness and Pentecost, and as soon as it was definitely settled that I was going through to Pentecost, he was let out of his job. I was working for a Hebrew concern, and they paid him the wages of a sterotyper to get him to feed a job press. God alone could have brought that about, and for the purpose of leading me into the truth and Holiness and Pentecost.
>
> Tuesday night May 3, 1913, I received the baptism of the Holy Ghost, speaking with other tongues as the Spirit gives utterance, and for eleven days I talked in other tongues in the church, on the job, at home, and in the stores. It became necessary for me to write to inform people what I wanted, and invariably they would write back to me. It was like heaven on earth.[1]

His first divine call was to do the work of a sexton. He offered his services as sexton to a surprised pastor, the Rev. Harry P. Lott, who gladly gave him the job which he had been doing himself. Contrary to Mr. Lott's guess, he proved faithful in the performance of this humble task. Before long he felt the call to preach renewed, and in August, 1913 he and Mrs. Muse both united with the Oklahoma Conference and began street services and working in jails. From there they went into "new field" evangelism and were miraculously and wonderfully blessed of God, being able to establish a number of churches. In 1918, when he attended the Annual Conference and made his report, a motion was offered and unanimously adopted that he be ordained. It was unusual to ordain a man who had not made application to be ordained, but that is what took place. He later served as President of the Sunday school work of the Conference, and as President of the Camp Meeting Association. From 1925 to 1934 he served as Secretary and Treasurer of the Oklahoma Conference, and in 1934 he was elected as Superintendent of the Conference, being re-elected unanimously for two years. In 1929 he was elected as a member of the General Board, and also as a member of the Board of Education. He has also served as Secretary

---

1 Loc. cit.

of Foreign Missions and Editor of the Missions Department in the Advocate. In 1933 he was elected General Secretary of the Church and served until 1937, when he was elected as one of the General Superintendents on the first ballot. In 1941 he was re-elected as General Superintendent, and also as Chairman of the General Board. In 1945 he was re-elected as General Superintendent, and upon the death of Bishop J. H. King in 1946 he again became Chairman of the General Board of Administration. According to all indications Bishop Muse will no doubt continue in this position of leadership for a long time to come. His popularity has continued to increase but it has made no difference in his humble attitude and brotherly consideration for all those who work under him. Of a truth he feels, "I am less than the least among the saints"; and he is a living example of the Scripture, "Humble yourselves therefore under the mighty hand of God, that he may exalt you in due time."[1]

Bishop J. A. Synan (1905—)

The Rev. J. A. Synan was elected to the office of Assistant General Superintendent at the General Conference which met at Franklin Springs, Georgia in 1941. Being 36 years old, he is the youngest man to hold such an office in the Church unless we consider the Rev. J. H. King who headed the Fire-Baptized Holiness Association at 31. He was born Feb. 18, 1905, in Tazewell County, Virginia. He joined the Methodist Church early in his teens but was not truly converted until sometime later at the age of sixteen. He was sanctified later that year, and in 1922, the following year he received the baptism of the Spirit. Mr. Synan entered the ministry in 1924, at 19 years of age, and at 21 he was ordained in the old Baltimore Conference, now called The Eastern Virginia Conference. He entered the pastorate the year after he was licensed to preach and served as a pastor from 1925 to 1943, with the exception of two years which were spent in evangelistic work. In 1934, at the age of 29 he was elected as Superintendent of the Baltimore Conference (East Virginia), serving in this position for a period of 11 years until 1945.

Besides being elected to the office of bishop in 1941, he was also elected as Chairman of the Home Missions Board which position he held during the quadrennium from 1941 to 1945. Bishop

---

[1] Ephesians 3:8; I Peter 5:6.

THE BISHOPS 417

Synan assisted in the organization of and became chairman of the Service Men's Commission in 1943 and continued to serve in that capacity until the General Conference met in 1945. After Bishop King died, Mr. Synan was elected as Vice-Chairman of the General Board of Administration.

Bishop Synan is a man of eminent qualifications although his formal education has been limited. He is what we often term "a self-made man." Quoting him, he says:

My motto has been to strive to be the best preacher it is possible for me to be, to do whatever may come to me in the line of duty to the very best of my ability, and to let those factors take me where they might in the matter of advancement and greater responsibilities.

Mr. Synan is one of the greatest preachers of his day, including men of all denominations. His diction is superb. His services are in demand in all parts of the Church. He is a man of pleasing personality and has the knack of making friends with all classes of people.

Bishop H. T. Spence (1898—)

The Rev. Hubert T. Spence was elected as fourth Bishop at the General Conference in 1945, and served for a period of one year until the annual meeting of the General Board of Administration in 1946. He felt that because of his health he should give up that work. The Rev. P. F. Beacham was elected in his place and Mr. Spence took the work of General Treasurer which Mr. Beacham had done for more than 20 years. Bishop Spence is a man of sterling character and exercises a wide influence over the entire church, and was well qualified for the office. His work as General Treasurer has been most commendable, especially in view of the fact that his reports have been exceptionally well-organized, simple and complete in every detail and are a reliable guide as to the financial status of the Church. He knows the art of making any task for Christ and the Church a dignified one, by amplifying the importance of even the smallest task.

Bishop Spence was born in Harnett County, N. C., August 27, 1898. He was converted in 1909 at the age of ten, but from 18 to 22 he was in a state of spiritual coldness. He had become worldly, but did not enter into immoral living. In June 1920, he was fully reclaimed under the ministry of the Rev. James F. Eppes, in September he was sanctified, and in February, 1921, received the baptism of the Holy Ghost. The next month Mr. Spence immediately felt a definite call to preach and was licensed to preach by the old Baltimore Conference. Since that time he has served as pastor of several churches, the most outstanding of which were the Richmond, Virginia church from 1930 to 1936, the Newport News, Virginia church from 1937 to 1940 and the Washington, D. C. Church from 1940 to 1945. His services have also been in demand as an evangelist and camp meeting speaker.

Bishop T. A. Melton

In 1945 at the General Conference which met in Oklahoma City the Rev. Thomas A. Melton was elected as an Assistant General Superintendent or Junior Bishop, and in 1946 when Bishop J. H. King died was elevated to the office of a bishop. Mr. Melton was born on a cotton farm in Gaston County, North Carolina, on September 5, 1893. At 55 he still seems young. He has been a member of the Pentecostal Holiness Church for 39 years and has a spotless record as a Christian and a minister. His parents were pious Christians and members of the Baptist Church of which he also became a member at the age of 9 but without being born again. It was not until he was 15 that he experienced a genuine conversion. He tells of his conversion in the following words:

> When I was fifteen years of age I went with two other boys to a tent meeting. It was the spring of 1909, and the Rev. J. C. Underwood was conducting a tent revival. They called the people who were worshipping in his tent the 'unknown tongues' people. I had never been to one of their services until that evening, and the people I saw there were the happiest worshippers I had ever seen. It looked as though they could sing without effort. The preacher preached without notes and with the greatest ease. The tent was full of people, and so was the grove where the tent stood. I was under strong conviction fifteen minutes after reaching the place. I left there that night with my mind fully made up that I would seek with all my heart to receive what those people had. I wanted to feel as they did for they were the happiest people I had ever seen. In a few weeks from that time they moved the gospel tent near our home. I went to the altar as soon as it was opened. I went three times but did not get saved. However, the next day after I had made the third trip to the altar the night before, I was saved at my work in the Ozark Cotton Mill at Gastonia, North Carolina. I had been working and praying for several days having eaten but little food, and had not been sleeping very well either for I was under deep conviction for my sins. On this afternoon I had caught up my work, and had seated myself on the

work bench tired, sleepy and praying to be saved. There I reached the point of surrender, it was there that I told the Lord I had done all that I knew to do and all that I had been told by others that I must do, and that I was no better, but by His help and grace I would not return to the sins that I had turned away from. It seemed to me that before I had fully finished that statement to God, the load of my guilt had been removed from my heart and I was very happy. I went from my work that same evening, and led family prayer for the first time in my life.[1]

This somewhat lengthy statement concerning Bishop Melton's conversion is quoted here to illustrate the depth and thoroughness of his experience which has characterized all of his experience as a Christian minister. He is of a happy and jovial nature, possessing lots of mother wit, but underneath is an impressive earnestness and determination which has brought him to the place he occupies in the Church today. He is extremely practical, sanely spiritual, and consistent.

After Mr. Melton graduated from the Holmes Bible and Missionary Institute in November, 1914, he was licensed to preach by the Southern Pentecostal Association in South Carolina on Dec. 11, 1914 as a Lay Evangelist. Soon after his conversion in 1909, he became a member of the Pentecostal Holiness Church in North Carolina and was a member of the same at the time of the consolidation in 1911. On November 29, 1917 he was ordained to preach. He did outstanding work as a pastor at Winston-Salem, Durham and Danville. In 1943 he was elected as Superintendent of the Western North Carolina Conference, and after Bishop King's death on April 23, 1946, he began his work as Bishop on June 15, 1946 and has served most admirably in that office. He will doubtless serve in that capacity for years to come.

Bishop Paul F. Beacham

The Rev. Paul F. Beacham was elected to the office of bishop in 1946, when Mr. Spence resigned because of ill health. He is known the Church over as a man of conservative and wise leadership. His mature judgment has been a ballast to the Church for years, and as a bishop he continues to guide in the making of important decisions which govern the destiny of the organization. Other biographical facts have been presented in connection with the History of Education in the Pentecostal Holiness Church.

---

[1] Letter received from Bishop T. A. Melton written March 24, 1948.

Part III
HISTORY OF EDUCATION AND PUBLICATIONS IN THE PENTECOSTAL HOLINESS CHURCH

SECTION I
EDUCATION

Chapter I
HOLMES BIBLE COLLEGE, GREENVILLE, S. C.

I. THE ADMINISTRATION OF NICKELS JOHN HOLMES,
THE FOUNDER, 1847-1919

A Brief Biographical Sketch

The Reverend Nickels John Holmes was the founder and first president of what is now known as the Holmes Bible College of Theology and Missions. He was converted in 1863 at Clinton, South Carolina, at the age of fifteen.[1] That great event in his life took place during a series of special evangelistic services conducted by the Rev. W. P. Jacobs in a Presbyterian church which had been organized and pastored a number of years by his father, Zelotes Lee Holmes.[2] It was on a previous occasion, however, that he had been deeply affected and was no doubt actually born-again of the Spirit. He tells of being in company with his father during the time he was conducting one of his protracted meetings up at the old Friendship Presbyterian Church. He says:

> My father, after moving back to Laurens County was pastor of several country churches, and used to carry me with him to his meetings and visiting around the churches. My parents gave their children religious training from the time they could take an impression. Mother taught us our prayers and heard us repeat them every night, and we could often hear her in her closet whispering her prayers to God for us. But the first real impression I remember, came to me on an occasion when I was about ten or twelve years old, when I was with my father at one of his protracted meetings up at old Friendship Presbyterian Church. I do not remember anything about the preaching, but we were staying at the home of Mr. Simpson Glen, one of his friends. Father took me out to walk one evening about sunset into the woods. We came to an old gate across an old road,

---

[1] N. J. Holmes and Wife, **Life Sketches and Sermons.** (Royston, Georgia: Press of the Pentecostal Holiness Church, 1920), p. 27.
[2] **Ibid.,** p. 108.

and he knelt down and prayed and talked to me and then he stood up beside the old gate and sang the old hymn:

> Jerusalem my happy home
> Name ever dear to me
> When shall my labors have an end,
> In joy and peace and thee?

He was a good singer and that song got down in my heart, and I did want to be good and go to heaven when I should die. I went back to the house thinking that I would live for heaven. The impression lingered for all these years in my memory.[1]

Though Brother Holmes, as he was affectionately known and as we will hereafter designate him, was never a member of any church other than the Presbyterian, he came to accept the doctrinal position of the Pentetcostal Holiness Church and devoted the major portion of his ministerial career to the espousal and promulgation of the full gospel for which it stands.

He was a man of eminent qualifications, a genuinely deep consecration, and a hereditary background of which he could be proud and thankful. There is not one blot against his immaculate Christian character. Those who knew him were impressed with two outstanding characteristics, his sweet humble spirit and his simple faith and trust in the all-wise providence of his heavenly Father. His influence, through the institution he established, came to be world-wide in scope. And in that Day of days no doubt many souls shall rise up and call him blessed. In order to properly appreciate and understand the sacrificial contribution he made to the cause of Christian education within the Pentecostal Holiness Church, it becomes necessary that we call attention to the general facts relating to his parentage, his education, his experience as a lawyer, and finally as a Presbyterian minister.

His Parentage

He was born September 9, 1847 in a small house some few miles from Spartanburg. He was the second child and oldest son of twelve children. His mother was Catherine Nickels the daughter of Dr. John Nickels, a practicing physician and farmer who was the owner of a number of slaves. Nickels John was thus named in honor of his maternal grandfather. It was one of these negro

---

1 Holmes and Wife, op. cit., pp. 25-27.

slaves, Mrs. Holmes writes, who influenced her in her early childhood to decide for Christ. We quote a few excerpts from her letter written to her son Nickels years later after she had become an octogenarian. The letter was dated November 21, 1906, the year before she died at eighty-four, and some eight years after Holmes Bible College had been established. She writes:

> When I was about seven years old there lived in our family a colored woman, a slave, who seemed to think that it was her duty to teach the children in the family, white and black, their religious duties. . . . The old woman continued to teach me and as soon as I could read, when she would go to church and hear a sermon she would have me get the Bible and read it for her, and she kept me reading for her until I was sent away to school. . . . At an early age I joined the church and then it was my desire to do good, and I studied a plan which I could never carry out, but still stayed on my mind until I married.
>
> The plan was this, I wanted a house of my own, and I filled it with young people that I could train to serve the Lord. And when I married, as your father was a minister, I thought I could carry out my plan, but I found out that the Lord was not ready for the plan. . . . In the course of twenty years I had a large family, but death entered and took four of the number in a short time, and one was the oldest . . .
>
> Now the Lord spared my oldest son, I knew not for what, but he was given to Him for service. But hope died in me when he chose the law as his profession. But in time he changed his mind for the ministry. And one day while at his house my mind ran over my life and his, and something has been fulfilled. My plan has been carried out. Praise the Lord! . . .
>
> Now if the African can teach us, why cannot some of the young people go to teach them? . . . I send you this hoping it may strengthen your faith in your work.
> Your loving mother,
N. C. Holmes.[1]

It is not difficult to appraise the value of his saintly Mother's influence. In 1909, he comments concerning her letter,

> I surely rejoice and thank God that He has led me, and enabled me in a measure to carry out what was on my Mother's heart, though I knew nothing of her plan or purpose of its fulfillment in me until she sent me the statement just a year before her death. . . .[2]

According to the Ministerial Directory of the Presbyterian Church, U. S., his father, Zelotes Lee Holmes was a student for two

---

1 Ibid., p. 126.
2 Ibid., pp. 188-192.

years at Mead College, and later at Columbia Theological Seminary at Columbia, S. C., from 1839 to 1842. During the same year he was licensed to preach and on July 28, 1844 he was ordained by the South Carolina Presbytery. He pastored a number of churches in the vicinity of Spartanburg and later at Laurens. In 1858 while living at Laurens he became a professor in the Laurenville Female College and in 1880 he taught at Clinton College. He died in 1885. His noteworthy ministerial and teaching career in the Presbyterian Church in South Carolina must have been transmitted in some measure to his illustrious son.[1]

Nickles J. Holmes' (Nickels is misspelled "Nickles") name also appears on the pages of the same Ministerial Directory—being licensed April 13, and ordained October 12, 1888. He was a member of the Presbytery of Enoree serving as Presbytery's evangelist, 1888-92. He was stated supply in Spartanburg in 1888 and was pastor of the Second Presbyterian Church of Greenville, S. C., 1892-95. In 1895 and 1896 he was engaged in evangelistic work, being appointed evangelist of the Synod of South Carolina, 1896 to 1898. Then there is the notation "not on roll 1898 and no further record."[2] It was in 1898 that he established the Holmes Bible College which he served as its president until his death in 1919.

His Call to Preach

In addition to the influence of his parents it should also be added that when he was sixteen his oldest sister, Olive, had died with the words on her lips—"You are to preach the gospel."[3] Brother Holmes, in speaking of the indelible impression it made upon him said, "The call through the words of my dying sister rang, ever and anon in my ears, like a bell. When anything occurred in my life for years that would suggest the subject of my future work, my mind would flash to that incident, as to the ringing of a bell and those words were still sounding."[4] At the tender age of seventeen he answered the call to arms for the cause of the Confederacy and was assigned to non-combat duty and

---
1 Rev. E. C. Scott, **Ministerial Directory of the Presbyterian Church, U. S., 1861-1941.** (Austin: Von Boeckmann-Jones Co.) p. 325.
2 Ibid., p. 32.
3 Holmes, op. cit., p. 28.
4 Ibid., p. 28.

served several months until the close of the War. During many of his experiences as a soldier he tells of hearing the ever recurring sound of the bell to "Preach the gospel." Years later he writes:

> I am thankful today as I look back over the forty years of peace that, God in His providence kept me away from the firing line, and that I have the full consciousness in my soul that I have no man's blood on my hands as an overt act . . .[1]

His Education

Because the best schools in the South were forced to suspend operations because of the desolation of war and the abject poverty to which many inhabitants had been reduced, his father at extreme sacrifice sent him to the University of Edinborough where he spent three years. While there he visited France and also spent five months in Gottingen, Germany studying the German language.

His Experience as a Lawyer, etc.

He returned from Scotland in the spring of 1869 but found it difficult to choose his life's vocation. He tried first to farm, then taught school for awhile, and later after much inward conflict decided to read law. This he did for a period of one year before being admitted to the bar. He formed a partnership with H. Y. Simpson, the son of W. D. Simpson. When Wade Hampton was elected governor, W. D. Simpson was also elected Lieutenant Governor and was later elected Chief Justice of the Supreme Court. Whereupon he turned over his law practice to his son and to young Holmes who had married his daughter, Lucy Elizabeth Simpson.[2]

Speaking of her forebears, she says, ". . . my ancestors on both sides were true blue Scotch Irish Presbyterians, sober, honest upright and conscientious Christians, a precious heritage for anyone. My father William Dunlap Simpson was the second son of Doctor John Wells Simpson, a successful and beloved physician, in the town of Laurens, and an elder of the Presbyterian Church, earnest and faithful in the discharge of every duty of his office."[3]

---

1 Loc. cit.
2 Ibid., pp. 29, 30.
3 Ibid., pp. 58, 59, 294, et passim.

After he had practiced law successfully for fourteen years he and his wife were settled comfortably at Laurens, South Carolina. And, in 1888, he decided to enter the race for the office of Solicitor. After entering that race he says: ". . . Those words came to me as if they had been sounded in my ears, 'You are seeking to prosecute men for crime. Had you not better seek to save them from the commission of crime?' I recognized that it was God speaking to me and renewing the call to preach!"[1] When he told his wife of the experience and unfolded to her his state of mind and heart she told him without hesitation, "Do as you feel led, and what God would have you do."[2] She became the first matron of the school he organized and was his constant companion and inspiration throughout his entire ministry. Her work was of such a nature and to such an extent that she can well be thought of as the joint-founder of the Bible College. Their only child, a baby boy of ten months, God saw fit to take to be with Him. Having no children of their own it became easy and natural for them to transfer their affections and parental love upon the members of their school family.

His Experience as a Presbyterian Minister

Though Mr. Holmes had served God as a Christian layman, he writes: "I knew there were matters in my life I would have to give up, if I preached the Gospel. Although I had been a member of the church for twenty-five years, and an elder for some years, I knew that my life would not measure up to the standard of the ministerial life. I would have to give up the social game of cards, and the social glass."[3] He also tells, somewhat at length, how he struggled to give up the tobacco habit before he was finally able to make a firm decision to leave it off for Jesus' sake.[4] No sacrifice, it seems, was too great for him to make for the cause of Him who made the supreme sacrifice. It is said that he disposed of an expensive watch-case and used the proceeds to help spread the gospel he loved. Though few people saw the cheaper case he had selected to replace the gold one, it is said that in the tarnished

---

1 Ibid., pp. 61, 62.
2 Ibid., p. 6".
3 Ibid., p. 64.
4 Ibid., pp. 65-67.

metal he had engraved as a personal reminder to continue his consecration—the words "Iron for Gold for Jesus' sake."

Other examples of his noble spirit will be seen in a later account of the early beginning and development of the Bible school which now memorializes his name.

Before he was licensed to preach and ordained in 1888 he wrote his father-in-law who was at the time Chief Justice of the Supreme Court, asking for counsel and advice. Chief Justice, W. D. Simpson's reply was in part as follows:

Columbia, S. C.
March 24, 1888.

Dear Nick:
Your letter received, I do feel a deep interest in your welfare, present and future, and earnestly wish that I were able to advise you in the matter about which you wrote. . . . But at last you must seek counsel from a higher power, and do what your good sense may determine. . . .[1]
Truly yours,
W. D. Simpson.

Since we have already given a brief outline of his ministerial activity as it appeared in the Ministerial Directory it will be unnecessary to reiterate, but during the time of his successful ministerial activity within the Presbyterian Church there are some outstanding experiences which finally led to his withdrawal and to the establishing of the school. Sometime before 1891 there fell into his hands a little book by D. L. Moody "The Secret of Power." He and his wife both read it with interest and became deeply impressed and spiritually hungry for the work of the Spirit to be wrought in their lives in a fuller measure. They later learned about the Northfield Bible Conference which Mr. Moody sponsored each year in July. It was there that they met with some who were preaching sanctification as a second work of grace, and that it might be received in this life.[2] He writes of this experience which we quote:

> Then we met up with some who were preaching sanctification as a second work of grace, and that it might be received in this life. That we might be sanctified by faith as an instantaneous experience; be made free from sin, have a pure clean heart, and be made holy now.

---

1 Ibid., p. 63.
2 Ibid., pp. 68, 69.

This was not as we had learned it, and I opposed it and preached against it, but at the same time I was not satisfied with my own experience, and thought sometimes that my life was more a theory than a real experience, but I could not then see the real death of the old man, or body of sin, and the consequent freedom from sin, as a definite work of grace wrought by the Holy Spirit, through faith and accomplished in this life. Yet I became more and more anxious to know more about the Holy Spirit and His work. I wanted to know more about the power for enduement for service that Mr. Moody spoke of in that little book, 'The Secret of Power,' and get something of the experience he had received. I could feel the lack of that power in my own life, see it in my own life and in the lives and work of my brethren in the ministry and in the whole church, but had not learned the remedy, and in fact, had not learned that there was a remedy.[1]

He tells of taking a buggy ride with Mr. Moody while they were there at which time Mr. Moody talked to him about the Holy Spirit and had a special prayer for him where he had reined up his horse and stopped in the middle of the road. B. F. Meyer, A. J. Gordon and others were invited speakers during the Conference.[2] Though he earnestly read his Bible and sought for the experience they taught that believers could have, he did not at that time receive it, though his wife did. He writes of her experience as follows:

My wife received a blessed experience, which we called the Baptism of the Holy Ghost under the teaching there, but which as we have since learned, was the baptism by the Holy Ghost with the blood cleansing away the body of sin and filling with the fruit of the Spirit, which is sanctification. Oh, how she was brought down and wept over herself, and renounced everything unlike God, and yielded herself to God and was flooded with a divine love that filled and permeated her whole being and seemed almost to consume her bodily. I saw and felt that a great crisis had come into her life. I felt that she had passed me by in experience like the flash of a great light. I could see it in her face, and feel it in the touch of her hand. God had done a great thing for her whereof we were glad.[3]

It was not until four years later on Sunday, July 7, 1895, that Brother Holmes received the experience of sanctification in a Methodist preacher's barn at Gray Court, S. C., while conducting evangelistic services there. He had preached on Romans 12:1 that morning, and while alone praying that afternoon in the pastor's

---
1 Ibid., p. 69.
2 Ibid., p. 71.
3 Ibid., pp. 76, 77.

barn he gave himself for life or death unto the Lord.[1] In speaking of the occasion later he writes: "There was a sudden flash of power that went through my body like an electric current, and passed away, and then there was a wonderful peace that came into my heart, like the peace that passeth understanding. . . . God had drawn so near to me and Christ was so precious. . . . I had accepted *by faith* the sanctifying grace and power of the Holy Spirit. I called it the baptism of the Holy Ghost, *received by faith*."[2]

He was at the time pastor of the Second Presbyterian Church which he had organized in Greenville, S. C. That fall, in 1895, he gave up that church and with the permission of the Presbytery entered again into evangelistic work. He writes of his experience as follows:

All the time since we left Northfield the Holy Spirit had been graciously working in my heart. He was revealing to me the truth of the Bible, on the subject of sanctification, holiness, divine healing and the work of the Spirit in a new light. As He did I tried to appropriate it to myself, and preach it to others. And as I did that my position began to be questioned by some of the brethren of the Presbytery.[3]

In referring to his church relation at this time he makes this further statement:

After I had been in the Synodical Evangelistic work for something over a year, and had visited a large part of the territory of the Synod, I began to find that my views on the subject of the Holy Ghost, sanctification, divine healing, etc., were being brought into question by some of the brethren of my Presbytery. I went to the committee that had the work in charge, and told them about my views, and that I did not want them to be embarrassed by my position and offered to resign. . . . Not long afterward some of the brethren of the Presbytery became disturbed about Brother S. C. Todd, and myself preaching sanctification, divine healing, etc., and brought the matter up before the Presbytery, and had a committee appointed to interview us as to our views. When we stated them, the committee advised us for the sake of peace to withdraw from the Presbytery, which we agreed to do upon letters of dismission being granted us by the Presbytery, which at the next meeting of the Presbytery were granted. After that I united with the Brewerton Independent Presbyterian Church which had also unanimously withdrawn from the jurisdiction

---

1 Ibid., pp. 83, 84.
2 Ibid., pp. 85, 86.
3 Ibid., p. 82.

of the Presbytery, because they held the same views on sanctification and healing that we did. I was called by that church to become its pastor, which I accepted and gave them one Sabbath a month and gave the rest of my time to evangelistic work. About a year after we were granted letters of dismissal by the Presbytery, and without complaint against the action, and without notice or summons of any kind to us, passed an exparte resolution purporting to divest us of our ministerial function. I did not recognize this action of the synod or its jurisdiction over me, being no party to Synod's action in any way, by summons or otherwise; and being a minister of another church and recognized by that church as a minister, and its pastor, and being in utter ignorance of the matter until it was over. I went right on exercising the functions of the ministry with a conscience void of offense before God and man, and with love and good will in my heart for the brethren.[1]

At a later date, on July 10, 1910, after he had erected a tabernacle at Greenville, S. C. in connection with the College which was later moved to the same location, a commission from the Brewerton Church organized the Tabernacle Presbyterian Church. This church organization was later consolidated with the Pentecostal Holiness Church at Canon, Georgia in 1915, though Brother Holmes for reasons which will be seen later did not himself unite with the new organization.

The Early Beginnings

In the year of 1892 while Brother Holmes was pastor of the Second Presbyterian Church in Greenville, he and his wife rented a cottage on Paris Mountain about nine miles from Greenville where they spent part of the summer. The salutary atmosphere, the beautiful scenery and the quiet meditative environment made such an appeal to them that by the following summer they had purchased several acres nearby and erected a cottage of their own. They felt that God would be pleased to bless their investment for His glory.

The Presbyterian Church made an exception in ordaining Brother Holmes to preach without his having had a formal seminary education. Since he had himself had a struggle to yield to his call to preach, he had for years desired to open some sort of Bible school to make it easier for others who might be halting along the way. Now he felt that this was his opportunity to realize in some

---

[1] Ibid., pp. 97, 98.

HOLMES BIBLE COLLEGE, GREENVILLE, S. C.   433

measure this fond dream. Whereupon, in the summer of 1893 he and his wife invited several promising young men to spend ten days or two weeks with them in Bible study and prayer. A tent was erected on the brow of the mountain which they used for their services and classes.[1] The first class was conducted in this tent at 6:30 A. M. on Wednesday, July 29, 1893, by the Rev. N. J. Holmes who was, as we have seen, a former lawyer of Laurens, S. C. and at that time the pastor of the Second Presbyterian Church in Greenville. Here it was that he read the 27 Psalm and in teaching this first Bible lesson he thus began an institution which was destined to afford untold blessings to a host of peoples throughout the earth. In the 1945-1946 Catalogue we quote the following paragraph relating to this historical background:

> There were only fifteen members of that institute, but for ten days they met classes from 6:30 A. M. to 9:00 P. M., and discussed such subjects as 'Prayer,' 'Have I Learned to Pray?' 'God in His Being, as Our God, as Our Father'; 'Is God My Father?' 'The Gift of the Holy Spirit to the Church.' Besides the Rev. N. J. Holmes, leaders of the classes were Rev. R. E. Henderson, Rev. S. E. Preston, D.D., J. C. Bailey, Jr., Rev. R. L. Walker, L. D. Bray, Geo. M. Howerton, Rhea Preston, W. W. Edge, C. P. Currie, Rev. W. R. Owings, Rev. W. L. Hoggs, and Rev. W. R. Minter. Miss M. B. Holmes and Mrs. N. J. Holmes also attended the institute, but there is no indication in the record that they conducted any classes.[2]

The following year, in 1894, they built an additional cottage for the purpose of housing the students, and also a little chapel to be used for the Bibly study and religious services. These were used each summer until 1898 at which time the school was formally organized and permanently opened on the first day of November.[3] Brother Holmes writes the following account in 1910:

> We, with Reverend S. C. Todd, then a Presbyterian minister, and Rev. M. H. Houston, D.D., returned missionary from China, after much prayer and waiting on God, arranged to open a permanent Bible and Missionary training institute in the fall of that year, 1898. It opened the first of November with one Bible teacher, Dr. Houston, and one student, Law M. Anderson. A few others came during the first month, and it increased in number up to, from fifty to seventy students.[4]

---

1 **Ibid.,** pp. 93, 94.
2 Catalogue of the Holmes Bible College, p. 1.
3 Holmes, **op. cit.,** pp. 94, 95.
4 **Ibid.,** p. 95.

In the above quotation it is indicated that the school was opened "after much prayer." At this point it is important that we recognize the solid foundation upon which this institution was founded and upon which it rests until this day. The following information is given to reveal the deep consecration which Brother Holmes made in 1895 and 1896, the years immediately preceding his final decision to give up evangelistic work and devote his time and energies to the training of young people for the work of the kingdom which led to the permanent opening of the school in 1898.

Several years ago this writer, while visiting in the home of a young minister by the name of A. M. Long, was told that he had a cherished possession in his personal library which he prized very highly. He related the following account of how he acquired it. He said:

> I was in school at Holmes Bible College and was using a Bible which had no concordance. My room-mate knowing of my handicap gave me a part-Bible which he had found in the attic of the old Boy's Dormitory where we roomed. It was the latter half of an old and worn Bible, but it had a good concordance. I gratefully accepted it and later discovered that it possessed considerable sentimental value. It was part of an old Bible which had belonged to N. J. Holmes, the founder of Holmes Bible College. I consider this to be the most prized volume I possess.[1]

Since then this valuable possession was sacrificed as a gift to the Bible College for its archives. The following four quotations in Brother Holmes' own handwriting were found on the fly leaf of this worn and discarded old volume. They are mentioned here to emphasize the prayerful caution which he exercised before making his final decision to devote himself exclusively to this sacrificial work which would require an unfaltering faith amid many discouragements. He earnestly desired to be sure before he acted. The following record of his intimate spiritual experiences was found written therein:

> Romans 12:1 Text Sabbath morning, Gray Court, July 7, 1895. Sabbath evening, I gave myself for life or death unto the Lord—soul and body, to be, or do, or suffer what He wills. (At Brother W. A. Shells, Gray Court. In his barn.) N. J. H.

---

[1] Rev. A. M. Long, Pastor of Pentecostal Holiness Church at Mullens, West Virginia.

The following day he had written these lines:

Thou wilt keep him in peace, peace whose mind is stayed on thee; because he trusteth in thee. (Isaiah 26:3, margin). Fear not for I am with thee; be not dismayed for I am thy God; I will strengthen thee; yea, I will uphold thee with the right hand of my righteousness. (Isaiah 41:10.) Know ye not that ye are the temple of God and that the Spirit of God dwelleth in you? (I Cor. 3:16.) And ye are not your own. (I Cor. 6:19.) For ye are bought with a price, therefore glorify God in your body, and in your spirit which are God's. (I Cor. 6:20.) But Christ is all in all. (Col. 3:11.) I am the bread of life. (John 6:35.) Which is Christ in you the hope of glory. (Col. 1:17.) Whose I am and whom I serve. (Acts 27:23.) The love God shed abroad in our hearts by the Holy Ghost, which is given to us. (Romans 5:5.) I am thine, O God, wilt thou keep me in the unity of the Spirit, in the bond of peace. Kept by the power of God. (I Peter 1:5) July 8, 1895.[1]

Another entry in this diary of important events is listed thus:

On the afternoon of the 27th of April, 1896, at Moundville, when I went out into the woods and prayed humbly and prostrated myself before God, He blessed me and caused my heart to burn within me. Also the next morning as I went to church it came into my heart. Bless His holy name. N. J. H.

On the same leaf also appears the following:

Bamberg, May 28, 1896. Prostrated on the floor of my room, counting myself dead with Christ, after reading 'Christ our Life' by Andrew Murray; and going over certain verses in God's Word; I poured out my soul in prayer. God wonderfully blessed me, and caused my heart to burn within me until I rejoiced aloud, in the ecstacy of joy and love. Glory to God. Praise His blessed name, Precious Savior. N. J. H.[2]

These experiences include and directly follow his experience of sanctification, received as a second definite work of grace. He was thus "sanctified, meet for the Master's use, and prepared unto every good work."[3] To know these facts is to better understand and properly appraise some of the events which will follow in our historical account.

The Changes in Location and Changes in Name

The school was first located on Paris Mountain where it remained for the first two years. It was at that time called "The Al-

---

1 N. J. Holmes' old Bible in the archives of Holmes Bible College at Greenville, S. C.
2 Op. cit., on fly leaf of Holmes' Bible.
3 II Timothy 2:21.

tamont Bible and Missionary Institute," taking its name from the old Altamont Hotel in which it was operated. Brother Holmes writes the following account in his book, "Life Sketches and Sermons.":

The first term of the Institute had been in the winter from November 1, 1898 to May 30, 1899, but was then changed from winter to summer for one term, April to October, 1900. And after that, was moved to Atlanta, Georgia, where it remained two years, January, 1901 to October, 1903. It was then moved to Columbia, South Carolina, to the Oliver Gospel Mission Building for two years, October, 1903 to June, 1905, after which it was moved back, October, 1905 to Altamont on Paris Mountain, eight miles from Greenville, South Carolina, where it was first opened. We had tried to sell the property on the mountain while we were away but failed and then felt it was the Lord's will for us to return to it.[1]

While the school was located in Atlanta from January, 1901 to October, 1903, it was called "The Bible and Missionary Institute of Atlanta."[2] After it was moved to Columbia, S. C., in October, 1903, where it operated until June, 1905, it was again called by the original name which it of course retained after it was moved again in October, 1905, to the original location on Paris Mountain. When the matter of moving was presented to the teachers and students in November, 1945, all but two, voted to move immediately to Greenville.[3] It has since been located on the corner of Buncombe Street and Briggs Avenue. After the opening of the session on October 1, 1916, at the new location it was decided by the Board of Trustees to change the name to "Holmes Bible and Missionary Institute" in honor of its founder. It continued under this name during his life-time and administration. The following chart will be helpful to present an over-all picture of these facts:

Date	Name	Location
Nov. 1, 1898 to Oct. 1900	Altamont Bible and Missionary Institute	Paris Mountain (8 miles from Greenville)
Jan. 1901 to Oct. 1903	The Bible and Missionary Institute of Atlanta	Atlanta, Georgia
Oct. 1903 to June 1905	Altamont Bible and Missionary Institute	Columbia, S. C.

---

1 Holmes and wife, op. cit., p. 117.
2 Catalogue, op. cit., p. 3.
3 Holmes, op. cit., p. 252.

Date	Name	Location
Oct. 1905 to Nov. 1915	Altamont Bible and Missionary Institute	Paris Mountain
Feb. 1, 1916 to May, 1940	Holmes Bible and Missionary Institute	Greenville, S. C.
May 23, 1940 to date	Holmes Bible College of Theology and Missions	Greenville, S. C.

(The last change of name took place under the Rev. Paul F. Beacham's administration after Brother Holmes' death in 1919.)

It will be observed from these dates that the terms appear to have been somewhat irregular. This was due to unfavorable climatic conditions. The winter weather on the mountain made the roads almost impassable and it was thus very difficult to bring in mail and supplies. The second term on the mountain was therefore changed from winter to summer, opening in April, 1900, and running until October, 1900.[1] While the school was operated in Atlanta and Columbia from January, 1901 until June, 1905, the terms began in the winter in regular fashion. From October, 1905 until March, 1910, the regular winter sessions, although with extreme discomfort, were continued. It was decided then that after a two months vacation the new term would open the first of May, 1910 and continue until December.[2] These summer sessions were made necessary every year until the school was moved to Greenville in 1916 where it has since opened each year in early October and closed the following May.

THE PROPERTY AND BUILDINGS

We have already mentioned the two cottages and a small chapel which were erected in 1893 and 1894 on the few acres of land which Brother Holmes and his wife purchased after their pleasant stay in the rented cottage in the summer of 1892. These buildings continued in use until 1898 when they had opportunity to purchase the Altamont Hotel property on the very top of Paris Mountain for the sum of $5,000. It had cost the original builders over $20,000. With the exception of a few negligible

---
1 Ibid., p. 117.
2 Ibid., p. 179.

amounts these entire obligations were assumed by Brother Holmes and his wife, individually.[1] This building was used for both dormitory and classrooms during the entire time the school operated on the mountain.

The Cross-Shaped Tabernacle

Sometime after the school had been moved from Columbia back to the mountain in 1905, Brother Holmes began to make it his custom to bring a few of the students each week-end to Greenville where they conducted religious services in a small rented room on Buncombe Street located near a large lot which he and his wife owned on the corner of Buncombe at Briggs Avenue.[2]

It was here, in 1909, that he built a cross-shaped tabernacle in which to conduct these services. There was, also, included within it a living quarters which were used on week-ends and during the winter months, after 1910, when the summer terms ended until the school was moved in 1916. Brother Holmes has this to say with reference to the building of the tabernacle:

> My wife and I had a good sized lot, about an acre, in the northwestern part of the city, just between the city and two of the large cotton mills, where we might if the Lord willed build a tabernacle for service, and eventually have a school or college where those who desired, might be taught the full gospel of Christ, along with other branches of learning. We went down and put up our little tents to live in while we worked. I had a small lot in another portion of the city which I traded to the West End Lumber Company. I got $400.00 for the lot in lumber, and then in the end added another hundred making the lumber cost $500.00.[3]

The plan was the shape of a cross thirty by sixty feet each way. Three rooms were cut off at the rear of the tabernacle and a porch and kitchen were added to make the top of the cross. A few friends helped with the construction of the tabernacle but the bulk of the work was done by the students. By the middle of July, in about two months after it was begun, a meeting was in progress in it. During these revival services a number were graciously blessed. It seemed that this was God's approval upon the work.[4]

---
1 Ibid., pp. 92-94.
2 Ibid., p. 171.
3 Ibid., p. 171.
4 Ibid., p. 171, 172.

The Administration Building, Etc.

In 1914, a nice two-story dwelling was purchased on the lot immediately contiguous to the original lot, on the south side and facing Briggs Avenue. This building was used for an administration building, and to house members of the faculty and from twenty to twenty-five girls after the school began operating in Greenville on February 1, 1916.

The Boys' Dormitory

It was on that date, also, that a three-story frame boys' dormitory was completed and occupied. Mr. John T. Dempsey, the faithful Superintendent of the Tabernacle Sunday School, still known to his many friends as "Brother Dempsey" was the foreman who supervised this work.

This building, which is located on the northwest corner of the property and faces on Buncombe Street had in it seventeen bedrooms, a boys' study hall and several other small rooms. It was used as the Boys' Dormitory until 1942 when the new Boys' Dormitory was occupied. It has since that time been conveniently divided into apartments for married couples and will perhaps serve a good purpose for some time to come. (The boys' study hall was later moved to the basement of the Holmes Memorial Church building which was constructed in 1925. And until it came to be occupied by married couples in 1941, this study hall space was used for an ironing room and students' barber shop.)

The Changes in Doctrinal Teaching

The opening of the school was postponed for two weeks in the fall of 1907 in order to allow Brother Holmes to attend the annual convention of the Pentecostal Mission at Nashville, Tennessee. He had attended these conventions for several years but this time there was a difference in doctrinal views expressed. Rev. J. O. McClurkin, the president of the mission, J. T. Benson, Tim H. Moore and others still claimed that they had received the baptism with the Holy Ghost in sanctification. But Brother Holmes had seen a number receive the Pentecostal Baptism, and had himself also received and had spoken in tongues. This made the difference.

He tells of special prayer and fastings during the school year 1904-1905 for an outpouring of God's Spirit. At that time the Institute was located at Columbia. In the fall of 1906, "The Way of Faith" a religious paper edited by J. M. Pipe, Columbia, S. C., carried accounts of similar spiritual activity among Christians at Los Angeles and other places. A number of them had received the baptism and had spoken in tongues, Brother Holmes had heard and read of these accounts and with mingled emotions of cautious fear and exultant rejoicing. He was at first both amazed and confused. Students in his school and teachers, alike, began to receive this strange "new blessing." Many of his friends in whom he had utmost confidence were also rejoicing and both speaking and singing in tongues. Some had visited the school and had left because Brother Holmes had been reluctant to accept fully their experiences with wholehearted enthusiasm. They left with somewhat the feeling that God's Spirit was grieved with Brother Holmes' attitude. Brother Holmes, being perturbed, anxiously sought to reconcile their theological differences, and began to consult the original Greek in an attempt to understand these strange happenings! Because of his position of leadership it was imperative that he should be absolutely sure before he accepted or endorsed this unusual experience.[1] We quote here what happened. He writes:

> When they were gone I told the Institute that I felt we should go on with the prayer services, and that we should fast and pray for the Lord to open up the truth. For my own part I was getting disturbed about my theology. I fasted three days without eating or drinking anything; and then for three more days with only one meal a day; then two more days with two meals a day. During these days we were praying, and reading and studying our Bible on the subject of Pentecost whether it was the same thing or different from sanctification. We had held that it was the same, but it seemed then that as the light of the Scriptures was turned on that God was undermining that position, and I became unsettled in the matter, and as I did not know at the time where I stood, in fact, I felt that I was not standing much anywhere. I felt unfit to teach or preach, or do anything until I could settle down someway, somewhere.[2]

It was not long until he clearly recognized that he had not received the baptism in sanctification, and was ready to seek

---
1 Ibid., p. 135 ff. et passim.
2 Ibid., p. 139.

earnestly and whole-heartedly for "Pentecost." On the night of April 27, 1907, the presence of God filled the chapel where prayer services were being conducted. While L. R. Graham, one of the teachers who had received the baptism of the Spirit, was leading in prayer, this glorious new experience came to be a reality in Brother Holmes' own heart and life. He, too, spoke in tongues, and in writing of the occasion later he says: "I had the witness with my tongue to the baptism, but not the gift of tongues, neither do I claim the gift of tongues yet, though I speak with tongues."[2] The evident conclusion is, that though he was still Presbyterian by church affiliation, he was now Pentecostal Holines in doctrinal experience. Throughout the history of the school until this time its students had been taught that in the experience of sanctification one receives the baptism of the Holy Ghost, and that the two experiences were synonymous. Both terms previously had been used to refer to the same experience. But, from henceforth, its doctrinal position was made to accord with their new found experience and their fuller understanding of the Scriptures. The Confession of Faith and Larger and Shorter Catechisms were amended by the Brewerton Independent Presbyterian Church to harmonize with these variant doctrinal teachings, and were later incorporated in the rules of faith accepted by the Tabernacle Presbyterian Church when it was organized in 1910.

When this organization was consolidated with the Pentecostal Holiness Church at Canon, Georgia in 1915, Brother Holmes did not himself become a member of the body. It was, however, not because of any disharmony or unwillingness to submit himself to ecclesiastical authority, but because of his relationship to the school. He felt that it would be unwise and would create some difficulties which would seriously hinder him in the prosecution of his school program. First of all, he desired that the school operate on a strictly interdenominational basis offering to worthy students of all denominations an equal opportunity for training. The school has always maintained this same policy of enrollment. Then, there was a second reason: to join the Conference would automatically require that he be subject to its appointing power, and such would likely at some time cause him to be moved from

---

2 Ibid., p. 145.

the Greenville church and hence away from his school work. The Greenville church, now known as the Holmes Memorial Church, nominally has been a part of the Pentecostal Holiness Church; but actually has operated on an independent basis, cooperating with the Conference only in such ways as would not interfere with but safeguard the avowed purposes of the institution with regard to its interdenominational character.

The relationship of the school to the Church has been somewhat parallel to the relationship which exists between the local church to the Conference. Though the school has always worked in close harmony with the Pentecostal Holiness Church and has advocated the same doctrinal teachings, it has never in the strictest sense been considered as being a Pentecostal Holiness church school. In recent years it has been brought under a closer supervision of the Church and coordinated with the overall educational program but its relation to the Church is still not on a parity with Emmanuel College and Southwestern Pentecostal Holiness College which are each church-sponsored, church-controlled and church-owned. A more complete explanation of these essential differences will appear later under another heading. It may as well be said here, that Holmes Bible College without question has made the greatest single contribution to this church in spite of its somewhat independent policy of operation. It has been one of the chief divine agencies which God has used in disseminating the full gospel truth on a world-wide scale. No other institution in the Pentecostal Holiness Church, and perhaps none in any Church has with the same facilities been able to boast of as many genuinely useful servants of God in the work of the Kingdom.

The Motto, The Purpose, The Policy, and The Rules

The motto of this school has always been to "Live for Others." The example of self-sacrifice exemplified by the sacrificial life and ministry of its founder who followed the example of Christ has unceasingly inspired and influenced those who knew him or who have learned of his sacrificial ministry of serving others. It is a distinguishing character trait of most of the students who have been trained within these sacred walls to willingly choose to enter fields of service where a ministry of sacrificial service is required.

The purpose of this institution is "to train Christian workers" and in so doing "To Give the Whole Bible to the Whole World." Its doors have been opened only to those who are Christians and who feel that God would have them to prepare themselves for some phase of Christian service either as a layman or a clergyman. It has never required that its students should feel definitely called to the ministry in order to be admitted for enrollment, but in a large percentage of the cases those who are not already called receive definite calls during the course of their training. The training and discipline to which the students are subjected is designed to develop Christian character and moral integrity as well as to meet certain scholastic standards.

The policy of the school has always been to operate as far as possible on a *strictly cash basis* and to never incur any indebtedness for which its president could not be personally responsible. For the first three years of the school's history there was a nominal charge made for room and board of from nine to ten dollars per month. But, it was later decided that beginning in October, 1902, the school would be operated *entirely by faith* and in utter dependence upon God's providence.[1] While the Institute was located at Atlanta, from 1901 to 1903, Brother Holmes wrote the following letter dated June 23, 1902, in which he listed the following eight reasons for putting the school on an entirely faith basis:

1. We believe the work is God's work.
2. It is for His glory.
3. We believe it is pleasing to Him to conduct and provide for His work.
4. We believe it honors God to rest upon Him for everything—Faith honors God.
5. We believe that it strengthens the worker to be dependent entirely upon God. He looks for God's strength, instead of human.
6. We believe God is calling out those who are willing to trust Him for witnesses, or examples, of faith.
7. We believe that God wants to train up young workers to learn to trust Him.

---

1 Ibid., pp. 117, 118.

8. It is according to the promise of the Master. 'Seek ye first the kingdom of God and his righteousness.'[1]

Now for almost a half century, since 1902, worthy Christian young men and women have been admitted as long as there has been room to receive them, irrespective of their financial ability to pay for either board or lodging. All the teachers, including the president, give their services without charge. Some of them are pastors of nearby churches. Others evangelize during the summer months. Brother Holmes, in speaking of this plan says:

We effected this change in the plan of work while in Atlanta, Georgia, in October, 1902. Stating that we would receive those who were consecrated to the service of God, and wanted to prepare for Christian work, whether they were able to contribute to the support of the work or not, but would expect those who had the means, with which they could contribute, to do so, as the Lord led them. We did not believe that it would be pleasing to God for those who had means to hold it back, and expect God to support them through the labor and means of others. We determined in the execution of this plan of trusting the whole work to God alone for its support, that we would look to Him alone, that we would not go in debt for supplies, but receive with thanksgiving what the Lord bestowed upon us. We went through the first month with about fifteen students with many trials and testings, but without missing a meal. We were indeed thankful that we had gone through our first month's experience with hearts full of praise, though the end of the month found us with an empty pantry and empty purse. The next day five new students came in and we had nothing on hand for them to eat. After giving them breakfast the next morning, one of them gave me five dollars saying that a friend had sent it, and said something else that I did not catch. I thought at the time it was for us, and rejoiced that we would have something for the next meal; but when I asked him again what he said was to be done with it, he said, 'For missions.' I said, 'All right, we will send it for missions,' but was a little disappointed that we still had nothing for dinner. The morning mail came with a letter from my Mother in South Carolina, with two dollars in it. I said, Praise God! He knows about us. Mother did not know of our need at that moment, but God did. He knew just when to move her to mail the letter at Laurens, just in time to reach Atlanta to meet our necessity. This is the way He dealt with us through the days, weeks, and years, until He has brought us up to the present time, with a household of fifty to seventy students, rejoicing in the providence of an ever faithful God.

Being in such an environment of a faith institution the students usually learn to trust God for their own personal needs as

---

1 Catalogue, op. cit., p. 2.

well as for those of the Institute which they are to remember daily in their private devotions as well as in public prayer. To learn such practical lessons while in training is particularly helpful when students enter mission fields and other types of work which require an explicit trust in God.

It is seldom that the president of the school makes any special mention regarding the pantry needs, and when such mention is made we all know that it means something out of the ordinary. This writer while a day student there, was in attendance on one such occasion during the second year of his course of study. He was after school hours working during spare time for a livelihood, buying and selling various articles, among which was a lady's wrist watch which he felt impressed during the prayer to give to the school. After the period of special prayer was over and the class dismissed it was learned from the president that there was a need among other things for meat either pork or beef, but preferably beef. The following experience is related as an illustration of how miraculously God has on numerous occasions answered prayer in behalf of this school.

Taking the watch with me, I went in my car in company with another student and drove across town. Stopping my car at the curb in the vicinity of west Greenville I took the watch from my pocket and holding it in my hand told him how I had been impressed while praying about the needs of the Institute. (It was then called Holmes Bible and Missionary Institute). We prayed together and asked that God accept the watch as a gift offering for which he had asked, and to bless us in finding someone who had either pork or beef who needed a watch, and who would accept it in exchange for what we needed. I, then, started the car, drove into the next filling station and asked the operator if he knew of anyone who dealt in hogs or cattle. It had not occurred to me that I might get the meat already butchered. He told us to drive a few blocks to West Greenville where we would find a man by the name of Nelson who operated Nelson's Cafe. After stopping and inquiring for him at the cafe we learned he was at home a few blocks to the north. Mr. Nelson came to the door and without any formal introduction, I asked him the question, 'Does your wife own a wrist watch?' He answered in the negative. I handed him the watch I had in my hand and told him to show it to her. He took it with a look of surprise and somewhat reluctantly carried it to show her. When he returned in a few minutes I asked him how she liked it. Then, I told him that I wanted to swap it 'even' for either pork or beef, but did not tell him my purpose in doing it. He carried me to an enclosure where he had a number of pigs and indicated one that he would be willing to swap for the watch, and then asked me if I had a permit to kill the pig which was required in the city limits. When I told him, No, he asked if I would just as soon have beef. He then took me to a cold storage plant where he kept his meat and showed me the hind quarter of a beef which he proposed to give me in exchange for the watch. I took it, drove him by his home, told him my address in case the watch did not prove satisfactory and then drove back to the school. It was a little less than thirty minutes from the time we had prayed at the curb until we had the meat in the school's kitchen.

This is not an unique example of such occurrences but is one of many even more miraculous ones which have gone to make up the thrilling history of this institution. Such landmark experiences in the lives of its students are of incalculable value in training them to live a life of faith and trust in God. Most of the students learn to trust God for both soul and body.

The Rules

With these facts in mind it is easier for the reader to understand the "stern rigidity" of the rules and discipline which have governed all alike, both students and faculty members, during its entire history. These rules, for the most part, seem unreasonable and arbitrary to those who are unacquainted with the institution, or who may not enter into the spirit in which they are given. It has been the conviction of its founder and his successor that God would not honor the prayers of those who were not wholeheartedly and unreservedly consecrated to Him. A young man, for example cannot be at his best in his studies, nor able to pray effectually who has his mind engaged in affairs of romance. There are times and places for all things but in a faith school of this kind, those who know it best believe it is better to leave such affairs in the background while such preparation is being made. It will be seen by the daily schedule and the rules which are listed below how that students are disciplined by a routine which has unfailingly affected all those who have been subjected to it. Very few of those who have been graduated have ever failed as Christians and a large percentage of them are today in places of authority and responsibility throughout the church. These facts testify to the value of the rules and daily schedule which we offer here as an outstanding reason for the continued existence of this faith institution. They are as follows:

1. All students are expected to furnish pillow cases, sheets and other coverings for the bed, and towels for their own use.

2. All students are required to care for their own rooms, and keep them sanitary and in good order all the time.

3. Everyone is required to rise when the 6:15 o'clock bell rings, and observe a quiet period of prayer and devotion until 7:15 o'clock. Students are not allowed to study any lessons during this hour. Everyone is expected to spend as much time in private prayer during the day as duties will allow.

4. All students are required to give due attention to special work assigned them, and also to report promptly to take part in the general work.

5. Everyone is requested to be careful in handling furniture, dishes, and tools, and required to make a report to the proper authorities if anything is broken, damaged or lost. All must give due attention to keeping everything in its proper place.

6. Students are not allowed to visit from room to room without permission. No one must receive relatives or visitors without permission of the President.

7. No one is allowed to sing aloud during quiet or study hours, or engage in anything that would infringe upon the rights and privileges of other members of the College.

8. Students are not allowed to gather in the halls and talk, nor talk unnecessarily loud in the buildings. Everyone is expected to be "swift to hear, and slow to speak."

9. No one is allowed to leave the grounds of the College without permission. The ladies must not go without proper attendants.

10. Students are not allowed to go in debt by purchasing things on time, or borrow money without permission from the President.

11. No one is expected to ask for permission to go to the city more than one time during the week, unless it is absolutely necessary. This permission must be granted by the President, or someone appointed by him.

12. Students are not allowed in the kitchen or dining room other than at meal time, except when engaged in appointed work.

13. Everyone is required to be prompt at classes, services, and meals, unless excused.

14. Students are not allowed to carry on correspondence of such a nature, or to such an extent, that it will hinder them in their school work.

15. Positively no communication is allowed between the young men and the ladies in the College, by writing or any other way. Members of the College are not allowed to engage in conversation about the opposite sex.

16. Students are not allowed to hold conversation with teachers of the opposite sex except on matters pertaining to their lessons, unless they get special permission from the President.

17. The young men are not allowed to walk on the campus around the girls' dormitory, or enter this building except on duty.

18. We are opposed to the lady students wearing their hair short; and the improper modern styles, such as short sleeves, low necks, and skirts immodestly short.

19. Everyone is required to be economical in using water, electricity, and all fuel, so as to keep expenses as low as possible. Lights must be out by 10:20 o'clock, unless permission is given to use them later.

20. It is not suitable for students to have radios in their rooms, and no special electrical appliances should be used without special permission from the President.

21. Students are expected to pay 5¢ an hour for current used while ironing or pressing; and everyone is required to disconnect irons when leaving the ironing room.

22. No one must leave garments scattered in the pressing room. The rooms must be left in good order for the convenience and benefit of others.

23. Garments must not be left on the clothes line over Sunday, nor too long at any time.

24. No one must take vessels or anything else which belongs to the dining room and kitchen, without permission, and when anything is borrowed it must be promptly returned.

25. When one is sick and needs a meal sent to the room, the dietician should be notified not later than fifteen minutes before the time for the meal.

26. Too much individual fixing of special dishes is not allowed, and girls must not expect to enjoy privileges boys cannot have in this matter. Eating in the rooms is not desirable and can only be permitted in a very limited way.

27. No one is allowed to stay out of classes without permission. Students who are absent from classes by not entering school on time at the opening of the term, or leaving before classes are dismissed for holidays, or at any other time, may not be able to pass their courses if in the judgment of the faculty the absences were unnecessary. Relatives should cooperate in this matter, and not expect students to be absent from school except in cases of emergency.

28. No one is allowed to drop a course of study without permission from the President.

29. Tests and examinations must be taken when appointed by the faculty.

30. Students are expected to be considerate of the management, and not ask for special privileges out of keeping with the general rules and principles of the College.

31. Every member of the College is required to report to the President if they have any knowledge of the disregard of any of these regulations by anyone.

32. These regulations are not imposed or to be observed as a matter of bondage, but enjoined for expediency and to safeguard the College and every member of its family. We, therefore, expect them to be observed in love, and cheerfulness as unto the Lord, that all things may be done to the glory of God.

DAILY SCHEDULE

Rising Bell	6:15 A. M.
Devotional	6:15 to 7:15 A. M.
Breakfast	7:15 A. M.
Worship and Bible	8:15 to 9:15 A. M.
Classes	9:15 A. M. to 12:50 P. M.
Dinner	1:00 P. M.
Classes	1:30 to 2:00 P. M.
Mission Prayer and Bible	2:00 to 3:00 P. M.
General Work	3:15 to 5:50 P. M.
Supper and Worship	6:00 to 7:00 P. M.
Study Period	7:00 to 10:00 P. M.
Lights Out	10:20 P. M.

THE ENROLLMENT, THE FACULTY, AND THE CURRICULUM

In the year when the school was opened, 1898, as we have previously mentioned, the Reverends S. C. Todd and M. H. Houston were associated with Brother Holmes as members of his teaching staff, and the school was opened with one student by the name of Law M. Anderson. By 1910, all of these brethren except Brother Holmes had passed to their eternal reward. Mrs. Holmes, in writing of the school in this beginning stage of its history relates the following facts:

This school was in the beginning a real pioneer work, starting indeed with a very small beginning. One boy the first day, and during the cold, hard winter of 1898-99 ten or a dozen boys and girls, gathered as close around the big heater in the large bleak dining room as they could get, listening to fine expositions of the Bible by our beloved teacher at that time, Dr. M. H. Houston, formerly a Presbyterian missionary to China.[1]

In the interim between the opening of the school in 1898 until 1910, the factual information as to the enrollment is indeed scanty. In the first month after the school had adopted the policy of operating by faith, in October 1902, there were fifteen

---
1 Holmes, op. cit., pp. 258, 259.

students. And at the beginning of the following month five additional students were accepted. In 1910, when Brother Holmes wrote his autobiography he states that there were on an average of from fifty to seventy in the student body. Very few of the names of these early students are mentioned. It seems that there would be some record extant which would reveal at least the names of these early students, but such is not the case.

He does mention the names of three of the most outstanding young men. They were converted under his influence as an evangelist during the summer of 1899. One of them, Starling A. Bishop became the pastor of one of the largest and strongest churches in Birmingham in the Alabama Conference. He also served as the Assistant General Superintendent of the whole church for a number of years. Another young man named L. R. Graham also became a prominent pastor of a church in Memphis, Tennessee, and was for years a general officer, serving as General Secretary of the Church. Homer Owings, the third of these young men mentioned, served for sometime as a faithful missionary to China. Others mentioned by name include Lewis Sagalsky, a Russian-German Jew, the first person saved in the New Tabernacle at Greenville, and who became an outstanding minister of the gospel; Miss Ella Brown, who became the wife of the prominent and venerable Rev. G. F. Taylor; T. A. Melton, who has since risen to the office of a Bishop; Miss Lucy Jones, who spent fourteen years in China as a missionary; Conway G. Anderson, who faithfully served several years in Central America and finally died as a result of disease he contracted while he labored for Christ in that fever infested area. He also mentions W. D. Reynolds, who for years remained at the Institute as the superintendent of work among the boys, and in more recent years has retired but is still living at the school. Mrs. Holmes writes of him building an outdoor furnace for cooking purposes at the site of the old abandoned school on Paris Mountain in 1918. (The same year Brother Holmes sold this property for $5,000 the price he had paid for it twenty years previously.) In company with his vacationing party just the year before Brother Holmes died is mentioned Miss Leta Coffee, H. H. Morgan and a nurse who combined their efforts to make it comfortable for Brother and Sister Holmes during three weeks of quiet rest and vacation.

W. H. Turner and the young lady he married, Miss Orine Entrekin, are also mentioned. They later spent years in China and were recently both prisoners of the Japanese in a concentration camp and are now home on furlough. Miss Julia Payne's name also appears. She, too, went to China as a missionary and later became the wife of the Rev. H. H. Morgan and with him is now in Birmingham, Alabama working as co-pastor of a church there. Then there are the names of the Rev. and Mrs. T. H. Rousseau who are still faithful missionaries to China; the Rev. and Mrs. Richard Anderson who went to Central America in company with Miss Fay Watson, the sister of Mrs. Anderson, Mrs. Nina Holmes who was Miss Nina Cotton, who became the bride of Zelotes Holmes before his untimely death in 1914, are both mentioned. She has remained a widow and has served as a teacher nearly forty years. The fragrance of her Christ-centered godly life has been a benediction to hundreds whom she has taught and hundreds of others who have known her as a Christian worker and friend. This brief list includes about all of the students mentioned who were in the school during Brother Holmes administration.[1]

The information regarding the *faculty* is also indeed scarce. In 1910, Brother Holmes writes the following information:

..... My wife and I with eight other teachers are trying by the grace and providence of God to carry the work on. The present teachers, January 10, 1910, are as follows: Reverend L. R. Graham and wife, Miss Lida Purkey, Mrs. Lorena Cotton, Miss Mary Smithson, Miss Mamie Leapard, and Mrs. S. B. Crozier, with ourselves. All working as unto the Lord without salary or remuneration, except that we eat at the Father's table with the students. The whole work rests upon faith in God.[2]

Miss Mary Smithson, the Rev. Oscar E. Taylor, Robert Pent and Miss Nell Lane, who later became the wife of the Rev. Paul F. Beacham, are also mentioned as teaching during the lifetime of the founder.

The *curriculum* requirements to begin with might be described as being designed to offer the student opportunity to gain a good

---

[1] Ibid., pp. 177, 242,, 243, 248, 257, 265, 269.
[2] Ibid., p. 95.

practical working knowledge of the Bible and missions, offering in addition only those subjects which would facilitate the study of these primal basic courses. This included regular grammar school work with some students beginning as low as the third or fourth grade. The major portion of the student's time has always been directed to the study and interpretation of God's Word. Students are repeatedly cautioned not to allow any other subject to interfere with their Bible assignments. During the entire history of the school, four hours in the morning each week have been devoted to the study of the New Testament and five hours during the afternoons have been given to the study of the Old Testament, making a total of nine hours per week of classroom lectures taught by the president. Only occasionally some other member of the faculty had substituted for him when it had become absolutely necessary. When Brother Holmes' health had begun to fail, in 1916, the Bible classes were under the direction of the Rev. Paul F. Beacham, one of the faithful teachers whom he had groomed for his successor. It was, however, Brother Holmes' custom as long as he was able, to attend these classes and offer any needed assistance when and if difficult passages and questions were under consideration.

During these Bible lectures all members of the faculty and student body alike are required to be in attendance. The course of study is designed to complete the Bible every three years. Those students who are the least advanced in their literary work are not required to take the Bible examinations until they are within three years of graduation. This gives to them the added advantage of hearing the Bible taught through sometimes two or more three-year periods. This is wisely intended to compensate for their academic deficiencies and give to them an equal chance with those students who enter after having had more advanced educational preparation.

Such an arrangement would allow those who felt a call to preach, even after they had reached mature years, the chance to prepare themselves without embarrassment. With few exceptions there have been no students accepted for enrollment who are younger than sixteen years of age. Many students have been above thirty.

The Certificates, Diplomas, and Degrees Offered

During the administration of the first president *certificates* were awarded to those students who satisfactorily completed the course of study offered in the Bible and a few additional subjects, such as, English, history, etc., provided, of course, that their Christian behaviour and character developments had also met with those standards to be expected of Christian workers.

The awarding of diplomas and degrees will be mentioned later.

The Alumni Organization and Contributions

There was no formal organization or meeting of the alumni during the founder's administration, although many of the former students have since 1912, attended the regular annual Camp Meetings which have usually been held in connection with the close of school each year.

The Voice and Camp Meetings

The *voice* of this institution was first heard in the publication of a standard size eight-page periodical approximately nine by eleven inches, and was increased by adding additional pages for special issues whenever it became necessary. It was called the "Altamont Witness" and represented "The Altamont Bible and Missionary Institute" by which name the school was then called. The Pentecostal Holiness Church at that time had no official organ. This monthly publication was therefore implemented to supplement the voice of other publications such as the "Apostolic Evangel" and "The Way of Faith" which were circulated in the interests of Pentecostal Holiness people. The "Altamont Witness" was fairly widely circulated, not only among its alumni, but also, among members and interested friends of the Church as a whole. Paul F. Beacham, who was then a teacher in the institution was the editor from the time of its initial appearance, in October of 1911, until the paper was discontinued, in May, 1918. There was no other such publication sponsored by the school until after Brother Holmes' earthly departure in 1919. These additional ventures will be discussed presently under Dr. Beacham's administration. The school has another means by which to publicize its activities, i. e., through the influence of its annual camp meetings.

The Holmes Bible College *camp meetings* have been a distinctive annual feature, since 1912, when the first one was conducted in October of that year. It was held in October at that time due to the fact that the school was operated during the summer months from 1910 to 1916, closing in October instead of May. Since that time these camp meetings have been conducted, for a period of from ten days to two weeks, immediately following the close of school and graduation exercises in May.

Former students and interested friends of the institution as a rule have gathered from a number of States and Canada each year, with a keen and eager anticipation of receiving spiritual benefit from these superb preaching services and periods of prayer and devotion. Such an occasion also gives an opportunity to renew old acquaintances and to form new ones. These camp meetings have offered a rich opportunity for Christian fellowship and spiritual enlightenment which is paralleled perhaps at no other place. Two special invited ministers, the very best that can be secured, conduct three preaching services daily at morning, afternoon and night. An early morning prayer group meets from six to seven o'clock to buttress these preaching services with prayer.[1]

Services Described

These camp meeting services are conducted in the informal atmosphere of a large gospel tent erected on the campus for the occasion. Amid the preaching, which is often characterized by earnest and powerful discourses, ejaculations and shouts can sometimes be heard among the congregations, punctuated often with a good old-fashioned Methodist-type of amen. At the close of these services congregations are invited to come forward to repent of their sins or to seek for the deeper experiences of sanctification or the baptism of the Holy Ghost, or to reconsecrate or rededicate their lives to God for Christian service. Great numbers are in attendance, especially during the week-end services. There are on many occasions a large percentage of these who gather around the altar for prayer and seeking God. Many are praying audibly at the same time and these congregational gatherings can be heard for quite a distance early and late. It might ordinari-

---

1 Ibid., p. 242.

ly be assumed that such worship technique would gender confusion and therefore become undesirable or even obnoxious, but such is not the case. Those who enter into the sacred spirit of these services receive incalculable spiritual benefit, and it is said by many even who are not Christians that the minute they set foot on these grounds they are conscious of the very presence of the Eternal. Being conducted at the close of each school year these camp meetings are a veritable source of spiritual dynamite for the students and other Christian workers to draw from for their anticipated summer evangelistic campaigns. Inspiration is gathered and earnest decisions are made here each year which change the course of many lives for spiritual betterment and sacrificial service.

II. THE ADMINISTRATION OF PAUL F. BEACHAM,
THE FOUNDER'S SUCCESSOR, 1919—

A Brief Biography

On December 17, 1919, when the venerable and aged Nickels John Holmes made his exit from this state of action, there departed from our midst a truly great Christian educator and humble follower of the Blessed Saviour. His successor, the Rev. Paul F. Beacham, had been in the making under his direct influence since he had entered the school as a student in November, 1908. There had been no break between the time of his graduation and the beginning of his experience as a teacher in this institution. He took up such duties immediately and has continued his career throughout his lifetime until this writing. In fact, his teaching experience in the classroom was begun to some extent even during his student days. For more than three years he had already been teaching the Bible classes regularly because of Brother Holmes' failing health. Mrs. Holmes in writing of the personnel and happenings in the school after Brother Holmes' home-going says:

Brother Beacham has also continued connected with the school, studying and trying to perfect his education in the face of difficulties, and as Mr. Holmes' health failed, and he had to give up teaching the Bible—Brother Beacham became teacher of one class, Brother O. E. Taylor of one, and when Brother Taylor felt he must leave the school, Brother Beacham became the teacher of both Old and New Testaments, and now he is the deserved and acceptable President of the school—made so by the will and appointment of Mr. Holmes, and we believe by the appointment of God also. Mr. Holmes was greatly attached to Brother Beacham, and once during his illness said to me, calling me by name, 'I love Brother Beacham.' He loved everyone, but especially loved those who had been so long with him and who were always kind and considerate of him. [1]

Under his able and conservative spiritual leadership the College and the Pentecostal Holiness Church, which he has so extensively and profoundly influenced, have grown from a very small and relatively insignificant organization of ten annual conferences and a few thousand in membership in 1919, to twenty-six annual conferences in 1945, and a total foreign and home church membership of 45,592. It is not the largest but it is unquestionably the sanest and most stable and substantial of the Pentecostal groups. This is largely attributable to the conservative and sane leadership of men like Paul F. Beacham and others of his calibre who have steadfastly held the reins amid turbulent mutations which have periodically impinged upon this church organization. He commands the respect and admiration of all who truly know him, and time has proved the wisdom of his counsel repeatedly, though it may at times have been questioned. It is difficult to gain much information about him by personal interview with him and for that reason this account may not appear to be altogether complete. Such a full biographical account is perhaps not expected while he is still our contemporary, but this noble and great man of God will without question occupy a prominent place in the history of the church when he has laid his armour down.

Dr. Paul F. Beacham in recent months had the honorary degree of Doctor of Divinity conferred on him upon the recommendation of Dr. Charles Haddon Nabors, Representative Joseph R. Bryson of the state of South Carolina and others. Dr. Nabors has known Dr. Beacham intimately during the long period he has been in Greenville as pastor of the First Presbyterian Church and accompanied him during his tour of Southern Europe and Bible lands in 1937.

The Reverend Beacham is fifty-nine years of age and is yet in excellent health, and should be able to render faithful service

---

1 Ibid., p. 243.

to the Church for an extended period of time. He entered the school as we have seen in 1908 at which time he was twenty years of age and has for now nearly forty years been connected with the school either as a student or as a teacher. Twenty-nine of these years he has served as its president. For the same length of time he has served the Holmes Memorial Church as its esteemed and loved pastor. His tolerant and sympathetic attitude has been coupled with a willingness to wait patiently for the fruit of righteousness. He has waited for such to show itself in the lives of even those who have stubbornly rejected moral instruction. This has won for him a goodly number who are his unyielding and staunch supporters and friends. His known reputation as a Bible scholar along with these personal character qualifications has drawn to both the church and the school students and parishioners who accept his teachings without mental reservation or question. Those who know him consider that he has a ready knowledge of the Bible above all others, at least above any within the ranks of his denomination. Testimony to the validity of this claim is evidenced by the position he occupies as president of this, our best school, and because for more than twenty years he has edited the Question Drawer; served as editor of the Bible Class Quarterly of the Sunday School literature, formulated two catechisms, and been called upon to write numerous sermons and several tracts which deal with doctrinal subjects.

Dr. Beacham served the Church as General Treasurer for more than two decenniums, and in recent years became the General Superintendent of the district including Eastern North Carolina, South Carolina, Georgia and Florida. This office carries the honorary title of Bishop. He is also Chairman of the Foreign Missionary Board.

His range of influence is not confined exclusively to the limited confines of his own Church, but embraces other denominations and civic organizations. Besides being Chairman of the Board of Trustees of the Greenville Rescue Mission, he is the third vice president of the South Carolina Federated Forces for Temperance and Law Enforcement and is chairman of the Greenville County unit of this organization. He has also served as president of the Greenville Ministerial Association.

Mr. Beacham has traveled considerably on church business and on preaching missions and Bible Conferences in Canada and Mexico, and extensively in the United States. And, as has been mentioned, in 1937, he made a tour of Bible lands and in parts of several other countries.

He was married on March 22, 1911, to Sarah Nell Lane who was herself a former student and at the time teaching in the school. Mrs. Holmes describes her as being "one of our most earnest and enthusiastic teachers, putting her heart and energy into the work of helping on the development of the students, doing with all her might what her hands find to do." Mrs. Beacham possessed unusual talents for teaching and was also a gifted public speaker, oftimes assisting her husband as a young minister with his preaching appointments and was also successful in evangelistic work, being an earnest soul-winner. She was the daughter of a Baptist minister and was born and reared at Marion, South Carolina, where she received her early education. She entered the Bible school in 1905 and after her graduation went elsewhere to teach for two years. When she returned in 1911 and married Mr. Beacham she became a member of the faculty and since that time has taught in the college. Bishop T. A. Melton, in writing of her after her recent death on August 2, 1947, makes the following appraisal of her work:

> She was a splendid teacher, having a storehouse of knowledge, and a vocabulary with which to impart it to her students. It seems that she is remembered for her ability as an English teacher more than any other subject. As I go from place to place over the nation, I hear both men and women telling of her classroom and of her having taught them English.[1]

Mrs. Beacham, like Mrs. Holmes was her husband's constant companion and co-laborer in the work of the school and therefore is due considerable recognition for her untiring sacrificial labors in the interest of Christian education.

The Bible College has made marvelous progress under the leadership of Dr. Beacham as will now be seen in subsequent paragraphs.

---

[1] T. A. Melton, An Article published in **The Voice of Holmes**, (A periodical published in Greenville, S. C., in interest of the Holmes Bible College, Nov., 1947), p. 7.

The Change in Name

At a joint meeting of the Pentecostal Holiness Church Board of Education and the Trustees of the Holmes Bible and Missionary Institute on May 27, 1942, it was decided to change the name from the "Holmes Bible and Missionary Institute" to its present name, "The Holmes Bible College" with subtitles of Theology and Missions. We have noticed that in all the school has had four different names in its history.

The Buildings

At the time of Brother Holmes' death in 1919, as we have noted, there were three buildings standing on the school property at Greenville. The Tabernacle had been erected in 1909, the Boys' Dormitory in 1916, and the Administration Building which also was used for a Girls' Dormitory and a faculty apartment—the building and lot being purchased in 1914. This was the extent of the school plant at that time. But there was no indebtedness left for Brother Holmes' successor to retire. The school, in every sense of the word, had been built on a solid and sure foundation. There had been no mushroom or ephemeral growth. It had been gradual and substantial in utter dependence upon God and without any human anxiety. No man or group of men had feverishly tried to keep it going but as God had opened the way his servants have followed. Dr. Beacham has had no different attitude about perpetuating its existence. He has been accused of being ultra-conservative because he has never tried, in the human sense, to make the school go by pushing any building program or any other phase of progress. He has patiently, but alertly, waited for God to open the way and indicate His will and purpose in all matters.

The Girls' Dormitory

Two years after Mr. Beacham became president in 1919, there was erected a Girls' Dormitory which was much needed to accommodate the increased enrollment. This building which was completed in 1922 was a large two-story frame structure erected on the lot adjoining the Administration Building, and wisely situated forty feet further from the street. It faces east on

Briggs Avenue and is on the southeast side of the campus. A large dining room and kitchen is on the south side of the building on the first floor. On this south side of the building is also a small library and faculty office. On the north side is a large classroom sufficient in size to accommodate the entire school for the Bible Classes for an hour each morning and afternoon. It is also used for other occasions as a chapel when needed. The second floor is used for the girls' dormitory and will accommodate about forty-five students.

Improved Girls' Dormitory Named Beacham Hall

In 1938, this frame building was brick veneered and completely remodeled, enlarging the dormitory space, the kitchen and dining room facilities, as well as adding the necessary room for the Bible Class and music rooms. This building has a colonial front and makes an imposing appearance. This elegant structure was then given the name of "Beacham Hall" in honor of the esteemed president of the institution. The enlargements which were made were commensurate with the increase in enrollment.

We have mentioned that the financial policy of the school has always been never to go in debt, and to make improvements only as God makes the way possible. Such improvements have not been begun until a substantial portion of the necessary funds have been provided, and has been brought to completion through the means of additional contributions so that no debt has been incurred beyond that for which the president could be personally responsible. During the time when this building was originally under construction in 1921, President Beacham made the following statements which were published in the official church organ. This is cited as an illustration of the business methods which have always been followed. He writes:

> We feel grateful to our heavenly Father that as a result of recent contributions to the building fund, we are able to go ahead with the construction of the new dormitory, and hope to have the first story completed and ready for use in the near future.
>
> Some consideration has been given to the matter of borrowing a sufficient amount to complete the new dormitory; but we certainly do not want to take such a step unless it should be God's plan. Surely He is just as able to supply the money now as He would be to pay it back if it should be borrowed, especially as it will be less to

pay as we go, as we have done up to this point. Please pray with us concerning the matter and that the Lord will guide in all things.[1]

The Holmes Memorial Church

The next building to be constructed was the Holmes Memorial Church in 1925. It is a neat and dignified building of brick and tile construction located on the northeast corner of school property facing on Buncombe Street. As soon as this building was ready for occupancy the Tabernacle, which was the original building, was razed, leaving considerable space between the new church and the girls' dormitory which had been erected in 1921. In this space the large camp meeting tent is erected each year. The first floor of this new church plant has since been used for classrooms for the Sunday School and also for the school during the week. The largest of these classrooms was used at night for the boys' study hall which had previously occupied a room on the first floor of what is now an apartment house for married couples and was originally the Boys' Dormitory. The study hall has since been moved to the basement of the new boys' dormitory. This church building is modern in every respect and has in it an excellent heating plant. The church auditorium will seat approximately seven to eight hundred, and is a lovely sanctuary with three beautiful murals at the front of the building, comfortable pews, and a superior quality rug covering the entire front of the church. The choir adapts itself readily for a stage when the seats are removed, and is used by the school for dramatic purposes and cantatas at special seasons of the church-year. The auditorium is well-lighted and well-ventilated and is on a parity with any average church of the larger denominations, and considerably above the average of those within the Pentecostal Holiness Church. But in spite of this more dignified atmosphere the services in the main are characterized by a free expression of emotion.

The New Boys' Dormitory

In 1942 the new boys' dormitory which has not been named was completed and occupied. In spite of the fact that it was built

---

[1] P. F. Beacham, **The Pentecostal Holiness Advocate,** (Franklin Springs, Ga., Publishing House of the Pentecostal Holiness Church, Oct. 17, 1921), p. 11.

during a period when the emergency of war had made many critical materials difficult to secure, God supplied both the money and the materials required to erect this much-needed building. It is three stories high with a roomy basement for classrooms, students' barber shop, and other necessary appointments including a large chapel which is adequate for the boys' study hall and to accommodate the ever increasing Bible classes. It is constructed of brick walls to the first floor line and is brick veneered from there to the roof. The attic is spacious and is approached by a wide stairway adapting itself readily for adequate storage purposes. It will accommodate 84 students, a few faculty members and a furnished guest room for visiting friends. It is 36 x 96 and fronts on Buncombe Avenue, being situated between the church and the apartment building for married couples.

The Lucy Holmes Memorial Building

The large two-story house and lot which was purchased in 1914, and has since been used first for the girls' dormitory, apartments for members of the faculty, and Administration Building is the next project for remodeling, enlarging and modernizing. When it is completed it will be three stories high instead of two, and will be brick-veneered in keeping with the other newer buildings on the campus. When completed it will take the name of the "Lucy Holmes Memorial Building" and will be a tribute to the wife of the school's founder who sacrificially labored at his side to make his work possible. This building improvement will cost approximately $25,000 and will be begun in the immediate future. For the details of this project we quote from an article which appeared in the January issue of "The Voice of Holmes" as follows:

In the providence of God nine surplus army building at Camp Sutton, Monroe, North Carolina, have been purchased by the college, and are being dismantled and hauled to Greenville by a group of students.

This material will enable the construction work on the $25,000 addition to the Lucy Holmes Memorial Building to begin right away. The present building which is estimated to be 40 x 50 feet will be extended back 46 feet. When completed the structure will be three stories high. On the first floor will be the administrative offices and classrooms, a new library on the second floor, and dormitory room for students on the third floor. The building will be brick veneered, and will include fixtures and heating material from the surplus army structure.

This addition will enable the dining room and chapel space to be enlarged later.[1]

Several thousand dollars are already in the building fund treasury and the prospects are that this building also will be erected on the usual "pay as you go" basis.

Veteran Education and Facilities (Special Housing)

It was announced through the church organ issued on July 19, 1945, that Holmes Bible College has been officially approved by the Director of the Division of Veteran's Education, Mr. W. A. Shiffley, being placed on the approved list of schools eligible to enroll veterans for special theological training. Afterward President Beacham purchased eleven lots suitably located within two blocks of the school. One of these lots is on the corner of Briggs Avenue and Pinkney Street, being the end lot of the same block where the school is located, and on the same side of the street. On it have been erected five veteran huts, four rooms each, and on the ten adjoining lots purchased in the next block there are twenty-five trailers with adequate plumbing facilities for toilet, bath, and laundry. All of this equipment was acquired from the government surplus war housing with special consideration being given to the school. It might well be mentioned here that two of the four houses in the same block with the school property are owned by individuals who have already made their wills providing that the property be transferred to the school at their decease. Indications are that other property in this block will be acquired in a similar manner, but that will be a matter to develop and be discussed in the future.[2]

THE ENROLLMENT, THE FACULTY, THE CURRICULUM

As we have noted, during Brother Holmes' lifetime, there was an average of from fifty to seventy students most of the time. With the building of the new girls' dormitory in 1922 they were able

---

1 Article by Editor, **Voice of Holmes**, (Greenville, S. C., a periodical published by the Alumni in interest of the school, January, 1948), p. 7.
2 **The Pentecostal Holiness Advocate**. (Franklin Springs, Ga., The Publishing House of the Pentecostal Holiness Church, July 19, 1945), p. 10.

to accommodate an average of 95 students. When this building was enlarged in 1938 there was an average of 115 until 1942 when the new boys' dormitory was built and when the average grew to more than 130. Since that time there has been a steady increase until in the 1947-1948 session there was a total of 260 enrolled.[1] Some of these are day students but the majority are in residence. With the government surplus facilities providing housing for the veterans and their wives there is a peak capacity and record enrollment. This institution has never experienced any difficulty in securing students but to the contrary has turned away a hundred or more every year during the past decade. There was an average of from five to eight teachers during Brother Holmes' Administration. There has been a corresponding increase in teachers with the relative increase in students. A helpful chart has been prepared to compare these averages as the new buildings made their appearance. It appears as follows:

Years	Buildings	Enrollment	Faculty Members
1898-1916	1916 Old Boy's Dormitory	50	5
1916-1922	1921 Girls' Dormitory	70	8
1922-1938	1938 Becomes "Beacham Hall"	95	10
1938-1942	1942 New Boy's Dormitory	115	12
1942-1948	1946-1948 Veteran Equipment and Day Students in private homes.	200	15

There are at present 18 on the school faculty with 260 students enrolled. The average attendance has been governed from time to time by the housing capacity of the institution entirely. A list of the present faculty and board of trustees is as follows:

FACULTY

Paul F. Beacham, D. D. _____ President and Bible Instructor
  Business College, Holmes Bible College, and Furman University
H. Ray Stewart, Th. B., B. A. _____ Theology, Public Speaking
  Holmes Bible College and Furman University
Alvin Rankin, Th. B., B. S. ___ Economics, Geometry, General Science
  Tri-State College and Holmes Bible College

---
1 Article. **Voice of Holmes,** op. cit., November, 1947, p. 13.

John R. Wells, J. D., LLD., S. T. D. .... Philosophy, Apologetics
    Burton College, Bethany Peniel College and Blackstone College
    of Law
James H. Taylor. Th. B. .... Holimetics
    Holmes Bible College and Anderson College, Erskine College
Nina C. Holmes, Th. B. .... Church History, Geography of Holy Land
    Holmes Bible College and Furman University
Pauline Rankin, Th. B. ....English, Commercial Law
    Business College and Holmes Bible College
Vera Ashford, Th. B. .... English
    Emmanuel College and Holmes Bible College
Ruth Heath, Th. B., B. A. ..... Dean of Girls, College Literature, Greek,
History, Missions
    Holmes Bible College and Furman University
Luetta Paschall, Th. B., B. A. .... History
    Holmes Bible College and Furman University
Emma Yeatts, Th. B. ....Algebra, Latin, Missions, Mathematics
    Holmes Bible College and Harrisburg State Teachers College
Lessie Green, Th. B., B. A .... Latin, Biology
    Emmanuel College, Holmes Bible College and Furman University
Florine Freeman, Th. B., B. A. .... English, History, Education,
    Music II
    Holmes Bible College and Furman University
Ruth Elliott, Th. B. .... Music, Theory, Piano
    Holmes Bible College and Furman University
Edna Harrell, B. A. .... Child Psychology, Sociology
    Emmanuel College and Eastern Carolina Teachers College
Gertrude Blake, Th. B. .... English
    Emmanuel College, Holmes Bible College and Furman University
Iva Thomas, Th. G., B. S. L. .... Spanish
    Oklahoma State Univ., Enid Business College, Holmes Bible College
Grace Andrews .... Evangelism, Psychology
    Wewoka Normal School, Holmes Bible College and Furman University

BOARD OF TRUSTEES

Paul F. Beacham .... Greenville, S. C.
Oscar E. Taylor .... Laurens, S. C.
W. D. Reynolds .... Greenville, S. C.
A. L. Jackson ....Tallapoosa, Ga.
B. S. Thompson .... Whiteville, N. C.
F. L. Bramblett .... Pelzer, S. C.
James H. Taylor .... Pelzer, S. C.
J. A. Synan .... Hopewell, Va.
T. T. Lindsay .... Danville, Va.

There is no record extant of the graduates of this institution prior to 1925-1926 term, but since that time the following have been graduated from year to year:

GRADUATES 1925-1926
G. H. Montgomery
T. T. Lindsey
G. A. Byus
J. H. Puckett
H. A. Probst
H. A. Brooks

GRADUATES 1926-1927
J. W. Warren
Celeta Kathleen Higdon
Mae Jane Grier
Mabel Cordelia Dell

GRADUATES 1927-1928
Emma Yeatts
Helen Dunkerly
Effie Barker

GRADUATES 1928-1929
Vinson Ellenberg
Vernon Ellenberg
Gano Hayes
E. B. Moss
G. C. Legge
Mrs. Edna Legge
Margaret Ingram
Mrs. Ethel Lamm

GRADUATES 1929-1930
W. E. Unthank
C. H. Herndon
H. B. Johnson
I. H. Webb
Horace Ward
Mavis Lee Oakley
Annie Fair Ward

GRADUATES 1930-1931
Silas Meeks
James Louis Coward
Ernest Leo McNeely
David Job Willoughby
James A. Green
Viola Stanley
Elda Jane Skinner

GRADUATES 1931-1932
R. L. McGougan
Andrew P. Mazur
Wm. Harvey Morris
Ralph R. Johnson
Effie Estelle Lanning
Sarah Eunice Bryant
Georgia Ruth Kirk
Myrtice L. Parks
Nancy Viola Leake
Clare Katie Godfrey

GRADUATES 1932-1933
Abner Scogin
Charles Walker
Bane Underwood
Annie Pearson
Elizabeth Arriet

GRADUATES 1933-1934
Dallas Tarkenton
John Few
L. T. Dunlap
Ray Taylor
Julius Green
Paul Love
Wesley J. Noble
S. J. Todd
Daniel Randolph
Ruth Pennington
Emma Britton
Dorothy Stroud

GRADUATES 1934-1935
Mary Sue Britton
Frances Brown
Leona Causey
Leslie Evans
Lucille Gaines
Mildred Johnson
Bonnie Price
Rachel Robinson
A. M. Herndon
O. T. Howard
Clemon Leviner
S. A. Merritt
Holmes Till
Victor Callahan
Joseph E. Campbell

GRADUATES 1935—1936
Mary E. Taylor
Margaret F. Britton

Nettie Mildred Barfield
Clara M. Looney
Eva B. Jewell
Nellie Magdalene Clower
Grady C. Collins
C. B. Edwards
Jack W. Johnson
Clifton J. Peyton
Julius W. Spain

GRADUATES 1936-1937
A. Grace McGraw
Mavis A. Barfield
Bertha M. Masters
S. Emma McGalliard
Esther B. Best
Mary E. Campbell
Pearl E. Branton
Rhoda H. Spain
C. Albert Barfield
Paul Virgil Hill
Earl T. Hoyle
Moody S. Johnson
Raymond O. Corvin
Kenneth Harrington
James L. Wall

GRADUATES 1937-1938
Don S. Whitfield
J. Elmo Hopkins
Mendel L. Moore
Vernon V. Pate
Levie Peyton
Mamie Hall
Esther Baker
Irene Gaskins
Margaret Powers
Lucile Swails
Corrie Lee Stewart
Dorothy Poteat
Ruth Malissa Masters

GRADUATES 1938-1939
Morrison Brown
Milford McPherson
L. Fred Jones
Arthur D. Beacham
Wayne V. Elliott, Jr.
E. L. Shirey

Woodrow Smith
Ruth N. Zaborouski
Oree N. McCants
Marjorie F. Newman
Evelyn D. Reid
Eula K. Staten
Hessie E. Moore

GRADUATES 1939-1940
Nora Moore
Velma Dickerson
Lorraine Shank
Mattie Britton
Margaret Smith
Remah Leviner
Fannie M. Morris
Marie Maloy
Earline Shelton
Eva Creech
Ada Lee Goff
Pearl Bordeaux
Mrs. Pauline Rankin
Mrs. Grace Andrews
Edward Boyce
L. D. Spence
Kenneth Dantzler
Aubrey Pate
Freeman Mashburn
Cline Atkinson
Carl W. Thurman

GRADUATES 1940-1941
Ruby Stewart
Weytona Johnson
Elsie Gordon
Mary Ellen Baity
Thelma Smith
Myrtice Shealy
Irene Lyon
Dorothy Bennett
Maggie Jeffcoat
Mary Evans
Margie Stephens
Mary Wood
Bonnie White
Elma Boykin
Grace Ellenberg
Mrs. Gladys Iverson
John W. Swails

468   HISTORY OF THE PENTECOSTAL HOLINESS CHURCH

H. P. Robinson
Robert Iverson
Ray Till
Lawrence English
George Fisher
H. Ray Stewart
William Ellenberg
Leopold M. Hayes
Charlie L. King—Bible Certificate

GRADUATES 1941-1942

Freda Atkinson
Loraine Barnette
Vera Blair
Ruth Evans
Leona Hearn
Daisy Jones
Zonell Jones
Eloise Lucas
Lucille Manley
Frances Moore
Etrulia Parker
Ruth Sharpe
Willie Maude Solesby
Rachel Yarbrough
Alvin Rankin
Clarence Blanchard
Phillip Genetti
Raymond Spain
Doyle Zachary

GRADUATES 1942-1943

Luetta Paschall
Kathleen Hearn
Ruth Heath
Winnie Ham
Violet Webb
Ruby Manuel
Lessie Dean Till
Ruth Jarrell
Mary Frances Holland
Juanita Williams
Louise Hallman
Myrtle Jernigan
Clare Louise Peel
Eleanor Carter
Harry Marley
Ben F. Jones
John B. Hutcherson

Curtis Wood
Muret Long
W. Garland Elliott
J. Robert Doby
L. E. Turpin
Russell Defibaugh

GRADUATES 1943-1944

Grace Barnette
Florine Freeman
Margaret F. Greene
Clydie M. Holt
Doris C. Lastinger
Wilodyn Malpass
Evelyn Propes
Louise Smith
Bettie Lee Taylor
Thelma R. Terrell
Annie Trent
Margaret West
Harold F. Blanchard
Harry B. Correll
Russel Frew
Charles M. King
Zeb D. Smith
Curtis Stowe
Lawrence A. Terrell

GRADUATES 1944-1945

Fannie J. Barbour
Donnie F. Bennett
Ruth Elliott
Beatrice Foley
Lessie Green
Florence O. Hamilton
Grace Hearn
Addie Lee Johnson
Ellen Murray
Marie A. Shirley
Ann Sykes
Juanita Taylor
Gladys E. Watts
Lucius T. Chappell
W. Revere Rhodes
Thomas C. Riddle
Elmer J. Rouse
Earl H. Shannon
Norva E. Skaggs
James H. Taylor

GRADUATES 1945-1946
(Th. B. & B. S. L.)

Gloria Ann Eason
Esther L. Evans
Sylvia Harvey
Gatha Hickman
Geraldine Jones
Rachel B. McGraw
Irene Morrison
Camilla R. Payne
Ruth Robinette
Mildred V. Smith
Rita Young
Floradell Baldwin
M. Gertrude Blake
Ruth Brown
D. Willene Burrell
Dott Caldwell
Myra Lou Callahan
William T. Cooke
Henry Goldsberry
James W. Jordan
J. T. Lastinger
James A. Sears
Andrew E. Spence, Jr.

GRADUATES 1946-1947
with degrees

Lois Dunn
Marie Elliott
Nellie Faye Fowler
Annie Mae Gainey
Louise E. Ginn
Mary Velma Hall
Bonnie Jones
Sanford Jones
Virginia Martin
Beatrice Monday
Gladys Myrick
John B. Parker
Christine Pratt
Reatha Mae Simpson
Beulah Taylor
Eulah Taylor
Walter Veasel
June Watson
Norma E. Webb
James Williams

HIGH SCHOOL DEPARTMENT

Vernon K. Clark
Adele E. Ellis
Marie R. Elliott
Nellie Faye Fowler
Eva Florine Freeman
Louise Elizabeth Ginn
Hal T. Goodman
Henry W. Goldsberry
Mary Velma Hail
Cary W. Higdon
Mary Alice Jenkins
Jesse L. Pruett
Lola R. Rankin
Mary Esther Rath
William N. Rogers
Walter Veasel
Norman E. Webb
Ruth Wiese
James A. Williams
Phyllis Jean Butler
Dorothy E. Page
Clara L. McNeill
Margaret A. Warren

No list of the faculty members has been kept but the following list of men are given from the common knowledge of this writer and others who know them as ministers who have since gained considerable recognition in various fields of activity in the Church. They are: G. H. Montgomery, J. Vinson Ellenberg, William E. Unthank, Dallas M. Tarkenton, Silas A. Meeks, Thomas T. Lindsey and others. Quite a number of faithful women have also made up this faculty, some of whom are: Mrs. Mae Grier Johndrow, Miss Emma Yeatts, Mrs. Effie Lanning Poole,

Mrs. Mae Puckett Wall, and the Rev. and Mrs. I. H. Pressley and others.

The curriculum had been developed and changed gradually and periodically during the founder's administration but in 1925, the year when diplomas began to be awarded instead of certificates, there was considerable improvement made in the curriculum. In addition to the usual eighth and ninth grade level there was now offered an additional three year course leading to graduation. Besides the regular tenth and eleventh grade work, Biblical, theological and music courses were required. No one in the student body or faculty may be excused from any of the Bible lectures, irrespective of their academic standing or the number of times they might repeat the same course of study. However, examinations are required only during the last three years immediately preceding graduation.

A study of the entire Bible is completed every three years and is conveniently divided into twelve courses which are equally divided over the three year period as follows:

OUTLINE FOR BIBLE STUDY COURSES
By The Year

FIRST YEAR
First Semester

COURSE I.—"Old Testament Introduction"
  Sec. 1.—Introduction to the Law. Genesis—Exodus.
  Sec. 2.—Introduction to Poetry. Proverbs.
  Sec. 3.—Introduction to History. Joshua, I Sam., II Sam., Ezra.
COURSE II.—"New Testament Introduction"
  An analysis of the Gospels.

Second Semester

COURSE III.—"The Prophetic Scriptures"
  Sec.. 1.—Major (Isaiah).
  Sec. 2.—Minor (Obadiah, Jonah, Micah, Nahum, Haggai).
COURSE IV.—"The Life and Ministry of Jesus Christ"
  Matthew, Mark, Luke, John.

SECOND YEAR

COURSE V.—"Old Testament History II"
  Sec. 1.—The Levitical Priesthood and Law. Leviticus—Numbers.
  Sec. 2.—Story of the Judges and Kings. Judges, I Kings, II Kings, Nehemiah.
COURSE VI.—"The Expansion of Christianity"
  Sec. 1.—Pentecost and Palestinian Christianity.
  Sec. 2.—Missionaries of the First Century (All in Acts).

COURSE VII.—"Old Testament Poetry and Prophecy"
Sec. 1.—Poets and their Work, Eccl., S. of S., Lamentations.
Sec. 2.—Major and Minor Prophets. Jer., Dan., Hab., Joel.
COURSE VIII.—"The Letters of St. Paul"
I Thess., II Thess., Gal., I Cor., II Cor., Romans.

THIRD YEAR

COURSE IX.—"Recapitulation of the Law"
Sec. 1.—By Moses—Deuteronomy.
Sec. 2.—By the Prophets—Hosea, Amos, Zephaniah, Zechariah, Malachi.
COURSE X.—"The Development of Christian Doctrine and Ideals"
Sec. 1.—Pauline Epistles and Hebrews.
Sec. 2.—The General Epistles.
Sec. 1 and 2, Eph., Phili., Col., Phile., I Tim., II Tim., Titus., Heb.; James, I Pet., II Pet., I, II, III John, Jude.)
COURSE XI.—"Review of God's Dealings with Israel"
Sec. 1.—Under the Judges (Ruth).
Sec. 2.—Under the Kings (1, II Chr.)
Sec. 3.—Under the Oppressors. (Esther and Ezekiel).
Sec. 4.—As Revealed in O. T. Poetry (Job and Psalms).
COURSE XII.—"The Apocalypse."[1]

In addition to the Bible, regular standard courses are offered in Greek, in the fields of theology, Apologetics, Literature, Music and practical work, as well as regular high school work all of which is fully described in the catalogue.[2]

CERTIFICATES, DIPLOMAS AND DEGREES

Some two hundred students have received diplomas, since 1925, when they began to be offered instead of the certificates, and in 1945, it was decided to graduate Holmes students on the following levels according to the varying curriculum requirements:

1. The Bachelor of Theology (Th.B.) degree is now awarded those students who have completed all the required courses in the Biblical, theological and practical fields, aggregating 90 semester hours.
2. The Bachelor of Sacred Literature (B. S. L.) degree is awarded to those students who complete all the work required to receive the Th.B. degree with the exception of the courses offered in Greek, Homiletics and Pastoral Theology.
3. A diploma is awarded those who complete the High School courses and the regular Bible courses.
4. A Certificate of Efficiency is awarded those who complete the

---
1 Catalogue, op. cit., p. 20.
2 Catalogue, op. cit., pp. 27-34.

regular Bible courses and a sufficient amount of other prescribed work to prepare them for acceptable Christian service.[1]

Each graduate is required to present a thesis on a suitable subject suggested by the faculty. The length of the thesis as well as the rules to be followed in writing it are commensurate with the academic level of the respective graduates. The type of award to be received is obviously determined by the previous preparation of the student before admission, and his individual aspiration.

It is the intended purpose of this institution to foster an educational program which will adequately prepare Christian workers for varying types of service in different fields of labor. The level of preparation, can be determined both according to the individual's special gifts, and the length of time he may have for preparation. In this way no person is excluded because of the rigid requirements which often discourage those who may feel a call to preach late in life, or who may be handicapped by their own personal limitations. While the Pentecostal Holiness Church is anxious to give its ministers sufficient preparation to meet the demands of a modern world, it is at the same time cautious not to set its requirements so high that good men who are called to preach may despair in making ready to enter the ministry.

When a student has completed all the work offered by the college, he has the equivalent of 30 hours offered in a standard liberal arts college, and in addition has forty-eight hours in Bible and the regular theological work. At the present time the school is neither a full-fledged college nor seminary but a combination of both. Some have questioned its authority to award degrees at its present stage of development, especially with relation to the Th.B degree, which is, for example, also offered by the school of religion at Harvard University. There are other Bible colleges, however, which offer the same degree without any more advanced curricula. Those of the Pentecostal Holiness Church who have had theological training in other denominational institutions unanimously affirm that the Bible course offered at Holmes Bible College is more thorough and that the college should rightfully grant some sort of degree. Further discussion on this point will be presented in the closing section of this chapter, under the caption, "The Future of the School."

---

[1] Ibid, pp. 6, 7.

THE ALUMNI AND ITS CONTRIBUTIONS

It was not until 1926 that the alumni were formerly organized into the Holmes' Student Association. It had its inception principally through the influential efforts of the Rev. T. A. Melton, a former student who became the first president of the alumni association.[1] The Rev. G. H. Montgomery has also played a prominent part in effecting and promoting this organization. Lee Braxton, a prominent layman who has become unusually successful in his business ventures, succeeded Mr. Melton and for the past several years has served the association most commendably. His business experience has enabled him to inject his promotional ideas into the alumni program.

Its Purpose

The H. S. A. was organized to serve a dual purpose, first to establish and maintain contact and fellowship between the members of the organization, second, to generate and keep alive a wholesome enthusiasm among the alumni and friends of the institution which would find expression in active participation and cooperation with a definite program to enlarge and improve the school.[2] It has been through the influence of this association that the building programs were launched to improve the Girls' Dormitory (Beacham Hall), in 1938, and to construct the New Boys' Dormitory, in 1942.

The Dollar Club

In 1936, the "Holmes Dollar Club" was begun and is intended to serve a useful purpose in providing a monthly income for the College by means of alumni members and friends contributing regularly the amount of one dollar each month. The funds thus raised are to be used for any needful purpose at the discretion of the college president. Such an arrangement made it possible for former students to make these small contributions without embarrassment if they were unable to make larger ones.

Contributions

The alumni of the Holmes Bible College have made a greater single contribution of Christian workers to the Pentecostal Holi-

---
1 T. A. Melton, **The Advocate, op. cit.,** Nov. 19, 1931, p. 5.
2 **Loc. cit.**

ness Church than that of any other school. Although there exists no accurate dependable record of the names of those enrolled before 1925, we can be sure that the majority of them rendered faithful service in various fields. According to reasonably reliable information, of the entire number graduated during the history of the school, until 1940, the following number have gone to different fields as missionaries: "Cuba—1; Palestine—1; Egypt 1; Hawaii—1; South America—4; Africa—10; Central America—12; India—12; and China—18. This is a fair illustration of the school's contribution to the foreign missionary field. Without the pastors, evangelists, church-officers and lay leadership which this institution has produced it is very doubtful whether the Pentecostal Holiness Church could have continued to exist. The Holmes Bible College has been God's primary agency in spreading the full gospel truth, especially within the Pentecostal Holiness Church.

THE VOICE

We have mentioned the "Altamont Witness" published from 1911 to 1918 which was the first voice of the college. In the interim, from 1918 until December, 1927, when the first issue of the "Herald of Truth" made its appearance, the school was without a voice. G. H. Montgomery was editor of the Herald of Truth, Wm. E. Unthank, its business manager, and Thomas T. Lindsey was its circulation manager. It was a first class dignified periodical 9" x 12" and was issued monthly. This publication, usually 32 pages in length, was filled with inspiring articles, sermons, editorials and theological discussions. Though the paper was well received it was short-lived due to insufficient funds with which to perpetuate its existence. It ceased to be published after 1928. There was no other publication in interest of the school until the winter of 1936 when the "Holmes Bulletin" ("News for the Institute Family and Friends") began to be published. It was for three years a mimeographed publication of some six or eight pages 8½ x 11 inches. It is, today, a modest but neat 6 x 9 printed publication usually aggregating about 12 pages. It has, since 1946, been called "The Voice of Holmes." It has been edited in the following order by Joe E. Campbell, J. Vinson Ellenberg, N. R. Beacham, Miss Frances Holland, and at present, is edited by Miss Gertrude Blake. It has a circulation of over 800 and like the "Herald of Truth" is sponsored by the Holmes Student Association.

THE FUTURE OF THE SCHOOL

Attention has been previously called to the fact that this school has never been in the fullest sense of the word the property of the Pentecostal Holiness Church. It has not been, strictly speaking, either church-owned nor church-controlled. It is true, however, that in more recent years it has come to be more and more under the control and under the ownership of the church, though not fully, and completely so. In 1936 and again in 1942 attempts were made with a perceptible degree of success to consolidate this school with Emmanuel College with the hope in view of unifying the educational program and activities of the church. At the General Board Meeting at Charlotte, N. C. in January, 1946, another effort was made to effect a better and more desirable relationship and understanding between the school and the church. There was a feeling among some in the church that the church should own and control the school in the same sense it does the Emmanuel College and the Southwestern Pentecostal Holiness College, if they were expected to give it a pro rata share of its support. A committee representing the General Board of Education of the Church composed of two members of the Eastern Zone and headed by Bishop J. A. Synan as chairman conferred with President Beacham to work out a mutually satisfactory agreement. The agreement was then submitted to the Board of Trustees of the Holmes Bible College and adopted in January, 1947, one year later. The agreement made the following provisions:

1. That the Board of Trustees of the Holmes Bible College should be composed of and perpetuated by competent members of the Pentecostal Holiness Church.

2. That the property could not be sold without the consent of the General Board of Administration who are the trustees of all general church property.

3. That the Board of Trustees of the Holmes Bible College be increased from 7 to 9 members and that the additional two members be chosen one each from the General Board of Education and the General Board of Administration. (This would establish a point of contact between these official bodies.)

4. That the purpose and intent of the Holmes Trust be safeguarded,

while the Pentecostal Holiness Church organization is to have their interest secured in their investment in this school property.

5. That the Holmes Bible College should become the Seminary of the Pentecostal Holiness Church, and that such should be developed as soon as possible.

Legal counsel was secured after which the Church was assured that their investment was absolutely safe, and for all practical purposes the Holmes Bible College is both church-owned and church-controlled, although technically this may not be a valid claim.

The General Board of Education functions to coordinate, oversee, and supervise the educational activities within the Church. The present over-all plans are to develop the Falcon Orphanage School into a full high school; to develop Emmanuel College from the junior college to the senior college level; and to develop Holmes Bible College into a church seminary. In the western zone, a coordinated program is also in progress. Although the western schools are yet in their inchoate stage of development, they are rapidly being brought into the total educational program. A more detailed account of the development of these schools will appear in separate histories.

The support of the church-owned schools has until recent weeks been derived from three sources: (1) the profits from Sunday School literature, (2) the general budget for education, and (3) from seasonal offerings for education promoted through the church organ.

The Emmanuel College and Southwestern Pentecostal Holiness College have thus far received amounts proportionately more than the Holmes Bible College. This fact indicates that the Church's attitude toward Holmes Bible College is not yet all that is to be desired. However, the church is unanimous in its wholehearted appreciation of the contribution this institute has made. At the General Board meeting which met, in January, 1948, in Memphis, a moratorium was declared on all publishing house profits which have heretofore been ear-marked for educational purposes. This is effective until June, 1949, when the next General Conference convenes.[1]

---

1 G. H. Montgomery, Editor and Business Manager of the Pentecostal Holiness Publishing House at Franklin Springs, Georgia, a personal letter, February 6, 1948.

Chapter II

THE EMMANUEL COLLEGE
FRANKLIN SPRINGS, GEORGIA
The Church Headquarters

The organization known as the Pentecostal Holiness Church had its inception around the turn of the century, and by the second decade of its history it had grown to somewhat sizeable proportions, counting a membership of some ten thousand. This constituency comprised ten annual conferences scattered over several states, but the major portion of this church population was geographically localized along the Atlantic seaboard from Virginia to Georgia. As yet there was no church-owned and church-operated school. There was, however, a growing demand for such a school. The more far-sighted leaders of the church had begun to cast about in search of a suitable location, while they earnestly besought God to direct them. The church not only needed a school, but also a publishing house, camp grounds, and other facilities necessary to accommodate and entertain their general conferences and other similar church-wide activities. But the immediate need was to organize and set in operation a church school.

The Property Purchased

The Franklin Springs Health Resort for more than a century had enjoyed a splendid reputation for the curative and salutary benefits which hundreds had derived from its healing and invigorating waters. The Springs were located in Franklin County, Georgia, in the northeastern part of the state lying in the Piedmont Belt. The property was two miles west of Royston on the main Atlanta highway. The Rev. G. O. Gaines, who for years was superintendent of the Georgia conference, prayed for five years that God would give the Franklin Springs property to the

Pentecostal Holiness Church.[1] He died shortly before the deal was consummated. This county contains the foot-hills of the Blue Ridge Mountains which traverse the state. There were 87 acres surrounding these springs, most of which commanded a magnificent view. The picturesque grandeur of the scenery, together with the medicinal water attracted any average individual. This property was offered for sale. On this tract there had been erected a power plant, two pavilions, two hotels and a skating rink, besides other buildings. One hotel had in it 32 rooms while the other had 36. These buildings were ideal for dormitories. The skating rink, 60 x 90, adapted itself with little change for a tabernacle suitable for both camp-meetings and conventions. Both an orphanage and a first class literary and Bible school could be located here. This property could be bought for the amazingly low sum of $9,000, but the church was not in position to consummate the deal.

Rather than let this opportunity slip The Pentecostal Benevolent Association was formed by George Oliver Gaines, Anderson Perry Sexton, Hugh Bowling, Josiah Allen, John W. Jordan, and Joseph C. Sorrow. This corporation was formed as a legal necessity and was pledged to deed this property to the Pentecostal Holiness Church when it became free of all incumberance. Five of these six men were members of the Georgia Conference and all were men of unimpeachable character. They gave their note conjointly for $9,000 to be paid within a year from the date of the transaction. A loan was negotiated from the Royston bank for $2,500 and the remaining $6,500 was to be paid to the owner of the property. A. P. Sexton obligated himself to be responsible for $500 personally. John W. Jordan matched this amount and others of the Association agreed to assume a liberal share of this obligation. Appeal was made through the church organ for contributions. The exact date of this purchase is not definitely stated though it is conclusive that it must have been on March 1, 1918. When the treasurer of the corporation made his report in January, 1919, he mentions that a note for $6,500 would fall due on March 1, 1919. The purchase of this property was the initial step toward the establishing of the school but there were

---

1 J. H. King, **Advocate**, op. cit., July 1, 1926, p. 1.

long, hard roads ahead. Someone must be chosen "full of faith and full of the Holy Ghost" who possessed both the vision and the determination to realize this objective.

A Brief Biographical Sketch of the Founder and First President

The founder and first president of the Emmanuel College was the venerable Reverend George Floyd Taylor who was also one of the fathers of the Pentecostal Holiness Church. A. E. Robinson describes him as "the most all-round servant" in the ranks of the church. F. A. Dail says of him, "I was greatly impressed by his deep piety." Byon A. Jones states that, "His life meant the world to me." C. F. Noble states that, "His life meant more to me than any other man I could mention in the early days of our church." W. C. McAbee in referring to his tender-heartedness, states that he heard him say that "He had shed enough tears to swim in." A. H. Butler says of him, "He was most conscientious and if he made a mistake he did not hesitate to correct it as soon as he discovered his error." His wife has repeatedly made this statement and seems to be impressed with this character trait above all others. These are a few statements about a truly great man who literally poured out his life for the cause of education (and also publications) in the Pentecostal Holiness Church, about whom too much could not be said in tribute. No history of education in the Church could be written without a biography of his life which was entwined in it. He it was who was selected to head Emmanuel College, which was opened on January 1, 1919.

G. F. Taylor was born in Duplin County, North Carolina, near Magnolia on August 10, 1891. In spite of an affliction which he suffered from infancy and which caused him to be a cripple for life, he possessed intellectual faculties which were equaled by few other men. His physical handicap in some sense perhaps drove him to excel in fields of mental activity. His inquiring, meditative mind revelled in the opportunity to be studious even early in life. The public school system in the community where he was born and reared was indeed sadly lacking, for there was no public school at all. He attended only eight months of public school, and from the time he was sixteen he worked to pay his own way and managed to finish the eleventh grade in exactly twenty-eight additional months, making thirty-six months in all of actual classroom instruction to finish from the first through the eleventh grade.

In 1901 he was accepted in the University of North Carolina without condition except in three courses in geometry, a condition which he soon removed. His wife remarked that he only had $25 when he entered the University, but somehow he managed to surmount the disheartening difficulties which confronted him and to struggle through the year. It was during his experiences of passing through the alembic of adversity that there was born within his heart and mind a God-given determination to someday establish a school and college where other boys and girls without financial resources could acquire an education with less difficulty. He wanted such training to be offered under the proper Christian influences.

After teaching in public school the following year, he then decided it might be possible to realize his avowed objective, and on October, 1903 near Rose Hill, N. C., and not far from Magnolia, the place of his birth, he opened his first private school and called it the "Bethel Holiness School." The school remained in operation for a period of four years until doctrinal difficulties arose which seriously threatened the continued existence of this venture. On January 15, 1907, Mr. Taylor had received the baptism of the Holy Ghost. It seemed to him providential that shortly before this time he made the acquaintance of J. A. Culbreth, who had opened a school about 75 miles Northwest of Rose Hill, at Falcon, N. C., where he had gone to attend a Camp Meeting in progress at the same location. Numbers of people all through this country had received the baptism of the Holy Ghost with the evidence of speaking in other tongues as the Spirit gave utterance, under the ministry of a man by the name of G. B. Cashwell who had, himself, gone to California and received the same experience. This experience was as old as the New Testament church but it was a brand new experience for people in that day. Many churchmen looked on with suspicion and doubt and were reluctant to submit to these questionable influences. Some withdrew themselves from the company of those who had accepted this new found experience and refused to further identify themselves with it. Such an attitude on the part of those who attended the Bethel Holiness School had caused its founder to wonder if God would be pleased for him to continue it. Shortly thereafter, he was invited by J. A. Culbreth to conduct a revival. He went to Falcon with his fleece out, asking that God would direct him in the matter of whether he should close the school or not. In the midst of the revival meeting at Falcon, the man whom Mr. Culbreth employed as head of the school he had opened there, had resigned without any notice and left unannounced in open protest against the "new experience" and had returned to Georgia, his native state. Mr. Culbreth and his wife then announced on Sunday night after it was learned of his defection that they would open classes on Monday as usual and continue until other arrangements could be made. Knowing of Mr. Taylor by repute, and being favorably impressed with him, having met and worked with him personally, Mr. Culbreth very cordially offered to him the opportunity to fill the vacancy in the school. This was interpreted as God's doings in answer to his prayer for guidance. He accepted immediately and began classes on the following Wednesday. Brother Taylor remained here from January, 1907 until December, 1918. These had been busy years in which he worked and prayed and studied. They were years of financial struggle and many disappointments in not being able to realize fully his desired objectives, but they were years rich in experiences which would prepare him for something bigger. He felt his work was finished at Falcon. What the next move would be, he did not know.

In a short time the Rev. J. H. King, who at the time was General Superintendent of the Pentecostal Holiness Church, came to visit him with the purpose in mind of telling him of the newly acquired property at Franklin Springs, Georgia, and to extend to him in the name of the Church an official invitation to come to Franklin Springs to open a church school there, and to build a publishing house for the Church. At the General Conference which convened during the preceding year, in 1917, it had been decided to publish an official church organ of which Mr. Taylor had been elected as its first editor. After much prayer and consideration, his wife says, they left Falcon, and on January 1, 1919, they opened Emmanuel College which was then called "The Franklin Springs Institute." The people of the Church knew him and had confidence in him and were willing to give to him their full whole-hearted support. All the notes which had been signed were paid before they matured.

G. F. Taylor's Administration

He remained here until 1926, when he resigned to return to the University of North Carolina in order to finish his education that he might be qualified to head a college for the Church. Having previously spent a year at the University from 1901-1902 he was able in two more years to satisfactorily complete the required course of study leading to the Bachelor of Arts degree, and in June, 1928, he was graduated. After taking a necessary rest which he felt was required after his strenuous activities as a student, he decided to take a two months tour of the Mediterranean countries and in Palestine. He sailed from New York on January 10, and upon his return entered the graduate school of the University of North Carolina at Chapel Hill in March, 1929, two months later. At the General Conference in 1929 he was again chosen to head the school at Franklin Springs, but was able to complete all the required work for his Master of Arts degree in time for graduation in 1931. According to a statement made by Rev. T. L. Aaron, his master's thesis on file in the library of the University is a masterpiece in its field. Numerous students whose research work has required information regarding the Reformation have repeatedly been directed to Mr. Taylor's scholarly work.

After his graduation in 1928, he was again chosen by the General Conference to head the school at Franklin Springs. For several reasons which will be seen later the school was forced to suspend operations and close its doors in 1931. When it was decided at the General Conference in 1933, to re-open the school, Thomas L. Aaron was elected as the new president. At that time the name of the institution was changed from "The Franklin Springs Institute" to "The Emmanuel College." Brother Taylor willingly and enthusiastically became a member of its faculty where he served faithfully until his untimely death on November 16, 1934.

The School's Struggle for Existence

This school like most others had a small beginning. God chose a busy man to assume a formidable task but he did it with a courageous enthusiasm that is seldom equaled. Soon after his arrival to open the school he wrote the following lines in an editorial which appeared in the church organ:

We are here at Franklin Springs ready for service. In counting up my duties and responsibilities, I find that I am Editor and Business Manager of the Pentecostal Holiness Advocate, Editor of the Pentecostal Sunday School Literature, Agent for Religious Literature, General Treasurer of the Pentecostal Holiness Church, Treasurer of the Benevolent Association, Superintendent of the Franklin Springs Institute, Manager of dormitory of said Institute, a Sunday School Superintendent, and a General Evangelist. I do not think that my duties are too many nor my responsibilities too great. I find that there now opens to me the greatest field for service that has ever presented itself to me before. My greatest desire is that I might have the strength to meet every call, and grace to do everything cheerfully, willingly, freely. There is nothing so sweet to me as service for Jesus. In all these places I just want to serve Him. My subscription list may run low, my finances may fail, but if I can just serve Him, it is all right. Life will soon be over anyway, and I want to meet Him with a finished work.

In fifteen short years his life was finished and his work was no doubt also finished. In speaking of the school enrollment this first month, he writes the following information:

The attendance of the Franklin Springs Institute is far beyond my expectations and calculations. Our boarders are few in number (only six students), but the community is furnishing us with twenty-four others. We are laboring under many disadvantages in the school room, and if we were only better prepared to entertain students, I know not how many we might have. This is only the beginning, and we are hoping to have things in far better shape within thirty days, and to be still better prepared by next fall. If you would like to send us your boy or girl we will do our very best for you.

The next term began on September 1, 1920, and closed on April 20, 1921, in order to allow ample time to make necessary preparations to be at the General Conference which was to convene in Roanoke, Virginia, on May 3, 1921. In speaking of the curriculum, board and tuition we quote from part of another editorial of Brother Taylor's which appeared in the church organ as follows:

Next, we wish to speak of the courses of study that we give. In the literary work we offer the regular course as given in the public schools of Georgia, with some variations according to our judgment.

We continue this line of work through the High School courses and preparation for college. We give eleven grades, including practically all things required for entrance into college or university work. We do not teach Greek, and only one year of French, but we give the regular four year course in Latin. In the Bible we are giving a three year course. . . . As to the music, we are going to use the University Course of Music Study, by the National Academy of Music, N. Y.

As to the expenses, we are giving the very lowest figures possible. When I first began to teach a Holiness School, the tuition in the literary branches ran from $1.00 to $2.00 per month. I taught from the eighth grade up for $2.00. I was also in charge of the dormitory, and for the year 1905-1906 I gave board for $3.67 per month. Music tuition was $2.00 per month. However, I found it impossible to run today on those figures. Our tuition begins with $1.50 per month and adds 25 cents for each additional grade up to the eleventh. The tuition for the Bible course will be governed by the grade of the pupil in his other work. We do not charge anything extra for Bible. We give only one Bible lesson a day. The music tuition will be $4.00 per month. The board at the dormitory will be $25.00 per month and lights included. The laundry is done by people in the community, and I cannot name the price. The rooms at the dormitory are furnished.

As to the price of the board, $25.00 per month may seem too high to some. I do wish I could make it lower. If I knew we would have twenty-five boarding students all the eight months, we might be able to furnish the board lower, but with only ten or fifteen, it is impossible for me to do so. Last year I lost money boarding for $20.00 per month. If provisions take a tumble, I shall be very glad to come off with the price of board, but at the present rate, it is impossible for me to give board any cheaper.[1]

Brother Taylor's naive, open and frank way of honestly giving the true facts spoken in language that all could understand reveals the bigness of his soul, and his earnest desire to serve his church and generation with the best he had to offer. He laments the fact that he had been unable to grant the urgent requests of a number who had written expressing a desire to work their way through school. He says, concerning the course of study offered: that none should come expecting to find a "Bible Training" school. He recommends the Holmes Bible School at Greenville, S. C. where such training is offered, explaining that the school at the Springs gives most of its time to literary work.[2]

The Franklin Springs school has never restricted its enrollment to Christians but opens its doors to the unsaved as well. It there-

---

[1] G. F. Taylor, Pentecostal Holiness Advocate, op. cit., p. 9.
[2] Loc. cit.

fore serves a purpose of enlisting many for the cause of Christ in this way which is not possible in a school where only Christians are admitted. In speaking of the purpose of the institution Mr. Taylor says, "We want to give the same course that is given in public schools, but we want to give it under the best influences."[1] The school made no promise that the student would be saved when he finished his year at the school, nor that unruly pupils would become tractable. If the parents had not accomplished these objects during the lives of their children it should not be expected that a miracle could be wrought in a year at this institution.

The school operated for four years until the fall of 1922, charging a reasonable amount for board and tuition. Every sacrifice that could be made was made by the faculty, and the policies of good business were strictly adhered to in order that students might receive their educational training at the lowest possible figure in spite of the pyramiding prices. But yet there was a growing dissatisfaction among those families whose children were of the grade and high school years, because it was cheaper for them to go to school at home than to send them to the Springs. In spite of this prevalent attitude the enrollment increased from year to year. By the third year, 1921-22, there were more than 100 enrolled and the average for the three years had been more than 50 each year.

Becomes Faith School

Although educational facilities had been provided at a nominal cost this plan had not yet reached the ideal which its founder had set up as a goal. It was therefore decided that with the opening of the term in 1922, the school should be operated on a faith basis, in a manner similar to the Holmes Bible and Missionary Institute which had adopted this policy and used it successfully since 1902. The school continued to operate under this newly adopted policy for three years. There were 105 students enrolled the first day and by the close of the term that year there were 150, the average attendance being 125 for the year. The following year the attendance reached 200 and many were turned away.[2]

---
[1] Ibid.
[2] G. F. Taylor, **Advocate, op. cit.**, Feb. 4, 1926, pp. 14, 15.

During this period the school was supported by free will offerings from churches and individuals over the organization; from voluntary contributions made by the students themselves who were able to contribute and who felt led to do so; from the arable land which was under cultivation and could be tended principally by the students; but the profits from the publishing house was the most substantial and lucrative source of income. A large per cent of the necessary funds came directly from the president's pocket, at least he contributed more than any single individual. The Sunday School Literature was written, published, owned and controlled by G. F. Taylor.

Because of the sudden increase in enrollment it became necessary to construct an additional school building for adequate classrooms. Mr. Taylor had begun the construction of such a building in 1924, and with the aid of the students along with other labor which was either hired or free labor, this building was sufficiently completed to be used during the fifth General Conference which convened at Franklin Springs in 1925. It was estimated to be worth some $40,000 though the actual cost was considerably less. A general appeal was made through the church organ to raise the necessary funds to retire this obligation. A special "dollar day" was suggested to be set by the pastors of the organization some convenient Sunday during July of 1924. The members of the local churches were expected to contribute at least one dollar for the purpose of paying for this new building. The indebtedness was a little over $10,000 and was to be paid in eleven notes, all of which were due by January 1, 1927. The interest during this period amounted to $67.00 per month.

G. F. Taylor Resigns to Further Education

This financial program was satisfactorily well under way when Brother Taylor resigned from the school in order to continue his education. This brought to an end the faith school project for there was no other leader who had the faith or the willingness to make the sacrifices necessary to carry on such an educational program. It would perhaps be better to say that there was no man so versatile as G. F. Taylor who had the capacity to carry on the necessary work which this project entailed.

A. M. Taylor was the head of the Franklin Springs Institute for a period of one year, 1926-1927, after which he resigned. The Executive Committee of the General Board at its regular meeting in Greenville, S. C., March 23, 1926, decided to create an Educational Fund to aid in the support of the school at Franklin Springs. This fund was intended to serve two purposes: to provide a small salary for the teachers and to create a fund from which to make loans to worthy students who were unable otherwise to complete their education. Every local church throughout the eighteen Annual Conferences were asked to take a special offering on every fifth Sunday for this educational fund.[1]

When the school opened that fall the new president announced that each student would be expected to pay $16.00 per month to cover the cost of board, light, fuel and room-rent. And if the pro rata expenses amounted to less than this amount, a refund would be made to cover the excess charge. A negligible amount in addition was charged for tuition.[2] This year there were a few more than 100 enrolled with only twenty dormitory students.[3]

A Great Loss

The front page of the Advocate carried the following account of the burning of the boys' dormitory:

Early Saturday morning, October 23, 1926, the Upper Hotel or Boys' Dormitory at Franklin Springs was destroyed by fire. It caught as far as we know from a defective flue and in less than one hour it lay in ashes. The building was dry and most of it consisting of heart pine the fire swept through it with greatest rapidity. No lives were lost. . . . The loss is great. It would require not less than $10,000 to replace the building as it stood, and we doubt whether it could be done for this sum. By the help of God and the heroic effort of men and boys all the buildings near the burning building were saved. For this we do thank God.[4]

There was no insurance to cover this loss. The loss which was thus sustained, together with the meager enrollment of dormitory students and other discouraging aspects such as the indebtedness, etc., cast a pall over the educational program of the church.

---

1 J. H. King, **Advocate, op. cit.,** May 20, 1926, pp. 1, 8.
2 A. M. Taylor, **Advocate, op. cit.,** July 29, 1926, pp. 3, 4.
3 A. M. Taylor, **Advocate, op. cit.,** Oct. 28, 1926, p. 8.
1 J. H. King, **Advocate, op. cit.,** October 28, 1926, p. 1.

During this year the General Board voted to sell the property and buy elsewhere. The proposition which they had under consideration which caused them to make this decision proved to be a spurious offer and as a result the deal never materialized. To augment the seriousness of an already critical situation came the resignation of Mr. A. M. Taylor, the president of the institution, after having served only one year. He was the only president up until this time who had a college degree.

Byon A. Jones' Administration

The Rev. Byon A. Jones took the school at a time when the odds were against him on all sides. He served for a period of two years from 1927-29, at which time G. F. Taylor had finished his education at the University of North Carolina, receiving his Bachelor of Arts Degree. The average enrollment during the period of Mr. Jones' administration was substantially the same as it had been under A. M. Taylor's, being slightly over 100. The curriculum was also unchanged.

Another Great Loss

In the midst of all the discouragements which have been mentioned another great loss was sustained when the only remaining dormitory was also burned. The front page of the Advocate carried the following notice in large bold-faced type:

The burning of the only school dormitory left at Franklin Springs, Georgia on March 23, 1928, creates a situation that demands the immediate attention of the General Board. Therefore, all members of the General Board are hereby requested to meet at Franklin Springs, Georgia, Tuesday, April 24, at 2:30 P. M.

We earnestly request all members of the Pentecostal Holiness Church everywhere to pray for the God of Wisdom to guide the Board in all its deliberations on this occasion.

J. H. King, Chairman.[1]

At this meeting of the General Board a motion was adopted to build another dormitory. A Building Committee and a Finance Committee were elected. Considerable pressure was brought to bear by the Finance Committee to raise the necessary funds, but with only a limited degree of success. The principals in charge of the educational work of the Church were in destitute

---

1 J. H. King, **Advocate, op. cit.,** March 29, 1928, p. 1.

need of financial aid to prosecute their program. On the other hand the constituency of the church was still being called upon to retire the indebtedness of the school building erected in 1924-25. It was not an impossible or unreasonable amount for which they had been asked, but under the circumstances it seemed so. People, generally had begun to wonder if perhaps there may have been a curse pronounced upon this whole lay-out.

A desperate attempt was made to secure the necessary funds to erect a dormitory. An indication of this is to be seen in an article that appeared in the Advocate captioned, "An Urgent Request" which read as follows:

> Thursday, August 9, 1928, is hereby proclaimed all over the Church as a day of fasting and prayer that we may beseech the God of heaven to move on hearts to supply the needed funds for the erection of the school dormitory.
> Let us meet in our churches at 10 o'clock.
> Please join us in humbly beseeching Almighty God to come to our rescue.
> We must have help now.
> > J. H. King, Chairman of General Board
> > Ralph Taylor, Chairman of Building Committee
> > Byon A. Jones
> > J. B. Todd[1]

By the following October the building was begun and hope was expressed that it might be ready by Christmas. The Rev. Byon A. Jones, at that time the president of the institution, wrote an article for the Advocate from which we quote:

> Well, we are moving slowly on the building. Most of the time there are only two of us at work, and I can only work half the time. Occasionally we have a little help. . . . Anyway we nearly have the roof on. At last it looks like a house, and it looks good too. . . .
> Cold weather is just around the corner. We must have the building ready by Christmas by all means. It gets terribly cold here about the first of the year. There are a number of things that ought to be going on now. The heating, plumbing and wiring should be going on now. They are expensive items. We are not buying anything only as we have the money to pay for same.[2]

These revealing lines give us at least some idea as to the grave problems which made it mandatory that someone should roll up his sleeves and take the lead. Byon A. Jones has many times

---
1 J. H. King, **Advocate, op. cit.,** Aug. 2, 1928, p. 12.
2 Byon A. Jones, **Advocate, op. cit.,** Oct. 25, 1928, p. 9.

demonstrated an undaunted courage and indomitable will, and the commendable way he tackled this herculean task amid discouragement deserves no little credit. He was on the job with both brain and brawn and by the help of God and God's people the school managed to weather the storms of adversity until G. F. Taylor could complete his education and return to take charge in the fall of 1929. It was a cherished hope that under his leadership the Church could eventually overcome all handicaps in its attempt to establish a church school.

THE GENERAL CONFERENCE IN 1929

In the meantime all eyes were turned toward the General Conference which was to convene in Oklahoma City, beginning May 2, 1929, wondering what steps would be taken to relieve this strained situation which existed throughout the church relative to the educational program. There were at the time four other institutions within the Church which were being at least partially supported by the Church, but the Franklin Springs Institute was the only one which was church-owned and church-controlled.

It was indeed a crucial period in the history of the Church. There was more than one school proposition to consider, and with each proposition there seem to have been many angles to consider. There were honest differences of opinion among the leaders of the Church, which seemed to be irreconcilable. The consideration of these matters imposed a tremendous responsibility upon the General Conference of the Church to choose the right course of action in this perplexing dilemma.

There had been two dormitories burned to the ground, there was an indebtedness on the school building which had been erected in 1924-25, and now an added obligation to raise money to complete the new boys' dormitory already under construction. It looked to some as though it might be wise to re-locate the school. A generous offer was made the Church by J. A. Culbreth to turn over the Falcon Holiness School and Orphanage if they would agree to locate their college at Falcon, N. C. and to perpetuate the work he had begun in operating the high school and orphanage. His offer was published in the Advocate for the whole Church to consider. He wrote, in part, the following:

Of course there are others who would have a voice in the legal transfer of the property and work which it is my purpose here to offer to the Church for its control and use, but I anticipate no trouble whatever in delivering the goods, if my proposition appeals to the Conference. (He meant the General Conference which was to meet in the following May.) There are no conditions of presentment which I make except that the college be located at Falcon. . . . The Church will be under no obligation to do anything personally for me in accepting my proposition. We now have an accredited High School, a nice ten room school dormitory and campus. The Falcon Orphanage has five buildings and a sixty-five acre farm, worth at least $30,000 above all its liabilities. The whole property together would amount to seventy acres of land and a value of from $50,000 to $60,000 and this property would be turned over to the Pentecostal Holiness Church upon the condition that the college be located here and that the work already established be perpetuated by the Church. By accepting this presentation, the Church would acquire a property of equal value of its church headquarters and eliminate the school here, which has a college as its ultimate goal, as a competitor of the educational work which it is about to launch.

The Franklin Springs property, which is more suitable for other uses than for the headquarters and educational work of the church, could be sold for $50,000 or more and the money used for endowment or building purposes at Falcon. This arrangement would hasten the establishment and beginning of our college work more than any action that the church might take at this time.[1]

In spite of the generosity and unselfishness of this offer, it was rejected. Bishop J. H. King wrote an article in reply in which he enumerated several reasons why he felt the Church should retain the property at Franklin Springs. One of the reasons given was that a dear brother, the Rev. George Oliver Gaines had earnestly prayed for five years that the property would be given to the Pentecostal Holiness Church. He died in 1918 just before the deal had been consummated and there had not lapsed sufficient time for the church to consider disposing of the property which they felt was theirs because of the prayers of so godly a man. It is thought by some that the Church made a colossal error in rejecting this offer. There were, however, other reasons for rejecting it. It would cost money to move the publishing house and school equipment. Employees who had been faithful would have to sell their property. Others who had invested in real estate at this church center would also be faced with the

---

[1] J. A. Culbreth, **Advocate**, op. cit., April 18, 1929, p. 11.

problem of re-locating, and take the chances of incurring heavy losses. There was no unified educational program in the church. A lack of appreciation and understanding and respect for personalities, tempered with genuine love and unselfish devotion to the cause of Jesus Christ, has hindered many organizations, and it seems there has been no church exempt from such deleterious and regrettable influences.

These and other articles had begun to appear in the pages of the church organ which had as their purpose to inform the constituency of the Church of the merits or demerits of various propositions. It was hoped that in some way this information might inspire the General Conference to take some definite action in outlining a workable program which would result in the establishment of an accredited junior college. Another offer was made by the Rev. G. F. Taylor in which he proposed to turn over to the church his privately-owned S. S. literature business, if in return they would give to him some place on the faculty of the proposed junior college and would use the proceeds from the Sunday School literature in supporting the Franklin Springs Institute. His records revealed that the profits from the literature business had averaged $2,000 per year.[1] It would be somewhat irrelevant and would not serve our present purpose to present the details here, but suffice it to say that a great and good man who had sacrificed more for the cause of the Pentecostal Holiness Church than perhaps anyone else was grossly misunderstood. His proposition to the Church was interpreted by some as a glaring example of self-seeking, while to others who knew him better and were acquainted with the tremendous sacrifices he had made in order to provide the Sunday School literature and the church organ, it seemed to be a calumnious vituperation. To have allowed articles to be printed which took so sharp an issue has since been recognized by all concerned as a serious mistake. But the reading of such articles caused such ferment among the constituency of the whole church that letters of protest began to stream into the publishing house, some of which were printed.[2] Before the General Conference met in May, a day of fasting and prayer was

---
1 G. F. Taylor, **Advocate, op. cit.**, Jan. 10, 1929, p. 10.
2 Various letters, **Advocate, op. cit.**, March 21, 1929, p. 11.

requested to be observed. An account of this occurrence appeared on the front page of the Advocate as follows:

> We earnestly request every member of the Pentecostal Holiness Church to observe Friday, April 19, 1929, as a day of fasting and prayer on behalf of the coming General Conference to be held at Oklahoma City, beginning May 2, 1929. We need the mighty hand of God to overrule and direct all business of the Conference. Let everyone fast and pray on that day.
>
> Yours in peace,
>
> J. H. King.[1]

While it is conceded that Mr. Taylor may have committed a blunder in formulating the conditions of presentation, his error in judgment did not emanate from a spirit of self-seeking, but was actually a zeal which issued from a godly concern for the cause of Christian education and publications in the Pentecostal Holiness Church for which he had literally poured out his very life. For example, in speaking of his work in connection with the school during the time it was operated by faith, from 1922-26, he writes of the following incident:

> Far beyond the tenth of my income has gone into the Lord's work, from forty to fifty percent some years, and in 1923, seventy-two percent. Feb. 23, 1923, I received orders not to borrow any more money on the building at Franklin Springs. At that time the seats for the auditorium were ready to ship, having been made by the factory to fit our floor, and I could not cancel the order, so I borrowed a thousand dollars to pay on the seats. . . . I borrowed no more in the name of the Church from that day till this, but I finished the auditorium on my personal responsibility.

The General Conference rejected his offer, but made a counter offer which he accepted in one hour after it was made. In substance it provided that instead of the Church granting the concession which he had stipulated, they offered to pay him the sum of $8,000 for his publishing business, to be paid in $500 installments each quarter. The further details of this agreement will be found in the discussion of the history of the Church in connection with the 1925 General Conference. Since he was re-elected editor of the Advocate and president of the Institute it actually amounted to him paying himself for his own business.

---

[1] J. H. King, Ibid., p. 1.

It is the opinion of some thoughtful leaders of the Church that the purchase of the property was not God's will, but His permissive will. If the leaders of the church had exercised enough forethought and tolerance and brotherly understanding as they might have, it would not have been necessary to have to move the school and publishing house to Franklin Springs; and the same offer which Mr. Culbreth made in 1929 it seems could have been agreed upon by all concerned in 1918 before the Franklin Springs property was purchased. This fact does not reflect on the Christian character of the principals involved, but it does indicate the lack of mature judgment and spiritual capacity which they later developed, and were then able to recognize their error. These facts are not mentioned with any measure of desire to be unduly critical, but to serve as a warning to those who are their successors.

When Brother Taylor took up his duties again at the Springs the dormitory which the former president, Byon A. Jones, had begun had been closed in by November, 1928, but was still unfurnished. Due to this fact only a few boarding students attended during the year 1929-30 and they were boarded in private homes. Although Mr. Taylor had been selected to head the school, and although he had the confidence of practically every person in the whole church, he was not able to engineer the project successfully. There remained an indebtedness on the school building which he had left in 1926, when he resigned to continue his education. The General Board of Administration and the Board of Religious Education for reasons which are not altogether clear saw fit to place the raising of money in other hands. It is believed by some that largely because of this action it eventually became necessary to close the school. The profits from the literature went to pay G. F. Taylor the quarterly installments. The 1929 depression kept away students who might have come, but had they come there were no dormitory facilities to accommodate them. All of these factors together added up made it clear, that there was no possible chance to continue the school under such circumstances. When all hope had vanished Brother Taylor offered his resignation on July 2, 1931[1] He gave up this project for the time being, but he did not give up the idea of establishing a Pentecostal

---

1 G. F. Taylor, **Advocate**, July 9, 1931, p. 9.

Holiness School to educate the children of Pentecostal Holiness families as will be seen in the last chapter of this section.

The Rev. J. B. Todd was chosen as the Rev. G. F. Taylor's successor, but never served. The Board of Education decided to close the school, and wait until the General Conference in 1933 to reopen it, and in the meantime to pay off the debts if possible.

THE ACTION OF THE GENERAL CONFERENCE (1933, 1941)

When the General Conference convened at Marion, N. C., in 1933, a Board of Education was elected, composed of five members. A program was set up by them for the ensuing quadrennium which called for the election of a new president of the revived Franklin Springs Institute, which was to be reopened in the fall of that year. A secretary-treasurer was also elected, and in so doing there was set up a depository for all funds which might be received. This Education Board was given the authority to employ or to dismiss members of the faculty. It was to be a separate Board from the General Board.

This Conference stipulated that all the net income derived from both the Sunday School literature and the literature published and sold to the Pentecostal Holiness Young People's Society should be earmarked for the educational fund to be disbursed by the Board of Education.[1]

The General Conference in 1941, stipulated that $6,000 annually should go to the support of the Emmanuel College, in addition to the returns which had been ordinarily derived from the publishing house profits and other associations. An assessment was made on each of twenty annual Conferences according to their numerical strength.[2] It was also agreed that no funds be diverted from the literature for Emmanuel College until this college is an accredited senior college.[3]

THE REV. THOMAS L. AARON'S ADMINISTRATION 1933—

The Rev. Thomas L. Aaron was chosen to head the Franklin Springs Institute when it was reopened in September of 1933. His

---

[1] Handbook of the Pentecostal Holiness Church (Franklin Springs, Ga.: Publishing House of the Pentecostal Holiness Church, 1933), pp. 30, 31.
[2] Minutes of the Ninth General Conference of the Pentecostal Holiness Church, (Franklin Springs, Ga., 1941), p. 20.
[3] **Ibid.**, p. 25.

academic qualifications were superior to any former president of the institution. He had received the A.B., B.D., and A.M. degrees and had finished most of the required work leading to the Ph.D. degree. He had come up the hard way, having also graduated from the "school of hard knocks," and was therefore ready for the obstacles which confronted him in reopening an institution that had been closed, and in assuming an old obligation of more than $5,000 which was still on the property. He had to face a discouraged church whose previous attempts had failed, but he did it with his head up and his eyes on a goal to make it succeed. He knew something about psychology, and how to work with people to gain their confidence and support. The school had at least one good thing in its favor, the debt which the Publishing House owed G. F. Taylor had been paid and there was the prospect of an annual income from the Sunday School and Young People's literature.

There were a total of 53 students enrolled, 41 of whom were in the high school deparment, and 12 in the junior college department. The grammar school grades had been discontinued. Students had come from nine different states. Twenty-three students were boarded in the dormitory.

Two Faculty Members Are Taken in Death

It was not long until discouragements came which were overwhelming and exceedingly difficult to understand. On July 13, 1934, the Rev. Merritt Thurman Ware, the leading instructor of the English department, made his earthly departure after he had suffered from an attack of fever. He was succeeded by the Rev. Claude Lee Goodrum. Then, the following November 16, 1934, the renowned Rev. George Floyd Taylor, the founder of the institution also passed to his eternal reward. He was at the time serving as professor of the new school system. Mr. W. G. Drum was selected as his successor.

Some Early Advances

During the year of 1935 the High School department was fully accredited by the State of Georgia.

The activities of the school were publicized with considerable enthusiasm through the medium of the church organ, and as a result it was not long until the interest and confidence of the Church were fully regained. The school was realizing a substantial income from various sources and was on a paying basis. The dormitory which Byon A. Jones had begun in 1928 was soon finished inside and brick veneered outside, at a cost of approximately $8,000.

The Junior College department, which had an enrollment of 12 students at the opening by 1937 had increased its enrollment to 48. There were 99 high school students enrolled by that time. In 1937 there was a total enrollment of 117 boarding students as compared with 23 when the school was opened. During the year of 1937-38 194 students were enrolled; and in 1940-41 there were 223 which has so far been the peak year in enrollment. In 1941-42 the enrollment decreased to 196, due principally to the outbreak of World War II. The enrollment has been more or less constant since that time and according to a recent report is slightly over the 200 mark.[1]

The Buildings and Improvements

In addition to the dormitory building already mentioned which was completed, there was also completed the first school building which had been erected in 1924-25. It was used as the administration building and girls'-dormitory combined, and also included faculty-apartments. It had in its classrooms, a vocational shop, and recreation-rooms in the basement. This first building, constructed during President Taylor's first administration, will accommodate approximately 100 students. In it, also, is a spacious auditorium which adapts itself for both school and church purposes. It is situated on the northeast side of the campus with a commanding view of the surrounding countryside. Since 1941 it has been used as a boys'-dormitory while the former boys'-dormitory is now occupied by the girls. The latter building is more conveniently located on the southeast corner of the campus and in closer proximity to the new three-story brick-veneered building, 52 x 154, which was built in 1940. On the first floor of this building are classrooms, on the second floor there are additional classrooms and faculty-apartments, and on the third floor there is adequate

---

[1] T. L. Aaron, **Advocate**, op. cit., Aug. 16, 1934, p. 4.

dormitory space to house 62 girls to supplement the girls' dormitory which is now used as both a dormitory and apartment house for married students.

Refectory

The refectory has had three different locations, first, in the basement of the building now used as the boys' dormitory, then, in a frame building on the south side of the campus which had formerly been used as a community church and which in recent months was destroyed by fire, and at present the dining room is temporarily located in the basement of the girls' dormitory.

Library

The library has since 1933 been located in the present boys' dormitory on the northeast side of the campus. This library which had in 1933 only a limited number of volumes has since that time been improved and new books have been added at frequent intervals. The greatest accretion was made in 1938, when 12,000 volumes were purchased at one time, together with considerable laboratory equipment for the ridiculously low figure of $1,000. This opportunity was made possible when the Summerland and Newberry Colleges were consolidated, and offered to sell these surplus books and equipment at this sacrifice price.

Buildings Now Under Construction

There is now under construction a three-unit combination chapel, library and refectory all under one roof. It is centrally located on the south side of the campus between and slightly to the north of the girls' dormitory and main administration building. It is being built so that the main entrance to the chapel will face west and will be 37 x 99 feet. On the south side of the chapel will extend a wing 40 x 108 which will be used as the library, and another wing of the same dimensions will accommodate the refectory. While all of the three units are well underway, the refectory will be completed first. It is expected that this unit will be completed and modernly equipped during the current school session. The walls of the chapel will be sufficiently high to provide a balcony which will increase the seating capacity for special occasions. It will take the place of the auditorium in the original building now used as the boy's dormitory.

The material for these buildings and others which will be mentioned presently was secured from the government surplus at a 95 per cent discount, i. e., 5 per cent of the fair value price. It is all first class heart lumber in good shape, including steam heat equipment, laundry and other facilities such as plumbing, etc. from officer's quarters and other types of government buildings which were at the Port of Embarkation in Charleston, S. C., and at Fort Oglethorpe, Georgia. These buildings cost the government more than $300,000, and when they are completed will be worth as much or more to the school. There is of course the cost of dismanteling, razing, moving, and reconstructing and brick-veneering these buildings on the school campus, but such cost is extremely reasonable in comparison with what the same buildings would cost to construct under normal circumstances. The Church is indeed grateful for this unusual opportunity which in God's providence has been made possible, and is straining every nerve to take advantage of it to prepare a set-up for the accredited senior college which is in prospect.

Additional Buildings In Immediate Future Prospect

There are three additional buildings to be begun immediately which are as follows:

Music Conservatory, 37½ x 132
Recreational Building, 37½ x 120.
Vocational Building, 29 x 120

Other buildings which are in prospect and are planned to be completed are:

Dormitory, 35 x 136, which will accommodate 82 students and will be a two-story brick-veneered structure.
Three Buildings, 30 x 80, which will be used as faculty living quarters.

A federal landscape gardener made the suggestion for locating these new buildings and improving the campus. A survey was made and the contour of the land has been mapped out. A landscape artist has drawn a picture of the proposed projects which will be indeed imposing when it has been finally completed. A beautiful church is also in prospect to be located on the highway where a suitable archway entrance is also planned. The county has agreed to hard surface all roads on the campus. This will add considerable value to the property, and will eliminate the unpleasant experience of walking in red mud during rainy seasons.

A Senior College

The junior college has already been accredited and it is planned in 1948 to add the third year's work and in 1949 to add the fourth year's to make it a fully accredited senior college. This will be the realization of a dream, after many years of toil and sacrifice for over thirty years by those to whom the church owes a great debt.

The Faculty and Officers of Administration

The present faculty members are all university or college graduates some of whom have also received graduate degrees. They are as follows:

THE FACULTY

Thomas L. Aaron
 A.B. Oglethorpe University; B.D. Atlanta Theological Seminary; A. M. George Washington University; Graduate Student University of Oklahoma; Graduate Student, George Washington University, where all classroom work for a Ph.D. has been completed.

Woodard G. Drum
 A.B. Asbury College; M.S. University of Georgia; Graduate Student Duke University.

C. L. Goodrum
 A.B. University of Georgia; A.M. University of Georgia.

D. C. Wilson
 A.B. Mississippi College; two years Graduate work at Southern Baptist Theological Seminary; All classroom work for an A. M. has been completed, University of Georgia.

Mrs. W. J. Nash
 A.B. University of Georgia.

E. H. Wirth
 A.B. Piedmont College.

Mrs. D. C. Wilson
 A.B. Piedmont College; Graduate Student University of Georgia.

Mrs. Grace Hardee
 A.B. Eastern Carolina Teachers College.

Miss Easter Lily King
 A.B. Asbury College.

This faculty is qualified to continue to serve after the school has become an accredited senior college.

The School's Purpose, and General Information

The purpose of this institution is to train young men and women for efficient Christian citizenship, leadership, and service in all vocations of life. Students are admitted from any denomination, and whether they are Christians or not. The tuition charge has always been comparatively lower than in any similar institution. Revivals have taken place practically every year during the regular school term and have resulted in many instances in every unsaved student becoming a Christian. Every year, since 1918, there has been conducted on the campus, a great camp meeting before the opening of school. These camp meetings have usually been well attended by people from various sections of the United States as well as by local people. They have proved to be an agency which God has used to bless the lives of many who have attended them, especially those of the students and their families. Scholarships have been provided on a limited scale by various individuals, churches and conferences. During the school term 1941-42 there were five scholarships granted as a means of stimulating drives among the churches in an attempt to completely retire all indebtedness on the property and buildings by the time the General Conference would be in session in June, 1941. The Alumni Association, which meets each year at commencement time, has served admirably to encourage and finance all programs for improvement of the institution, many of which they have themselves formulated and set up. A school annual has been edited each year since 1935. At first it was an unpretentious publication but in more recent years has progressively improved commensurate with the other phases of development.

The school took the name of Emmanuel College in 1938 and is church-owned and church-controlled in the fullest sense of the terms. It functions as part of a coordinated over-all church program, and is destined to serve the Church in the future in an even greater measure by helping develop a denomination which will ultimately make a substantial contribution to the whole Church and to God's great kingdom.

Chapter III
SOME EDUCATIONAL PROJECTS WHICH WERE ATTEMPTED AND HAVE FAILED

It is quite often true that in the history of infant church organizations there is usually a lack of unified, organized effort so vitally necessary for the prosecution of different phases of church activity. This may result from the lack of capable leadership to set up a workable program, or it may grow out of a failure to secure the necessary cooperation in the carrying out of a given program. As a rule either one or both of these two main causes can be made to account for subsequent failure.

The history of Christian education in the Pentecostal Holiness Church is spotted here and there with examples of attempted projects which have failed, no doubt because of the reasons mentioned. Such failures do not necessarily reflect upon the leadership qualities or the good judgment of those who were involved. Although such may have been true in some instances, it should be kept in mind that even in such cases, those who were involved were good and sincere men who were motivated by a zeal and earnestness which deserves commendation rather than criticism. The record of their failure should be interpreted as an evidence of their love and devotion for a cause which they were trying so desperately to promote. And yet their unfortunate experiences should demonstrate the value and the necessity of an all-out, well-organized, unified and coordinated educational program if genuine success is to be achieved.

With these prefatory remarks in mind it will be less difficult to appreciate and sympathize with the courageous and valiant souls whom God chose to pioneer. Their sacrificial and unselfish service for the great cause of Pentecostal Holiness to which they had dedicated themselves should be a living inspiration to all those who follow in their steps.

THE BETHEL HOLINESS SCHOOL (1903-1907)

This school and others which will be mentioned were not sponsored by the Pentecostal Holiness Church on a church-wide basis,

EDUCATIONAL PROJECTS ATTEMPTED AND FAILED 503

but were operated either by private individuals, individual conferences, or by a group of conferences. In every instance, however, they existed primarily for the express purposes of serving the Pentecostal Holiness Church in the field of Christian education and to teach the doctrines of that church.

The Bethel Holiness School was a private institution which the Rev. George Floyd Taylor opened on October 12, 1903, near Rose Hill, North Carolina. He had formerly been a member of the Methodist Church, but after he received the experience of sanctification it became necessary to change his church affiliation. On the second Sunday in March, 1903, he thus united with the Pentecostal Holiness Church which had been organized in 1900, but in 1901 had changed its name to "The Holiness Church," which name was retained until 1909, when it was again called the "Pentecostal Holiness Church." Since "The Holiness Church" was only three years old and had no church school Mr. Taylor opened his private school in the interest of the new church. The Falcon Holiness School had been opened in the fall of 1902, but it was not a church school, being privately operated by J. A. Culbreth.

After finishing one year's work at the University of North Carolina, 1901-1902, Mr. Taylor taught for two years in public schools. In a previous section it has been indicated that during his early struggles to get an education he had purposed in his heart and mind that, God being his helper, he would establish a college or school that would enable other young people to gain an education under Christian influences without similar difficulties.

His school had been in operation for about four years when, on January 15, 1907, Mr. Taylor received the baptism of the Holy Ghost with the evidence of speaking with other tongues. Because of the opposition thus engendered by this "new doctrine" he questioned the advisability of trying to continue the school, and began to seek divine guidance in making some decision in the matter. He could not afford to compromise what he believed to be the truth, and yet it was difficult to continue the holiness school otherwise. A few days after he had received this new experience he was invited by J. A. Culbreth to conduct revival services at Falcon, North Carolina, in the octagon-shaped church at the same location where the Falcon Holiness School was located.

The man who had been employed as principal of the school was in bitter opposition to the Pentecostal baptism of the Spirit, and it was during this meeting that he left unannounced, the details of which we have already recorded. When Mr. Taylor was offered the opportunity to become the principal of this school, he accepted and thus the Bethel Holiness School ceased to exist.

King's College (1925-1932)

In 1924, the Oklahoma Conference and Camp Meeting were concurrently held at Benson Park on the property belonging to the Shawnee Street Railway Company, located two miles from the city. This was the occasion of the Rev. Paul F. Beacham's first visit to preach among the brethren on the west side of the Mississippi, which fact largely accounts for this camp meeting being better attended than on any previous occasion. The interest and enthusiasm ran high, and many souls were blessed during this meeting. Among the number was an ordained minister of another denomination whose name and church affiliation it is not necessary to mention. He had been divinely healed of tuberculosis under the ministry of a young minister who had conducted a series of revival services in a community near a church of which he was pastor in a little town not far from Chattanooga, Tennessee. This young minister was a member of the Oklahoma Conference, and it was through his influence that this minister came to attend the camp meeting. He professed to have received the baptism of the Holy Ghost with the evidence of speaking with tongues. On the strength of his testimony and his apparent interest in the Pentecostal Holiness Church he was admitted to the Conference as an ordained minister. He is mentioned here because of his connection with a school that was later opened at Checotah, a small town in east Oklahoma.

Several months before this conference opened, the Rev. Dan W. Evans, Superintendent of the Conference, and two of his coadjutors had bought an option on two tracts of land located near Shawnee which consisted of more than 200 acres, and would cost $30,000. This tentative transaction was made in the hope that the Conference would approve their actions, and that the property could be procured for the purpose of building a school. The Conference failed to take favorable action, feeling that such a financial undertaking would not be wise, especially in view of the fact that it would cost an additional $30,000 to erect the necessary buildings. The Superintendent was much discouraged and chagrined by the Conference's refusal to accept his proposition, especially since he felt so great a zeal to accomplish something for the Conference and the cause of Christ. When the preacher in question sensed the situation, he went to him with words of assurance that something could be done, perhaps at another location, and that he would render him assistance in doing it. Time has since proved that the minister was evidently not prompted by the best motives.

This minister was instrumental in securing the services of another man by the name of George M. Ryder who was a minister of still another denomination. He likewise made a profession, and in time became a member of the Pentecostal Holiness Church and was placed at the head of the school which was opened in 1925, at Checotah, Oklahoma, and given the name of King's College. A public school was rented and the school was operated at this location for about two years, when it became known that some of the faculty were rank materialists and evolutionists, and that there were other doctrinal differences believed and taught which could not be condoned or tolerated by the Pentecostal Holiness Church. The school, until 1926 was sponsored by the East Oklahoma Conference and the Texas Conference both of which had been carved out of the Oklahoma Conference in 1924 and 1925 respectively.

It was then decided to move the school to Kingfisher, Oklahoma where it remained until it closed in 1932. The King's College was operated, after 1926, by four conferences, viz., Kansas, Oklahoma, Texas and East Oklahoma. The property in Kingfisher which was purchased in 1927 had formerly belonged to the New England Congregational Church where they had operated what was one of the leading colleges in the West, having produced several Rhodes scholars. It had been abandoned after it was forced to close because of bad management and had stood vacant for a time. The campus covered 150 acres and had on it three dormitories, an administration office, a large stone dwelling and a frame dwelling for teachers.

While it remained vacant the property, of course, deteriorated somewhat, and the conferences were therefore able to purchase it for the relatively small amount of $10,000. Five thousand dollars was given by the town and the remaining amount of $5,000 was paid by a prominent layman of the Pentecostal Holiness Church, named G. W. Frazier, who took a mortgage on the property. Five thousand dollars was raised among the churches which was used to renovate the buildings and condition them for occupancy.

The Rev. Thomas L. Aaron was elected as the second president in 1927 and served until 1931, when he was succeeded by the Rev. C. H. Williams who had just received his A.B. degree from the Oklahoma City University. Mr. Aaron was transferred to the Baltimore Conference where he pastored the Washington, D. C. church and continued his education at George Washington University working toward his Ph. D. degree.

After the administration building burned in 1932, the school remained open a little while, and it was decided that it would not be wise to try to continue its operation. Mr. Frazier offered to cancel the mortgage on the building if the school would deed to him all the property except 20 acres and the buildings. There was, however, a "conditional deed" providing that the property should go back to the original owners if it ceased to be used for a school. It therefore became necessary to close the school because of these and other complications.

OZARK INDUSTRIAL COLLEGE 1928-1931, MONTE NE, ARK.

This institution, it seems, was organized and operated on a somewhat independent basis, although the 1929 minutes of the Arkansas Conference have in them the record of two motions which were as follows:

By motion the Arkansas Conference endorses the Ozark Industrial College.

By motion Dean Smith is elected as a Board Member of the Ozark Industrial College for one year.[1]

This information indicates that there was some measure of Conference backing given. Large buildings were purchased, much

---

[1] Minutes of Second Annual Session of Arkansas Conference of Pentecostal Holiness Church, (Franklin Springs, Ga., The Publishing House of the Pentecostal Holiness Church, 1929), p. 4.

EDUCATIONAL PROJECTS ATTEMPTED AND FAILED   507

money was spent, and good men united their efforts but the school had to suspend operations after three years.

A last desperate attempt was made to save the property. Brother G. F. Taylor had resigned as president of Franklin Springs Institute on July 2, 1931, and was asked to take over this school, which he agreed to do and announced the same. Arrangements had been made to entertain a new political party which was to be organized in the West, and had agreed to meet at Monte Ne for their convention. The convention for the political organization was appointed to meet August 25-29, 1931. It was estimated that the attendance at this convention would be quite large, and would provide a way whereby the neceesary funds could be raised to pay off the mortgage. With this in prospect Mr. Taylor decided to take hold of the school, but in having made his announcements relative to the opening of the school he had explained there were some obstacles in view. He was aware of the fact that his success depended on the success of the convention. The attendance of the convention was so small that nothing in the way of profit was realized from having entertained it.

A High School faculty, all of whom had college degrees, had been secured; and 50 dormitory students had been accepted, but the project could not be carried further due to the reasons given.

TRIANGLE INDUSTRIAL COLLEGE (1932, attempted organization)

Brother Taylor tried to lease the property at Franklin Springs to reopen and continue independently, the school which had been closed after his resignation, but was unable to effect a lease agreement. He then attempted to buy the property from the church and conducted a straw vote through the Advocate to determine the sentiment of the voting constituency of the Church. Although it was revealed that of all who voted there were 95% in favor of it,[1] he did not press the matter further because some were censoriously critical because he had left a debt on the school in constructing the school building. His offer to buy the school and thus assume the obligation of the debt, he felt would relieve the church and at the same time provide them a school. He was again grossly misunderstood when his offer was interpreted by

---
1 G. F. Taylor, **Advocate**, op. cit., September 15, 1932, p. 8.

some as an evidence of his self-seeking spirit. But actually his attitude was diametrically opposite. When all efforts had failed to lease or buy the property he then wrote an article which was published in the Advocate explaining his position in which he said:

I am called to build a college for our people, and I know nothing to do but to keep right on at it.[1]

Emmanuel College of Milford, Texas (1933)

Will H. Evans of Sherman, Texas, a real esate broker offered for sale a school plant at Milford, Texas, 50 miles north of Dallas and 52 miles south of Waco. There were six buildings three of which were three-story, one one-story, one, one and one-half story, and one one-story building with a central heating plant. The deal to purchase this property was consummated and some payments were made, but the project Mr. Taylor had in mind by which to finance it failed to function, and he was forced to abandon the attempt. In 1933 the Rev. Mr. Taylor was selected as a member of the faculty of the reopened Franklin Springs Institute where he served until his death in 1934. The institution there afterwards adopted the name "Emmanuel" in 1938.

Practically all of the unsuccessful attempts to establish schools have been made in the West where the Pentecostal Holiness Church population was considerably less than in the East. In more recent years there have been, however, three schools established in western territory, the history of which we will now consider in the closing chapter of this section.

The history of the Falcon School is presented in the chapter dealing with the Falcon Orphanage.

The Holiness Bible School, Beulah, Oklahoma (1906-1910)

Sometime during the latter part of 1906, a band of independent holiness people called the Indian Creek Band originated near Beulah, Oklahoma on what is now the Rock Island Railroad midway between Elk City and Sayre in western Oklahoma. Under the leadership of the Rev. Frank P. Alexander they purchased a tract of land and established a Holiness Bible School.

---

1 G. F. Taylor, Advocate, op. cit., p. 10.

which continued to operate until 1910 when it was sold. The famous Daniel Awrey, who was widely known in both home and foreign lands, taught here for three years beginning in 1907, while he continued his preaching ministry during the summer months. After the school was closed he went as a missionary to Liberia, West Africa where he died on December 4, 1913.

While this Indian Creek Band institution, strictly speaking, was never actually operated by people of the Pentecostal Holiness Church, it taught the same doctrines, and invited men like F. M. Britton and others of that communion to conduct services at Bethel, which were miraculously blessed of God. It is mentioned here because it influenced many individuals who now comprise Pentecostal Holiness Church membership in Western Oklahoma having become charter members when the Church and Conference was organized in that section. The names of some of them familiar to many are: the Dunlaps, the Robert Aarons, the Chesters, the Reeders, the Knights, the Taylors, the Starks, the Odens, the Hills, the Bealls, the Reinkings, the Millers, the Kennys, the Andersons, the Dodds, the Moores, the Bridges, the Kerns, the Herrells, the Starchers, the Martins, the Colsons, the Davises, the Peters, the Kerseys, the Neals, the Boles, the Quintals, the Colliers, the Higginbothams, the Stewarts, the Thurmans, and many others. These came into the Church either directly or indirectly because of the influence of this school or the meetings which this independent holiness group sponsored.

Chapter IV

THE EDUCATIONAL INSTITUTIONS IN WESTERN TERRITORY

I. *Conference Sponsored Schools*

In addition to the schools sponsored by the whole church there have been, in recent years, two other schools organized to meet the need of outlying territories in somewhat isolated areas of the Church. Although these schools are not supported by the whole Church, they are not in any sense in disharmony with the overall church educational program. There has always existed a close cooperation between them and the General Board of Education, as well as with the other church schools. These educational leaders confer with one another periodically in working out their kindred problems, and in coordinating their efforts in realizing some common objective. No formal resolutions had been adopted to establish such a relationship until a recent meeting of the General Board of Administration at Memphis, Tennessee, in January, 1948, when the following resolutions were submitted by the General Board of Education and were approved and adopted by the General Board of Administration:

1. With regard to the Pacific Coast Bible Institute and the Sharon Bible and High School, we recognize them as an integrated part of the educational system of the Pentecostal Holiness Church.
2. We recommend that funds from the conferences in which these schools are located be used in the development of these schools, and that said funds be reported to the General Treasurer quarterly, and to the General Board of Education in its annual sessions.
3. We accept and approve the systems adopted by the California and British Columbia Conferences providing for two western members of the General Board of Administration to be allowed to serve with the Regional Board of Education, thus coordinating our educational program into one great whole.
4. We recommend that the curricula of these schools be coordinated in order that students transferring from one of these schools to another may not suffer a loss of credit unnecessarily.[1]

---

[1] Minutes of the General Board of Administration meeting, January, 1948, in Memphis, Tennessee.

While the adoption of these resolutions does not in any way alter the original status of these schools, it does effect a satisfactory understanding of their relationship to the educational program and relieve these two conferences of their responsibility to contribute financially to the support of those schools which are supported by the whole church. There are several valid reasons why these schools are justified in their existence as an integral part of the whole church educational program, some of which are as follows:

1. God has blessed and supplied the needs of these institutions and neither of them have any indebtedness.

2. The Church's limited financial ability will not justify assuming any additional encumbrance which would be entailed in attempting to support other schools. Emmanuel and Southwestern are each in debt and have recently incurred additional obligations necessary in their expansion programs designed to provide adequate facilities to become accredited four year colleges.

The item of transportation necessary for students to make the round trip to the nearest church schools is an expenditure proportionately large enough to defray the expenses of a part of the regular school term in their own locality. For example, to travel by plane would cost approximately $500.00. By train would cost approximately $250.00. In the case of Canadian students travelling from the far West, the immigration authorities will not permit them to remain in the States during vacation periods to work.

4. These schools also enjoy the advantages of training students who are familiar with the immediate territory where there is a special need for trained workers. Educational programs and emphases have been adapted to the particular needs of these specific localities.

5. The funds contributed for the support of the schools would not likely be invested in the regular Church-school programs anyway.

6. A number of schools in different localities provides a wholesome competition which vitalizes the whole program and prevents stagnation and inertia.

So far, two such schools have been organized since 1944, to the history of which consideration will now be given.

SHARON BIBLE AND HIGH SCHOOL

The Need and Purpose

For a considerable time prior to 1944 it was in the minds of many of the California Conferences, ministers and laymen, that there should be organized a school within the bounds of the

Conference. There came to be developed a general feeling that there should be some means provided to train Christian young people for Christian work, and at the same time to make it possible to give children of the Church regular high school training in an environment which would be conducive to spirituality. Such an institution would eliminate the necessity of their being subjected to the temptations ordinarily associated with the average public school system. Money was raised, plans were made, and property was purchased. A location was selected near the central section of the Conference on the famous 99 Highway two miles north of Madera which is the county seat of Madera County. The school was opened in the fall of 1944.

The Buildings

The campus consists of 27 acres on which have been erected two dormitories, a refectory, teacher's quarters, president's house, school building, music studio, and library. The property at a conservative estimate is worth $75,000 on which there is no indebtedness.

The Curriculum

This institution has so far been developed into a regular four year high school with additional courses in Bible, Missions and Music. The courses offered in music include both instrumental and vocal training. Future plans call for the addition of other courses in the field of both theology and business administration.

The Faculty

So far the school has had four presidents, The Rev. C. Edwin Ditto served the first two years; the Rev. Arthur P. Holley the third year; and the Rev. Ben F. Jones began the fourth year but was forced to resign because of the illness and death of his father. The Official Board of the Conference and the School Board then invited the Rev. George A. Byus to become president of the institution. He accepted, and since October, 1947, has headed the school. Mr. Byus is a man of unusual ability and wide experience, having organized and served the California Conference for a number of years as its superintendent. He also served the Pentecostal Holiness Church faithfully as a missionary in India.

Other members of the present faculty are: Mrs. George A. Byus, Miss Vesta Edson, Mrs. Chessie Skaggs, Miss Shirley Ann Kemper, Mrs. Gertrude Hedrick, the Rev. and Mrs. M. W. Maudin and Mrs. Clarence Johnson. Others who have served in the past include: the Rev. William Hopkins, Mrs. C. E. Ditto, Mrs. A. P. Holley, Miss Vera Colthar, Mrs. May Sibley, Miss Edith Selby, Miss Hazel Marie Keele, Miss Zonell Jones, the Rev. Thomas E. Bigby, the Rev. Jack O'Neal, Mrs. Myrtle Norcross, Mrs. John Bunnell, Mrs. Walter Honeywell, Mrs. Gertrude Morgan and the Rev. and Mrs. Elmer Rouse.

This school has served a useful purpose in the Church and it gives promise of making a still greater contribution in the future.

PACIFIC COAST BIBLE INSTITUTE, CHILLIWACK, B. C.

The Pacific Coast Bible Institute was opened in 1945 as a conference sponsored school of the British Columbia Conference. Thousands of miles separate it from other Pentecostal Holiness Church schools. For reasons already mentioned it was virtually impossible and highly impracticable for students in this far western section of Canada to attend the existing church institutions.

The Organization

Miss Florence Hamilton was selected as the first principal of this school. She had served formerly as a principal in the Vancouver City Schools and held a Th.B. degree from Holmes Bible School. For twenty years she was a Pentecostal Holiness Church missionary to China and during that time she had taught in the public schools of Hanchow, China. She was a woman of deep consecration and was eminently qualified for this principalship. Serving with her as members of the faculty were also well qualified teachers, including an Oxford-trained Episcopal Rector, the Rev. Dr. Wesley Bruce, Ph.D. of the Methodist Church, Miss Bessie E. Cartmell, a returned missionary from China, and Mrs. L. N. MacAuley who had taught in Canadian public schools. The school was operated in a splendid building, a former mansion, which had been occupied formerly by a member of Parliament. It was bought for the small sum of $6,000. A large garage was converted into a school chapel. It was located in the heart of

Chilliwack, the "Garden of British Columbia," situated on the beautiful Fraser Valley, about sixty-five miles from the city of Vancouver, easy access by train, bus and air line. This is a rich dairy, orchard, fishing, farming, cattle and lumber country.

Sixteen students attended the first year. Twenty dollars per month was charged for board and tuition. There was no indebtedness remaining on the property by the end of the first term. None of the teachers received any salary except the dean, who was paid $90.00 per month. The Dean moved away after the first year, and Miss Florence Hamilton was returned to China as a missionary.

The Expansion and Change of Policy

The Rev. H. Ray Stewart was chosen to head the school the second term in 1946. He had for some years taught at Holmes Bible College after he was graduated from that school and also Furman University, holding the B.A. and Th.B. degrees. Mr. Stewart had had a wide range of experience as a pastor, evangelist and teacher and could both do and supervise construction work. He had been influenced by the Holmes Bible College policies and sought to operate this school somewhat on the same faith basis. He immediately secured the cooperation, and gained the favor of those connected with the Conference, school, and the local church.

He had left Holmes Bible College on a sort of furlough, and agreed to remain in Canada for one year, and to do the best he could to promote the interests of the school and local church to the best of his ability. During the summer a large truck was secured to haul produce, cattle, fish, fruits, etc. The church people helped with the work of canning, dressing and preserving such items as could be bought while the harvest was in abundance. Potatoes were in the hills, meat in refrigerator lockers, and dried and canned fruit and produce filled the pantry shelves when the school term opened, and forty students were enrolled in response to a prospectus which had been circulated during the summer. Sixteen of these had attended the first year.

Buildings

During the year, after students arrived, the large veranda of the building was enclosed and made into a spacious dining room, the garage which had been converted into a chapel was enlarged and made into a boys' dormitory, plumbing installed, and other necessary improvements were made. The boys' dormitory had previously been on one floor of the main building which also housed the Dean, Principal and female students. The church, five blocks away, was modernized and enlarged inside and outside, increasing the seating capacity from less than 100 to accommodate 200. There was again no indebtedness on the property at the close of this term.

Radio and Practical Work

Mr. Stewart directed a regular Sunday broadcast which elicited an amazing number of responses from the citizenry of Chilliwack, and the vicinity included in the station coverage. Students were trained to participate in these services, and also members of the local church group. This, with Mr. Stewart's dynamic preaching and southern accent, went a long way toward introducing and popularizing the new school.

In addition to this work students and parishioners conducted Sunday schools in outlying communities, and on Saturday nights street services were conducted on the main square up town. These services were well attended and were greatly respected. The conservative Canadians had not seen it on this wise before. Invitations were extended to the Rev. Mr. Stewart and his group of singers to conduct preaching and singing services in a number of the local churches and to actively participate in the Youth for Christ Movement of which Mr. Stewart was elected Vice President. Besides being a good preacher he is a gifted song-leader which made his services in demand in many quarters.

The Future

When Mr. Stewart resigned to return to his post at Holmes Bible College, the Rev. Mr. Harold Paul, who holds a M.A. degree, was chosen to continue this work. He was also superintendent of the British Columbia Conference and widely known as a minister in this section, being a native Canadian and having labored in this territory for many years. Around 50 students were enrolled for the 1947-48 session under his leadership. A great revival has recently been in progress among the students, and within the local church which has extended its influence far and wide. The future of this school is without doubt destined to be, it seems, bright and prosperous.

The Institute depends entirely upon faith in the providence of God for its support, and opens its doors to fully consecrated Christian workers everywhere who feel God is leading them in that direction. Both provisions and money are sent in by those who feel impressed that God would have them make such contributions. The zeal and earnestness which have characterized the attitude of many Canadians has indeed been touching and impressive. One example of sacrificial giving is to be seen in Robert Kennedy and his wife who sold their home and are living in a barn in order to give to the support of this school. Miss Bessie Cartmell has also given 10 acres and a house which she owned on the edge of town. Mr. Robert Armstrong, a retired contractor, has promised $5,000 to the church. With such zeal success is certain.

The Curriculum and Rules

The curriculum and disciplinary requirements closely parallel those of the Holmes Bible College. A three year Bible course is the main emphasis. Along with it are offered courses in Missions, General Theology, Pastoral Theology, Homiletics, Evangelism, Church History, Psychology, English, Public Speaking, Philosophy, Religious Education, Geography of the Holy Land, Sociology and Music. Each day's schedule begins at 6:15 A. M. and follows rigid program of prayer, study and work until bedtime at 10:25 P. M.

SOUTHWESTERN PENTECOSTAL HOLINESS COLLEGE

The Purchase

This institution is the newest and the fastest growing institution in the Church at the present time. It had its inception on July 1, 1946, when the former Abe Hale's Night Club, 5000 N. W. Tenth Street was purchased by the Western Board of Education of the Pentecostal Holiness Church for the sum of $37,500. Fifteen thousand dollars was paid in cash and the remaining $22,500 was to be paid all or in part every three months, beginning October 1, 1946, at six per cent interest. The signatories who signed the purchase agreement were the members of the Western Board of Education as follows: The Rev. R. O. Corvin, Chairman, the Rev. Oral Roberts, Secretary, the Rev. C. H. Williams, the Rev. J. M. Lemmon and the Rev. A. M. Herndon. A loan for $2,500 was negotiated to complete the down payment on the property which lacked $1,000, and the remaining portion was used for remodeling and procuring the necessary equipment to begin operation that fall.

The Need and Initial Steps

The need for this institution rose out of a situation which developed in and around Shawnee in 1944, which had been agitated as a result of unfavorable circumstances that existed in the public schools of that vicinity, and which threatened the spiritual well being of Pentecostal Holiness children. The Rev. Oral Roberts, at that time pastor of the Shawnee Pentecostal Holiness Church, Mr. B. B. Scrivner, a prominent layman of that church, and others, immediately began to raise funds to establish a school. Other communities over Oklahoma and other states were influenced to take up the torch in their areas where similar conditions existed. After the property had been purchased a tour of the churches was conducted by a dozen or so men who had been selected to raise funds to liquidate the indebtedness. A systematic drive was scheduled which began September 8, 1946. Preceding this special drive, the Rev. Oral Roberts had made a tour of the Kansas Conference, beginning July 5, informing them of the purchase of the property and receiving offerings. The response was encouraging and enthusiastic. The Rev. R. O. Corvin, who had been selected to head the institution, raised $1,075 at the Falcon Camp Meeting in late August, 1946, which was to be applied to the cost of building a music hall to be named "Falcon Music Hall." The Rev. Oral Roberts turned the first shovel of dirt for the foundation of this building on September 2, 1946. In the meanwhile, during the first week in August, a crew of volunteer workers was engaged in remodeling, renovating and painting the buildings, and conditioning the grounds to make ready for the grand opening that fall.

The Announcement of the Opening and Seasonal Drive for Funds

Bishop J. A. Synan, Chairman of the General Board of Education, wrote the following account which appeared in the Advocate.

The Western Board of Administration for Education has announced the opening of the Southwestern Pentecostal Holiness College for October, 1946.

The Board has purchased the spacious Abe Hale property and will use its two buildings in which to launch the Bible Department of the college this fall. The High School Department is to be opened one year from this fall, and the College Department as soon thereafter as possible.

The brethren had not planned to open the school 'till 1947. The fact that they were able to secure this property with some buildings already adaptable for school purposes, together with a considerable amount of practical equipment, will enable them to start teaching Bible courses with the opening of the fall term this year. . . .

The Board has unanimously elected the Rev. R. O. Corvin and the Rev. C. H. Williams, as President and Dean, respectively, of the Western school.

The Board is going to promote a Southwest-wide seasonable drive during the month of September to raise funds for the school. The goal is $100,000 for the purpose of paying the balance due on the property and constructing one new building by the time of the 1947 opening of the high school.

Wide publicity has been given the school over the largest radio stations and in the leading newspapers in Oklahoma. Many applications have already come in from young people who have heard these newscasts over the radio. Applications are coming in daily, and the present indications point toward an enrollment of 100 ministerial students for the fall term. . . .[1]

Junior College

There were actually 110 students during this term according to a statement from the president of the institution. For a number of reasons it was deemed unwise to open the high school department to begin with. By opening the first year as a junior college the institution gained recognition from the State and approval from the government for training G. I.'s which enabled it to secure the needed facilities for the development of both the high school and college departments. On February 4, 1947, the government approved the school for G. I. Training and made it to apply retroactively as of the opening date, October 8, 1946.

The school officials have been in constant contact with the State officials regarding the possibility of accreditation. In a recent educational meeting in Oklahoma City, and in a more

---

[1] J. A. Synan, **Advocate,** op. cit., Aug. 1, 1946, p. 13.

recent national educational meeting in St. Louis, Southwestern officials learned that only five out of twenty-eight junior colleges in the state of Oklahoma have a larger attendance and that Southwestern ranks first among denominational junior colleges in enrollment. In a brief period of time it is altogether possible and highly probable that this school will take first place. Officials from the State Accrediting Agency have visited the institution and given suggestions which will guide it toward meeting the standards for accreditation. The future plans call for a four-year Bible College offering two degrees, the Th. B. to those who plan to become ministers and missionaries, and the Bachelor of Music degree to those who desire to prepare themselves in the field of church music, hymnology and choir-training techniques.

The Property

The original Abe Hale Night Club property consisted of one large building, 44 x 96, one garage apartment, and a few outbuildings and seven and one-half acres of land, located on a city bus line one and one-half miles from the city limits of Oklahoma City. Oklahoma City is the central hub of all the Southwest. Transportation by highways, railways, and airways reaches all parts of the nation from this metropolis. The school site is in an exclusive residential section surrounded by beautiful homes valued at from $30,000 to $50,000. The improvements, enlargements and new buildings which have been developed since the property was purchased bring the total assets of Southwestern Pentecostal Holiness College to more than $150,000 according to a recent statement from the Rev. R. O. Corvin. A total of $73,000 had been raised during the year ending December 4, 1947. Negotiations are now being made to secure government surplus property which will prepare the institution to construct all necessary buildings to accommodate students in the high school and a four-year college department. In December, 1947, the current indebtedness totaled $17,000 which had been refinanced at 4½% interest.[1] A dollar club has been organized with 1100 members who are pledged to pay $1.00 per month according to a report from Bishop J. A. Synan recently.

---

1 Letter from the Rev. R. O. Corvin, Oklahoma City, Dec. 4. 1947.

The Curriculum, The Cost, The Faculty, and The Enrollment

The freshman year requires courses in Old Testament, American History, English Grammar and Composition, Mathematics, Spanish, Music Theory, Shorthand, Typing, Bookkeeping and Band. These courses are continued during the sophomore year except Mathematics for which Chemistry is substituted.

The cost for boarding students is $195.50 per semester and $391.00 per year. The cost for day students totals $63.00 per semester and $126.00 per year.

The present faculty is as follows: The Rev. R. O. Corvin, A.B., M.A., B.D., President; W. B. Corvin, A.B., the Rev. C. H. Williams, A.B., W. T. Jeffers, B. Mus., Scott T. Muse, Band, Mrs. Margaret Muse Odom, Miss Cara Mae Stark, Registrar, and Miss Ruth Lutman, Counselor.

The present enrollment is 122.

Prior to the General Conference which met in Oklahoma City in 1945, it as thought that there would be a consolidating of the church schools in the East with the proposed school in the West. At the Conference the following recommendations were made:

> That a four-year accredited college and Theological Seminary shall be located in a geographical center that will best serve the entire Pentecostal Holiness Church.
>
> That the Board of Education shall make investigations of prospective locations for the College and Seminary. A report of these investigations shall be made to a joint session of the General Board at its first annual session. These two Boards shall have the authority to choose the final location.[1]

As has been seen, it was afterward decided because of a revulsion of public opinion within the Church to retain the existing schools at their present locations and to allow the West to begin a church-sponsored school of their own. The Holmes Bible College was selected as the institution to develop into the Church seminary. The Educational Board was divided according to the Eastern and Western Zones, new members were elected to complete these Boards, and the entire church educational program

---

[1] Minutes of the Tenth General Conference of the Pentecostal Holiness Church. (Franklin Springs, Ga., July 7 to 14, 1945), p. 43.

was coordinated and unified. There should be smooth sailing in the future.

A recent editorial in the Advocate reflects the progress of this coordinated program in the following statements:

> Both Emmanuel and Southwestern College are in the midst of an ambitious and vigorous program for advancement. Holmes Bible College moves steadily on its course, saying little about its operations and its needs, but ever showing improvements in both the plant and the system. Across the continent from us, Sharon Bible College and Pacific Coast Bible Institute are striving to meet educational needs of the Church in their particular territories. It is our duty to give liberal support to the needs of these institutions. . . .[1]

The educational emphasis in the Pentecostal Holiness Church has in recent years focused the eyes of other Pentecostal Groups upon the progress that is being made. Some have looked on with suspicion, while others have sought to emulate its programs. It is to be wondered if this new emphasis does not indicate another step in the development into another phase of the evolutionary cycle *from a* radical, emotional sect with an emphasis on the crisis-conversion experience *to* the more staid denomination which has become educated and set up rational inhibitions which prohibit emotional expression and the crisis-conversion experience, and have come to rely more on educational evangelism. There is such a danger which should be guarded against, lest the Pentecostal Holiness Church lose its appeals to the socially-disinherited groups, and in the process forfeit its right to exist as another sect different to the established churches who are on the whole unable to minister to the economically-disfranchised and socially-inferior groups.

---

1 G. H. Montgomery, **Advocate, op. cit.,** Feb. 12, 1947, p. 2.

Section II

PUBLICATIONS

CHAPTER I

Periodicals and Sunday School Literature Since 1899

THE IMPORTANCE OF THE PRINTED PAGE

The greatest single agency of evangelism came into being in 1456 when Guttenberg invented the printing press. It happened in ample time to prepare the way for the spread of the Protestant Reformation. After Luther's memorable stand at the Diet of Worms he was taken captive by friendly hands on his way home, to protect his life after he had been put under the imperial ban of the Emporer. His friend, Frederick the Wise, had him secretly taken to the Castle of Wartburg, near Fisenach for safe keeping. Luther took advantage of his three months of seclusion and translated the New Testament into the German vernacular so that it could be read by the ordinary layman. Here it was that he threw the inkpot at the devil who opposed him. It was Luther, Melanchthan, Calvin and others who made prolific use of their pens to promote the cause of the Reformation. Luther's book on Galatians fell into John Bunyan's hands and resulted in his conversion. The 138th translation of Bunyan's Pilgrim's Progress was recently issued, this time in an African dialect. Spurgeon's sermons have been circulated in more than 150,000 copies.[1] Wesley wrote over 400 booklets and pamphlets. The Methodist frontier circuit rider made it his habit to carry with him in his saddle-bags, journals and books calculated to minister to the spiritual needs of the people.[2]

Dr. Benjamin R. Lacy refers to the effects of the Revival of 1800, among which he mentions the new emphasis on the printing

---

[1] Samuel M. Zwemer, **Evangelism Today: Message, Not Method.** (New York: Fleming H. Revell Co., 1944), p. 96.
[2] Catherine C. Cleveland, **The Great Revival in the West 1797-1805.** (Chicago: The University of Chicago Press, 1916), pp. 27, 28.

of religious literature which was tremendous.[1] Bible Societies and other agencies came into being to foster the cause of the Gospel. When the deists wanted to spread their damaging doctrine they sent thousands of copies of Tom Paine's "Age of Reason" to America to be sold for a few pence, and if they could not be sold they were given away. The modern-day Jehovah's Witnesses have printed and circulated millions of copies of Pastor Russell's Bible expositions and sermons, as well as millions more of Judge Rutherford's. Both Christians and non-Christians have long since recognized the unsurpassed value of the printed page as an agency to spread various philosophies.

When Jonathan Edwards was dismissed from his church at Northfield at the age of forty-seven, with ten living children to support, he spent seven years, from 1751-58, as a missionary to the Housatonic Indians at Stockbridge, Massachusetts. Dr. W. W. Sweet refers to these years as the "harvest time of his intellectual activity".[2] No wonder that John Erskine of Edinborough states that the British Isles have produced no such writers on Divinity in the 18th century as Dickinson and Edwards. During this seven-year period Edwards wrote his famous treatise on "The Freedom of the Will" and many other books. He took advantage of his opportunity to write while he was limited by being placed in this humble field of labor.[3] It was the Apostle Paul who wrote from the Roman prison, "The Word of God is not bound."[4] Isaiah has told that God's Word shall not return unto Him void, but it shall accomplish that which pleases God.[5]

A most striking example of the far reaching effect of God's printed word is to be seen in the experience of a wounded young Frenchman centuries ago. While he lay languishing on a pallet in a hospital a tract on the coverlet caught his eye. He was converted. Today, his statue graces the entrance to the Church of the Consistory in Paris. He was Admiral Coligny, the leader of the Reformation in France. His nurse was also converted

---
[1] Benjamin R. Lacy, **Revivals in the Midst of the Years.** (Richmond, Virginia, John Knox Press, 1943), p. 82.
[2] W. W. Sweet, **The Story of Religion in America.** (New York: Harper and Brothers, 1939), p. 197.
[3] **Loc. cit.**
[4] II Timothy 2:9.
[5] Isaiah 55:11.

and penitently passed the tract into the hands of Lady Abbess, and she too, was converted. She later became the wife of a young Hollander. The influence she had upon the life of her husband reacted upon the whole continent of Europe, for he was William of Orange, who became the champion of liberty and Protestantism in the Netherlands.[1]

An article recently appeared in the Advocate entitled, "Two Books and a Boy" which tells the story of the Editor's experience as a poor lad living in the mountains of Virginia, of reading two religious books that his mother ordered through an agent who came through that country. The effect these books had on his life was both profound and lasting.[2] Volumes could be written on the powerful influence the printed page has had in the lives of many individuals. The following needful information which Arthur V. Casselman gives in his book is worthy of close attention.

> A billion people in the world cannot read and write. In India's 398 million, only twelve out of every one hundred can read; in China's 450 million, only ten . . . . Literacy has a most essential corollary, literature. Of what avail is the ability to read if the newly literate had nothing to read. . . . Christianity has long recognized literacy and literature as twin hand maids in the production of strong Christian leadership among the younger churches of the world. In a notable talk, Vice-President Henry A. Wallace said that the missionary has been 'the most outstanding foe to oriental illiteracy for a century and a half.' . . . The meeting of the International Missionary Council at Madras in 1938 helped the Christian forces to see the need of united effort to rout illiteracy and provide suitable literature. The oldest churches had thought in terms of preachers, doctors, and teachers. The imagination of the younger churches had leaped ahead to additional new tools, to the evangelizing power of the printed word, to authors, translators and distributors, to pamphlets, magazines, pictures, posters, books and films—**News Letter**, Committee on World Literacy and Christian Literature on the Foreign Missions Conference of North America.[3]

A striking example of a most outstanding and different publication of this type is to be found in Clyde Dennis's recently inaugurated periodical, "The Christian Life and Times," a

---

1 Samuel M. Zwemer, **Evangelism Today: Message, not Method.**
2 G. H. Montgomery, **Advocate**, op. cit., August 7, 1947, p. 1.
3 Arthur V. Caaselman, **Into All the World.** (Philadelphia: The Christian Education Press, 1943), p. 4.

monthly magazine which he began in 1945. His original ideas and methods of presenting suggestive materials have won for his unique publication a subscription list, unparalleled in size for so young a publication and which continues its phenomenal growth and far reaching effect.

The whole history of civilization began when man began to write records. All that happened previous to that time is obscured or lost in the midnight of illiteracy. God commanded Moses, David, Jeremiah and other holy men to write. The history of the expansion of the early church had its apologists and writers, including the Apostles, Clement, Barnabas, Justin Martyr, Tertullian, Cyprian and others. Their successors have likewise taken up the pen, Thomas A. Kempis, Jerome Wycliff, Luther, Calvin, Wesley and hundreds more. The ubiquitous missionary since the fifteenth century has been the printing press. Every church organization has sooner or later seen the need of an official church organ, and prior to its own publications used the voice of other publications to promote its interests and propagate the truths for which it stood.

PUBLICATIONS IN INTEREST OF THE PENTECOSTAL HOLINESS CHURCH

The Pentecostal Holiness Church and the related groups which were brought into this organization in 1911 and 1915 have through the entire history of these different organizations either sponsored or supported some sort of publication or publications. However, the consolidated church as we know it today had no official church organ until May 3, 1917. These facts would indicate that there has been constantly some appreciation and awareness of the value of literature as a means whereby the public could become acquainted with the tenets of the Church. In more recent years there has been a growing appreciation of this valuable means of communicating the truths for which the Church stands. Pamphlets, booklets, tracts, and some books have found their way into circulation along with a full assortment of graded Sunday School literature. More will be said of such publications in due time, but our present consideration will include the various periodicals which have been used to voice the cause of Pentecostal Holiness. Some of these are not actually to be considered as being periodicals published by those who were members of the organization in every case, but they were publications which the Church could make use of because they were in sympathy with the same gospel at least in some measure. The chart which appears in this same chapter will serve to give an outline of the various developments in this field during the history of the Church.

Some brief history or mention of these periodicals will be presented in subsequent paragraphs according to the order in which they have been listed on this chart.

Live Coals of Fire

"The Live Coals of Fire" was founded in 1898 soon after the organization of the Fire-Baptized Holiness Church which had been founded by the Rev. Benjamin H. Irwin, who also became editor of the paper. This was in some sense the official church organ of the Church which Mr. Irwin headed. It was issued semi-monthly and was circulated principally among the constituency of the Fire-Baptized Holiness Church, although it also had some wider circulation. The subscription price was one dollar per year. The format called for an eight page periodical approximately 11" x 15" printed on newspaper in newspaper print, which was the popular size and general make-up of such papers in that day.

The small printing press was located in the rear of the residence which B. H. Irwin owned in Lincoln, Nebraska, Albert Ernest Robinson was at that time in charge of this printing plant, having moved to that section from Toronto, Canada. This was for him the beginning of a long and useful career in printing church periodicals. He was also employed a number of years in the Government Printing Office in Washington, D. C., but his primary interest has been in printing gospel literature.

B. H. Irvin's Defection.

The Rev. B. H. Irwin continued to edit the paper until April 13, 1900, when he appointed the Rev. Joseph Hillery King as acting editor. Mr. King assumed these duties until July 2, 1900, when he automatically became the Editor-in Chief. Mr. Irwin who had been the General Overseer of the Fire-Baptized Holiness Church, because of questionable conduct, relating the details of which would serve no worthwhile purpose, resigned his office and withdrew from the church organization. After the Rev. Mr. Irwin's defection, the leadership of the entire organization soon fell upon the youthful shoulders of the Rev. Mr. King. As acting editor he had the authority to call a special session of the General Council. During this special session he was elected as General Overseer of the infant organization. (Mr. Irwin's defection has already been recorded in connection with the early history of the Fire-Baptized Holiness Church organization.)

Efforts to Relocate.

It then became necessary to move the printing equipment away from Mr. Irwin's residence. Because of this necessary change, and also because of other complications which were the natural outgrowth of such a situation, the printing of this publication was suspended for a two-year period, from 1900 to 1902. However, the press was moved to Chariton, Iowa, where it was stored for the period mentioned.

In 1902, Mr. King secured a suitable place and arranged to relocate the plant at Mercer, Missouri, where it continued to operate for two years until it was forced to cease operations again, this time for lack of funds. Mr. Robinson had managed to keep in touch with the church publication program amid every vicissitude of its turbulent struggle for existence. He had just married in 1902 and with his young wife, for two years until 1904, fought a losing, but courageous, battle to keep alive the "Live Coals" periodical. It was called by that name after 1902. In spite of their faithfulness and sacrifice they were forced to close the door of the little printing plant.

It was soon arranged, however, to move the plant to Royston, Georgia, where it resumed operations under difficult financial circumstances. A location was chosen in the basement of what is now the Pentecostal Holiness Church in that town. It was at that time a Fire-Baptized Holiness Church, but its name was later changed when the organization to which it belonged was consolidated with the Pentecostal Holiness Church in 1911. Brother A. E. Robinson and his frugal and enterprising young wife made a desperate attempt to continue its operation from 1904 to 1907 when the panic forced them to close for good.

The machinery was sold to the Rev. Richard Anderson, a missionary from Central America. While the paper was still being published at Royston, perhaps during the last year, its name was changed to "The Apostolic Evangel." The Apostolic Evangel was not published again until 1909.[1] The further details of its history will be recorded in a later paragraph.

THE HOLINESS ADVOCATE (1900-1908)

Not long after the Rev. B. H. Irvin had begun the publication of his paper "Live Coals of Fire" at Lincoln, Nebraska, the Rev. A. B. Crumpler, the leader of another holiness group, called the Pentecostal Holiness Church, had also begun to publish a periodical called "The Holiness Advocate." The paper which he published had the same general appearance and format as Mr. Irwin's paper. It was also issued bi-monthly for the subscription price of one dollar annually. While it existed to promote the cause of the Pentecostal Holiness Church, it was not the official organ, but was owned and edited exclusively by A. B. Crumpler. In one sense it may have been considered the official organ. It is commonly agreed that during the period of seven years while it was published that no other paper carried more fundamental and inspiring articles than did Mr. Crumpler's. It enjoyed a rather wide circulation outside as well as inside the ranks of his own church. In the interim, from 1900-1902, while the "Live Coals of Fire" was not being printed for reasons mentioned above, A. B. Crumpler's paper was substituted for Mr. Irwin's paper during that two year period. The Holiness Advocate was also circulated during the entire period of its existence among the Methodist, Free-Will Baptist, and other church groups.

When the Ninth Annual Convention of the Holiness Church met at Dunn, North Carolina on November 26, 1908, Mr. Crumpler was unanimously chosen as president. He had succeeded himself each year since the church had been organized in 1900. But before the business session had closed the first day, the Rev. Crumpler saw fit to withdraw from the Convention and to resign from his office and membership in the Church.[2] He was bitterly

---

1 J. H. King, **Advocate, op. cit.,** May 2, 1940, p. 3.
2 Minutes of the Proceedings of the Ninth Annual Convention of the Holiness Church of North Carolina. Nov. 26-28, 1908.

CHART OF PUBLICATIONS

Date Published	Periodical	Editor	Place
1899-1900	"Live Coals of Fire'	Benjamin H. Irwin, Editor	Lincoln, Nebraska
1900-1902	(Remained idle for two years) changed to "Live Coals",		Chariton, Iowa
1902-1907	and later to "Apostolic Evangel"	J. H. King, Editor	Mercer, Mo., 1902-1904 Royston, Ga., 1904-1907
1900-1908	"The Holiness Advocate"	A. B. Crumpler, Editor	Clinton, N. C.
1907-1909	"The Bridegroom's Messenger"	Mrs. A. E. Sexton, Editor	Atlanta, Ga.
1903-1918	"The Way of Faith"	J. M. Pike, Editor	Columbia, S. C.
1909-1928	"The Apostolic Evangel"	J. H. King, J. A. Culbreth, C. B. Strickland, J. D. Messick, A. E. Robinson	Falcon, N. C.
1907	"The Intercessory Missionary"	Not known	Fort Wayne, Indiana
1910	"Victory"	Not known	Not known
1913	"The Christian Evangel"	Not known	Plainfield, Indiana
1911-1918	"The Altamont Witness"	Paul F. Beacham	Greenville, S. C.
1917-1948	"The Pentecostal Holiness Advocate"	G. F. Taylor, Paul F. Beacham, Acting Editor, J. H. King, G. H. Montgomery	Franklin Springs, Ga.

Other Publications in Recent Years

1931-1937	"The Bible Standard"	G. H. Montgomery	Greenville, Pa.
1943-1945	"Gospel News Review"	Sam Wicks	Newnan, Georgia
1935	"Gospel Temple News"	Byon A. Jones.	Portsmouth, Va.

Conference Papers (various and special independent publications).

opposed to the experience of the baptism of the Holy Ghost "with the evidence of speaking with other tongues" which a majority of the ministers of this Convention had received either during or since the Rev. G. B. Cashwell's great revival at Dunn, N. C., in January, 1907. The details of his withdrawal will appear in connection with the early history of the Pentecostal Holiness Church, which was called the Holiness Church from 1901 to 1909. After Mr. Crumpler withdrew from the church, he no longer published "The Holiness Advocate."

The Bridegroom's Messenger and The Way of Faith

During the interim, from 1907-1909, while the Apostolic Evangel had suspended operations because of financial failure, and had ceased to be published at Royston, Georgia; and after November, 1908 when Mr. Crumpler's paper was discontinued and until February, 1909, neither of those two holiness groups had any publication which they could claim as their own in any sense. During this period of inactivity in the field of publications within their immediate ranks, however, they did have a strong holiness voice on which to rely. "The Way of Faith," published by J. M. Pike from about 1903 until 1918, had for years served the cause of various holiness groups. Mr. Pike was connected with the Oliver Gospel Mission in Columbia, S. C. where he also published his paper. It was through this paper that many Holiness people read the inspiring accounts of G. B. Cashwell's meetings and the great Azuza Street Pentecostal outpouring in Los Angeles, California. Mrs. A. E. Sexton was editor of the "Bridegroom's Messenger" which was published in Atlanta, Georgia. (This paper was begun by G. B. Cashwell in 1908.) These two papers were a great blessing to those people who were seeking light and information regarding the outpouring of the Spirit at that time. They served a very special purpose for the Fire-Baptized and Pentecostal Holiness groups, although they had no official voice within their ranks, as has been said.

Apostolic Evangel

We have noted that the "Live Coals of Fire" took the name of "Apostolic Evangel" perhaps during the last year it was printed at Royston, Georgia, in 1907. At that time the printing press equipment was sold, and the printing office permanently closed.

During the latter part of December, 1908, the Rev. J. H. King in company with the Rev. G. F. Taylor talked over and considered the possibility of issuing the paper which also took the name of the "Apostolic Evangel." Mr. King made the decision to begin the first issue on February 15, 1909. He went with Brother G. F. Taylor to Goldsboro where they contracted with Nash Brothers to print the paper monthly for a sum mutually agreeable. Sample copies were then sent all over the United States to the former subscribers of the paper when it was printed at Royston, Georgia. It was not long until many subscriptions were sent in by former subscribers. But in addition to these many were sent in by itinerant ministers and pastors who volunteered their services to secure subscriptions. Mr. King continued to serve as editor until he began his tour of the world in the fall of 1910. At that time he arranged for J. A. Culbreth to assume his duties as editor. Others who succeeded Mr. Culbreth have been the Rev. C. B. Strickland, J. D. Messick, A. E. Robinson, and A. C. Holland.

The Falcon Publishing Company was organized by J. H. King, in 1909, for the purpose of publishing the Apostolic Evangel and other religious literature. Arrangements were first made to have another firm to print this paper and other literature by job contract, but in 1913 a plant was purchased and the paper was published at Falcon until August of 1927, when the Falcon Publishing Company sold its plant to the Cape Fear Printing Company of Falcon, N. C. This firm continued to print the Evangel until it was discontinued some months later and merged with the Pentecostal Holiness Advocate.

The purpose of this publication was to spread the doctrines of conversion, sanctification and the baptism of the Holy Ghost, divine healing, and the imminent pre-millennial second coming of Christ, for which the Pentecostal Holiness Church stood. It was not however a church-sponsored or church-owned publication. Being published at Falcon, it was used for the organ of the Falcon Camp Meeting Association, the Falcon Orphanage and the Falcon Holiness School. It was the standard periodical size and never exceeded sixteen pages, but was usually an eight page publication. It was at first issued twice each month but after August, 1927 it became a monthly. The subscription price was $1.00 per year.

Other Publications

There were quite a number of other papers which were circulated among Pentecostal Holiness churchmen until the time they began their official church organ in 1917. Information regarding the exact time of publication of most of these is not available, but according to single issues which have been gathered here and there, "The Intercessory Missionary" was published at Fort Wayne, Indiana during 1907. A paper called "Victory" was published in 1910. "The Christ-Evangel" was published in Plainfield, Indiana during 1913. Mention has already been made of "The Altamont Witness" in connection with the history of Holmes Bible College. It was published from 1911 to 1918. In the early beginnings of the Church there were also other mediums which were implemented to spread the teaching it sought to communicate through the printed pages, among which were "The Christian Pathway," "Living Waters" and others.

Early Sunday School Literature

After the Falcon Publishing Company was organized in 1909 its Board of Directors were reluctant and hesitant about becoming too involved in business ventures such as would become necessary in order to be able to furnish an adequate supply of printed matter needed for the rapidly growing new Pentecostal Holiness organization. To meet this urgent requirement there seemed to be but one alternative, i. e., that some enterprising and courageous individual would take the responsibility to do what neither the publishing company nor the infant church organization had been willing to take the risk of doing. There was needed some person who had caught the vision of the dire need, and an appreciation of the virtually unlimited possibilities which were to be developed in the field of religious publications in the Pentecostal Holiness Church.

G. F. Taylor, the founder

Such a person was found in the Rev. G. F. Taylor, to whom must be accorded the high honor of beginning the Sunday school literature, and also the building and operating of the first Pentecostal Holiness Publishing House. He had begun to agitate for the publication of our church literature as early as 1904, the year after he had united with this organization.

Although Mr. Taylor had a congenital physical handicap which hindered him throughout life, he possessed unusual intellectual capacities which approximated those of a genius. At the early age of four he could add and substract with a facility far in advance of those of much older years. He did not attend school until he was nine years of age, then over a scattered period of thirty-six short months of actual classroom work he had finished the eleventh grade work and was admitted to the University of North Carolina, which had one of the best academic ratings of any school in the nation. His mind was kept active throughout his lifetime. He liked to study and was fond of reading. He finished reading the Bible through 100 times on his 53 birthday. These facts reveal something as to the qualifications of the man who was destined to make by far the greatest single contribution to the field of literature in the Pentecostal Holiness Church.

Since 1904 he had continuously grasped every possible opportunity to promote the cause of publication within the Church, with an ever-increasing zeal as time went by. In January of 1913, when the Second General Conference (then called the General Convention) convened at Toccoa, Georgia, Mr. Taylor spoke in interest of beginning some sort of Sunday school literature. Although he made recommendations that steps be taken for its publication, there was not a sufficient number of others who shared the vision of such a project. As a consequence there was no definite action taken at that time. However, there was a "Committee on Books and Periodicals" elected, which made certain recommendations that were significant in that they seemed to be prophetic of what was to be accomplished later. Among the recommendations submitted was the following one:

> Since many unscriptural and false teachings and false doctrines are being taught and disseminated in the Pentecostal movement at this time, we deem it a necessity to do our utmost to circulate sound and wholesome literature among our own people. . . .[1]

Such a recommendation reflected the dire need for a church

---

[1] Minutes of the Second General Convention of the Pentecostal Holiness Church held at Toccoa, Ga., Jan. 28-30, 1913.

organ and Sunday-school literature, as well as other types of publications which would set forth the teachings of the Church.

Since the Rev. Mr. Taylor was president of the Falcon Publishing Company he took it upon himself to call together the Board of Directors, and put the matter before them regarding the publishing of suitable Sunday-school literature. After a majority of the Board of Directors had voted against the proposition he had suggested, Mr. Taylor then asked if any one of them would be willing to share with him the responsibility of the project with the prospect in view of dividing any profits which might accrue from such a venture. Despite the fact that no person accepted his offer, Brother A. E. Robinson, one of the Board of Directors, stated that he would be willing to do the printing at the lowest possible cost.

This courageous Christian brother had previously gone to Mercer, Missouri with Brother J. H. King in 1902 to publish the "Live Coals" periodical. They had entered the property which they had leased, although their lives were threatened by the owner's sons. Mr. Robinson and his newly-wed wife spread towels over one of their two trunks for a table, and served the first meal to the three of them, which consisted of bread, syrup and green onions. They began housekeeping here with no furniture in a vacant farm dwelling. Parts of an old fence were made into improvised beds which were nailed to the walls on one side and supported by crude wooden legs on the outer side. Dry grass was gathered to fill in the "box-like beds." Canvas was tacked over the grass and then the bedclothing placed on top. With the promise of help from a man who had weathered such stormy experiences as these, Brother Taylor felt inspired to tackle the job. He and his wife had also lived with scarcely the bare necessities of life for most of the years of their married life, especially since their coming to the Falcon Holiness School in 1907. His good wife expressed her readiness and willingness to continue to help him in every way possible.

Mr. Taylor at the time expressed a distaste for an individual to become the head of such a project for the Church. But since the Church had failed to take any definite action at the General Conference which had just convened, and since the Falcon Publishing Company had likewise declined the opportunity, he felt that he should assume the task personally. In referring to the occasion later, he wrote:

... I much preferred that some organization take it up; but if neither the Church nor Publishing Company would, I felt that I should undertake it. I asked to use the name of the Falcon Publishing Company on the Literature, and a resolution was passed that G. F. Taylor be allowed to publish Sunday School Literature in the name of the Falcon Publishing Company, with the strict understanding that he must not involve the company in any financial way. A trial was made with the cards for the Third Quarter, 1913, and with cards and leaflets for the Fourth Quarter, but it did not pay expenses. However with the First Quarter, 1914, a full line of literature was opened, and that year the profits were $150.00. Soon the plant of the Falcon Publishing Company was no longer in a position to print this literature, and I had to look elsewhere to have the printing done. I then asked the Board of Directors to give their consent to me to publish the literature in my own name. The majority gave their consent, and the literature of the Second Quarterly, 1918, was the first to be published in my own name.[1] (The Richmond Press published it until the second quarter in 1920 when the Pentecostal Holiness Publishing House began its publication.)

These were days of extreme sacrifice for all concerned, but these lusty pioneers had learned the simple but great lesson that it takes sacrifice to gain. Mrs. G. F. Taylor, the widow of the late Rev. G. F. Taylor in reminiscing of these eventful days said:

Mr. Taylor had a great struggle during the early days of printing the Sunday school literature. He had to assume practically the whole responsibility of that work. There was no one else to do it, it seemed, and the burden of it laid heavily on his heart. Mr. Taylor got very little money in those days, but somehow God provided for us and helped us to rear our growing family. Early and late Mr. Taylor was on the job writing, printing, studying, preaching and praying. Financial problems were heavy. His income was small.

The Sunday school literature was folded in our home. There was not enough room in the little printing office. When I could find a few minutes to spare from my household duties during the day, and at night when the children had gone to sleep, I helped with the folding of the literature. The literature began with a circulation of about 300, and reached about 60,000 by the time he turned it over to the Church in 1929.[2]

THE OFFICIAL ORGAN OF THE PENTECOSTAL HOLINESS CHURCH

The meeting of the Third General Conference of the Pentecos-

---

1 G. F. Taylor, **Advocate, op. cit.,** Jan. 10, 1929, p. 9.
2 Mrs. G. F. Taylor, A personal interview.

tal Holiness Church at Abbeville, South Carolina, January 23-29, 1917 was a memorable occasion in the history of the Church for several reasons, among which were the recommendations submitted which were adopted in the "Report of the Committee on Publications" part of which was as follows:

We, your Committee on Publications, beg leave to submit the following report. We recommend:
1. A complete exposition of our Basis of Union.
2. Tracts for general distribution in harmony with the teachings of the Pentecostal Holiness Church.
3. A periodical published in interest of the work of the Pentecostal Holiness Church, to be known as the official organ of said church.
4. We recommend further that our preachers and people be urged to give due reverence to that publication of all publications, the Bible. . . .[1]

A. E. Robinson
Ralph Taylor
M. H. Clower

With the adoption of this committee report the official organ of the Church was ordered to be brought into existence. On motion G. F. Taylor was elected editor of the official organ. On motion Mr. Taylor was also elected business manager of the official organ. There was unanimity of opinion that no other man in the Church was better qualified to assume these duties with greater enthusiasm and courageous faith than George Floyd Taylor. In every way he met the challenge and demonstrated his ability to prosecute every phase of the work connected with this prodigious program. While it was somewhat insignificant in size when compared with many other such projects it represented a formidable undertaking under the circumstances which attended this effort. It was indeed unfortunate that no one in this young organization seemed to recognize the need of setting forth any adequate financial program to initiate or foster the development of this new venture. On the other hand, it may have been the members of the Committee on Publications and the leaders of the Conference realized that their report would not be passed if such a provision had been incorporated in their recommendations. The subscrip-

---

[1] **Minutes of the Third Session of the General (Convention) Conference of the Pentecostal Holiness Church**, (Abbeville, S. C.; Jan. 23-29, 1917), p. 9.

tion price of $1.50 per year was the only provision for financial support which the Conference made. The date of the first issue was set for May 1, 1917.¹

Mr. Taylor was living at Falcon, N. C., at the time and was already publishing the Sunday School literature for the Church. Arrangements were then made with the Falcon Publishing Company to issue this new periodical. Mr. A. E. Robinson was the manager of this company, and this fact guaranteed that no stone would be left unturned which would in any wise contribute toward the success of this undertaking. He had years of experience behind him, and had been connected with not less than thirteen other periodicals. Some of his experiences have already been mentioned. When the first copy was received for publication it was an occasion which stimulated profound emotion within the hearts of the entire printing staff, which had finally come to realize a cherished ambition of many years of struggle and sacrifice. The Rev. R. H. Lee, who served the church most faithfully for more than twenty-five years, and was associate editor and business manager for most of that time, was one of the members of that little group of printers which produced the first issue of the Advocate on May 3, 1917. In speaking of the occasion he wrote this thrilling account:

It was a day of rejoicing, with the entire staff of the Falcon Publishing Company, when the copy arrived for the first issue. They were anxious to do all they could to make it a success. By sacrifice, consecration, grace and suffering, mixed with grit and courage, had this corps of workers been carrying on since the establishing of the printing plant four years prior to that time. The manager as well as the helpers worked long hours in the cold and the heat, without proper light, heat, and power for driving the machinery, in an effort to get the printed gospel to the lovers of the Pentecostal way. Financial remuneration for such work was of little or 'no consideration, for weeks and months passed when the worker received not even as much as a postage stamp to apply on board and other actual necessities of life. It would eventually come in, and the promised wages, though small, were paid. There must be sacrifices on the part of everyone connected with getting out the paper and Sunday school literature (the editor bearing the brunt), if they should survive and grow, and they did.²

1 **Op. cit.**, pp. 21, 22, et passim.
2 R. H. Lee, **Advocate, op. cit.**, May 1, 1941, p. 10.

The First Issue Described

The format of the paper was to be exactly the same as the Apostolic Evangel, the popular periodical size being approximately 9" x 12". The record of the proceedings of the Third General Conference (Convention) yields the following information, "On motion, we shall have an official organ, dimensions of The Apostolic Evangel sixteen pages, to be issued weekly."[1] This was a distinct improvement in the frequency of the issues. The Apostolic Evangel had from its beginning in 1909 been issued only twice a month.

Some attention will now be given to the content of the first issue which was a sort of prototype. Subsequent issues followed the same general form for quite some time, with some occasional variation adapted to meet some new requirement when such a demand arose. On the first page was a section captioned "Editorial Thoughts." In it were listed various types of information regarding the important happenings within the Church, or any other information which reflected the thought and experiences of the editor. The simple, naive, humble and sincere way which characterized the spirit and writing of the new editor was indeed impressive, and played no small part in winning many friends for the Advocate. His unique way of introducing and explaining the purpose of the new periodical can hardly be improved upon. An example of these editorial thoughts which were attractively arranged is as follows:

In the beginning God! In the beginning was the Word! The Word was God. God alone has no beginning; everything else had to begin. The Pentecostal Holiness Advocate, the Official Organ of the Pentecostal Holiness Church, has begun. It extends greetings to all its subscribers and friends. Its purpose in the world is to help forward the work of the Lord which He has committed into the hands of the Pentecostal Holiness Church.

Are you a part of that church? If so, will you welcome me, and help me to help you? You were here first, but you should give me a place when I come. I am seeking a place in your home! I want to be at your fireside! I can't be one of your children, but I do want to help your children. In fact, I have come for your children. I want to lead them to Jesus. If already they love Jesus, I want to teach them His Word. Do you object? The Word and God go together! The Advocate

---

1 Minutes of the Third Session of the General (Convention) Conference of the Pentecostal Holiness Church, (Abbeville, S. C.; Janury 23-29, 1917), p. 2.

puts God first, and takes the Word as its guide. With God and the Word in the lead, we expect to move forward with victory.

The Pentecostal Holiness Advocate is now a part of The Pentecostal Holiness Church. It is a part that has long been lacking. The church has been lame at this point. The Advocate comes to fill the vacancy.

The Advocate then is your paper. We expect to find friends outside the church, but we are not looking to them for support. We do not come for the purpose of crowding out other papers. We do not ask that any leave your paper, and take up The Advocate. It would be selfish to ask such a thing. We have a field distinctly our own. In our own field, we choose to live. This we have a perfect right to do. Others are welcome to live with us.

The Pentecostal Holiness Advocate is not launched as the Official Organ of the church because we think we have "The Church," and that other churches are failures for God and that they belong to Babylon. We take no such position. Far from it. We believe that all other churches have a right to exist as we do; we believe that they have as much right to their official organ as we have to ours. We are sure it is granted to us by all.

The Advocate wishes to bring you news each week from the different parts of our work. Surely you will be glad to know just what is going on in the different conferences, and in the different localities of your own conference? Well, the Advocate will tell you. Do you want to hear a sermon each week, preached by the different preachers throughout the church? Take the Advocate! Would you be glad to see photographs of the different tabernacles owned by our people from Virginia to Florida, and from the Atlantic Ocean to Oklahoma? The Advocate will show them to you. Would you like to have information concerning the best methods of Sunday school work, and to read about the management of other Sunday schools? Would you like to write something concerning your own Sunday school? Would you like to discuss these points with other Sunday schools? Here is the channel, The Advocate gives it.

Do you want to see the monthly report of the general treasurer of your church, showing all money received and all paid out? You will have to look into the Advocate to find it. Do you want to know how your fellow pastor is getting along with his flock? The Advocate will tell you! Would you like to learn of our best evangelists, where they are holding meetings, and whom you need to help you in your own meeting? You will find it in the Advocate. Do you want to hear news direct from the mission field? Here's your chance. Do you want a monthly program for your missionary society, containing information as to missionary work in general? You will find it in the Advocate. Would you like to keep posted concerning the Quarterly meetings, Annual Conferences, Bible Conference, State Camp Meetings, etc., of the Pentecostal Holiness Church? The Advocate is the only paper that will give them all.

Did you say you wanted your chidren to take a simple Bible course, and have a paper to which they can write their discoveries of Bible truth, and in which they can give their testimony if they like? This is what the Advocate is for. Have you any question you would like to ask concerning the Bible, concerning your church, or touching any other religious topic? There is a question department in the Advocate. Do you understand the Basis of Union of your church? Would you like to read an exposition of it? It is coming soon in The Advocate.

Would you like a good Bible, or would you like to know where you can get the very best books for yourself or children? They will be advertized in the Advocate. Would you like to give your testimony, read other testimonies, write concerning your dead, or announce your wedding? The Advocate gives you space. Do you want to buy or sell a gospel tent? The Advocate will tell you about it.

Stop! Think! Listen! Can you tell us how you have gone so long without THE PENTECOSTAL HOLINESS ADVOCATE?[1]

$1.50 answers all the above for one year.

It would be redundant to attempt any further explanation as to the content or purpose of the Advocate. These various departments sometimes have been given different names but, in the main, they have remained substantially the same. For example, "The Question Box" was later called, "The Question Drawer" and is now called, "Light on the Subject." The "Missionary Department" is now called "Foreign Missions." The "Children's Corner" was later called "The Young People's Department" from 1925 to July, 1929 after which time it was published separately from the Advocate and called "The Youth's Leader." The "Home Missions" department which was added in 1940 is edited by the Rev. Hubert T. Spence. The "Among the Women" is an even more recent department edited by Mrs. Blanche King since the organization of "The Woman's Auxiliary" in 1944. "Education" department is now edited by Bishop J. A. Synan, and previously when it was inaugurated in 1933 was edited by the Rev. T. L. Aaron. There have periodically been other departments such as "News Items," "From the Field," "Evangelism," "Sunday School Lesson," "Teaching the Lesson," "For the Prayer Meeting," "Wayside Thoughts" and others. However, there has been no substantial change in the content or format since this first issue.

Turning through it, one would find an article from the Rev. S. A. Bishop, pastor of the Pentecostal Holiness Church in Bir-

---

[1] The first issue of the Official Church Organ—**Pentecostal Holiness Advocate**, (Falcon, N. C., May 3, 1917), p. 1-16 et passim.

mingham. In it is given a brief sketch of his pastoral experiences there since he accepted the work on Feb. 25, 1910. He tells of many disappointments that awaited him during the first years of this pastorate. Then he adds:

> We have truly found that Bud Robinson is correct when he says, 'The way to make a success of life when you meet with disappointment is just to drop the letter "d" and put the letter "H" instead, and then it reads, "His appointment."'

Then there is a notice of the Greenville Camp Meeting announced to begin May 23, 1917. Next is a notice from the editor, stating that Evangelistic, Pastoral, Sunday School, Official Announcements, Testimonies, etc. are not for the editor to fill, but that their success depends upon the evangelists, pastors, officers, Sunday school superintendents, laymen, etc. Looking in the next column is a picture and brief history of the tabernacle at Wagoner, Oklahoma; then a sermon, "Wisdom is Strength," by Bishop Joseph H. King. Following that there is the question box, answering practical questions relating to pastoral counseling, Bible questions, etc.; an editorial on journalism; the Missionary Department; a report from the mission field, The Children's Corner with a letter from Paul Bishop, the Birmingham pastor's son, asking a question of all the other children. Here also is a notice from the Western North Carolina Superintendent, the Rev. F. A. Dail and Jas. H. Capps, Secretary, announcing a Bible conference to be held at Durham, N. C., from June 2 to 19, 1917. Then, a notice that the Catechism by G. F. Taylor is ready; another notice that the supply of Sunday School literature for that quarter has been exhausted, and an offer to send any old literature free of charge to any new Sunday school that might organize; a statement that the Rev. J. H. King, General Superintendent of the Pentecostal Holiness Church has resigned the pastorate of the Memphis, Tennessee Church in order to be able to attend to the General Business of the church connected with his office. A number of books are also advertized, including G. F. Taylor's book on "The Second Coming of Christ" and a pamphlet on "Daniel's Seventy Weeks," etc.[1]

Finally, here is also an expression of thanks which reads as follows:

---

1 First Issue, op. cit., p. 15.

We wish to thank the many preachers and friends who have so kindly secured subscribers for us for the first issue of the paper. We are sorry that we cannot now financially remunerate you, but we hope to recompense you with a good paper at least. It costs us a good deal to start, and we trust that all our friends will help us to get started. Do your best to get subscribers before our next issue[1]

Changes in Subscription Price

Brother Taylor began at the General Convention at Abbeville to take money for subscriptions immediately after the report of the Committee on Publications had been adopted. In the same alert and enthusiastic style he continued his work against all the odds that came against him. Sometimes it became necessary to announce that "there would be no issue the next week due to lack of funds" but this was seldom. However, at somewhat more frequent intervals it became necessary to reduce some issues to eight pages instead of sixteen. As a necessary expedient the subscription price was raised to $2.00 per year on July 4, 1918 where it remained nearly four years until it was again reduced to $1.50 per year on January 12, 1922. (Beginning with the Dec. 15, 1932 issue the subscription price was further reduced to $1.00 per year, where it has stayed until recently. When the General Board of Administration met in Memphis, Tennessee in January, 1948, it was decided to advance the subscription to $1.50 per year to become effective in 60 days following that meeting.)[2]

In 1924 Mr. Taylor wrote an editorial in which he reported the work of the Advocate for the seven years it had existed. During 1924, it became necessary to print nine half-size issues because of the lack of funds. During the first quadrennium in the history of the Advocate 87.5% of the entire number of expected pages were printed. The following table will give the number of subscribers at the close of each year:

First Year	1,605
Second Year	1,488
Third Year	1,850
Fourth Year	1,692
Fifth Year	1,461
Sixth Year	1,785
Seventh Year	1,615

---

1 G. F. Taylor, **Advocate** (First Issue) May 3, 1917, p. 15.
2 The information regarding the subscription prices was secured by consulting the issues of each year from the beginning in 1917.

The facts which have been presented give a limited insight into some of the hardships and problems which attended the efforts of those who pioneered in the field of publications in the Pentecostal Holiness Church.

The Publishing House Built and Dedicated

Before the quadrennium had expired after the 1917 General Convention had authorized the official church organ to be published, it was possible to erect a simple, modest brick structure on the southeast side of the property which had been purchased for the church headquarters in March of 1918, to be used for the publishing house of the Pentecostal Holiness Church. In this unpretentious little building which could boast of only one room 24 x 50 feet the Advocate was printed for the first time in its own home on October 16, 1919. After Mr. Taylor moved from Falcon, N. C. in December of 1918, the paper was printed beginning with the first issue in January, 1919 through October 9, 1919 by the Royston Record, the local newspaper of Royston, Georgia. Some additions have been made from time to time to this original building. The editor, Brother G. F. Taylor, received no salary for his work as editor and on numerous occasions made contributions toward the publishing fund. The printers worked at a minimum wage or less, many volunteered their services to secure new subscribers. Through the Advocate's pages the constituency of the church was acquainted with the needs and given opportunity to make free will offerings to build the printing plant. Because of the candid and open way Brother Taylor presented the facts about the need, he was able to win the confidence and gain the support of officials and laymen alike. The following letter was written to the Conference officials and later published in the Advocate with the report of their vote:

> The Pentecostal Holiness Church needs a printing plant and needs it at once. It is our desire to take steps at once toward purchasing a printing plant with the view of locating it at Franklin Springs, Royston, Georgia. It is not our purpose to load the Pentecostal Holiness Church with debt against its wishes, nor to ask anyone of its members for one cent against his free will to give; but we do desire permission from the different official boards for us to purchase a printing plant in the name of the Pentecostal Holiness Church, we two, J. H. King and G. F. Taylor, taking the responsibility of securing our

creditors against loss, and then have the liberty to collect from the church to pay for such plant. Also we desire to erect on the property at Frankln Springs a brick building suitable for the care of said plant and then ask the church to pay for same.

It is not our plan to organize a stock company for this business, but invite all to give to it as God may direct each one. Then the plant will belong to the church as a whole as the other church property, and will be under the control of the Official Board.

We are writing to you this letter in order to secure your vote as a member of the Official Board of the (———) Conference, either for or against this project. Please feel perfectly free to cast your vote entirely according to your own judgment. Kindly fill either one or the other of the blanks below, and return in the enclosed envelope as soon as possible, to G. F. Taylor, Royston, Georgia.

Thanking you for this favor, we remain

Yours in Him,
J. H. King
G. F. Taylor[1]

Fifty-three of the total fifty-seven officials voted in favor while the other four did not reply. With such an official backing it was not difficult to secure the backing of an overwhelming majority of the entire constituency of the church. In a report of the Franklin Springs Camp Meeting the editor included the following statement:

August 2, at 11 A. M., the printing office was dedicated to God for His service. Many have remarked that it was a very impressive service. Talks were made from the ten conferences, and the remarks were very encouraging to me in this line of the work. The dedication of the office witnessed the building free of debt, all that was lacking being supplied in the last moments. . . .

The building was to cost $3,190.00 but by being able to retire this obligation before the notes matured it cost exactly $3,085.44. After giving the report of the financial status the building was dedicated by the Rev. J. H. King.[2] The detailed account of this happy occasion is as follows:

After giving this report, and hearing talks from several, the congregation marched from the tabernacle to the printing office where the services were completed. Brother King had charge of the services there. His remarks were timely and impressive. There were deposited a list of the donors, a discipline of the Church, a copy of the Advocate of the date August 7, 1919, and a few grains of wheat, a vial of oil,

---

1 G. F. Taylor, Advocate, op. cit., Jan. 23, 1919, p. 8.
2 G. F. Taylor, Advocate, op. cit., August 19, 1919, p. 8.

and a vial of grape juice. Brother King explained the significance of each article deposited.

God was with us and all seemed to be happy.¹

G. F. Taylor Asks to be Relieved

It should be kept in mind that the Rev. Mr. Taylor was not only engaged in the strenuous man-size job of carrying on the pressing duties connected with the infant publishing house, but had also opened the Franklin Springs Institute on January 1, 1919. In 1922, the school was changed to a faith institution and that naturally intensified the burden of administration. By 1924 Mr. Taylor was beginning to feel the impact of these twin responsibilities tremendously. In one more year it would be time for the Fifth General Conference to meet. Having had the publishing house responsibility for seven years, and having had the additional responsibility of the school for five of the seven years, he asked to be relieved of the editorship in 1925 when this Conference was scheduled to convene. Because of these unusual circumstances, and great responsibility attached to such colossal undertakings, it seems fitting that the exact nature of his appeal requesting to be relieved should be recorded here in order to more fully appreciate the sacrificial contribution he made in both of these fields. Part of his editorial which appeared in the Advocate read as follows:

> One more year will bring us to the close of the second quadrennium, and to the next General Conference. It is my sincere desire to make this year the best in the history of this paper, but I do not know that I shall be able to do it. So far as I know I have the same interest in journalism that I had seven years ago when I began, but I may not have as much zeal. For the last two years I have felt a greater interest in school work than usual, and this is detracting my efforts to some extent from the zeal I need in regard to the paper. It may be that the thought could be expressed better by saying that I have as great an interest in the paper as ever, but do not find the time to put to the editorial work that should be given it. I am very happy to know that we have been able to make the run successful for seven years, and I see nothing in the way of a successful run in the future. However, I do hope that the General Conference will find a suitable person to take the editorship of this paper, and permit me to give my attention more directly to the school work. If no such is available, I am willing to continue in this position until such a one is

---

1 Ibid., p. 9.

available, or until Jesus comes or I leave the world; but I realize much success would attend this work if there was one person to give his entire time to it. I would be perfectly willing to do so if some one else could be found to take the school, but it is time the church was giving me relief at some point. I am willing to work at either post, but I prefer that my task be lightened. I will hold to all until I die rather than any part of it to fail, but surely there are others who might take a part of it. I have put forth a number of efforts to select persons myself who would assist me in this editorial work, or to prove to be my successor, but all my selections have been in vain. I now call upon the church, giving them one year's notice, to pray for and look forward to a new editor of the Advocate to be selected a year from now. In the meantime I shall do my best to make this the best year in our history, and ask you to cooperate with us in the same, that the new editor may find things in the very best shape when he enters upon his task.[1]

The Rev. Mr. Taylor was relieved at that Conference. Mr. R. H. Lee who had been a long time faithful employee was elected as associate editor and business manager. The Rev. J. H. King was elected to serve as editor for the coming quadrennium for 1925 to 1929. Though Mr. King stated that he did not feel qualified to do this work, which to him was a laborious task, he served faithfully and very commendably. He likewise asked to be relieved at the close of the quadrennium.

G. F. Taylor's Offer and The Church's Counter Offer

During the same interim Mr. Taylor had attended the University of North Carolina, after he had resigned from the Franklin Springs Institute, and was awarded the Bachelor of Arts degree in 1928. Before the General Conference convened Mr. Taylor felt that he would like to turn over his S. S. Literature business to the Church, if in so doing, he could be guaranteed that the cause of education in the Church could be assured by the transaction. He had not begun the literature business in his own name except for the reason that neither the Church nor the Falcon Publishing Company were willing to assume the responsibility. He and his family particularly, as well as others connected with the publishing of the literature, had made untold sacrifices. He had also made similar sacrifices in interest of the educational program of the Church, and had used a major portion

---

1 G. F. Taylor, **Advocate,** op. cit., May 1, 1924, p. 9.

of his literature profits to support the Franklin Springs Institute. No more unselfish contribution was possible to make for either cause. Brother Taylor felt that he had a right to protect the interest of the school by asking that the profits from the sale of Sunday school literature be ear-marked for a church college and that an endowment should be created to perpetuate its existence. He also felt that in view of his sacrifices and his jealous concern for such a school that he should be given some place on its teaching staff so that he could continue to make a personal contribution by serving on its faculty. He had dedicated himself early in life to the cause of founding such a college and for seven years from January 1, 1919 until he resigned to complete his education in 1926, he had given himself to this task. He still had no selfish motive prompting him in his proposed agreement, but some in the Church interpreted it that he did. Thus it was that a truly great and good man was grossly misunderstood and suffered virtually a broken heart because of it. It is conceded however, that those few who opposed him apparently had some grounds to justify their position, and took their stand in all sincerity and honesty. Good men are often mistaken and live to regret their errors in judgment.

The details of the agreement which Mr. Taylor proposed, together with the counter-offer which was submitted by the 1929 General Conference are presented here for its historic value in order that the reader may know the complete detailed facts involved in the transaction.

The Rev. G. F. Taylor's proposed agreement was as follows:

1. That our next General Conference appoint a Board of Religious Education, entirely separate and distinct from all other general boards.

2. That all religious literature and religious education in control of the general organization of the church be placed in the hands of the Board, including Sunday School literature, disciplines, report blanks, song books, etc., but excluding the official organ of the church, and including at least one institution for secondary and higher education.

3. The Publishing House of said church be controlled by a Board of Religious Education, just as Editor of Sunday School literature now promised to do, and that arrangements then be made whereby the Publishing House shall do the printing for this Board of Religious Education.

4. That this Board take off my hands at wholesale prices all religious

literature stock at the time transfer is made, including the books of which I am author.

5. That all clear-cut profits obtained from the publication and sale of this religious literature be turned to the support of an institution for secondary and higher education, as presented below.

6. That the church designate some common center at which shall be located an accredited institution for secondary and higher education, offering in its curricula courses covering four years of high school and two years of Junior College work, from which the grammar grades shall be either eliminated or taught under separate arrangement.

7. That arrangements be made by which the minimum annual operating income for the Junior College work shall be $10,000, a part of which shall be derived from endowments.

8. That subscriptions for endowment be opened; when endowment is complete, interests and profits accruing therefrom shall be placed to the support of this Junior College, to which shall be added all the profits of the Board of Religious Education, as described in paragraph 5 above, and to this shall be added tuition, registration fees, incidentals, etc., charged to college students, until the required annual income of $10,000 is reached.

9. That the boarding plan of the school be so arranged as to secure the number of students required for an accredited institution.

10. That all the editors of the Sunday School literature and the P. H. Y. S. literature be selected from the college faculty, so as not to divide nor subtract from the funds for the college.

11. That the present Editor and Publisher of the Sunday School literature be offered a place on the college faculty, that he be allowed to hold the literature as it is until the required endowment be raised, and that until it is raised, he be allowed to remain at Chapel Hill to pursue graduate work, to prepare himself for a position on this faculty.[1]

Some of the provisions of this sales agreement may doubtlessly be interpreted as in some sense lacking in sound business judgment, yet the motive which prompted their formulation cannot justly be questioned when the entire facts relating to the matter have been taken into full consideration. When the Conference submitted their counter-proposal Mr. Taylor accepted their proposition in one hour after the offer had been made. Thus it was that the literature business was transferred to the Pentecostal Holiness Church on August 25, 1929, in consideration of the sum of $8,000 to be paid in $500.00 installments every three months without interest.[2]

---

[1] R. H. Lee, **Advocate, op. cit.,** May 23, 1929, pp. 8, 9.
[2] J. H. King, **Advocat, op. cit.,** June 20, 1929, p. 9.

A summary of the Report of the Committee on Education as adopted by the Conference is as follows:

Sec. 1. The Pentecostal Holiness Church shall establish an educational institution.
  (a) This institution shall contain an elementary department and a high school of accredited rating. The said elementary and high school shall begin operation as early as preparations can be made.
Sec. 2. The educational institution shall be located at Franklin Springs, Georgia.
Sec. 3. At least one-third of the General Board shall be elected by this Conference to serve as an educational committee to aid the institution of the Pentecostal Holiness Church. (Five members of the Board were elected on this committee.)
  The duties and privileges of the Educational Committe shall be:
  (a) To employ and dismiss members of the school faculty.
  (b) It shall devise a plan by which the school may be operated on a well-organized, systematic basis.
  (c) It shall have access to the columns of The Advocate in making efforts to further the educational work of the Church.
  (d) It shall have authority to make distribution of all funds raised for educational purposes. The one entrusted with said funds shall be under an adequate indemnity bond. This committee shall report annually to the General Board.
  (e) It shall not borrow money nor take other actions which would involve the Church in debt without the written consent of the General Board.
Sec. 4. A ministerial course shall be provided by the faculty of the school and suggested for all candidates for ordination.
Sec. 5. The following offer shall be made to G. F. Taylor for his entire religious literature business and good will:
  (a) Five Hundred ($500) Dollars every three months for the next four years, without interest.
  (b) That G. F. Taylor inform the Board within sixty days as to his decision.
  (c) The Church shall purchase all of the acceptable stock of G. F. Taylor at prevailing wholesale prices.
Sec. 6. That net income of all religious literature of the Church shall go to the Church school except payments in Division (a) of Sec. 5.
Sec. 7. Each Annual Conference shall cooperate with the educational committee in any plan to raise funds for the educational work of the Church.[1]

The Rev. Mr. Taylor was again elected to serve as editor in 1929 after which time he served until his death November 16, 1934. It seemed to be difficult for some to understand why the

---

[1] G. F. Taylor, Advocate, op. cit., Jan. 10, 1929. pp. 8, 9.

Church should be obligated to pay anything for his literature business which they felt had been made possible because of the patronage received from the Church. The $8,000 he received in $500.00 installments beginning Aug. 15, 1929 until 1933 was paid out of the literature business he had turned over to the Church. Actually, in a sense, he was paying himself.

An analogy of such a case may be seen in a supposed parallel situation. Let us say a certain man is in business who sells groceries to people of a given neighborhood. Through hard work and sacrificial toil he had over a period of years been able to show a net profit from his business of $2,000 per year. Because he appreciates his patrons and wishes to establish for them a school, he makes an offer to give them his business with its yearly income which must be used for educational purposes pertaining to such an institution, provided they will help to create an endowment by their additional contributions, and will give him a job of some kind on the faculty of the institution. We will suppose then that the people do not like his offer, and a few said that he is a selfish old man, and that his business is theirs anyway for he could not have built it up at all had they not patronized his enterprise. They then elect him to continue to head the business which has been transferred to them, and to use the proceeds from his former business to pay him each quarter in $500.00 installments.

Although those involved in making the counter offer at the 1929 General Conference were honest, sincere, Christian men who desired to be fair in their dealings, it must have been a sore trial for the owner of the literature business to suffer the criticism which came from a few individuals in the Church who utterly misunderstood and misinterpreted his intentions. The Church as a whole, however, loved and respected Mr. Taylor and deeply appreciated his sacrificial labors.

Such may seem to some to be overdrawing the facts in the case, but actually this is a fair analogy. Mr. Taylor accepted the offer the Church made and took the criticism some of them offered, and the debt has been long since paid. He has gone to his eternal reward in peace, but the Pentecostal Holiness Church owes to him a great debt which cannot be measured in material terms. His faithful and beloved widow and the family of children are due the satisfaction of these lines being incorporated into the history of the church he loved and into which he literally emptied his life in service. He and other such men of his calibre are responsible for the founding of the organization known as the Pentecostal Holiness Church. When God's books are balanced every man shall receive according as his work shall be.[1]

The Rev. Paul F. Beacham was appointed immediately as acting editor and served until the meeting of the General Board, January 9, 1935, when the Rev. J. H. King was again elected as editor and served until June, 1937 when the General Conference met at Roanoke, Virginia, at which time the Rev. G. H. Montgomery was elected. He has been re-elected at each General Conference since that time and is now in the eleventh year of service in this capacity.

The Present Editor and Future Plans

The Rev. Granville H. Montgomery was 34 years of age in 1937, the year when he was elected to the high office of editor of the Pentecostal Holiness Advocate. Although he was youthful in years he was quite mature in experience as an editor. He had been editor of the "Herald of Truth" which will be found mentioned in connection with the history of Holmes Bible College. At the time of his election he was editor of the Bible Standard, the official organ of the Pennsylvania Conference of the Pentecostal Holiness Church, which he owned and operated. Over a considerable period of years he had made substantial contributions to these papers as well as to the pages of the Advocate itself. Mr. Montgomery is also author of several booklets which have been widely circulated.

He took over his new duties as editor of the Advocate with a zest and enthusiasm which indicated his appreciation of having been elected, and which in addition seemed to indicate that God had ordained him for that special work. There was an immediate improvement perceptible in the character of the editorial work, as well as other features, and distinct improvement in the general appearance. Today, it is a more dignified periodical which has continued to improve, especially since 1945 when he began to

---

[1] Revelation 22:12.

give all of his time to editorial work. Since January, 1947, he has also served as the business manager, Brother R. H. Lee having resigned after more than twenty years of faithful service as associate editor and business manager, in addition to having served for eight years previous to that time as a faithful employee in the printing plant. Brother Lee is due no little credit for the success of the Advocate and the publishing house for more than two decenniums. His service to the church and the cause of the full gospel was far greater than most of the church perhaps have yet been able to realize. Mr. Montgomery has also demonstrated his business ability in managing the affairs of the publishing house admirably well. He has been keenly alert to adopt any new method which he deemed practical to improve the entire publishing house set-up. Under his progressive and astute leadership it appears that this important phase of the total church program will make great strides in the future.

The present building and printing equipment are woefully inadequate although they have served a useful purpose in the past. The building floor-space since additions have been added is about three times as great as when the original building was constructed, but it is yet far less than what is desperately needed. Old machinery has been replaced and new machinery added only when it has become absolutely necessary. It has been nothing less than remarkable that so much progress has been made in spite of the conditions which have thrust themselves upon this vital agency in the church. It should be kept in mind that all of the profit from the sale of Sunday school literature has been allocated for the purpose of supporting the educational institutions of the church. Since this is a principal source of income from the publishing house business, it has seriously handicapped the progress that might have been made if these funds could have been put back into the business. It is doubtful whether the educational program of the church could have functioned without this subsidy, but it has now become doubtful whether the publishing house can continue to operate any longer under these circumstances. Mr. Montgomery, seeing this inevitable collapse impending, recently made recommendations to the Official Board of the Church at the board meeting in Memphis, Tennessee, in January, 1948, which were adopted. This Board declared a moratorium on the Publishing House payments to the Board of Education until the next General Conference in 1949 when that body will permanently dispose of the matter. An editorial reporting and explaining the action of this Board appeared in a recent issue of the Advocate, part of which was as follows:

> We spare you some of the details which were discussed at the General Board meeting. It is sufficient to say, that the diversion of this great fund from the Publishing House to another department of the Church has been largely responsible for the fact that we have come to the place where we need at least $30,000 worth of new equipment, and have not one cent with which to purchase it. This is not a fact that commends the ability of our church authorities to conduct the affairs of the Publishing House. This institution may truly be said to be the nerve center of the Pentecostal Holiness Church, for from it stems the life-line of good will, fellowship, cooperation and understanding which are so vital to the very life of the entire Church. In 1947 we paid Emmanuel College and Southwestern College more than $4,000 profits from the Publishing House. . . . However, because of the accrued deficit from past years, and because of the installation of new equipment that had to be paid for in some way we came to the end of the year with a deficit of more than $5,000 owing to the schools.
>
> When these facts were presented to the General Board of Administration, the brethren voted in majority for the moratorium. This simply means that the Publishing House has a legal right to delay payment of profits from the Sunday school literature and supplies until the General Conference has opportunity and time to review the situation in the light of circumstances that have developed in the last eighteen years, and then decide what shall be done in the future. . . .[1]

An interesting reaction to the General Board's action in declaring a moratorium on these payments is to be seen in a published statement by Mr. Seiss N. Taylor who is a son of the late Rev. G. F. Taylor, and who has also been a publishing house employee for a number of years. He writes:

> We can't believe that there is anyone who wants to see the program of our Church schools halted, and too, we don't believe anyone should want to see them grow hale and hearty at the expense and hindrance of another department that is equally as important.
>
> In view of these facts, our manager met with the General Board to get their consent to use the profits of the literature for the needs of the Publishing House until the meeting of the next General Conference, and the request was granted. Therefore, in consideration of the great needs of the Publishing House, and in consideration of what

---

[1] G. H. Montgomery, **Advocate**, op. cit., February 12, 1948, p. 3.

she may be able to do for the Church if she has an opportunity to expand, I think the Board did a wise thing.[1]

In 1947, more than $8,000 worth of equipment was purchased, and yet there is an imperative need for $30,000 more to be spent, to anything like modernize the plant. The amount of printed matter produced even with the limited equipment at their disposal during 1947 has astonished experts in the field. To those who know the facts about this equipment it is almost unbelievable that the denominational production for 1947 was as follows:

40,000 books of sixteen titles
2,000 copies of the discipline
2,500 copies of a drama
53,500 copies of the Youth's Leader
298,850 copies of the Advocate
2,492,300 pieces of Sunday School literature
2,000 copies of the Pentecostal Pulpit.

This makes a grand total of 2,988,300 pieces of Pentecostal Holiness literature. This does not include any of the commercial work such as the conference minutes, conference newspapers or printing for the local churches.[2]

In order to be able to meet the demands of the expansion program which has been inaugurated as a result of these urgent recommendations, the General Board has also authorized an advance in the subscription price of the Advocate from $1.00 to $1.50 per year; the Youth's Leader from 75c. to $1.00 per year; and an advance of two cents on the following Sunday School publications: Bible Grade, Intermediates, Primary and Pentecostal Visitor's Leaflet.[3]

A fund was created some few months ago for the purpose of relocating the Publishing House. Some money was raised for that purpose by selling life-time subscriptions for $25.00 each. However, since the General Board of Administration met the major emphasis has been made in a different direction toward repairing worn and defective equipment, and modernizing the plant.

To compare the Pentecostal Holiness Publishing House facilities with those of other denominations of the same size, it is only fair to say that the comparison is unfavorable. This fact grows

---
1 Seiss N. Taylor, **Advocate, op. cit.,** Feb. 19, 1948, p. 2.
2 G. H. Montgomery, Personal Letter dated Feb 6, 1948.
3 G. H. Montgomery, **Ibid.,** Feb. 5, 1948, p. 4.

out of the circumstances that have just been described, which have made normal progress impossible. The future history of publications in the Pentecostal Holiness Church will no doubt be quite different.

The back page of a March, 1948 issue of the Advocate reads as follows and this gives some idea of the progress being made.

The First Quarter of 1948 we printed the greatest supply of literature ever to come off our presses in one quarter. Yet in spite of this abundant supply, our stocks are running so low that we wonder if we will have enough to last the quarter out. More and more schools are turning to us for help. Recently two other denominations and an independent Publishing House have contacted us on the possibility of supplying them with Sunday School helps. At the present time we are supplying twice as many Sunday Schools as the total number of our local churches. What is the answer? There must be a reason.

Scriptural, clear, dynamic presentation of truth by our editors. Painstaking, attractive, colorful work by our printers. Prices reasonable almost to the point of sacrifice, fixed by our Board of Publications. These make REASON ENOUGH.[1]

OTHER PUBLICATIONS IN THE PENTECOSTAL HOLINESS CHURCH

There have been from time a number of other publications of various types to appear and disappear periodically in the Pentecostal Holiness Church. Mention has already been made of the "Altamont Witness," "The Herald of Truth," "The Bible Standard," etc. In addition to these many of the Conferences have their conference newspapers which are edited usually by their respective Superintendent. An example of these may be seen in the "Virginia Messenger," edited by the Rev. W. W. Carter; "The Southwestern Pentecostal Holiness News," edited by the Rev. Oscar Moore; the "Co-Worker," edited by the Rev. T. T. Lindsey; the "Upper South Carolina Conference News," edited by the Rev. James H. Taylor, and "Monthly Rays," edited by the Rev. Alpheus Noseworthy. A large per cent of the conferences have discovered the need for, and have seen the value of, using this medium of contact to prosecute their programs.

The Pentecostal Holiness Herald

The Pentecostal Holiness Herald was a standard size eight page periodical approximately 9 x 12 which was published monthly at Toronto, Canada at a subscription price of $1.00 per year. It

---

1 G. H. Montgomery, **Advocate, op. cit.,** March 4, 1948, p. 16.

was the official organ of the Pentecostal Holiness Church in Canada for a six year period, from June, 1931 until it was discontinued in 1937. The Rev. Alpheus Noseworthy was its only editor, and associated with him was the late Rev. Edward D. Reeves. The format of this paper was much the same as that of the Advocate, except that it was limited to eight pages instead of sixteen. It contained editorials, sermons and other articles, but the main emphasis seems to have been given to Home and Foreign Missions. Mr. Noseworthy performed a noteworthy task as its editor, but it was eventually decided that the Pentecostal Holiness Advocate could be substituted to serve the same purpose.

The Gospel Temple News

For the past several years, since 1935, the Rev. Byon A. Jones has owned, edited, and published a small ten to twenty page monthly periodical, approximately 5 x 7 inches in size. This little paper which has a somewhat home-made appearance is Brother Jones' hobby, but it has also served to publicize the Portsmouth, Virginia Pentecostal Holiness Church of which he has been pastor for more than a decade. There are other such church papers issued by a number of other churches, but his is unique in the character of its content, and has a more or less general appeal for readers over the entire church. Mr. Jones manages to get the news from all over the church, and in his own inimitable way says what he pleases. His comments often provoke laughter, and quite often are somewhat caustic and irritating. If he makes a mistake he is quite ready to apologize, and whatever he may have said is said in a good-natured way, all for the thrill he seems to get out of upsetting somebody's applecart, or to goad someone into doing what he thinks he should do. Nobody takes his remarks too seriously. He gets lots of criticism and enjoys it, but those who criticize him are also eager to read his paper every month to discover what his capricious mind has spun. He humorously charges $2.00 for three months, $1.00 for six months, or 50¢ per year, and then he adds, "If you will send us your address, and the address of your friends, we will mail the Gospel Temple News free of charge." He calls it the "Itch' because it irritates people. He says what he wants to because he depends on no one to elect him as editor, or pay for his subscription although a number of people do pay, some of them on the basis of a three months subscription. The strange thing is that regardless of the amount you pay, or whether you pay anything or not, the paper keeps coming every month. Everybody that gets it reads it, every word, before they turn it loose. It is an insignificant thing to say so much about, but a history of publications in the Pentecostal Holiness Church would not be quite complete without these remarks.

Healing Waters Magazine

This eight page 9 x 12 inch periodical is very attractively printed in colors on a smooth glazed surface paper and is filled with pictures of the activities of its owner and editor, the Rev. Oral Roberts, who founded it in December, 1947. He is now publishing 10,000 copies monthly and states that the subscription list after three months was 1500, and 200 new subscriptions are being added weekly. Its purpose is intended to publicize the special divine healing campaigns which Mr. Roberts has conducted with phenomenal success during the past several months.

Pictures of the large auditoriums and the crowds which thronged to these services are cleverly arranged with the pictures and testimonies of many who have been divinely healed under his ministry, and of the pastors with whom he has worked. Instructions are given how to wire, telephone or write for special prayer for healing. Advertisements of the "Healing Waters Radio Schedule" are listed as to the time and kilocycle number of the various stations over which the broadcasts originate. Interesting accounts of recent services are given. "Partners for Deliverance" are urged to enlist themselves as volunteers to help Mr. Roberts in this ministry by purchasing and circulating his book, "If You Need Healing—Do These Things"; and by engaging in fasting and prayer for God's blessings to attend these efforts. Donations are asked for various purposes in order to raise the necessary funds to carry on his extensive work. Although some have questioned the Scriptural validity of this new emphasis on healing, as well as the sincerity of its director, Mr. Roberts continues to count hundreds who are converted, as well as healed, in his campaigns, and numbers friends by the thousands who are his loyal supporters. This is the only periodical of its kind that has been published in the Pentecostal Holiness Church. This new type of ministry has caused many to look on with mingled wonder and suspicion.

Gospel News Review

The Gospel News Review was a regular eight page standard size newspaper published by a former newspaperman from 1943 to 1945. It was a monthly publication published in the interest of the Pentecostal Holiness Church, but owned, published and controlled by Mr. Sam Wicks of Newnan, Georgia. Mr. Wicks was the husband of Mrs. Mildred Wicks, a prominent woman preacher of the Pentecostal Holiness communion whose ministry he brought into sharp focus. His ideas were somewhat original, and met with the approval of the Church in many quarters. His paper carried regular large print newspaper headlines of important happenings. The general appearance of the newspaper seemed to suggest to the reader that the whole world was Christian, and that the only news was that which pertains to current events in the Church. Many pictorial representations of various church activities, and pictures of church leaders were made prominent. Newsy accounts of revivals, local church programs and some social happenings were published. The paper gradually lost its popularity when its editor unwisely began to make critical and personal remarks in giving expression to his own opinion about matters which many felt he was incompetent to appraise or judge. After a period of about two years it soon disappeared. The subscription price was one dollar per year.

Preacher's Helper

The "Preacher's Helper," a magazine edited by the Rev. Oral Roberts, was issued in May, June, and August of 1944. Contributions to its columns were made by a number of Pentecostal Holiness Ministers, but it was short-lived. Its author claims, however, that it is the direct forerunner of a new quarterly minister's magazine called "The Pentecostal Pulpit," which is edited by the Rev. Granville H. Montgomery and published at Franklin Springs, Georgia.

The Pentecostal Pulpit

This preacher's magazine was first issued in October, 1947. It is a quarterly publication by Pentecostal preachers for Pentecostal preachers, priced at twenty-five cents per copy.

Chapter II
BOOKS, BOOKLETS, TRACTS AND PAMPHLETS IN THE PENTECOSTAL HOLINESS CHURCH

There have been relatively few books, booklets, pamphlets and tracts written or published in the ranks of the Pentecostal Holiness Church. This is attributable to several causes, one of which is perhaps the lack of necessary funds to finance such publication; or the lack of a proper appraisal of the value of such a ministry; but, principally, because those who are capable of writing have not recognized their gift and made use of it. The average person of the Pentecostal Holiness communion is not the type of person who has cultivated an appreciation for reading. On the whole they have not obeyed Paul's instruction to "give attendance to reading." This fact has likely hindered some in writing who otherwise might have.

A hopeful new feature which has been added to the Advocate pages recently is the column, "Let's Talk About Books," which is edited by the Rev. Harry B. Correll. In this column each week he attractively presents two book reviews, one of which deals with a book of the lighter vein, while the other reviews a book of the heavier type. Through these stimulating and suggestive columns a perceptible interest in reading has come to be developed, i. e., if we are to be guided by the steady increase in the publishing house sales of the books which he has reviewed. In the future the demand for good books written by men of the Pentecostal Holiness Church will no doubt be greater because of this current emphasis.

If the distinctive doctrines of this church are to be preserved, then it is mandatory that Pentecostal Holiness writings must take their place among Pentecostal Holiness people along side the writings which have been produced by men of other faiths, lest they imbibe that which will attenuate their witness, and eventually they come to the place where their existence as a denomination can no longer be justified.

The Pentecostal Holiness Church can be thankful for the writing which has been done, and these successes should demonstrate the fact that others can follow in the steps of those who have blazed the trail. In considering what has been done there will be no attempt to deal with the publications in their various categories as to the type and size, but these will be listed each with their respective author. By following this method, a fair comparison can be made of the individual contributions which have been made. Such information will also help those of the Church who have not exercised their gifts to respond to the wholesome competition which such a comparison should stimulate, and get to work writing something themselves.

G. F. Taylor

Perhaps the first publications to appear in the Church were those of the Rev. G. F. Taylor, for the reason that he was likely more publication-conscious than any other single individual at that time. His first booklet written in 1906 consisted of 76 pages and was titled, "The Devil," which dealt with his origin, his fall, his personality, his names, his influence and his final punishment. In 1907, his booklet, "The Spirit and the Bride," was published. This helpful treatise dealt with the preparation and qualification necessary for those who might expect to constitute this elect number, especially with relation to the baptism of the Holy Ghost as a needed preparation. In 1916 one of the first hardback full-sized books to be published in the Pentecostal Holiness Church made its appearance under the title of, "The Second Coming of Jesus." It had in it 264 pages and was 6 x 9 inches in size. In a very able and masterful way, Mr. Taylor presents the doctrine of the Second Coming of Christ, comprehensively covering all of the important phases of the subject as taught by the Pentecostal Holiness Church. Later, 1924, this book was abridged and published in a 5 x 7 inch booklet, consisting of 223 pages which carried a new title, "The Rainbow." This smaller size enabled the author to offer it for considerably less price and thus to give the book a wider circulation. He is the author of another book called, "A Tour in Bible Lands." G. F. Taylor wrote almost incessantly for the Advocate on many subjects, but the abovementioned publications were the extent of his writings which were issued in book form, except "Daniel's Seventy Weeks," "The Sabbath," and "A Primary Catechism," which appeared as pamphlets.

Bishop J. H. King

The late Bishop J. H. King wrote the first hard-back clothbound book to be published in the Pentecostal Holiness Church. It was 6 x 9 inches in size and ran over 200 pages, being titled "Passover to Pentecost." The main object of the book was to present a Scriptural exposition of the distinctive doctrines taught by the Pentecostal Holiness Church especially as they are reflected in the Levitical Feasts, and in the symbolic significance to be seen in the experience of the Children of Israel. The study of these Old Testament Scripture passages is presented in such a way as to reveal their particular relationship to New Testament teachings. This book is considered by Pentecostal Holiness people to be a classic in its field, and has for a number of years been listed among the required books to be read for prospective licentiates and candidates for ordination. Bishop King was also the author of a book called, "Twelve Select Sermons."

G. H. Montgomery

"Steps to the Upper-Room" was the first booklet to be written by the Rev. G. H. Montgomery. It is a handy 5 x 7 size, intended for the average layman, as well as ministers, to read. This booklet contained a series of sermons dealing with the experiences of Salvation step by step to the Pentecostal experience of "the upper-room." It has met with a somewhat wide acceptance and has reappeared in several editions. Mr. Montgomery is also the author of three other booklets: "Art Thou Sanctified?" "Practical Holiness," and "After Armageddon What?" The latter of these is an outline discussion of the Book of Revelation, containing a glossary to aid in the interpretation of the symbolic language of the Book. Besides these he has written several tracts and pamphlets among which are: "Bible Holiness, As Exemplified by the Heroes of Faith," "The Speckled Bird" and "A Natural Road to a Spiritual Blessing," which deals with the subject of tithing.

Hubert T. Spence

The Rev. Hubert T. Spence is the author of a 61 page booklet entitled, "The Person, Work and Witness of the Holy Spirit," which has been widely used by Bible classes as a guide to the study of the Holy Spirit. It is also suggested for the reading of those preparing for the ministry. Its chapters which appear in separate lessons have a list of questions at the close of each chapter. This booklet, written in simple language, is a clear exposition which both clerical and lay members have read with appreciation. Mr. Spence has also published a booklet titled, "Twelve Radio Sermons" as preached over Station WINX, while he was pastor of the Washington, D. C. Pentecostal Holiness Church.

A. E. Robinson

Mr. A. E. Robinson is perhaps the most prominent layman in the Pentecostal Holiness Church of which he is a charter member. He has read the Bible through consecutively more times than any other person in the Church, and as many times perhaps as any living person among the laity of any denomination. He is the author of "A Layman and the Book" which has been published with both a cloth and paper binding. He presents in it the doctrines taught by the Pentecostal Holiness Church in a unique way—easy and interesting, especially for laymen to read. He is also the author of a widely circulated booklet, "Problem Helps for Young People." Both of these have found a wide usefulness in the Church, particularly because those who know this great layman have utmost confidence in his integrity and Christian character.

Bishop Dan T. Muse

Bishop Dan T. Muse has lectured on the Song of Solomon in various sections all over the Pentecostal Holiness Church, expounding this portion of Scripture in such a way as to prove a spiritual blessing to every Christian who has listened. The growing appreciation for these lectures resulted in the appearance of his book, "The Song of Songs" which was published in 1947. It contains 231 pages and is beautifully cloth-bound and very dignified in appearance. This is considered by many in the Church as one of the best books which has so far been presented. It is an exposition of the Song of Solomon which has few equals. Bishop Muse is also the author of the tract, "I Have Sealed My Own Doom."

D. D. Freeman

The Rev. D. D. Freeman who has served as a faithful missionary to Africa for most of his lengthy ministerial career has written an interesting account of his experiences in which he graphically describes the native African. The title of his book is "Observe the African." He is also the author of a more recent publication, "Native Customs in Africa."

John W. Warren

Another booklet which closely parallels the Rev. Mr. Freeman's writings is to be found in the Rev. John W. Warren's account of his experiences as a missionary to Africa, in which he discusses the customs of the tribesmen among whom he labored. The title of this book is, "Answering God's Call to Africa."

J. W. Kelley

"The Temptation, and the Spirit's Leadership in the Wilderness" is the title of a little booklet, written by the Rev. J. W. Kelley in which he presents a helpful analysis of Jesus' experience, pointing out the value to be derived for believers.

May Gould Johnson

A 1948 publication is a 71 page booklet entitled, "Stories to Tell," intended to fill a need in helping those who are interested in training children in the Christian way of life. It is adapted for use in the home or church. The author is the wife of the Rev. Harvey E. Johnson, a widely known evangelist and pastor of the Pentecostal Holiness Church. This booklet is dedicated to their daughter, Janis.

N. J. Holmes and Wife

The Rev. Nickels J. Holmes and his wife, Lucy Holmes, are co-authors of a cloth-bound volume which is titled "Life Sketches and Sermons." This simply written book is especially valuable to give an insight into the history of the Holmes Bible College around which most of his ministerial labors were centered. Mr. Holmes was the author of "The Baptism by the Spirit, The Baptism by Christ and Other Topics," "God's Provision for Holiness" and other booklets.

F. M. Britton

The Rev. F. M. Britton who was a pioneer preacher of the

Pentecostal Holiness Church is the author of a 255 page booklet approximately 4½ x 6½ inches in size. This booklet, the title of which is "Pentecostal Truth," includes a brief sketch of the author's life and experience, with twenty-three of his choice sermons dealing principally with the distinctive doctrines taught by the Pentecostal Holiness Church. Among his experiences are thrilling accounts of several most remarkable healings which took place under his ministry.

W. M. Hayes

"Memoirs of Richard Baxter Hayes" is a cloth-bound book containing 204 pages which was edited by his son, the Rev. W. M. Hayes. It is a sketch of the life and ministerial experience of the Rev. Richard Baxter Hayes who was one of the most outstanding pioneer preachers of the Pentecostal Holiness Church. Included in the book are accounts of marvelous healings and other miraculous manifestations of divine power which attended his ministry. The latter half of the book includes quite a number of panegyrics written by ministers and laymen who knew him intimately.

Paul F. Beacham

Dr. Paul F. Beacham has written a "Primary" and "Advanced Catechism," a widely read tract on "Scriptural Sanctification," and a tract on "That Blessed Hope." It is to be hoped that so great a Bible scholar may yet make a major contribution to the field of publications in the Pentecostal Holiness Church.

Mrs. K. E. M. Spooner, et al

"Sketches of the Life of K. E. M. Spooner, Missionary to South Africa" is a booklet comprised of materials collected by Mrs. K. E. M. Spooner, the Rev. Paul F. Beacham, and Mr. A. E. Robinson. It is paper bound and 108 pages in length, and contains a fine running account of the active, untiring ministry of perhaps the most successful missionary the Pentecostal Holiness Church has sent to South Africa. He established 60 churches there. Accounts of his sacrificial work are related in the booklet by several of his friends who worked with him, and those who knew him most intimately.

Oral Roberts

The Rev. Oral Roberts is the author of the following booklets:

"Salvation by the Blood," the "Drama of the End-Time," "If You Need Healing—Do These Things." The first printing of this last mentioned booklet was 3,000 in 1947, but when issued in the second edition, in 1948, 20,000 copies were printed. This booklet is circulated in connection with Mr. Roberts' healing ministry either in his campaigns, or to supply the orders elicited from his radio ministry.

William H. Turner

The most prolific writer in the Pentecostal Holiness Church, if one is to judge from the number of books circulated as well as written, is the Rev. William H. Turner. The Rev. Mr. Turner has spent two long terms of service as a Missionary to China. His services have constantly been in demand also as an evangelist during periods he spent in this country on furlough. The books and booklets and tracts which he has written have been widely read both in this country and in China.

There have been a total of 400,000 copies of his writings published as compared to an estimated total of some 150,000 copies of the writings of all others in the Pentecostal Holiness Church combined. These figures are based on the author's recent statement. The major portion of his writings have dealt with doctrinal subjects in which Pentecostal Holiness people are interested. A number of these booklets have been printed in recent months. Some of his books have dealt with Missionary Work, and others his experiences as a prisoner of the Japanese. A list of most of the books he has written is as follows: (All of these have been paper-bound.)

Pentecost and Tongues
Relationship of the Pastor and Foreign Missions
Pioneering in China
Christ, The Great Physician
I Was a Prisoner of the Japanese
I Was Exchanged for a Jap
Six Thousand Years of Tithing
Building for God in Blood, War and Death

A list of the booklets which average from 40 to 50 pages are as follows:

Pentecostal Manifestations
5,000 Years of Healing
What Must I Do to Be Healed?
I Am the Lord Thy God that Healeth Thee

2,000 Years of Pentecost
Is Pentecost Scriptural?
What the Churches Say About Sanctification as a Second Blessing.
The Difference Between Regeneration, Sanctification and the Pentecostal Baptism
The Finished Work of Calvary or the Second Blessing—Which?
How May the Experience of Sanctification be Obtained?
Are We Baptized With the Holy Ghost When Converted?
Is it the Will of God to Heal All Who Are Sick?
Shall God's People Take Medicine?
Why are Not All Healed?

Sarah Nell Beacham

Mrs. Sarah Nell Beacham, the late wife of the Rev. Paul F. Beacham, is the author of a very splendid book titled "Men and Missions." It is used as a text book on missions in Holmes Bible College where she ably taught the subject for several years.

Joe E. Campbell

Joe E. Campbell is the author of two booklets dealing with doctrinal subjects. One of these titled, "What to Believe and Why?" is an exposition of the doctrine of Sanctification. This booklet is 6 x 9 in size and contains 97 pages. In it is also included a brief sketch of the author's life and experience. The other booklet, of 80 pages, is 5 x 7, bearing the title, "Can a Man Live Above Sin?"

Tracts

A number of other individuals have written tracts, some of which are listed as follows:

Thomas T. Lindsey, "Try Holiness"
R. H. Lee, "Can a Man Be Born Again?" "A Passion for Lost Souls," "Your Friend"
Alpheus Noseworthy, "The Deathless Blood of Atonement"
James F. Eppes, "A Lieutenant's Miraculous Escape from Death"
L. J. Oliver, "Is Jesus the Father?" "Are the 'Jesus Only' People Correct?" "What Saith the Scriptures?" "The Golden Age"
W. Eddie Morris, "War and the Soldier's Hope," "The Scripture on Tongues"

The major portion of these publications were printed by the Pentecostal Holiness Publishing House while some of them were not. With the adding of the proposed additional facilities to improve the Pentecostal Publishing House, it is altogether probable that this field of activity will be in the future one of the most fruitful in the Church.

BIBLIOGRAPHY

Books

Atkins, Glenn Gaius, *Religion in Our Times.* Round Table Press, 1932.

Bates, Ernest Southerland, *American Faith.* New York: W. W. Norton and Company, Inc., 1940.

Beardsley, Frank G., *A History of American Revivals.* New York: American Tract Society, 1912.

Binder, Louis Richard, *Modern Religious Cults and Society.* Boston: Richard G. Badger, The Gorham Press, 1933.

Brooks, John R., *Scriptural Sanctification.* Nashville Publishing House of the M. E. Church, South, 1899.

Brown, Charles Ewing, *The Meaning of Sanctification.* Anderson Indiana: The Warner Press, 1945.

Byrum, Russell R., *Holy Spirit Baptism and The Second Cleansing.* Anderson, Indiana: Gospel Trumphet Company, 1923.

Caldwell, Ernest and White, Margaret Bourke, *You Have Seen Their Faces.* New York: Modern Age Books, Ind., 1937.

Carroll, H. K., *The Religious Forces of the United States.* New York: Charles Scribner's Sons, 1912.

Cartwright, Peter, *Autobiography of Peter Cartwright.* Cincinnati: Cranston and Curtie, 1856.

Casselman, Arthur V., *Into All the World.* Philadelphia: The Christian Education Press, 1943.

Clark, Elmer T., *The Small Sects in America.* Nashville: Cokesbury Press, 1937.

Cleveland, Catherine C., *The Great Revival in the West 1797- 1805.* Chicago: The University of Chicago Press, 1916.

Cole, Stewart G., *History of Fundamentalism.* New York: Richard R. Smith, Inc., 1931.

Conant, J. E., *Every Member Evangelism.* New York: Harper and Brothers, 1922.

Curran, Francis X., *Major Trends in American Church History*. New York: The American Press, 1946.

Cutten, George Barton, *The Psychological Phenomena of Christianity*. New York: Charles Scribner's Sons, 1908.

Dalton, Robert Chandler, *Tongues Like As of Fire*. Springfield: The Gospel Publishing House, 1945.

Davenport, Frederick Morgan, *Primitive Traits in Religious Revivals*. New York: MacMillan Company, 1917.

DeHaan, M. R., *The Second Coming of Christ*. Grand Rapids: Zondervan Publishing House, 1944.

Dimond, Sidney G., *The Psychology of the Methodist Revival*. Nashville: Whitmore and Smith, August 3, 1934.

Evans, John, *History of All Christian Sects*. New York: James Moffatt and Company, 1844.

Frodsham, Stanley F., *With Signs Following*. Springfield: Gospel Publishing House, 1946.

Garrison, Winifred Ernest, *The March of Faith*. New York: Harper and Brothers, 1933.

Gewehr, Wesley M., *The Great Awakening in Virginia*, 1740-1790 Durham: Duke University Press.

Gilbert, George Holley, *The American Journal of Theology*. Chicago: The University of Chicago Press, 1910.

Gordon, Ernest, *The Leaven of the Pharisees*. Chicago: The Bible Colportage Associaition, 1926.

Hayes, W. M., *Memoirs of Richard Baxter Hayes*. Philadelphia: The Dunlap Printing Company, 1945.

Holmes, N. J. and Wife, *Life Sketches and Sermons*. Royston, Georgia: Press of the Pentecostal Holiness Publishing House, 1920.

Homrighuasen, Elmer G., *Choose Ye This Day*, Philadelphia: The Westminister Press, 1943.

Hood, Edwin Paxton, *The Great Revival of the Eighteenth Century*. Philadelphia: American Sunday School Union, 1882.

Horsh, John, *Modern Religious Liberalism*. Chicago: Bible Institute Colportage Association, 1924.

Hurst, John F., *Short History of the Church in the United States.* New York: Chautauqua Press, 1890.

Jarratt, Devereau, *The Life of the Reverend Devereau Jarratt.* SDH SDA.

Jefferson, Charles E., *The Minister As Prophet.* Grand Rapids: Zondervan Publishing House, 1933.

Johnson, Thomas Cary, *Some Modern Isms.* Richmond: Presbyterian Committee of Publications, 1919.

Jones, Clarence W., *Radio The New Missionary.* Chicago: Moody Press, 1946.

Jordan, G. Ray, *The Emerging Revival.* New York: Abingdon-Cokesbury Press, 1946.

Lacy, Benjamin Rice, Jr., *Revivals in the Midst of the Years.* Richmond: John Knox Press, 1943.

Latourette, Kenneth Scott, *The First Five Centuries (A History of the Expansion of Christianity).* New York: Harper and Brothers, 1937.

Loud, Grover C., *Evangelized America.* New York: Dial Press, 1928.

Lyon, William H., *A Study of Christian Sects.* Boston: The Beacon Press, Inc., 1926.

Machen, J. Gresham, *Christianity and Liberalism.* New York: The MacMillan Company, 1924.

McComus, Henry C., *The Psychology of Religious Sects.* New York: H. Holt and Company, 1929.

Miller, Randolph Crump, Editor, *Interseminary Series,* Volume II. New Harper and Brothers, 1946.

Monsma, N. J., *The Trial of Denominationalism.* Grand Rapids: Wm. B. Erdmans Publishing Company, 1932.

Moore, Arthur J., *Central Certainties.* New York: Abingdon-Cokesbury Press, 1942.

Moore, Edward Caldwell, *The Spread of Christianity in the Modern World.* Chicago: University of Chicago Press, 1919.

Morison, James, *St. Paul's Teaching on Sanctification.* London: Hodder and Stoughton, 1886.

Muncy, W. L., Jr., *A History of Evangelism in the United States.* Kansas City: Central Seminary Press, 1945.

Munro, Harry C., *Educational Evangelism.* Chicago: National Christian Teaching Mission, 1946.

Neve, J. L., *Churches and Sects of Christendom.* Burlington, Iowa: The Lutheran Literary Board, 1940.

Niebehr, H. Richard, *Social Sources of Denominationalism.* New York: H. Holt and Company, 1929.

Page, Jesse, *David Brainard.* Kilmarnock, Scotland: John Ritchie Ltd., (no date given).

Pethrus, Lewi, *The Wind Bloweth Where It Listeth.* Chicago: Philadelphia Book Concern, 1945.

Pierce, Earle V., *The Church and World Conditions.* Philadelphia: The Blakiston Company (Distributed by Fleming H. Revell Company, N. Y.) 1943.

Pope, Liston, *Millhands and Preachers,* New Haven: Yale University Press, 1942.

Price, R. N. *Holston Methodism.* Nashville: Publishing House of the M. E. Church, South, 1904.

Reeves, Mrs. E. D., *Edward D. Reeves, His Life and Message.* Franklin Springs, Georgia: Publishing House of the Pentecostal Holiness Church, 1940.

Rice, John R., *Revival Appeals.* Wheaton, Illinois: Sword of the Lord Publishers, 1945.

Scott, E. C., *Ministerial Directory of the Presbyterian Church, 1861-1941.* Austin Von Boekmann-Jones Company, 1941.

Smith, Wilbur M., *Therefore Stand.* Boston: W. A. Wilde Company, 1945.

Spooner, Mrs. K. E. M. et al, *Sketches of the Life of K. E. M. Spooner, Missionary, South Africa.* Franklin Springs, Georgia: 1945.

Spurr, Frederic C., *The Evangelism for Our Time.* London: The Epworth Press, 1937.

Stewart, I. D., *The History of the Freewill Baptist, Vol. I, From 1780-1830.* Dovers Free-Will Baptist Printing Establishment, 1862. (Reprinted 1943.)

Strickland, Arthur B., *The Great American Revival*. Cincinnati. Standard Press, 1934.
Sweet, William Warren, *Men of Zeal*. New York: Abingdon Press, 1935.
——————, *Religion on the American Frontier, The Baptist, 1783-1830*. New York: Henry Holt and Company, 1931.
——————, *Revivalism in America*. New York: Charles Scribner's Sons, 1944.
——————,*The Story of Religion in America*. New York: Harper and Brothers, Publishers, 1939.
——————, *Matters of American Christianity*. New York: Henry Holt and Company, 1937.
Swift, Arthur L., *New Frontiers of Religion*. New York: The Macmillan Company, 1938.
——————, *Religion Today*. New York: McGraw-Hill Book Company, Inc., 1933.
Thom, W. T., *Struggle For Religious Freedom in Virginia*. Baltimore: John Hopkins University Press, 1900.
Tracy, Joseph, *The Great Awakening*. New York: Dayton and Newman, 1942.
Walker, Williston, *A History of the Christian Church*. New York: Charles Scribner's Sons, 1945.
Warfield, Benjamin Breckinridge, *Perfectionism*, Volume I. New York: Oxford University Press, 1931.
Wentz, Abdel Ross, *The Lutheran Church in American History*. Philadelphia: The United Lutheran Publishing House, 1933.
Wyrick, Hubert M., *Seven Religious Isms*. Grand Rapids: Zondervan Publishing Company, 1940.
Zwemer, Samuel M., *Evangelism Today* (Message, Not Method). New York: Fleming H. Revell Company, 1944.

B. PERIODICAL ARTICLES

The Pentecostal Holiness Advocate (The Official Organ of the Pentecostal Holiness Church), Entire files from May 3, 1917 until 1948, the latest issue. Also copies of the following periodicals were read:

The Pentecostal Evangel.
The Apostolic Evangel.
The Bible Standard.
The Pentecostal Holiness Herald.
The Holiness Advocate.
Intecessory Missionary.
Christian and Missionary Alliance.
God's Revivalist.
Victory.
The Way of Faith.
The Voice of Holmes.[1]
Pressman, Corrine, "Southern Revival," *Salute,* Nov., 1947.
Boisen, A. T., *Social Action.* Article.
Baptist Quarterly Review, IX. (1875).

C. CATALOGUES

Holmes Bible School, 1947-1948.
Emmanuel College, 1947-1948.
Franklin Springs Institute, 1933 Handbook.

D. MINUTES AND YEAR BOOKS

General Conference Minutes, 1911 to 1945.
Annual Conference Minutes, Numerous, various and sundry copies.
Year Books, 1929 to 1947.

E. ENCYCLOPEDIAS

Encyclopedia Americana, Volume 22.
Encyclopedia Britannica, Volume 7.

F. UNPUBLISHED MANUSCRIPT

J. H. King's Account of His Life and Experience.

---

[1] The Above list of periodicals beginning with the Pentecostal Evangel were either single issues, parts of issues or at the most a limited number of issues.

G. LETTERS

Personal letters were received from numbers of individuals, and quite a number of old personal letters were read in search of historical information.

H. PERSONAL INTERVIEWS

Numerous personal interviews were made with men in states ranging from Florida to Canada.

www.ingramcontent.com/pod-product-compliance
Lightning Source LLC
Chambersburg PA
CBHW052042290426
44111CB00011B/1595